THE

LITERARY LIFE AND CORRESPONDENCE

OF THE

COUNTESS OF BLESSINGTON.

BY

R. R. MADDEN, M.R.I.A.,

AUTHOR OF

"TRAVELS IN THE EAST," "INFIRMITIES OF GENIUS," "THE MUSSULMAN,"
"SHRINES AND SEPULCHRES," "THE LIFE OF SAVONAROLA," ETC.

"L'homme marche vers le tombeau, trainant après lui, la chaine de ses esperances trompées."

IN TWO VOLUMES.

VOL. I.

NEW YORK:
HARPER & BROTHERS, PUBLISHERS,
329 & 331 PEARL STREET,
FRANKLIN SQUARE.
1855.

DEDICATION.

TO DOCTOR FREDERICK QUIN, M.D.

I DEDICATE, my dear Quin, this work to you—one of the most intimate friends of that gifted lady who is the subject of it, and whose entire confidence was possessed by you. I inscribe it to you in remembrance of old and happy days, of kind friends, and of many intimate acquaintances of our early days in Italy—of people we have met in joyous scenes and memorable places; some highly gifted, subsequently greatly distinguished, most of whom have passed away since you and I first became acquainted with the late Countess of Blessington in Naples, upward of thirty years ago.

Perhaps these pages may recall passages in our young days which, in the turmoil of the cares and struggles of advanced years, it may be a sort of recreation to our wearied minds and jaded energies to have presented to us again in a life-like form.

In treading on this old Italian ground once more, and that portion of it especially best known to us—a fragment of some bright star dropped from heaven :

"That, like a precious gem, Parthenopè
Smiles as of yore—the syren of the sea"—*

* The Heliotrope, or the Pilgrim in Italy, a Poem, by Dr. W. Beattie.

we may have many graves to pass, and memories, not only of dear friends, but of early hopes, to make us thoughtful.

But I trust we shall have also some pleasing recollections renewed by these Memoirs, and our old feelings of affectionate regard revived by them.

I am, my dear Quin, faithfully yours,

R. R. MADDEN.

LONDON, NOV. 1, 1854.

CONTENTS OF VOL. I.

CHAPTER XIX.

CHAPTER XX.

CHAPTER XXI.

CHAPTER XXII.

CHAPTER XXIII.

CHAPTER XXIV.

CHAPTER XXV.

CHAPTER XXVI.

CHAPTER XXVII.

APPENDIX.

No. I.

No. II.

A MEMOIR

OF THE

LITERARY LIFE AND CORRESPONDENCE

OF THE

COUNTESS OF BLESSINGTON.

INTRODUCTION.

The task of Biography is not comprised only in an attempt to make a word—picture, and likeness of a person that can be identified by its resemblance to the original; to narrate a series of striking passages in the life of an individual, whose career it is intended to illustrate; to record dates of remarkable events, and particulars of important occurrences; to give a faithful account of signal failures and successes; to delineate the features of the individual described, and to make deportment and demeanor, manner of thought, and mode of expression, clearly perceptible to those for whom we write or paint in words. These are essential things to be done, but they are not all that are essential in human life-history, which should be descriptive not only of external appearance and accidental circumstances, but of the interior being, dispositions, and actual peace of mind of those of whom it treats. The great aim to be accomplished is to make the truthful portraiture of the person we describe and present to the public, stand out in a distinct shape and form, distinguishable from all other surrounding objects, an instructive, directive, suggestive, encouraging, or admonitory representation of a character and career, as the case may be. The legitimate aim and end of that representation of a life will be gained if the biographer, in accomplishing his task, makes the portraiture of the individual described advantageous to the public, renews old recollections agreeably as well as usefully; looks to the future in all his dealings with the past; draws away attention from the predominant materialism of the present time; violates no duty to the dead, of whom he treats; no obligation to the living, for whose benefit he is supposed to write; if, without prejudice to truth or morals, he indulges his own feelings of kindness, and tenderness of regard for the memory of those who may have been his friends, and who have become the subjects of his inquiries and researches; if he turn his theme to the account of society at large, of literature also, and of its living votaries; if he places worth and genius in their true position, and, when the occasion calls for it, if he manfully puts forward his strength to pull down unworthy and ignoble pretensions, to unmask selfishness, to give all due honor to noble deeds and generous aims and efforts; if he sympathizes sincerely with struggling merit, and seeks earnestly for truth, and speaks it boldly. And if he has to deal with the career of one who has played an important part in public life or in fashionable circles, and would attain the object I have referred to, he will have to speak freely and fearlessly of the miseries and vexations of a false position, however splendid that position may be—miseries which may not be escaped from by any efforts to keep them out of sight or hearing, either in the turmoil of a fashionable life, in the tumult of its pleasures, or in the solitude of the dressing-room, the stillness of which is often more intolerable than the desert-gloom, the desolation of Mar Saba, or the silence of La Trappe.

All this can be done without composing homilies on the checkered life of man, or pouring forth lamentations on its vicissitudes, and pronouncing anathemas on the failings of individuals, on whose conduct we may perhaps be wholly incompetent or unqualified to sit in judgment. There is often matter for deep reflection, though requiring no comment from the biographer, to be found in a single fact seasonably noticed, in a passage of a letter, a sentence in conversation, nay, even at times in a gesture, indicative of weariness of mind in the midst of pomp and pleasure, of sickness of spirit at the real aspect of society, wreathed though it may be with smiles and blandishments, at the hollowness of its friendships, and the futility of one's efforts to secure their happiness by them. I am much mistaken if this work can be perused without exciting feelings of strong conviction, that no advantageousness of external circumstances, no amount of luxury, no *entourage* of wit and learning, no distinction in fashionable or literary life, no absorbing pursuits of authorship, or ephemeral enjoyments in exclusive circles of *haut ton*, constitute happiness, or afford a substitute for it, on which any reliance can be placed for the peace and quiet of one's life.

An intimate acquaintance and uninterrupted friendship with the late Countess of Blessington during a period of twenty-seven years, and the advantage of possessing the entire confidence of that lady, are the circumstances which induced the friends of Lady Blessington to commit to me the task of editing an account of her Literary Life and Correspondence. To many other persons familiarly acquainted with her ladyship, eminent in different walks of literature and art, distinguished for abilities and acquirements, and well known in the world of letters, this task might have been confided with far more service to the execution of it in every literary point of view. But, in other respects, it was considered I might bring some advantages to this undertaking, one of no ordinary difficulty, and requiring no ordinary care and circumspection to surmount. The facilities I refer to are those arising from peculiar opportunities enjoyed of knowing Lady Blessington at an early period of that literary career which it is intended to illustrate, and the antecedents of that position in literature and the society of intellectual celebrities which she occupied in London.

The correspondence and other papers of Lady Blessington that have been made use of in these volumes are connected by a slender thread of biographical illustration, which may serve to give some idea of the characters and position, and prominent traits or peculiarities of those who are addressed or referred to in this correspondence, or by whom letters were written which are noticed in it.

In doing this, I trust it will be found I am not unmindful of the obligations I am under to truth and charity, as well as to friendship—obligations to the living as well as to the dead; but, on the contrary, that I am very sensible that literature is never more profaned than when, such claims being forgotten or unfelt, statements or sentiments expressed in confidence to private persons that are calculated to hurt the feelings, to injure the character, or prejudice the interests of individuals in any rank of life, are wantonly, malevolently, or inconsiderately disclosed.

Such sentiments seem to have been acted on by a late eminent statesman, and were well expressed in a codicil to his will, wherein he bequeathed to Lord Mahon and E. Cardwell, Esq., M.P., "all the unpublished papers and documents of a public or a private nature, whether in print or in manuscript, of which he should, at the time of his decease, be possessed," &c. "Considering that the collection of letters and papers referred to in this codicil included the whole of his confidential correspondence for a period extending from the year 1817 to the time of his decease, that during a considerable portion of that period he was employed in the service of the crown, and that when not so employed, he had taken an active part in parliamentary business, it was highly probable that much of that correspondence would be interesting, and calculated to throw light upon the conduct and character of public men, and upon the political events of the times." This was done in the full assurance that his trustees would so exercise the discretion given to them, that no honorable confidence should be betrayed, no private feelings be unnecessarily wounded, and no public interests injuriously affected.

I think it is Sir Egerton Brydges who observes, "It is not possible to love literature and to be uncharitable or unkind to those who follow its pursuits." Nothing would certainly be more uncharitable and unkind to literary people than to publish what they may occasionally say in private of one another in the way of raillery, banter, or *persiflage*, a ridicule-aiming turn, as if such *badinage* on paper, and escapades of drollery, with a dash of sarcasm, in conversation, were deliberate expressions of opinion, and not the smartness of the sayings, but the sharpness of the sting in them, was to be taken into account in judging of the motives of those who gave utterance to things spoken in levity and not in malice.

There is no necessity, indeed, with such materials as I have in my hands, to encumber my pages with any trivialities of this kind, or the mere worthless tittle-tattle of epistolary conversation.

There is an abundance of thought-treasure in letters of people of exalted intellect in this collection; ample beauties in their accounts of scenery and passing events, and in their references to current literature—the works of art of the day, the chances and changes of political life, the caprices of fashion of the time, and the vicissitudes in the fortune of the celebrities of all grades in a great city—to furnish matter well worthy of selection and preservation; matter that would perish if not thus collected, and published in some such form as the present.

I have no sympathies with the tastes and pursuits of the hangers-on of men of genius in literary society, who crawl into the confidence of people of exalted intellect to turn their acquaintance with it to a profitable account; to drag into notice failings that may have hitherto escaped attention, or were only suspected to exist, and to immortalize the errors of gifted individuals, whose credulity has been taken advantage of with a deliberate purpose of speculating on those failings that have been diligently observed and drawn out.

Censure, it is said, is the tax which eminence of every kind pays for distinction. The tendency of our times especially is to pander to a morbid taste, that craves continually for signal spectacles of failings and imperfections of persons in exalted stations, for exhibitions of eminent people depreciated or defamed. The readiness of men to minister to the prevailing appetite for literary gossip, by violating the sanctity of private life, and often even the sacred ties of friendship, is not only to be lamented, but the crime is to be denounced. I have given expression to such opinions on those subjects at the onset of my career in literature, and they have undergone no change since the publication of them, upward of twenty years ago.*

We naturally desire to know every thing that concerns the character or the general conduct of those whose productions have entertained or instructed us, and we gratify a laudable curiosity when, for the purposes of good, we inquire into their history, and seek to illustrate their writings by the general tenor of their lives and actions. But when biography is made the vehicle of private scandal, the means of promoting sordid interests, and looks into every infirmity of human nature through a magnifying medium, which makes small imperfections seem to be large, and exaggerates large ones, it ceases to be a legitimate inquiry into private character or conduct, and no infamy is greater than the baseness of revealing faults that possibly had never been discovered had no friendship been violated, no confidence abused by exaggerated representations of failings and defects, which take away from the reputation of the living, or dim the bright fame of the illustrious dead.

"Consider," says a learned German, "under how many aspects greatness is scrutinized; in how many categories curiosity may be traced, from the highest grade of inquisitiveness down to the most impertinent, concerning great men! How the world never wearies striving to represent to itself their whole structure, conformation outward and inward. Blame not the world for such curiosity about its great ones: this comes of the world's old-established necessity to worship. Blame it not; pity it rather with a certain loving respect. Nevertheless, the last stage of human perversion, it has been said, is when sympathy corrupts itself into envy, and the indestructible interest we take in men's doings has become a joy over their faults and misfortunes: this is the last and lowest stage—lower than this we can not go."

"Lower than this we can not go!" says the German moralist.

* The Infirmities of Genius, &c., in 2 vols. 8vo, London, 1833.

But suppose we do more than exult in these failings and misfortunes; that we sit in judgment on them, and judge not justly, but in an unchristian manner—that is to say, with false weights and measures of justice, having one scale and standard of judicial opinion for the strong and the unscrupulous in evil doing, and another for the weak, and ill-directed, and unfortunately circumstanced; lower then I say men can go in the downward path of hypocrisy, when those most deserving of pity have more to fear from pretenders to virtue than from religion itself. At the tribunal of public opinion, there are some failings for which there must be an acquittal on every count of the indictment, or a condemnation on all.

With respect to them, it is not for the world to make any inquiries into the antecedents of error; whether they included the results of the tyranny, the profusion, the profligacy, and the embarrassments of an unworthy father, the constant spectacle of the griefs and wrongs of an injured mother, mournful scenes of domestic strife, of violence and outrage even at the domestic hearth, and riotous displays of ill-assorted revelry and carousing in the same abode, every-day morning gloom and wrangling, temporary shifts to meet inordinate expenses tending to eventual ruin, meannesses to be witnessed to postpone an inevitable catastrophe, and provide for the carousing of another night, the feasting of military friends, of condescending lords and squireen gentlemen of high rank and influence, justices of the peace of fiery zeal in provincial politics, men of mark in a country town, ever ready to partake of hospitality and to enjoy society set off with such advantages as beauty, and mirth, and gayety unrestricted can lend to it.

It is not for the world to inquire into the circumstance that may have led to an unhappy union or its unfortunate result; whether the home was happy, the society that frequented the parental abode was safe and suitable for its young inmates; the father's example was edifying in his family—the care of his children sufficient for their security—his love and tenderness the crown of their felicity; whether he watched over his daughters as an anxious father should do, and treated them with kindness and affection, bearing himself quietly and amiably toward their mother and themselves; whether their youth and innocence were surrounded with religious influences, and the moral atmosphere in which they lived from childhood and grew up to womanhood was pure and wholesome!

It matters not, in the consideration of such results, whether their peace and happiness were made things of sale and barter by a worthless father! whether, in forcing them to give their hands where they could not give their hearts, they had been sold for a price, and purchased for a consideration in which they had no share or interest!

The interests of religion, of truth, and morality, do not require that we should throw aside all considerations of this sort, and come to a conclusion on a single fact, without any reference to the influences of surrounding circumstances.

The grave has never long closed over those who have been much admired and highly extolled in their day; who have been in society formidable competitors for distinction, or in common opinion very fortunate in life and successful in society, or some particular pursuit, before the ashes of those dead celebrities are raked for error. Those tombs, indeed, are seldom ransacked unsuccessfully; but those who sit in judgment on the failings of their fellow-creatures are never more likely to be erroneous in their opinions than when they are most harsh and uncharitable in their judgments. Those persons who stand highest in the opinion of their fellow-men may rank very low in the estimation of the Supreme Judge of all; and those for whose errors there is here no mercy, may have fewer advantages of instruction and example, of position, and of favorable circumstances that have been thrown away to account for, than the most spiritually proud of the complacent self-satisfied, self-constituted judges and arraigners of their fellow-creatures.

It has been said that "a great deal has been told of Goldsmith (in the early and incidental notices of his career) which a friendly biographer would have concealed, or at least silently passed over; he would have felt bound in duty to respect the character which he took on himself to delineate; and while he withheld nothing that could have enabled the public to form a right estimate of the subject, he would not have drawn aside the curtain that concealed the privacy of domestic intercourse, and exposed to view the weakness and inconsistency of the thoughtless and confidential hours of a checkered and too fortuitous life. The skillful painter can preserve the fidelity of the resemblance, while he knows how to develop all becoming embellishments. In heightening what is naturally beautiful, in throwing a shade over the less attractive parts, he presents us with a work that is at once pleasing and instructive. The biographer must form his narrative by selection. All things belonging to a subject are not worth telling; when the circle of information is once completed, it is often the wisest part to rest satisfied with the effect produced. Such, evidently, was the rule which guided Mason in the very elegant and judicious account which he gave of his illustrious friend Gray; and though later inquirers have explored and unlocked some channels which he did not wish to open, they have left the original sketch very little altered, and hardly at all improved. In this he followed, though with a more liberal allowance to rational curiosity than had before been granted, the general practice of all biographers; but Boswell's Life of Johnson opened at once the floodgates of public desire on this subject, and set up an example, too faithfully imitated, of an indiscriminate development of facts, gratifying not a very honorable or healthy curiosity, with the minutest details of personal history, the eccentricities of social intercourse, and all the singularities of private life. The original work, however defective we may think it in its plan, derived a lustre from the greatness of its subject; but it has been the cause of overwhelming literature with a mass of the most heavy and tiresome biographies of very moderate and obscure men; with cumbersome details of a life without interest, and character without talent, and a correspondence neither illuminated with spirit nor enriched with fact. 'Vous me parlez,' says D'Olivet, 'd'un homme de lettres; parlez moi donc de ses talens, parlez moi de ses ouvrages, mais laissez moi ignorer ses foiblesses, et à plus forte raison ses vices.'"*

* Gent. Mag., March, 1837. Notice of Prior's Life of Goldsmith, p. 229.

Those who are desirous to be acquainted with the parentage, education, and incidents in the early career of the subject of this memoir, will find the information they require, gracefully given, and with a tender feeling of affectionate regard for the memory of the deceased lady of whom this work treats, in a Memoir written by her niece, Miss Power. Extracts from that Memoir, by the kind permission of Miss Power, I have been allowed to avail myself of, and they will be found subjoined to this Introduction, with such additional matter of mine appended to them as Lady Blessington's communications to me, both oral and written, and my own researches, enable me to offer.

The task I have undertaken is to illustrate the literary life of Lady Blessington. Her acquaintance with the literary men and artists of England, and foreign countries, dates from the period of her marriage with Lord Blessington, and her application to literature, as a pursuit and an employment, from the time of the first continental tour, on which she set out in 1822.

It is not necessary for me here, at least, to enter at large into her early history, though, with one exception, I am probably better acquainted with it than any other person living. The whole of that history was communicated to me by Lady Blessington, I believe with a conviction that it might be confided to me with safety, and, perhaps, with advantage at some future time to her memory.

EXTRACTS FROM A MEMOIR OF THE COUNTESS OF BLESSINGTON BY MISS POWER, WITH ADDITIONAL MATTER IN BRACKETS INSERTED BY THE AUTHOR OF THIS WORK.

"Marguerite Blessington was the third child and second daughter of Edmund Power, Esq., of Knockbrit, near Clonmel, in the county of Tipperary, and was born on the first of September, 1790. Her father, who was then a country gentleman, occupied with field-sports and agricultural pursuits, was the only son of Michael Power, Esq., of Curragheen, and descended from an ancient family in the county of Waterford. Her mother also belonged to a very old Roman Catholic family, a fact of which she was not a little proud, and her genealogical tree was preserved with a religious veneration, and studied till all its branches were as familiar as the names of her children: 'My ancestors, the Desmonds,' were her household gods, and their deeds and prowess her favorite theme."

[Mr. Edmund Power, the father of Lady Blessington, was the son of a country gentleman of a respectable family, once in tolerable circumstances. His father, Mr. Michael Power, left him a small property, eight miles distant from Dungarvan, called Curragheen.

He married, at an early age, a daughter of an ill-fated gentleman, Mr. Edmund Sheehy, descended from one of the most respectable Roman Catholic families in the county of Tipperary.

In 1843 Lady Blessington presented me with an account of the Sheehy family, drawn up with great care, and from that document, in the handwriting of Lady Blessington, which is in my possession, the following notice is taken verbatim.

Pedigree of the Sheehy Family.

"This ancient family possessed a large estate on the banks of the River Deel, in the county of Limerick, from the time that Maurice, the first Earl of Desmond's daughter, was married to Morgan Sheehy, who got the said estate from the earl as a portion with his wife.

"From the above Morgan Sheehy was lineally descended Morgan Sheehy, of Ballyallenane. The said Morgan married Ellen Butler, daughter of Pierce, Earl of Ormond, and the widow of Connor O'Brien, Earl of Thomond, and had issue, Morgan Sheehy. The said Morgan Sheehy married Catherine Mac Carthy, daughter to Donnough Mac Carthy-More, of Dunhallow, in the county of Cork; and had issue, Morgan Sheehy, who married Joan, daughter of David, Earl of Barrymore, in the county of Cork, and Lady Alice Boyle, eldest daughter of Richard, Earl of Cork; and had issue, Morgan Sheehy, and Meanus, from whom the Sheehys of Imokilly, and county of Waterford, are descended. The said Morgan married Catherine, the eldest of the five daughters of Teige O'Brien, of Ballycorrig, and of Elizabeth, daughter of Maurice, Earl of Desmond. He had issue, three sons, John, Edmund, and Roger, and five daughters. Of the daughters, Joan married Thomas Lord Southwell; Ellen married Philip Magrath, of Sleady Castle, in the county of Waterford, Esq.; Mary married Eustace, son of Sir John Brown, of Cammus, Bart.; and Anne married Colonel Gilbrern, of Kilmallock.

"Of the five daughters of the above Teige O'Brien, Catherine married the above Morgan Sheehy, Esq.; Honoria married Sir John FitzGerald, of Cloyne, Bart.; Maudin married O'Shaughnessy, of Gort; Julia married Mac Namara, of Cratala; and Mary married Sir Thurlough Mac Mahon, of Cleana, in the county of Clare, Bart.

"Of the three sons of Morgan Sheehy, Esq., and Catherine O'Brien, John, the eldest, married Mary, daughter of James Casey, of Rathcannon, in the county of Limerick, Esq. (It was in this John's time, about 1650, that Cromwell dispossessed the family of their estates.) The said John had issue John Sheehy, who married Catherine, daughter of Donough O'Brien, of Dungillane, Esq. He had issue Charles Sheehy, who married Catherine Ryan, daughter of Matthew Ryan, Esq., and of Catherine FitzGerald, daughter of Sir John FitzGerald, of Clonglish, Bart., and had issue John and William Sheehy, Esqs., of Spittal. The said John married Honoria O'Sullivan, maternal grand-daughter to McBrien, of Sally Sheehan, and had issue one son and two daughters, viz., William Sheehy, Esq., of Bawnfowne, county Waterford, and Eleanor and Ellen. (Here there is an omission of any mention of William Sheehy's marriage.) The said Eleanor married William Cranick, of Galbally, Esq., and had issue Ellen, who married Timothy Quinlan, Esq., of Tipperary. Edmund Sheehy,* Esq., son of the above-named William Sheehy, and brother to Eleanor and Ellen, married Margaret O'Sullivan, of Ballylegate, and had issue Robert and James Sheehy, and two daughters, Ellen and Mary. The said Ellen married Edmund Power, Esq., of Curragheen, in the county of Waterford; and had issue, Anne, who died in her tenth year; Michael, who

* Executed in 1766 for alleged rebellion. Edmund Sheehy was called Buck Sheehy, and lived at Bawnfowne, county Waterford.

died a Captain in the 2d West India Regiment at St. Lucia, in the West Indies; Marguerite, who married, firstly, Captain St. Leger Farmer, of the 47th Regiment, who died in 1817, and secondly, the Earl of Blessington; Ellen, who married John Home Purves, Esq., son of Sir Alexander Purves, Bart., of Purves Hall, in the county of Berwick, and secondly, to Viscount Canterbury; Robert, who entered the army young, and left it a Captain in the 30th Regiment of Foot in 1823. The said Robert married Agnes Brooke, daughter of Thomas Brooke, Esq., first member of council at St. Helena; and Mary Anne, married, in 1831, to Count de St. Marsault."*

In the Appendix will be found a detailed account of the persecutions of several members of the Sheehy family in 1765 and 1766. It commenced with the prosecution, conviction, and execution of a priest, Father Nicholas Sheehy, who was a cousin of Edmund Sheehy, the grandfather of Lady Blessington.

If ever affrighted justice might be said to "swing from her moorings," and, passion-driven, to be left at the mercy of the winds and waves of party violence, it surely was in these iniquitous proceedings; and for innocence it might indeed be affirmed that there was no anchorage in the breasts of a jury, in those times, packed as it was for the purpose of conviction, or in the sanctuary of a court, surrounded by a military force to overawe its functionaries, and to intimidate the advocates and witnesses of the accused. The unfortunate Father Sheehy was found guilty of the murder of a man named John Bridge, and sentenced to be hanged, drawn, and quartered, and the sentence was carried into execution at Clonmel. The head of the judicially murdered priest was stuck on a spike, and placed over the porch of the old jail, and there it was allowed to remain for upward of twenty years, till at length his sister, Mrs. Burke, was allowed to remove it.

The next victim of the Sheehy family was the cousin of the priest, Edmund Sheehy, the grandfather of Lady Blessington; and he, equally innocent, and far less obnoxious to suspicion of

* Here ends the genealogical account of the Sheehy family, given me by Lady Blessington.—R. R. M.

any misprision of agrarian outrage, was put to death a little later than his relative.

Edmund Sheehy, the maternal grandfather of Lady Blessington, who perished on the scaffold in May, 1766, and was buried in Kilronan church-yard, left four children, Robert, James, Ellen, and Mary. One of his sisters had married a Dr. Gleeson, of Cavehill, near Dungarvan. His eldest son, Robert, was murdered on his own property in 1831, at Bawnfowne, in the parish of Kilronan; his eldest daughter, Ellen, married Edmund Power, Esq., of Curragheen, in the county of Waterford. This lady was not in anywise remarkable for her intellectual qualities. She was a plain, simple woman, of no pretensions to elegance of manners or remarkable cleverness. She died in Dublin upward of twenty years ago. The second son, James, went to America at an early age, and was never afterward heard of. His youngest daughter, Mary, married a Mr. John Colins, the proprietor of a newspaper in Clonmel.

Robert Sheehy, who was murdered in 1831, left a son (Mr. John Sheehy, first cousin of Lady Blessington), whom I knew about two years ago in Clonmel, filling the situation of Master of the Auxiliary Workhouse (named Keyward Workhouse). Shortly after his marriage, Mr. Power removed to Knockbrit, a place about two miles from Cashel, and there, where he resided for many years, all his children were born.]

"Beauty, the heritage of the family, was, in her early youth, denied to Marguerite: her eldest brother and sister, Michael and Anne, as well as Ellen and Robert, were singularly handsome and healthy children, while she, pale, weakly, and ailing, was for years regarded as little likely ever to grow to womanhood; the precocity of her intellect, the keenness of her perceptions, and her extreme sensitiveness, all of which are so often regarded, more especially among the Irish, as the precursive symptoms of an early death, confirmed this belief, and the poor, pale, reflective child was long looked upon as doomed to a premature grave.

"The atmosphere in which she lived was but little congenial to such a nature. Her father, a man of violent temper, and little given to study the characters of his children, intimidated and shook the delicate nerves of the sickly child, though there were moments—rare ones, it is true—when the sparkles of her early genius for an instant dazzled and gratified him. Her mother, though she failed not to bestow the tenderest maternal care on the health of the little sufferer, was not capable of appreciating her fine and subtile qualities, and her brothers and sisters, fond as they were of her, were not, in their high health and boisterous gayety, companions suited to such a child.

"During her earliest years, therefore, she lived in a world of dreams and fancies, sufficient, at first, to satisfy her infant mind, but soon all too vague and incomplete to fill the blank within. Perpetual speculations, restless inquiries, to which she could find no satisfactory solutions, perpetually occupied her dawning intellect; and, until at last accident happily threw in her way an intelligence capable of comprehending the workings of the infant spirit, it was at once a torment and a blessing to her.

"This person, a Miss Anne Dwyer, a friend of her mother's, was herself possessed of talents and information far above the standard of other country women in those days.

"Miss Dwyer was surprised, and soon interested by the reflective air and strange questions which had excited only ridicule among those who had hitherto been around the child. The development of this fine organization, and the aiding it to comprehend what had so long been a sealed book, formed a study fraught with pleasure to her; and while Marguerite was yet an infant, this worthy woman began to undertake the task of her education.

"At a very early age, the powers of her imagination had already begun to develop themselves. She would entertain her brothers and sisters for hours with tales invented as she proceeded; and at last, so remarkable did this talent become, that her parents, astonished at the interest and coherence of her narrations, constantly called upon her to *improviser* for the entertainment of their friends and neighbors, a task always easy to her fertile brain; and, in a short time, the little neglected child became the wonder of the neighborhood.

"The increasing ages of their children, and the difficulty of obtaining the means of instruction for them at Knockbrit, induced Mr. and Mrs. Power to put into practice a design long formed, of removing to Clonmel, the county town of Tipperary. This change, which was looked upon by her brothers and sisters as a source of infinite satisfaction, was to Marguerite one of almost unmingled regret. To leave the place of her birth, the scenes which her passionate love of nature had so deeply endeared to her, was one of the severest trials she had ever experienced, and was looked forward to with sorrow and dread. At last, the day arrived when she was to leave the home of her childhood, and sad and lonely she stole forth to the garden to bid farewell to each beloved spot.

"Gathering a handful of flowers to keep in memory of the place, she, fearing the ridicule of the other members of the family, carefully concealed them in her pocket; and with many tears and bitter regrets, was at last driven from Knockbrit, where, as it seemed to her, she left all of happiness behind her."

[The removal of the Powers from Knockbrit to Clonmel must have been about the year 1796 or 1797. Their house in Clonmel, which I lately visited, is a small, incommodious dwelling, near the bridge leading to the adjoining county of Waterford, at a place called Suir Island.]

"At Clonmel, the improving health of Marguerite, and the society of children of her own age, gradually produced their effect on her spirits; and though her love of reading and study continued rather to increase than abate, she became more able to join in the amusements of her brothers and sisters, who, delighted at the change, gladly welcomed her into their society, and manifested the affection which hitherto they had little opportunity of displaying.

"But soon it seemed as if the violent grief she had experienced at quitting the place of her birth, was prophetic of the misfortunes which, one by one, followed the removal to Clonmel.

"Her father, with recklessness too prevalent in his day, commenced a mode of living, and indulged in pleasures and hospitality, which his means, though amply sufficient to supply necessary expenses, were wholly inadequate to support.

"In an evil hour he was tempted by the representations of a certain nobleman, more anxious to promote his own interest and influence than scrupulous as to the consequences which might result to others, to accept the situation of magistrate for the counties of Tipperary and Waterford, a position from which no pecuniary advantage was to be obtained, and which, in those times of trouble and terror, was fraught with difficulty and danger.

"Led on by promises of a lucrative situation and hints at the probability of a baronetcy, as well as by his own fearless and reckless disposition, Mr. Power performed the painful and onerous duties of his situation with a zeal which procured for him the animosity of the friends and relatives in the remotest degree of those whom it was his fate, in the discharge of the duties of his office, to bring to punishment, and entirely precluded his giving the slightest attention to the business which had bid so fair to re-establish the fortunes of his family. His nights were spent in hunting down, with troops of dragoons, the unfortunate and misguided rebels, whose connections, in turn, burned his store-houses, destroyed his plantations, and killed his cattle; while for all of these losses he was repaid by the most flattering encomiums from his noble friend, letters of thanks from the Secretary for Ireland, acknowledging his services, and by the most gratifying and marked attention at the Castle when he visited Dublin.

"He was too proud to remind the nobleman he believed to be his friend of his often-repeated promises, while the latter, only too glad not to be pressed for their performance, continued to lead on his dupe, and, instead of the valuable official appointment, &c., &c., proposed to him to set up a newspaper, in which his lordship was to procure for him the publication of the government proclamations, a source of no inconsiderable profit. This journal was, of course, to advocate only his lordship's political views, so that, by way of serving his friend, he found a cheap and easy method of furthering his own plans. The result may be guessed; Mr. Power, utterly unsuited in every respect to the conduct of such an undertaking, only became more and more deeply involved, and year by year added to his difficulties."

[Alderman H——, of Clonmel, a schoolfellow of one of the sons of Mr. Power, and well acquainted with the latter, informs me, "When Mr. Power came to Clonmel, he was about thirty years of age; he was a good-looking man, of gentlemanly appearance and manners. He was then married. His first wife was a Miss Sheehy, of a highly respectable family. He engaged in the business of a corn-merchant and butter buyer. Subsequently he became proprietor of the Clonmel Gazette, or Munster Mercury. The editor of it was the well-known Bernard Wright. The politics of the paper were liberal—Catholic politics—Power was then a Catholic, though not a very strict or observant one.* The paper advocated the electioneering interests of the Landaff or Matthew family.

"Bernard Wright," continues Alderman H——, "the editor of the Clonmel Gazette, was my guardian. He was a man of wit, a poet, and an accomplished gentleman. He had been educated for the Church in France. He was the only member of his family who was a member of the Roman Catholic religion. He had to fly from Paris at the time of the French Revolution. In the Irish rebellion of 1798, he was one of the victims of the savagery of Sir Thomas Judkin Fitzgerald, and the only one of those victims who made that ferocious man pay for his inhumanity after 1798."

In January, 1844, when residing in Portugal, Mr. Jeremiah Meagher, Vice-consul at Lisbon, a native of Clonmel, and a clerk of Lady Blessington's father at the time the latter edited the Clonmel Gazette in that town, informed me of many particulars relating to his connection with Mr. Power, and his great intimacy with Lady Blessington and her sister, which account Lady Blessington subsequently confirmed when I visited her in London, and spoke of my friend, the vice-consul, in the warmest terms of affectionate regard.

* Power's family were Roman Catholics, but it seems that he had conformed to the Protestant religion, and had stipulated that his sons should be brought up in that faith, and had consented that his daughters should be of the religion of their mother, who was a Catholic. Mr. Power, however, when he had nothing more to expect from his great patrons, came back to the old church, lived for many years in it, and died, it may be said with perfect truth, "a very unworthy member of it."

Mr. Meagher, in reference to the torture inflicted on Bernard Wright in 1798, said, "He was flogged severely for having a letter in the French language in his pocket, which had been addressed to him by one of his friends, he being a teacher of the French language. Poor Wright used to furnish articles of a literary kind for the paper, and assist in the management, but he had no political opinions of any kind. Of that fact he, Mr. Meagher, was quite certain. In 1804, the paper was prosecuted for a libel on Colonel Bagwell, written at the instigation of Mr. Watson, in the interest of Lord Donoughmore. There was a verdict against Power, and he was left to pay the costs."

The newspaper concern was a ruinous affair to Mr. Power. Mr. Meagher says, "Of all the children of Mr. Power, Marguerite was his favorite. He never knew a person naturally better disposed, or of such goodness of heart." He knew her subsequently to her marriage in 1804, when living at Cahir.

Lady Blessington informed me that "her father's pursuits in carrying out the views of his patron, Lord Donoughmore, caused him to neglect his business. His affairs became deranged. To retrieve them, he entered into partnership, in a general mercantile way, with Messrs. Hunt and O'Brien, of Waterford. He expended a great deal of money there in building stores and warehouses. Those buildings, however, were burned by the people (it was imagined), in revenge for the cruelties he had practiced on them.

"His violence," continued her ladyship, "which had formerly been of a political kind only, now became a sort of constitutional irascibility, his temper more and more irritable, his habits irregular and disorderly—he became a terror to his wife and children. He treated his wife with brutality, he upbraided her frequently with her father's fate, and would often say to her, '*What more could be expected from the daughter of a convicted rebel?*'

"His mercantile career was unfortunate; his partners got rid of him after many fruitless remonstrances. He had overdrawn the capital he had put into the house by several thousand pounds. His next speculation was a newspaper, called the Clonmel Mercury, which was set up by him at the instance of Lord Donoughmore, for the support of his lordship's electioneering interests in the county, and of his political opinions. Bernard Wright, the person who was flogged in 1798 by Sir John Judkin Fitzgerald for having a French letter in his pocket, was for some time the manager and editor of that paper. The paper was at length prosecuted for a libel written by Lord Donoughmore; but his lordship left her father to bear the brunt of the action, and to pay the expense of the suit and the damages. The paper then went to ruin; Mr. Power for some years previously had given himself up to dissipation, and his affairs had become involved in difficulties even previously to his settling up the paper, so much so, that she (Lady Blessington) and her sister Ellen, while at school, had often felt the humiliation of being debarred from learning certain kinds of work, tambour embroidery, &c., on account of the irregularity of the payment of their school charges."

Mr. Power was a fair, though not, perhaps, a very favorable specimen of the Irish country gentleman of some sixty years ago, fond of dogs, horses, wine, and revelry, and very improvident and inattentive to all affairs of business. He was a fine-looking man, of an imposing appearance, showy, and of an aristocratic air, very demonstrative of frills and ruffles, much given to white cravats, and the wearing of leather breeches and top boots. He was known to the Tipperary bloods as "a buck," as "shiver the frills," "Beau Power," and other appellations complimentary to his sporting character, rollicking disposition, and very remarkable costume.

When the times were out of joint in 1798, and for some years succeeding that disastrous epoch, Mr. Power, having thrown himself into local politics, and becoming deeply engaged in public affairs, acquired in a short time the character of a terrorist in the district that was the sphere of his magisterial duties. The hunting of suspected rebels, of persons thought to be disloyal in the late rebellion, even so long as four and five years after its complete suppression, became a favorite pursuit of Mr. Power. At length the energy of his loyalty went beyond the law. In scouring the country in pursuit of suspected rebels, he took it into his head to arrest a young man whom he met on the road.

The unfortunate man fled at the approach of the armed gentleman with his pistol leveled at him. Mr. Power shot the flying peasant, seized the wounded man, set him on a horse, and carried his dying prisoner first to his own house, and from thence to the jail at Clonmel. The unfortunate man died. Mr. Power was tried for the murder, and was acquitted.

The particulars of this frightful affair were given me in 1843 by Lady Blessington, and more recently by other parties having a very intimate knowledge of the circumstances referred to.

The account given me by Lady Blessington in some respects differs from the others; but, though it contradicts them in some minor details, it must be borne in mind her ladyship's account is evidently derived from that put forward by her father in his defense.

Though at the risk of being somewhat prolix, it seems best, in a matter of this kind, to give the several statements which seem deserving of attention separately.

Lady Blessington, in speaking to me of this catastrophe, said, "On one occasion (when her father went out scouring the country for suspected rebels) he took his son Michael out with him. After riding along the road for some time, he informed the young man he was going to apprehend a very desperate fellow in the neighborhood, whom none of the constables dare lay hands on. The son, whose principles were altogether opposed to the father's, was reluctant to go on this mission, but dared not refuse. The father, approaching the cabin of the suspected peasant, saw a person at work in an adjoining field. Mr. Power galloped into the field, attended by his son and a servant, and leveling a pistol at the man's head, called on him to surrender (but exhibited no warrant for his apprehension). The man flung a stone at his assailant, whereupon Mr. Power, taking deliberate aim, mortally wounded the man in the body. This was not sufficient; he placed the wounded man on horseback behind his servant, and thus conveyed him to town, and in the first instance to his own place of abode, and then to jail."

Lady Blessington added, that "she remembered with horror

the sight of the wounded man mounted behind the servant, as the party entered the stable-yard of her father's house; pale and ghastly, his head sunk on his breast, his strength apparently exhausted, his clothes steeped with blood, when in this condition he was brought into the court-yard bound to the servant. The horror of this deed never left the mind of Michael Power; it haunted him during his short career. He died at an early age in St. Lucia, one of the most noble-minded and tender-hearted of human beings. Such was the influence of his character over the unfortunate wounded man, that when he was dying, he besought his family to take no steps against Mr. Power, and this was solely in consideration of the humanity exhibited by the son. The man died, and Bagwell, from animosity to Power, on account of his alliance with the Donoughmore interest, persuaded the family to prosecute Power. Proceedings were commenced against him, but the grand jury threw out the bill. A second bill was sent up subsequently and found, but Power fled to England, and returned in time to take his trial for murder. He was acquitted; but the judge, even in those unhappy times (it was about 1803), thought this murder going a little too far with the system of terror; he reprobated the conduct of Power, and had his name expunged from the magistracy."

Alderman H—— states that Mr. Power, in and after the rebellion of 1798, was what was called "an active magistrate, and when patrolling the country, he shot a young man named Lonergan, the son of a widow, a peasant. This poor fellow Power called a rebel, and had his dead body brought into town and hung out of the old court-house, or, as the place was called long subsequently, the main guard."

This gentleman adds, "There the body was first seen by his mother after the boy's death, and after she had gazed on the body for a few instants, she knelt down and cursed her son's murderer."

A lady, upon whose accuracy every dependence can be placed, Mrs. Ryan, a native of Tipperary (and nearly connected by marriage with Mr. John O'Connell), who knew Lady Blessington when a child, her father and Mr. Power being near neighbors, states that Mr. Power, in the stormy period of 1798 and some succeeding years, sought to obtain local influence and distinction by hunting down the peasantry at the head of a troop of mounted yeomanry. He succeeded in being made a magistrate. He was in the habit of scouring the country for suspected parties around his residence.

At a period when martial law was in full force throughout the country, Mr. Power, in one of his scouring expeditions in his district, met a young lad going along the road, with a pitchfork in his hand, the son of an old widow woman living on the property of Mr. Ryan's father. Mr. Power, on seeing the lad, at once decided he was a rebel, and his pitchfork was an evidence of treasonable intentions. The sight of the well-known terrorist and his troopers was at once sufficient to put the lad to flight —he ran into a field. Mr. Power fired at him as he was running; the shot took effect, and death shortly afterward was the result. Mrs. Ryan states, the widow and her son (her only child) were harmless, honest, well-disposed people, much liked in the neighborhood. The lad, having broken the prong of his fork, was proceeding to the smith's forge in the evening of the day referred to to get it mended, when he had the misfortune to fall in with Mr. Power at an angle of a road, and was murdered by him. Before the poor lad had left the cabin, his mother subsequently stated that she had said to him, "Johnny, dear, it's too late to go: maybe Mr. Power and the yeomen are out." The lad said, "Never mind, mother, I'll only leave the fork and come back immediately; you know I can't do without it to-morrow. The widow watched for her son all night long in vain. He returned to her no more. She made fruitless inquiries at the smith's. She went into Clonmel in the morning, and there she learned her son had been shot by Mr. Power.

The usual brutality of exposing the mutilated body of a presumed rebel in front of the jail was gone through in this case. The widow recognized the remains of her only child. Her piercing shrieks attracted attention. They soon ceased; some of the bystanders carried away the old creature senseless and speechless. She had no one now of kith or kin to help her, no one at home to mind her, and she was unable to mind herself. Mrs. Ryan's father, a humane, good-hearted man, took pity on the poor old forlorn creature. He had her brought to his own home, and she remained an inmate of it to the day of her death. The children of this good man have a rich inheritance in his memory to be proud of and thankful to God for. The old woman never wholly recovered the shock she had sustained; she moped and pined away in a state of listless apathy, that merged eventually into a state of hypochondria, and in a paroxysm of despondency she attempted to put an end to her existence by cutting her throat.

Strange to say, although the windpipe was severed, and she lost a great deal of blood, the principal arteries being uninjured, with timely assistance and the best medical care she partially recovered, and was restored, not only to tolerable bodily health, but to a comparatively sound state of mind also. She died after a year or two. Scarcely any one out of Ryan's house cared for her or spoke about her; nothing more was heard of her or hers, but the voice of her innocent son's blood went up to heaven.

The ways and wisdom of heaven are inscrutable indeed. Mr. Power, who shed that innocent blood, lived for some years in the midst of revelry and riot, and eventually died in his bed, not wanting for any of the necessaries or comforts of life, with ample time, but with no disposition for repentance for an ill-spent life.

But the eldest son of Mr. Power, Michael, a noble-minded, generous, kindly-disposed youth, who looked with horror on the acts of his father, and was forced to witness the last barbarous outrage of his, to which reference has been just made, who never spoke to his sister Marguerite of that terrible outrage without shuddering at its enormity—he died in a distant land, in the prime of life, suddenly, without previous warning or apprehension of his untimely fate.]

"About this time," says Miss Power, "Anne, the eldest of the family, was attacked by a nervous fever, partly the result of the terror and anxiety into which the whole of the family were plunged by the misfortunes which gathered round them, aggravated by the frequent and terrible outbreaks of rage to which their father, always passionate, now became more than ever subject. In spite of every effort, this lovely child, whose affectionate disposition and endearing qualities entirely precluded any feeling of jealousy which the constant praises of her extreme beauty, to the disparagement of Marguerite, might have excited in the breast of the latter, fell a victim to the disease, and not long after, Edmund, the second son, also died.*

"These successive misfortunes so impaired the health and depressed the spirits of the mother, that the gloom continued to fall deeper and deeper over the house.

"Thus matters continued for some years, though there were moments when the natural buoyancy of childhood caused the younger members of the family to find relief from the cloud of sorrow and anxiety that hung over their home. The love of society still entertained by their father brought not unfrequent guests to his board, and enabled his children to mix with the families around. Among those who visited at his house were some whose names have been honorably known to their country. Lord Hutchinson and his brothers, Curran, the brilliant and witty Lysaght, Generals Sir Robert Mac Farlane, and Sir Colquhoun Grant—then lieutenant colonels—officers of various ranks, and other men of talent and merit, were among these visitors, and their society and conversation were the greatest delight of Marguerite, who, child as she was, was perfectly capable of understanding and appreciating their superiority."

[Among those also, in 1804, who were intimately acquainted with the Powers, were Captain Henry Hardinge, of the 47th Regiment of Foot, Captain Archibald Campbell, Major Edward Blakeney, and Captain James Murray of the same regiment.]

"At fourteen, Marguerite began to enter into the society of grown-up persons, an event which afforded her no small satisfaction, as that of children, with the exception of her brothers and sisters, especially Ellen, from whom she was almost inseparable, had but little charm for her. Ellen, who was somewhat

* Lady Blessington, in the account of the family given to me by her ladyship, makes no mention of a son named Edmund.—R. R. M.

more than a year her junior, shared the beauty of her family, a fact of which Marguerite, instead of being jealous, was proud, and the greatest affection subsisted between the sisters, though there was but little similarity in their dispositions or pursuits. In order that they might not be separated, Ellen, notwithstanding her extreme youth, was permitted to accompany her sister into the society of Tipperary, that is to say, to assemblies held there once a week, called *Coteries*. These, though music and dancing were the principal amusements, were not considered as balls, to which only girls of riper years were admitted. Here, though Ellen's beauty at first procured her much more notice and admiration than fell to the lot of her sister, the latter, ere long, began to attract no inconsiderable degree of attention. Her dancing was singularly graceful, and the intelligence of her conversation produced more lasting impressions than mere physical beauty could have won.

"About this period the 47th Regiment arrived, and was stationed at Clonmel, and, according to the custom of country towns, particularly in Ireland, all the houses of the leading gentry were thrown open to receive the officers with due attention.

"At a dinner given to them by her father, Marguerite was treated with marked attention by two of them, Captain Murray and Captain Farmer, and this attention was renewed at a juvenile ball given shortly after.

"The admiration of Captain Murray, although it failed to win so very youthful a heart, pleased and flattered her, while that of Captain Farmer excited nothing but mingled fear and distaste. She hardly knew why; for young, good-looking, and with much to win the good graces of her sex, he was generally considered as more than equal to Captain Murray in the power of pleasing.

"An instinct, however, which she could neither define nor control, increased her dislike to such a degree at every succeeding interview, that Captain Farmer, perceiving it was in vain to address her personally, applied to her parents, unknown to her, offering his hand, with the most liberal proposals which a good fortune enabled him to make. In ignorance of an event which was destined to work so important a change in her destiny, Marguerite received a similar proposal from Captain Murray, who at the same time informed her of the course adopted by his brother officer, and revealed a fact which perhaps accounted for the instinctive dread she felt for him."

[Captain Farmer was subject to fits of ungovernable passion, at times so violent as to endanger the safety of himself and those around him; and at all times there was about him a certain wildness and abruptness of speech and gesture, which left the impression on her mind that he was insane.]

"Astonishment, embarrassment, and incredulity were the feelings uppermost in the girl's mind at a communication so every way strange and unexpected.

"A few days proved to her that the information of Captain Farmer's having addressed himself to her parents was but too true; and the further discovery that these addresses were sanctioned by them, filled her with anxiety and dismay. She knew the embarrassed circumstances of her father, the desire he would naturally feel to secure a union so advantageous in a worldly point of view for one of his children, and she knew, too, his fiery temper, his violent resistance of any attempt at opposition, and the little respect, or consideration, he entertained for the wishes of any of his family when contrary to his own. Her mother, too, gave but little heed to what she considered as the foolish and romantic notions of a child who was much too young to be consulted in the matter. Despite of tears, prayers, and entreaties, the unfortunate girl was compelled to yield to the commands of her inexorable parents; and, at fourteen and a half, she was united to a man who inspired her with nothing but feelings of terror and detestation."*

[Captain Maurice St. Leger Farmer entered the army in February, 1795; he had been on half pay in 1802, and obtained his company the 9th of July, 1803, in the 47th Regiment of Foot.† In 1805 he continued in the same regiment, but in 1806

* The brideman of Captain Farmer was a *Captain Hardinge*, of the 47th Regiment. The captain became a general, and is now a lord.—R. R. M.

† Vide Army Lists for 1804, 5, 6.

his name is not to be found in the Army List, neither of officers on full or on half pay.]

"The result of such a union may be guessed. Her husband could not but be conscious of the sentiment she entertained toward him, though she endeavored to conceal the extent of her aversion; and this conviction, acting upon his peculiarly excitable temperament, produced such frequent and terrible paroxysms of rage and jealousy, that his victim trembled in his presence. It were needless to relate the details of the period of misery, distress, and harrowing fear through which Marguerite, a child in years, though old in suffering, passed. Denied in her entreaties to be permitted to return to the house of her parents, she at last, in positive terror for her personal safety, fled from the roof of her husband to return no more."

[There is a slight mistake in the passage above referred to. On Lady Blessington's own authority I am able to state, that she did return to her father's house, though she was very reluctantly received there. The particulars of this unhappy marriage had best be given in the words of Lady Blessington, and the following is an account of it, furnished me by her ladyship on the 15th of October, 1853.

"Her father was in a ruined position at the time Lady Blessington was brought home from school, a mere child, and treated as such. Among his military friends, she then saw a Captain Farmer for the first time; he appeared on very intimate terms with her father, but when she first met him, her father did not introduce her to him; in fact, she was looked on then as a mere school-girl, whom it was not necessary to introduce to any stranger. In a day or two her father told her she was not to return to school: he had decided that she was to marry Captain Farmer. This intelligence astonished her; she burst out crying, and a scene ensued in which his menaces and her protestations against his determination terminated violently. Her mother unfortunately sided with her father, and eventually, by caressing entreaties and representations of the advantages her father looked forward to from this match with a man of Captain Farmer's affluence, she was persuaded to sacrifice herself, and to marry a man for whom she felt the utmost repugnance. She had not been long under her husband's roof before it became evident to her that her husband was subject to fits of insanity, and his own relatives informed her that her father had been acquainted by them that Captain Farmer had been insane; but this information had been concealed from her by her father. She lived with him about three months, and during this time he frequently treated her with personal violence; he used to strike her on the face, pinch her till her arms were black and blue, lock her up whenever he went abroad, and often has left her without food till she felt almost famished. He was ordered to join his regiment, which was encamped at the Curragh of Kildare. Lady Blessington refused to accompany him there, and was permitted to remove to her father's house, to remain there during his absence. Captain Farmer joined his regiment, and had not been many days with it, when, in a quarrel with his colonel, he drew his sword on the former, and the result of this insane act (for such it was allowed to be) was, that he was obliged to quit the service, being permitted to sell his commission. The friends of Captain Farmer now prevailed on him to go to India (I think Lady Blessington said in the Company's service); she, however, refused to go with him, and remained at her father's."

Such is the account given to me by Lady Blessington, and for the accuracy of the above report of it I can vouch; though, of course, I can offer no opinion as to the justice of her conclusions in regard to the insanity of Captain Farmer. But it must be stated fully and unreservedly that the account given by her ladyship of the causes of the separation, and those set forth in a recent communication of a brother of Captain Farmer to the editor of a Dublin evening paper are in some respects at variance.

But in one important point the statement of the brother of Captain Farmer, in contradiction of the account given by Lady Blessington's niece of the habits of Captain Farmer, must be erroneous, if the finding of the jury at the inquest held on his body, and the evidence of the deputy marshal of the prison be correct.

Mr. John Sheehy, now residing in Clonmel, the cousin of Lady

Blessington, informs me that "he has a perfect recollection of the marriage of Lady Blessington with Captain Farmer. His father considered it a forced marriage, and used to speak of the violence done to the poor girl by her father as an act of tyranny. It was an unfortunate marriage," says Mr. Sheehy, "and it led to great misfortunes. It was impossible for her to live with Captain Farmer. She fled from him, and sought refuge in her father's house.

"She refused to return to her husband, and a separation was agreed on by the parties. Mrs. Farmer found herself very unhappily circumstanced in her former home. Her father was unkind, and sometimes more than unkind to her. She was looked on as an interloper in the house, as one who interfered with the prospects and advancement in life of her sisters. It was supposed that one of the military friends of Mr. Power's, and a frequent visitor at his house, Captain Jenkins, then stationed at Tullow, had been disposed to pay his addresses to Miss Ellen Power, and to have married her, and was prevented by other stronger impressions made on him by one then wholly unconscious of the influence exerted by her."* The supposition, however, was an erroneous one.

Captain Jenkins was brought up in the expectation of inheriting a large fortune in Hampshire, and was ultimately disappointed in that expectation. For several years he had a large income, and having expended a great deal of money previously to his marriage, had been for many years greatly embarrassed. His embarrassments, however, did not prevent him from retain-

* The officer referred to by Mr. Sheehy was a Captain Thomas Jenkins, of the 11th Light Dragoons, a gentleman of a good family in Hampshire, and of very large expectations of fortune.

By the Army List we find this gentleman entered the army in December, 1801. He held the rank of lieutenant in the 11th Light Dragoons in January, 1802. In December, 1806, he obtained a captaincy, and continued to hold the same rank in that regiment till after the peace in 1815. In 1809 he was domiciled in Dublin, in Holles Street, and Mrs. Farmer was then also residing in Dublin. In 1816 his name disappears from the Army Lists. He had an establishment at Sidmanton, in Hampshire, for three or four years previously to 1814. He served with his regiment in the latter part of the Peninsular campaign, and was absent from Sidmanton nearly two years.—R. R. M.

ing the esteem and regard of all who had known him in his more prosperous circumstances. He was a generous man, an amiable and high-minded gentleman, of elegant manners and pleasing address. He married, when rather advanced in years, the Baroness Calabrella—a sister of a gentleman of some notoriety in his day, Mr. Ball Hughes—the widow first of a Mr. Lee, and secondly of a Mr. De Blaquiere. This lady, who was possessed of considerable means, purchased a small property on the Continent, with some rights of seigniorage appertaining to it, from which the title is derived which she now bears.

She resided for some years in Abbeville, up to a short period, I believe, of her second husband's death, which took place in Paris.

This lady is the talented authoress of several remarkable productions, was long intimately acquainted with Lady Blessington, and held in very high estimation by her ladyship.

"The house of Mr. Power," Mr. Sheehy states, "was made so disagreeable to Mrs. Farmer, that she might be said to have been driven to the necessity of seeking shelter elsewhere.

"He remembers Mrs. Farmer residing at Tullow, in the county of Waterford, four miles from Lismore. His own family was then living at Cappoquin, within seven miles of Tullow. Mrs. Farmer wrote to her uncle and his daughters, but he disapproved of her separation from Captain Farmer, and refused on that account to allow his daughter to visit her.

"Previously to her marriage with Captain Farmer," he adds, "idle persons gossiped about her alleged love of ball-room distinction and intimacy with persons remarkable for gayety and pleasure. But there was no ground for the rumor."

Another gentleman well acquainted with the family, Alderman H——, says: "Mrs. Farmer lived for nearly three years with her husband at different places. After the separation, she sojourned for some time with her aunt, Mrs. Gleeson, the wife of Dr. Gleeson, who lived at Ringville, near Dungarvan. She resided also occasionally at her father's with her sister Ellen, *sans reproche* (but not without great trials); her husband treated her badly."

Mr. Jeremiah Meagher, British Vice-Consul at Lisbon, informed me that he was in the employment of Mr. Power, in connection with the Clonmel Gazette, in 1804, at the period of the marriage of Marguerite Power with Captain Farmer; that subsequently to it he knew her when she was residing at Cahir.

Mr. Meagher speaks in terms of the strongest regard for her. "He never knew a person so inclined to act kindly toward others, to do any thing that lay in her power to serve others; he never knew a person naturally better disposed, or one possessing so much goodness of heart. He knew her from childhood to the period of her marriage, and some years subsequently to it; and of all the children of Mr. Power, Marguerite was his favorite."

This is the testimony of a very honest and upright man.

Mr. Meagher says: "She resided at Cahir so late as 1807. He thinks Captain Jenkins' intimacy with the Power family commenced in 1807." And another informant, Mr. Wright, son of Bernard Wright, states that Mrs. Farmer, while residing at Cahir, visited frequently at Lord Glengall's. Other persons have a recollection of Colonel Stewart, of Killymoon, being a favorite guest at the house of Mr. Power at many entertainments between 1806 and 1807.

The Tyrone militia was stationed at Clonmel or in its vicinity about the period of Captain Farmer's marriage with Miss Power, or not long after that event.

The colonel of this regiment was the Earl of Caledon (date of appointment, 11th of August, 1804). The lieutenant colonel, Lord Mountjoy (date of appointment, 28th of September, 1804). His lordship was succeeded in the lieutenant colonelcy by William Stewart, Esq., son of Sir J. Stewart, of Killymoon (date of appointment, 16th of April, 1805), and he continued to hold that rank from 1805 to 1812. As an intimate friend of Lady Blessington and her sister, Lady Canterbury, a few words of Colonel Stewart may not be out of place.

He was a descendant of the junior branch of the Stewarts of Ochiltree, who were related to the royal line, and who received large grants from James I. after his accession to the British throne. Colonel Stewart's splendid seat and magnificent demesne of Killymoon were hardly equaled, for elegant taste and beauty of situation and scenery, in the county of Tyrone. The library, the remains of which I saw immediately after the sale of the property in 1850, was one of the richest in Ireland in Italian literature. The colonel had been much in Italy, and had carried back with him the tastes and habits of an accomplished traveler, and a lover of Italian lore. His personal appearance and manners were remarkable for elegance, and were no less prepossessing and attractive than his mental qualities and accomplishments.

Sir John Stewart, the father of the late Colonel Stewart, died in October, 1825, at his seat, Killymoon. He had been a distinguished member of the Dungannon volunteer convention. "Sir John had been returned six times for the county Tyrone, and had been a member of the Irish and Imperial Parliament for forty years, during which time he was a steady, uniform, and zealous supporter of the Constitution in church and state. He filled the offices of counsel to the Revenue Board, Solicitor General, and Attorney General; and of him it was truly observed by an aged statesman, 'that he was one of the few men who grew more humble the higher he advanced in political station.' Sir John was married in the year 1790 to Miss Archdale, sister of General Archdale, M.P. for the county of Fermanagh, by whom he had two sons and a daughter."*

In the several notices of Lady Blessington that have been published, there is a hiatus in the account given that leaves a period of about nine years unnoticed.

In 1807 she was living at Cahir, in the county Tipperary, separated from her husband; in 1809 she was sojourning in Dublin; a little later she was residing in Hampshire; in 1816, we find her established in Manchester Square, London; and at the commencement of 1818, on the point of marriage with an Irish nobleman.

The task I have proposed to myself does not render it necessary for me to do more than glance at the fact, and to cite a few passages more from the Memoir of Miss Power.]

"Circumstances having at last induced Mrs. Farmer to fix

* Annual Register, Appendix to Chronicle, 1825, p. 286.

upon London as a residence, she established herself in a house in Manchester Square, where, with her brother Robert (Michael had died some years previously), she remained for a considerable period.

"Notwithstanding the troublous scenes through which she had passed, the beauty denied in her childhood had gradually budded and blossomed into a degree of loveliness which many now living can attest, and which Lawrence painted, and Byron sung."

[Among the visitors at her house, we are told by Miss Power, was the Earl of Blessington, then a widower. And on the occurrence of an event in 1817 which placed the destiny of Mrs. Farmer in her own hands, his lordship's admiration was soon made known, and proposals of marriage were offered to her, and accepted by her, in 1818.

The event above referred to was the death of Captain Farmer. Captain Farmer, subsequently to the separation about 1807, having left his regiment, still serving in Ireland, went to the East Indies, obtained an employment there, and remained in it a few years. He returned to England about 1816, and being acquainted with persons involved in pecuniary embarrassments, who had been thrown into prison during their confinement within the rules of the Fleet, he visted them frequently, lived freely, and, I believe it may be added, riotously, with his imprisoned friends.

On one occasion, of a festive nature, after having been regaled by them, and indulging to excess, in the act of endeavoring to sally forth from the room where the entertainment had been given, he rushed out of the room, placed himself on the ledge of the window to escape the importunities of his associates, fell to the ground in the court-yard, and died of the wounds he received a little later.

From the "Morning Herald" of October 28th, 1817, the following account is taken of the inquest on Captain Maurice Farmer:

"An inquisition has been taken at the Bear and Rummer, Wells Street, Middlesex Hospital, on the body of Captain Maurice Farmer, who was killed by falling from a window in the

King's Bench Prison. The deceased was a captain in the army, upon half pay; and having received an appointment in the service of the Spanish Patriots, went, on Tuesday week, to take leave of some friends confined in the King's Bench Prison. The party drank four quarts of rum, and were all intoxicated. When the deceased rose to go home, his friends locked the door of the room to prevent him. Apprehensive that they meant to detain him all night, as they had done twice before, he threw up the window and threatened to jump out if they did not release him. Finding this of no avail, he got upon the ledge, and, while expostulating with them, lost his balance. He hung on for some minutes by his hands, but his friends were too much intoxicated to be able to relieve him. He consequently fell from the two pair, and had one thigh and one arm broken, and the violence with which his head came in contact with the ground produced an effusion of blood on the brain. He was taken up in a state of insensibility, and conveyed to the Middlesex Hospital, where he died on Tuesday last. The deputy marshal of the King's Bench Prison attended the inquest. He stated that the friends of the deceased had no intention of injuring him; but, from the gross impropriety of their conduct, the marshal had committed them to Horsemonger Lane Jail, to one month's solitary confinement.

"The jury came to the following verdict: 'The deceased came to his death by accidentally falling from a window in the King's Bench Prison when in a state of intoxication.'"

In that statement made to me by Lady Blessington in 1843, to which I have previously referred, I was informed, "In a few days after Captain Farmer's death, Perry, of the Morning Chronicle (then unknown to Lord Blessington), addressed a note to Lord Blessington, inclosing a statement, purporting to be an account of the death of Captain Farmer, sent to him for insertion in his paper, throwing an air of mystery over the recent catastrophe, asserting things that were utterly unfounded, and entering into many particulars in connection with his marriage. The simple statement of the facts on the part of Lord Blessington to Perry sufficed to prevent the insertion of this infamous slander, and laid the foundation of a lasting friendship between Lord and Lady Blessington, and the worthy man who was then editor of the 'Morning Chronicle.'"

Mr. Power, in the mean time, had become a ruined man, bankrupt in fortune, character, and domestic happiness. He removed to Dublin from Clonmel, and there, in Clarendon Street, Mrs. Power died, far advanced in years. Her husband married a second time, upward of twenty years ago, a Mrs. Hymes, widow of a brewer of Limerick. This lady, whose maiden name was Vize, was a native of Clonmel. He had been supported for a great many years previously to his death by his two daughters, Lady Blessington and Lady Canterbury, who jointly contributed the sum of one hundred and twenty pounds a year toward his maintenance. He possessed no other means of subsistence, having assigned over to his son a small farm which he possessed in the county of Waterford at the time the arrangement was entered into by his daughters to contribute each sixty pounds a year for his maintenance.

The claims on Lady Blessington were more extensive than can be well conceived. One member of her family had an annual stipend paid monthly, from the year 1836 to 1839 inclusive, of five pounds a month. In 1840 it was increased to eight pounds a month. From 1841 to 1847, inclusive, it was seven pounds a month. These payments, for which I have seen vouchers, amounted, in all, to the sum of seven hundred and eighty-four pounds. I have reason to believe the stipend was continued to be paid in 1848, which additional sum would make the amount eight hundred and sixty-eight pounds devoted to the assistance of one relative alone, exclusive of other occasional contributions on particular occasions.

Miss Mary Anne Power, the youngest sister of Lady Blessington, married, in 1831, an old French nobleman of ancient family, the Count Saint Marsault. The disparity of years in this alliance was too great to afford much expectation of felicity. The count returned to his own country, and his wife returned to her native land, preserving there, as elsewhere, a character for some eccentricity, but one uniformly irreproachable.

Mrs. Dogherty, to whom allusion is made in the letters of Lady Blessington, was a relative of a Mr. Edward Quinlan, of Clonmel, an old gentleman of considerable means, who had been connected by marriage with Lady Blessington's mother (vide genealogical account of the Sheehy family). Mr. Quinlan died in November, 1836, leaving large fortunes to his daughters. On the occasion of the trial of Edmund Power for the murder of the boy Lonergan, till Mr. Quinlan came forward with a sum of fifty pounds as a loan to Power, the latter was actually unable at the time to engage counsel for his defense.

The Countess St. Marsault went to reside with her father on her arrival in Ireland, first at Arklow, afterward in lodgings at No. 18 Camden Street, Dublin, and next at 5 Lower Dorset Street, where, in the latter part of October, 1836, Mr. Power was reduced to such a helpless state of bodily debility and suffering, that he was "unable to make the slightest movement without screaming and groaning with agony." He was attended in Dublin by a relative of his, a Dr. Kirwan, a first cousin. He appears to have died in the early part of 1837. On the 30th of January, 1837, the Countess of St. Marsault was no longer residing in Dublin, but was then domesticated at the abode of an old lady of the name of Dogherty, a relative of hers, at Mont Bruis, near Cashel, in the county of Tipperary. There she remained for nearly a year. "After an absence of thirty years she visited Clonmel." The date of this visit was April, 1837. She must then have quitted Clonmel in 1807, in very early childhood. In 1839 she returned to England.

Mr. Power, at the time of his decease, was seventy years of age. A youth passed without the benefit of experience, had merged into manhood without the restraints of religion, or the influences of kindly home affections, and terminated in age without wisdom, or honor, or respect, and death without solemnity, or the semblance of any becoming fitness for its encounter. The day before he died, the only thing he could boast of to a friend who visited him was, that he had been able to take his four or five tumblers of punch the evening before.

This brief outline brings us to the period of the marriage of

Lord and Lady Blessington, at which it will be my province to commence the history of the literary career of her ladyship.

Of Lockhart's "Life of Scott," it has been observed, "There we have the author and the man in every stage of his career, and in every capacity of his existence—Scott in his study and in court—in his family and in society—in his favorite haunts and lightest amusements. There he is to be seen in the exact relation in which he stood to his children, his intimates, his acquaintances, and dependants—the central figure, and the circle which surrounded it (Constable, the Ballantynes, Erskine, Terry, and a score or two besides), all drawn with such individuality of feature, and all painted in such vivid colors, that we seem not to be moving among the shadows of the dead, but to live with the men themselves."*

I hope, at least in one particular, it will be found I have endeavored to follow, even at an humble distance, the example of Scott's biographer, in placing before my readers the subject of my work in a life-like, truthful manner, as she was before the public in her works and in her saloons, and also in her private relations toward her friends and relatives.]

CHAPTER I.

NOTICE OF THE EARL OF BLESSINGTON—HIS ORIGIN, EARLY CAREER, FIRST AND SECOND MARRIAGE, ETC.

THE first Earl of Blessington was a descendant of the Walter Stewart, or Steward, who, "on account of his high descent, and being the nearest branch of the royal family of Scotland," we are told by Lodge,† "was created Seneschal, or Lord High Stuart of Scotland, or Receiver of the Royal Revenues, from which office his family afterward took and retained their surname of Stewart." This office and dignity were created by Malcolm the Third, of Scotland, after the death of Macduffe, in 1057. The descendants of the Lord High Constable became the founders of

* Literary Gazette, February 15, 1851.

† Irish Peerage, vol. ii., p. 196, ed. 8vo, 1754.

the house of Lenox, and one of them, by intermarriage with the daughter of King Robert Bruce, the founder of many noble families in England and Ireland. The first Stewart of this race who settled in Ireland was Sir William Stewart, of Aughentean and of Newtown Stewart, in the county of Tyrone, and his brother, Sir Robert Stewart, of Culmore, knights, "both very active and able gentlemen in the distracted times of King Charles the First." Sir Robert came into Ireland in the reign of James the First. He received from that monarch, for his Irish services, various grants of rectories and other Church property in Leitrim, Cavan, and Fermanagh, and subsequently a large tract of country of the confiscated lands of Ulster was obtained by his brother William. In 1641 he raised and commanded a troop of horse and a regiment of foot of one thousand men. He was made Governor of Derry in 1643, and in that year totally routed the Irish under Owen O'Neill at Clones. He and his brother, having refused to take the Covenant, were deprived of their command, and sent, by Monck's orders, prisoners to London. After many vicissitudes, Sir Robert returned to Ireland, and was appointed governor of the city and county of Derry in 1660. Sir William, "being in great favor with James the First, became an undertaker for the plantation of escheated lands in Ulster." He was created a baronet in 1623. He assisted largely in the plantation of Ulster, and profited extensively by it. He was a member of the Privy Council in the time of King James the First and Charles the First. At the head of his regiment, he, with his brother's aid, routed Sir Phelim O'Neill at Strabane. He left many children; his eldest son, Sir Alexander Stewart, sided with the Covenanters in 1648. He was killed at the battle of Dunbar, in Scotland, in 1653. By his marriage with a daughter of Sir Robert Newcomen, he had issue Sir William Stewart, who was made Custos Rotulorum of the county of Donegal in 1678, and was advanced to the dignity of Baron Stewart of Ramaltan, and Viscount Mountjoy, in 1682, being constituted at the same time Master General of the Ordnance and colonel of a regiment of horse.

William Stewart, first Viscount Mountjoy, was slain at the

battle of Steinkirk, in Flanders, in 1692. He was succeeded by his son William, Viscount Mountjoy, who died in Bordeaux, without issue.*

Alexander, brother of the preceding William, died during the lifetime of his brother, leaving an only daughter.

The Right Honorable Luke Gardiner, member of Parliament and privy councilor, married, in 1711, Anne, sole daughter and heiress of the Honorable Alexander Stewart, second son of William, first Viscount Mountjoy.†

Lord Primate Boulter recommended Mr. Luke Gardiner as a fit and proper person to be made a privy councilor. His views of fitness for that high office led him to look out for a sturdy *parvenu* of Irish descent, without regard to ancestry, who was capable of curbing the degenerate lords of the English Pale, and gentlemen in Parliament descended from English undertakers, too influential to be easily managed, who had become "Hiberniores quam Hibernis ipsis;" in a few words, "such a one as Mr. Gardiner, to help to keep others in order" in the Privy Council.

Primate Boulter, in a communication to the English minister recommending Mr. Gardiner, said:

"There is another affair which I troubled the Duke of Dorset about, and which I beg leave to lay before your grace, which is the making Mr. Gardiner a privy councilor. He is deputy to the vice-treasurer of this kingdom, and one of the most useful of his majesty's servants here, as your grace will be fully satisfied when you do us the honor to be with us. There is nobody here more against increasing the number of privy councilors than I am, who think they are by much too numerous; but it

* Exshaw's London Magazine, 1754, p. 259.

† Luke Gardiner's generally supposed origin and rise in the world from a menial station in the service of Mr. White, of Leixlip Castle, a descendant of Sir Nicholas White, the owner and occupier of the castle in 1666, were subjects of some satirical pasquinades and witticisms in the early part of the last century. In reference to his alleged former servile situation, it was said that a noble friend of his, in embarrassed circumstances, once observed to him, on seeing him enter his carriage, "How does it happen, Gardiner, you never make a mistake and get up behind?" To which Gardiner replied, "Some people, my lord, who have been long accustomed to going in, remain at last on the outside, and can neither get in nor up again."

is because many have been brought in without any knowledge of business or particular attachment to his majesty's service, merely for being members of either house of Parliament, that we want such a one as Mr. Gardiner to help to keep others in order; as he is most zealously attached to his majesty by affection as well as by interest, and is a thorough man of business, and of great weight in the country."*

The practice of making Jews officers in the Inquisition was thought to have worked well in Spain, and to have served to keep the grandees in order.

Luke Gardiner died at Bath in 1753, and was succeeded in his estates by his son, Charles Gardiner, who, on the demise of his maternal grandfather (when the male line of the Stewart family ceased), succeeded to all the property of the late lord. He married in 1741, and at his death left several children.

His oldest son, the Right Honorable Luke Gardiner, inherited the Mountjoy estates. He was born in 1745, represented the city of Dublin in Parliament, was made a privy councilor, and held the rank of colonel in the Dublin volunteers, and subsequently in the Dublin militia. He held a command, also, in a volunteer corps in his native county. The Mountjoy title was renewed in his person. In 1789 he was created a baron, and in 1795 was advanced to the dignity of Viscount Mountjoy. He married, in 1773, the eldest daughter of a Scotch baronet, Sir William Montgomery, and sister of Anne, Marchioness of Townsend, by whom he had issue two sons, Luke and Charles John, and several daughters.

1st. Luke, who died in 1781, in infancy.

2d. Charles John, who succeeded his father, second Viscount Mountjoy, the late Earl of Blessington, born the 19th July, 1782.

3d. Florinda, who died in 1786, aged twelve years.

4th. Louisa, born in 1775, who married the Right Reverend Robert Fowler, D.D., Bishop of Dromore, and died in 1848, aged seventy-three years.

5th. Harriet, born in 1776, died in 1849, aged seventy-three years.

* Boulter's Letters.

6th. Emily, who died in 1788.

7th. Caroline, who died in 1782.

8th. Elizabeth, who died in 1791, aged eight years.

His lordship married, secondly, in 1793, Margaret, the eldest daughter of Hector Wallis, by whom he had issue,

9th. Margaret, born in 1796, married the Honorable Hely Hutchinson, died in 1825.

The father of the late Earl of Blessington, the Right Honorable Luke Gardiner, Viscount Mountjoy, was an able and energetic man. In his zeal for the public weal, he was by no means unmindful of his own interests. He advocated warmly the claims of the Roman Catholics; he was one of the earliest and most zealous champions of their cause in the Irish Parliament. He took a very active and prominent part in the suppression of the rebellion of 1798; and on the 5th of June of that disastrous year, fell at the head of his regiment at the battle of New Ross.

Mr. John Graham, a small farmer, still living on the Mountjoy Forest estate, in the county of Tyrone, now in his eighty-sixth year, informs me the first Lord Mountjoy, in the year 1798, induced him to join his lordship's regiment, and to accompany him to Wexford. He was close to his lordship, at Three Bullet Gate, at the battle of New Ross, when the king's troops were attacked by a party of rebels, who lay in wait for them in the ditches on either side of the road, and commenced a heavy fire, which threw the troops into complete disorder. The general who was there in command ordered the troops to retreat; and they did retreat, with the exception of Lord Mountjoy and a few soldiers of his regiment. Graham saw his lordship fall from his horse mortally wounded, and when he next saw him he was dead, pierced by several balls and with many pike-wounds also.

Lord Mountjoy enjoyed several sinecures of considerable emolument. The two principal ones were hereditary. The caricaturists of his day devoted their sarcastic talents to the illustration of his supposed sinecurist propensities.*

* In one of these productions, inquiry is made "why a gardener is the most extraordinary man in the world," and the following reasons are assigned in reply to the query:

The Right Honorable Charles John Gardiner, second Viscount and Baron Mountjoy, in the county of Tyrone, at the time of his father's death in 1798, was in his seventeenth year. He was educated at Eton and at Christ Church, Oxford, where he obtained the honorary degree of Master of Arts.* In 1803 he was appointed lieutenant colonel of the Tyrone militia, and in 1807 a deputy lieutenant of the county of Tyrone; in 1809 he was elected a representative peer for Ireland, and advanced to the Earldom of Blessington, June 22d, 1816.

The origin of this latter title dates from 1763. Michael, Archbishop of Armagh (of the family of Boyle, Earl of Cork and Orrery), in 1665 was constituted Lord High Chancellor of Ireland, and in 1671 was sworn one of the lords justices. In 1689 his house at Blessington was plundered by the Irish. He died in 1702, and was buried in St. Patrick's church. His eldest son, Murrogh, by his second marriage with a daughter of Dermod, Earl of Inchiquin, was created Lord Viscount Blessington, in the county of Wicklow, by patent, in 1673. He died in 1718, and was succeeded by his son Charles. One of the daughters of the preceding Viscount, Anne, in 1696, married Sir William Stewart, third Viscount Mountjoy, born in 1709. Charles, the second Viscount Blessington, was member of Parliament for Blessington in the reigns of Queen Anne and George the First. The title became extinct by his lordship's death near Paris, without issue, in 1733.

The Sir William Stewart, third Viscount Mountjoy above mentioned, who married a daughter of Murrogh, Viscount Blessington, had been advanced to the dignity of an earl by the title of Earl of Blessington in 1745.†

"Because no man has more business upon *earth*, and he always chooses good *grounds* for what he does. He turns his *thyme* to the best account. He is master of the *mint*, and fingers *penny royal;* he raises his *celery* every year, and it is a bad year, indeed, that does not bring him in a *plum;* he has more *boughs* than a minister of state, does not want *London pride*, rakes a little under the *rose*, but would be more sage to keep the *Fox* from his inclosures, to destroy the rotten *Burroghs*, and to avoid the blasts from the North, and not to *Foster* corruption, lest a *Flood* should follow."

* Among Lord Blessington's contemporaries at Christ Church, Oxford, in 1798, were the late Lord Dudley, Lord Ebrington, Bishop Heber, &c.

† Archdall's Peerage, vol. vi., p. 256.

Few young noblemen ever entered life with greater advantages than the young Viscount Mountjoy; he was possessed of a fine fortune at the time of his coming of age; he had received an excellent education, was possessed of some talents, and a great deal of shrewdness of observation, and quickness of perception in the discernment of talents and ability of any intellectual kind. He had a refined taste for literature and arts. In politics he was a faithful representative of his father's principles. From the commencement of his career to the close of it, he supported the cause of the Roman Catholics.

The first time that the Viscount Mountjoy spoke in the House of Lords, after having been elected a representative peer for Ireland in 1809, was in favor of a motion for the thanks of the House to Lord Viscount Wellington, and the army under his command, for the victory of Talavera; when Lord Mountjoy, in reply to the Earl of Grosvenor's opposition to the motion, said that "no general was better skilled in war, none more enlightened than Lord Viscount Wellington. The choice of a position at Talavera reflected lustre on his talents; the victory was as brilliant and glorious as any on record. It was entitled to the unanimous approbation of their lordships, and the eternal gratitude of Spain and of this country."

His lordship seldom attended his Parliamentary duties, and very seldom spoke.

On the queen's trial in 1820, in opposing the bill of pains and penalties, Lord Blessington spoke in vindication of the character of Mr. Powell (who had been engaged in the Milan commission, and was assistant solicitor for the bill), "and expressed much regret that that person had any thing to do with the Milan commission."

John Allan Powell, Esq., was an intimate acquaintance of the Blessingtons.

The young lord's manners, deportment, and demeanor were all in keeping with the qualities of his mind and the amiability of his disposition. That calamity was his, than which few greater misfortunes can befall a young man of large expectations—prided, courted, flattered and beset by evil influences, the loss of a father's care, his counsel and control at the very age when these advantages are most needful to youth and inexperience.

The taste of all others which the young nobleman, on coming into his ample fortune, gave himself up to, was for the drama.

He patronized it liberally, and was allured into all the pleasures of its society. The green-room and its affairs—the interests, and rivalries, and intrigues of favorite actors and actresses, the business of private theatricals, the providing of costly dresses for them, the study of leading parts for their performance (for his lordship was led to believe his talents were of the first order for the stage), engaged the attention of the young nobleman too much, and gave a turn in the direction of self-indulgence to talents originally good, and tastes naturally inclined to elegance and refinement.

In 1822, Byron thus spoke of Lord Blessington as he remembered him in early life: "Mountjoy (for the Gardiners are the lineal race of the famous Irish viceroy* of that ilk) seems very good-natured, but is much tamed since I recollect him in all the glory of gems and snuff-boxes, and uniforms and theatricals, sitting to Strolling, the painter, to be depicted as one of the heroes of Agincourt."

His father's great fondness for him had contributed in some manner to the taste he had acquired in very early life for gorgeous ornaments, gaudy dresses, theatrical costumes, and military uniforms. At the period of the volunteering movement in Ireland, about 1788 or 1789, when the boy was not above six or seven years of age, his father had him equipped in a complete suit of volunteer uniform, and presented him thus to a great concourse of people with a diminutive sword in the poor child's hand, on the occasion of a grand review at Newtown Stewart, at the head of the corps that was commanded by his lordship.

* The famous lord deputy to whom Byron alludes was a fierce marauder and *conquistador* in the good old times of raid and of rapine of the good Queen Bess. Morrison, an English writer on Irish affairs (fol. 43), says, "Lord Mountjoy (the deputy) never received any to mercy but such as had drawn blood upon their fellow-rebels. Thus McMahon and McArt both offered to submit, but neither would be received without the other's head."

His lordship had been unfortunately allowed to think, almost from his boyhood, that no obstacle stood between him and the gratification of his desires that could not be removed; and the result was what might be expected.

This evil tendency to self-indulgence impeded the growth of all powers of self-control, and nourished a disposition to unrestrained profusion and extravagance, whenever the gratification of the senses or allurements of pleasure were in question.

His lordship, in the latter part of 1808 or the beginning of 1809, made the acquaintance of a lady of the name of Browne (née Campbell), remarkable for her attractions, and indebted to them chiefly, if not solely, for her distinction.

The young lord found some difficulties in the way of the resolution he had formed of marrying this lady, but the obstacles were removed; and while means were being taken for their removal and the marriage that was to follow it, Warwick House in Worthing was taken by his lordship for her abode, and there she resided for several months.

Mrs. Browne belonged to a Scotch family of respectability, of the name of Campbell, and, as I am informed, a brother of hers represented in Parliament the borough in which his native place was situated, and was connected with a baronet of the same name.

While the residence was kept up at Worthing, another place of abode was occasionally occupied in Portman Square, where his son Charles John was born. In 1811, his lordship took a house in Manchester Square, and there his daughter Emilie Rosalie was born. The following year he removed to Seymour Place, where he resided till the latter part of 1813.

In 1812, the death of Major Browne (long expected) having taken place, Lord Mountjoy married "Mary Campbell, widow of Major Browne," as we are informed by the Peerage.

Lord Mountjoy had not long resided in Seymour Place when he determined on going on the Continent. The health of Lady Mountjoy must have been at that period impaired. His lordship's friend and medical attendant, Mr. Tegart, of Pall Mall, recommended a young physician of high character to accompany the tourists; and accordingly Dr. Richardson (an old and valued friend of the author's) proceeded to France with them.

The circumstances are to be kept in mind of this marriage, the impediment to it, the waiting for the removal of it, the accomplishment of an object ardently desired, without reference to future consequences, without any regard for public opinion, or feelings of relatives; the restlessness of his lordship's mind, manifested in changes of abode, and the abandonment of his residence in London for the Continent soon after he had married, and had gone to considerable expense in fitting up that place of abode.

Lady Mountjoy did not long enjoy the honors of her elevated rank and new position. She died at St. Germain's, in France, the 9th of September, 1814. The legitimate issue of this marriage was, first, Lady Harriet Anne Frances Gardiner, born the 5th of August, 1812 (who married the Count Alfred D'Orsay the 1st of December, 1829; and, secondly, the Hon. Charles Spencer Cowper, third son of the late Earl Cowper, the 4th of January, 1853, the Count D'Orsay having died the 4th of August, 1852);* second, the Right Hon. Luke Wellington, Viscount Mountjoy, born in 1814, who died in 1823, at the age of nine years and six months.

The children of whom mention is not made in the Peerage were:

First, Charles John, born in Portman Square, London, the 3d of February, 1810, now surviving, who retains a small portion of the Mountjoy Forest estate (the income from which is about £600 a year); all that remains, with a trifling exception, of the wreck of that once vast property of the Earl of Blessington.

Second, Emilie Rosalie, commonly called Lady Mary Gardiner, born in Manchester Square, London, on the 24th of June, 1811 (who married C. White, Esq., and died in Paris without issue about 1848).

* The Honorable Charles Spencer Cowper is the youngest son of the late Earl Cowper, who married in 1805 the Honorable Emily Mary Lamb, eldest daughter of Penniston, first Viscount Melbourne. Lord Cowper died at Putney in June, 1837. His widow married secondly Lord Palmerston, in 1839. The Honorable Charles Spencer Cowper, born in 1816, filled the office of Secretary of Legation in Florence.

Lord Mountjoy's grief at the loss of his lady was manifested in a funeral pageant of extraordinary magnificence on the occasion of the removal of her remains to England, and from thence to Ireland. One of the principal rooms in his lordship's Dublin residence, in Henrietta Street, was fitted up for the mournful occasion at an enormous cost. The body, placed in a coffin, sumptuously decorated, had been conveyed to Dublin by a London undertaker of eminence in the performance of state funerals, attended by six professional female mourners, suitably attired in mourning garments, and was laid out in a spacious room hung with black cloth, on an elevated catafalque, covered with a velvet pall of the finest texture, embroidered in gold and silver, which had been purchased in France for the occasion, and had recently been used at a public funeral in Paris of great pomp and splendor, that of Marshal Duroc. A large number of wax tapers were ranged round the catafalque, and the six professional female mutes, during the time the body lay in state, remained in attendance in the chamber in becoming attitudes, admirably regulated; while the London undertaker, attired in deep mourning, went through the dismal formality of conducting the friends of Lord Blessington who presented themselves to the place where the body was laid out; and as each person walked round the catafalque, and then retired, this official, having performed the lugubrious duties of master of the funeral solemnities, in a low tone expressed a hope that the arrangements were to the satisfaction of the visitor.

They ought to have been satisfactory; the cost of them (on the authority of the late Lady Blessington) was between £3000 and £4000.

The remains of the deceased lady were conveyed with great pomp to St. Thomas's Church, Marlborough Street, Dublin, and were deposited in the family vault of Lord Blessington, and are now mingled with the dust of the latest descendants of the illustrious Lord President Mountjoy.

One of the friends of Lord Blessington, who witnessed the gorgeous funeral spectacle, well acquainted with such pageants, informs me the magnificence of it was greater than that of any similar *performance* of private obsequies he ever saw.

But this great exhibition of extravagant grief, and the enormous outlay made for its manifestation, was in the bright and palmy days of Irish landlordism, when potatoes flourished, and people who had land in Ireland lived like princes. The Scotch haberdasher who now lords it over a portion of the broad lands of the Mountjoys will live, however, and bury his dead after a very different fashion.

The once gorgeous coffin, covered with rich silk velvet and adorned with gilt mounting, in which the remains of the "Right Hon. Mary Campbell, Viscountess Mountjoy," were deposited, is still recognizable by its foreign shape from the other surrounding receptacles of noble remains above it and beneath it. But the fine silk velvet of France, and the gilt mountings of the coffin of the Viscountess Mountjoy, have lost their lustre. Forty years of sepulchral damp and darkness have proved too much for the costly efforts of the noble Earl of Blessington to distinguish the remains of his much-loved lady from those of the adjacent dead.

About the latter part of 1815 Lord Blessington was in Ireland. He gave a dinner-party at his house in Henrietta Street, which was attended by several gentlemen, among whom were the Knight of Kerry, A. Hume, Esq., Thomas Moore, Sir P. C., Bart., James Corry, Esq.,* Captain Thomas Jenkins, of the 11th Light Dragoons, and one or two ladies. His lordship, on that occasion, seemed to have entirely recovered his spirits; and to one of the guests, who had not been in the house or the room, then the scene of great festivity, since the funeral solemnities which have been referred to had been witnessed by him there less than two years previously, the change seemed a very remarkable one. Captain Jenkins left the company at an early hour, to proceed that evening to England, and parted with his friends, not without very apparent feelings of emotion.

* James Corry, Esq., who figures a good deal in Moore's Journals, was a barrister, whose bag had never been encumbered with many, I believe I might say with any, briefs. He was admitted to the bar in 1796. For many years he filled the office of Secretary to the Trustees of the Linen Manufacture, in their offices in Lurgan Street. He was a man of wit and humor, assisted in all the private theatricals of his time, not only in Dublin, but in the provinces, and particularly those at the abode of Lord Mountjoy at Rash, near Omagh.

Lord Mountjoy did not long remain a widower. His lady died in September, 1814, and on the 16th of February, 1818, his lordship was united to a lady of the name of Farmer, who had become a widow four months previously—in 1817.

The marriage of Lord and Lady Blessington took place by special license, at the church in Bryanston Square. There were present Sir W. P. Campbell, Baronet, of Marchmont, William Purves, Esq., Robert Power, Esq., and F. S. Pole, Esq.

This work is not intended to be a biography of Lady Blessington, but to present a faithful account of her literary life and correspondence.

From the period of her marriage with the Earl of Blessington, that intercourse with eminent men and distinguished persons of various pursuits may be said to date; and from that period I profess to deal with it, so far as the information I have obtained, and the original letters and manuscripts of her ladyship in my hands, will enable me to do.

Mrs. Farmer had been separated from her husband, Captain Maurice St. Leger Farmer, of Poplar Hall, county Kildare, for upward of twelve years, resided much in England, at Sidmanton, in Hampshire, for several years previously to the termination of the war, and in the latter part of 1815 had made London her place of residence, and had a house taken for her in Manchester Square in 1816.*

Lord Mountjoy's second marriage was entered into after an acquaintance that had commenced may years previously in Ireland, and had been long interrupted.

The lady of his love was then twenty-eight years of age, in the perfection of matured beauty—that bright and radiant beauty which derives its power not so much from harmony of features

* There, in 1816, I am informed by one of the most eminent medical men in London, he had met Lord Blessington at dinner. I have likewise been informed by the late Mr. Arthur Tegart, of Pall Mall, then intimately acquainted with the parties, that he also had frequently met Lord Blessington at Mrs. Farmer's, but never unaccompanied by some mutual friend or acquaintance. Mr. Tegart, the intimate and medical attendant of Curran, Grattan, and Ponsonby, a gentleman most highly respected by all who knew him, and by none more than the writer of these lines, died in 1829, in his sixty-ninth year.

and symmetry of form, as from the animating influences of intelligence beaming forth from a mind full of joyous and of kindly feelings and of brilliant fancies—that kind of vivid loveliness which is never found where some degree of genius is not. Her form was exquisitely moulded, with an inclination to fullness; but no finer proportions could be imagined; her movements were graceful and natural at all times, in her merriest as well as in her gravest moods.

The peculiar character of Lady Blessington's beauty seemed to be the entire, exact, and instantaneous correspondence of every feature, and each separate trait of her countenance, with the emotion of her mind, which any particular subject of conversation or object of attention might excite. The instant a joyous thought took possession of her fancy, you saw it transmitted as if by electrical agency to her glowing features; you read it in her sparkling eyes, her laughing lips, her cheerful looks; you heard it expressed in her ringing laugh, clear and sweet as the gay, joy-bell sounds of childhood's merriest tones.

There was a geniality in the warmth of her Irish feelings, an abandonment of all care, of all apparent consciousness of her powers of attraction, a glowing sunshine of good humor, and of good nature in the smiles and laughter, and the sallies of the wit of this lovely woman in her early and her happy days (those of her Italian life, especially from 1823 to 1826), such as have been seldom surpassed in the looks, gesture, or expression of any other person, however beautiful. The influence of her attraction was of that kind described by the poet:

> "When the loveliest expression to features are joined,
> By nature's most delicate pencil designed,
> And blushes unbidden, and smiles without art,
> Speak the softness and feeling that dwell in the heart."

Her voice was ever sweetly modulated and low—"an excellent thing in woman!" Its tones were always in harmonious concord with the traits of her expressive features. There was a cordiality, a clear, silver-toned hilarity, a correspondence in them, apparently with all her sensations, that made her hearers feel "she spoke to them with every part of her being," and that their communication was with a kindly-hearted, genial person, of womanly feelings and sentiments. The girlish-like joyousness of her laugh, the genuine gayety of her heart, of her "*petit ris follatre*," the *éclats* of those Jordan-like outbursts of exuberant mirthfulness which she was wont to indulge in—contributed not a little to her power of fascination. All the beauty of Lady Blessington, without the exquisite sweetness of her voice, and the witchery of its tones in pleasing or expressing pleasure, would have been only a secondary attraction.

Mirabeau, in one of his letters, descants on the perfections of a French lady—*une dame spirituelle*, of great powers of attraction:

"When she talks, she is the art of pleasing personified. Her eyes, her lips, her words, her gestures, are all prepossessing; her language is the language of amiableness; her accents are the accents of grace; she embellishes a trifle; interests upon nothing; she softens a contradiction; she takes off the insipidity of a compliment by turning it elegantly; and when she has a mind, she sharpens and polishes the point of an epigram better than all the women in the world.

"Her eyes sparkle with pleasure; the most delightful sallies flash from her fancy; in telling a story she is inimitable—the motions of her body and the accents of her tongue are equally genteel and easy; an equable flow of sprightliness keeps her constantly good-humored and cheerful, and the only objects of her life are to please and be pleased. Her vivacity may sometimes approach to folly, but perhaps it is not in her moments of folly she is least interesting and agreeable."

Mirabeau goes on enlarging on one particular faculty which she possessed, and for which she was remarkable, beyond all comparison with other women—a power of intellectual excitation which roused up any spark of talent in the minds of those around her:

"She will draw wit from a fool; she strikes with such address the chords of self-love, that she gives unexpected vigor and agility to fancy, and electrifies a body that appears non-electric."*

* Mirabeau's Letters during his residence in England, translated, in 2 vols. London, 1832.

Lady Blessington might have sat for the portrait of the spiritual French woman that Mirabeau has sketched with so much animation!

Soon after their marriage, Lord Blessington took his bride over to Ireland, to visit his Tyrone estates; but that was not the first occasion of the lady's visit to Mountjoy Forest.

The marriage had been so far kept a secret that many of Lord Blessington's friends were not aware of it at the time of his arrival in Dublin. He invited some of those with whom he was most intimately acquainted to a dinner at his house in Henrietta Street.*

Some of those first mentioned were only made acquainted with the recent marriage when Lord Blessington entered the drawing-room with a lady of extraordinary beauty, and in bridal costume, leaning on his arm, whom he introduced as Lady Blessington.

Among the guests, there was one gentleman who had been in that room only four years before, when the walls were hung in black, and in the centre, on an elevated platform, was placed a coffin, with a gorgeous velvet pall, with the remains in it of a woman, once scarcely surpassed in loveliness by the lady then present—radiant in beauty, and decked out in rich attire—all in white, in bridal costume. Stranger events and more striking contrasts are often to be encountered in brilliant circles and in noble mansions than are to be met with even in books of fiction.

The Blessingtons proceeded from Dublin to the county of Tyrone; but preparations were previously made by his lordship for the reception of his bride at Mountjoy Forest of a most costly description.

* The Gardiner family owned the fee simple of the whole street nearly, and the house No. 10, at the west end, and north side of Henrietta Street, which now constitutes the Queen's Inns Chambers, formerly held by the Right Honorable Luke Gardiner, Lord Mountjoy, and subsequently in the possession of the late Right Honorable Charles John, Earl of Blessington. The house was sold in 1837 to Tristram Kennedy, Esq., for £1700. Immediately in front of Lord Blessington's abode, the noted Primate Boulter erected his palace, which he makes mention of in his letters. The worthy primate wanted only the scholarship and munificence of Wolsey, and the great intellectual powers and political wisdom of Richelieu, to be a very distinguished temporally-minded churchman, and unspiritualized sacerdotal statesman.

Speaking of these extravagant arrangements of her husband, Lady Blessington has observed in one of her works, "The only complaint I ever have to make of his taste is its too great splendor; a proof of which he gave me when I went to Mountjoy Forest on my marriage, and found my private sitting-room hung with crimson Genoa silk velvet, trimmed with gold bullion fringe, and all the furniture of equal richness—a richness that was only suited to a state-room in a palace."*

Some of the frieze-coated peasantry of the Mountjoy Forest estate, still surviving on the wrecked property (that has lately gone through the Encumbered Estates Court), but now living in penury in wretched hovels, who remember the great doings in the house of their lord on the occasion referred to, speak of "the wonderful doings" of his lordship, and of "the terrible waste of money," and "the great folly of it," that was witnessed by them.

Folly, indeed, there were abundant proofs of, in the lavish expenditure, which Lady Blessington attributed to rather too great a taste for splendor. I consider these things as evidence of a state of insanity of Lord Blessington, partially developed, even at the early period referred to, manifested subsequently on different occasions, but always pointing in one direction. The acts of Lord Blessington on several occasions, in matters connected with both his marriages, it always appeared were the acts of a man of an unsound judgment, that is to say, of a man insane on subjects which he had allowed to obtain entire possession of his mind, and with respect to objects which he had devoted all his energies to attain, wholly irrespective of future consequences.

At the time of Lord Blessington's marriage, his fortune was embarrassed to some extent, as he imagined, through the mismanagement of his agents, but, in point of fact, by his lordship's own extravagances, and the numerous encumbrances with which he had already charged his estates.

It was owing, in no small degree, to Lady Blessington's advice, and the active steps she had caused his lordship to take for the retrieval of his affairs, that his difficulties were to some ex-

* The Idler in France, vol. i., p. 117.

tent diminished, and his rental increased considerably. From £30,000 a year it had decreased to £23,000 or £24,000; but for two years previously to his departure from England it rather exceeded that amount.

I visited several of the surviving tenants of Lord Blessington, still living on the Mountjoy estate, near Armagh, in March, 1845. All concurred in one statement, that a better landlord, a kinder man to the poor, never existed than the late Lord Blessington. A tenant was never evicted by him; he never suffered the tenants to be distressed by an agent, however much in need he might stand of money; he would not suffer them to be pressed for rent, to be proceeded against, or ejected. Graham, one of the oldest and most respectable tenants on the estate, says he is aware of his lordship, at a period when he was in great want of money, having written to the agent not to press the tenants too much, even for arrears that had been long due; that, rather than they should be dealt harshly with, he would endeavor to obtain money on mortgage in London; and Graham adds, the money his lordship then required was thus obtained by him. "*He took after his father in this respect. He looked on his tenants as if he was bound to see they suffered no injury at the hands of any person acting for him on his estate.*"

The residence of the father of the late Lord Blessington, on the Mountjoy Forest estate in Tyrone, was on the town land of Rash, near the "Church of Cappagh," on the opposite side of the river, about a quarter of a mile from the cottage residence to which Lord Blessington subsequently removed.

The Dowager Lady Mountjoy resided at Rash for some years after the death of her husband in 1798.

And here, also, prior to 1814, the late Lord Blessington resided when he visited his Tyrone estates; and about 1807, expended a great deal of money in enlarging the offices, building an extensive kitchen and wine-cellars, and erecting a spacious and elegantly decorated theatre, and providing "properties," and a suitable wardrobe of magnificent theatrical dresses for it.

The professional actors and actresses were brought down by his lordship, for the private theatricals at Mountjoy Forest, from

Dublin, and some even from London. But there were amateur performers also, and two of the old tenants remember seeing his lordship act " some great parts ;" but what they were, or whether of a tragic or a comic nature, they can not say ; they only know " he was thought a fine actor, and the dresses he wore were very grand and fine."

The ladies who acted were always actresses from the Dublin theatres, and during the performances at Rash, his lordship had them lodged at the house of the school-mistress, in the demesne near the avenue leading to the house.

The " quality" who came down and remained at Rash during the performances, which generally lasted for three or four weeks each year, were entertained with great hospitality by his lordship.

The expenditure was profuse in the extreme for their entertainment, and the fitting up and furnishing of places of temporary accommodation for them during their brief sojourn.

The dwelling-house of Rash was more a large cottage, with some remains of an older structure, than a nobleman's mansion.

Moore, in his Diary, September 11th, 1832, alludes to the theatricals of Lord Blessington, but without specifying time or place. He refers to a conversation with Corry about the theatricals of his lordship. " A set of mock resolutions, one of which was the following, chiefly leveled at Crampton, who was always imperfect in his part—' That every gentleman shall be at liberty to avail himself of the words of the author in case his own invention fails him.' "

These theatricals were at Rash, in Tyrone.

To an inquiry addressed to Sir P. C—— on the subject of these theatricals, I received a note informing me he had never heard of any theatricals in Dublin got up by the Blessingtons, and that, if there had been any such there, he must have heard of it, nor was he the person alluded to in the mock resolutions ; " he had neither hand, act, nor *part* in theatricals of any description." The observation might possibly allude, for any thing he knew to the contrary, to a brother, who had been dead many years.

The taste for theatricals survived the theatre in Mountjoy Forest. In June, 1817, Lord Blessington took a leading part in the public entertainment and testimonial given to John Philip Kemble on his retirement from the stage. At the meeting which took place at the Freemasons' Tavern, when a piece of plate was presented to Kemble, Lord Holland presided; on his right hand sat Mr. Kemble, and on his left the Duke of Bedford. Lords Blessington, Erskine, Mulgrave, Aberdeen, Essex, and many other noblemen were present; and among the literary and artistic celebrities were Moore, Campbell, Rogers, Croker, and the great French tragedian, Talma. Lord Blessington assisted also in the well-known Kilkenny theatricals. He took parts which required to be gorgeously appareled; on one occasion, he played the part of *the Green Knight*, in "Valentine and Orson."

The theatricals at Rash lasted from 1808 to 1812. The first Lady Blessington was there during one season, and remained for several months.

The period selected for the theatricals at Rash was usually the shooting season. But the guests were not confined to sportsmen; the latter came occasionally accompanied by their ladies, and what with their field-sports and the stage amusements, there was no dearth of enjoyments and gayety for a few weeks in a place that all the rest of the year was a dull, solitary, lifeless locality, in the midst of a forest some fourscore miles from the metropolis.

The second Lady Blessington did not visit Mountjoy Forest during the period of the theatricals. It was the peculiarity of Lord Blessington to throw himself with complete *abandon* into any passion or pursuit that came in his way, and to spare no expense or sacrifice of any kind to obtain, as soon as possible, the fullest enjoyment that could possibly be derived from it; and no sooner was the object so ardently desired accomplished, the expense encountered, and the sacrifice made for its attainment, than the zest for its delight was gone; other phantoms of pleasure were to be pursued, and no sooner grasped than to be relinquished for some newer objects of desire.

The delights of the chase in Mountjoy Forest, and of the theatre at Rash, after a few years, became dull, tame, and tiresome amusements to the young lord. He went to England, contracted engagements there which led to his making London principally his place of abode, and Mountjoy Forest and the theatre at Rash were allowed to go to ruin.

The Dowager Lady Mountjoy had left Rash, and fixed her abode in Dublin prior to 1807. The house became in a short time so dilapidated as to be unfit to live in. His lordship gave directions to have extensive repairs and additions made to a thatched house of middle size, about a quarter of a mile distant from Rash. The furniture was removed to this place, which Lord Blessington called "the Cottage," and the old home at Rash was left to go to ruin.

When I visited the place recently, nothing remained but some vestiges of the kitchen and the cellars. The theatre had utterly disappeared, and nothing could be more desolate than the site of it. The grounds and garden had been broken up, the trees had been all cut down in the vicinity. Here and there, trunks and branches, yet unremoved, were lying on the ground. The stumps of the felled trees, in the midst of the debris of scattered timber, gave an unpleasant and uncouth aspect to a scene that had some melancholy interest in it for one who had known the noble owner of this vast property.

The extent of the estate appears almost incredible; I am told its extreme length exceeded ten miles.

But though the theatre erected by Lord Blessington on his estate has wholly disappeared, one structure on it exists: a vault beneath the chancel of the church of Cappagh, on the estate, which he intended for his tomb, and which, in several notices of his lordship's death, and some memoirs of Lady Blessington, is erroneously stated to have been the place of sepulture of his remains. I was misled by those accounts, and visited the vault, in the expectation of finding his remains there. But no interment had ever taken place there, though it was constructed by his lordship with the intention above-mentioned; and at his death, orders had been sent down from Dublin to have the vault prepared for his interment: these orders, however, had been countermanded, for what reason I know not, and the remains of his lordship were deposited in St. Thomas's Church, in Marlborough Street, along with the remains of his father.

It has been also erroneously stated that the remains of his lordship's first wife were deposited in the vault beneath the chancel of Cappagh Church; such, however, is not the fact.

In September, 1816, Lord Blessington visited his estate of Mountjoy Forest. His first wife had been then dead nearly two years. He brought down some friends of his from Dublin, and invited others from the neighborhood of his estate to come on a visit to "the Cottage."

Among the guests, I was informed by tenant farmers on the estates who have a recollection of these circumstances, were Mr. Corry, *Major* and Mrs. Purvis, Colonel Stewart of Killymoon, Mrs. Farmer, and also Captain Jenkins.*

The most extravagant expense was gone into in fitting up and decorating the Cottage for some weeks previously to the arrival of his lordship and his guests.

The walls were hung with costly drapery. The stairs and passages were covered with fine baize. Nothing could exceed the elegance of the decorations, and furnishing of an abode that was destined only for a residence of a few weeks.

During the sojourn of Lord Blessington and his friends at the Cottage, several gentlemen of the neighborhood were entertained.

Among the visitors was an old clergyman, Father O'Flagherty, parish priest of Cappagh, a simple-minded, good man, who was the dispenser of the bounty of Lord Blessington among the poor of the estate, long subsequently to this visit, to a very large amount.

Lord Blessington had no sectarian feelings—it never entered his mind what the religion of a man was by whom assistance was needed; and his worthy Roman Catholic almoner, although a man by no means highly cultivated, polished in his manners, or peculiarly happy in his style of epistolary correspondence, en-

* A Capt. Montgomery, of the Navy, a very intimate friend of the Blessingtons, at some period was on a visit to the Cottage, but the precise date I do not know.

joyed the full confidence and strong regard of Lord Blessington, and also of his lady.

Lady Blessington, on her subsequent visit, was the means of procuring for her great favorite, Father O'Flagherty, a donation from his lordship that enabled the good padre either to repair or rebuild the Catholic place of worship of his parish. He continued to correspond with the Blessingtons when they resided in London, and for some time while they were on the Continent, and the epistles of the good old man were very great literary curiosities.

In 1823, Lord Blessington, unaccompanied by Lady Blessington, visited his Tyrone estates; he came to the Cottage accompanied by Colonel Stewart of Killymoon.

In 1825, his lordship again and for the last time visited his Tyrone estates. He was accompanied then by General Count D'Orsay, the father of the Count Alfred D'Orsay, and also by a young French nobleman, the Count Leon.

From some cause or other, Lady Blessington appeared to have formed a strong antipathy, on the occasion of her last visit, to Mountjoy Forest as a place of residence even for a few weeks. She prevailed on Lord Blessington to return to London, perhaps earlier than he had intended, and expressed her determination never again to return to Mountjoy Forest, if she could help it.

After a few weeks spent in Tyrone, the Blessingtons returned to London. The new-married lady, having exchanged her abode in Manchester Square for the noble mansion in St. James's Square, found herself suddenly, as if by the magic wand of an enchanter, surrounded by luxuries, gorgeous furniture, glittering ornaments, and pomp and state almost regal. The transition was at once from seclusion and privacy, a moderate establishment, and inexpensive mode of life, into brilliant society, magnificence, and splendor—to a condition, in short, little inferior to that of any lady in the land.

The *éclat* of the beauty of Lady Blessington and of her remarkable mental qualities, of the rare gifts and graces with which she was so richly endowed, was soon extensively diffused over the metropolis.

Moore, in his Diary of April, 1822, mentions visiting the Blessingtons in London at their mansion in St. James's Square. The fifth of the month following, he says he called, with Washington Irving, at Lady Blessington's, " who is growing very absurd! 'I have felt very melancholy and ill all this day,' she said. 'Why is that?' I asked. 'Don't you know?' 'No.' 'It is the anniversary of my poor Napoleon's death.'"

Any one acquainted with Lady Blessington will perceive in this remark a great want of knowledge of her character and opinions, and will not fail to discover in her observation evidences of that peculiar turn for grave irony which was one of her characteristics. I have seldom met a literary person so entirely free from all affectation of sentimentality as Lady Blessington.

In the new scenes of splendor and brilliancy which her ladyship had been introduced into on her marriage with Lord Blessington, she seemed as if it was her own proper atmosphere, to which she had been accustomed from infancy, in which she now lived and moved.

Greatness and magnificence were not thrust upon her—she seemed born to them. In all positions she had the great art of being ever perfectly at home. There was a naturalness in her demeanor, a grace and gentleness in her mind and manner—a certain kindliness of disposition and absence of all affectation—a noble frankness about her, which left her in all circles at her ease—sure of pleasing, and easily amused by agreeable and clever people.

In 1818, when Lady Blessington was launched into fashionable life, and all at once took her place, if not at the head of it, at least among the foremost people in it, she was twenty-eight years of age.

For three years, her mansion in St. James's Square, nightly thronged by men of distinction, was the centre of social and literary enjoyments of the highest order in London. Holland House had its attractions for the graver spirits of the times, but there was no lack of statesmen, sages, scholars, and politicians at the conversaziones of Lady Blessington.

Charleville House, too, had its charms for well-established authors—for blue-stocking ladies especially, of all lines of authorship—for distinguished artists and noble amateurs, for foreign ministers and their attaches.

But Lady Blessington had certain advantages over all *Aspasian* competitors in society—she was young and beautiful, witty, graceful, and good-humored; and these advantages told with singular effect in the salon; they tended largely to establish her influence in society, and to acquire for her conversations in it a character it might never otherwise have obtained.

The Blessingtons' splendid mansion in St. James's Square in a short time became the rendezvous of the *élite* of London celebrities of all kinds of distinction; the first literati, statesmen, artists, eminent men of all professions, in a short time became habitual visitors at the abode of the new-married lord and lady.

Among the distinguished foreigners who visited the Blessingtons in St. James's Square in the latter part of 1821 or the commencement of 1822, were the Count de Grammont (the present Duc de Guiche) and his brother-in-law, a young Frenchman of remarkable symmetry of form and comeliness of face, and of address and manners singularly prepossessing, the Count Alfred D'Orsay, then in the prime of life, highly gifted, and of varied accomplishments, truly answering Byron's designation of him, a "*cupidon déchainé.*" The count's sojourn in London at that time was short; but the knowledge he seems to have gained of its society, if the account given of his diary be true, must have been considerable. This was the beginning of an intimate acquaintance with the Blessingtons, one in many respects of great moment to his lordship and to others—an intimacy which terminated only in death.*

Two royal English dukes condescended, not unfrequently, to do homage at the new shrine of Irish beauty and intellect in St. James's Square. Canning, Lord Castlereagh, the Marquis of Lansdowne, and Lords Palmerston and Russell, Burdett and Brougham, Scarlett and Jekyll, Erskine, and many other celebrities, paid their devoirs there. Whig and Tory politicians and

* This acquaintance did not commence, as it has been generally asserted, by accident, in a French hotel, when the Blessingtons were on their way to Italy.

lawyers, forgetful of their party feuds and professional rivalries for the nonce, came there as gentle pilgrims. Kemble and Matthews, Lawrence and Wilkie—eminent divines too, Dr. Parr and others. Rogers, Moore, and Luttrel were among the votaries who paid their vows in visits there, not angel-like, for theirs were neither "few nor far between." But among all the distinguished persons who visited Lady Blessington, none were more *devoués* in their attachment, or ardent in their admiration of the talents and traits, intellectual and personal, of the fair lady, than the late Earl Grey.

CHAPTER II.

DEPARTURE OF THE BLESSINGTONS FROM LONDON ON A CONTINENTAL TOUR, SEPTEMBER, 1822.

The love of change, of travel, of excitement—the necessity for distraction, for novelty, and new effects, not only in scenery, but in society, seems to have led to Lord Blessington's determination to abandon his magnificent abode in St. James's Square at a time when nothing appeared wanting that wealth, beauty, and brilliant society could supply, to render that abode every thing that could be desired by those who think such necessaries all that can be desirable to make homes happy.

But Lord Blessington, although yet a young man, had drained his cup of pleasure and enjoyments of every kind to the dregs, and the taste of the draught that remained on his palate required new cordials, and other stimulants of increasing strength continually, to keep down the loathing he already felt for all the allurements of fashion, the follies of the day, the foil and tinsel glories of the green-room, and the life behind the scenes of the drama, and of that other theatre of society, with its *tableaux vivants*, and its varied performances by the real actors on the stage of aristocratic life. Lord Blessington was palled and satiated with pleasure, and no kind of *éclat* or of distinction in English society had now any charm for him. And yet this young nobleman, thus early *blazé* and exhausted, prematurely impaired in mental energies, was fitted for better things, and was naturally amiable, and possessed many eminent qualities which might have rendered him, under other circumstances of education and position, a most estimable and a very useful man to his country and to society.

The 22d of August, 1822, the Blessingtons, accompanied by Miss Mary Ann Power, the youngest sister of Lady Blessington, and Mr. Charles James Matthews, the only son of the celebrated comedian, set out on a Continental tour, and made their arrangements for an intended sojourn of some years in the south of Europe.

Miss Mary Ann Power was then about one-and-twenty, bearing no resemblance to her sister in face or form, but, nevertheless, far from unattractive. She was remarkably slight, rather of low stature, of small, regular features, good complexion, light brown hair, always tastefully arranged; an extremely pretty and girlish-looking young lady, with bluish laughing eyes, and altogether a piquant expression of countenance, *une petite mignon*, pleasingly original and *naïve* in her modes of thinking and acting, always courted and complimented in society, and coquetted with by gentlemen of a certain age, by humorists in single blessedness, especially like Gell, and by old married bachelors like Landor and the Duke Laval de Montmorency.

Charles Matthews could hardly then have been twenty years of age. He had been intended for the profession of an architect, and was articled to a person of eminence in London in that profession. Lord Blessington had kindly offered his father to take charge of the young man, and to afford him every facility of pursuing his professional studies in Italy. That offer was accepted, and for upward of two years young Matthews remained with the Blessingtons on the Continent, and was no slight acquisition to their party. A merrier man within the limits of becoming mirth it would be difficult to find. He was an admirable mimic, had a marvelous facility in catching peculiarities of manners, picking up the different dialects of the several parts of Italy he passed through. But with all his comic talents, love of fun and frolic, ludicrous fancies, and overflowing gayety of heart, he never ceased to be a gentleman, and to act and feel like a man well-bred, well-disposed, and well-principled.

The writer's reminiscences of Charles Matthews are of an old date—upward of thirty years; but they are of too pleasurable a kind to be easily effaced.

In her journals Lady Blessington makes frequent allusions to her "happy home" in St. James's Square, and at the moment of departure, of "the almost wish" she was not going from it; and some dismal forebodings take the form of exclamations: "What changes! what dangers may come before I again sleep beneath its roof!" Many changes, indeed, came before she returned from the Continent. She never beheld her husband beneath that roof again!

Lord Blessington's preparations in Paris for the approaching touring *campaign* in Italy were of a very formidable description. The commissariat department (including the culinary) was amply provided for; it could boast of a *batterie de cuisine* on a most extensive scale, which had served an entire club, and a cook who had stood fire in the kitchen of an emperor. No Irish nobleman, probably, and certainly no Irish king, ever set out on his travels with such a retinue of servants, with so many vehicles and appliances of all kinds to ease, comfort, and luxurious enjoyment in travel.

Byron's traveling equipage, according to Medwin, when he arrived in Florence, accompanied by Rogers, consisted of seven servants, five carriages, five horses, a monkey, a bull-dog, and a mastiff, nine live cats, three pea-fowls, and some hens; his luggage, or what Cæsar would call "his impedimenta," consisted of "a very large library of modern books, a vast quantity of furniture," with trunks and portmanteaus of apparel—of course to correspond to the other parts of the equipage.

Lord Blessington set out with an abundance of "impediments;" but in his live-stock he had no bull-dogs, mastiffs, monkeys, cats, pea-fowls, or hens.

On her arrival in Paris, Lady Blessington mentions in her diary receiving a visit from her old friend the Baron Denon, and finding "all her French acquaintances charmed to see her."

Mention is made of two previous visits of hers to Paris. Her former sojourn there must have been of some duration, and previously to her second marriage; in her letters of this period we find a familiarity with French idiom, and the conversational terms of French society, which could only have been acquired by a good deal of intercourse with French people in their own country.

In her Italian journal of the 31st of August, 1822, she speaks of her "old friend the baron," "a most amusing man," "a compound of *savant* and *petit maitre*, one moment descanting on Egyptian antiquities, and the next passing eulogiums on the *joli chapeau*, or robe of his female visitors, who seems equally at home in detailing the perfections of a mummy, or in describing 'le mignon pied d' une charmante femme,' and not unfrequently turns from exhibiting some *morceau d' antiquite bien remarquable* to display a cast of the exquisite head of Pauline Borghese."*

September 1st, the diary opens with the words "my birthday." Her ladyship could be sad and sentimental, but is obliged to smile and seem joyful at receiving the congratulations of her friends that she had added another year to her age, and at a period of woman's life, too, when one had passed thirty.

During the short sojourn of the Blessingtons in Paris, Tom Moore was frequently with them at a restaurateur's: Lady Blessington descended "La Montagne Russe;" but then Tom Moore often visited the spot, and greatly enjoyed her descent, and it was pleasant to observe with what a true zest he entered into every scheme of amusement, though the buoyancy of his spirits and resources of his mind rendered him so independent of such means of passing time.† Lady Blessington descants on the agreeable excitement of the extreme velocity of this locomotive amusement; but we need not marvel at Tom Moore's true zest in entering into it, accompanied with her ladyship, when we find Dr. Johnson dwelling on the enjoyment of traveling fast in a post-chaise with a pretty woman among the great pleasures of life.

Perhaps it was one of those rapid journeys on the "Montagne

* The Idler in Italy, Par. ed., 1839, p. 8. † Ibid., p. 28.

Russe," that Moore's conversation reminded her ladyship "of the evolutions of some bird of gorgeous plumage, each varied hue of which becomes visible as he carelessly sports in the air."

In her observations on art, literature, and society, there are ample evidences of originality of mind, of true feeling, of refined taste, and an intimate acquaintance with the light literature of France and Italy. Many of her passing remarks have the merit of those short and memorable sayings which get the name of maxims and apothegms. Speaking of the Louvre, which she had visited "at least thirty times," and that was her third visit to Paris, she found, "like fine music, fine sculptures and fine pictures gain by long acquaintance."

"There is something that stirs the soul and elevates the feelings in gazing on those glorious productions of master minds, where genius has left its ineffaceable impress to bear witness to posterity of its achievements.".........

The excellence of art, like every thing that is exquisite in workmanship and spiritual in conception, is to be appreciated by an intuitive sense, that gives a true perception of the sublime and beautiful; "it is to be felt, and not reasoned upon."

In the galleries of the Louvre, she sickens of the "cant of criticism," she turns away from the connoisseurs, "to meditate in silence on what others can talk about, but can not comprehend."

"Here Claude Lorraine, seems to have imprisoned on canvas the golden sunshine in which he bathes his landscapes. There Raphael makes us, *though stern Protestants*, worship a Madonna and child, such is the innocence, sweetness, and beauty with which he has imbued his subjects."

Poor Lady Blessington's "stern Protestantism" is lugged in, head and shoulders, into a criticism which really stood in no need of the intrusion of any religious opinions. Her faith in Raphael's perfections required no apology. In qualifying her admiration of the exquisite portraiture of innocence, sweetness, and beauty of the Virgin and child, it must have been rather painful to her (not a Protestant) to have to descend to the cant of criticism, which was so justly odious to her.

While the fair countess was absorbed in art, and occupied

with the sublime and beautiful, in the most glorious works of the ancient masters in the Louvre and the gallery of Versailles, my lord was securing the services of the culinary artist of great celebrity, already referred to, who had been the cook of an emperor, and providing a very extensive *batterie de cuisine*—a complete equipage of a cooking kind, *en ambulance*, for their Italian tour.

After a sojourn of twelve days in Paris, the Blessingtons and their party set out for Switzerland.

The customary pilgrimages were made to Ferney, the many shrines at the base of Mount Jura, on the borders of the Lake of Geneva, the birth-place and haunts of Rousseau, the homes for a time of Gibbon, Shelley, Byron, and De Staël, then the place of abode of John Philip Kemble, and a little later, his place of burial in the cemetery of Lausanne. Several days were spent in visiting monuments and other marvels of Lyons, Vienne, Grenoble, Valence, Orange, and on the 20th of November they arrived at Avignon. Here they remained till the 12th of February, 1823, mixing a good deal in the fashionable circles of the town and its environs, making frequent excursions to the celebrated fountain of Vanclure, the site of the chateau of Laura, and visiting that of her tomb, in the ruins of the Church of the Cordeliers, those of the Palace of the Popes, and the Inquisition with all its horrors. Lady Blessington speaks of the repugnance, the feelings of "a native of dear, free, happy England," at the sight of such a place, and in the heat of her abhorrence of the crimes committed in it, fancies herself a native of England.

In her diary of the 20th of December, Lady Blessington says, "Spent last evening at Madame de C.'s; met there the Duc and Duchess de C—— G——. Madame was dame d'honneur to Marie Louise, and has all the air and manner of one accustomed to find herself at home in a court."

The persons indicated by the initials C—— G—— were the Duc and Duchesse de Caderousse Grammont, who then resided in their chateau in the vicinity of Avignon. But no mention is made of any other member of their family in the Avignon society of the Blessingtons, though there was one who was an object of some interest to the party.

After a prolonged stay of two months and upward at Avignon, Lady Blessington says in her diary, "It is strange how soon one becomes habituated to a place. I really feel as much at home at Avignon as if I had spent years there."

On the 12th of February, 1823, Lady Blessington and her party, increased by a young Frenchman of a noble family, previously known in England, lately met with in Paris, and subsequently at Valence and Avignon, now a compagnon de voyage, set out for Italy, via Marseilles, Toulon, and Nice, and on the 31st of March they arrived at Genoa.

In the diary of that day, the uppermost thought in Lady Blessington's mind is thus recorded: "And am I, indeed, in the same town with Byron! And to-morrow I may perhaps behold him!"

There are two works of Lady Blessington's, "the Idler in Italy"* and "the Idler in France,"† in which an account is given of her tours, and her observations on the society, manners, scenery, and marvels of all kinds of the several places she visited and sojourned in.

CHAPTER III.

BYRON AND THE BLESSINGTONS AT GENOA.

The 1st of April, 1823, Lady Blessington's strong desire was gratified—she saw Byron. But the lady was disappointed, and there is reason to believe that the lord, always indisposed abroad to make new acquaintances with his countrymen or women, was on the occasion of this interview taken by surprise, and not so highly gratified by it as might have been expected, when the

* The Idler in Italy, in 3 vols. 8vo, was published in 1839, and is descriptive of her visit to Paris, and sojourn there from the first of September to the 12th of the same month, 1822; her route through Switzerland, and extensive tour in Italy, extended over a period of five years, the greater portion of which was spent in Naples.

† The Idler in France, subsequently published, is descriptive of her residence in Paris for a period of two years and a half, from the autumn of 1828 to the end of November, 1830, when she returned to England.

In her manuscript memoranda and commonplace books there are also frequent references to persons whom she had met with in her travels, and observations on places she had visited, several of which are almost identical with passages in "the Idlers."

agrèmens and personal attractions of the lady are taken into consideration.

Lady Blessington's expression of disappointment has a tincture of asperity in it which is seldom, indeed, to be found in her observations. There are very evident appearances of annoyance of some kind or another in the account given by her of this interview, occasioned either by the reception given her by Byron, or at some eccentricity, or absence of mind, that was unexpected, or apparent want of homage on his part to her beauty or talents on this occasion, to which custom had habituated her.

It must also be observed, that the interview with her ladyship is described as having been sought by Lord Byron. It is more than probable, however, a little ruse was practiced on his lordship to obtain it. It is stated by one who has a good knowledge of all the circumstances of this visit, that a rainy forenoon was selected for the drive to Byron's villa; that shelter was necessitated, and that necessity furnished a plea for a visit which would not have been without some awkwardness under other circumstances. Lord Blessington, having been admitted at once on presenting himself at Byron's door, was on the point of taking his departure, apologizing for the briefness of the visit on account of Lady Blessington being left in an open carriage in the court-yard, the rain then falling, when Byron immediately insisted on descending with Lord Blessington, and conducting her ladyship into his house.

"When we arrived," says Lady Blessington, "at the gate of the court-yard of the Casa Saluzzo, in the village of Albano,* where he resides, Lord Blessington and a *gentleman of our party* left the carriage and sent in their names.† They were admitted immediately, and experienced a very cordial reception from Lord Byron, who expressed himself delighted to see his old acquaintance. Byron requested to be presented to me, which led to Lord Blessington's avowing that I was in the carriage at the gate, with my sister. Byron immediately hurried out into the

* About a mile and a half from Genoa.—R. R. M.

† The gentleman's name will be found in a letter of Byron to Moore, dated 2d April, 1823.

court, and I, who heard the sound of steps, looked through the gate, and beheld him approaching quickly toward the carriage without his hat, and considerably in advance of the other two gentlemen."

The visit was a long one; and many questions were asked about old friends and acquaintances. Lady Blessington says Byron expressed warmly, at their departure, the pleasure which the visit had afforded him—and she doubted not his sincerity; not that she would arrogate any merit in her party to account for his satisfaction, but simply because she could perceive that Byron liked to hear news of his old associates, and to pass them *en revue*, pronouncing sarcasms on each as he turned up in conversation.

In a previous notice of this interview, which bears some internal evidence of having been written long after the period it refers to, lamenting over the disappointment she felt at finding her beau ideal of a poet by no means realized, her ladyship observes: "Well, I never will allow myself to form an ideal of any person I desire to see, for disappointment never fails to ensue."

Byron, she admits, had more than usual personal attractions, "but his appearance nevertheless had fallen short of her expectations." There is no commendation, however, without a concomitant effort at depreciation. For example, her ladyship observes, "His laugh is musical, but he rarely indulged in it during our interview; and when he did, it was quickly followed by a graver aspect, as if he liked not this exhibition of hilarity. Were I asked to point out the prominent defect of Byron's manner, I should pronounce it to be a flippancy incompatible with the notion we attach to the author of Childe Harold and Manfred, and a want of self-possession and dignity that ought to characterize a man of birth and genius. Notwithstanding this defect, his manners are very fascinating—more so, perhaps, than if they were dignified; but he is too gay, too flippant for a poet."*

Lady Blessington was accompanied on this occasion by her

* Idler in Italy, p. 392.

sister, Miss Mary Anne Power, now Comtesse de St. Marsault. Byron, in a letter to Moore, dated April 2d, 1823, thus refers to this interview:

"Your other allies, whom I have found very agreeable personages, are Milor Blessington and *épouse*, traveling with a very handsome companion in the shape of a 'French count' (to use Farquhar's phrase in the Beaux Stratagem), who has all the air of a Cupidon *déchainé*, and is one of the few specimens I have seen of our ideal of a Frenchman *before* the Revolution, an old friend with a new face, upon whose like I never thought that we should look again. Miladi seems highly literary, to which, and your honor's acquaintance with the family, I attribute the pleasure of having seen them. She is also very pretty, even in a morning—a species of beauty on which the sun of Italy does not shine so frequently as the chandelier. Certainly English women wear better than their Continental neighbors of the same sex. Mountjoy seems very good-natured, but is much tamed since I recollect him in all the glory of gems and snuff-boxes, and uniform, and theatricals, and speeches in our house—'I mean of Peers'—I must refer you to Pope, whom you don't read and won't appreciate, for that quotation (which you must allow to be poetical)—and sitting to Stroelling, the painter (do you remember our visit, with Leckie, to the German?), to be depicted as one of the heroes of Agincourt, 'with his long sword, saddle, bridle, Whak fal de," &c., &c.

We thus find, from the letter of Byron to his friend Moore, that the Blessingtons were accompanied by the Count Alfred d'Orsay in their visit to his lordship, and that he was one of the party on their arrival and at their departure from Genoa.

It is probable that the arrangements for the count's journey to Italy with the Blessingtons had been made in Paris, though he did not accompany them from that city, but joined them first at Valence on the Rhone, and subsequently at Avignon.

D'Orsay, who had been attached to the French army of the pretended expedition against Spain, abandoned his profession in an evil hour for the career of a mere man of pleasure and of fashion.

Byron and the Blessingtons continued to live on the most intimate terms, we are told by Lady Blessington, during the stay of the latter at Genoa; and that intimacy had such a happy influence on the author of Childe Harold, that he began to abandon his misanthropy. On the other hand, I am assured by the Marquise de Boissy, formerly Countess of Guiccioli, that the number of visits of Byron to Lady Blessington during the entire period of her sojourn in Genoa did not exceed five or six at the utmost, and that Byron was by no means disposed to afford the opportunities that he believed were sought, to enable a lady of a literary turn to write about him. But D'Orsay, she adds, at the first interview, had struck Byron as a person of considerable talents and wonderful acquirements for a man of his age and former pursuits. "Byron from the first liked D'Orsay; he was clever, original, unpretending; he affected to be nothing that he was not."

Byron sat for his portrait to D'Orsay, that portrait which subsequently appeared in the New Monthly Magazine, and afterward as a frontispiece of her ladyship's work, "Conversations with Lord Byron."

His lordship suffered Lady Blessington to lecture him in prose, and, what was worse, in verse. He endeavored to persuade Lord Blessington to prolong his stay in Genoa, and to take a residence adjoining his own named "Il Paradiso." And a rumor of his intention to take the place for himself, and some good-natured friend observing, "Il diavolo è ancora entrato in Paradiso," his lordship wrote the following lines:

> Beneath Blessington's eyes
> The reclaimed Paradise
> Should be free as the former from evil;
> But if the new Eve
> For an apple should grieve,
> What mortal would not play the devil?

But the original conceit was not in poetry.

Lady Blessington informed me that, on the occasion of a masked ball to be given in Genoa, Byron stated his intention of going there, and asked her ladyship to accompany him: *en badinant* about the character she was to go in, some one had suggested that of Eve—Byron said, "As some one must play the devil, I will do it."

Shortly before her departure from Genoa, Lady Blessington requested Byron to write some lines in her album, and, accordingly, he composed the following stanzas for her:

TO THE COUNTESS OF BLESSINGTON.

1.

You have ask'd for a verse: the request
In a rhymer 'twere strange to deny;
But my Hippocrene was but my breast,
And my feelings (its fountain) are dry.

2.

Were I now as I was, I had sung
What Lawrence has painted so well;
But the strain would expire on my tongue,
And the theme is too soft for my shell.

3.

I am ashes where once I was fire,
And the bard in my bosom is dead;
What I loved I now merely admire,
And my heart is as gray as my head.

4.

My life is not dated by years—
There are moments which act as a plow;
And there is not a furrow appears,
But is deep in my soul as my brow.

5.

Let the young and the brilliant aspire
To sing what I gaze on in vain;
For sorrow has torn from my lyre
The string which was worthy the strain.

Moore speaks of the happy influence of Lady Blessington's society over the mind of Byron:

"One of the most important services conferred upon Lord Byron by Lady Blessington during this intimacy was that half reviving of his old regard for his wife, and the check which she contrived to place upon the composition of Don Juan, and upon the continuation of its most glaring immoralities. He spoke of Ada; her mother, he said, 'has feasted on the smiles of her infancy and growth, but the tears of her maturity shall be mine.' Lady Blessington told him that if he so loved his child, he should never write a line that could bring a blush of shame to her cheek, or a sorrowing tear to her eye; and he said, 'You are right; I never recollected this. I am jealously tenacious of the undivided sympathy of my daughter; and that work (Don Juan), written to beguile hours of *tristesse* and wretchedness, is well calculated to loosen my hold on her affections. I will write no more of it—would that I had never written a line.' In this gentler mind, with old loves, old times, and the tenderest love that human heart can know, all conducing to soothe his pride and his dislike of Lady Byron, he learned that a near friend of her ladyship was in Genoa, and he requested Lady Blessington to procure for him, through this friend, a portrait of his wife. He had heard that Lady Byron feared he was about to come to England for the purpose of claiming his child. In requesting the portrait and in refuting the report, he addressed the following letter to Lady Blessington:

"'May 3, 1823.

"'Dear Lady Blessington,—My request would be for a copy of the miniature of Lady B. which I have seen in possession of the late Lady Noel, as I have no picture, or indeed memorial of any kind of Lady B., as all her letters were in her own possession before I left England, and we have had no correspondence since—at least on her part. My message with regard to the infant is simply to this effect, that in the event of any accident occurring to the mother, and my remaining the survivor, it would be my wish to have her plans carried into effect, both with regard to the education of the child, and the person or persons under whose care Lady B. might be desirous that she should be placed. It is not my intention to interfere with her in any way on the subject during her life; and I presume that it would be some consolation to her to know (if she is in ill health, as I am given to understand), that in *no* case would any thing be done, as far as I am concerned, but in strict conformity with Lady B.'s own wishes and intentions, left in what manner she thought proper. Believe me, dear Lady B., your obliged,'" &c.

At length, in the early part of June, 1823, the Blessingtons took their departure from Genoa, and Moore tells us how the separation affected Byron:

"On the evening before the departure of his friends, Lord and Lady Blessington, from Genoa, he called upon them for the purpose of taking leave, and sat conversing for some time. He was evidently in low spirits, and after expressing his regret that they should leave Genoa before his own time of sailing, proceeded to speak of his own intended voyage in a tone full of despondence. 'Here,' said he, 'we are all now together; but when, and where, shall we meet again? I have a sort of boding that we see each other for the last time; as something tells me I shall never again return from Greece.' Having continued a little longer in this melancholy strain, he leaned his head upon the arm of the sofa on which they were seated, and, bursting into tears, wept for some minutes with uncontrollable feeling. Though he had been talking only with Lady Blessington, all who were present in the room observed, and were affected by, his emotion, while he himself, apparently ashamed of his weakness, endeavored to turn off attention from it by some ironical remark, spoken with a sort of hysterical laugh, upon the effects of nervousness. He had, previous to this conversation, presented to each of the party some little farewell gift—a book to one, a print from his bust by Bartolini to another, and to Lady Blessington a copy of his Armenian Grammar, which had some manuscript remarks of his own on the leaves. In now parting with her, having begged, as a memorial, some trifle which she had worn, the lady gave him one of her rings; in return for which he took a pin from his breast, containing a small cameo of Napoleon, which he said had long been his companion, and presented it to her ladyship. The next day Lady Blessington received from him the following note:

"'Albaro, June 2, 1823.

"'My dear Lady Blessington,—I am *superstitious*, and have recollected that memorials with a *point* are of less fortunate augury: I will, therefore, request you to accept, instead of the *pin*, the inclosed chain, which is of so slight a value that you need not hesitate. As you wished for something *worn*, I can only say that it has been *worn* oftener and longer than the other. It is of Venetian manufacture, and the only peculiarity about it is that it could only be obtained at or from Venice. At Genoa they have none of the same kind. I also inclose a ring, which I would wish *Alfred* to keep; it is too large to *wear;* but it is formed of *lava*, and so far adapted to the fire of his years and character. You will perhaps have the goodness to acknowledge the receipt of this note, and send back the pin (for good luck's sake), which I shall value much more for having been a night in your custody.

" 'Ever faithfully your obliged, &c.

" 'P.S.—I hope your *nerves* are well to-day, and will continue to flourish.' "

Some fourteen years only had elapsed since that criticism appeared in the Edinburgh Review on his (Byron's) juvenile poems, which began with these words: "The poesy of this young lord belongs to the class which neither gods nor men are said to tolerate."

And in the interval between the date of the publication of "English Bards and Scotch Reviewers" in 1809, and that of the visit of the Blessingtons to Genoa in June, 1823, and his departure for Greece a little later, the poesy of the young lord manifested to the world that it belonged to a class which all the powers of criticism could not decry or crush. A few months only had elapsed since Byron parted with Lady Blessington and bade adieu to Italy, and the career of the poet was near its close in Greece.

In 1828, again at Genoa, Lady Blessington, alluding to Byron's death, writes: "I sat on the chair where I had formerly been seated next him; looked from the window whence he had pointed out a beautiful view; and listened to Mr. Barry's graphic description of the scene, when, becalmed in the Gulf of Genoa, the day he sailed for Greece, he returned and walked through the rooms of his deserted dwelling, filled with melancholy forebodings. He had hoped to have found in it *her* whom he was destined never more to behold—that fair and young Italian lady, the Contessa Guiccioli—whose attachment to him had triumphed over every sentiment of prudence and interest, and by its devotion and constancy half redeemed its sin. But she, overwhelmed by grief at the sad parting, had been placed in a traveling carriage while almost in a state of insensibility, and was journeying toward Bologna, little conscious that he whom she would have given all she possessed on earth to see once more was looking on the chamber she had left and the flowers she had loved, his mind filled with a presentiment that they should never meet again.

"*Such is one of the bitter consequences resulting from the violation of ties never severed without retribution.*"*

Lady Blessington's feelings of regard for Byron's memory were by no means such as might have been desired.

Moore's sentiments with respect to the reputation of his departed friend were not altogether those which might have been expected.

Campbell's feelings in relation to the fame of a brother bard, who had only recently been a living rival, were those which some who knew him well always feared they would prove; they were something more than merely cold and unkindly—they were passionately inimical. At a period when most other literary men who ever had an acquaintance with Byron, or sympathy with his literary pursuits, would have avoided entering into a controversy with his enemies, and espousing the views of his opponents, Campbell with avidity seized an opportunity of rushing into print to wound the reputation of a brother bard, whose fame during his lifetime he might not with impunity have assailed. A periodical of the time, commenting on this ill-advised proceeding, observed: "This strange matter has now assumed another and a darker shade from the interference of Mr. Campbell, who, assuming to be the personal champion of Lady Byron, has stepped forward to throw the most odious imputations upon the character of Lord Byron which can possibly be left to the worst imaginations to conceive. Against this course we protest, in the name of all that is honorable in human nature. We were the undeviating censurers of the poet's injurious productions during his lifetime; but we can not do otherwise than condemn, in far stronger terms, any attempt, after he is laid in his grave, to blast him forever by mysterious and voiceless whisperings. Of what monstrous crime was he guilty? for, unless he was guilty of some monstrous crime, a foul wrong is done to his memory. His accusers are bound by every moral and sacred tie to be definite in their charge: against such there is a possi-

* The Idler in Italy, vol. iii., p. 365.

bility of defense; but there can be no shield against the horribly vague denunciation which has been so intemperately hurled at the unprotected and unanswering dead. And what called this forth? A very slight surmise by Mr. Moore against the parents of Lady Byron; to repel which, she comes rashly out with a statement that damns the husband of her bosom; and, as if this were not enough, the zeal of Mr. Campbell advances to pour additional suspicion and ignominy upon his mouldering ashes. The fame of a Byron is public property; and, after what has passed, it is imperative on his adversaries either to fix some eternal brand upon it, such as can justify their language, or confess that they have used expressions which no conduct of his could authorize. And we are persuaded that they must do the latter; for it is incredible that any woman of the spirit and honor of Lady Byron could have lived an hour with a man whom she knew to be a detested criminal, and far less that she should have corresponded with him in playful and soothing letters. The plea of insanity itself can not reconcile this with any thing like the atrocious guilt now by circumstance imputed; and we do earnestly trust that an explanation will be vouchsafed, which will set this painful discussion at rest in a manner more satisfactory to the world. Having, in these few remarks, grappled with the main point at issue, we abstain from saying a syllable on minor affairs; and we do not deem ourselves in a condition to blame any one of the parties we have been obliged to name."*

Lord Byron's yacht, "the Bolivar," was purchased by Lord Blessington previously to his departure from Genoa, and it was subsequently considered by Lady Blessington that the poet drove a hard bargain with her husband.

Medwin, however, as a proof of Byron's lavish and inconsiderate expenditure, and his incongruity of action in regard to money matters, states that he gave £1000 for a yacht which he sold for £300, and yet refused to give the sailors their jackets.

The 2d of June, 1823, the Blessingtons set out from Genoa for Naples, via Lucca, Florence, Vienna, and Rome; took their departure from the Eternal City the 13th of the same month, and arrived at Naples on the 17th.

* Literary Gazette.

CHAPTER IV.

THE CITY AND BAY OF NAPLES.—THE BLESSINGTONS AND THEIR SOCIETY IN NAPLES.—JUNE, 1823, TO FEBRUARY, 1826.

JUNE 2d (1823), the Blessingtons left Genoa, and passed through Lucca, where they stayed a few days, and arrived in Florence on the 8th of the same month. Here they remained till the 1st of July. Lady Blessington spent her whole time visiting monuments of antiquity, churches, galleries, villas, and palaces, associated with great names and memories. In no city in Italy did she find her thoughts carried back to the past so forcibly as at Florence. A thousand recollections of the olden time of the merchant princes, the Medici, and the Pazzi—of all the factions of the republic, the Neri and Bianchi, the Guelphs and Ghibellines, recurred to memory in her various visits to the different localities of celebrity in the noble city, the grandeur and beauty of which far surpassed her expectations. After a sojourn of about three weeks in Florence, the party set out for Rome. On the 5th of July, the first view of the Eternal City burst on the pilgrims from St. James's Square.

As they entered the city, the lone mother of dead empires, all appeared wrapped in silent solemnity, not wanting, however, in sublimity. "Even the distant solitude of the Campagna," says Lady Blessington, "was not divested of the latter. But in the evening the Corso was crowded with showy equipages, occupied by gayly-dressed ladies, and thronged with cavaliers on prancing steeds riding past them. Nothing could surpass the gayety of the evening scene, or contrast more strangely with the gloom of the morning aspect of the sombre suburbs."

The mournful contemplations awakened by the ruins of ancient Rome are frequently spoken of by Lady Blessington.

I can not help thinking they were of too mournful a character for her ladyship to make that city of the dead, of shattered thrones and temples, of shrines and sepulchres, a place of abode congenial to her feelings, tastes, and predilections.

The Eternal City and its everlasting monuments appear to have made less impression on the mind of Lady Blessington than might have been expected by those acquainted with her refined tastes and literary acquirements.

The gloom of the sombre monumental city seemed oppressive to her spirits; the solemn aspect of the sites of palaces renowned of old, and those sermons in stones of crumbling monuments, and all the remaining vestiges of a people, and their idols of long past ages, speaking to the inmost soul of decay and destructibility, were not in accordance with her turn of mind, and her natural taste for objects and scenery that exhilarated the senses, and communicated joyousness to every faculty. Naples, in Lady Blessington's opinion, and not Rome, was the appropriate locality for an elysium that was to last forever, and for any sojourn of English tourists of *haut ton* that was intended to be prolonged for the enjoyment of Italian skies and sunshine, scenery and society.

On the 14th of July, nine days after her arrival in Rome, Lady Blessington writes in her diary, "Left Rome yesterday, driven from it by oppressive heat, and the evil prophecies dinned into my ears of the malaria. I have no fears of the effect of either for myself, but I dare not risk them for others."

There were other circumstances besides those referred to, in all probability, which determined the precipitate departure from Rome. All the appliances to comfort, or rather to luxury, which had become necessary to Lady Blessington, had not been found in Rome. Her ladyship had become exceedingly fastidious in her tastes. The difficulties of pleasing her in house accommodation, in dress, in cookery especially, had become so formidable, and occasioned so many inconveniences, that the solicitude spoken of for the safety of others was only one of the reasons for the abrupt departure referred to.

With the strongest regard for Lady Blessington, and the fullest appreciation of the many good qualities that belonged to her, it can not be denied that, whether discoursing in her salons, or talking with pen in hand on paper in her journals, she occasionally aimed at something like stage effects, acted in society and in her diaries, and at times assumed opinions, which she abandoned a little later, or passed off appearances for realities. This was done with the view of acquiring esteem, strengthening her position in the opinion of persons of exalted intellect or station, and directing attention to the side of it that was brilliant and apparently enviable, not for any unworthy purpose, but from a desire to please, and perhaps from a feeling of uncertainty in the possession of present advantages.

The first impressions of Lady Blessington of the beauty of the environs of Naples, the matchless site of the city, its glorious bay, its celebrated garden, the Villa Reale, its delightful climate, and exquisite tints of sea and sky, and varied aspect of shore and mountain, of isles and promontories, are described by her, in her diaries, in very glowing terms.

Her hotel, the Gran Bretagna, fronted the sea, and was only divided from it by the garden of the Villa Reale, filled with plants and flowers, and adorned with statues and vases. The sea was seen sparkling through the openings of the trees, with numbers of boats gliding along the shore. In the "Idler in Italy," Lady Blessington thus speaks of the delightful climate and its cheering influences:

"How light and elastic is the air! Respiration is carried on unconsciously, and existence becomes a positive pleasure in such a climate. Who that has seen Naples can wonder that her children are idle, and luxuriously disposed? To gaze on the cloudless sky and blue Mediterranean, in an atmosphere so pure and balmy, is enough to make the veriest plodder who ever courted Plutus abandon his toil, and enjoy the delicious *dolce far' niente* of the Neapolitans."*

A few words of this epitome of Paradise may be permitted to one who enjoyed its felicity of clime, and site, and scenery for upward of three years.

The city of Naples retains no vestiges of Greek or Roman antiquity. It occupies the site of two ancient Greek towns, Palæ-

* The Idler in Italy, p. 244. Par. ed., 1839.

opolis, founded by Parthenope, and Neapolis, or the New Town. Eventually they merged into one city, which became a portion of the Roman Empire, and obtained the name of Neapolis. The Bay of Naples, for the matchless beauty of its situation and its surrounding scenery, is unrivaled. Its circling beach extends from the promontory of Pausilippo to Sorrento, a line of more than thirty miles of varied beauty and magnificence. This city, with its churches, palaces, villas, and houses, luxuriant gardens and vineyards, with the surrounding hills and grounds thickly planted in the vicinity, backed by the Apennines, well deserves its poetical designation, "*Un pezzo di cielo caduto in terra.*" Naples, it is truly said, "viewed by moonlight, is enchanting. The moon, pouring out an effulgence of silvery light from a sky of the deepest azure, through a pure and transparent atmosphere, places all the prominent buildings in strong relief; and while it makes every object distinctly visible, it mellows each tint, and blends the innumerable details into one vast harmonious whole, throwing a bewitching and indescribable softness and repose on the scene."

From the time that this city and territory fell under the power of the Romans, to the period of the destruction of Pompeii in the year of our Lord 79, Neapolis, on account of the beauty of its situation and excellence of its climate, became the favorite place of residence in the winter season, and the chosen sojourn for a continuance of several of the magnates of the Eternal City, of the Emperor Tiberius for the last years of his iniquitous reign—of many of the most illustrious sages and philosophers of Rome. For some centuries subsequently to the destruction of Pompeii, Naples shared the calamitous fate of the other Italian cities: it was ruled, harassed, pillaged, and devastated successively by Goths, Vandals, Saracens, Lombards, and Parmans, and ultimately by Germans, French, and Spaniards. The flight of the King of Naples in 1799—the short reign of Joseph Bonaparte—the rule of Murat—his deposition, execution—and other modern vicissitudes, it is hardly necessary to refer to.

The Castello dell Novo, standing on a projecting insulated rock, commands the entire of the two semicircular bays on which the city stands. In one direction extends the long line of shore on which are the Chiatamone, the Marino and Chiaja, with numerous ascending terraces of streets behind them, crowned by Fort St. Elmo and Castello Nuovo, the convent of Camaldole, the Palazzo Belvidere, and the hill of the Vomero; and still farther westward, the Promontory of Pausilippo terminates the land view, and in this vicinity lie the beautiful little islands of Ischia and Procida. In the other direction, to the eastward of the Castello dell Novo, are semicircular clusters of houses, convents, and churches, with the mole, the light-house, and harbor, the quay of Santa Lucia, surmounted by the Palace of Capo di Monte, and the eminence of Capo di Chino, and in the distant background the bold outlines of the Apennines, with their tints of purple varying with the atmosphere, and presenting a different aspect with the several changes of the setting sun. Still farther by the eastern shore is the Ponte Madelena leading to Portici and Torro del Græco, the sites and ruins of Pompeii and Herculaneum, and rising up in the vicinity, in the plains of the Campagna Felice, Vesuvius of portentous aspect, sombre and majestic, with all its associations of terror and destruction, and the traditionary horrors of its history, from those of 79 A.D. to the latest eruptions of signal violence in 1821, are recalled as we approach its base or ascend the dreary foot-path in the ravines of molten lava or ragged scoriæ and masses of huge rock that have been torn from the sides of the crater in some past eruptions.

Still farther along the shore to the southeast stands Castellamare, a place of resort noted for its coolness and refreshing sea-breezes, the site of the ancient Stabia, the summer retreat of the *élite* of Naples. A little farther is the delightful scenery of Monte S. Michel, Sorrento, the birth-place of Tasso, and the Cape Campanello, the ancient Athenæus, or Promontory of Minerva, terminate the land view to the eastward. At the entrance to the bay, where the expanse is greatest between the eastern and western shore, in a southern direction, is the island of Capri, the ancient Capreæ, eighteen miles distant from the opposite extremity of the Bay of Portici, about four miles from the nearest shore. The extreme length of the island is about four miles;

in breadth it is about two miles. The peak of the southern mountain of the island is about 2000 feet high. Several ruins, supposed to be of palaces of the imperial monster Tiberius, exist on this island.

The extreme length of Naples is from the Ponte Madelena to Pausilippo, along the sea-shore, a distance of about four miles. The breadth is unequal; at the west end it is contracted between the hills of the Vomero and the Belvidere and the sea-side, and in the interval there are only three or four streets. Toward the centre it extends from the Castello dell Novo northward to the Capo di Monte and Monte di Chino, and in this direction the breadth of this most ancient part of the city, and most densely populated from the quay of St. Lucia to the eminences of Capo di Monte and Capo di Chino, is about two miles. The main street, Strada del Toledo, runs nearly parallel with the shore. It is broad, and fronted with large houses, five or six stories high, in which are the principal shops of the city. The population amounts to about 380,000 inhabitants; there are upward of 300 churches; the lazzaroni are estimated at 40,000; the clergy, monks, and nuns, at 7800.

The Castello dell Novo is built on a rock, which projects into the sea from the Chiatamone, which separates it from Pizzo Falcone. It was formerly called Megera, then Lucullanum. The last of the Roman Emperors, Romulus Augustulanus, is said to have been imprisoned here in 476. The fortress consists now of a composed mass of buildings, ancient and modern. In one of the old gloomy apartments, the Queen Joanna was for some time confined. Its venerable commandant in 1822–4, and for many years previously, was a brave old Irish officer, General Wade.

Willis has happily sketched the Bay of Naples in a few words, not destitute of poetry or of graphic talent.

"The bay is a collection of beauties, which seems to me more a miracle than an accident of nature. It is a deep crescent of sixteen miles across, and little more in length, between the points of which lies a chain of low mountains, called the island of Capri, looking from the shore like a vast heap of clouds brooding at sea. In the bosom of the crescent lies Naples. Its palaces and principal buildings cluster around the base of an abrupt hill crowned by the castle of St. Elmo, and its half million of inhabitants have stretched their dwellings over the plain toward Vesuvius, and back upon Posilippo, bordering the curve of the shore on the right and left with a broad white band of city and village for twelve or fourteen miles. Back from this, on the southern side, a very gradual ascent brings your eye to the base of Vesuvius, which rises from the plain in a sharp cone, broken in at the top ; its black and lava-streaked sides descending with the evenness of a sand-hill, on one side to the disinterred city of Pompeii, and on the other to the royal palace of Portici, built over the yet unexplored Herculaneum. In the centre of the crescent of the shore, projecting into the sea by a bridge of two or three hundred feet in length, stands a small castle, built upon a rock, on one side of which lies the mole with its shipping. The other side is bordered, close to the beach, with the gardens of the royal villa, a magnificent promenade of a mile, ornamented with fancy temples and statuary, on the smooth alleys of which may be met, at certain hours, all that is brilliant and gay in Naples. Farther on, toward the northern horn of the bay, lies the Mount of Posilippo, the ancient coast of Baiæ, Cape Misenum, and the mountain isles of Procida and Ischia ; the last of which still preserves the costumes of Greece, from which it was colonized centuries ago. The bay itself is as blue as the sky, scarcely ruffled all day with the wind, and covered by countless boats fishing or creeping on with their picturesque lateen sails just filled ; while the atmosphere over sea, city, and mountain is of a clearness and brilliancy which is inconceivable in other countries. The superiority of the sky and climate of Italy is no fable in any part of this delicious land ; but in Naples, if the day I have spent here is a fair specimen, it is matchless even for Italy. There is something like a fine blue veil of a most dazzling transparency over the mountains around, but above and between there seems nothing but viewless space—nothing like air that a bird could rise upon. The eye gets intoxicated almost with gazing on it."*

* Pencilings by the Way, p. 32.

"I can compare standing on the top of Vesuvius and looking down upon the bay and city of Naples to nothing but mounting a peak in the infernal regions overlooking Paradise. The larger crater encircles you entirely for a mile, cutting off the view of the sides of the mountain; and from the elevation of the new cone, you look over the rising edge of this black field of smoke and cinders, and drop the eye at once upon Naples, lying asleep in the sun, with its lazy sails upon the water, and the green hills inclosing it clad in the indescribable beauty of an Italian atmosphere. Beyond all comparison, by the testimony of every writer and traveler, the most beautiful scene in the world—the loveliest water and the brightest land lay spread out before us. With the stench of hot sulphur in our nostrils, ankle deep in black ashes, and a waste of smouldering cinders in every direction around us, the enjoyment of the view certainly did not want for the heightening of contrast."*

The Bay of Naples, long after the departure of Lady Blessington from its shores, ceased not to be a favorite theme both in conversation and composition with her ladyship.

The sketch of its beauties appeared in the "Book of Beauty" for 1834, and again came out, retouched, in one of her later publications, "The Lottery of Life."

THE BAY OF NAPLES

In the Summer of 1824.

"It is evening, and scarcely a breeze ruffles the calm bosom of the beautiful bay, which resembles a vast lake, reflecting on its glassy surface the bright sky above, and the thousand stars with which it is studded. Naples, with its white colonnades seen amid the dark foliage of its terraced gardens, rises like an amphitheatre: lights stream from the windows and fall on the sea beneath like colums of gold; the castle of St. Elmo crowning the centre; Vesuvius, like a sleeping giant in grim repose, whose awakening all dread, is to the left; and on the right are the vine-crowned heights of the beautiful Vomero, with their palaces and villas peeping forth from the groves that surround

* Pencilings by the Way, p. 43.

them ; while rising above it, the convent of Camaldoli lifts its head to the skies. Resina, Portici, Castelamare, and the lonely shores of Sorrento, reach out from Vesuvius as if they tried to embrace the isle of Capri, which forms the central object; and Pausilipo and Misenum, which, in the distance, seemed joined to Procida and Ischia, advance to meet the beautiful island on the right. The air, as it leaves the shore, is laden with fragrance from the orange-trees and jasmine, so abundant round Naples; and the soft music of the guitar, or lively sound of the tambourine, marking the brisk movements of the tarantella, steals on the ear. But hark! a rich stream of music, silencing all other, is heard, and a golden barge advances; the oars keep time to the music, and each stroke of them sends forth a silvery light; numerous lamps attached to the boat give it, at a little distance, the appearance of a vast shell of topaz floating on a sea of sapphire. Nearer and nearer draws this splendid pageant, the music falls more distinctly on the charmed ear, and one sees that its dulcet sounds are produced by a band of glittering musicians clothed in royal liveries. This illuminated barge is followed by another with a silken canopy overhead, and the curtains drawn back to admit the balmy air. Cleopatra, when she sailed down the Cydnus, boasted not a more beautiful vessel; and, as it glides over the sea, it seems impelled by the music that precedes it, so perfectly does it keep time to its enchanting sounds, leaving a bright trace behind, like the memory of departed happiness. But who is he that guides this beauteous bark? His tall and slight figure is curved, and his snowy locks, falling over ruddy cheeks, show that age has bent, but not broken him; he looks like one born to command—a hoary Neptune steering over his native element; all eyes are fixed, but his follow the glittering barge that precedes him. And who is she that has the seat of honor at his side? Her fair, large, and unmeaning face wears a placid smile, and those light blue eyes and fair ringlets speak her of another land; her lips, too, want the fine chiseling which marks those of the sunny clime of Italy; and the expression of her countenance has in it more of earth than heaven. Innumerable boats, filled with lords and ladies, follow, but intrude not on the privacy of this royal bark, which passes before us like a vision in a dream. He who steered was Ferdinand, King of the Sicilies, and she who was beside him Maria Louisa, ex-Empress of France."

Many a glorious evening have I passed with the Blessingtons in 1823 and in the early part of 1824, sailing in the Bay of Naples, in their yacht, the Bolivar, which had belonged to Lord Byron; and not unfrequently, when the weather was particularly fine, and the moonlight gave additional beauty to the shores of Portici and Castelamare, Sorrento, and Pausilippo, the night has been far advanced before we returned to the Mole.

The furniture of the cabin of the Bolivar reminds one of its former owner. The table at which he wrote, the sofa on which he reclined, were in the places in which they stood when he owned the yacht. Byron was very partial to this vessel. It had been built for him expressly at Leghorn. On one occasion I was of the party, when, having dined on board, and skirted along the shores of Castelamare and Sorrento, the wind fell about dusk, and we lay becalmed in the bay till two or three o'clock in the morning, some six or eight miles from the shore. The bay was never more beautiful than on that delightful night; the moonlight could not be more brilliant. The pale blue sky was without a cloud, the sea smooth and shining as a mirror, and at every plash of an oar glittering with phosphorescent flashes of vivid light. But all the beauties of the bay on that occasion wasted their loveliness on the weary eyes of poor Lady Blessington that long night in vain.

"Captain Smith," *capitaine par complaisance*, a lieutenant of the navy, who had the command of the Bolivar, a very great original, on that as well as many other occasions served to relieve the tedium of those aquatic excursions, which were sometimes a little more prolonged than pleased Lady Blessington. Her ladyship had a great turn and a particular talent for grave banter, for solemn irony, verging on the very borders of obvious hoaxing. It was a very great delight to her to discover a prevailing weakness, vanity, absurdity, prejudice, or an antipathy in an extravagant or eccentric, vain or peculiar person, and then to draw out that individual, and seem to read his thoughts, throwing out catch-words and half sentences to suggest the kind of expression she desired or expected to solicit, and then leading the party into some ridiculous display of oddity or vanity, and exceedingly absurd observations.

But this was done with such singular tact, finesse, and delicacy of humor, that pain never was inflicted by the mystification, for the simple reason that the badinage was never suspected by the party on whom it was practiced, even when carried to the very utmost limit of discretion. This taste for drawing out odd people, and making them believe absurd things, or express ridiculous ones, was certainly indulged in, not in a vulgar or coarse manner, but it became too much a habit, and tended, perhaps, to create a penchant for acting in society, and playing off opinions, as other persons do jokes and jests, for the sake of the fun of the performance.

The Count D'Orsay, who was a man of genuine wit and wonderful quickness of perception of the ridiculous wherever it existed, also possessed this taste for mystifying and eliciting absurdity to a very great extent, and rendered no little aid to Lady Blessington in these exhibitions of talent for grave irony and refined banter, which ever and anon, of an evening, she was wont to indulge in. In Naples, poor "Captain Smith's" anxiety for promotion, and high sense of fitness for the most exalted position in his profession, furnished the principal subjects for the display of this kind of talent.

The poor captain was "fooled to the very top of his bent." He was drawn out in all companies, in season and out of season, on the subject of *posting*. The Admiralty were regularly lugged into every argument, and it invariably ended with an inquiry "why he was not *posted*." The same observations in reply were always produced by an allusion to the Lords of the Admiralty; and the same replies, with unerring precision, were sure to follow the inquiry about post rank. "There was no patronage for merit." "He ought to have been posted fifteen years ago." "Half the post-captains in the navy were his juniors, though all got posted because they had patrons." "But the

Lords of the Admiralty never posted a man for his service, and—" The disconcerted lieutenant would then be interrupted by D'Orsay with some such good-natured suggestion as the following, in his broken English: "Ah, my poor Smid, tell miladi over again, my good fellow; once more explain for Mademoiselle Power, too, how it happens Milords of the Admirals never posted you?"

Then would the lieutenant go over the old formula in a querulous tone, without the slightest change of voice or look.

In July, 1823, the Blessingtons established themselves at the Palace or Villa Belvidere, on the Vomero, one of the most beautiful residences in Naples, surrounded by gardens overlooking the bay, and commanding a most enchanting view of its exquisite features. Though the palace was furnished suitably for a Neapolitan prince, Lady Blessington found it required a vast number of comforts, the absence of which could not be compensated by beautifully decorated walls and ceilings, marble floors, pictures, and statues, and an abundance of antiquated sofas, and chairs of gigantic dimensions, carved and gilt. The Prince and Princess Belvidere marveled when they were informed an upholsterer's services would be required, and a variety of articles of furniture would have to be procured for the wants of the sojourners who were about to occupy their mansion for a few months. The rent of this palace was extravagantly high; but nothing was considered too dear for the advantage of its sight and scenery.

Lady Blessington thus describes her new abode: "A long avenue, entered by an old-fashioned archway, which forms part of the dwelling of the *intendente* of the Prince di Belvidere, leads through a pleasure ground filled with the rarest trees, shrubs, and plants, to the palazzo, which forms three sides of a square, the fourth being an arcade that connects one portion of the building with the other. There is a court-yard and fountain in the centre. A colonnade extends from each side of the front of the palace, supporting a terrace covered with flowers. The windows of the principal salons open on a garden formed on an elevated terrace, surrounded on three sides by a marble balustrade, and inclosed on the fourth by a long gallery, filled with pictures, statues, and alti and bassi relievi. On the top of this gallery, which is of considerable length, is a terrace, at the extreme end of which is a pavilion, with open arcades, and paved with marble. This pavilion commands a most enchanting prospect of the bay, with the coast of Sorrento on the left; Capri in the centre, with Nisida, Procida, Ischia, and the promontory of Misenum to the right; the foreground filled up by gardens and vineyards. The odor of the flowers in the grounds around this pavilion, and the Spanish jasmine and tuberoses that cover the walls, render it one of the most delicious retreats in the world. The walls of all the rooms are literally covered with pictures; the architraves of the doors of the principal rooms are of Oriental alabaster and the rarest marbles; the tables and consoles are composed of the same costly materials; and the furniture, though in decadence, bears the traces of its pristine splendor. Besides five *salons de réception* on the principal floor, the palace contains a richly-decorated chapel and sacristy, a large *salle de billard*, and several suites of bed and dressing rooms."*

Never did English lady of refined tastes make a sojourn in the neighborhood of Pompeii and Herculaneum, visit the various localities of Naples and its vicinity, carry out researches of antiquarian interest, and inquire into the past amid the ruins of Pæstum and Beneventum, Sorrento, Amalfi, Salerno, Ischia, and Procida, and Capri, under such advantageous circumstances as Lady Blessington.

When she visited Herculaneum she was accompanied by Sir William Gell; when she examined museums and galleries devoted to objects of art, ancient or modern, she was accompanied by Mr. Uwins, the painter, or Mr. Richard Westmacott, the sculptor, or Mr. Millingen, the antiquarian, who "initiated her into the mysteries of numismatics." If she made an excursion to Pæstum, it was with the same erudite cicerone; or when she had an evening visit to the Observatory, it was in the company of Mr. Herschel (now Sir John), or the famous Italian astronomer Piazzi. Or if she went to Beneventum, or the Torre di

* The Idler in Italy, p. 247. Par. ed., 1839.

Patria, the site of the ancient Liternum, it was in the agreeable society of some celebrated savant.

The visit to Pompeii, with Sir William Gell as cicerone, has been immortalized by Lady Blessington in some admirable stanzas, the first and last of which I present to my readers:

"Lonely city of the dead!
Body whence the soul has fled,
Leaving still upon thy face
Such a mild and pensive grace
As the lately dead display,
While yet stamped upon frail clay,
Rests the impress of the mind,
That the fragile earth refined.

* * * * *

"Farewell, city of the dead!
O'er whom centuries have fled,
Leaving on your buried face
Not one mark time loves to trace!
Dumb as Egypt corpses, you
Strangely meet our anxious view;
Showing to the eager gaze
But cold still shades of ancient days."

Among the papers of Lady Blessington, I found some beautifully written verses on the ruins of Pæstum, without name or date, which appear to have been sent to her by the author of them.

Her ladyship visited Pæstum in May, 1824, accompanied by Mr. Millingen, Mr. C. Matthews, and Lord Morpeth; and probably these lines may have been composed by one of her companions on that occasion.

PÆSTUM.

"'Mid the deep silence of the pathless wild,
Where kindlier nature once profusely smiled,
Th' eternal temples stand; unknown their age,
Untold their annals in historic page!
All that around them stood, now far away,
Single in ruin, mighty in decay!
Between the mountains and the neighb'ring main,
They claim the empire of the lonely plain.
In solemn beauty, through the clear blue light,
The Doric columns rear their awful height!

Emblems of strength untamed! yet conquering time
Has mellowed half the sternness of their prime;
And bade the richer, mid their ruins grown,
Imbrown with darker hues the vivid stone.
Each channeled pillar of the fane appears
Unspoiled, yet softened by consuming years.
So calmly awful! so serenely fair!
The gazers rapt still mutely worship there.
Not always thus, when full beneath the day,
No fairer scene than Pæstum's lovely bay;
When her light soil bore plants of every hue,
And twice each year her beauteous roses blew;
While bards her blooming honors loved to sing,
And Tuscan zephyrs fanned th' eternal spring.
When in her port the Syrian moored his fleet,
And wealth and commerce filled the peopled street;
While here the trembling mariner adored
The seas' dread sovereign, Posidonia's lord;
With native tablets decked yon hallowed walls,
Or sued for justice in her crowded halls;
There stood on high the white-robed Flamen, there
The opening portal poured the choral prayer;
While to the searching heaven swelled loud the sound,
And incense blazed, and myriads knelt around.

'Tis past! the actors of the plain are mute,
E'en to the herdsman's call, or shepherd's flute!
The toils of art, the charms of nature fail,
And death triumphant rules the tainted gale.
From the lone spot the affrighted peasants haste,
A wild the garden, and the town a waste.

But they are still the same: alike they mock
The invader's menace and the tempest's shock;
And ere the world had bowed at Cæsar's throne,
Ere yet proud Rome's all-conquering name was known,
They stood, and fleeting centuries in vain
Have poured their fury o'er the enduring fane.
Such long shall stand, proud relics of a clime
Where man was glorious, and his works sublime;
While in the progress of their long decay,
Thrones shrink to dust, and nations pass away."*

* I visited Pæstum in company with Mr. Greenough, one of the Vice Presidents of the Geographical Society, and Mr. Burton, the architect, in 1823, a short

I accompanied Lady Blessington and her party on the occasion, I think, of their first visit to Mount Vesuvius. The account in the "Idler in Italy" of the ascent is given with great liveliness and humor, but the wit and drollery of some of the persons who were of this party contributed to render the visit one of the merriest, perhaps, that ever was made to a volcano, and to the joyousness of the expedition altogether I think her ladyship has hardly done justice.

I had previously made a very singular excursion to Vesuvius, accompanied by a blind gentleman, who used to boast of his having come from England expressly to *see* an eruption. He was certainly recompensed for his pains by having an opportunity afforded him, during his sojourn in Naples, of hearing the bellowing of the disemboguing volcano, of the greatest violence that had occurred in recent times.

The great eruption of June, 1821, was witnessed by me. I accompanied to the mount the celebrated blind traveler, Lieutenant Holman, the evening on which the violence of the eruption was at its greatest height. He has given an account of our night ascent, and adventures by no means free from peril, in his "Narrative of a Journey in France, Italy, Savoy, &c., in the years 1819, 1820, and 1821," page 234. We set off from Naples about five o'clock in the afternoon, as my blind companion says in his work, "with the view of *seeing* the mountain by

time only before the murder of Mr. and Mrs. Hunt in that vicinity. No traveler has said so much to the purpose of Pæstum in so few words as Forsyth.

"On entering the walls of Pæstum I felt all the religion of the place. I trod as on sacred ground. I stood amazed at the long obscurity of its mighty ruins. They can be descried with a glass from Salerno, the high road of Calabria commands a distant view, the city of Capaccio looks down upon them, and a few wretches have always lived on the spot; yet they remain unnoticed by the best Neapolitan antiquaries. Pelegrino, Capaccio, and Sanfelice wrote volumes on the beaten tracks of topography, but they never traveled.

"I will not disturb the dreams of Paoli, who can see nothing here but the work of Tuscans and the Tuscan order; nor would I, with other antiquaries, remount to the Sybarites, and ascribe these monuments—monuments the most simple, sage, austere, energetic—to a race the most opposite in character. Because the Pæstan Doric differs in all its proportions from that of the exaggeration of mass which awes every eye, and a stability which, from time unknown, has sustained in the air these ponderous entablatures. The walls are fallen, and the columns stand; the solid has failed, and the open resists."

moonlight." Passing through Portici, we reached Resina about seven o'clock, and at the base of the mountain took a conductor from the house of Salvatori. Visitants usually ascend on asses two thirds of the way toward the summit, but my blind friend preferred walking, "to see things better with his feet." We reached the hermitage by eight or nine o'clock, where we supped, and did great justice to the hermit's fare. The eruption was chiefly of light ashes, when we proceeded upward from the hermitage, and the road or path, at all times difficult, was now doubly so from the heavy dust and scoriæ, interspersed with large and dark stones, which lay all along it. The shower of ashes was succeeded, as we ascended, by torrents of red-hot lava, that streamed over the crater in the direction of the wind, and, like a river of molten lead, as it descended, and lost its bright red heat, flowed down not impetuously, but slowly and gradually, in a great broad stream, perhaps sixty or eighty feet wide, toward the sea to the east of Resina. We proceeded along the edge of this stream for some distance, and my blind friend formed his notions of its consistence, rate of flowing, and temperature by poking his staff in this stream of lava, and feeling the charred stick when he removed it. The great crater was then in repose. At length we reached the spot where a great fissure, somewhat lower than the crater, was emitting torrents of lava and sulphurous vapors. My blind friend would not be persuaded to remain behind when the guide conducted us to any spot particularly perilous, and especially to one where fire and ashes were issuing from clefts in the rock on which we walked. He insisted on walking over places where we could hear the crackling effects of the fire on the lava beneath our feet, and on a level with the brim of the new crater, which was then pouring forth showers of fire and smoke, and lava, and occasionally masses of rock of amazing dimensions, to an enormous height in the air. A change of wind must inevitably have buried us, either beneath the ashes or the molten lava. The huge rocks generally fell back into the crater from which they issued. The ground was glowing with heat under our feet, which often obliged us to shift our position. Our guide conducted us to the edge of a crater, where a French gentleman had thrown himself in about two months previously. He had written some lines in the travelers' book at the hermitage on his ascent, indicative of the old fact that "the course of true love never did run smooth."

The view of the Bay of Naples and of the distant city from the summit of Vesuvius on a beautiful moonlight night, without a cloud in the sky, such as we had the good fortune to enjoy, was almost magic in its effect; such serenity, and repose, and beauty in perfect stillness, formed a striking contrast with the lurid glare of the red-hot masses that were emitted from the volcano, and the frightful bellowings of the burning mountain on which we stood.

I should have observed that there are, properly speaking, two summits, one westward, called Somma, the other South Vesuvius. In 1667, an eruption had added two hundred feet to the crater's elevation. But in the present eruption a very large portion of this crater had fallen in.

We got back to Portici at three o'clock in the morning, and to Naples at four.

Lady Blessington has given some account of her "descents into the graves of buried cities," and her ascent also to the summit of Mount Vesuvius. In some of these visits and excursions I had the pleasure of accompanying her, when the admirable and erudite cicerone of her ladyship was Sir William Gell.*

Among the English who frequented the Palazzo Belvidere, the following may be enumerated as the *élite*, or most highly esteemed of the visitors there: Sir William Drummond, Sir William Gell, the Honorable Keppel Craven, Mr. William Ham-

* Herculaneum was founded A.M. 2757, sixty years before the siege of Troy, about 3092 years ago. It was destroyed by the same eruption of Vesuvius, in the year 79 A.D., which buried Pompeii. Scarcely any more than a mere reference to the fact of the destruction of either city is to be found in Pliny, or any ancient author.

The buried cities remained undiscovered till 1641 years after their destruction. Herculaneum had been successively ruled by the Etruscans, Oscians, Samnites, Greeks, and, when destroyed, by the Romans. The original founder was said to be the Theban Hercules. Portici and Resina are built over the buried city.

ilton, the British minister to the Neapolitan court; Colonel Chaloner Bisse, the Honorable R. Grosvenor, Captain Gordon, brother of Lord Aberdeen; Mr. Matthias, the author of "the Pursuits of Literature;" Lord Guilford, Count (now Prince) Paul Lieven, Lord Ashley, Mr. Evelyn Denison, Mr. Richard Williams, Signor Salvaggi, a distinguished *litterateur;* the Duc de Rocco Romano, Marchese Guiliano, Duc de Cazarano, Lord Dudley and Ward, Lord Howden, and his son Mr. Cradock; later, if I mistake not, Colonel Caradoc, the Honorable George Howard, the present Lord Morpeth, Mr. Millingen, the eminent antiquarian; Mr. Charles Matthews, the son of the celebrated comedian; Lord Ponsonby, Prince Ischitelli, Mr. J. Strangways, the brother of Lord Ilchester; Mr. H. Baillie, Mr. Herschel, the astronomer; Mr. Henry Fox (now Lord Holland), Mr. J. Townsend (now Lord Sydney), Count de Camaldole, General Church, General Florestan Pepe, Mr. Richard Westmacott, the Duc de FitzJames, Casimir Delavigne, Filangiere (Prince Satriani), son of the well-known writer on jurisprudence; Mr. Bootle Wilbraham, Jun., the Abbé Monticelli, an eminent geologist; the Archbishop of Tarento, Sir Andrew Barnard, Signor Piazzi, a celebrated astronomer, the discoverer of the planet Ceres.

The situation of the villa Belvidere—the lovely prospect from the terrace that communicated with the principal saloon—the classic beauty of the house, the effect of the tasteful laying out of the grounds—the elegance of the establishment, and the precious objects of modern art, of an ornamental kind, of bijouterie, porcelain, ivory, gems of great rarity, and vases of exquisite form and workmanship, and relics too of antiquity, of great value, collected by Lady Blessington throughout Italy, or presented to her by connoisseurs and *dilettante* like Gell, and Millingen, and Dodswell, and Drummond—it would be difficult to exaggerate the merits of, or to describe adequately the effects of, so many excellences were combined in the admirable *tout ensemble* of that villa, when it was the abode of the Countess of Blessington.

Who ever enjoyed the pleasures of her elegant hospitality in that delightful abode, and the brilliant society of the eminent persons by whom she was habitually surrounded there, and can forget the scene, the hostess and the circle, that imparted to the villa Belvidere some of the Elysian characteristics that poetry has ascribed to a neighboring locality?

Difficulties with the proprietor of this mansion obliged the Blessingtons to quit their Neapolitan paradise on the Vomero for the villa Gallo, situated on another eminence, that of Capo di Monte, the end of March, 1825, and there they remained till February the following year.

CHAPTER V.

DEPARTURE FROM NAPLES, SOJOURN IN ROME, FLORENCE, MILAN, VENICE, AND GENOA.—RETURN TO PARIS.—FEBRUARY, 1826, TO JUNE, 1829.

THE Blessingtons and their party having made Naples their head-quarters for upward of two years and a half, took their departure the end of February, 1826, and arrived at Rome the beginning of March following.

The departure from Naples was sudden, and the cause for that suddenness is not explained in the journals of Lady Blessington.

The Blessingtons arrived in Rome from Naples the beginning of March. They remained in Rome till about the middle of the month, and then set out for Florence.

We find them in the month of April in that city, where Lord and Lady Normanby were then entertaining the inhabitants with theatricals. They remained in Florence nearly nine months. In December they were once more at Genoa, but he who had made their previous sojourn there so agreeable was then numbered with the dead. Before the close of the month we find them established at Pisa, where they had the pleasure of meeting the Duc and Duchesse de Guiche.

Lady Blessington had met Lord John Russell in Genoa. She had known his lordship in England, and thought very highly both of his talents and the amiability of his disposition. With the exception of the Duke of York, who was an especial favorite of her ladyship, Lord Grey, and perhaps Lord Durham, none of the persons who frequented the abode of the Blessingtons in St. James's Square were spoken of in such warm terms of regard and esteem by Lady Blessington as Lord John Russell. She thus speaks of him in her Naples diary:

"He came and dined with us, and was in better health and spirits than I remember him when in England. He is exceedingly well read, and has a quiet dash of humor, that renders his observations very amusing. When the reserve peculiar to him is thawed, he can be very agreeable; and the society of his Genoese friends having had this effect, he appears here to much more advantage than in London. Good sense, a considerable power of discrimination, a highly-cultivated mind, and great equality of temper, are the characteristics of Lord John Russell; and these peculiarly fit him for taking a distinguished part in public life. The only obstacle to his success seems to me to be the natural reserve of his manners, which, by leading people to think him cold and proud, may preclude him from exciting that warm sentiment of personal attachment rarely accorded, except to those whose uniform friendly demeanor excites and strengthens it; and without this attraction, it is difficult, if not impossible, for a statesman, whatever may be the degree of esteem entertained for his character, to have devoted friends and partisans, accessories so indispensable for one who would fill a distinguished *rôle* in public life.

"Lord John Russell dined with us again yesterday, and nobody could be more agreeable. He should stay two or three years among his Italian friends, to wear off forever the reserve that shrouds so many good qualities, and conceals so many agreeable ones; and he would then become as popular as he deserves to be. But he will return to England, be again thrown into the clique which political differences keep apart from that of their opponents, become as cold and distant as formerly; and people will exclaim at his want of cordiality, and draw back from what they consider to be his haughty reserve."*

The Blessingtons remained in Pisa till the latter part of June, 1827. We find them again in Florence from July to the November following.

* The Idler in Italy, Par. ed., 1839, p. 370.

At Florence, in 1826 and 1827, Lady Blessington was acquainted with Demidoff, "the Russian Crœsus;" with Lord Dillon, the author of an epic poem, "Eccelino, the Tyrant of Padua," a production more complacently read aloud by his lordship on various occasions than often patiently listened to by his hearers; the Prince Borghese, a "noble Roman," remarkable for his obesity, the number and size of his gold rings, and the circumstance of his being the husband of the sister of Napoleon—"La petite et Mignonne Pauline;" Lamartine, "very good-looking and distinguished in his appearance, who dressed so perfectly like a gentleman that one never would suspect him to be a poet;" Comte Alexandre de la Borde, and his son M. Leon de la Borde; Mr. Jerningham, the son of Lord Stafford; Henry Anson, "a fine young man, on his way to the East" (and never destined to return from it); Mr. Strangways, in the absence of Lord Burghersh officiating as Charge d'Affaires; Mr. Francis Hare, "gay, clever, and amusing;" and in May, 1827, Walter Savage Landor, "one of the most remarkable writers of his day, as well as one of the most remarkable and original of men." This was the first time of meeting with Mr. Landor, and during the sojourn of the Blessingtons in Florence there were few days they did not see him. The strongest attachment that comes within the legitimate limits and bonds of literary friendships was soon formed between Lady Blessington and the celebrated author of "Imaginary Conversations."

Hallam, the historian, the young Lord Lifford, "formed for the *dolce far niente* of Italian life," with his imploring expression of *Laissez moi tranquille* in his good-natured face, were then likewise residing there; and Lord and Lady Normanby also were still sojourning there in 1827. Lord Normanby, during his sojourn there, was a frequent visitor at the Blessingtons'. His taste for theatricals was quite in unison with Lord Blessington's, while his taste for literature, his polished and fascinating manners, his desire to please, and disposition to oblige, and most agreeable conversation, furnished peculiar attractions for Lady Blessington. Lord Normanby was then thirty years of age, in the incipient stage of fashionable authorship, beginning to write novels, in the habit of contributing to albums, ambitious of politics, and exhibiting his turn for them by occasional prose articles for reviews and magazines.

The Blessingtons, though they had retraced their steps toward the North, were now veering between Florence, Genoa, and Pisa, and seem to have seldom turned their thoughts homeward. St. James's Square was beginning to disappear from their recollections. Those connected with Lord Blessington by the ties of blood residing in his own country were seldom thought of; new scenes and new acquaintances appear to have taken fast hold of his tastes and feelings.

When Lord Blessington quitted England in September, 1822, he had four children; his eldest son, Charles John Gardiner, born in Portman Square, London, the 3d of February, 1810, was then twelve years of age.

His eldest daughter, Emilie Rosalie Hamilton, commonly called Lady Mary Gardiner, born in Manchester Square the 24th of June, 1811, was then (in 1822) eleven years of age. His legitimate daughter, the Hon. Harriet Anne Jane Frances, commonly called Lady Harriet Gardiner, born in Seymour Place the 5th of August, 1812, was then ten years of age; and his legitimate son, the Hon. Luke Gardiner, commonly called Lord Mountjoy, born in 1813, was then nine years of age. The eldest son, Charles John Gardiner, had been placed at school; the two daughters and the young Lord Mountjoy had been left under the care of Lady Harriet Gardiner, the sister of Lord Blessington, who was then residing in Dublin, at the house of the Bishop of Ossory, the brother-in-law of Lord Blessington, in Merrion Square, South.

The Dowager Lady Mountjoy (the second wife of the first Lord Mountjoy) was then also living in Dublin.*

The 6th of April, 1823, Lady Blessington mentions in her diary at Genoa the news, having just reached Lord Blessington by

* In August, 1839, the Right Hon. Margaret Viscountess Mountjoy died in Dublin at an advanced age. She was the second wife of the Right Hon. Luke Gardiner, Lord Viscount Mountjoy, father of the late Earl of Blessington by a former marriage. She married Viscount Mountjoy in 1793, and became a widow in 1798. She resided chiefly in Dublin for many years previous to her decease.

courier from London, of the death of his son and heir, the young Lord Mountjoy, on the 26th of March preceding.

The boy was only in his tenth year. He was the only legitimate son of Lord Blessington, and by his death his lordship was enabled to make a disposition of his property of a very strange nature—a disposition of it which it is impossible to speak of in any terms except those of reprehension, and of astonishment at the fatuity manifested in the arrangements made by his lordship, and in the contemplated disposal of a daughter's hand without reference to her inclinations or wishes, or the feelings of any member of her family.

Within a period of three months from the time of the death of his only son, on the 22d of June, 1823, Lord Blessington signed a document purporting to be a codicil to a former will, making a disposition of his property and a disposal of the happiness of one or other of his then two living daughters—an arrangement at once imprudent, unnatural, and wanting in all the consideration that ought to have been expected at the hand of a father for the children of a deceased wife. Partial insanity might explain the anomalies that present themselves in the course taken by Lord Blessington in regard to those children; and my firm conviction, the result of my own observation, is, that at the period in question, when this will was made, Lord Blessington could not be said to be in a state of perfect sanity of mind; but, on the contrary, was laboring under a particular kind of insanity, manifested by an infatuation and infirmity of mind in his conduct with respect to his family affairs, though quite sane on every other subject, which unfitted him to dispose of his children at that juncture, and had assumed a more decided appearance of monomania after that disposal was made.

At Genoa, June the 22d, 1823, Lord Blessington made a codicil to his will, wherein it is set forth that General Albert D'Orsay (the father of the Count Alfred) had given his consent to the union of his son with a daughter of his lordship. But it is evident, from the terms of this document, that it was then optional with the count to select either of the daughters of his lordship.

CODICIL.

"GENOA, June 2d, 1823.

"Having had the misfortune to lose my beloved son Luke Wellington, and having entered into engagements with Alfred, Comte D'Orsay, that an alliance should take place between him and my daughter, which engagement has been sanctioned by Albert, Count D'Orsay, general, &c., in the service of France, this is to declare and publish my desire to leave to the said Alfred D'Orsay my estates in the city and county of Dublin (subject, however, to the annuity of three thousand per annum, which sum is to include the settlement of one thousand per annum to my wife, Margaret, Countess of Blesinton, subject also to that portion of debt, whether by annuity or mortgage, to which my executor and trustee, Luke Norman, shall consider them to be subjected), for his and her use, whether it be Mary (baptized Emilie) Rosalie Hamilton, or Harriet Anne Jane Frances, and to their heirs male, the said Alfred and said Mary, or Harriet, forever in default of issue male, to follow the provisions of the will and testament.

"I make also the said Alfred D'Orsay sole guardian of my son Charles John, and my sister, Harriet Gardiner, guardian of my daughters, until they, the daughters, arrive at the age of sixteen, at which age I consider that they will be marriageable.

"I also bequeath to Luke Norman my estates in the county of Tyrone, &c., in trust for my son, Charles John, whom I desire to take the name of Stewart Gardiner, until he shall arrive at the age of twenty-five, allowing for his education such sums as Alfred D'Orsay may think necessary, and one thousand per annum from twenty-one to twenty-five.

"Done at Genoa, life being uncertain, at eight o'clock on the morning of Monday, June the second, one thousand eight hundred and twenty-three. BLESINTON."

I find in the papers of Lady Blessington a letter of a noble lord, dated September 20th, 1836, inclosing a copy of the codicil above mentioned, sent to him for an opinion; and the following reference to it of the great legal authority. "Inclosed is the opinion. I regret that it is not, and can not be more favorable:

"I have read the statement, will, and codicil, and am of opinion that the legatee is liable for the rent and taxes, and subject to all the covenants of the lease."

At the date of this letter, Lord Blessington had been dead about six years.

On the 31st of August, 1823, Lord Blessington executed his last will and testament, formally carrying out the intentions, in respect to the marriage of one of his daughters, briefly expressed in the preceding codicil. This will was executed only two months later than the document above referred to; and it merits attention, that the provision made for the Countess of Blessington, in the former codicil, of an annuity of £3000, inclusive of a preceding marriage settlement of £1000 a year, is reduced in the will of the 31st of August to £2000 a year, including the marriage settlement of £1000 per annum; so that in after years, when it was generally believed that Lady Blessington had an income of £3000 a year, she in reality had only £2000.

EXTRACTED FROM THE REGISTRY OF HIS MAJESTY'S COURT OF PREROGATIVE IN IRELAND.

"This is the last will and testament of me, Charles John, Earl of Blessington, of that part of the united kingdom called Ireland. I give Luke Norman, Esquire, for and during the time he shall continue agent of my estates, in the county and city of Dublin, and in the county of Tyrone, twelve hundred pounds per annum, in lieu of receivers' fees. I appoint Alfred D'Orsay, Count of [ ], in France, Luke Norman, Esquire, and Alexander Worthington, Esquire, my executors; and I give unto each of them one thousand pounds. I give to Isabella Birnly, Michael McDonough, and John Bullock, one hundred pounds each. I give and devise my real and personal estate to said Alfred D'Orsay, Luke Norman, and Alexander Worthington, for the following purposes: First, for the payment of two thousand pounds, British, per annum (inclusive of one thousand pounds settled on her at the time of my marriage), to my wife Margarette, or

Margaret, Countess of Blessington; and I give to her all her own jewels, requesting that she may divide my late wife's jewels between my two daughters at the time of her decease. I give to Robert Power and Mary Anne Power one thousand pounds each. I give to my daughter Harriet Anne Jane Frances, commonly called Lady Harriet, born at my house at Seymour Place, London, on or about the 3d day of August, 1812, all my estates in the county and city of Dublin, subject to the following charge. Provided she intermarry with my friend, and intended son-in-law, Alfred D'Orsay, I bequeath her the sum of ten thousand pounds only. I give to my daughter Emilie Rosalie Hamilton, generally called Lady Mary Gardiner, born in Manchester Square, on the 24th June, 1811, whom I now acknowledge and adopt as my daughter, the sum of twenty thousand pounds.

"In case the said Alfred D'Orsay intermarries with the said Emilie, otherwise Mary Gardiner, I bequeath to her my estates in the county and city of Dublin. The annuity of two thousand pounds per annum, British, to be paid to my beloved wife out of the said estates. I give to my son Charles John, who I desire may take the name of Stewart Gardiner, born in Portman Square, on the 3d day of February, 1810, all my estates in the county of Tyrone, subject to the following charges; also the reversion of my Dublin estates, in case of male issue of said daughters. In case of male issue, lawfully begotten, I leave these estates to the second son of Alfred D'Orsay and my daughter; or if only one son, to him, in case of failure to male issue, to go to the male issue of my other daughter. My estates are to be subject in the first instance to the payment of my debts. I give to my wife the lease of my house in London, at the expiration of which the furniture, books, &c., &c., are to be removed to the intended residence at Mountjoy Forest; and I direct that the said house be built according to the plan now laid down, and do empower my said executors to borrow money for the said purpose. I give to my wife all my carriages, her paraphernalia and plate. I give to my son Charles John my plate, wardrobe, swords, &c., &c., &c. I appoint Alfred D'Orsay guardian of my son Charles John until he arrives at the age of twenty-five years, the settlement of twelve thousand pounds to be null and void on his obtaining the Tyrone estates. I appoint my beloved wife guardian of my daughter Harriet Anne; and I appoint my sister Harriet guardian of my daughter commonly called Lady Mary. I give to Isabella McDougal, of Perth, one hundred pounds per annum for her life, it being bequeathed her by my first wife, Mary Campbell, Viscountess Mountjoy. I give to the National Gallery, intended to be formed in London under royal protection, my picture of the 'Three Graces,' by Sir Joshua Reynolds, with a desire that 'The gift of Charles John, Earl of Blessington,' may be affixed to the said picture, as an encouragement to others to contribute to the said collection. I give to my sister, Harriet Gardiner, five hundred pounds per annum for her natural life. I revoke all other wills by me made, and declare this to be my last will and testament. In witness whereof, I have to this my last will, contained in five sheets of paper, set to the first four my hand, and to this, the fifth and last, my hand and seal, this 31st day of August, 1823. Blessington seal."

The marriage, then, of Count D'Orsay with a daughter of Lord Blessington we find determined on at Genoa so early as the 2d of June, 1823; and it was not till the 1st of December, 1827, four years and a half subsequently to that determination, that the long-contemplated event took place.

In December, 1827, the Blessingtons returned to Rome from Florence, after a sojourn there of upward of four months.

They engaged the two principal floors of the Palazzo Negroni, for six months certain, at the rent of 100 guineas a month (at the rate of 1200 guineas a year).* This abode though nominally furnished, had to be further provided with hired "*meubles*," the cost of which was about twenty pounds a month. The seeds of the Encumbered Estates Court were being sown in Italy, as well as in other Continental countries, pretty extensively some thirty years ago by our Irish landed proprietors.

* While this enormous expenditure for house accommodation was going on in Italy, the noble mansion in St. James's Square, in London, and the Irish residence, Mountjoy House, on the Tyrone estate, were kept up by Lord Blessington.

In the month of March, 1828, on my return from the East, I visited the Blessingtons at the Palazzo Negroni, and there, for the first time, I beheld the recently married daughter of the Earl of Blessington.

Had I been a member of their family, I could not have been received with greater kindness and warmth of feeling.

During my stay in Rome, I dined with them most days, and passed every evening at their *conversaziones.*

Their salons, as at Naples, were regularly filled every evening with the *élite* of the distinguished foreigners and natives, artists and *literati* of the Eternal City.

The Count D'Orsay had been married the 1st of December, 1827, to Lady Harriet Frances Gardiner, who was then fifteen years of age and four months.

It was an unhappy marriage, and nothing to any useful purpose can be said of it except that Lord Blessington sacrificed his child's happiness by causing her to marry, without consulting her inclinations or her interests.

Taken from school without any knowledge of the world, acquaintance with society, or its usages and forms, wholly inexperienced, transferred to the care of strangers, and naturally indisposed to any exertion that might lead to efforts to conciliate them, she was brought from her own country to a distant land, to wed a man she had never seen up to the period of her arrival in Italy, where, within a few weeks of her first meeting with that foreign gentleman, who had been on terms of intimacy with her father, she was destined to become his bride.

Lady Harriet was exceedingly girlish-looking, pale and rather inanimate in expression, silent and reserved; there was no appearance of familiarity with any one around her; no air or look of womanhood, no semblance of satisfaction in her new position were to be observed in her demeanor or deportment. She seldom or never spoke, she was little noticed, she was looked on as a mere school-girl; I think her feelings were crushed, repressed, and her emotions driven inward by the sense of slight and indifference, and by the strangeness and coldness of every thing around her; and she became indifferent, and strange and cold, and apparently devoid of all vivacity and interest in society, or in the company of any person in it. People were mistaken in her, and she, perhaps, was also mistaken in others. Her father's act had led to all these misconceptions and misconstructions, ending in suspicions, animosities, aversions, and total estrangements.

In the course of a few years, the girl of childish mien and listless looks, who was so silent and apparently inanimate, became a person of remarkable beauty, *spirituelle*, and intelligent, the reverse in all respects of what she was considered where she was misplaced and misunderstood.*

A few days before I quitted Rome for England, I received a kind letter from Lord Blessington to his friend John Galt, which I never had an opportunity of delivering. This letter of his lordship was dated Rome, March, 6, 1828.

"Rome, March 6, 1828.

"My dear Galt,—The bearer of this letter, Mr. Madden, is a gentleman of literary acquirement and talent. He has lately returned from the East, and, besides an account of deserts and Arabs, Turks and Greeks, he will be able to give you an account of your old friends at Rome.

"Believe me, yours most truly, Blessington.

"John Galt, Esq."

May the 7th, 1828, Mr. Mills gave a farewell dinner to the Blessingtons at his villa Palatina, a day or two before their departure from Rome. A party of the friends of the Blessingtons were invited to meet them, and the final meeting and separation were any thing but joyous.

"Schemes of future meeting, too faintly spoken to cheat into hope of their speedy fulfillment, furnished the general topic; and some were there, already stricken with maladies, the harbingers of death—and they, too, spoke of again meeting! Yet who

* Lady Harriet D'Orsay and her aunt, Miss Gardiner, visited the Continent in the latter part of 1833 or beginning of 1834. In September, 1835, Lady Harriet and her sister, Miss Emily Gardiner, were in Dublin, residing with their aunt. Shortly after, Miss Emily Gardiner was married to a Mr. Charles White. Mr. White some years ago traveled a good deal, principally in the East, wrote some works of light literature, and an account of his travels. As a gentleman of good education, agreeable manners and conversation, he was known to the frequenters of Gore House many years ago. He had resided in many parts of the Continent, and latterly altogether in Belgium. Mrs. White died in Paris about ten years ago.

can say whether the young and the healthy may not be summoned from life before those whose infirmities alarm us for their long continuance in it?

"And there were with me two persons, to whom every ruin and every spot in view were 'familiar as household words;' men who had explored them all, with the feelings of the historian, the research of the antiquarian, and the reflections of the philosopher—Sir William Gell and Mr. Dodwell; both advanced toward the downward path of life, every step of which rapidly abridges the journey, and consequently reminds parting friends of the probability that each farewell may be the last. There was our host, seated in a paradise of his own creation, based on the ruins of the palace of the Cæsars, yet, forgetful for the moment of the mutability of fortune of which such striking memorials were before his eyes, thinking only that we were on the eve of parting. Mrs. Dodwell was there, her lustrous eyes often dimmed by a tear of regret at our separation, but her rare beauty in no way diminished by the sadness that clouded a face always lovely."

Sir William Gell and Count Paul Esterhazy came to the Palazzo Negroni to see the Blessingtons take their departure. "Poor Gell!" says Lady Blessington in her diary, "I still seem to feel the pressure of his hand, and the tears that bedewed mine, as he pressed it to his lips, and murmured his fears that we should meet no more.

"'You have been visiting our friend Drummond's grave today,' said he, 'and if you *ever* come to Italy again, you will find me in mine.'"

This was in the early part of May, 1828, and in the month of April, 1836, the accomplished, witty, ever jocund and facetious Sir William Gell was in his grave.

Lady Blessington, quitting Rome, speaks of her sad presentiment that she should see the Eternal City no more. She descants in her diary on the uncertainty of life, and especially in the case of those older or more infirm than ourselves, as if *we* were more exempt from danger and death than they. "Strange delusion! that while we tremble for those dear to us, the conviction of the irrevocable certainty of our own dissolution is less vividly felt! we picture our own death as remote, and consequently less to be dreaded; and even when most impressed with the awful conviction that we, like all other mortals, must pass away, though our reason acknowledges the truth, our hearts refuse to believe that the event may be near."

The "event" was then twenty-one years distant from her own door of life.

From Rome the Blessingtons proceeded to Loretto, where they visited the shrine of the Santa Casa. "The pious votaries of superstition," the folly of their munificence, wasting jewels "to decorate an idol," the tawdry appearance of "the glittering toy-shop," "the heterogeneous mixture of saints and sybils," of pagan rites and superstitious practices, came in for a pretty large share of the customary reprehension of English travelers from Lady Blessington, the value of which, of course, mainly depends on the sincerity of the reprover.

In the present instance, however, Lady Blessington was certainly not so much proclaiming her own sentiments as writing up to the readable mark of those who were to be her public.

From Loretto the travelers proceeded to Ancona and Ravenna, and in the latter place a spectacle was witnessed which Lady Blessington has described in her published diary; but one very striking circumstance connected with it is not mentioned in the diary, but was told to me by her ladyship.

"Various were the conjectures we formed as to the probable cause of the desertion of the silent and solitary city through which we were pacing, and vainly did we look around in search of some one of whom to demand an explanation of it; when, on turning the corner of a larger street or place than we had hitherto passed, the mystery was solved in a manner that shocked our feelings not a little, for we suddenly came almost in personal contact with the bodies of three men hanging from bars erected for the purpose of suspending them. Never did I behold so fearful a sight! The ghastly faces were rendered still more appalling by the floating matted locks and long beards, which, as the bodies were agitated into movement by the wind, moved backward and forward. The eyes seemed starting from their sockets, and the tongues protruded from the distended lips, as if in horrid mockery. I felt transfixed by the terrible sight, from which I could not avert my gaze; and each movement of the bodies seemed to invest them with some new features of horror. A party of soldiers of the Pope guarded the place of execution, and paced up and down with gloomy looks, in which fear was more evident than disgust. Within view of the spot stood the tomb of Dante, whose 'Inferno' offers scarcely a more hideous picture than the one presented to our contemplation. The papal uniform, too, proclaiming that the deaths of these unfortunate men had been inflicted by order of him who professed to be the vicar of the Father of Mercy on earth, added to the horror of the sight."*

Lady Blessington informed me there was another person who witnessed this horrid spectacle, and who was more strongly affected by it than any of the party. That person was a noble marquis, of some celebrity in Ireland, who, traveling the same route as the Blessingtons, had left his own calêche, and entered that of Lord and Lady Blessington; and beholding the dead bodies suspended from the gallows, became deadly pale and almost insensible.

Ferrara and Padua were next visited by the Blessingtons on their route to Venice. In the latter city they fixed their residence for several weeks; and the journals of Lady Blessington abound with evidence of the excellent use she made of her time and talents in visiting remarkable monuments and recording her observations.

At Venice the Blessingtons again made the acquaintance of their old friend, Walter Savage Landor. Verona was next visited by them on their route to Milan.

In her diary she speaks of having spent several hours in the Ambrosian Library, conducted through it by the Abbé Bentivoglio, a man of great erudition, whom Lady Blessington had known in Naples, a friend of the good Archbishop of Tarento. The library contains 50,000 volumes and 10,000 manuscripts;

* The Idler in Italy, vol. iii., p. 33.

and among its treasures, the "Virgil" that had belonged to Petrarch, in which is his note to Laura. The next object that excited Lady Blessington's attention was a lock of golden hair of Lucretia Borgia, the daughter of Alexander the Sixth. Once before she saw a lock of that same golden hair on the breast of Byron, consisting of about twenty fair hairs, resembling fine threads of gold, which he had obtained from the ringlet at the Ambrosian Library, and always wore.

Nine or ten letters from Lucretia Borgia to the Cardinal Bembo are placed in a casket, with the lock of hair she sent to him. Lady Blessington makes no mention in her journal of having been given a small tress of this golden hair of the too celebrated Lucretia; but that precious gift came into my hands among the other papers of Lady Blessington; and in her hand-writing of the envelope that incloses it, it is stated, that the hair in question was given to her by the Abbé Bentivoglio, of the Ambrosian Library, a descendant of the Bembo family.

There is a remarkable reference to the hair of Lucretia Borgia in the "New Monthly Magazine:"

"Auburn is a rare and glorious color, and I suspect will always be more admired by us of the North, where the fair complexions that recommend golden hair are as easy to be met with as they are difficult in the South. Ovid and Anacreon, the two greatest masters of the ancient world in painting external beauty, both seem to have preferred it to golden, notwithstanding the popular cry in the other's favor: unless, indeed, the hair they speak of is too dark in its ground for auburn.

"Perhaps the true auburn is something more lustrous throughout, and more metallic than this. The cedar, with the bark stripped, looks more like it. At all events, that it is not the golden hair of the ancients has been proved to me beyond a doubt by a memorandum in my possession, worth a thousand treatises of the learned. This is a solitary hair of the famous Lucretia Borgia, whom Ariosto has so praised for her virtues, and whom the rest of the world is so contented to call a wretch. It was given me by a wild acquaintance, who stole it from a lock of her hair preserved in the Ambrosian Library at Milan. On the envelope he put a happy motto,

"'And beauty draws us with a single hair.'

"If ever hair was golden, it is this. It is not red, it is not yellow, it is not auburn; it is golden, and nothing else; and, though natural-looking too, must have had a surprising appearance in the mass. Lucretia, beautiful in every respect, must have looked like a vision in a picture—an angel from the sun."*

As an example of the happy style, and just views, and correct judgment of Lady Blessington, I may cite the following passage, in reference to a visit to the subterranean shrine of St. Carlo Borromeo, in the Duomo, the sarcophagus of rock crystal which preserves the mortal remains of the renowned prelate in pontifical attire:

"Carlo Borromeo was one of the most remarkable men to whom Italy has ever given birth; and those who might be disposed to undervalue the canonized saint, must feel a reverence for the memory of the man, whose patriotism, courage, and charity entitle his name to the esteem of posterity. Elevated to the rank of cardinal at the early age of twenty-two, his conduct justified the partiality of his uncle, Pope Pius IV., who conferred this dignity on him. As a scholar no less than as a divine was this excellent man distinguished; but his courageous and unceasing exertions during the plague that ravaged his country in 1576 are beyond all praise. These are remembered with a feeling of lively admiration, that the costly trappings and brilliant diamonds which decorate his remains might fail to awaken for the saint; and we turned from the crystal sarcophagus and its glittering ornaments to reflect on the more imperishable monument of his virtues—the fame they have left behind.

"I could not contemplate the crucifix borne by this good and great man in the procession during the fearful plague without a sentiment of profound reverence. It is carefully preserved under a glass case, and, I confess, appears to me to be a far more befitting monument than the costly sarcophagus of rock crystal to the glory of him who, actuated by his deep faith in it, was enabled to fulfill duties from which the less pious and charitable shrank back in terror."†

* New Monthly Mag., part iii., 1825. † The Idler in Italy, vol. iii., p. 299.

From Milan the Blessingtons turned their steps at length in a homeward direction, at least toward Paris, and at the close of 1828 once more found themselves in their old quarters at Genoa. Five years previously, Byron often stood conversing with Lady Blessington on the balcony of her hotel, or walked about the gardens of it with her. The several spots where she remembered to have seen him distinctly recalled him to her memory. She again seemed to look upon him, to see his features, to perceive his form, "to hear the sound of that clear, low, and musical voice, never more to be heard on earth." But one day, while these sweet and bitter fancies were presenting themselves to her imagination, she saw a young lady, an English girl, who resembled Byron in an extraordinary degree, accompanied by an elderly lady. That English girl was "Ada, sole daughter of my house and heart," and the elderly lady was her mother, the widow of Lord Byron.

The City of Palaces had few attractions on this last visit for Lady Blessington.

One episode more in the Italian journals is narrated, and we come to the concluding line: "We have bidden farewell to our old and well-remembered haunts at Genoa, and to-morrow we leave it, and perhaps forever!"

Here ends the second phase in the career I have before referred to—the Italian life of Lady Blessington.

CHAPTER VI.

RETURN TO PARIS IN JUNE, 1828.—RESIDENCE THERE.—DEATH OF LORD BLESSINGTON.—DEPARTURE OF LADY BLESSINGTON FOR ENGLAND IN NOVEMBER, 1830.

In June, 1828, the Blessingtons arrived in Paris, at the expiration of six years from the period of their former sojourn there. Their first visitors were the Duc and Duchesse de Guiche; the latter "radiant in health and beauty," the Duc looking, as he always did, "more *distingué* than any one else—the perfect *beau ideal* of a gentleman."

The Blessingtons took up their abode in the Hotel de Terasse, Rue de Rivoli. After some time they rented the splendid mansion of the Marechal Ney, in the Rue de Bourbons, the principal apartments of which looked on the Seine, and commanded a delightful view of the Tuilleries Gardens. This hotel was a type of the splendor that marked the dwellings of the imperial noblesse.

The rent of this hotel was enormously high, and the expense which the new inmates went to in adding to the splendor of its decorations and furniture was on a scale of magnificence more commensurate with the income of a prince of some *vielle cour* than with that of an Irish landlord.

With the aid of "those magicians," the French upholsterers, the Hotel Ney soon assumed a wonderful aspect of renewed splendor. The principal drawing-room had a carpet of dark crimson, with a gold-colored border, with wreaths of flowers of brightest hues. The curtains were of crimson satin, with embossed borders of gold color, and the sofas, *bergeres*, *fauteuils*, and chairs, were richly carved and gilt, and covered with satin, to correspond with the curtains. Gilt *consoles* and *chiffonieres*, on which marble tops were placed wherever they could be disposed; large mirrors, gorgeous buhl cabinets, costly *pendules* of bronze, magnificent candelabras, abounded in the long suite of salons, boudoirs, and sitting-rooms. The furniture of the bedroom was kept a secret by Lord Blessington till quite completed, in order to give a surprise to her ladyship—when its surpassing splendor was to burst upon her all at once—at the first view of this apartment. "The only complaint I ever have to make of his taste," observes her ladyship, "is its too great splendor. . . . . . . We feel like children with a new plaything in our beautiful house; but how, after it, shall we ever be able to reconcile ourselves to the comparatively dingy rooms in St. James's Square, which no furniture or decoration could render any thing like the Hotel Ney?"*

At length, "the scheme laid by Lord Blessington" to surprise his lady—"for he delighted in such plans"—was revealed on

* The Idler in France, vol. i., p. 117.

the doors of the *chambre à coucher* and dressing-room being thrown open. "The whole fitting up," says Lady Blessington, "is in exquisite taste; and, as usual, when my most gallant of all gallant husbands that it ever fell to the happy lot of woman to possess interferes, no expense has been spared. The bed, which is silvered instead of gilt, rests on the backs of two large silver swans, so exquisitely sculptured that every feather is in alto-relievo, and looks as fleecy as those of the living bird. The recess in which it is placed is lined with white fluted silk, bordered with blue embossed lace; and from the columns that support the frieze of the recess, pale blue silk curtains, lined with white, are hung, which, when drawn, conceal the recess altogether."

In one of her letters she enlarges on this subject.

"A silvered sofa has been made, to fit the side of the room opposite the fire-place, near to which stands a most inviting *bergere*. An *escritoire* occupies one panel, a book-stand the other, and a rich coffer for jewels forms a pendant to a similar one for lace or India shawls. A carpet of uncut pile, of a pale blue, a silver lamp, and a Psyche glass; the ornaments, silvered, to correspond with the decorations of the chamber, complete the furniture. The hangings of the dressing-room are of blue silk, covered with lace, and trimmed with rich frills of the same material, as are also the dressing-stands and chaire longue, and the carpet and lamp are similar to those of the bed. A toilet-table stands before the window, and small jardinieres are placed in front of each panel of looking-glass, but so low as not to impede a full view of the person dressing in this beautiful little sanctuary. The salle de bain is draped with white muslin, trimmed with lace; and the sofa and the *bergere* are covered with the same. The bath is of marble, inserted in the floor, with which its surface is level. On the ceiling over it is a painting of Flora, scattering flowers with one hand, while from the other is suspended an alabaster lamp in the form of a lotus."

Poor Lady Blessington, summing up the wonderful effects of the various embellishments and decorations, the sensations produced by such luxuriant furniture, coffers for jewels and India shawls, gorgeous hangings, and glittering ornaments of every kind, observes: "The effect of the whole is chastely beautiful, and a queen could desire nothing better for her own private apartments."

The gilt frame-work of the bed, resting on the backs of the large silver swans, it does not do to think of when visiting the Mountjoy Forest estate in Tyrone, that did belong to the late Earl of Blessington, when one enters the cabin of one of the now indigent peasantry, from the sweat of whose brow the means were derived that were squandered in luxury in foreign lands, luxury on a par with any Oriental voluptuousness of which we read in the adornment of palaces.

Lord Blessington, when fitting up the Hotel Ney in this sumptuous manner, was co-operating very largely indeed with others of his order, equally improvident and profuse, in laying the foundation of the Encumbered Estates' Court Jurisdiction in Ireland.

We are reminded, by the preceding account of the fitting up of the Hotel Ney for the Blessingtons, of the imperial pomp of one of the palaces of Napoleon, a short time only before his downfall. At Fontainebleau, soon after the abdication of the emperor, Haydon visited the palace, and thus describes the magnificence which was exhibited in the decoration and furniture of that recent sojourn of imperial greatness:

"The chateau I found superb, beyond any palace near Paris. It was furnished with fine taste. Napoleon's bed hung with the richest Lyons green velvet, with painted roses, golden fringe a foot deep; a footstool of white satin, with gold stars; the top of the bed gilt, with casque and ostrich plumes, and a golden eagle in the centre grappling laurel. Inside the bed was a magnificent mirror, and the room and ceiling were one mass of golden splendor. The panels of the sides were decorated in chiaroscuro with the heads of the greatest men.

"No palace of any sultan of Bagdad or monarch of India ever exceeded the voluptuous magnificence of these apartments."

Shortly before the passing of the Catholic Emancipation Act, Lady Blessington received at Paris a letter from Lord Rosslyn, urging the attendance of Lord Blessington in his place in Parliament, and his support of the Emancipation Act.

Lord Blessington, on receipt of Lord Rosslyn's letter, immediately proceeded from Paris to London, expressly to give his vote in favor of the great measure of Emancipation.

"His going to England," observes Lady Blessington, "at this moment, when he is far from well, is no little sacrifice of personal comfort; but never did he consider self when a duty was to be performed. I wish the question was carried, and he safely back again. What would our political friends say if they knew how strongly I urged him not to go, but to send his proxy to Lord Rosslyn?"*

While Lord Blessington remained in London, I had the pleasure of seeing him on several occasions. A day or two before his departure from London, I breakfasted with him at his residence at St. James's Square.

I never saw him to more advantage, or more deeply interested on any public matter, than he seemed to be in the measure he had come over to support, and which he deemed of the highest importance to the true interests of Ireland.

Whatever the defects may have been in his character, in one respect he was certainly faultless: he had a sincere love for his country and for his countrymen.

The following statement of his opinions on the means of bettering the condition of the country was made to me four years previously to the period above-mentioned, when presenting me with a letter of introduction to the British minister at Constantinople.†

"I wish you would, at Constantinople or Smyrna, turn your thoughts to the subject of Ireland; but it is a difficult task to

* The Idler in France, vol. ii., p. 6.

† "Naples, August 15th, 1824.

"My dear Sir,—I send you the letter for Lord Strangford, which I hope may be useful to you. I trust the experiment you are about to make will be successful. You will have the advantage, at least, of seeing the world; and a medical man has very great opportunities of seeing the interior of Turkish modes of life. Wishing you health and prosperity, I remain, yours very truly,

"Blessington.

"R. R. Madden, Esq."

encounter, as you say, for an Irishman indignant at many acts of former oppression and injustice. Upon the subject of repeal of the Union, I fear it would be worse than a negative measure. We are impoverished in money and talent. England has a superabundancy of the one, and a sufficiency of the other, if she will apply her materials to our good. Send the Parliament back to Dublin, and that city will, perhaps, flourish again; but I fear the same effect could not be produced through the kingdom; and if, to forward the views which I think absolutely necessary for Ireland, the Commons imposed heavy taxes, being refused aid from England, the people would have cause for dissatisfaction, and an Irishman's mode of expressing it is blows, and not words. Let the Roman Catholic Church of Ireland separate itself in toto from the Pope, and receive from the British Parliament a respectable revenue. Establish a better mode of educating the priesthood, take away the tithes, and pay the Reformed Church out of the public purse. Admit Catholics to the houses of Parliament and the Bench, at the same time establishing throughout Ireland an extensive gendarmerie, not for political, but policial purposes. Make the nobility and gentry live on their estates or sell them. Give a grant sufficient to cut canals in all directions. Establish colonies of industrious citizens in what are now barren districts. Let there be neither Ribbonmen, Free-masons, or Orangemen. Let the offenders against the public peace, of whatever party, be sent to the colonies. Let the middling classes be taught that public money is levied for the public good, and not for individual advantage, and then Ireland will be, what it should be from its situation and with its natural advantages, a gem in the ocean."

His lordship had returned from London only a few days, when, one forenoon, feeling himself slightly indisposed, he took some spoonfuls of eau de Melisse in water, and rode out, accompanied by his servant, in the heat of the day, along the Champs Elysées.

He had not proceeded far when he was suddenly attacked by apoplexy, and was carried home in a state of insensibility, where all means were resorted to in vain for his relief.

On the 23d of May, 1829, thus suddenly died Charles James Gardiner, second Lord Blessington, in his forty-sixth year. He was the only surviving son of the first marriage of Viscount Mountjoy.

At the age of sixteen he succeeded his father, who was slain at Ross, June 5th, 1798. He was elected a representative Peer for Ireland about 1809, and was advanced to his earldom, June 22d, 1816.

Lord Blessington's remains were conveyed to Ireland, and deposited in the family vault, in St. Thomas's Church, Marlborough Street, where his father's remains were buried, and also those of his first wife; of his son and heir, the Hon. Luke William Gardiner; of his sister Margaret, the wife of the Hon. John Hely Hutchinson; of his sister Louisa, wife of the Right Rev. Dr. Fowler, Lord Bishop of Ossory; and of his sister, the Hon. Harriet Gardiner. In the church there is only one mural tablet bearing an inscription in memory of any member of the Blessington family.

To the loved Memory
Of the HONORABLE MARGARET, Wife of
JOHN HELY HUTCHINSON, Esq.,
Daughter of Luke Gardiner, Viscount Mountjoy,
Who fell at New Ross, in 1798,
At the head of his Regiment:
She died October 13, 1825, aged 29 years.

The remains of the husband of this lady, the Right Hon. John Hely Hutchinson, third Earl of Donoughmore, were deposited in the same vault, September 17, 1851. The earl died in his sixty-fourth year.

In one of Mr. Landor's unpublished "Imaginary Conversations," in which the discoursers are Lord Mountjoy, the father of the Earl of Blessington, and Lord Edward Fitzgerald, there are two notes written in 1829, immediately after the death of Lord Blessington. In the first note Mr. Landor observes:

"Lord Mountjoy was killed in the beginning of the insurrection of 1798; he left an only son, the Earl of Blessington, who voted for the Union in the hope that it would be beneficial to

Ireland,* though the project had suspended the erection of several streets and squares on his estate in Dublin, and it was proved to him that he must lose by it two thirds of his rent-roll; he voted likewise in defense of Queen Caroline, seeing the insufficiency of the evidence against her, and the villainy of the law officers of the crown: he esteemed her little, and was personally attached to the king. For these votes, and for all he ever gave, he deserves a place, as well as his father, in the memory of both nations."

The second note thus refers to the recent death of Lord Blessington.

"Scarcely is the ink yet dry upon my paper, when intelligence reaches me of the sudden death of Lord Blessington.

"Adieu, most pleasant companion! Adieu, most warm-hearted friend! Often and long, and never with slight emotion, shall I think of the many hours we have spent together; the light seldom ending gravely; the graver always lightly.

"It will be well, and more than I can promise to myself, if my regret at your loss shall hereafter be quieted by the assurance which she, who best knew your sentiments, has given me, that by you, among the many, I was esteemed and beloved among the few."

On the news of the death of Lord Blessington reaching Mr. Landor, he addressed the following lines to the countess:

"Baths of Lucca, June 6.

"DEAR LADY BLESSINGTON,—If I defer it any longer, I know not how or when I shall be able to fulfill so melancholy a duty. The whole of this day I have spent in that torpid depression, which you may feel without a great calamity, and which others can never feel at all. Every one that knows me knows the sentiments I bore toward that disinterested, and upright, and kind-hearted man, than whom none was ever dearer or more delightful to his friends. If to be condoled with by many, if to be esteemed and beloved by all whom you have admitted to your society, is any comfort, that comfort at least is yours. I know how inadequate it must be at such a moment, but I know too that the sentiment will survive when the bitterness of sorrow shall have passed away. Yours very faithfully, W. S. LANDOR."

* Mr. Landor is mistaken. Lord Blessington did not vote for the Union.—R. R. M.

In another letter to Lady Blessington, Mr. Landor thus expressed himself on the same subject:

"July 21, 1289.

"DEAR LADY BLESSINGTON,—Too well was I aware how great my pain must be in reading your letter. So many hopes are thrown away from us by this cruel and unexpected blow. I can not part with the one, of which the greatness and the justness of your grief almost deprives me, that you will recover your health and spirits. If they could return at once, or very soon, you would be unworthy of that love which the kindest and best of human beings lavished on you. Longer life was not necessary for him to estimate your affection for him, and those graces of soul which your beauty in its brightest day but faintly shadowed. He told me that you were requisite to his happiness, and that he could not live without you. Suppose, then, he had survived you, his departure, in that case, could not have been so easy as it was, unconscious of pain, of giving it, or leaving it behind. I am comforted at the reflection that so gentle a heart received no affliction from the anguish and despair of those he loved.

"You have often brought me over to your opinion after an obstinate rather than a powerful contest; let me, now I am more in the right, bring you over by degrees to mine.

"And believe me, dear Lady Blessington, your ever devoted servant,

"W. S. LANDOR."

Dr. Richardson, the Eastern traveler, and former traveling physician of Lord Blessington, in writing to Lady Blessington from Ramsgate, the 25th of April, 1832, on the death of her husband, says,

"YOUR late lord is never absent from my mind; during life he occupied the largest share of my affections, his friendship was my greatest honor and pride, and his memory is the dearest of all in the keeping of my heart. I feel his loss every day of my life, and shall never cease to feel it till my eyes close on all this scene of things till we meet again in another and a better world.

"Yours, my dear Lady Blessington, very sincerely,

"R. RICHARDSON."

At the time of the decease of Lord Blessington, his affairs were greatly embarrassed. The enormous expenditure in France and Italy, and in London also, previously to his departure for the Continent in 1822, was not met by the rental of his vast estates.

It will be seen by the schedules appended to the act of Parliament for the sale of the Blessington estates (to be found in the Appendix), that the rental of the properties referred to in the act was estimated, in 1846, at £22,718 14*s.* 7*d.* But when his lordship succeeded to the title and estates, the rental was about £30,000 a year.

In 1814 he sold a valuable property in the barony of Strabane, in the county of Tyrone, the rental of which was very considerable. The remaining estates, by mismanagement, constant changes of agents, the pressure of mortgages, and other causes of ruin, arising out of absenteeism, improvidence, and embarrassments, became much reduced.

The extent of the Mountjoy territory in Tyrone and Donegal, into which Lord Blessington came to possession, may be imagined, when the extreme length of one of the Tyrone properties could be described as "a ride of several miles."

The three estates of Lord Blessington in Tyrone were the following:

1st. The Newtown Stewart estate, called Mountjoy Forest, on which property the residence of Lord Blessington, "the Cottage," was situated, which was sold in 1846 or 1847.

2d. The Mountjoy estate near Killymoon produced £5000 or £6000 a year. The demesne, comprising one thousand nine hundred acres, according to Mr. Graham's account, "the largest demesne in Europe of any private gentleman's property," was sold four or five years ago.

3d. Aughertain estate, near Clogher, the first portion of the estreated Ulster lands which came into the possession of one of the first adventurers in Ireland of the Stewart family, comprised fourteen town lands; it was sold for £98,000. The produce of the sale of a large portion of the territory of the O'Neil of the Red Hand went to pay the debts of a French count to the Jews and money-lenders of London.

In the county of Donegal there was another estate of the Mountjoy family, named "Conroy;" but this valuable property had been sold previously to the death of Lord Blessington.

In 1813 Lord Blessington obtained advances of money from the Globe Insurance Company, for which he gave them an annuity for one young life. Amount of annuity, £526.

In 1813 he got money again from the same company, for

which he gave an annuity for the life of A. Mocatta, a youth, of £520.

In 1813 he got money from the company, for which he gave an annuity for the life of William Coles, of £510.

In 1813 he obtained money from the same company, for which he gave an annuity for the life of A. Angelo Tremonando, of £527.

In 1814 he obtained money from A. Tremonando, and gave a life annuity of £880.

In 1814, for other pecuniary accommodation, he gave an annuity to Alexander Nowell, for the lives of Frances and Henry Josias Stracy, and Rev. T. Whittaker, of £1000.

In 1816 he obtained money advances from Henry Fauntleroy, for which he gave an annuity for the lives of John Fauntleroy, and William and James Watson, of £500.

In 1817 Lord Blessington borrowed largely money on mortgages. In that year he raised on mortgage to Conyngham M'Alpine, Esq., £11,076.

In 1821 he borrowed from the Westminster Insurance Company, on mortgage, £25,000.

In 1825 he borrowed from the same company, on mortgage, £5000.

In 1823 he borrowed from Thomas Tatham, Esq., on mortgage, £4000.

The following items give the principal amounts of annuities, mortgages, judgments, and other debts, legacies, sums of money, and incumbrances charged upon or affecting the estate of Charles John, Earl of Blessington, at the time of his decease:

Mortgages from 1783 to 1823 inclusive, £47,846.

Legacies of the late earl, £23,353.

Legacy to the Honorable Harriet Gardiner, to be raised only on certain contingencies set forth in the will, £9230.

Settlement on marriage of Lady Harriet with Count D'Orsay, £40,000.

Judgments, £13,268. Bond debts, £10,357.

Promissory notes, letters of acknowledgments, and I. O. U.'s, from 1808 to 1828, £10,122.

Simple contract debts due, or claimed to be due, to parties by the Earl of Blessington, £6878.

Total of debts, incumbrances, and legacies of the Earl of Blessington, set forth in the fourth schedule, £161,044.

But to this sum there is to be added that of annuities given by Lord Blessington to various parties, bankers, Jews, and others, to the amount of £7887.

By the fifth schedule appended to the act, it appears the mortgages and sums of money which had been charged by the Count D'Orsay on the estates of Lord Blessington from 1837 to 1845 amounted to £20,184.

An act of Parliament (Vict. 9, cap. 1) was passed the 18th of June, 1846, "for vesting the real estates of the Earl of Blessington in trustees for sale, for the payment of his debts, and for other purposes."

The act sets out with reciting a deed of settlement, dated 3d of August, 1814, made shortly after the first marriage of the earl.

By this deed, Josias Henry Stracey, Esq., of Berners Street, a partner of Fauntleroy, the banker, was appointed a trustee over all the Tyrone estates, for the purpose of securing to Lord Blessington's son, Charles John Gardiner, a sum of £12,000 on his coming of age, and the interest of that sum till he had obtained the age of twenty-one.

The next deed recited is one of lease and release, dated 16th of February, 1818, on the occasion of the intended marriage of the earl with Margaret Farmer, of "Manchester Square, widow," settling one thousand a year on that lady in the event of that marriage taking place; which marriage eventually took place the 16th of February, 1818.

The will of the earl, dated 31st of August, 1823, is next recited, bequeathing "£2000 British per annum to Lady Blessington (inclusive of £1000 settled on her at the time of his marriage), to Robert Power £1000, and Mary Anne Power £1000 each. To his daughter, Lady Harriet, all his estates in the county of Dublin, subjected to certain charges," provided she intermarried with his "friend and intended son-in-law, Alfred

D'Orsay;" and in the event of her refusal, he bequeathed to her only the sum of £10,000. To his daughter Emilie Rosalie Gardiner, commonly called Lady Mary Gardiner, whom he hereby acknowledged and adopted as his daughter, he left the sum of £20,000; but in case she married Alfred D'Orsay, he bequeathed all his Dublin estates to her, chargeable, however, with the payment of the annuity before mentioned to Lady Blessington. To his son, Charles John Gardiner, he left all his estates in Tyrone, subject to certain charges, also the reversion of his Dublin estates in case of failure of male issue, lawfully begotten, of said daughters.

[It is to be borne in mind, when this will was made, the 31st of August, 1823, his lordship's daughter Harriet, whose marriage he provided for, being born the 3d of August, 1812, was just eleven years of age.]

The act then goes on to recite a deed of settlement made in contemplation of the marriage between Count and Countess D'Orsay, dated 2d of November, 1827; the parties to this deed being Lord Blessington of the first part, Count D'Orsay of the second part, Lady Harriet Gardiner of the third part, the Duc de Guiche, lieutenant general and premier (ecuyer) of his royal highness the Dauphin, and Robert Power, formerly captain of the 2d Regiment of Foot, then residing at Mountjoy Forest, of the fourth part.

The deed is stated to be for the purpose of making a provision for the said Alfred, Count D'Orsay, and Lady Harriet Gardiner, who is described as "*then an infant of the age of fifteen years or thereabouts.*"

Lord Blessington bound himself by this deed to pay, within twelve months after the solemnization of this marriage, the sum of £20,000 British to the trustees, the Duc de Guiche and Robert Power; and bound his executors, within twelve months after his decease, to pay said trustees £20,000 more, to be invested in the funds, and the interest thereof to be paid to Count D'Orsay, and after his decease to the said Lady Harriet during her life; the principal at her death to go to any issue by that marriage; and in the event of failure of issue, to be held in trust for the executor and administrator of the said Alfred, Count D'Orsay.

Then the act recites the marriage of the Count D'Orsay with Lady Harriet during the lifetime of the said earl, of there being no issue by that marriage, *and of their being separated in the year* 1831, and having lived wholly separate from that time.*

The death of the earl is then mentioned, having occurred on the 25th of May, 1829, and the fact of the will being duly proved in the Prerogative Court; and it is also stated that his lordship was possessed of estates in Kilkenny which were not devised by his will; that his lordship's son, Charles John Gardiner, had filed a bill against Lady Blessington, Count and Countess D'Orsay, in 1831; that the will was declared by a decree in Chancery well proven, and that the trusts therein specified should be carried into execution; that receivers should be appointed; that Luke Norman should continue agent of the estates, and that an account should be taken of all debts and incumbrances on the same; that the 18th of June, 1834, the Master in Chancery reported on the charges and debts on the estates, and on the 14th of July, 1834, an order was made directing a sum of £500 to be paid yearly to the Count D'Orsay, and £450 to the Countess D'Orsay, for their maintenance.

Various bequests of his lordship are recited in this document: to Lady Blessington he bequeathed the léase of his house in London (in St. James's Square); at the expiration of the lease, the furniture, books, &c., were to be removed to Mountjoy Forest estate in Tyrone, where a house was to be built according to plans then laid down, empowering executors to borrow money for the purpose. "All his carriages, *her* paraphernalia and plate," he left also to his wife; to his son John "*his* plate, wardrobe, swords," &c., &c. He appointed Alfred D'Orsay guardian of his son Charles John Gardiner till he came of age, the previous settlement of £12,000 to be null and void on his obtaining the Tyrone estates. "He appointed his beloved wife guardian of his daughter Harriet Anne, and appointed his sister

* The date of the deed of separation between the Count and Countess D'Orsay is the 15th and 16th of February, 1838.

Harriet guardian of his daughter commonly called Lady Mary." To his sister, Miss Harriet Gardiner, he left an annuity for life of £500.

A deed of separation between the Count and Countess D'Orsay is referred to, setting forth that Count D'Orsay had granted several annuities for his life to his creditors, with power to repurchase the same, and had charged the interest on the two sums of £20,000 settled on him at the period of his marriage by Lord Blessington, and that he required a sum to redeem the same amounting to about £23,500.

That Countess D'Orsay also had incurred some debts, and required a sum of £10,000, or thereabouts, to discharge the same; that Charles John Gardiner had incurred some debts, secured by judgments on the Tyrone estates, amounting to £10,000; and that Countess D'Orsay had entered into an agreement to purchase all the interests and claims of the several parties to whom bequests were made and debts were due, and that to pay off said incumbrances and liabilities a sum of £120,500, applicable to the purchase of Count D'Orsay's annuities and some other purposes, would be required. By a subsequent agreement, the latter sum was raised to £180,000, "and such other sums as might be found necessary" among other objects for securing to Count D'Orsay, within a period of ten years, a sum of £42,000.

Eventually, by two orders of the Court of Chancery, one of the 6th of February, 1845, and another the 13th of February, 1846, it was decreed the trustees, when the sanction of an act should be procured, would be empowered to make sales of several estates to the amount of £350,000, to pay off all incumbrances and claims.

The act for the sale of the Blessington estates was passed in 1846. Its provisions have been duly carried into execution. Of the vast properties of the Mountjoys, there remains a remnant of them, producing about £6000 a year, to be still disposed of.

Lord Blessington by his will put an end to the wealth, honor, and territorial greatness of the ancient race of the Mountjoys.

Thus passes away the glory of "the English Pale" in Ireland.

CHAPTER VII.

CONVERSATIONAL POWERS OF DISTINGUISHED PERSONS.—SEAMORE PLACE AND GORE HOUSE LITERARY CIRCLES.—RIVAL SALONS OF HOLLAND HOUSE, AND RÉUNIONS AT THE COUNTESS OF CHARLEVILLE'S.—RESIDENCE OF LADY BLESSINGTON AT SEAMORE PLACE FROM 1832 TO 1836, AND AT GORE HOUSE, KENSINGTON GORE, FROM 1836 TO APRIL, 1849.

ABOUT twenty years ago there were three circles of fashionable society in London, wherein the intellectual celebrities of the time did chiefly congregate. Three very remarkable women presided over them: the Countess of Blessington, the Countess of Charleville, and Lady Holland. The qualities, mental and personal, of the ladies, differed very much; but their tastes concurred in one particular: each of them sought to make society in her house as agreeable as possible, to bring together as much ability, wit, and intellectual acquirements as could be assembled and associated advantageously; to elicit any kind, or any amount, however small, of talent that any individual in that society might possess, and to endeavor to make men of letters, art, or science, previously unacquainted, or estranged, or disposed to stand aloof, and to isolate themselves in society, think kindly and favorably of one another. I am not quite sure, however, that a very kindly feeling toward each other prevailed among the rival queens of London literary society.

The power and influence of Lady Blessington's intellectual qualities consisted chiefly in her conversational talents. It would be difficult to point out any particular excellence, and to say that one constituted the peculiar charm of her conversation.

It was something of frankness and archness, without the least mixture of ill nature, in every thing she said, of *enjouement* in every thought she uttered, of fullness of confidence in the outspeaking of her sentiments, and the apparent absence of every *arriere pensée* in her mind, while she laughed out unpremeditated ideas, and *bon mots* spontaneously elicited, in such joyous tones, that it might be said she seldom talked without a smile at least on her lips; it was something of felicity in her mode of expression, and freedom in it from all reserve, superadded to the effect produced by singular loveliness of face, expressiveness of look and gesture, and gracefulness of form and carriage, that constituted the peculiar charm of the conversation of Lady Blessington.

She seldom spoke at any length, never bored her hearers with disquisitions, nor dogmatized on any subject, and very rarely played the learned lady in discourse. She conversed with all around her in "a give and take" mode of interchange of sentiments. She expressed her opinions in short, smart, and telling sentences; brilliant things were thrown off with the utmost ease; one *bon mot* followed another, without pause or effort, for a minute or two, and then, while her wit and humor were producing their desired effect, she would take care, by an apt word or gesture, provocative of mirth and communicativeness, to draw out the persons who were best fitted to shine in company, and leave no intelligence, however humble, without affording it an opportunity and an encouragement to make some display, even in a single trite remark or telling observation in the course of conversation.

How well Lady Blessington understood the excellencies and art of brilliant and effective conversation, may be noticed in the following observation:

"The conversation of Lamartine," says Lady Blessington, "is lively and brilliant. He is, I am persuaded, as amiable as he is clever, with great sensibility, which is indicated in his countenance as well as it is proved in his works; he possesses sufficient tact to conceal, in general society, every attribute peculiar to the poetical temperament, and to appear only as a well-informed, well-bred, sensible man of the world. This tact is probably the result of his diplomatic career, which, compelling a constant friction with society, has induced the adoption of its usages."*

* The Idler in Italy, Par. ed., p. 372, 1839.

We are told that "books which make one think" are most valued by people of high intelligence; but conversation which makes one think I do not think is the description of discourse which would tell best in the salons, even of Gore House, when it was most frequented by eminent literary men, artists, and state politicians. Conversation which makes one laugh, which tickles the imagination, which drives rapidly, pleasantly, and lightly over the mind, and makes no deep impression on the road of the understanding, which produces oblivion of passing cares, and amuses for the time being, is the enjoyment in reality that is sought in what is called the brilliant circles of literature and of art, *à la mode*. How does the conversation of such circles tally with the taste for reading referred to in the following passage?

"I, for my own part," says Archdeacon Hare, "have ever gained the most profit, and the most pleasure also, from the books which have made me think the most; and when the difficulties have once been overcome, these are the books which have struck the deepest root, not only in my memory and understanding, but likewise in my affections. If you would fertilize the mind, the plow must be driven over and through it. The gliding of wheels is easier and rapider, but only makes it harder and more barren. Above all, in the present age of light reading, that is, of reading hastily, thoughtlessly, indiscriminately, unfruitfully, when most books are forgotten as soon as they are finished, and very many sooner, it is well if something heavier is cast now and then into the midst of the literary public. This may scare and repel the weak; it will rouse and attract the stronger, and increase their strength by making them exert it. In the sweat of the brow is the mind as well as the body to eat its bread. Are writers, then, to be studiously difficult, and to tie knots for the mere purpose of compelling their readers to untie them? Not so. Let them follow the bent of their own minds. Let their style be the faithful mirror of their thoughts. Some minds are too rapid, and vehement, and redundant to flow along in lucid transparence; some have to break over rocks, and to force a way through obstacles which would have dammed them in. Tacitus could not write like Cæsar. Niebuhr could not write like Goldsmith."*

Goldsmith's conversation, however, was not calculated to make men in society either think or laugh much.

"Mr. Fox," we are told, in a recent biography, "declared that he learned more from conversation than all the books he had ever read. It often happens, indeed, that a short remark in conversation contains the essence of a quarto volume."†

Lady Blessington had a particular turn for cramming a vast deal of meaning into an exceeding small number of words. She not only had a natural talent for condensing thoughts, and producing them in terse, vigorous, and happily-selected terms, but she made a study of saying memorable things in short, smart sentences, of conveying in a remark some idea of the import, essence, and merits of an entire book.

Lord John Russell, in his Preface to the fifth volume of Moore's "Memoirs," makes an observation, very just and singularly felicitous in its expression, in reference to the conversational powers of Sir James Mackintosh and Sidney Smith:

"There are two kinds of colloquial wit which equally contribute to fame, though not equally to agreeable conversation. The one is like a rocket in a dark air, which shoots at once into the sky, and is the more surprising from the previous silence and gloom; the other is like that kind of fire-work which blazes and bursts out in every direction, exploding at one moment, and shining brightly in its course, and changing its shape and color to many forms and many hues.

"The great delight of Sidney Smith was to produce a succession of ludicrous images; these followed each other with a rapidity that scarcely left time to laugh; he himself laughing louder and with more enjoyment than any one. This electric contact of mirth came and went with the occasion; it can not be repeated or reproduced; any thing would give occasion to it.......

"Of all those whose conversation is referred to by Moore, Sir James Mackintosh was the ablest, the most brilliant, and the

* Guesses at Truth. † Moore's Memoirs.

best informed. A most competent judge in this matter has said, 'Till subdued by age and illness, his conversation was more brilliant and instructive than that of any human being I ever had the good fortune to be acquainted with.' His stores of learning were vast, and of those kinds which, both in serious and in light conversation, are most available."

It would be idle to compare the conversational talents of Lady Blessington with those of Sidney Smith or Sir James Mackintosh in any respect but one, namely, the power of making light matters appear of moment in society, dull things brilliant, and bright thoughts, given utterance to even in sport, contribute to the purposes of good humor, tending to enliven, amuse, and exhilarate people's minds in society when sought for amusement and relaxation.

The perfection of conversational talent is said "to be able to say something on any subject that may be started, without betraying any anxiety or impatience to say it." The Prince de Ligne, a great authority in conversational matters, said, "Ce qui coute le plus pour plaire, c'est de cacher que l' on s'ennuie. Ce n'est pas en amusant qu'on plait. On n'amuse pas même si l'on s'amuse ; c'est en faisant croire que l'on s'amuse."

Madame de Staël spoke of conversation emphatically as an art:

"To succeed in conversation, we must possess the tact of perceiving clearly, and at every instant, the impression made on those with whom we converse ; that which they would fain conceal, as well as that which they would willingly exaggerate—the inward satisfaction of some, the forced smiles of others. We must be able to note and arrest half-formed censures as they pass over the countenance of the listeners, by hastening to dissipate them before self-love be engaged against us. There is no arena in which vanity displays itself under such a variety of forms as in conversation."*

Of all the women of our age, Madame de Staël was the most eminently intellectual. With genius, and judgment, and powers of mental application of the highest order, she was imbued with

* L'Allemagne.

poetry and enthusiasm, she was of a sanguine, impulsive nature, wonderfully eloquent, chivalrous, patriotic, a lover of liberty and glory, and, withal, womanly in her feelings and affections. She delighted in society; with her large heart, and well-stored head, and remarkable powers of conversation, it is no wonder the circles of a metropolis that was in that day the great centre of civilization should have peculiar attractions for her; Paris, with its brilliant society, where her literary reputation had its birth, became her world. She gloried in society, and was the chief grace, glory, and ornament of it.

Byron said to Lady Blessington that "Madame de Staël was certainly the cleverest, though not the most agreeable woman he had ever known; she declaimed to you instead of conversing with you, never pausing except to take breath; and if, during that interval, a rejoinder was put in, it was evident that she did not attend to it, as she resumed the thread of her discourse as though it had not been interrupted."

His lordship went on to say that she was in the habit of losing herself in philosophical disquisitions, and although very eloquent and fluent when excited in conversation, her language was sometimes obscure, and her phraseology florid and redundant.

Lady Blessington's love for London and its celebrities was of the same all-absorbing nature as that of Madame de Staël for Parisian society.

The exile of the illustrious baroness from the French capital was "a second death" to her, we are told in a recent admirable memoir.

"It appears strange that banishment from Paris should thus have been looked upon by Madame de Staël as an evil, and cause of suffering almost beyond her endurance. With her great intellectual resources, her fine heart, capable of attaching itself to whatever was lovable or excellent, and the power she possessed of interesting others, and of giving the tone to whatever society she entered, one would have supposed that she, of all people, ought not to have depended for her happiness upon any clique or association, however brilliant. But, though she viewed with deep interest and philosophical curiosity every form of human society, she only seems to have *loved* that to which she had been accustomed, and to have felt herself *at home* only in the midst of the bustle and excitement among which her life had begun. She was not yet fully alive to the beauties of nature. Like Charles Lamb, she preferred the 'sweet security of streets' to the most magnificent scenery the world contained, and thought, with Dr. Johnson, that there was no scene equal to the high tide of human existence in the heart of a populous city. When guests who came to visit her at Geneva were in ecstasies with its lovely scenes, 'Give me the Rue de Bac,' she said: 'I would rather live in Paris in a fourth story, and with a hundred a year. I do not dissemble: a residence in Paris has always appeared to me, under any circumstances, the most desirable of all others. French conversation excels nowhere except in Paris, and conversation has been, since my infancy, my greatest pleasure.'"

One who knew her peculiar talents and characteristics well has observed of her in later years: "An over-stimulated youth, acting on a temperament naturally ardent and impassioned, had probably aggravated these tendencies to a morbid extent; for in the very prime of her life, and strength of her intellect, it would have seemed to her almost as impossible to dispense with the luxury of deep and strong emotions, as with the air which sustained her existence."

Madame de Staël had this advantage over all the learned and literary women of her time—she was born and bred in the midst of intellectual excitement, conversational exhibitions, triumphs of imagination, and all the stirring scenes of a grand drama, which opened with bright visions of freedom, and renewed vigor and vitality for the human race, though it terminated in a terrible denouément of revolution and widely-extended phrensy.

Madame de Staël lacked one great source of influence and power in conversation, namely, beauty. Her features were flexible, but strongly marked and somewhat masculine; but her eyes were full of animation, vivacity, and expression, and her voice was finely modulated and harmonious, peculiarly touching and pleasing to the ear, while her movements were graceful and dignified. She entered on life at the beginning of a mighty revolution, with lofty aspirations and glorious inspirations, animated by enthusiastic feelings of love of liberty, of humanity, of glory, and exalted virtue. There was no affectation in these heroic sentiments and chivalrous imaginings: they were born with her; they were fostered in her; the times in which her lot was cast developed them most fully.

It would be vain to look for intellectual power in the literary women of other lands, of our time, that could have produced "Thoughts on the French Revolution," "Ten Years of Exile," "Sophia, or Secret Sentiments," "On the Influence of Passions in Individuals and National Happiness," "Literature, considered in its connection with Social Institutions," "Delphine," "Corinne," "Germany," &c., &c., &c.

The labor of her great works on the French Revolution, after her return to her beloved Paris, at the period of the restoration of Louis the Eighteenth, contributed, it is supposed, to the breaking down of her health, after a short but memorable career of wonderful literary toil and application of the mental faculties. She died in 1817, at the age of fifty-one years.

Of Holland House society, Mr. Macauley, in an article in the "Edinburgh Review," has commemorated the brilliancies; and Lord John Russell has likewise recorded its attractions in terms worthy of a man of letters and a lover of the amenities of literature. In his preface to the six volumes of "Moore's Memoirs," he seems to revel in the short snatches of literary occupation which he has indulged in, at the expense of politics and affairs of state, when he describes the conversational powers of Lord Holland, and the display of them in those circles which his lordship and his friend Moore were in the habit of frequenting. He characterizes the charms of Lord Holland's conversation as combining a variety of excellencies of disposition, as well as of mental endowments, generous sentiments and principles, kindliness of nature, warmth of feeling, remarkable cheerfulness of disposition, toleration for all opinions, a keen sense of the ridiculous, good memory, an admirable talent for mimicry, a refined taste, an absence of all formality, a genial warmth and friendliness of intercourse in society. "He won," says Lord John, "without seeming to court, he instructed without seeming to teach, and he amused without laboring to be witty. But of the charm which belonged to Lord Holland's conversation future times can form no adequate conception:

"'The pliant muscles of the varying face,
The mien that gave each sentence strength and grace,
The tuneful voice, the eye that spoke the mind,
Are gone, nor leave a single trace behind.'"*

I find among the papers of Count D'Orsay a few slight but graphic sketches of Lord Holland and some of his contemporaries worthy of the writer, and possibly these may be all that now remain of those delineations of London celebrities by the count which Byron refers to in his letters.

"It is impossible," says the count, "to know Lord Holland without feeling for him a strong sentiment of affection; he has so much goodness of heart, that one forgets often the superior qualities of mind which distinguish him; and it is difficult to conceive that a man so simple, so natural, and so good, should be one of the most distinguished senators of our days."

Holland House was the well-known place of réunion of the most eminent men of the time for nearly a century; the scene of innumerable wit combats, and keen encounters of intelligence and talent.

The late Lord Holland's reputation for classical attainments and high intelligence, fine tastes and cultivated mind, his encouragement of art and literature, conversational talents, and elegant hospitality, are not better known than his amiability of disposition, kindliness of heart, and genial, noble, loving nature, prompting him ever to generous conduct, and liberal, and sometimes even heroic acts of benevolence.

One evidently well acquainted with Lady Holland thus speaks of the brilliant circles over which she so long presided, and of the qualities of heart and mind which enabled her to give to the réunions of men of letters, wit, art, and science, the attractions which characterized them.

* Moore's Memoirs, vol. v.

"Beyond any other hostess we ever knew, and very far beyond any host, she possessed the tact of perceiving and the power of evoking the various capacities which lurked in every part of the brilliant circles she drew around her. To enkindle the enthusiasm of an artist on the theme over which he had achieved the most facile mastery; to set loose the heart of the rustic poet, and imbue his speech with the freedom of his native hills; to draw from the adventurous traveler a breathing picture of his most imminent danger, or to embolden the bashful soldier to disclose his own share in the perils and glories of some famous battle-field; to encourage the generous praise of friendship when the speaker and the subject reflected interest on each other, or win the secret history of some effort which had astonished the world, or shed new lights on science; to conduct those brilliant developments to the height of satisfaction, and then to shift the scene by the magic of a word, were among her daily successes. And if this extraordinary power over the elements of social enjoyments was sometimes wielded without the entire concealment of its despotism—if a decisive check sometimes rebuked a speaker who might intercept the variegated beauty of Jeffrey's indulgent criticism, or the jest announced and self-rewarded in Sidney Smith's delighted and delighting chuckle, the authority was too clearly exerted for the evening's prosperity, and too manifestly impelled by an urgent consciousness of the value of those golden hours which were fleeting within its confines, to sadden the enforced silence with more than a momentary regret. If ever her prohibition, clear, abrupt, and decisive, indicated more than a preferable regard for livelier discourse, it was when a depreciatory tone was adopted toward genius, or goodness, or honest endeavor, or when some friend, personal or intellectual, was mentioned in slighting phrase.

"Habituated to a generous partisanship by strong sympathy with a great political cause, she carried the fidelity of her devotion to that cause into her social relations, and was ever the truest and fastest of friends. The tendency, often more idle than malicious, to soften down the intellectual claims of the absent, which so insidiously besets literary conversation, and teaches a superficial insincerity even to substantial esteem and regard, found no favor in her presence; and hence the conversations over which she presided, perhaps beyond all that ever flashed with a kindred splendor, were marked by that integrity of good nature, which might admit of their exact repetition to every living individual whose merits were discussed without the danger of inflicting pain.

"Under her auspices, not only all critical, but all personal talk was tinged with kindness; the strong interest which she took in the happiness of her friends shed a peculiar sunniness over the aspects of life presented by the common topics of alliances, and marriages, and promotions; and not a promising engagement, or a wedding, or a promotion of a friend's son, or a new intellectual triumph of any youth with whose name and history she was familiar, but became an event on which she expected and required congratulation as on a part of her own fortune.

"Although there was naturally a preponderance in her society of the sentiment of popular progress, which once was cherished almost exclusively by the party to whom Lord Holland was united by sacred ties, no expression of triumph in success, no virulence in sudden disappointment, was ever permitted to wound the most sensitive ear of her conservative guests. It might be that some placid comparison of recent with former time spoke a sense of peaceful victory, or that on the giddy edge of some great party struggle, the festivities of the evening might take a more serious cast as news arrived from the scene of contest, and the pleasure be deepened with the peril; but the feeling was always restrained by the present evidence of permanent solaces for the mind which no political changes could disturb. If to hail and welcome genius, or even talent which revered and imitated genius, was one of the greatest pleasures of Lord Holland's life, to search it out and bring it within the sphere of his noble sympathy was the delightful study of hers. How often, during the last half century, has the steep ascent of fame been brightened by the genial appreciation she bestowed, and the festal light she cast on its solitude! How often has the assurance of success received its crowning delight amid the genial luxury of her circle, where renown itself has been realized in all its sweetness!"*

CHARLEVILLE HOUSE, CAVENDISH SQUARE.

The late Dowager Lady Charleville was a remarkable person, eminently gifted, and highly accomplished. The author had the honor of knowing her ladyship intimately about twenty years ago. Few women possessed sounder judgment, or were more capable of forming just opinions on most subjects.

Dublin and its society at the time of the Union, and for some years before, as well as after that measure, was a frequent subject of conversation with her. All the Irish celebrities of those times were intimately known by her; Clare and Castlereagh, young Wesley and Lord Edward Fitzgerald, Lord Moira, and the Beresfords, cum multis aliis, of most dissimilar political elements. Throughout her whole career, it seemed to be a settled plan of hers to bring persons of worth, of opposite opinions, together, and to endeavor to get them to think justly and favorably of one another, as if she considered one of the chief causes of half the estrangements and animosities that exist was the groundless misapprehensions of unacquainted people of the same class, pursuits in life, or position in society.

The Countess Dowager of Cork, at the same period that Ladies Blessington, Holland, and Charleville collected round them their several celebrities of fashion and literary eminence, was the centre of a brilliant circle of London celebrities. From 1820 to 1840 was frequently to be seen at the London theatres this genuine representative, in all but one respect, of the celebrated Ninon de l'Enclos.

The Right Hon. Mary, Countess Dowager of Cork and Derry, resided for a great many years in New Burlington Street. Her ladyship's *soirées* were not on so extensive a scale as those of Lady Blessington and Lady Holland, but still they were crowded with fashionable and distinguished people. Lady Cork, when Miss Monckton, was one of Dr. Johnson's favorites. "Her vivacity," we are told, "exhilarated the sage;" and they used to talk

* Remarks on the character of Lady Holland, in the "Morning Chronicle."

together with all imaginable ease. Frequent mention of her is made by Boswell. She was born in 1746; her father was John Monckton, first Viscount Galway. In 1784 she married the Earl of Cork. For a large portion of her life she occupied a conspicuous place in London society. Her residence in New Burlington Street was a rendezvous of wits, scholars, sages, and politicians, and *bas bleux* of celebrity. "Her social reputation dates from her attempts, the first of the kind (in England), to introduce into the routine and formation of our high life something of the wit and energy which characterized the society of Paris in the last century. While still young, she made the house of her mother, Lady Galway, the point of rendezvous where talent and genius might mingle with rank and fashion, and the advantages of intellectual endowments be mutually interchanged."

The endeavors of Miss Monckton to give a higher tone to the society in which she found herself in the latter part of the last century had the beneficial effect of thinning the crowds round the faro-tables, then the nightly excitement of both sexes. Her Sunday parties were the first that were attempted without this accompaniment. Her ladyship, to the last enjoying society; "ready for death, but not wishing to see him coming," died at the age of ninety-four, in her house in Burlington Street, the 20th of May, 1840.

SEAMORE PLACE.

Lady Blessington, in one of her novels, "The Victims of Society," wherein abundance of sarcasm was bestowed on the lionizing tendencies of English fashionable society, refers to "the modern Mecænases of May-fair" (in which locality her ladyship resided when this novel was written by her), "who patronise poets and philosophers, from association with whom they expect to derive distinction. . . . . . . A few of the houses, with the most pretensions to literary taste, have their tame poets and *petits litterateurs,* who run about as docile and more parasitical than lap-dogs; and, like them, are equally well fed, ay, and certainly equally spoiled. The dull pleasantries, thrice-told anecdotes, and *resumés* of the scandal of each week, served up *rechauffés* by these pigmies of literature, are received most graciously by their patrons, who agree in opinion with the French writer,

> "'Nul n'aura de l'esprit,
> Hors nous et nos amis.'"

Not even, we may add, in Seamore Place or Kensington Gore, where the experience was chiefly gained which enabled poor Lady Blessington to delineate "The Victims of Society."

Lady Blessington returned to London from the Continent in November, 1830. In the latter part of 1831 she took up her abode in Seamore Place, May Fair. The mansion in St. James's Square, which had been bequeathed to her by Lord Blessington, was far too expensive an establishment to be kept up by her on an income of two thousand a year. Having disposed of her interest in it, she rented the house in Seamore Place from Lord Mountford, and fitted it up in a style of the greatest magnificence and luxury.* Here, in the month of March, 1832, I found her ladyship established. The Count and Countess D'Orsay were then residing with her. The salons of Lady Blessington were opened nightly to men of genius and learning, and persons of celebrity of all climes, to travelers of every European city of distinction. Her abode became a centre of attraction for the beau monde of the intellectual classes, a place of réunion for remarkable persons of talent or eminence of some sort or another, and certainly the most agreeable resort of men of literature, art, science, of strangers of distinction, travelers, and public characters of various pursuits, the most agreeable that ever existed in this country.

Perhaps the *agrémens* of the Seamore Place society surpassed those of the Gore House *soirées*. Lady Blessington, when resid-

* The house in St. James's Square, which had been bequeathed to Lady Blessington by her husband, it was expected, would have added £500 a year to her income for the few years of the unexpired term of the lease. The head rent, however, was very high, £840 a year. It had been let to the Windham club, furnished, for £1350 a year; but the mode in which the property in the furniture had been left by Lord Blessington, and the conditions imposed by the will with respect to its ultimate transfer to Ireland, and the fault, moreover, found with the bad state of it, had led to such difficulties, that eventually she relinquished her right and interest in the house to the executors, Messrs. Norman and Worthington.

ing in the former street, had not then long commenced the career of authorship as a pursuit and a speculation.

In the twelfth letter of "the Pencilings," dated 1834, Mr. Willis gives an account of his first visit to Lady Blessington in London, then residing in Seamore Place, certainly more graphic than any other description of her *réunions* that has been given:

"A friend in Italy had kindly given me a letter to Lady Blessington, and with a strong curiosity to see this celebrated authoress, I called on the second day after my arrival in London. It was 'deep i' the afternoon,' but I had not yet learned the full meaning of town hours. 'Her ladyship had not come down to breakfast.' I gave the letter and my address to the powdered footman, and had scarce reached home, when a note arrived inviting me to call the same evening at ten.

"In a long library, lined alternately with splendidly-bound books and mirrors, and with a deep window, of the breadth of the room, opening upon Hyde Park, I found Lady Blessington alone. The picture, to my eye, as the door opened, was a very lovely one—a woman of remarkable beauty, half buried in a *fauteuil* of yellow satin, reading by a magnificent lamp suspended from the centre of the arched ceiling; sofas, couches, ottomans, and busts arranged in rather a crowded sumptuousness through the room; enamel tables, covered with expensive and elegant trifles in every corner, and a delicate white hand relieved on the back of a book, to which the eye was attracted by the blaze of its diamond rings. As the servant mentioned my name, she rose and gave me her hand very cordially; and a gentleman entering immediately after, she presented me to Count D'Orsay, the well-known Pelham of London, and certainly the most splendid specimen of a man, and a well-dressed one, that I had ever seen. Tea was brought in immediately, and conversation went swimmingly on.

"Her ladyship's inquiries were principally about America, of which, from long absence, I knew very little. She was extremely curious to know the degrees of reputation the present popular authors of England enjoy among us, particularly Bulwer and D'Israeli (the author of 'Vivian Grey'). 'If you will come to-morrow night,' she said, 'you will see Bulwer. I am delighted that he is popular in America. He is envied and abused—for nothing, I believe, except for the superiority of his genius, and the brilliant literary success it commands; and knowing this, he chooses to assume a pride which is only the armor of a sensitive mind afraid of a wound. He is to his friends the most frank and noble creature in the world, and open to boyishness with those who he thinks understand and value him. He has a brother Henry, who is also very clever in a different vein, and is just now publishing a book on the present state of France.

"'Do they like the D'Israelis in America?'

"I assured her ladyship that the 'Curiosities of Literature,' by the father, and 'Vivian Grey' and 'Contarini Fleming,' by the son, were universally known.

"'I am pleased at that, for I like them both. D'Israeli the elder came here with his son the other night. It would have delighted you to see the old man's pride in him, and the son's respect and affection for his father. D'Israeli the elder lives in the country, about twenty miles from town; seldom comes up to London, and leads a life of learned leisure, each day hoarding up and dispensing forth treasures of literature. He is courtly, yet urbane, and impresses one at once with confidence in his goodness. In his manners, D'Israeli the younger is quite his own character of "Vivian Grey;" full of genius and eloquence, with extreme good nature, and a perfect frankness of character.'

"I asked if the account I had seen in some American paper of a literary celebration at Canandaigua, and the engraving of her ladyship's name with some others upon a rock, was not a quiz.

"'Oh, by no means. I was much amused by the whole affair. I have a great idea of taking a trip to America to see it. Then the letter, commencing, "Most charming Countess—for charming you must be, since you have written the 'Conversations of Lord Byron'"—oh, it was quite delightful. I have shown it to every body. By-the-way, I receive a great many letters from America from people I never heard of, written in the most extraordinary style of compliment, apparently in perfect good faith. I hardly know what to make of them.'

"I accounted for it by the perfect seclusion in which great numbers of cultivated people live in our country, who, having neither intrigue, nor fashion, nor twenty other things to occupy their minds, as in England, depend entirely upon books, and consider an author who has given them pleasure as a friend. 'America,' I said, 'has probably more literary enthusiasts than any country in the world; and there are thousands of romantic minds in the interior of New England who know perfectly every writer on this side of the water, and hold them all in affectionate veneration, scarcely conceivable by a sophisticated European. If it were not for such readers, literature would be the most thankless of vocations; I, for one, would never write another line.'

"'And do you think these are the people which write to me? If I could think so, I should be exceedingly happy. A great proportion of the people of England are refined down to such heartlessness; criticism, private and public, is so much influenced by politics, that it is really delightful to know there is a more generous tribunal. Indeed, I think many of our authors now are beginning to write for America. We think already a great deal of your praise or censure.'

"I asked if her ladyship had known many Americans.

"'Not in London, but a great many abroad. I was with Lord Blessington in his yacht at Naples when the American fleet was lying there ten or eleven years ago, and we were constantly on board your ships. I knew Commodore Creighton and Captain Deacon extremely well, and liked them particularly. They were with us frequently of an evening on board the yacht or the frigate, and I remember very well the bands playing always "God save the King" as we went up the side. Count D'Orsay here, who spoke very little English at the time, had a great passion for "Yankee Doodle," and it was always played at his request.'

"The count, who still speaks the language with a very slight accent, but with a choice of words that shows him to be a man of uncommon tact and elegance of mind, inquired after several of the officers, whom I have not the pleasure of knowing. He seems to remember his visits to the frigate with great pleasure. The conversation, after running upon a variety of topics, turned very naturally upon Byron. I had frequently seen the Countess Guiccioli on the Continent, and I asked Lady Blessington if she knew her.

"'Yes, very well. We were at Genoa when they were living there, but we never saw her. It was at Rome, in the year 1828, that I first knew her, having formed her acquaintance at Count Funchal's, the Portuguese embassador.'

"It would be impossible, of course, to make a full and fair record of a conversation of some hours. I have only noted one or two topics which I thought most likely to interest an American reader. During all this long visit, however, my eyes were very busy in finishing for memory a portrait of the celebrated and beautiful woman before me.

"The portrait of Lady Blessington in the 'Book of Beauty' is not unlike her, but it is still an unfavorable likeness. A picture by Sir Thomas Lawrence hung opposite me, taken, perhaps, at the age of eighteen, which is more like her, and as captivating a representation of a just matured woman, full of loveliness and love, the kind of creature with whose divine sweetness the gazer's heart aches, as ever was drawn in the painter's most inspired hour. The original is no longer *dans sa première jeunesse.* Still she looks something on the sunny side of thirty. Her person is full, but preserves all the fineness of an admirable shape; her foot is not pressed in a satin slipper, for which a Cinderella might long be sought in vain; and her complexion (an unusually fair skin, with very dark hair and eyebrows) is of even a girlish delicacy and freshness. Her dress, of blue satin (if I am describing her like a milliner, it is because I have here and there a reader in my eye who will be amused by it), was cut low, and folded across her bosom, in a way to show to advantage the round and sculpture-like curve and whiteness of a pair of exquisite shoulders; while her hair, dressed close to her head, and parted simply on her forehead with a rich *feronier* of turquoise, enveloped in clear outline a head with which it would be difficult to find a fault. Her features are regular, and her mouth, the most expressive of them, has a ripe fullness and freedom of play peculiar to the Irish physiognomy, and expressive of the most unsuspicious good-humor. Add to all this a voice merry and sad by turns, but always musical, and manners of the most unpretending elegance, yet even more remarkable for their winning kindness, and you have the prominent traits of one of the most lovely and fascinating women I have ever seen. Remembering her talents and her rank, and the unenvying admiration she receives from the world of fashion and genius, it would be difficult to reconcile her lot to the 'doctrine of compensation.' *

"In the evening I kept my appointment with Lady Blessington. She had deserted her exquisite library for the drawing-room, and sat, in full dress, with six or seven gentlemen about her. I was presented immediately to all; and when the conversation was resumed, I took the opportunity to remark the distinguished *coterie* with which she was surrounded.

"Nearest me sat Smith, the author of 'Rejected Addresses'—a hale, handsome man, apparently fifty, with white hair, and a very nobly-formed head and physiognomy. His eye alone—small, and with lids contracted into an habitual look of drollery, betrayed the bent of his genius. He held a cripple's crutch in his hand, and, though otherwise rather particularly well-dressed, wore a pair of large India-rubber shoes—the penalty he was paying, doubtless, for the many good dinners he had eaten. He played rather an *aside* in the conversation, whipping in with a quiz or witticism whenever he could get an opportunity, but more a listener than a talker.

"On the opposite side of Lady Blessington stood Henry Bulwer, the brother of the novelist, very earnestly engaged in a discussion of some speech of O'Connell's. He is said by many to be as talented as his brother, and has lately published a book on the present state of France. He is a small man; very slight and gentlemanlike; a little pitted with the small-pox, and of

* Pencilings by the Way, p. 355, 356.

very winning and persuasive manners. I liked him at the first glance.

"A German prince, with a star on his breast, trying with all his might—but, from his embarrassed look, quite unsuccessfully—to comprehend the drift of the argument; the Duke de Richelieu; a famous traveler just returned from Constantinople; and the splendid person of Count D'Orsay, in a careless attitude upon the ottoman, completed the *cordon*.

"I fell into conversation after a while with Smith, who, supposing I might not have heard the names of the others in the hurry of an introduction, kindly took the trouble to play the dictionary, and added a graphic character of each as he named him. Among other things, he talked a great deal of America, and asked me if I knew our distinguished countryman, Washington Irving. I had never been so fortunate as to meet him. 'You have lost a great deal,' he said, 'for never was so delightful a fellow. I was once taken down with him into the country by a merchant to dinner. Our friend stopped his carriage at the gate of his park, and asked us if we would walk through his grounds to the house. Irving refused, and held me down by the coat, so that we drove on to the house together, leaving our host to follow on foot. 'I make it a principle,' said Irving, 'never to walk with a man through his own grounds. I have no idea of praising a thing whether I like it or not. You and I will do them to-morrow morning by ourselves.' The rest of the company had turned their attention to Smith as he began his story, and there was a universal inquiry after Mr. Irving. Indeed, the first question on the lips of every one to whom I am introduced as an American is of him and Cooper. The latter seems to me to be admired as much here as abroad, in spite of a common impression that he dislikes the nation. No man's works could have higher praise in the general conversation that followed, though several instances were mentioned of his having shown an unconquerable aversion to the English when in England. Lady Blessington mentioned Mr. Bryant, and I was pleased at the immediate tribute paid to his delightful poetry by the talented circle around her.

"Toward twelve o'clock Mr. Lytton Bulwer was announced, and enter the author of 'Pelham.' I had made up my mind how he *should* look, and, between prints and descriptions, thought I could scarcely be mistaken in my idea of his person. No two things could be more unlike, however, than the ideal of Mr. Bulwer in my mind and the real Mr. Bulwer who followed the announcement. I liked his manners extremely. He ran up to Lady Blessington with the joyous heartiness of a boy let out of school; and the 'how d'ye, Bulwer?' went round, as he shook hands with every body, in the style of welcome usually given to 'the best fellow in the world.' As I had brought a letter of introduction to him from a friend in Italy, Lady Blessington introduced me particularly, and we had a long conversation about Naples and its pleasant society.

"Bulwer's head is phrenologically a fine one. His forehead retreats very much, but is very broad and well masked, and the whole air is that of decided mental superiority. His nose is aquiline. His complexion is fair, his hair profuse, curly, and of a light auburn. A more good-natured, habitually-smiling expression could hardly be imagined. Perhaps my impression is an imperfect one, as he was in the highest spirits, and was not serious the whole evening for a minute—but it is strictly and faithfully my impression.

"I can imagine no style of conversation calculated to be more agreeable than Bulwer's. Gay, quick, various, half-satirical, and always fresh and different from every body else, he seemed to talk because he could not help it, and infected every body with his spirits. I can not give even the substance of it in a letter, for it was in a great measure local or personal.

"Bulwer's voice, like his brother's, is exceedingly lover-like and sweet. His playful tones are quite delicious, and his clear laugh is the soul of sincere and careless merriment.

"It is quite impossible to convey in a letter, scrawled literally between the end of a late visit and a tempting pillow, the evanescent and pure spirit of a conversation of wits. I must confine myself, of course, in such sketches, to the mere sentiment of things that concern general literature and ourselves.

"'The Rejected Addresses' got upon his crutches about three o'clock in the morning, and I made my exit with the rest, thanking Heaven that, though in a strange country, my mother tongue was the language of its men of genius.

"Letter June 14, 1834. I was at Lady Blessington's at eight. Moore had not arrived, but the other persons of the party—a Russian count, who spoke all the languages of Europe as well as his own; a Roman banker, whose dynasty is more powerful than the Pope's; a clever English nobleman, and the 'observed of all observers,' Count D'Orsay, stood in the window upon the park, killing, as they might, the melancholy twilight half hour preceding dinner.

"Dinner was announced, the Russian handed down 'miladi,' and I found myself seated opposite Moore, with a blaze of light on his Bacchus head, and the mirrors with which the superb octagonal room is paneled reflecting every motion.... The soup vanished in the busy silence that beseems it, and as the courses commenced their procession, Lady Blessington led the conversation with the brilliancy and ease for which she is remarkable over all the women I ever met....

"O'Connell was mentioned.

"'He is a powerful creature,' said Moore; 'but his eloquence has done great harm both to England and Ireland. There is nothing so powerful as oratory. The faculty of "*thinking on his legs*" is a tremendous engine in the hands of any man. There is an undue admiration for this faculty, and a sway permitted to it which was always more dangerous to a country than any thing else. Lord A—— is a wonderful instance of what a man may do *without* talking. There is a general confidence in him—a universal belief in his honesty, which serves him instead. Peel is a fine speaker, but, admirable as he had been as an Oppositionist, he failed when he came to lead the House. O'Connell would be irresistible, were it not for the two blots on his character—the contributions in Ireland for his support, and his refusal to give satisfaction to the man he is still willing to attack. They may say what they will of dueling: it is the great preserver of the decencies of society. The old school, which made a man responsible for his words, was the better. I must confess I think so. Then, in O'Connell's case, he had not made his vow against dueling when Peel challenged him. He accepted the challenge, and Peel went to Dover on his way to France, where they were to meet; and O'Connell pleaded his wife's illness, and delayed till the law interfered.* Some other Irish patriot, about the same time, refused a challenge on account of the illness of his daughter, and one of the Dublin wits made a good epigram on the two:

> " Some men, with a horror of slaughter,
> Improve on the Scripture command,
> And 'honor their' wife and their daughter,
> 'That their days may be long in the land.' "

The great period of Ireland's glory,' continued Moore, 'was between '82 and '98, and it was a time when a man almost lived with a pistol in his hand. Grattan's dying advice to his son was, "Be always ready with the pistol!" He himself never hesitated a moment....'

" Talking of Grattan, is it not wonderful, with all the agitation in Ireland, we have had no such man since his time? You can scarcely reckon Shiel of the calibre of her spirits of old, and O'Connell, with all his faults, stands alone in his glory.

"The conversation I have given is a mere skeleton, of course ...

" This discussion may be supposed to have occupied the hour after Lady Blessington retired from the table; for with her vanished Moore's excitement, and every body else seemed to feel that light had gone out of the room. Her excessive beauty is less an inspiration than the wondrous talent with which she draws from every person around her his peculiar excellence. Talking better than any body else, and narrating, particularly, with a graphic power that I never saw excelled, this distinguished woman seems striving only to make others unfold themselves; and never had diffidence a more apprehensive and en-

* There are many statements made and opinions expressed by Mr. Willis in the extracts above given, with regard to which, silence, it is hoped, will not be taken for acquiescence in their justice.—R. R. M.

couraging listener. But this is a subject with which I should never be done.

"We went up to coffee, and Moore brightened again over his *chasse-café*, and went glittering on with criticisms on Grisi, the delicious songstress now ravishing the world, whom he placed above all but Pasta; and whom he thought, with the exception that her legs were too short, an incomparable creature. This introduced music very naturally, and with a great deal of difficulty he was taken to the piano. My letter is getting long, and I have no time to describe his singing. It is well known, however, that its effect is only equaled by the beauty of his own words; and, for one, I could have taken him into my heart with my delight. He makes no attempt at music. It is a kind of admirable recitative, in which every shade of thought is syllabled and dwelt upon, and the sentiment of the song goes through your blood, warming you to the very eyelids, and starting your tears, if you have a soul or sense in you. I have heard of women's fainting at a song of Moore's; and if the burden of it answered by chance to a secret in the bosom of the listener, I should think, from its comparative effect upon so old a stager as myself, that the heart would break with it.

"We all sat around the piano, and after two or three songs of Lady Blessington's choice, he rambled over the keys a while, and sang 'When first I met thee' with a pathos that beggars description. When the last word had faltered out, he rose and took Lady Blessington's hand, said good-night, and was gone before a word was uttered."*

In a former edition of "the Pencilings," there are some references to one of the literary men of distinction he met on the occasion above referred to which do not exist in the later edition. In these references there are some remarks, intended to be smart sayings, exceedingly superficial and severe, as well as unjust; but there are other observations which are no less true than happily expressed, especially with regard to the descriptive and conversational powers of one of the most highly gifted of all the celebrities of Gore House society.

* Pencilings by the Way, p. 360 to 367.

"D'Israeli had arrived before me at Lady Blessington's, and sat in the deep window, looking out upon Hyde Park, with the last rays of daylight reflected from the gorgeous gold flowers of a splendidly embroidered waistcoat. Patent leather pumps, a white stick, with a black cord and tassel, and a quantity of chains about his neck and pockets, served to make him, even in the dim light, rather a conspicuous object. D'Israeli has one of the most remarkable faces I ever saw. He is lividly pale, and, but for the energy of his action and the strength of his lungs, would seem a victim to consumption. His eye is black as Erebus, and has the most mocking and lying-in-wait sort of expression conceivable ....

"His hair is as extraordinary as his taste in waistcoats. A thick, heavy mass of jet black ringlets falls over his left cheek almost to his collarless stock, while on the right it is parted and put away with the smooth carefulness of a girl's, and shines most unctuously

"'With thy incomparable oil, Macassar.'

D'Israeli was the only one at table who knew Beckford, and the style in which he gave a sketch of his habits and manners was worthy of himself. I might as well attempt to gather up the foam of the sea as to convey an idea of the extraordinary language in which he clothed his description. There were at least five words in every sentence that must have been very much astonished at the use they were put to, and yet no others apparently could so well have conveyed his idea. He talked like a race-horse approaching the winning post, every muscle in action, and the utmost energy of expression flung out in every burst. Victor Hugo and his extraordinary novels came next under discussion; and D'Israeli, who was fired with his own eloquence, started off, *apropos des bottes*, with a long story of impalement he had seen in Upper Egypt. It was as good, and, perhaps, as authentic as the description of the chow-chow-tow in 'Vivian Grey.' The circumstantiality of the account was equally horrible and amusing. Then followed the sufferer's history, with a score of murders and barbarities, heaped together, like Martin's feast of Belshazzar, with a mixture of horror and splendor that was unparalleled in my experience of improvisation. No mystic priest of the Corybantes could have worked himself up into a finer phrensy of language."

My recollection of the scene to which I think Mr. Willis alludes is of a very different kind, so far as relates to the impression made by the truly extraordinary powers of description of Mr. D'Israeli.

Haydon, in his diary, 27th of February, 1835, writes, "Went to Lady Blessington's in the evening; every body goes to Lady Blessington. She has the first news of every thing, and every body seems delighted to tell her. No woman will be more missed. She is the centre of more talent and gayety than any other woman of fashion in London."*

In the summer of 1833, Lady Blessington met with a severe loss. Her house in Seamore Place was broken into at night by thieves, and plate and jewelry to the value of about £1000 were carried off, and never afterward recovered. This was the first disaster in the way of loss of property that occurred to her. A few years later, she was destined to see every thing swept away she was accustomed to set a store on, every object of luxury that had become a necessity to the splendid misery of her mode of life—costly furniture, magnificent mirrors, adornments of salons, valuable pictures, portraits by the first masters, all the literary baubles of the boudoir and precious ornaments of the person, rarities from every land, books elegantly bound, and perhaps more prized than all her other treasures.

Lady Blessington removed from Seamore Place to the more spacious and elegant mansion of Gore House, Kensington Gore, the former abode of William Wilberforce, in the early part of 1836. And here her ladyship remained till the 14th of April, 1849.

GORE HOUSE.

Any person acquainted with Lady Blessington when residing at the villa Belvidere at Naples, the Palazzo Negrone at Rome,

* Memoirs of B. R. Haydon, vol. iii., p. 12.

her delightful residence at Seamore Place in London, and her latest English place of abode in Gore House, must have observed the remarkable changes that had come over her mind at the different epochs of her career in intellectual society and in fashionable life from 1823 to 1849.

In Naples, the charm of Lady Blessington's conversation and society was indescribably effective. The genial air, the beautiful scenery of the place, and all the "influences of the sweet South," seemed to have delighted, soothed, and spiritualized her feelings. A strong tendency to fastidiousness of taste, to weariness of mind in the enjoyment of any long-continued entertainment or amusement, to sudden impulses of hastiness of temper (as distinguished from habitual ill-humor), had been subdued and softened by those changes of scenery and "skiey influences;" and, above all, there was observable in her animal spirits a flow of hilarity, a natural vivacity, such as those who knew her in early life were well aware had belonged to her childhood, and which, having been restrained and checked to some extent, had resumed, in the south of Italy, its original character of outbursting *gaité du cœur*. The ringing laugh of joyous girlhood, which Mrs. Jordan used to act to such perfection, was a reality with Lady Blessington in those merry moods of hers in Naples, which were then, indeed, neither "few nor far between."

In society Lady Blessington was then supremely attractive; she was natural and sprightly, and *spirituelle* in proportion to her naturalness, and utter absence of all appearance of an effort to be effective in conversation.

At the distance of a period of three years from the time of my departure from Naples, when I next met Lady Blessington at Rome, that vivacity to which I have referred seemed to me to have been considerably impaired. She had become more of a learned lady, a queen regnant in literary circles, expected to speak with authority on subjects of art and literature, and less of the agreeable woman, eminently graceful, and full of gayety, whom I had parted with in Naples in 1824. But she was at all times attractive and triumphant in her efforts to reign in the society she moved in; and she was, moreover, at all times kindly disposed and faithful in her friendships.

After an interval of nearly five years, I renewed my acquaintance with Lady Blessington in Seamore Place. It was evident that another great "change had come over the spirit of her dream" of life since I had last seen her. Cares, and troubles, and trials of various kinds had befallen her, and left, if not visible external traces, at least perceptible internal evidence of their effects.

After a lapse of two or three years, my acquaintance with Lady Blessington was renewed at Gore House. The new establishment was on a scale of magnificence exceeding even that of Seamore Place.

The brilliant society by which she was surrounded did not seem to have contributed much to her felicity. There was no happiness in the circles of Gore House comparable to that of the Palazzo Belvidere in Naples. There was manifestly a great intellectual effort made to keep up the charm of that society, and no less manifest was it that a great pecuniary effort was making to meet the large expenditure of the establishment that was essential for it. That society was felt by her to be a necessity in England. It had been a luxury in Italy, and had been enjoyed there without anxiety for cost, or any experience of the wear and tear of life that is connected with arduous exertions to maintain a position in London *haut ton* society, acquired with difficulty, and often supported under continually increasing embarrassments.

But, notwithstanding the symptoms of care and anxiety that were noticeable in Lady Blessington's appearance and conversation at that period of her Gore House celebrity, her powers of attraction and of pleasing had lost none of their influences. There were a higher class of men of great intellect at her *soirées* than were formerly wont to congregate about her. Lady Blessington no longer spoke of books and bookish men with diffidence, or any marked deference for the opinions of other persons: she laid down the law of her own sentiments in conversation rather dogmatically; she aimed more at saying smart things than heretofore, and seemed more desirous of congregating celebrities of distinction in her salons than of gathering round her people solely for the *agrèmens* of their society, or any peculiarities in their characters or acquirements.

There was more of gravity and formality in her *conversaziones* than there had been wont to be, and the conversation generally was no longer of that gay, enlivening, cheerful character, abounding in drollery and humor, which made the great charm of her *réunions* in the villa Belvidere, and in a minor degree in Seamore Place.

In Gore House society, Lady Blessington had given herself a mission, in which she labored certainly with great assiduity and wonderful success—that of bringing together people of the same pursuits, who were rivals in them for professional distinction, and inclining competitors for fame in politics, art, and literature, to tolerant, just, and charitable opinions of one another. This, most assuredly, was a very good and noble object, and in her efforts to attain it she was well seconded by Count D'Orsay.

The count, indeed, not only devoted his talents to this object, but extended his aims to the accomplishment of a purpose calculated to do a great deal of good; to remove the groundless misapprehensions of unacquainted intellectual people of neighboring countries, the fruitful cause of national jealousies and antipathies; to remove the prejudices which had raised barriers even in the best societies between English people and foreigners, to level distinctions on account of difference of country, and to unite the high intelligences of various nations in bonds of social intercourse.

The party warfare that is waged in art, literature, and politics, it seemed to be the main object of the mistress of Gore House, in the high sphere in which she moved, to assuage, to put an end to, and, when interrupted, to prevent the recurrence of. It was astonishing with what tact this object was pursued; and those only who have seen much of the correspondence of Lady Blessington can form any idea of the labor she imposed on herself in removing unfavorable impressions, explaining away differences, inducing estranged people to make approaches to an accommodation, to meet and to be reconciled. These labors were not confined to people of the studio or of literary pursuits;

grave politicians and solemn statesmen, great legal functionaries, and even divines, have been largely indebted to them. She threw herself into those labors with an earnestness which seemed almost incredible to those who were accustomed to the reserve and absence of all demonstrativeness of feeling that is supposed to characterize the *haut ton* of English society.

Mackintosh, in his beautiful "Life of Sir Thomas More," enforcing the virtue of moderation and tolerance of opinion, and reprobating the vulgar brutality of "hating men for their opinions," said, "All men, in the fierce contests of contending factions, should, from such an example, learn the wisdom to fear, lest in their most hated antagonist they may strike down a Sir Thomas More; for assuredly virtue is not so narrowed as to be confined to *any party*, and we have in the case of More a signal example, that the nearest approach to perfect excellence does not exempt men from mistakes which we may justly deem mischievous. It is a pregnant proof that we should beware of hating men for their opinions, or of adopting their doctrines because we love and venerate their virtues."

But the high purposes to which I have referred as actuating Lady Blessington and the Count D'Orsay, namely, of bringing together eminent and estimable people of similar pursuits, who had been estranged from one another, at variance, or on bad terms, did not interfere occasionally with the exercise of the peculiar talents and inclinations of both for drawing out absurd or eccentric people for the amusement of their visitors.

One of the visitors who frequented Gore House about 1837 and 1838 was a very remarkable old French gentleman, then upward of seventy years of age, whom I had known intimately both in France and England—"Monsieur Julien le jeune de Paris," as he styled himself.

He had figured in the great French Revolution—had been patronised by Robespierre, and employed by him in Paris and in the south of France in the Reign of Terror. It was generally asserted and believed that he had voted for the death of Louis the Sixteenth. That, however, was not the fact. It was Monsieur Julien l'ainè who gave his voice for the execution of his sovereign. I believe, moreover, that Monsieur Julien le jeune, though employed under Robespierre, and at one time even acting as his secretary, was not a man of blood *de son grè*, though a very ardent Republican at the period of the regime of terror.

If my poor friend, Monsieur Julien le jeune, was for some time a minister of that system, he certainly repented of it, and made all the atonement, as he thought, that could be made by him, by his connection with a number of philanthropical societies, and the advocacy of the abolition of the punishment of death, the slave-trade, and slavery, and also by the composition of various works of a half moral, part political and polemical kind, and a considerable quantity of lachrymose poetry, chiefly devoted to the illustration of the wrongs and persecutions he had suffered for his country and his opinions. His pieces on this subject, which were extremely lengthy and doleful, he called "*Mes Chagrins Politiques*."

Julien had commenced "patriotic declamation" at a very early period of his career, on the great stage of the Revolution of 1789. Touchard la Fosse, in his "Souvenirs d'un demi siècle," makes mention of him at Bordeaux, at the time that Tallien, one of the leading Terrorists, was there on his mission of extermination, seeking out the last remains of the fugitive Girondists. The future Madame Tallien, an enchantress of the Corinne school, daughter of the Spanish banker Monsieur Cabarrus, then bearing the name of Madame Fontenay, was also at Bordeaux, at that time "in the dawn of her celebrity."

"It was one day announced," says Touchard la Fosse, "that a beautiful citizeness had composed a wonderfully patriotic oration, which would be delivered at the club by a young patriot named Julien (who subsequently, during the Empire, held several important posts in the military administration, and who, since the Restoration better known as Julien de Paris, was, in conjunction with the estimable Amaury Duval, the founder of the 'Revue Encyclopedique').

"The following *decade* was the time fixed for the delivery of his discourse. The club was full. All eyes were bent upon a young woman dressed in a riding habit of dark blue kerseymere faced and trimmed with red velvet. Upon her beautiful black hair, cropped *à la Titus*, then a perfectly new fashion, was lightly set, on one side, a scarlet cap trimmed with fur. Madame Fontenay is said to have been most beautiful in this attire.

"The oration, admirably well read by Citizen Julien, excited wonderful admiration. Its commonplace patriotic declamation, lighted up by a reflection of the admiration felt for the author, gained it the utmost praise. Unanimous applause, flattering address of the president, honors of the sitting—in short, all the remunerations of popular assemblies, were launched upon this beautiful patriot."

"Le Cher Julien" thus, we find, had commenced his *metier* of patriotic recitations some forty-three or four years previously to his exhibitions in Seamore Place. The first performance was in the presence of a very celebrated French enchantress, who reigned in Revolutionary circles, and the latest was in the presence of an Irish enchantress, who reigned over literary fashionable society in London.

At the period of his sojourn in London his head was filled with these "Chagrins." As regularly as he presented himself in the evenings at the salons of Lady Blessington, he brought with him, on each occasion, a roll of paper in his side pocket, consisting of some sheets of foolscap filled with his "Chagrins," which would be seen projecting from the breast of his coat, when, on entering the room, he would stoop to kiss the hand of Lady Blessington, after the manner of the polished courtiers of *la Vielle Cour;* for Monsieur Julien le jeune, in his old age at least, was a perfect specimen of French courtesy, and preserved very little of the burly bearing, or the sturdy manners or opinions of a Republican.

Poor Julien le jeune, like D'Alembert, had the gift of shedding tears at pleasure, to which *don de larmes* of D'Alembert, La Harpe was indebted for the success of one of his dramatic pieces.

"C'est à ce don de larmes que La Harpe dut le succès de sa Melanie. L'etiquette voulait qu'on eut pleuré à ce drame. D'Alembert ne manquait jamais d'accompagner La Harpe. Il prenait un air sérieux et composé, qui fixait d'abord l'attention.

Au premier acte il faisait remarquer les aperçues philosophiques de l'ouvrage ; en suite profitant du talent qu'il avait pour la pantomine, il pleurait toujours aux mêmes endroits, ce qui imposait aux femmes la nécessité, de s'attendrir—et comment auraient elles eu les yeux secs lorsqu'un philosophe fondait en larmes?" Tom. ii., 10.

It used to be a scene that it was most difficult to witness with due restraint, and certainly not without great efforts at external composure, when Monsieur Julien le jeune, all radiant with smiles and overflowing with urbanity, having paid his devoirs to her ladyship, would be approached by Count D'Orsay, and with the eyes of the whole circle fixed on him (duly prepared to expect amusement), the poor old man would be entreated to favor Lady Blessington with the recital of another canto of his political afflictions. Then Julien would protest he had read all that was worth reading to her ladyship, but at length would yield to the persuasions of Lady Blessington with looks and gestures which plainly said, "Infandum Regina jubes renovare dolorem."

On the first occasion of my witnessing this scene, Julien had just gone through the usual formula of praying to be excused, and had made the protestation above referred to, when D'Orsay, with a gravity that was truly admirable, and surprising how it could be maintained, overcame all the reluctance assumed by poor old Julien le jeune to produce the poem expressly brought for recital, by renewed supplications, and on a novel plea for the reading of it.

There was one present, the count observed, who had never heard the "Chagrins," long and earnestly as he desired that gratification, "N'est pas Madden vous n'avez jamais entendu les Chagrins Politiques de notre cher ami Monsieur Julien?"

All the reply that could be given was in a single word, "Jamais."

"Allons mon ami," continued D'Orsay. "Ce pauvre Madden a bien besoin d'entendre vos chagrins politiques—il a les siens aussi—(I had been recently reviewed and reviled in some periodicals)—Il a souffert—oui—il a des sympathies pour les blessés, il faut le donner cette triste plaisir—N'est ce pas Madden?"

Another dire effort to respond in the affirmative, "Oui, Monsieur le Comte."

Monsieur Julien, after playing off for some minutes all the diffident airs of a bashful young lady dying to sing and protesting she can not, placed himself at the upper end of the room, near a table with wax lights, pulled the roll of paper from his breast pocket, and began to recite his "Chagrins Politiques" in a most lugubrious tone, like Mademoiselle Duchesnois—avec les pleurs dans la voix. The saloon was crowded with distinguished guests. On the left hand of the tender-hearted poet and most doleful reciter of his own sorrows—this quondam secretary of Robespierre—was Lady Blessington, in her well-known *fauteuil*, looking most intently, and with apparent anxious solicitude, full in the face of the dolorous reciter. But it would not do for one listening to the "Chagrins" to look too curiously into the eyes of that lady, lest he might perceive any twinkling there indicative of internal hilarity of a communicative kind. On the other side of Monsieur Julien, but somewhat in front of him, sat Count D'Orsay, with a handkerchief occasionally lifted to his eyes; and ever and anon a plaudit or an exclamation of pain was uttered by him at the recital of some particular "Chagrin." At the very instant when the accents of the reciter were becoming most exceedingly lugubrious and ludicrous, and the difficulty of refraining from laughter was at its height, D'Orsay was heard to whisper in a *sotto voce*, as he leaned his head over the back of the chair I sat on, "Pleurez donc!"

Doctor Quin, who was present at this scene, one of the richest, certainly, I ever witnessed, during the recital contributed largely to its effect. Whenever D'Orsay would seize on some particular passage, and exclaim, "Ah que c'est beau!" then would Quin's "magnifique!" "superbe!" "vraiement beau!" be intonated with all due solemnity, and a call for that moving passage over again would be preferred and kindly complied with, so that there was not one of Monsieur Julien's "Chagrins Politiques" which was not received with the most marked attention and applause.

At the conclusion of each "Chagrin," poor Julien's eyes were always sure to be bathed with tears, and as much so at the latest recital of his oft-repeated griefs as at the earliest delivery of them.

It was always in this melting mood, at the conclusion of a recital, he was again conducted by the hand to the fauteuil of Lady Blessington by D'Orsay, and there bending low, as the noble lady of the mansion graciously smiled on him, he received compliments and consolations, most liberally bestowed on his "Chagrins Politiques."

Of one of those displays of D'Orsay's peculiar power in drawing out absurd, eccentric, or *outre* people of a similar kind, one of the most distinguished writers of his time thus writes in April, 1838:

"Count D'Orsay may well speak of an evening being a happy one to whose happiness he contributed so largely. It would be absurd, if one did not know it to be true, to hear Dickens tell, as he has done ever since, of Count D'Orsay's power of drawing out always the best elements of the society around him, and of miraculously putting out the worst. Certainly I never saw it so marvelously exhibited as on the night in question. I shall think of him hereafter unceasingly, with the two guests that sat on either side of him that night. But it has been impossible for me to think of him at any time since I have known him but with the utmost admiration, affection, and respect, which genius and kindness can suggest to every one."

The last time I met Monsieur Julien was at a breakfast given by Colonel Leicester Stanhope, on which occasion many remarkable persons were assembled. Julien, at that period, had abandoned his "Chagrins Politiques," and adopted a new plan of attracting attention. He exhibited a small dial, on the circumference of which, in opposite directions, moral and evil tendencies were marked, and to these a movable index pointed, showing the virtue to be cultivated when any particular defect in character was referred to. This instrument Monsieur Julien called his "Horloge Moral." The old man was lapsing fast into second childhood, but with his senility a large dash of *charla-*

tanerie was very obviously combined. On the occasion I allude to, a brother of Napoleon, one of the ex-kings of the Bonaparte family, was present for a short time, but on seeing Monsieur Julien he immediately departed. Poor L. E. L., who was one of the guests, was singled out by Julien for special instruction in the use of the "Horloge Moral," and she allowed herself to be victimized with most exemplary patience and good humor, while Monsieur Julien was showing off the latest product of his ethical and inventive faculties.

CHAPTER VIII.

THE BREAK-UP AT GORE HOUSE.

Poor Lady Blessington, when she launched into the enormous expenditure of her magnificent establishments, first in Seamore Place, next in Kensington Gore, had little idea of the difficulties of her position in the fashionable world, with a jointure of £2000 a year, to meet all the extensive and incessant claims on her resources, and those claims on them also of at least seven or eight persons, members of her family, who were mainly dependent on her. Little was she aware of the nature of those literary pursuits, and the precariousness of their remuneration, from which she imagined she could derive secure and permanent emolument, that would make such an addition to her ordinary income as would enable her to make head against the vast expenditure of her mode of life—an expenditure which the most constant anxiety to reduce within reasonable limits, by an economy of the most rigid kind in small household matters, was wholly inadequate to accomplish.*

A lady of quality, who sits down in fashionable life to get a livelihood by literature, or a large portion of the means neces-

* Lady Blessington's punctuality and strictness in examining accounts at regular periods, inquiring into expenditure by servants, orders given to tradesmen, and the use made of ordinary articles of consumption, were remarkable. She kept a book of dinners, in which the names of all persons at each entertainment were set down; this register of guests served a double purpose, as a reference for dates, and a check on the accounts of her maître d'hotel.

sary to sustain her in that position, at the hands of publishers, had better build any other description of castles in the air, or, if she must dream of "chateaus en Espagne," let it be of some order of architecture less visionary.

Charles Lamb, the inimitable quaint teller of solemn truths, in amusing terms, in a letter to Bernard Barton, the Quaker poet, in 1823, thus speaks of "literature as a calling to get a livelihood."

"What! throw yourself on the world without any rational plan of support beyond what the chance of employment of booksellers would afford you? Throw yourself rather, my dear sir, from the steep Tarpeian rock slap-dash, headlong down upon iron spikes.

"I have known many authors want bread: some repining, others enjoying the sweet security of a spunging house; all agreeing they had rather have been tailors, weavers, what not, rather than the things they were! I have known some starved—some go mad—one dear friend literally dying in a work-house.

"O! you know not, may you never know, the miseries of subsisting by authorship! 'Tis a pretty appendage to situations like yours or mine, but a slavery worse than all slavery to be a bookseller's dependent; to drudge your brains for pots of ale and breasts of mutton; to change your free thoughts and voluntary numbers for ungracious task-work! The booksellers hate us."

If Lamb had been an Irishman, one might imagine that the "h" in the penultimate word was an interpolation of some sarcastic copyist, who had been infelicitous in authorship, and that we should read *ate*, and not *hate*. Emolument from literature must have been looked to by Lady Blessington, not in the sense of Lamb's pretty appendage to his situation, but as a main resource, to meet an expenditure which her ordinary income could not half suffice for.

The establishment of Gore House, and the incidental expenditure of its noble mistress, could not have been less than £4000 a year. Lady Blessington's jointure was only £2000. But then it must be borne in mind, a very large portion of that expenditure was incurred for aid and assistance given to members of her family, and that she frequently stated in her letters, particularly in those to Mr. Landor, that nothing would induce her to continue her literary labors but to be enabled to provide for those who were dependent on her.

There is a passage in a letter of Sir Walter Scott, in reference to the costly efforts made by a lady of literary tastes to maintain a position in literary society, or rather to be the centre of a literary circle, which well deserves attention.

In his diary while in Italy, Sir Walter makes mention of "Lydia White." "Went to poor Lydia White's, and found her extended on a couch, frightfully swelled, unable to stir, rouged, jesting, and dying. She has a good heart, and is really a clever creature; but unhappily, or rather happily, she has set the whole staff of her life in keeping literary society about her. The world has not neglected her; it is not always so bad as it is called. She can always make up her circle, and generally has some people of real talent and distinction. She is wealthy, to be sure, and gives *petits diners*, but not in a style to carry the point *à force d'argent*. In her case the world is good-natured, and perhaps it is more frequently so than is generally supposed."*

Of the false position of distinguished women in society, it has been very justly observed, in a notice of the life of Madame de Staël:

"The aspect of ill-will makes women tremble, however distinguished they may be. Courageous in misfortune, they are timid against enmity. Thought exalts them, yet their character remains feeble and timid. Most of the women in whom the possession of high faculties has awakened the desire of fame, are like Erminia in her warlike accoutrements. The warriors see the casque, the lance, the shining plume; they expect to meet force, they attack with violence, and with the first stroke reach the heart."

Troubles and afflictions of various kinds had fallen on Lady Blessington, in quick succession, from the year 1843. The loss of fortune and the loss of friends, trials of different kinds, pe-

* Lockhart's Life of Sir W. Scott.

cuniary difficulties, and humiliations, had followed each other with little intermission of late years. In the latter part of 1845, the effects of the potato blight and the famine in Ireland made themselves felt in the magnificent salons in London and on the Continent, even in the place of sojourn of the Irish aristocracy. The sumptuous apartments of Gore House were made intimately acquainted with them.

By the robbery of plate, jewelry, and other valuables, that was committed in Lady Blessington's house in Seamore Place, a loss of upward of £1000 had been sustained. By the failure of Charles Heath, the engraver, she incurred a loss of £700.

The difficulties of Count D'Orsay had contributed also not in a small degree to the derangement of her affairs; and those difficulties had commenced at a very early period of his career in London, while Lady Blessington was residing in Seamore Place, and the count in a small house in Curzon Street, nearly opposite Lord Chesterfield's. The count was arrested, soon after his arrival in England, for a debt of £300 to his boot-maker in Paris, Mr. McHenry, and was only saved from imprisonment by the acceptance, on the part of his creditor, of bail on that occasion.*

In October, 1846, when difficulties were pressing heavily on Lady Blessington, she received a letter (in the handwriting of a lady who signs herself M. A.), from which the following extract appears to have been taken:

"Well may it be said, 'Sweet are the uses of adversity,' which, like the toad, ugly and venomous, bears yet a precious jewel in its head!! and its chief advantage is, that it enables us to judge our real friends from false ones. Rowland Hill on one occasion (preaching to a large congregation on men's trust in the friendship of the world) observed, that his own acquaint-

* I have been informed by Mr. McHenry that he had allowed that debt to remain unsettled for many years, and had consented to accept the security finally offered to him on account of the very large obligations he felt under to the count; for the mere fact of its being known in Paris that Count D'Orsay's boots were made by McHenry, had procured for him the custom of all the tip-top exquisites of Paris. Similar obligations existed in London, with similar relations between the debtors and the indebted; and similar results there between the count and his tradesmen, but sometimes not of a nature so agreeable, frequently took place.

ances would probably fill the church; and he was quite certain that his friends, at the most, would only fill the pulpit. Thus many may say, and those, too, who may have expended thousands in entertaining selfish and cold-hearted men, who would not render them a real service if they wanted one, or give a sigh to their memory on hearing of their decease."

Poor Lady Blessington's mind was ill at ease when she set down the following observations in her commonplace book:

"Great trials demand great courage, and all our energy is called up to enable us to bear them. But it is the minor cares of life that wear out the body, because, singly and in detail, they do not appear sufficiently important to engage us to rally our force and spirits to support them...... Many minds that have withstood the most severe trials have been broken down by a succession of ignoble cares."

How much bitter experience must it have required to say so much in so few words? "When the sun shines on you, you see your friends. It requires sunshine to be seen by them to advantage. While it lasts, we are visible to them; when it is gone, and our horizon is overcast, they are invisible to us."

And elsewhere, another "Night Thought" is to a similar effect:

"Friends are the thermometers by which we may judge the temperature of our fortunes."

"There is no knowledge for which so great a price is paid as a knowledge of the world; and no one ever became an adept in it except at the expense of a hardened or a wounded heart.

"M. B."

Lady Blessington makes reference to "a friend of long standing, and deeply interested in her welfare," who had been consulted by her at the period of her most serious embarrassments, and who had addressed the following letter to her ladyship, without date or name, but probably written in 1848:

"My dearest Friend,—You do not do me more than justice in the belief that I most fully sympathize with all your troubles, and I shall be only too happy if my advice can in any way assist you.

"First. As to your jointure, nothing in law is so indisputable as that a widow's jointure takes precedence of every other claim on an estate. The very first money the agent receives from the property should go to the discharge of this claim. No subsequent mortgages, annuities, encumbrances, law-suits, expenses of management, &c., can be permitted to interfere with the payment of jointure; and as, whatever the distress of the tenants or the embarrassments of the estate, it is clear that some rents must have come in half-yearly, so, on those rents, you have an indisputable right; and I think, on consulting your lawyer, he will put you in a way, either by a memorial to Chancery or otherwise, to secure in future the regular payment of this life-charge. Indeed, on property charged with a jointure, although the rents are not paid for months after the proper dates, the jointure must be paid on the regular days; and if not, the proprietor would become liable to immediate litigation. I am here presuming that you but ask for the jointure, due quarterly or half-yearly, and not in advance, which, if the affairs are in Chancery, it would be illegal to grant.

"Secondly. With respect to the diamonds, would it be possible or expedient to select a certain portion (say half), which you least value on their own account, and, if a jeweler himself falls too short in his offer, to get him to sell them on commission? You must remember that every year, by paying interest on them, you are losing money on them, so that in a few years you may thus lose more than by taking at once less than their true value. There are diamond merchants, who, I believe, give more than jewelers; and if you know Anthony Rothschild, and would not object to speak to him, he might help you.

"Thirdly. With respect to an illustrated work, I like your plan much; and I think any falling off is to be attributed to a relaxation in Heath himself, of proper attention to the interests of the illustrations. You have apparently some idea as to the plan and conception. I fancy that illustrations of our most popular writers might be a novelty. Illustrations from Shakspeare—not the female characters only, but scenes from the plays themselves—by good artists, and the letter-press bearing upon the subject, might make a very saleable and standard work. Again (and I think better), in this day, illustrations from English scenery, ruins, and buildings might be very popular; in fact, if you could create a rational interest in the subject in the plates, your sale and profit would be both larger and more permanent on the first demand, and become a source of yearly income.

"You do perfectly right not to diminish your income by loans; ——— will wait your time, and I am sure that, with proper legal advice, you can insure the regular payments of your jointure in future.

"I think I have thus given you the best hints I can on the different points on which you have so kindly consulted me. I know well how, to those accustomed to punctual payments, and with a horror of debt, pecuniary embarrassments prey upon the mind. But I think they may be borne, not only with ease, but with some degree of complacency, when connected with such generous devotions and affectionate services as those which must console you amid all your cares. In emptying your purse, you have at least filled your heart with consolations, which will long outlast what I trust will be but the troubles of a season."

In April, 1849, the clamors and importunate demands of Lady Blessington's creditors harassed her, and made it evident that an inevitable crash was coming. She had given bills to her bankers, and her bond likewise, for various advances, in anticipation of her jointure, to an amount approaching to £1500. Immediately after the sale, the bankers acknowledged having received from Mr. Phillips, the auctioneer, by her order, the sum of £1500, leaving a balance only in their hands to her credit of £11. She had the necessity of renewing bills frequently as they became due, and on the 24th of April, 1849, she had to renew a bill of hers to a Mr. ——— for a very large amount, which would fall due *on the* 30*th of the following month of May*, four days only before "the great debt of all debts" was to be paid by her.

In the spring of 1849, the long-menaced break-up of the establishment of Gore House took place. Numerous creditors, bill-discounters, money-lenders, jewelers, lace-venders, tax-collectors, gas-company agents, all persons having claims to urge, pressed them at this period simultaneously. An execution for a debt of £4000 was at length put in by a house largely engaged in the silk, lace, India shawl, and fancy jewelry business. Some arrangements were made, a life insurance was effected, but it became necessary to determine on a sale of the whole of the effects for the interest of all the creditors.* Sev-

* For about two years previous to the break-up at Gore House, Lady Blessington lived in the constant apprehension of executions being put in, and unceasing precautions in the admission of persons had to be taken both at the outer gate and hall-door entrance. For a considerable period, too, Count D'Orsay had been in continual danger of arrest, and was obliged to confine himself to the house and grounds, except on Sundays, and in the dusk of the evening on other days. All those precautions were, however, at length baffled by the ingenuity of a sheriff's officer, who effected an entrance in a disguise, the ludicrousness of which had some of the characteristics of farce, which contrasted strangely and painfully with the denouément of a very serious drama.

Lady Blessington was no sooner informed, by a confidential servant, of the fact

eral of the friends of Lady Blessington urged on her pecuniary assistance, which would have prevented the necessity of breaking up the establishment. But she declined all offers of this kind. The fact was, that Lady Blessington was sick at heart, worn down with cares and anxieties, wearied out with difficulties and embarrassments daily augmenting, worried with incessant claims, and tired to death with demands she could not meet. For years previously, if the truth was known, she was sick at the heart's core of the splendid misery of her position—of the false appearances of enjoyment in it—of the hollow smiles by which it was surrounded—of the struggle for celebrity in that vortex of fashionable life and luxury in which she had been plunged, whirling round and round in a species of continuous delirious excitement, sensible of the madness of remaining in the glare and turmoil of such an existence, and yet unable to stir hand or foot to extricate herself from its obvious dangers.

The public sale of the precious artices of a boudoir, the bijouterie and beautiful objects of art of the salons of a lady of fashion, awakens many reminiscences identified with the vicissitudes in the fortunes of former owners, and the fate of those to whom these precious things belonged. Lady Blessington, in her "Idler in France," alludes to the influence of such lugubrious feelings, when she went the round of the curiosity shops on the Quai D'Orsay, and made a purchase of an amber vase of rare beauty, said to have belonged to the Empress Josephine.

"When I see the beautiful objects collected together in these shops, I often think of their probable histories, and of those to whom they belonged. Each seems to identify itself with the former owner, and conjures up in my mind a little romance."

of the entrance of a sheriff's officer, and an execution being laid on her property, than she immediately desired the messenger to proceed to the count's room, and tell him that he must immediately prepare to leave England, as there would be no safety for him, once the fact was known of the execution having been levied. The count was at first incredulous—*bah!* after *bah!* followed each sentence of the account given him of the entrance of the sheriff's officer. At length, after seeing Lady Blessington, the necessity for his immediate departure became apparent. The following morning, with a single portmanteau, attended by his valet, he set out for Paris, and thus ended the London life of Count D'Orsay.

"Vases of exquisite workmanship, chased gold *etuis*, enriched with Oriental agate and brilliants that had once probably belonged to some *grandes dames* of the court; pendules of gilded bronze, one with a motto in diamonds on the back—'Vous me faites oublier les heures'—a nuptial gift; a flacon of most delicate workmanship, and other articles of bijouterie, bright and beautiful as when they left the hands of the jeweler. The gages d'amour are scattered all around; but the givers and receivers, where are they? Mouldering in the grave long years ago.

"Through how many hands may these objects have passed since death snatched away the persons for whom they were originally designed! And here they are, in the ignoble custody of some avaricious vendor, who, having obtained them at the sale of some departed amateur for less than their first cost, now expects to extort more than double the value of them! . . . . . 'And so will it be when I am gone,' as Moore's beautiful song says; the rare and beautiful bijouteries which I have collected with such pains, and looked on with such pleasure, will probably be scattered abroad, and find their resting-places, not in gilded salons, but in the dingy coffers of the wily *brocanteurs*, whose exorbitant demands will preclude their finding purchasers."*

The property of Lady Blessington offered for sale was thus eloquently described in the catalogue composed by that eminent author of auctioneering advertisements, Mr. Phillips:

"Costly and elegant effects, comprising all the magnificent furniture, rare porcelain, sculptures in marble, bronzes, and an assemblage of objects of art and decoration, a casket of valuable jewelry and bijouterie, services of rich chased silver and silver-gilt plate, a superbly-fitted silver dressing-case, collection of ancient and modern pictures, including many portraits of distinguished persons; valuable original drawings and fine engravings, framed and in the portfolio; the extensive and interesting library of books, comprising upward of 5000 volumes; expensive table-services of china and rich cut glass, and an infinity of valuable and useful effects, the property of the Right Honorable the Countess of Blessington, retiring to the Continent."

* The Idler in France, vol. ii., p. 53.

On the 10th of May, 1849, I visited Gore House for the last time. The auction was going on. There was a large assemblage of people of fashion. Every room was thronged; the well-known library-saloon, in which the conversaziones took place, was crowded, but not with guests. The arm-chair in which the lady of the mansion was wont to sit was occupied by a stout, coarse gentleman of the Jewish persuasion, busily engaged in examining a marble hand extended on a book, the fingers of which were modeled from a cast of those of the absent mistress of the establishment.

People, as they passed through the room, poked the furniture, pulled about the precious objects of art and ornaments of various kinds that lay on the table; and some made jests and ribald jokes on the scene they witnessed.

It was a relief to leave that room: I went into another, the dining-room, where I had frequently enjoyed, "in goodly company," the elegant hospitality of one who was indeed a "most kind hostess." I saw an individual among the crowd of gazers there who looked thoughtful and even sad. I remembered his features. I had dined with the gentleman more than once in that room. He was a humorist, a facetious man—one of the editors of "Punch;" but he had a heart, with all his customary drollery, and penchant for fun and raillery. I accosted him, and said, "We have met here under different circumstances." Some observations were made by the gentleman, which showed he felt how very different indeed they were. I took my leave of Mr. Albert Smith, thinking better of the class of facetious persons who are expected to amuse society on set occasions, as well as to make sport for the public at fixed periods, than ever I did before.

In another apartment, where the pictures were being sold, portraits by Lawrence, sketches by Landseer and Maclise, innumerable likenesses of Lady Blessington by various artists; several of the Count D'Orsay, representing him driving, riding out on horseback, sporting, and at work in his studio; his own collection of portraits of all the frequenters of note or mark in society of the villa Belvidere, the Palazzo Negroni, the Hotel

Ney, Seamore Place, and Gore House, in quick succession, were brought to the hammer. One whom I had known in most of those mansions, my old friend Dr. Quin, I met in this apartment.

This was the most signal ruin of an establishment of a person of high rank I ever witnessed. Nothing of value was saved from the wreck, with the exception of the portrait of Lady Blessington by Chalon, and one or two other pictures. Here was a total smash, a crash on a grand scale of ruin, a compulsory sale in the house of a noble lady, a sweeping clearance of all its treasures. To the honor of Lady Blessington be it mentioned, she saved nothing, with the few exceptions I have referred to, from the wreck. She might have preserved her pictures, objects of *virtù*, bijouterie, &c., of considerable value, but she said all she possessed should go to her creditors.

There have been very exaggerated accounts of the produce of the sale of the effects and furniture of Lady Blessington at Gore House.

I am able to state, on authority, that the gross amount of the sale was £13,385, and the net sum realized was £11,985 4*s*.

When it is considered that the furniture of this splendid mansion was of the most costly description—that the effects comprised a very valuable library, consisting of several thousand volumes, bijouterie, ormolu candelabras and chandeliers, porcelain and china ornaments, vases of exquisite workmanship, a number of pictures by first-rate modern artists, the amount produced by the sale will appear by no means large.

The portrait of Lady Blessington, by Lawrence, which cost originally only £80, I saw sold for £336. It was purchased for the Marquis of Hertford. The portrait of Lord Blessington, by the same artist, was purchased by Mr. Fuller for £68 5*s*.

The admirable portrait of the Duke of Wellington, by Count D'Orsay, was purchased for £189, for the Marquis of Hertford.*

* This picture was D'Orsay's *chef-d'œuvre*. The duke, I was informed by the count, spoke of this portrait as the one he would wish to be remembered by in future years. He used frequently, when it was in progress, to come of a morning, in full dress, to Gore House, to give the artist a sitting. If there was a crease or a fold in any part of the dress which he did not like, he would insist on its being

Landseer's celebrated picture of a spaniel sold for £150 10*s.*
Landseer's sketch of Miss Power was sold for £57 10*s.*
Lawrence's pictures of Mrs. Inchbald were sold for £48 6*s.*

The following letter, from the French valet of Lady Blessington, giving an account of the sale at Gore House, contains some passages, for those who make a study of human nature, of some interest.

"Gore House, Kensington, May 8th, 1849.

"My Lady,—J'ai reçu votre lettre hier, et je me serais empressé d'y repondre le même jour, mais j'ai eté si occupé etant le premier de la vente qu'il m'a eté impossible de la faire. J'ai vu Mr. P—— dans l'après midi. Il avait un commis ici pour prendre le prix des differents objets vendu le 7 May, et que vous avez sans doute reçu maintenant, au dire des gens qui ont assisté a la vente. Les choses se sont vendus avantageusement, et je dois ajouter que Mr. Phillips n'a rien negligé pour rendre la vente interessante a toute la noblesse d'ici.

"Lord Hertford a acheté plusieurs choses, et ce n'est que dimanche dernier fort tard dans l'après midi, qu'il est venu voir la maison, en un mot je pense sans exageration, que le nombre de personnes qui sont venus a la maison pendant les 5 jours quelle a eté en vue, que plus de 20,000 personnes y sont entrées une tres grande quantité de catalogue ont eté vendu, et nous en vendons encore tout les jours, car vous le savez, personnes n'est admis sans cela. Plusieurs des personnes qui frequantent la maison sont venus les deux premiers jours.

"Je vous parle de cela my lady parceque j'ai su que Mr. Dick avait dit a un de ses amis dans le salons qu'il y avait dans la maison une quantité d'articles envoyé par Mr. Phillips, et comme j'etais certain du contraire, je me suis addressé a Mr. Guthrie, qui etait en ce moment dans le salon, et qui lui meme s'en est plaint a Mr. Dick. Il a nié le fait, mais depuis j'ai acquit la certitude qu'il avait avancé ce que je viens de vous dire. Je n'ai pas hesité a parler tres haut dans le salon, persuadé que je désabuseraît la foule qui s'y trouvait.

"Le Dr. Quin est venu plusieurs fois et a paru prendre le plus grand interet a ce qui se passait ici. M. Thackeray est venu aussi, et avait les larmes aux yeux en partant. *C'est peut etre la seule personne que j'ai vu réellement affectè en votre depart.*

"J'ai l'honneur d'etre, my lady, votre très humble serviteur,

"F. Avillon."

One of Lady Blessington's most intimate friends, in a note to her ladyship, dated the 19th of May, 1849 (after the break-up at

altered. To use D'Orsay's words, the duke was so hard to be pleased, it was most difficult to make a good portrait of him. When he consented to have any thing done for him, he would have it done in the best way possible.

Gore House and departure from London), writes, "I have not been without an instinct or an impression for some time that you were disturbed by those preoccupying anxieties which make the presence of casual visitors irksome.....

"But, now that the change is once made, may it yield you all that I hope it will. I trust now that what there is of pain will remain for those who lose you. You can not but be enlivened by those new objects and scenes of your new place of abode, turbulent as it is. When that charm is done, you will come back to us again. Meanwhile, what a time to be looking forward to! One becomes absolutely sick wondering what is to be the end of it all. I could fill books with tales which one new courier after another brings of dismay, and misery, and of breaking-up abroad."

On the same sad subject came two letters, worthy of the kind and noble-hearted person who wrote them.

From Mrs. T——:

"Chesham Place, Friday, April, 1849.

"My dearest ——,

* * * * * * *

"Is it true that you are going to Paris? If so, I hope I shall see you before you go, for it would grieve me very much not to bid you good-by by word of mouth, for who can tell when we may meet again! Dearest ——, I hardly like to say it, because you may think it intrusive, but M—— told me some time ago that you were in difficulties, owing to the Irish estates not paying, and told me to-day that a rumor had reached her to this effect. If it be true, I need not say how it grieves me. You have *so often* come forward in our poor dearest mother's difficulties, so often befriended her, and *us through her*, that it goes to my heart to think you are harassed as she was, and that I am so poor that I can not act the same generous part you did by her. But, dearest ——, I am at this moment in communication with Mr. P——, through another lawyer, on the subject of the money left me by my mother. * * * * Dearest ——, do not be offended with me, but in case I receive my money (£1600) down, do make use of *me*. Remember I am your own ——, and believe me I am not ungrateful, but love you dearly, and can not bear to think of your being in trouble. I am offering what, alas! Mr. P—— *may* create a difficulty about, but I trust he will not, and that you will not be angry or mistrust me, and consider me intrusive. Possibly there is no truth in the rumor. If so, forget that I have ever seemed intrusive, and only rest assured of my affection. May God bless you, my dearest ——.

"Ever your most affectionate ——, Marguerite ——."

From Mrs. T——:

"28th April, 1849.

"I was very glad to receive your affectionate note, my dearest ———, and to know you are not offended with mine to you. I wrote to you from my heart, and one is seldom misinterpreted at those times. While I live, dearest ———, I shall have a heart to care for you, and feel a warm interest in your happiness; you must never let any thing create a doubt of this. Will you promise me this?

"I doubt not you will be *happier* in Paris. It saddens me, however, to feel that, perhaps, we shall never meet again, and I am *very, very* sorry not to have seen you, and bid you at least good-by.

"I can not say how much I have thought of you, and felt for you, dearest ———, breaking up your old house. I know how poor dearest mamma felt it, when such was her lot; and you resemble each other in so many things! Every one says you have acted most admirably in not any longer continuing to run the chance of not receiving your annuity duly, but selling off, so as to pay all you owe and injure no one. I think there is some little comfort in feeling that good acts are appreciated, so I tell you this. I am half ashamed of my little paltry offer. Dearest ———, I am so glad you were not affronted with me, for I know you would have done the same over and over again by me; but then *you* always *confer* and never accept, and I have much to thank you for, as well as my sisters, for you have been a *most unselfish* friend to each and all of us.

* * * * * * * *

"I should so like to know what is become of poor old Comte S——. I wrote to him at the beginning of the year, but have never had an answer. If you meet him, do be kind to him, poor old man, in spite of his deafness and blindness, which make him neglected by others, for he is a very old friend of ours, and I feel an interest in the poor old man, knowing so many good and kind acts of his.

"Ever, dearest, yours most affectionately, MARGUERITE."

Lady Blessington and the two Misses Power left Gore House on the 14th of April, 1849, for Paris. Count D'Orsay had set out for Paris a fortnight previously.

For nineteen years Lady Blessington had maintained a position almost queenlike in the world of intellectual distinction, in fashionable literary society, reigning over the best circles of London celebrities, and reckoning among her admiring friends and the frequenters of her salons the most eminent men of England, in every walk of literature, art, and science, in statesmanship, in the military profession, and every learned pursuit. For nineteen years she had maintained establishments in London seldom surpassed, and still more rarely equaled in all the appliances to a state of society brilliant in the highest degree ; but, alas! it must be acknowledged at the same time, a state of splendid misery, for a great portion of that time, to the mistress of those elegant and luxurious establishments.

And now, at the expiration of those nineteen years, we find her forced to abandon that position, to relinquish all those elegancies and luxuries by which she had been so long surrounded, to leave her magnificent abode, and all the cherished works of art and precious objects in it, to become the property of strangers, and, in fact, to make a departure from the scene of all her former triumphs, which it is in vain to deny was a flight effected with privacy, most painful and humiliating to this poor lady to be compelled to have recourse to.

Lady Blessington began her literary career in London in 1822, with a small work in one vol. 8vo, entitled "Sketches of Scenes in the Metropolis." It commences with an account of the ruin of a large establishment in one of the fashionable squares of the metropolis, and of an auction in the house of the late proprietor, a person of quality, the sale of all the magnificent furniture and effects, costly ornaments, precious objects of art, and valuable pictures.

And, strange to say, as if there was in the mind of the writer a sort of prevision of future events of a similar nature occurring in her own home at some future period, she informs us the name of the ruined proprietor of the elegant mansion in the fashionable square, the effects of which were under sale, was B——. The authoress says, sauntering through the gilded salons, crowded with fashionables, brokers, and dealers in bijouterie, exquisites of insipid countenances and starched neckcloths, elderly ladies of sour aspects, and simpering damsels, all at intervals in the sale occupied with comments, jocose, censorious, sagacious, or bitterly sarcastic on the misfortunes and extravagance of the poor B——'s, she heard on every side flippant and unfeeling observations of this kind: "Poor Mrs. B—— will give no more balls;" "I always thought how it would end;" "The B——'s gave devilish good dinners, though;" "Capital feeds, indeed;" "You could rely on a perfect *supreme de volaille*" (at their table); "Where could you get such *cotellettes des pigeons à la Champagne?*" "Have you any idea of what has become of B——?" "In the Bench, or gone to France, but (yawning) I really forget all about it;" "I will buy his Vandyke picture;" "It is a pity that people who give such good dinners should be ruined;" "A short campaign and a brisk one for me;" "Believe me, there is nothing like a fresh start, and no man, at least no dinner-giving man, should last more than two seasons, unless he would change his cook every month, to prevent repetition of the same dishes, and keep a regular *roaster* of his invitations, with a mark to each name, to prevent people meeting twice at his house the same season." The elderly ladies were all haranguing on "the follies, errors, and extravagances of Mrs. B——." "Mr. B——, though foolish and extravagant in some things, had considerable taste and judgment in some others; for instance, his books were excellent, well chosen, and well bought;" "His busts, too, are very fine;" "Give me B——'s pictures, for they are exquisite;" "That group, so exquisitely colored and so true to nature, could only be produced by the inimitable pencil of a Lawrence."

"And this is an auction!" says the authoress, at the end of the first sketch in her first work; "a scene," she continues, "that has been so often the resort of the young, the grave, and the gay, is now one where those who have partaken of the hospitality of the once opulent owner of the mansion now come to witness his downfall, regardless of his misfortune, or else to exult in their own contrasted prosperity."*

This sketch would indeed have answered for the auction scene at Gore House in 1849, seven-and-twenty years after it had been penned by Lady Blessington.

Her ladyship thus commenced her literary career in 1822 with a description of the ruin of an extravagant person of quality in one of our fashionable squares in London, with an account of the break-up of his establishment and the auction of his effects, and a similar career terminates in the utter smash and the

* The "Magic Lantern," &c., p. 1, 2, 3. London: Longman, 1822.

sale at Gore in 1849. There are many stranger things 'twixt heaven and earth than are dreamed of in the philosophy of our Horatios of fashionable society.

CHAPTER XI.

ARRIVAL OF LADY BLESSINGTON IN PARIS THE MIDDLE OF APRIL, 1849.—HER LAST ILLNESS, AND DEATH ON THE 4TH OF JUNE FOLLOWING.—NOTICE OF HER DECEASE.

Lady Blessington and her nieces arrived in Paris in the middle of April, 1849. She had a suite of rooms taken for her in the Hotel de la Ville d'Eveque, and there she remained till the 3d of June. The jointure of £2000 a year was now the sole dependence of her ladyship, and the small residue of the produce of the sale of her effects at Gore House, after paying the many large claims of her creditors and those of Count D'Orsay.

Soon after her arrival in Paris, she took a moderate-sized but handsome *appartement* in the Rue du Cerq, close to the Champs Elysées, which she commenced furnishing with much taste and elegance; her preparations were at length completed, but they were destined to be in vain. In the brief interval between her arrival in Paris and her taking possession of her new apartment on the 3d of June, she received the visits of many of her former acquaintances, and seemed in better spirits than she had been for a long time previously to her departure from London.

The kindness she met with in some quarters, and especially at the hands of several members of the Grammont family, was at once agreeable and encouraging. But the coolness of the *accueil* of other persons who had been deeply indebted to her hospitality in former times was somewhat more chilling than she had expected to find, and the warm feelings of her generous heart and noble nature revolted at it.

Prince Louis Napoleon, on Lady Blessington's arrival in Paris, requested her to come to the palace of the Elysée, where he then resided; she went, accompanied by Count D'Orsay and the two Misses Power. He subsequently invited them to dinner. He had been one of the most constant and intimate guests at Gore House, both before and after his imprisonment at Ham. He used to dine there whenever there were any distinguished persons, whether English or foreign. He was on the most familiar and intimate terms with Lady Blessington and her circle, joining them in parties to Greenwich, Richmond, &c.; and all his friends, as well as himself, were made welcome, and on his escape from Ham he came to Gore House straight on his arrival in London, giving Lady Blessington the first intimation of his escape.

On that occasion, at Count D'Orsay's advice, he wrote at once to Monsieur St. Aulaire, then embassador in London, stating that he had no intention of creating any ferment or disturbance, but meant to reside quietly as a private individual in London. Lady Blessington proffered some pecuniary assistance to the prince, and both Lady Blessington and Count D'Orsay manifested their earnest desire and willingness to aid him in any way they could be made serviceable to him. While he needed their services, and influence, and hospitality, the prince expressed himself always most grateful for them. But with the need, the sense of the obligations ceased.

There is no doubt on the minds of some of the friends even of Prince Louis Napoleon but that the active and unceasing exertions and influence of Count D'Orsay and his friends and connections in Paris went far to aid his election as President. D'Orsay rallied to his party Emile de Girardin, one of the ablest and boldest journalists of the day, but who subsequently became a formidable opponent. The chief cause of his ingratitude to Count D'Orsay was believed to have been his apprehension of being supposed to be advised or influenced by any one who had been formerly intimate with him; a fear which has induced him to surround his person with men of mean intellect and of servile dispositions, pliant, indigent, and unscrupulous followers, of no station in society, or character for independence or integrity of principle.

Lady Blessington began to form plans for a new literary career: she engaged her thoughts in projecting future works, in making new arrangements for the reception of the *beau monde*. She employed a great deal of her time daily in superintending the furnishing of her new apartment; in the way of embellishments, or luxuries, or comforts, some new wants had to be supplied every day. The old story of unsatisfied desires ever seeking fulfillment, and never contented with the fruition of present enjoyments, applies to every phase in life, even the most checkered:

> "Like our shadows,
> Our wishes lengthen as our sun declines."

The sun of Lady Blessington's life was now declining fast; and even when it had reached the verge of the horizon, its going down was unnoticed by those around her, and the suddenness of its disappearance occasioned no little surprise, and gave rise to many vague surmises and idle rumors.

There were some striking coincidences in the circumstances attending the deaths of Lord and Lady Blessington.

In May, 1829, Lord Blessington returned to Paris from England, purposing to fix his abode there for some months at least; and on the 23d of the same month, a few weeks after his arrival, without previous warning or indisposition, "appearing to be in good health," he was suddenly attacked by apoplexy, while riding on the Champs d'Elysée, and died the same day, in a state of insensibility.

Twenty years from that date, Lady Blessington arrived in Paris from London, purposing to fix her abode there; and on the 4th of June, having made all suitable preparations for a long residence in Paris, and after a sojourn there of about five weeks, without previous warning or indisposition, she was suddenly attacked by an apoplectic malady, complicated with disease of the heart, and was carried off suddenly, at her abode adjoining the Champs d'Elysée, being quite unconscious, during the brief period of the struggle, of the fatal issue that was about to take place.

A few weeks before that event, a British peeress, whom I have had the pleasure of meeting at Gore House in former days, wrote to Lady Blessington at Paris, reminding her of a promise that had been extorted from her, and entreating of her to remember her religious duties, and to attend to them.

Poor Lady Blessington always received any communication made to her on this subject with respect, and even with a feeling of gratitude for the advice given by her. She acted on it solely on one or two occasions, in Paris, when she accompanied the Duchess de Grammont to the Church of the Madeleine on the Sabbath.

But no serious idea of abandoning the mode of life she led had been entertained by her. Yet she had a great fear of death, and sometimes spoke of a vague determination, whenever she should be released from the chief cares of her career—the toils and anxieties of authorship, the turmoil of her life in salons and intellectual circles—that she would turn to religion, and make amends for her long neglect of its duties by an old age of retirement from society, and the withdrawal of her thoughts and affections from the vanities of the world. But the proposed time for that change was a future which was not to come; and the present time was ever to her a period in which all thoughts of death were to be precluded, and every amusing and exciting topic was to be entertained which was capable of absorbing attention for the passing hour.

An extract of a letter from Miss Power to the author, on the death of Lady Blessington, will give a very accurate and detailed account of her last illness and death:

"Rue de la Ville l'Eveque, No. 38, February 18th, 1850.

"On arriving in Paris, my aunt adopted a mode of life differing considerably from the sedentary one she had for such a length of time pursued; she rose earlier, took much exercise, and, in consequence, lived somewhat higher than was her wont, for she was habitually a small eater. This appeared to agree with her *general* health, for she looked well, and was cheerful; but she began to suffer occasionally (especially in the morning) from oppression and difficulty of breathing. These symptoms, slight at first, she carefully concealed from our knowledge, having always a great objection to medical treatment; but as they increased in force and frequency, she was obliged to reveal them, and medical aid was immediately called in. Dr. Léon Simon pronounced there was 'energie du cœur,' but that the symptoms in question proceeded probably from bronchitis—a disease then very prevalent in Paris; that they were nervous, and entailed no danger; and as, after the remedies he prescribed, the attacks diminished perceptibly in violence, and that her general health seemed little affected by them, he entertained no serious alarm.

"On the 3d of June she removed from the hotel we had occupied during the seven weeks we had passed in Paris, and entered the residence which my poor aunt had devoted so much pains and attention to the selecting and furnishing of, and that same day dined *en famille* with the Duc and Duchesse de Guiche (Count D'Orsay's nephew). On that occasion, my aunt seemed particularly well in health and spirits, and it being a lovely night, and our residences lying contiguous, we walked home by moonlight. As usual, I aided my aunt to undress—she never allowed her maid to sit up for her—and left her a little after midnight. She passed, it seems, some most restless hours (she was habitually a bad sleeper), and early in the morning, feeling the commencement of one of the attacks, she called for assistance, and Dr. Simon was immediately sent for, the symptoms manifesting themselves with considerable violence; and, in the mean time, the remedies he had ordered—sitting upright, rubbing the chest and upper stomach with ether, administering ether internally, &c.—were all resorted to without effect. The difficulty of breathing became so excessive, that the whole of the chest heaved upward at each inspiration, which was inhaled with a loud whooping noise, the face was swollen and purple, the eyeballs distended, and utterance almost wholly denied, while the extremities gradually became cold and livid, in spite of every attempt to restore the vital heat. By degrees, the violence of the symptoms abated; she uttered a few words: the first, 'The violence is over, I can breathe freer;' and soon after, 'Qu'elle heure est-il?' Thus encouraged, we deemed the danger past; but, alas! how bitterly were we deceived; she gradually sunk from that moment; and when Dr. Simon, who had been delayed by another patient, arrived, he saw that hope was gone; and, indeed, she expired so easily, so tranquilly, that it was impossible to perceive the moment when her spirit passed away.

"The day but one following, the autopsy took place, when it was discovered that enlargement of the heart to nearly double the natural size, which enlargement must have been progressing for a period of at least twenty-five years, was the cause of dissolution, though incipient disease of the stomach and liver had complicated the symptoms. The body was then embalmed by Dr. Ganal, and deposited in the vaults of the Madeleine, while the monument was being constructed, a task to which Count D'Orsay devoted the whole of his time and attention. He bids me to say that he is about to have a daguerreotype taken of the place, a drawing of which we shall have forwarded to you.*

"The mausoleum is a pyramid of granite, standing on a square platform, on a level with the surrounding ground, but divided from it by a deep fosse, whose sloping sides are covered with green turf and Irish ivy, transplanted from the garden of the house where she was born. It stands on a hill-side, just above the village cemetery, and overlooks a view of exquisite beauty and immense extent, taking in the Seine, winding through the fertile valley and the forest

* From that *daguerreotype*, the sketch given in this work has been exactly copied by an artist very highly gifted.

of St. Germain; plains, villages, and far-distant hills; and at the back and side it is sheltered by chestnut-trees of large size and great age: a more picturesque spot it is difficult to imagine. M. A. POWER."

From Mrs. Romer's account of this monument the following passages are taken:

"Solid, simple, and severe, it combines every requisite in harmony with its solemn destination; no meretricious ornaments, no false sentiment, mar the purity of its design. The genius which devised it has succeeded in cheating the tomb of its horrors, without depriving it of its imposing gravity. The simple portal is surmounted by a plain massive cross of stone, and a door, secured by an open-work of bronze, leads into a sepulchral chamber, the key of which has been confided to me. All within breathes the holy calm of eternal repose; no gloom, no mouldering damp, nothing to recall the dreadful images of decay. An atmosphere of peace appears to pervade the place, and I could almost fancy that a voice from the tomb whispered, in the words of Dante's Beatrice,

"'Io sono in pace!'

"The light of the sun, streaming through a glazed aperture above the door, fell like a ray of heavenly hope upon the symbol of man's redemption—a beautiful copy, in bronze, of Michael Angelo's crucified Savior—which is affixed to the wall facing the entrance. A simple stone sarcophagus is placed on either side of the chamber, each one surmounted by two white marble tablets, incrusted in the sloping walls."

The monument was visited by me a few weeks before the death of Count D'Orsay. It stands on a platform or mound, carefully trenched, adjoining the church-yard, and approached from it. The sepulchral chamber is on a level with the platform from which you enter. Within are two stone sarcophagi (side by side), and in one of these is deposited the coffin containing the remains of Lady Blessington, covered with a large block of granite. On the wall above (on the left hand side of the vault) are the two inscriptions; one by Barry Cornwall, the other—that which has led to a correspondence.

The first inscription above referred to is in the following terms:

"IN MEMORY OF
MARGUERITE, COUNTESS OF BLESSINGTON,
WHO DIED ON THE 4TH OF JUNE, 1849.

In her lifetime
She was loved and admired
For her many graceful writings,
Her gentle manners, her kind and generous heart.
Men, famous for art and science
In distant lands,
Sought her friendship:
And the historians and scholars, the poets, and wits, and painters,
Of her own country,
Found an unfailing welcome
In her ever hospitable home.
She gave cheerfully to all who were in need,
Help, and sympathy, and useful counsel;
And she died
Lamented by her friends.
They who loved her best in life, and now lament her most,
Have raised this tributary marble
Over the place of her rest."

BARRY CORNWALL.

The other inscription, altered from one written by Walter Savage Landor, is as follows:

"Hic est *depositum*
Quod superest mulieris
Quondam pulcherrimæ
Benefacta celare potuit
Ingenium *suum* non potuit
Peregrinos *quoslibet*
Gratâ hospitalitate convocabat
Lutetiæ Parisiorum
Ad meliorem vitam abiit
Die IV mensis Junii
MDCCCXLIX."

The original inscription, by W. S. Landor, is certainly, in all respects but one, preferable to the substituted; and that one is the absence of all reference to a future state:

"Infra sepvltvm est id omne qvod sepeliri potest
mvlieris qvondam pvlcherrimæ.
Ingenivm svvm svmmo stvdio colavit,

aliorvm pari adjvvit.
Benefacta sva celare novit; ingenivm non ita.
Erga omnis erat largâ bonitate
peregrinis eleganter hospitalis.
Venit Lvtetiam Parisiorvm Aprili mense:
qvarto Jvnii die svpremvm svvm obiit."

The following English version of the above inscription has been given by Mr. Landor:

TO THE MEMORY OF MARGUERITE, COUNTESS OF BLESSINGTON.

"Underneath is buried all that *could* be buried of a woman once most beautiful. She cultivated her genius with the greatest zeal, and fostered it in others with equal assiduity. The benefits she conferred she could conceal—her talents not. Elegant in her hospitality to strangers, charitable to all, she retired to Paris in April, and there she breathed her last, on the 4th of June, 1849."*

There is an epitaph on the tomb of a daughter-in-law of Dryden, who died in 1712, and was buried in Kiel Church, in Staffordshire—(see "Monumenta Anglic.," p. 154)—where some expressions occur somewhat similar to those which Mr. Landor has taken exception to in the substituted inscription. It runs thus:

"Hæc quo erat, forma et genere illustrior,
eo se humiliorem præbuit maritum honorando
familiam præcipue Liberos fovendo
pauperes sublevando, peregrinos omnes decorè

* On the subject of this inscription, Mr. Landor addressed a long letter to the "Athenæum," complaining of the alterations which had been made in the Latin lines he had written, from which I will only extract the concluding paragraphs.

"It may be thought superfluous to remark that epitaphs have certain qualities in common; for instance, all are encomiastic. The main difference and the main difficulty lie in the expression, since nearly all people are placed on the same level in the epitaph as in the grave. Hence, out of eleven or twelve thousand Latin ones, ancient and modern, I find scarcely threescore in which there is originality or elegance. Pure latinity is not uncommon, and is perhaps as little uncommon in the modern as in the ancient, where certain forms exclude it, to make room for what appeared more venerable. Nothing is now left to be done but to bring forward in due order and just proportions the better peculiarities of character composing the features of the dead, and modulating the tones of grief.

"WALTER SAVAGE LANDOR."

proximosque et vecinos humaniter excipiendo,
ut neminem reperisses decidentum:
non prius devinctum, mira hujus
et honesta morum suavitate."

The age of Lady Blessington has been a subject of some controversy. She was born, we are informed by her niece (on the authority, I have reason to believe, of her aunt) the 1st of September, 1790. She died the 4th of June, 1849; hence it would appear her age was fifty-eight years and nine months. From inquiries that were made by me in Clonmel, and examination of the marriage registry, it was ascertained that Lady Blessington had been married the 7th of March, 1804. She must then have been about fifteen years of age; but, according to the first account, she would have been only fourteen years of age the 1st of September, 1804.*

Lady Blessington stated to me that she was married in 1804, and was then under fifteen years of age. Had she been born the 1st of September, 1789, she would have been fifteen years of age on the 1st of September, 1804.

The probability then is that she was born in 1789, and not in 1790, and was therefore sixty years of age, less by two months, when she died.

Ellen, Lady Canterbury (her youngest sister), in the account of her death in "the Annual Register," is stated to have died in her fifty-fourth year, the 16th November, 1845. From this it would appear that she was born in the latter part of 1791.

Mary Anne, Countess St. Marsault, the youngest of all the children of Edmund Power, I am informed was fifteen years younger than Lady Blessington. If this be the case, and Lady Blessington was born in 1789, the Countess of Marsault must have been born in 1804, and would be now fifty years of age.

But if I might hazard an opinion on so delicate a subject as

* A person intimately acquainted with Lady Blessington's family is the editor of a Clonmel paper, in which the following paragraph appeared:

"THE LATE LADY BLESSINGTON.—A Dublin solicitor has just been in Clonmel, for the purpose of exactly ascertaining the age of the late Countess of Blessington, in reference to an insurance claim. She was not so old at her death as the newspapers said, having been married in 1804, at the early age of fifteen years, so that she was only sixty years old at her decease."

a lady's age, I would venture to set down the date of that event as 1801, and not 1804.

In a letter from Miss Power, dated 12th of July, 1849, then residing at Chambourcy Près de St. Germain-en-Laye (the seat of the Duchesse de Grammont, the sister of Count D'Orsay), the loss of Lady Blessington is thus referred to:

"Count D'Orsay would himself have answered your letter, but had not the nerve or the heart to do so; although the subject occupies his mind night and day, he can not speak of it but to those who have been his fellow-sufferers; it is like an image ever floating before his eyes, which he has got, as it were, used to look upon, but which he can not yet bear to grasp and feel that it is real: much as she was to us, we can not but feel that to him she was all; the centre of his existence, round which his recollections, thoughts, hopes, and plans turned; and just at the moment she was about to commence a new mode of life, one that promised a rest from the occupation and anxieties that had for some years fallen to her share, death deprived us of her."

On D'Orsay's first visit to the tomb where the remains of Lady Blessington had been deposited, his anguish is said to have been most poignant and heart-rending. He seemed almost phrensied at times, bewildered and stupefied; and then, as if awakened suddenly to a full consciousness of the great calamity that had taken place, he would lament the loss he had sustained as if it had occurred only the day before. His state of mind might be described in the words of an Arabic poem, translated by Sir William Jones:

"Torn from loved friends, in Death's cold caverns laid,
I sought their haunts with shrieks that pierced the air;
'Where are they hid? oh! where?' I wildly said;
And Fate, with sullen echo, mocked, 'O where?'"*

A notice of the death of Lady Blessington appeared in "the Athenæum" of June 9th, 1849, written by one who appears to have known Lady Blessington well, and to have appreciated fully her many excellent qualities.

"Only a fortnight since, the journals of London were laying

* Translation from an Arabic poet, by the late Sir William Jones.

open to public gaze the relics of a house which for some dozen years past has been an object of curiosity, and a centre of pleasurable recollection to many persons distinguished in literature and art, abroad and at home.

"The Countess of Blessington, it appears, lived just long enough to see her gates closed and her treasures dispersed; for on Tuesday arrived from Paris tidings that, within a few hours after establishing herself in her new mansion there, she died suddenly of apoplexy on Monday last.

"Few departures have been attended with more regrets than will be that of this brilliant and beautiful woman in the circle to which her influences have been restricted. It is unnecessary to sum up the writings published by Lady Blessington within the last eighteen years, commencing by her 'Conversations with Lord Byron,' and including her lively and natural French and Italian journals, half a score of novels, the most powerful among which is 'The Victims of Society,' detached thoughts and fugitive verses, since these are too recent to call for enumeration.

"As all who knew the writer will bear us out in saying, they faintly represent her gifts and graces, her command over anecdote, her vivacity of fancy, her cordiality of manner, and her kindness of heart. They were hastily and slightly thrown off by one with whom authorship was a pursuit assumed rather than instinctive—in the intervals snatched from a life of unselfish good offices and lively social intercourse.

"From each one of the vast variety of men of all classes, all creeds, all manner of acquirements, and all color of political opinions, whom Lady Blessington delighted to draw around her, she had skill to gather the characteristic trait, the favorite object of interest, with a fineness of appreciation to be exceeded only by the retentiveness of her memory.

"Thus, until a long series of family bereavements and the pressure of uncertain health had somewhat dimmed the gayety of her spirits, her conversation had a variety of reminiscence, a felicity of *a propos*, and a fascination, of which her writings offer faint traces. In one respect, moreover, her talk did not resemble the talk of other *beaux esprits*. With the eagerness of a child, she could amuse and persuade herself as entirely as she amused and persuaded others. Among all the brilliant women we have known, she was one of the most earnest—earnest in defense of the absent, in protection of the unpopular, in advocacy of the unknown; and many are those who can tell how generously and actively Lady Blessington availed herself of her widely-extended connections throughout the world to further their success or to promote their pleasures. In her own family she was warmly beloved as an indefatigable friend, and eagerly resorted to as an unwearied counselor. How largely she was trusted by some of the most distinguished men of her time, her extensive and varied correspondence will show, should it ever be given to the world. Into the causes which limited her gifts and graces within a narrower sphere than they might otherwise have commanded, we have no commission to enter."*

CHAPTER X.

NOTICE OF THE CAREER, LITERARY TASTES, AND TALENTS OF LADY BLESSINGTON.

WITH respect to the influence exercised in society over persons of exalted intellect by fascinating manners, personal attractions, liveliness of fancy, quickness of apprehension, closeness of observation, and smartness of repartee, among the literary ladies of England of the present or past century, it would be difficult to find one with whom Lady Blessington can be fitly compared. The power of pleasing, of engaging attention, of winning, not only admiration, but regard and friendship, which the latter lady possessed, and long and successfully exerted over men of genius and talents of the highest order, and of every profession and pursuit, has been seldom surpassed in any country.

It would not be difficult to point out ladies of celebrity as *bas bleus* of far superior abilities as authoresses, of imaginations with richer stores of wit and poetry, of more erudition, and better cultivated talents; but we shall find none who, for an equal length of time, maintained an influence of fascination in litera-

* The Athenæum, June 9th, 1849.

ry and fashionable society over the highest intellects, and exercised dominion over the feelings as well as over the faculties of those who frequented her abode.

Grimm, in his "Mémoires Littéraires et Anecdotaires," makes mention of a Madam Geoffrin, the friend of D'Alembert, Marmontel, Condorcet, Morellet, and many other illustrious *littéraires*, whose character and mental qualities, *agréments*, *esprit*, *finesse de l'art*, *bonté de cœur*, *et habitudes de bienfaisance*, would appear, from his account of them, very remarkably *en rapport* with the qualities of mind and natural dispositions of Lady Blessington. Those of Lady Mary Wortley, Lady Craven, Lady Holland, and Lady Morgan, present no such traits of resemblance fitly to be compared with the peculiar graces, attractions, and kindly feelings of Lady Blessington.

D'Alembert has consecrated some lines of homage to his friend and benefactress, in a letter published in the "Mémoires Littéraires et Historiques." We learn from it that Madam Geoffrin's salons were open nightly to the artists, literati, ministers of state, grandees, and courtiers. Authors were not assured of the success of their new works till they had been to Madam Geoffrin's *soirées*, and a smile and an encouraging expression of the sovereign of the salons set their hearts at ease on the subject of their productions.

Helvetius, when he published his book "De l'Esprit," felt no confidence in its reception by the public till he had consulted Madam: ce thermometre de l'opinion.

"Madam Geoffrin n'avoit guerre des ennemis que parmi les femmes." She had all the tastes, we are told, of a sensitive, gentle creature, of a noble and a loving nature. "La passion de donner qui fut le besoin de sa vie, etoit née avec elle et la tourmenta pour ainsi dire de ses premières années." She had aptly taken for her device the words "Donner et pardonner."

There was nothing brilliant in her talents, but she was an excellent sayer of good things in short sentences. She gave dinners, and there was a great *éclat* in her entertainments: "*Mais il faut autre choses que des diners pour occuper dans le monde la place que cette femme estimable s'y etait faite.*"

Monsieur Malesherbes was happily characterized by her, "*l'homme du monde le plus simplement simple.*" She said, among the weaknesses of people, their vanity must be endured, and their talk, even when there was nothing in it. "I accommodate myself," she said, "tolerably well to eternal talkers, provided they are chatterers, and that only, who have no idea of any thing but talking, and do not expect to be replied to. My friend Fontenelle, who bears with them as I do, says they give his lungs repose. I derive another advantage from them; their insignificant gabble is to me like the tolling of bells, which does not hinder one from thinking, but often rather invites thought."

When her friends spoke of the enmity to her of some persons, and made some allusion to her many generous acts, she turned to D'Alembert and said, "When you find people have feelings of hatred to me, take good care not to say any thing to them of the little good you know of me. They will hate me for it all the more. It will be a torment to them, and I have no wish to pain them." When this amiable and lovely woman died, D'Alembert uttered words very similar to those which D'Orsay addressed to me on the first occasion of my meeting him after the recent loss of that friend, who had so many qualities of a kindred nature to those of Madame Geoffrin. "Her friendship," said D'Alembert, "was my consolation in all troubles. The treasure which was so necessary and precious to me has been taken away, and in the midst of people in society, and the filling up of the void of life in its circles, I can speak to none who will understand me. I spent my evenings with the dear friend I have lost, and my mornings also. I no longer have that friend; for me there is no longer evening or morning."*

It has been truly said of Lady Blessington's uniform kindness and generosity under all circumstances,

"In the midst of her triumphs, the goodness of her heart, and the fine qualities that had ever distinguished her, remained wholly unimpaired. Generous to lavishness, charitable, compassionate, delicately considerate of the feelings of others, sincere, forgiving, devoted to those she loved, and with a warmth

* Mémoires Lit. et Anecdotes, vol. ii., p. 64.

of heart rarely equaled, her change of fortune was immediately felt by every member of her family. The parents whose cruel obstinacy had involved her in so much misery, but whose ruined circumstances now placed them in need of her aid, were comfortably supported by her up to the period of their deaths. Her brothers and sisters (the youngest of whom, Marianne, she adopted and educated), and even the more distant of her relatives, all profited by her benefits, assistance, and interest."

A lady of very distinguished literary talents, and highly esteemed by Lady Blessington, well acquainted, too, with many of her benevolent acts, Mrs. A. M. Hall, thus wrote of her very recently, in answer to some inquiries of the author:

"Firfield, Addlestone, Surrey, June 7, 1854.

"I never had occasion to appeal to Lady Blessington for aid for any kind or charitable purpose that she did not *at once*, with a grace peculiarly her own, come forward cheerfully, and 'help' to the extent of her power.

"I remember one particular instance of a poor man who desired a particular situation which I thought Lady Blessington could obtain. All the circumstances I have forgotten; but the chief point was, that he entreated employment, and had some right to it in one department. Lady Blessington made the request I entreated, and was refused. Her ladyship sent me the refusal to read, and, of course, I gave up all idea of the matter, and only felt sorry that I had troubled her; but she remembered it, and in a month accomplished the poor man's object; her letter was indeed a sunbeam in his poor home, and he, in time, became prosperous and happy."

In a subsequent communication of the 3d of August, Mrs. Hall adds:

"When Lady Blessington left London, she did not forget the necessities of several of her poor dependents, who received regular aid from her after her arrival, and while she resided in Paris. She found time, despite her literary labors, her anxieties, and the claims which she permitted society to make upon her time, not only to do acts of kindness now and then for those in whom she felt an interest, but to give what seemed perpetual thought to their well-doing; and she never missed an opportunity of doing a gracious act or saying a gracious word. My acquaintance with Lady Blessington was merely a literary one, commencing when, at my husband's suggestion, she published much about Lord Byron in the pages of the 'New Monthly Magazine,' which at that time he edited. That acquaintance continuing till her death, I wrote regularly for her Annuals, and she contributed to those under our care.

"I have no means of knowing whether what the world said of this beautiful woman was true or false, but I am sure God intended her to be good, and there was a deep-seated good intent in whatever she did that came under my observation.

"Her sympathies were quick and cordial, and independent of worldliness; her taste in art and literature womanly and refined—I say 'womanly,' because she had a perfectly feminine appreciation of whatever was delicate and beautiful. There was great satisfaction in writing for her whatever she required; labors became pleasures, from the importance she attached to every little attention paid to requests which, as an editor, she had a right to command. Her manners were singularly simple and graceful; it was to me an intense delight to look at beauty, which, though I never saw it in its full bloom, was charming in its autumn time; and the Irish accent, and soft, sweet Irish laugh, used to make my heart beat with the pleasures of memory. I always left her with an intense sense of enjoyment, and a perfect disbelief in every thing I ever heard to her discredit. Her conversation was not witty nor wise, but it was in good tune and good taste, mingled with a great deal of humor, which escaped every thing bordering on vulgarity. It was surprising how a tale of distress or a touching anecdote would at once suffuse her clear, intelligent eyes with tears, and her beautiful mouth would break into smiles and dimples at even the echo of wit or jest.

"The influence she exercised over her circle was unbounded, and it became a pleasure of the most exquisite kind to give her pleasure.

"I think it ought to be remembered to her honor that, with all her foreign associations and habits, she never wrote a line that might not be placed on the book-shelves of any English lady.

"Yours sincerely, A. M. HALL."

From Mr. Hall I have received the following account of an act of kindness and beneficence of Lady Blessington which fell under his own observation:

"I once chanced to encounter a young man of good education and some literary taste, who, with his wife and two children, was in a state of absolute want. After some thought as to what had best be done for him, I suggested a situation in the Post-office as a letter carrier. He seized at the idea, but, being better aware than I was of the difficulty of obtaining it, expressed himself to that effect.

"I wrote to Lady Blessington, telling her the young man's story, and asking if she could get him the appointment. Next day I received a letter from her, inclosing one from the secretary, regretting his utter inability to meet her wishes; such appointments, although so comparatively insignificant, resting with the Postmaster General. I handed this communication to the young man, who was by no means disappointed, for he had not hoped for success. What was my surprise and his delight, however, when, the very next day, there came to me another letter from Lady Blessington, inclosing one from the Postmaster General, conferring the appointment on the young man. This appointment I believe he still holds—at least, he did so a year or two ago.

"S. C. HALL."

Lady Blessington was quick to discover talent or worth of any kind in others, sure to appreciate merit, and generous in her sentiments, and ardent in the expression of approbation in regard to it.

She was by no means indiscriminate in her praise; one of the class whose judgment is to be distrusted on account of the lavish bestowal of encomium: "Defiez vous de ces gens qui sont a tout le monde et ne sont a personne." Nor, on the other hand, did she belong to that most despicable of all cliques, the sneering, depreciatory, would-be aristocratic clique of small intellectual celebrities in literature and art, whose members are niggards in acknowledgment of all worth and merit which do not emanate from their own little circle of pretentious cleverness.

There is a sentiment of envy discoverable in the recognition of intellectual advantages in such circles not confined to low or vulgar people, a sense of something burdensome in the claims to commendation of other people, which seems to oppress the organs pulmonary, sanguineous, and cerebral of that class of small celebrities, be they artists, authors, savans, doctors, or divines, or patronesses in literary society, when merit that has any affinity with the worth supposed or self-estimated of the parties present is brought to the notice of that clique. There is a "je ne sais quoi" of an indisposition to let it be perceived that they admit the existence of any ability superior to their own. The most vulgar-minded, the least highly-gifted, are sure to be most on their guard not to be betrayed into any terms of commendation of an enthusiastic kind that might lead people to suppose they acknowledged any excellence in others they were incapable of manifesting in their own works, words, or writings.

A member of this clique, of a waspish mind and an aspish tongue, is never more entertaining in it than when he is most sneering in his remarks, and churlish of praise in dealing with the intellectual advantages of other people. He is unaccustomed to think favorably or to speak well of his absent literary neighbors. He is afraid of affording them a good word; he would be ashamed to be thought easily pleased with his fellow-men—having any bookish tastes; he can not hear them eulogized without feeling that his own merits are overlooked. Or, if he does chime in with any current praise, the curt commendation and scanty applause are coupled with a sneer, a scoff, some ribald jest, or ridiculing look or gesture, intended to depreciate or to give a ludicrous aspect to a subject that might turn to the advantage of another if it had been gravely treated. In fine, it is not in his nature to be just or generous to any man behind his back who has any kindred tastes or talents with his own.

The subject of this memoir was not of the clique in question, or of their way of dealing with literary competitors in the acknowledgment of worth or merit in other people of literary pursuits.

Lady Blessington was naturally lively, good-humored, mirthful, full of drollery, and easily amused. Her perception of the ridiculous was quick and keen. If there was any thing absurd in a subject or object presented to her, she was sure to seize on it, and to represent the idea to others in the most ridiculous aspect possible. This turn of mind was not exhibited in society alone; in private it was equally manifested. One of the class proverbially given to judge severely of those they come most closely into contact with, after a service of fifteen years, thus speaks of the temper and disposition of her former mistress, Lady Blessington;

"Every one knew the cleverness of this literary lady; but few, very few knew all the kindness of heart of the generous, affectionate woman, but those who were indebted to her goodness, and those who were constantly about her as I was—who saw her acts, and knew her thoughts and feelings.

"My lady's spirits were naturally good; before she was overpowered with difficulties and troubles on account of them, she was very cheerful, droll, and particularly amusing. This was natural to her. Her general health was usually good; she often told me she had never been confined to her bed one whole day in her life; and her spirits would have continued good, but that she got so overwhelmed with care and expenses of all kinds. The calls on her for assistance were from all quarters. Some depended wholly on her (and had a regular pension quarterly paid)—her father and mother for many years before they died; the education of children of friends fell upon her. Now one had to be fitted out for India—now another to be provided for. Constant assistance had to be given to others (to the family, in particular, of one poor lady, now dead some years, whom she loved very dearly). She did a great many charities; for instance, she gave very largely to poor literary people—poor artists; something yearly to old servants; she contributed thus also to Miss Landor's mother—in fact, to several, too many to mention; and from some whom she served, to add to all her other miseries, she met with shameful ingratitude.

"Laboring night and day at literary work, all her anxiety was to be clear of debt. She was latterly constantly trying to curtail all her expenses in her own establishment, and constantly toiling to get money. Worried and harassed at not being able to pay bills when they were sent in—at seeing large expenses still going on, and knowing the want of means to meet them, she got no sleep at night. She long wished to give up Gore House, to have a sale of her furniture, and to pay off her debts. She wished this for two years before she left England; but when the famine in Ireland rendered the payment of her jointure irregular, and every succeeding year more and more so, her difficulties increased, and at last H—— and J—— put an execution in the house, which proved the immediate cause of her departure from England in 1849.

"Poor soul! her heart was too large for her means. Oh! the generosity of that woman was unbounded! I could never tell you the number of persons she used her influence with her friends to procure situations for—great people as well as small. I can not withhold my knowledge of these things from you, one of Lady Blessington's particular friends; nor would I say so much, but knowing that her ladyship esteemed you so highly, she would not have scrupled to have told you all that I have done, and a great deal more."

Queen Catherine's language to "honest Griffith" might have been applied by Lady Blessington to the person from whom I have received the preceding communication:

> "After my death I wish no other herald,
> No other speaker of my living actions,
> To keep mine honor from corruption,
> But such an honest chronicler as Griffith."*

It would occupy a considerable portion of this volume were all the charitable acts, the untiring efforts of this truly generous-minded woman recorded, to bring her influence to bear on friends in exalted station in behalf of people in unfortunate circumstances, and of persons more happily situated, yet needing her services, seeking employment or appointments of some kind or another for them.

There was this peculiarity, too, in the active benevolence of Lady Blessington: whether the person for whom she interested herself was rich or poor, of the upper or the humble class of society, her exertions were equally strenuous and unremitting till they were successful. I have on many occasions seen her, after receiving a letter from some important personage in Parliament, or perhaps some friend of hers in power, intimating the inability of the party to render the service required by her for a *protegé* of hers, when, for a few moments, she would seem greatly disappointed and discouraged. Then there would be a little explosion of anger on account of the refusal or non-compliance with her application.

But this was invariably followed by a brightening up of her looks, a little additional vehemence of tone and gesture, but accompanied with some gleams of returning good-humor and gayety of manner, mingled at the same time with an air of resolution; and then throwing herself back in her fauteuil, and planting her foot rather firmly on the footstool, still holding the letter that annoyed her rolled up tightly, and apparently grasped somewhat energetically, she would declare her firm determination, in spite of the refusal she had met with, that her application should be successful in some other quarter. The poor person's friends

* Henry the Eighth, Act iv., Sc. 2.

or family were counting on her efforts, and they should not be disappointed.

The subject from that time would be uppermost in her mind, whoever the people were who were about her. But when any influential person entered the salon, many minutes would not elapse before he would be put in possession of all the worth of the individual to be served, and all the wants of the poor family dependent on him; and this would be done with such genuine eloquence of feelings strongly excited, finding expression in glowing words, spoken with such pathos, and in accents of such sweetness, that an impression was generally sure to be made, and the subject in view was either directly or indirectly promoted or attained.

The embarrassments of Lady Blessington for some years before her departure from England had made her life a continual struggle with pecuniary difficulties, which, for the maintenance of her position, it was necessary to conceal, and to make a perpetual study of concealing. The cares, anxiety, and secret sorrows of such a situation it is easier to conceive than to describe. Suffice it to say, they served to embitter her career, and, latterly, to give a turn to her thoughts in relation to society, and a taste for the writings of those who have dealt with its follies, as philosophers, without faith in God or man, which tended by no means to her peace of mind, though she attached great importance to that sort of worldly wisdom which teaches us how to lay bare the heart of man, but leaves us in utter ignorance of all things appertaining to his immortal spirit.

It is in vain to seek, in the worldly wisdom of Rochefoucault, for remedies for the wear and tear of literary life; the weariness of mind, the depression of physical energies, occasioned by long-continued literary labors, and the anxieties, cares, and contentions of authorship. The depression of spirits consequent on disappointments in the struggle for distinction, the sinking of the heart at the failure of arduous efforts to obtain success, the blankness of life's aim after the cooling down of early enthusiasm—for these ills, the remedies that will soothe the sick at heart are not to be found in the philosophy of moralists who are materialists professing Christianity. There is a small book ascribed to a religious-minded man, named Thomas à Kempis, which, in all probability, Lady Blessington never saw, in which there are germs of greater thoughts, and fraught with more consoling influences, than are to be discovered in the writings of Rochefoucault or Montaigne, and from which better comfort and more abundant consolation are to be derived than from any of their most successful efforts in laying bare the surface and sounding the depths of the selfishness of the human heart.

Rochefoucault deems selfishness the *primum mobile* of all humane and generous actions. Humanity, in the opinion of this philosopher, is like physic in the practice of empirics. They admit of no *idiosyncrasies;* no controlling influence in nature; no varieties of character determined by temperament, fortuitous circumstances, external impressions, alteration or diversity of organization. Yet the knowledge of human nature is a science to which no general rules can be applied. There is no certainty in regard to the law that is laid down for its government, no uniformity of action arising from its operation, no equality of intellect, passion, disposition, in individuals, to make its general application just or possible.

But, granting that all men feel only for the distresses of others from selfish motives—from a sense of the pain they would feel if they suffered like those with whom they spmpathize—still their sympathy with misfortune or misery is beneficial to others and themselves.*

* In a discussion on the subject of "the selfishness of the motives of benevolent actions," the following anecdote was related, in opposition to the advocates of the theory of Rochefoucault:

"A poor woman, with three children, dressed in black, was observed in Regent Street, standing at the edge of the flags, not asking, but silently standing there, for alms. A lady in deep mourning (widow's weeds), of the middle class, a coarse, hard-featured, and even unfeminine-looking person, passed on; but after she had gone nearly to the end of the street, she turned back, took out her purse, and, with some evident appearances of feeling, gave money to the poor woman. There can be little doubt but that the black gown of the pauper had reminded the passenger in widow's weeds of her bereavement, and made her feel for one, in all probability, deprived like herself of a husband. But, however much of feelings of self, and for self, might enter into her emotions, there was sympathy shown with the sorrows of another that were like her own. And what mattered it to the

It is exceedingly painful to observe the undue importance that Lady Blessington attached to the writings of Rochefoucault, and the grievous error she fell into of regarding them as fountains of truth and wisdom—of deep philosophy, which were to be resorted to with advantage on all occasions necessitating reflection and inquiry. Satiated with luxuries, weary with the eternal round of visits and receptions, and entertainments of intellectual celebrities, fatigued and worn out with the frivolous pursuits of fashionable literary life, and fully sensible of the worthlessness of the blandishments of society and the splendor of its salons, she stood in need of some higher philosophy than ever emanated from mere worldly wisdom.

Literature and art have their victims as well as their votaries, and those who cater for the enjoyments of their society, and aspire to the honor (ever dearly purchased by women) of reigning over it, must count on many sacrifices, and expect to have to deal with a world of importunate pretensions, of small ambitions, of large exigencies, of unbounded vanity, of unceasing flatteries, of many attachments, and of few friendships.

The sick at heart and stricken in spirit, the weary and the palled in this society, have need of other philosophy than that which the works of Rochefoucault can supply. The dreariness of mind of those jaded intellectual celebrities is manifest enough to the observant; in their works and in their conversation, even when they appear in the midst of the highest enjoyments, with bright thoughts flashing from their eyes, with laughter on their lips, and with sallies of wit, sarcasm, or drollery coming from their tongues.

It has been observed of Rochefoucault by a French writer, Monsieur de Sacy, in a review of that author's works:

"His moral has every thing in it that can humble and depress the heart of man, that is to be found in the rigorous doctrine of the Gospel, with the exception of that which exalts man's na-

poor woman, who was relieved by her, how that sympathy was associated? and to herself, was it of no advantage to be reminded of being subject to the same sorrows as the beggar in her tattered weeds, with her fatherless children beside her in the street?"

ture and uplifts his spirit. It is the destruction of all the illusions, without the hopes which should replace them. Rochefoucault, in a word, has only taken from Christianity the fall of man; he left there the dogma of the Redemption . . . Rochefoucault believes no more in piety than he does in wisdom; no more in God than he does in man. A penitent is not more absurd in his eyes than a philosopher. Every where pride —every where *self*, under the hair shirt of the monk of La Trappe, as well as under the mantle of the cynic philosopher. Rochefoucault permits himself to be a Christian only in order to pursue the emotions of the heart into their last intrenchments. He condescends to seem to be a Christian only to poison our joys, and cast a deadly shade on the most cherished illusions of life's dreams. What remains for man then? For those resolute minds, there remains nothing but a cold and daring contempt of all things human and divine—an arid and stoical contentment in confronting—annihilation: for others differently constituted, there remains despair or abandonment to the enjoyment of brutalizing pleasures as the only aim and ultimate object of life."

There remains for women of cultivated minds and of elevated notions of a literary kind—women who are the disciples of Rochefoucault—a middle course to pursue, which Monsieur de Sacy has not noticed; and that course is to shine in the society of intellectual people. The pursuit, indeed, is a soul-wearying one, but there is a kind of glory in it that dazzles people, and makes them exceedingly eager for it.

Those to whom amusement becomes a business, the art of pleasing a drudgery that is daily to be performed, pass from the excitement of society, its labors and its toils, into the retirement and privacy of domestic life, in exhaustion, languor, irksomeness, and ennui; and from this state they are roused to new efforts in the salons by a craving appetite for notice and for praise.

> "Their breath is *admiration*, and their life
> A storm whereon they ride."

Lady Blessington had that fatal gift of pre-eminent attractiveness in society which has rendered so many clever women distinguished and unhappy. The power of pleasing people indiscriminately, in large circles, is never long exercised by women with advantage to the feminine character of their fascinations.

The facility of making one's self so universally agreeable in literary salons as to be there "the observed of all observers," "the admired of all admirers," "the pink and rose" of the fair state—of literature, *à la mode*, "the glass of fashion and the mould of form," becomes in time fatal to naturalness of character, singleness and sincerity of mind. Friendship that becomes so diffusive as to admit of as many ties as there are claims of literary talents to notice in society, and to be considered available for all intimacies with remarkable persons and relations with intellectual celebrities, must be kept up by constant administrations of cordial professions of kindness and affection, epistolary and conversational, and frequent interchange of compliments and encomiums, that tend to invigorate sentiments of regard that would fade away without such restoratives. "*On ne loue d'ordinaire que pour être loué.*" The praiser and the praised have a nervous apprehension of depreciation; and those who live before the public in literature or society get not unfrequently into the habit of lavishing eulogies, less with reference to the deserts of those who are commended than with a view to the object to be gained by flattery, namely, the payment in its own coin, and with good interest, of the adulation that has been bestowed on others.

Lady Blessington exercised the double influence of beauty and intellectuality in society, in attracting attention, to win admiration, and to gain dominion over admirers.

In effecting this object, it was the triumph of her heart to render all around not only pleased with her, but pleased with themselves. She lived, in fact, for distinction on the stage of literary society before the foot-lights, and always *en scene*. Lady Blessington was very conscious of possessing the hearts of her audience. She had become accustomed to an atmosphere of adulation, and the plaudits of those friends, which were never out of her ears, at last became a necessity to her. Her abode was a temple, and she the Minerva of the shrine, whom all the votaries of literature and art worshiped.

The swinging of the censer before her fair face never ceased in those salons, and soft accents of homage to her beauty and her talents seldom failed to be whispered in her ear, while she sat enthroned in that well-known *fauteuil* of hers, holding high court in queen-like state—"the most gorgeous Lady Blessington."* The desire for this sort of distinction of a beautiful woman bookishly given—in other words, "*the coquetterie d'un dame des salons litteraires*"—in many respects is similar to that common sort of female ambition, of gaining the admiration of many without any design of forming an attachment for one, which Madam de Genlis characterizes, "*Ce que les hommes meprisent et qui les attire.*"

But, in one respect, the intellectual species of coquetry is of a higher order than the other; it makes the power of beauty, of fascination, of pleasing manners, auxiliary only to the influence of intellect, and seeks for conquests over the mind, even while it aims at gaining an ascendency over the feelings of the heart. The chief aim of it, however, is to achieve triumphs over all within its circle, and for this end, the lady ambitious of reigning in literary society must live to be courted, admired, homaged by its celebrities. The queen-regnant in its salons must at length cease to confide in the natural gifts and graces which belong to her—the original simplicity of her character or sweetness of her disposition. She must become an actress there, she must adapt her manners, fashion her ideas, accommodate her conversation to the taste, tone of thought, and turn of mind of every individual around her.

She must be perpetually demonstrating her own attractions or attainments, or calling forth any peculiarities in others calculated to draw momentary attention to them. She must become a slave to the caprices, envious feelings, contentions, rivalries, selfish aims, ignoble sacrifices, and *exigeants* pretensions of lite-

* Dr. Parr was introduced to Lady Blessington by Mr. Pettigrew, and shortly after that introduction, the doctor, writing to Mr. Pettigrew, spoke of her ladyship as "the most gorgeous Lady Blessington."

rati, artists, and all the notabilities of fashionable circles, *les amis des hommes des lettres, ou les amants imaginaires des dames d'esprit.*

In a word, she must part with all that is calculated to make a woman in this world happy—peace of mind, the society of true friends, and pursuits which tend to make women loved and cherished; the language of sincerity, the simplicity and endearing satisfaction of home enjoyments. And what does she gain when she has parted with all these advantages, and has attained the summit of her ambition? a name in the world of fashion, some distinction in literary circles, homage and admiration so long as prosperity endures, and while means are to be found for keeping up the splendor of a vast establishment and its brilliant circles.

And when the end of all the illusion of this state of splendid misery comes at last, the poor lady who has lived in it so long awakens from it as from a dream, and the long delirium of it becomes manifest to her. She has thrown away fortune, time, and talents in obtaining distinction, in surrounding herself with clever people, in patronising and entertaining artists and literati. She has sacrificed health and spirits in this pursuit. Her establishment is broken up—nothing remains to her of all its treasures; she has to fly to another country, and, after a few weeks, she is suddenly carried off, leaving some persons that knew her well and long to lament that one so generous, kindly disposed, naturally amiable and noble-minded, so highly gifted, clever, and talented, should have been so unhappily circumstanced in early life and in more advanced years, as well as at the close of her existence, and that she should have been placed so long in a false position; in a few words, that the whole course of her life should have been infelicitous.

The wear and tear of literary life leave very unmistakable evidence of their operation on the traits, thoughts, and energies of bookish people. Like the eternal rolling of the stone of Sisyphus, the fruitless toiling up the hill, and the conscious failure of each attempt on coming down, are the ceaseless struggles for eminence of authors, artists, and those who would be surrounded by them in society as their patrons or influential admirers, and would obtain their homage for so being.

Like those unceasing tantalizing efforts on which the energies of Sisyphus were expended in vain, are the tiring pursuits of the literati, treading on the heels of one another day after day, tugging with unremitting toil at one uniform task—to obtain notoriety, to overcome competition, to supplant others in public favor, and, having met with some success, to maintain a position at any cost, with the eminence of which perhaps some freak of fortune may have had more to do than any intrinsic worth or superior merit of their own. And then they must end the labors which have consumed their health and strength without any solid advantage in the way of an addition to their happiness, a security to their peace of mind, or a conviction that those labors have tended materially to the real good of mankind, and thereby to the glory of God, and of His cause on earth, namely, the promotion of the interests of truth, justice, and humanity.

In no spirit of unkindness toward the memory of Lady Blessington, in no cynical mood, or momentary forgetfulness even, of the many estimable qualities and excellent talents which she possessed, let us ask, did her literary career, and position in literary society, secure for her any of those advantages which have been just referred to, or was that position attended with any solid benefits to those high interests which transcend all others in this world in importance?

Or, apart from her literary career, if the question be asked, Was her life happy? assuredly the answer must be, It was not happy.

In the height of her success, in the most brilliant period of her London life, in St. James's Square, in Seamore Place, in Gore House, in the midst of the luxuries by which she was surrounded, even at the period of her fewest cares—in Italy and France —*the present enjoyments were never unaccompanied with reminiscences of the past that were painful.*

But who could imagine that such was the case who knew her only in crowded salons, so apparently joyous, animated, and exhilarated by the smiling looks and soft accents of those who paid such flattering homage to her beauty and her talent, fully conscious as she was of the admiration she excited, and so accustomed to it that it seemed to have become essential to her being?

Ample evidence is to be found in the detached thoughts of Lady Blessington, scattered through her papers or among those records of reflection to which she gave the appropriate name of "Night Thought Books." The following extracts from them may serve to show the truth of the preceding observation.

WRONGS AND WOES OF WOMEN.

"Men can pity the wrongs inflicted by other men on the gentler sex, but never those which they themselves inflict (on women)."

"Quelle destinée que cette de la femme! A l'etre le plus foible le plus entouré des seductions, le plus mal elevé, pour les resister, les juges les plus severes, les peines les plus dures la vengeance la plus inflexible. Quand le ciel chasse de son Paradis notre pere et notre mere coupables, la glaive de l'ange les frappa tous deux: pour tous deux son feu impitoyable brula devant la porte du lien des delices, sans que la femme fut plus puni, plus malheureux que l'homme. Si elle eut les douleurs de la maternité, son compagnon d'infortune eut les sueurs du travail et les horribles angoisses qui accompagnent le spectacle des souffrances de celle qu'on aime. Il n'y eut point entre eux un inegal partage de punition, et Adam ne put pas à l'exclusion d'Eve rentrer dans ce jardin qui lui fermait la colere du ciel! Hommes vous vous êtes faits pour nous plus inflexible que Dieu, et quand nous sommes tombées par vous, à cause de vous, pour nous seules brille l'epée qui met hors du monde, hors de l'honneur, hors de l'estime, et qui nous empêche à jamais d'y rentrer."!!!—*Brisset.*

"The whole system of female education is to teach women to allure and not to repel, yet how much more essential is the latter?"

"England is the only country in Europe where the loss of

one's virtue superinduces the loss of all. I refer to chastity. A woman known to have violated this virtue, though she possess all the other virtues, is driven with ignominy from society into a solitude rendered insupportable by a sense of the injustice by which she is made a victim to solitude, which often becomes the grave of the virtues she brought to it."

"Passion! Possession! Indifference! What a history is comprised in these three words! What hopes and fears succeeded by a felicity as brief as intoxicating—followed in its turn by the old consequence of possession—indifference! What burning tears, what bitter pangs, rending the very heart-strings—what sleepless nights and watchful days form part of this every-day story of life, whose termination leaves the actors to search again for new illusions to finish like the last!"

"A woman who exposes, even to a friend, her domestic unhappiness, has violated the sanctity of home and the delicacy of affection, and placed an enduring obstacle to the restoration of interrupted domestic peace and happiness."

"The youth of women is entitled to the affectionate interest of the aged of their own sex."

"Women who have reached old age should look with affectionate interest on those of their own sex who are still traveling the road scattered with flowers and thorns over which they have already passed themselves, as wanderers who have journeyed on through many dangers should regard those who are still toiling over the same route."

BEAUTY WITHOUT THE SECURITY OF FIXED PRINCIPLE.

"A beautiful woman without fixed principles may be likened to those fair but rootless flowers which float in streams, driven by every breeze."

"Whenever we make a false step in life, we take more pains to justify it than would have saved us from its commission, and yet we never succeed in convincing others—nay, more, ourselves—that we have acted rightly."

"The happiness of a woman is lost forever when her husband ceases to be its faithful guardian. To whom else can she confide the treasure of her peace who will not betray the trust? and it is so precious, that, unless carefully guarded, it is soon lost."

"Love-matches are made by people who are content, for a month of honey, to condemn themselves to a life of vinegar."

"There are some chagrins of the heart which a friend ought to try to console without betraying a knowledge of their existence, as there are physical maladies which a physician ought to seek to heal without letting the sufferer know that he has discovered their extent."

"In some women modesty has been known to survive chastity, and in others chastity to survive modesty. The last example is the most injurious to the interests of society, because they who believe, while they preserve chastity inviolate, that they may throw aside the feminine reserve and delicacy which ought to be its outward sign and token, give cause for suspicions, and offend the purity of others of their sex with whom they are brought in contact much more than those who, failing in chastity, preserve its decency and decorum."

"The want of chastity is a crime against one's self, but the want of modesty is a crime against society."

"A chaste woman may yield to the passion of her lover, but an unchaste woman gives way to her own."*

Lines on various subjects, from the "Night Thought Book" of Lady Blessington:

NIGHT.

1.

"Yes, night! I love thy silence and thy calm,
That o'er my spirits shed a soothing balm,
Lifting my soul to brighter, purer spheres,
Far, far removed from this dark vale of tears.

2.

"There is a holiness, a blessed peace
In thy repose, that bids our sorrow cease;
That stills the passions in the hallowed breast,
And lulls the tortured feelings into rest."

* Some of the sentiments expressed in these observations I do not think true or just, in a moral or religious point of view.—R. R. M.

FLOWERS.

"Flowers are the bright remembrances of youth;
They waft back, with their bland and odorous breath,
The joyous hours that only young life knows,
Ere we have learned that this fair earth hides graves.
They bring the cheek that's mouldering in the dust
Again before us, tinged with health's own rose;
They bring the voices we shall hear no more,
Whose tones were sweetest music to our ears;
They bring the hopes that faded one by one,
Till naught was left to light our path but faith,
That we, too, like the flowers, should spring to life,
But not, like them, again e'er fade or die."

Lines of Lady Blessington, unfinished, written on the back of a letter of Lord Durham, very much injured and defaced, dated July 28, 1837:

"At midnight's silent hour, when hushed in sleep,
They who have labored or have sorrowed lie,
Learning from slumber how 'tis sweet to die,
I love my vigils of the heart to keep;
For then fond memory unlocks her store,
Which in the garish noisy . . . . . .
Then comes reflection, musing on the lore
And precepts of pure, mild philosophy.
Sweet voices—silent now, ...
Bless my charmed ear; sweet smiles are seen,
Though they who wore them long now dwell on high,
Where I shall meet them, but with chastened mien,
To tell how dull was life where they were not,
And that they never, never were forgot."

Unfinished lines in pencil, with numerous corrections and alterations, in the hand-writing of Lady Blessington, apparently of a recent date:

"And years, long, weary years have rolled away,
Since youth with all its sunny smiles has fled,
And hope within this saddened breast is dead,
To gloomy doubts and dark despair a prey,
Turning from pleasure's flow'ry path astray,
To haunts where melancholy thoughts are bred,
And meditation broods with inward dread
Amid the shades of pensive twilight gray.

Yet has this heart not ceased to thrill with pain,
Though joy can make its pulses beat no more;
Its wish to reach indifference is vain,
And will be, till life's fitful fever's o'er,
And it has reached the dim and silent shore,
Where sorrow it shall never know again.
Like to a stream whose current's frozen o'er,
Yet still flows on beneath its icy . . . . . ."

* * * * *

On the same sheet of paper as that on which the preceding lines are written, there are the following fragments of verse, evidently composed in the same thoughtful mood as the previous lines of a retrospective character:

"But though the lily-root in earth
Lies an unsightly thing,
Yet thence the flow'ret had its birth,
And into light will spring.
So when this form is in the dust,*
Of mortals all, the lot,
Oh, may my soul its prison burst,
Its errors all forgot!"

Other lines unfinished, in a MS. book of Lady Blessington, in her ladyship's hand-writing:

"The smile that plays around the lips
When sorrow preys upon our hearts,
Is like the flowers with which we deck
The youthful corpse ere it departs
Forever to the silent grave,
From those who would have died to save."

A fragment in penciling, in another commonplace book of Lady Blessington, in her ladyship's hand-writing, but no date or signature:

"Pardon, O Lord! if this too sinful heart,
Ingrate to thee, did for a mortal feel
Love all too pure for earth to have a part.
Pardon—for lowly at thy feet I kneel:
Bowed to the dust, my heart, like a crushed flower,
Yields all remaining sweetness at thy shrine.

* A line has here been erased.

Thou only, Lord of mercy, now hath power
  To bid repose and hope again be mine.
Chase from this fond and too long tortured breast
  Thoughts that intrude to steal my soul from thee ;
Aid me within a cloister to find rest,
  When I from sin and passion shall be free."

No one who ever knew Lady Blessington, and perhaps few persons who may chance to read these pages, would refuse to say "Amen" to that sweet prayer.

CHAPTER XI.

NOTICES OF THE WRITINGS OF LADY BLESSINGTON, ETC.

It would be absurd to lay claim for Lady Blessington to the great attributes of first-rate intellectual powers, creative and inventive, namely, concentrativeness, originality, vigor, and elevation of mind, genius of the highest order, combining intensity of thought, strength of imagination, depth of feeling, combinative talents, and mastery of intellect in delineation and description; excellence, in short, in literature, that serves to give a vivid look and life-like appearance to every thing it paints in words.

It would be a folly to seek in the mental gifts and graces of Lady Blessington for evidences of the divine inspirations of exalted genius, endowed with all its instincts and ideality, favored with bright visions of the upper regions of poetry and fiction, with glimpses of ethereal realms, peopled with shadowy forms and spiritualized beings, with glorious attributes and perfections, or to imagine we are to discover in her keen perception of the ridiculous the excellent in art, literature, or conversation, or in her ideas of the marvelous or admirable in striking effects, sublime conceptions of the grand, the beautiful, the chivalrous, or supernatural. The power of realization of great ideas, without encumbering the representation of ideal objects with material images and earthly associations, belongs only to genius of the first order, and between it and graceful talent, fine taste, shrewdness of mind, and quickness of apprehension, there are many degrees of intellectual excellence.

It is very questionable if any of the works of Lady Blessington, with the exception of the "Conversations with Lord Byron," and perhaps the "Idler in Italy," will maintain a permanent position in English miscellaneous literature. The interest taken in the writer was the main source of the temporary interest that was felt in her literary performances.

The master-thinker of the last century has truly observed: "An author bustling in the world, showing himself in public, and emerging occasionally, from time to time, into notice, might keep his works alive by his personal influence; but that which conveys little information, and gives no great pleasure, must soon give way, as the succession of things produces new topics of conversation, and other modes of amusement."*

Lady Blessington commenced her career of authorship in 1822. Her first work, entitled "The Magic Lantern; or, Sketches of Scenes in the Metropolis," was published by Longman in that year, in one volume 8vo.

The work was written evidently by one wholly inexperienced in the ways of authorship. There were obvious marks in it, however, of cleverness, quickness of perception, shrewdness of observation, and of kindly feelings, though occasionally sarcastic tendencies prevailed over them. There were evidences in that production, moreover, of a natural turn for humor and drollery, strong sensibility also, and some graphic powers of description in her accounts of affecting incidents.

The sketches in the "Magic Lantern" are the Auction, the Park, the Tomb, the Italian Opera.

A second edition of the "Magic Lantern" was published soon after the first. There is a draught of a preface, in her ladyship's hand-writing, intended for this edition, among her papers, with the following lines:

"If some my Magic Lantern should offend,
The fault's not mine, for scandal's not my end;
'Tis vice and folly that I hold in view:
Your friends, not I, find likenesses to you."

It is very questionable if more indications of talent are not to

* Dr. Johnson. Life of Mallet.

be found in the first work written by Lady Blessington, "The Magic Lantern," than in the next production, or, indeed, in any succeeding performance of hers, though she looked so unfavorably on "The Magic Lantern" in her later years as seldom or never to make any reference to it.

"Sketches and Fragments," the second work by Lady Blessington, was also published by Longman in 1822, in one small 12mo volume. The preface to it is dated June 12, 1822. The contents of this volume are the following:

Blighted Hopes, Marriage, the Ring, Journal of a Week of a Lady of Fashion, an Allegory, Fastidiousness of Taste, Coquetry, Egotism, Reflections, Sensibility, Friendship, Wentworth Fragments.

In the "Sketches and Fragments," Lady Blessington began to be somewhat affected and conventional, to assume a character of strait-laced propriety and purism, that made it incumbent on her to restrain her natural thoughts and feelings, and to adopt certain formulas expressive of very exalted sentiments, and of a high sense of the duties she had imposed on herself as a censor of society—its manners, morals, and all externals affecting the decorum of its character. The fact is, Lady Blessington was never less effective in her writings than when she ceased to be natural. And with respect to her second production, though in point of style and skill in composition it was an improvement on her former work, in other respects it was hardly equal to it.

Lady Blessington received no remuneration from either of the works just mentioned. From the produce of the sale of the second production, after defraying all the expenses of publication, there was a small sum of £20 or £30 available, which was applied, by her ladyship's directions, to a charitable purpose.

The necessity of augmenting her income by turning her literary talents to a profitable account brought Lady Blessington before the public as a writer of fashionable novels. The peculiar talent she exhibited in this style of composition was in lively descriptions of persons in high life, in some respect or other *outre* or ridiculous, in a vein of quiet humor, which ran throughout her writings—a common-sense, and generally an amiable way of viewing most subjects; a pleasant mode of effecting an *entente cordiale* with her readers, an air of good-nature in her observations, and an apparent absence of malice or malignity in the smart sayings, sharp and satirical, which she delighted in giving utterance to.

The great defect of her novels was want of creative power, and constructive skill in devising a plot, and carrying on any regularly planned action from the beginning of a work to its close, and making the *denouément* the result that ought to be expected from the incidents of the story throughout its progress.

The characters of her mere men of fashion are generally well drawn. Many of her sketches of *scenes* (in one of the French acceptations of the word) in society, not of scenes in nature, are admirably drawn.

Lady Blessington, in novel-writing, discarded the services of "gorgons, hydras, and chimæras dire." She had no taste for horrors of that kind; and if she had ventured into the delineation of them, the *materiel* of her imagination would not have enabled her to deal with them successfully.

The characters of her women are generally naturally delineated, except when in waging war with the follies or vices of fashionable society. She portrayed its female members in colors rather too dark to be true to nature, or even just to her own sex. But she always professed to have a great dislike to works of fiction in which humanity was depicted in a revolting aspect, and individuals were represented without any redeeming trait in their characters. We find in several of her novels, in the character of the personages, a mixture of good and evil, and seldom, except in "the Victims of Society," evidence of unmitigated, unredeemable baseness and villainy in the character of any person she writes of. Books that give pain, and are disagreeable to think of after they had been read, she had a strong objection to. One of her literary correspondents in 1845, writing to her, referring to a recent work which gave a painful and disagreeable portraiture of several characters, said, "It is a sin against art, which is designed to please even in the terrors which it evokes. But the highest artists—Sophocles, Shakspeare, and

Goëthe—have departed from that rule on certain occasions and for certain ends. I should have compromised with the guilt depicted if I had abated the pain the contemplation of such guilt should occasion. It is in showing by what process the three orders of mind, which, rightly trained and regulated, produce the fairest results of humanity, may be depraved to its scourge and pestilence, that I have sought the analysis of truths which, sooner or later, will vindicate their own moral utilities. The calculating intellect of D——, which should have explored *science;* the sensual luxuriance and versatility of V——, which should have enriched *art;* the conjunction of earnest passion with masculine understanding in L——, which should have triumphed for good and high ends in *active practical* life, are all hurled down into the same abyss of irretrievable guilt, from want of the one supporting principle—brotherhood and sympathy with others. They are incarnations of egotism pushed to the extreme. And I suspect those most indignant at the exposition are those who have been startled with the likeness of their own hearts. They may not have the guilt of the hateful three, but they wince from the lesson that guilt inculcates. The earnestness of the author's own views can alone console him in the indiscriminate and lavish abuse, with all its foul misrepresentations, which greets his return to literature, and, unless he is greatly mistaken, the true moral of his book will be yet recognized, though the vindication may be deferred till it can only be rendered to dust—a stone and a name."

In 1832, in "Colburn's New Monthly Magazine," Lady Blessington's "Journal of Conversations with Lord Byron" made its first appearance. The Journal contains matter certainly of the highest and most varied interest, and would convey as just an account of Byron's character, and as unexaggerated a sketch as any that has been ever published, if some secret feeling of pique and sense of annoyance were not felt by her, and had not stolen into her "Conversations."

The "Journal" was published in one vol. 8vo, a little later, and had a very extensive sale.

"Grace Cassidy, or the Repealers," a novel in 3 vols., was published by Bentley in 1833.

From all Irish political novels, including "The Repealers," the English public may pray most earnestly to be delivered.*

"Meredyth," a novel in 3 vols., was published by Longman, 1833.

In October, 1833, Mr. William Longman wrote to Lady Blessington, stating that "Meredyth" had not hitherto had the success that had been anticipated. £45 had been spent in advertising, and only 380 copies sold, 300 of which had been subscribed.

KEY TO THE REPEALERS.

(WRITTEN IN 1833.)

Duchess of Heaviland—Duchess of Northumberland.
Marchioness of Bowood—Marchioness of Lansdowne
Countess of Grandison—Countess of Grantham.
Lord Albany—Lord Alvanley.
Lord Elsinore—Lady Tullamore.
Lady Rodney—Lady Sidney.
Duke of Lismore—Duke of Devonshire.
Mrs. Grantley—Mrs. Norton.
Countess of Guernsey—Countess of Jersey.
Lord Rey—Earl Grey.
Marchioness of Stewartville—Marchioness of Londonderry.
Lord Montague—Lord Rokeby.
Duchess of Lennox—Duchess of Richmond.
Marchioness of Burton—Marchioness of Conyngham.
Marquess of Mona—Marquess of Anglesey.
Lady Augusta Jaring—Lady Augusta Baring.
Marchioness of Glanricarde—Marchioness of Clanricarde.
Lady E. Hart Burtley—Lady E. S. Wortley.
Lady Yesterfield—Lady Chesterfield.
Mrs. Pranson—Hon. Mrs. Anson.
Lady Lacre—Lady Dacre.
Lady Noreley—Lady Moreley.
Mr. Manly—Mr. Stanley.
Sir Robert Neil—Sir Robert Peel.
Mr. Hutter Serguson—Mr. Cutlar Ferguson.
Mr. Enice—Mr. Edward Ellice.
Mr. Theil—Mr. R. L. Sheil.
Lord Refton—Lord Sefton.
Lady Castlemont—Lady Charlemont.
Lord Leath—Lord Meath.
Duke and Duchess of Cartoun—Duke and Duchess of Leinster.

"The Follies of Fashion, or the *Beau Monde* of London in 1835"—a sketch by Lady Blessington, appeared in one of the periodicals of the time.

"The Belle of the Season," a much later production, was a lively sketch of an episode in fashionable society.

"The Two Friends," a novel in 3 vols., was published by Saunders and Ottley in 1835.

"The Victims of Society," a novel in 3 vols., Saunders and Ottley, published in 1837. If the delineation of high life given in this work be correct, the experience which qualified the author to produce such a performance was very terrible. If it be not true, the wholesale pulling-down process, the utter demolition of the reputation of people in fashionable society, of women as well as men, in this work, is much to be regretted.

"The Confessions of an Elderly Lady," in one vol., Longman, 1838.

"The Governess," a novel in 3 vols., Longman, 1839.

"Desultory Thoughts and Reflections," in one thin 16mo vol., appeared in 1839, published by Longman.

"The Idler in Italy" was published in 2 vols. 8vo, Colburn, in 1839; the most successful and interesting of all the works of Lady Blessington.

"The Idler in France" appeared in 2 vols. 8vo, Longman, in 1841.

"The Lottery of Life, and other Tales," in 3 vols., appeared in 1842.

"Strathern, or Life at Home and Abroad," a story of the present day. This novel appeared first in "The Sunday Times;" afterward it was published by Colburn, in 1845, in 4 vols. Between the two publications, Lady Blessington is said to have realized nearly £600. It was the most read of all her novels, as she imagined; yet the publisher, in a letter to Lady Blessington, several months after publishing, complained that he only sold 400 copies, and had lost £40 by the publication, and that he must decline a new work proposed by her. In this work, the writer drew, as in her other novels, her illustrations of society from her own times; and her opportunities of studying human nature in a great variety of its phases, but particularly in what is called "the fashionable world," afforded her ample means of giving faithful portraitures of its society. These portraitures in "Strathern" are graphic, vivid, and not without a dash of humor and sarcastic drollery in her delineation of fashionable life at home and abroad. But the representation is certainly not only exceedingly unfavorable to the class she puts *en scene* in Rome, Naples, Paris, and London, but very unpleasing on the whole, though often amusing, and sometimes instructive.

In "The Memoirs of a Femme de Chambre," a novel in 3 vols., published by Colburn and Bentley in 1846, Lady Blessington availed herself of the privileges of an imaginary servant-maid to penetrate the inner chambers of temples of fashion, to discover and disclose the arena of aristocratic life. The follies and foibles of persons in high life, the trials and heart-sicknesses of unfortunate governesses, and the vicissitudes in the career of ladies'-maids, and, in particular, in that of one *femme de chambre*, who became the lady of a bilious nabob, are the subjects of this novel, written with great animation, and the usual piquancy and liveliness of style of the writer.

"Lionel Deerhurst, or Fashionable Life under the Regency," was published by Bentley, 1846.

"Marmaduke Herbert," a novel, was published in 1847. Of this work, a very eminent *litterateur* wrote in the following terms to Lady Blessington, May 22d, 1847:

"It seems to me, in many respects, the best book you have written. I object to some of the details connected with the 'fatal error,' but the management of its effects is marked by a very high degree of power; and the analytical subtlety and skill displayed throughout the book struck me very much.

"I sincerely and warmly congratulate you on what must certainly extend your reputation as a writer."

"Country Quarters," a novel, first appeared in the columns of a London Sunday paper in 1848, and was published separately, and edited by Lady Blessington's niece, Miss Power, after her ladyship's death, in 3 vols. 8vo, Shoberl, 1850.

"Country Quarters," the last production of Lady Blessington, is illustrative of a state of society and of scenes in real life in provincial towns, in which young English military Lotharios and tender-hearted Irish heroines, speculative and sentimental, are the chief performers, for the delineation of which Lady Blessington was far more indebted to her recollection than to her imagination. There is no evidence of exhausted intellect in this last work of Lady Blessington's. But the drollery is not the fun that oozed out from exuberant vivacity in the early days of Lady Blessington's authorship; it is forced, strained, "written up" for occasion; and yet there is an air of cheerfulness about it, which, to one knowing the state of mind in which that work was written, would be very strange, almost incredible, if we did not call to mind the frame of mind in which the poem of John Gilpin was written by Cowper.

The literary friends of Lady Blessington were in the habit of expressing to her ladyship their opinions on her performances as they appeared, and sometimes of making very useful suggestions to her.

The general tone of opinions addressed to authors by their friends, must, of course, be expected to be laudatory; and those, it must be admitted, of many of Lady Blessington's friends were no exception to the rule.

Of "The Repealers," a very distinguished writer thus wrote to the authoress:

"My dear Lady Blessington, I have read your 'Repealers;' you must be prepared for some censure of its politics. I have been too warm a friend to the Coercive Bill to suffer so formidable a combatant as you to possess the field without a challenge. I like many parts of your book *much*; but—will you forgive me?—you have not done yourself justice. Your haste is not evident in style, which is pure, fluent, and remarkably elegant, but in the slightness of the story. You have praised great ladies and small authors too much; but that is the fault of good nature. Let your next book, I implore you, be more of passion, of sentiment, and of high character. You are capable of *great things*, of beating many of the female writers of the day in prose, and you ought to task your powers to the utmost; your genius is worthy of application.

"Forgive all this frankness; it is from one who admires you too much not to be sincere, and esteems you too highly to fear that you will be offended at it."

Another eminent literary writer writes to her on the subject of another recent production of hers:

"You have only to write passions instead of thoughts in order to excel in novel writing. But you fear too much; you have the prudes before you; you do not like to paint the *passions* of love, you prefer painting its sentiment. The awe of the world chills you. But perhaps I am wrong, and in 'The Two Friends' I shall find you giving us another 'Corinne' or a better 'Admiral's Daughter,' both being works that depend solely on passion for their charm. You have all the tact, truth, and grace of De Staël, and have only to recollect that while she wrote for the world, the world vanished from her closet. In writing, we should see nothing before us but our own wild hearts, our own experience, and not till we correct proofs should we remember that we are to have readers."

One fully authorized to speak on the subject of authorship thus writes to her ladyship on the appearance of a recent novel of hers:

"People often say to me, I shall write a novel; if I question them 'on what rule?' they state they know of no rules. They write history, epic, the drama, criticism, by rules; and for the novel, which comprises all four, they have no rules; no wonder that there is so much of talent *manqué* in half the books we read. In fact, we ought to do as the sculptors do, gaze upon all the great master-pieces till they sink into us, till their secrets penetrate us, and then we write according to rules without being quite aware of it.

"I have been trying to read some fashionable French books. Sue and Balzac seem most in vogue, but the task is too heavy. Rant run mad, and called, God wot, philosophy! I feel as if these writers had taken an unfair advantage of us, and their glittering trash makes common sense too plain and simple to be true."

Of "The Victims of Society," a friendly critic writes:

"I have finished the whole of 'The Victims of Society.' The characters are drawn with admirable tact and precision, and a knowledge of human nature that is only too fine for the obtuse. You are, indeed, very severe in the second volume, more so than I had anticipated; but it is severe truth, finely conceived, boldly attempted, and consummately executed. You have greatly retrieved and fined down Miss Montresor's character by her touches of penitence and remorse. Lord C—— is perfect. W——, an English dandy throughout. I can not conceive that you have any thing to dread. You have attacked only persons whom the general world like to hear attacked; the few who wince will pretend not to understand the application."

Of "The Idler in Italy," one of her most distinguished friends says:

"I have already nearly finished the two volumes of 'The Idler in Italy,' and am delighted with the sparkling and graceful ease. You interest us in every thing, even in the 'bed resting on pillar swans,' and the 'terrace that is to be turned into a garden:' your observations on men and things are, as usual, excellent. All the account of the Revolution is highly animated and original; I am sure the work will be UNIVERSALLY liked."

On the appearance of "The Two Friends," Lady Blessington received the following notice of it from one of her literary acquaintance:

"I have just finished your work, 'The Two Friends,' and I may congratulate you on a most charming publication, which can not fail to please universally, and to increase your reputation. It is true that there is nothing exaggerated in it, but it is written in a thoroughly good tone and spirit, very elegant, and sustained with great knowledge of character, many dramatic situations, abounding with profound observations and much playful wit. The happiest and newest character of the kind I know is the Count de Bethune. He is admirable. His bearing his griefs like 'a man and a Frenchman,' his seeing to his dinner, and reproving his daughter for her want of feeling in disturbing his digestion, are exquisite traits of character, and remind us of the delicate touches of Manzoni in 'I Promessi Sposi.'

Lord Scamper is very humorous, and I laughed heartily at some of the scenes in which he appears, though in one part his verisimilitude is a little injured by your making him talk sense about the Revolution. Your politics there, by-the-by, are shockingly Tory, and will please Lord Abinger. There are some beautiful discriminative reflections, not dragged in per force, nor tedious and extraneous, but natural and well timed. In your story you have improved prodigiously since 'The Repealers;' it is more systematic and artful. Altogether, you have exceeded my hopes, and may reckon here on complete success. Lady Walmer is very harsh, but a very true portrait. Cecile is charming, and pleases me more than Lady Emily, I scarcely know why. The only fault I see in your book is, that it is a little too prudent. But perhaps you are quite right, and a man does not allow for the fears of a woman; at all events, such prudence will make you more popular. There is no doubt of your having greatly excelled 'The Repealers.'"

Another novel of her ladyship's called forth the following observations from another quarter:

"I have received your book ('Marmaduke Herbert'), and I must candidly tell you that I think you have outdone yourself in this most interesting and effective work. It has a grave, sustained solemnity of power about it, of which I can not speak too highly.

"It reminds me greatly of Godwin's earlier writings. The same minute and faithful analysis of feeling, the same patience in building up the interest, and the same exhibition of strength and weakness in one motley volume.

"I did not think, when you spoke to me of the story long ago, that you could have made so fine a thing of it. The first volume and a half are extremely thrilling, and without effort."

"The Belle of a Season" brought several letters to Lady Blessington. The following one is most deserving of being cited:

"I read your 'Belle of the Season' with sincere admiration; the very lightness of the subject makes the treatment so difficult, and it is surprising how much actual interest you have given to the story, while the verification is so skillful, so graceful and easy, as to be a model in its way.

"I was charmed from the first few lines, and indeed the opening of the story is one of the happiest parts.

"The whole partakes of the character of the subject, and is a true picture of what a London season is to a young lady—opening those views that are new to her of life and society. A London season wears different faces to different classes; the politician, the author, the actor, the artist, the tradesman, the pickpocket, the boy who wants to " 'old your 'oss', each has his own London season. But no doubt the happiest of all, for a year or two, is the young lady's, beginning with court, and ending with a fancy ball, to say nothing of the declaration, for that is the drop scene.

"Your style is peculiarly fluent and appropriate, and very original. I do not remember any specimen of the 'Rambler' like it.

"I then went from poetry to prose, and read your 'Governess.' The story is very interesting, and the character of the poor child so exquisite a sketch, that I regret much that it was not more elaborate; it alone would have furnished matter for three volumes. The Williamsons are extremely well hit off, and so are the Manwarings; the poets, and characters I like best, are those which belong to what is now the popular class of literature, very *caricature.* To this class I think the Mondens, and some of the scenes at Mr. V. Robinson's, belong. But they are amusing, and will, no doubt, please generally.

"I am delighted to see that you improve and mature in your charming talent with every new work. I never saw a more striking improvement in any writer since the date, not a long one, of the 'Repealers.' I ought, as I am on the subject, to add how much I was struck with the little tale of the Dreamer; if a very few lines, a little too English and refined, were toned down into the Irish coloring of the rest, it would be a perfect gem in composition, as it is now in sentiment and conception."

THE ANNUALS.

The late Frederick Shoberl, Esq., who died in March, 1853,

originated in 1823, in conjunction with the late Mr. Ackermann, the first of the English annuals, "The Forget-me-not." For several years he was the editor of it. The last of these annuals was the volume for 1834. This periodical paved the way for the numerous illustrated works that have since issued from the press.

These luxuries of literature were got up especially for the entertainment of ladies and gentlemen of fashionable circles, but not exclusively for the *élite* of English society. The tastes of belles and beaux of the boudoir of all grades aspiring to distinction were to be catered for, and the contributors, in general, were sought for among the aristocracy, not in the republic of letters.

It was necessary, however, to enliven a little dullness of noble amateur authorship with the sparkling gems of genius, with more regard to brilliancy of talent than to advantages of ancestry, and these adventitious aids of professional literati were very largely paid for.

In 1828, Moore makes mention of the editor of "The Keepsake" offering him £600 for 120 lines of either prose or poetry, which he declined.

Persons known as popular writers had likewise to be employed as editors of those periodicals, and were largely paid in general; some for their name alone, and others for their services.

In those palmy days of annual periodicals, when the name of a literary notability as editor was so important to success, we find "The Scenic Annual" for 1838 edited by Thomas Campbell.

"The Keepsake" for 1833 was edited by F. Mansel Reynolds. The contributors were the Countess of Blessington, Lord Dover, Leitch Ritchie, Esq., John Carne, Esq., J. H. Louther, Esq., M.P., Hon. Grantley Berkley, Hon. W. Liddell, Ralph Bernal, Esq., M.P., Lord Morpeth, James Boaden, Esq., Lord Mahon, Mrs. C. Gore, Colley Grattan, Esq., Mrs. Shelley, Hon. H. Craddock, author of "Hajji Baba;" Archdeacon Spencer, Miss L. E. Landon, &c., &c.

"The Court Journal" for 1833 was edited by the Hon. Mrs. Norton.

"Heath's Book of Beauty" for the same year was edited by L. E. L.

"Portraits of the Children of the Nobility" was edited by Mrs. Fairlee in 1838, and in the same year, "The Picturesque Annual" by Leitch Ritchie.

Fisher's "Drawing-Room Scrap-Book" for 1838 was edited by L. E. L.

"Flowers of Loveliness," with poetical illustrations by L. E. L., also appeared the same year.

Finden's "Tableaux; or, Picturesque Scenes of National Character, Beauty, and Costume," edited by Mary Russell Mitford, was published in 1838. The poetical contributions were by Mr. Kenyon, Mr. Chorley, and Barry Cornwall.

The greatest and first promoter, in his day, of illustrated annuals, was Mr. Charles Heath.

This eminent engraver was the son of Mr. James Heath, a distinguished artist also, whose engravings have been the studies on which the two Findens are said to have employed days and nights.

The success of the Findens in working for the booksellers in the illustration of periodicals and popular publications did not satisfy themselves. They became the publishers of their own works, and the works of those whose productions were illustrated by them. Their Byron Illustrations turned out advantageous, but in their other speculations they were less fortunate. Mr. William Finden's "Gallery of British Art" proved a ruinous undertaking; he died in very poor circumstances, September 20, 1852, in his sixty-fifth year.

Mr. Charles Heath had, like the Findens, entered on the publication of periodicals illustrated by him, and with the same unfortunate result. He excelled in small plates, and in his hands that sort of artistic talent exhibited in the embellishment of annuals reached its greatest perfection.

Heath's "Book of Beauty" for 1834, edited by the Countess of Blessington, contained nine pieces by her ladyship. The following are the contents of this volume, and the names or signatures of the authors:

1. The Choice of Phylias, a tale. Sir E. L. B.
2. Francesca, a poem. Dr. William Beattie.

3. Margaret Carnegie, a tale. Viscount Castlereagh.
4. The Phantom Guest, a poem. Anonymous.
5. Mary Lester, a tale. Countess of Blessington.
6. To a Jasmine Tree, lines. Viscount Morpeth.
7. Amy, lines. Countess of Blessington.
8. The Friends, a tale. Henry Lytton Bulwer, Esq., M.P.
9. On the Portrait of Lady C. A. W. Villiers, lines. Lady E. S. Wortley.
10. An Irish Fairy Fable, a tale. Mrs. S. C. Hall.
11. Phœbe, or my Grandmamma West, lines. James Smith.
12. Imaginary Conversations, Rhadamistus and Zenobia. W. S. Landor.
13. To Memory, stanzas. The Countess of Blessington.
14. The Desert, lines. John Galt, Esq.
15. Bianca Vanezzi, lines. Dudley West, Esq.
16. Rosalie, lines. Countess of Blessington.
17. Epochs, lines. H. L. Bulwer, Esq.
18. Imaginary Conversations, Philip II. and Donna Juana Coelho. W. S. Landor.
19. The Coquette, a tale. The Countess of Blessington.
20. The Deserted Wife, lines. R. Bernal, Esq., M.P.
21. Farewell forever, lines. J. H. Lowther, Esq.
22. The Bay of Naples in the summer of 1824, a sketch. The Countess of Blessington.
23. To Matilda sketching, lines. The Countess of Blessington.
24. Rebecca, a tale. Anonymous.
25. To Lucy reading, lines. The Countess of Blessington.
26. What art thou, life? stanzas. Idem.

As one of the most favorable specimens of those illustrated works, the following notice of "the Book of Beauty" for 1835, under the editorship of Lady Blessington, may not be out of place. The principal beautiful celebrities of whom engraved portraits are given in this volume are "The Marchioness of Abercorn," by E. Landseer; "Lucilla," by Parris; "Nourmahal," by Meadows; "Habiba," by Chalon. The gem of the volume is "Juliet," by Bostock.

Among the contributors we find the distinguished literary names of Viscount Strangford, Sir William Gell, E. L. Bulwer, M.P., Lord Nugent, the Hon. K. R. Craven, Lady Emmeline S. Wortley, Lord Albert Conyngham, R. Bernal, M.P., Lady Charlotte Bury, Lord William Lennox, Miss Louisa H. Sheridan, H. L. Bulwer, M.P., Sir Aubrey de Vere, Bart., Hon. G. Berkely, Hon. J. Lester, Sir William Somerville, Bart., Hon. K. Talbot, Mr. Sergeant Talfourd, M.P., &c., &c.

The fair editress contributed a lively and graceful illustration of an excellent plate, named "Felicité," by M'Clise, representing a pretty pert lady's maid trying on a fine dress before the glass, and looking perfectly satisfied with the result.

FELICITE.

BY THE COUNTESS OF BLESSINGTON.

"Oh! would I were a lady,
In costly silks to shine;
Who then could stand beside me?
What figure match with mine?

"Who'd rave about my mistress,
With her pale and languid face,
If they could see *my* pink cheeks,
Edged round with Brussels lace?

"How well her cap becomes me!
With what a jaunty air
I've placed it off my forehead,
To show my shining hair!

"And I declare, these ribands
Just suit me to a shade;
If Mr. John could see me,
My fortune would be made.

"Nay, look! her bracelets fit me,
Though just the least too tight;
To wear what costs so much, must
Afford one great delight.

"And then this pretty apron,
So bowed, and frill'd and laced—
I hate it on my mistress,
Though well it shows my waist.

"I must run down one minute,
That Mr. John may see
How silks, and lace, and ribands
Set off a girl like me.

"Yet all of these together,
Ay, pearls and diamonds too,
Would fail to make most ladies look
As well as—I know who."

Another of these periodicals, edited by her ladyship from 1835 to 1840, was entitled "Gems of Beauty, designs by E. T. Parris, Esq., with fanciful illustrations in verse by the Countess of Blessington."

Her ladyship was gifted with a great facility for versification; poetry of a high order hers certainly was not. But she could throw great vivacity, much humor, and some pathos into her *vers de societé*, and many of her small published pieces in verse were quite equal to the ordinary run of "*bouts rhymées*" in the literature of annuals, and some far superior to them. But it must be observed, Lady Blessington's poetry derived considerable advantage from the critical care, supervision, and correction of very eminent literary men, some certainly the most eminent of their day. Of this fact there are many evidences, and some proofs of extensive services of this sort.

"The Book of Beauty for 1843," edited by the Countess of Blessington, contained only two pieces by her ladyship.

1. On a Picture of Her Majesty and Children, lines. Dr. W. Beattie.
2. An Episode in Life, a tale. Sir E. L. Bulwer, Bart.
3. On Portrait of Princess Esterhazy, lines. Countess of Blessington.
4. Love, lines. Mrs. Edward Thomas.
5. To ———, lines. A. Baillie Cochrane, Esq., M.P.
6. Inez de Castro, a sketch. Lord William Lennox.
7. Mens Divinior, lines. Barry Cornwall.
8. On Portrait of Mrs. Craven, lines. Anonymous.
9. Medora, a fragment. C. G. H.
10. On Portrait of Mrs. Kynaston, lines. Anonymous.

11. Ministering Angels, lines. Adelaide.
12. Poets die in Autumn, lines. Mrs. C. B. Wilson.
13. A sketch in the Tuilleries. Hon. George Smythe, Esq.
14. On the 25th of January, 1842, lines. Lord John Manners.
15. The Venetian Glass, a tale. Baroness de Calabrella.
16. On Portrait of Miss Dormer, lines. Miss Power.
17. In Midland Ocean, a sketch. B. D'Israeli, Esq., M.P.
18. William of Ripperda, lines. Anonymous.
19. Third Imaginary Letter, Earl of Chesterfield to his daughter. Viscount Powerscourt.
20. The Fairy Ring, lines. Miss A. Savage.
21. On Portrait of Miss Meyer, lines. Miss Power.
22. The Two Flowers, lines. Miss M. H. Acton.
23. Rail-roads and Steam-boats, a sketch. Lady Blessington.
24. On the Civic Statue of the Duke of Wellington, Latin lines. Marquis Wellesley.
25. On Portrait of the Hon. Mrs. Spalding. A. H. Plunkett.
26. Ye Gentlemen of England. Sir J. Hanmer, Bart., M.P.
27. Her I dearly love, lines. R. Bernal, Esq., M.P.
28. The Teacher, a sketch. Mrs. S. C. Hall.
29. Ellen, a tale. Major Mundy.
30. The Great Oak, lines. Lord Leigh.
31. Night breezes, lines. Miss Ellen Power.
32. Death, song. Lady Emmeline Stuart Wortley.
33. Edward Clinton, a tale. Sir Hesketh Fletwood, Bart.
34. On Portrait of Mrs. C. Coape. Anonymous.
35. A Children's Fancy Ball, lines. Lady Stepney.
36. Imaginary Conversation, Vittoria Colonna and M. A. Buonarotti, by W. S. Landor.
37. On Portrait of Mrs. Burr, lines. Camilla Toulmin.
38. To Leonora, lines. Mrs. Torre Holme.
39. Can I e'er cease to love thee? lines. J. D'Oyley, Esq.
40. Gratitude, a sketch. Captain Marryatt.
41. On the launching of a Yacht, lines. Richard Johns, Esq.
42. Morna, Adieu, lines. Hon. Grantley F. Berkeley, M.P.
43. Claudia, a tale. Virginia Murray.
44. On Portrait of Miss Bellew, lines. A. Hume Plunkett.

45. Yes, peace should be there, lines. A. H. T.
46. The Stone-cutter Boy, a sketch. Miss Grace Aguilar.
47. The Closed Gate, lines. Marchioness of Hastings.
48. I love the Oak, lines. Sir W. Somerville, Bart., M.P.
49. Lines on Portrait of Mrs. G. Wingfield. Miss Power.
50. The two Soldiers, a sketch. Barry Cornwall.
51. The Song of a Bird, lines to Miss E. Power. Anonymous.
52. Sleeping and waking Dreams, lines. Mrs. Abdy.
53. An agreeable *Tête-à-tête*, sketch. Isabella F. Romer.
54. Field Flowers, lines. Miss E. Scaife.

For several years Lady Blessington continued to edit both periodicals, " the Keepsake" and " the Book of Beauty." This occupation brought her into contact with almost every literary man of eminence in the kingdom, or of any foreign country, who visited England. It involved her in enormous expense, far beyond any amount of remuneration derived from the labor of editing those works. It made a necessity for entertaining continually persons to whom she looked for contributions, or from whom she had received assistance of that kind. It involved her, moreover, in all the drudgery of authorship, in all the turmoil of contentions with publishers, communications with artists, and never-ending correspondence with contributors. In a word, it made her life miserable.

In 1848, Heath died in insolvent circumstances, heavily in debt to Lady Blessington, to the extent nearly of £700. His failure had taken place six or seven years previously. From that time the prosperity of the annuals was on the wane, and Lady Blessington's receipts from them became greatly reduced. The prices she received for her novels had likewise been much diminished. In fact, of late years it was with the utmost difficulty she could get a publisher to undertake, at his own risk, the publication of a work of hers.

The public were surfeited with illustrated annuals. The taste for that species of literature had died out. The perpetual glorification even of beauty had become a bore. The periodical pæans sung in honor of the children of the nobility ceased to be amusing. Lords, and ladies, and right honorables, ready to write on any subject at the command of fashionable editors and editresses, there was no dearth of, but readers were not to be had at length for love or money.

When Lady Blessington's income from the annuals and her novels began to fall off largely, she hoped to be able to derive some emolument from other sources.

In 1845, a newspaper project on a grand scale was entered into by the eminent printers, Messrs. Bradbury and Evans, with the co-operation of some of the most distinguished literary men of England. The "Daily News" was established, and the literary services of Lady Blessington were solicited for it in January, 1846. Her ladyship was to contribute, in confidence, "any sort of intelligence she might like to communicate, of the sayings, doings, memoirs, or movements in the fashionable world." Her contributions were supposed to consist of what is called "Exclusive Intelligence."

Lady Blessington estimated the value of the services required of her at £800 per annum; the managers, however, considered the amount more than could be well devoted to that branch of intelligence. They proposed an arrangement at the rate of £500 a year for the term of half a year, but at the rate of £400 a year for a year certain; and the arrangement was carried into effect.

In May, 1846, Lady Blessington wrote to the managers, stating "it was not her intention to renew her engagement with the 'Daily News.'"

The sum of £250 for six months' services was duly paid by the proprietors.

Mr. Dickens retired from the management of the paper in July, 1846, and was replaced by Mr. Forster, who gave up the management in November following.*

* There are some observations that have reference to the writings of Forster and Dickens, in a letter of Lady Blessington on literary subjects, addressed to a very dear friend and a very distinguished writer, which are deserving of notice. "I have read with delight the article of F—— on the 'Life of Churchill.' It is the most masterly review I ever read, and places Churchill in a so much better point of view as to excite a sympathy for him. Every one is speaking of this review. All the papers have taken it up. It is generally attributed to Macaulay,

Mr. Jerdan, formerly editor of the "Literary Gazette," who was intimately acquainted with the publishing affairs of Lady Blessington, thus speaks in his "Autobiography" of the income she derived from her literary labors:

"As an author and editor of 'Heath's Annual' for some years, Lady Blessington received considerable sums. I have known her to enjoy from her pen an amount somewhere midway between £2000 and £3000 per annum, and her title, as well as talents, had considerable influence in 'ruling high prices,' as they say in Mark Lane and other markets. To this, also, her well-arranged parties with a publisher now and then, to meet folks of a style unusual to men in business, contributed their attractions; and the same society was in reality of solid value toward the production of such publications as the annuals, the contents of which were provided by the editor almost entirely from the pens of private friends, instead of being dearly bought from the 'Balaam' refuse of celebrated writers."

On this subject Miss Power says:

"I never heard her say the exact amount of her literary profits any particular year. I believe that for some years she made, on an average, somewhat about a thousand a year; some years a good deal above that sum."

WAIFS AND STRAYS OF THOUGHTS AND OBSERVATIONS; OR, ODDS AND ENDS OF IMPRESSIONS AND REFLECTIONS, FROM LADY BLESSINGTON'S UNPUBLISHED PAPERS, VERSES, AND MEMORANDA, IN COMMONPLACE BOOKS.

Lady Blessington was in the habit for some time of writing

and is said to be the best of his articles. F—— has crushed Tooke by the dextrous exposure of his mistakes, ignorance, and want of comprehension. I assure you that Count D'Orsay and I are as proud of the praises we hear of this article on every side, as if we had a share in it. F——'s notice of 'The Chimes' is perfect. It takes the high tone it ought for that book, and ought to make those ashamed who cavil because its great author had a nobler task in view than writing to amuse Sybarites, who do not like to have their selfish pleasures disturbed by hearing of the miseries of the poor. You will smile to see me defending our friend Mr. Dickens from charges of wishing to degrade the aristocracy. I really have no patience with such stupidity. I now clearly perceive that the reading world of a certain class imagine that an author ought to have no higher aim than their amusement, and they account as a personal insult any attempt to instruct them."

down her thoughts and observations at the close of every day, after she retired from her drawing-room, and the book in which this record was made of her reflections on the passing events of the day, the conversations of the evening, the subjects of her reading or research, she called her "Night Book." The earliest of these books commences with an entry of the 21st of March, 1834; the second of them with the year alone, 1835.

The following extracts from these books, in which the *pensées* are given as they were written (word for word, and signed with the initials M. B.), will clearly show that her ladyship's extensive acquaintance with society, her quickness of perception, acumen, and felicitous mode of compressing her ideas, and giving expression to them in laconic, piquant, and precise terms, enabled her to give an epigrammatic turn to sentiments, which could only be similarly done by one thoroughly conversant with the writings of Rochefoucault and Montaigne.

The reader will hardly fail to notice in these *pensées* evident relationship between the ideas of many cynics of celebrity of France, the images too of several of our own most popular poetical writers, and the smart short sayings of her ladyship, with all the air of originality, neatness of attire, and graceful liveliness of language which she has given them.

But the "Night Book" gives only a very poor and inadequate idea of the thoughts which were productive of such effect, when given expression to by her ladyship with all that peculiar charm of *naiveté*, natural turn for irony, admirable facility of expression, clearness of intonation and distinctness of enunciation, joyousness of spirits, beaming in those beautiful features of hers (when lit up by animated conversation, the consciousness of the presence of genius, and contact with exalted intellect), that spontaneous outpouring of felicitous thoughts and racy observations, ever accompanied with an exuberant good humor, often supplying the place of wit, but never degenerating into coarseness or vulgarity, which characterized her conversational powers, and, in fact, constituted the chief fascination of her society

GENIUS AND TALENT.

"Genius is the gold in the mine, talent is the miner who works and brings it out."

"Genius may be said to reside in an illuminated palace of crystal, unapproachable to other men, which, while it displays the brightness of its inhabitant, renders also any blemishes in her form more visible by the surrounding light, while men of ordinary minds dwell in opaque residences, in which no ray of brightness displays the faults of ignoble mediocrity."

TALENT.

"Talent, like beauty, to be pardoned, must be obscure and unostentatious."

GREAT INTELLECTUAL POWERS.

"In many minds, great powers of thinking slumber on through life, because they never have been startled by any incident calculated to take them out of the common routine of every-day occurrence."

CLEVER WOMEN ENVIED.

"It is less difficult, we are told by Brissot, for a woman to obtain celebrity by her genius than to be pardoned for it."

EFFECTS OF CONTACT WITH GENIUS.

"It is doubtful whether we derive much advantage from a constant intercourse with superior minds. If our own be of equal calibre, the contact is likely to excite the mind into action, and original thoughts are often struck out; but if any inferiority exists, the inferior mind is quelled by the superior, or loses whatever originality it might have possessed by unconsciously adopting the opinions and thoughts of the superior intelligence."

LITERATURE AND LITERATI.

"On reading a work, of how many faults do we accuse the

author when they are only to be found in ourselves. If the story is melancholy, and yet we feel not the sadness of it, we lay the blame of our insensibility on the author's want of pathos. If it be gay, and yet it fails to amuse us, we call in question the writer's want of power."

JUDGMENT OF BOOKS.

"The frame of mind in which we read a work often influences our judgment upon it. That which for the moment predominates in our minds colors all that we read: and we are afterward surprised, on a reperusal of works of this kind, under other circumstances and with different feelings, to find no longer the merit we formerly attributed to them."

SUPPOSED CORRESPONDENCE BETWEEN THE WRITINGS OF AUTHORS AND THEIR LIVES.

"The world is given to indulge in the very erroneous supposition that there exists an identity between the writings of authors and their actual lives and characters.

"Men are the slaves of circumstances in the mass; but men of genius, from the excitability of their temperament, are peculiarly acted on by surrounding influences. How many of them, panting after solitude, are compelled to drag on existence in crowded cities, and how many of them, sighing for the excitement of busy life, and the friction of exalted intelligence with kindred intellect, pass their lives in retirement, because circumstances, which they were too indolent or too feeble to control, had thrown them into it. Such men in their writings will have the natural bias of their feelings and tastes frequently mistaken by those around them. The world judges falsely when it forms an estimate of an author from the life of the man, and the life and conduct of the man from the writings of the author, and finding discrepancies between them, may often bring forward accusations of insincerity, making comparisons between their works and lives."

POETS AND POETRY.

"Poets make a book of nature, wherein they read lessons unknown to other minds, even as astronomers make a book of the heavens, and read therein the movements of the planets.

"The poetry in our souls is like our religion, kept apart from our every-day thoughts, and, alas! neither influence us as they ought. We should be wiser and happier (for wisdom is happiness) if their harmonizing effects were permitted more to pervade our being."

WIT AND CENSORIOUSNESS.

"Half the reputations for wit that pass current in fashionable life are based on ill-natured sayings of persons who would have found it difficult to have obtained any notice in society, except by censorious observations; they are of the class of whom mention is made in the French verse:

"'S'il n'eut mal parlé de personne
On n'eut jamais parlé de lui.'"

PLAIN-SPEAKING GENTLEMEN.

"Your plain speakers are usually either of obtuse intellect or ill-natured dispositions, wounding the feelings of others from want of delicacy of mind and sensibility, or from intentional malice. They deserve to be expelled from the society of enlightened people, because they are likely to give annoyance to all who are not of their own level in it."

MISCELLANEOUS THOUGHTS.

"Borrowed thoughts, like borrowed money, only show the poverty of the borrower."

"A poor man defended himself when charged with stealing food to appease the cravings of hunger, saying, the cries of the stomach silenced those of the conscience."

"A woman should not paint sentiment till she has ceased to inspire it."

"A woman's head is always influenced by her heart, but a man's heart is always influenced by his head.

"Catherine the First of Russia was called the mother of her people; Catherine the Second, with equal justice, might be denominated the wife."

"Memory seldom fails when its office is to show us the tombs of our buried hopes."*

"It would be well if virtue was never seen unaccompanied by charity, nor vice divested of that grossness which displays it in its most disgusting form, for the examples of both would then be more beneficial."

"Some good qualities are not unfrequently created by the belief of their existence, for men are generally anxious to justify the good opinion entertained of them."

THE WORST OF SEPARATIONS.

"The separation of friends by death is less terrible than the divorce of two hearts that have loved, but have ceased to sympathize, while memory is still recalling what they once were to each other."

ENGLISH RESERVE.

"Distrust is the most remarkable characteristic of the English of the present day. None but the acknowledged wealthy are exempted from the suspicions of our society. The good, the wise, the talented, are subject to the scrutinizing glances of this policy of suspicion; and those by whom it is carried out seldom fail to discover cause of distrust and avoidance in all that they will not or can not comprehend. But on the poor their suspicions fall, if not with all their malice, at least with all their uncharitableness. Hence they are shunned, and regarded

* Young's ideas sometimes furnish the matter of Lady Blessington's "Night Thoughts."

> "Thought—busy thought—too busy for my peace,
> Through the dark postern of Time long elapsed,
> Led softly by the stillness of the night—
> Led like a murderer—
> . . . Meets the ghosts
> Of my departed joys."

as dangerous or doubtful neighbors by the sons and daughters of prosperity."

WORLDLY WISDOM, SOCIETY, ETC.

"Society seldom forgives those who have discovered the emptiness of its pleasures, and who can live independent of it and them."

"Great men direct the events of their times; wise men take advantage of them; weak men are borne down by them."

"In the society of persons of mediocrity of intellect, a clever man will appear to have less *esprit* than those around him who possess least, because he is displaced in their company."

"Those who are formed to win general admiration are seldom calculated to bestow individual happiness."

"Half the ill-natured things that are said in society are spoken, not so much from malice as from a desire to display the quickness of our perception, the smartness of our wit, and the sharpness of our observation."

"A man with common sense may pass smoothly through life without great talents; but all the talents in the world will not enable a man without common sense to do so."

"——— expends so much eulogy on himself, that he has nothing but censure and contempt to bestow on others."

"The poor, in their isolation in the midst of civilization, are like lepers in the outskirts of cities, who have been repulsed from society with disgust."

"There is a difference between the emotions of a lover and those of a husband: the lover sighs, and the husband groans."

"There are some persons who hesitate not to inflict pain and suffering, though they shrink from witnessing its effects. In the first case it is another who suffers; in the second, the suffering being presented to the sight, is thus brought home to the feelings of those who inflict it."

SYMPATHIES AND ANTIPATHIES.

"On sympathies and antipathies, how much might be written without defining either any better than by the pithy lines—

"'The reason why I can not tell,
I do not like thee, Dr. Fell.'

And yet all feel, in a greater or less degree, what none can adequately describe or define. A dog knows by instinct that certain herbs in a field will relieve him in a sickness, and he devours them. We know that certain physiognomies repel or attract us, and we avoid or seek them; and this is all we know of the matter."

ALL THE WORLD'S A STAGE, ETC.

"The great majority of men are actors, who prefer an assumed part to that which Nature had assigned them. They seek to be something, or to appear something which they are not, and even stoop to the affectation of defects rather than display real estimable qualities which belong to them."

"A German writer observes: 'The noblest characters only show themselves in their real light. All others act comedy with their fellow-men even unto the grave.'"

"Men's faults will always be better known than their virtues, because their defects will find more persons capable of forming a judgment of them than their noble qualities—persons fit to comprehend and to appreciate them."

COLDNESS OF MANNER.

"There are some persons in the world who never permit us to love them except when they are absent; as, when present, they chill our affection by showing a want of appreciation of it."

"Coldness of manner does not always proceed from coldness of heart, but it frequently produces that effect in others."

CONSCIENCE.

"Conscience is seldom heard in youth, for the tumultuous throbbing of the heart and the strong suggestions of the passions prevent its still small voice from being audible; but in the decline of life, when the heart beats languidly and the passions slumber, it makes itself heard, and on its whispers depend our happiness or misery."

BEAUTY AND FEMININE PERFECTIONS.

"Even as a fountain, in whose clear waters are seen the reflections of the bright stars of heaven, so in ——'s face was reflected the divine spirit that animated it and shone through its pure lineaments."

"A young woman ought, like an angel, to pardon the faults she can not comprehend, and an elderly woman like a saint, because she has endured trials."

"One of the old painters always painted the object of his love as a goddess."

"People are seldom tired of the world till the world are tired of them."

"If over-caution preserves us from many dangers, of how much happiness may it not deprive us, by closing our hearts against the sympathy which sweetens life. 'The heart,' says Pascal, 'has its arguments as well as the understanding.'"

STRONG PASSIONS.

"Strong passions *belong only to strong minds*, and terrible is the struggle that *Reason* has to make to subdue them. The victory is never a bloodless one, and many are the scars that attest the severity of the conflict before *her* opponents are driven from the field."*

"In the 'Memoirs of Mackintosh,' page 115, we find a passage from the MS. Lectures on the Law of Nature and Nations: 'It was his course to make wonders plain, not plain things wonderful.'"

"It is not sufficient for legislators to close the avenues to crime, unless they open those which lead to virtue."

A POET TRULY CRACKED.

"Jeremy Taylor finds a moral in the fable that Æschylus sat

* Once for all, I may observe, in many of the writings of Lady Blessington there are but too many evidences of the undue importance attached to *Reason*, as a power all-sufficient for the repression of vice, the support of virtue, and consolation of affliction; and proofs of an absence of all reliance on religion for the objects in question.

beneath the walls of his abode with his bald head uncovered, when an eagle, hovering over the house, unfortunately mistook the shining cranium for a large round stone, and let fall a tortoise he had just seized to break the shell, but cracked the skull of the poor poet instead of the shell of the tortoise."

THE DISLIKED MISUNDERSTOOD.

"The moment we are not liked, we discover that we are not understood; when probably the dislike we have excited proceeds altogether from our being perfectly understood."

THE IDOLS OF THE HEART.

"We make temples of our hearts, in which we worship an idol, until we discover the object of our love was a false god, and then, when it falls, it is not the idol only that is destroyed—the shrine is ruined."

LOVE AND JEALOUSY.

"Love often reillumes his extinguished flame at the torch of jealousy."

A FALSE POSITION.

"A false position is sustained at a price enormously expensive. Sicard truly said, 'Une fausse position coute enormement car le societé fait payer fort cher aux gens, le tort, qu'ils ont, de ne pas être d'accord avec eux.'"

JESTERS—FUNNY PEOPLE.

"*We never respect persons who condescend to amuse us.* There is a vast difference between those we call amusing men and others we denominate entertaining. We laugh with the former, we reflect with the others."

COURAGE, PHYSICAL AND MORAL.

"We find in all countries multitudes of people physically brave, but few persons in any land morally courageous."

SELF-DEPENDENCE.

"We acquire mental strength by being left to our own resources; but when we depend on others, like a cripple who accustoms himself to a crutch, we lose our own strength, and are rendered dependent on an artificial prop."

GENEROSITY AND SELFISHNESS.

"A generous mind identifies itself with all around it, but a selfish one identifies all things with self. The generous man, forgetting self, seeks happiness in promoting that of others. The selfish man reduces all things to one—his own interest."

"The good and generous, who look most closely into their own hearts and scrutinize their own defects, will feel most pity for the frailties of others."

"Advice, like physic, is administered with more pleasure than it is taken."

ESTIMATION OF MEN OF THE WORLD.

"Those who give abundant dinners,
Are never deemed by guests great sinners."

"Your *bon vivants*, who are such 'good livers,' make very bad *diers*."

"Shiel describes one of our statesmen as a man who united the maximum of coldness with the minimum of light; 'he was an iceberg with a farthing rushlight on the summit.'"

"Those who judge of men of the world from a distance are apt to attach an undue importance to them, while those who are in daily contact with them are prone to underrate them."

"We are never so severe in dealing with the sins of others as when we are no longer capable of committing them ourselves."

"Extremes of civilization and of barbarism approach very nearly—both beget feelings of intense selfishness."

"Inferior minds have as natural an antipathy to superior ones, as insects have to animals of a higher organization, whose power is dreaded by them."

"The chief requisites for a courtier are a flexible conscience and an inflexible politeness."

"The genius and talents of a man may generally be judged of by the large number of his enemies, and his mediocrity by that of his friends."

THE YOUNG TO BE KINDLY TREATED.

"Childhood should not be a season of care and constant attention, incessant teaching and painful acquisition: Puisque le jour peut lui manquer bientôt, laissons le un peu jouir de l'aurore."

SPARTAN MORALISTS.

"Society, in its Spartan morality, punishes its members severely for the detection of their vices, but crime itself has nothing but detection to apprehend at its hands."

"Some people seem to consider the severity of their censures on the failings of others as an atonement for their own."

THE VICTIMS OF SOCIETY.

"Society is like the sea monster to which Andromeda was devoted by the oracle. It requires for its worship many victims, and the fairest must be occasionally given to its devouring jaws. But we now find no Perseus in its circles for the rescue of the doomed ones; and the monster is not converted into a rock, though we might show him many gorgons hideous enough to accomplish the transformation."

"In society we learn to know others, but in solitude we acquire a knowledge of ourselves."

SHORT NOTICES OF NOTABILITIES.

"——'s conversation resembles a November fog—dense, oppressive, bewildering, through which you can never see your way."

"The poetry of —— is like a field with wild flowers, many of them beautiful and fragrant."

"The poetry of —— resembles a bouquet of artificial flowers, destitute of odor, and possessing none of the freshness of nature."

"It was said of —— that his conversation was a tissue of *bon mots*, and was overlaid by them: a few spangles may ornament a garment, but if the texture of it is wholly covered by them, the dress is spoiled."

"—— formed few friendships in life, but he cultivated many enmities."

"—— in his old age might be said to resemble a spent thunderbolt."

"The difference between the minds of —— and —— is this: the one is introspective, and looks into the vast recesses of its intelligence for the treasures of deep thought; the other looks behind the shelves of others' thoughts, and appropriates all he finds there. The intellect of one is profound and solid, that of the second sparkling and versatile."

"The works of —— do not exhibit the overflowings of a full mind, but rather the dregs of an exhausted one."

"When I see Lady ——'s wrinkles daubed with rouge, and her borrowed ringlets wreathed with flowers, I am reminded of the effigies of the dead, which in ancient times were introduced at festivals, to recall the brevity of life, and give a keener zest to the pleasures of existence."

BIGOTRY AND FANATICISM.

"Men who would persecute others for religious opinions, prove the errors of their own."

"In fighting for the Church, religion seems generally to be quite lost sight of."

SUPERSTITION.

"Superstition is but the fear of belief; religion is the confidence."

SKEPTICS.

"Skeptics, like dolphins, change when dying."

"We render ourselves the ministers of the fatality which our weakness imagines."

"It is difficult to decide whether it is most disagreeable to live with fanatics, who insist on our believing all they believe, or with philosophers, who would have us doubt every thing of which they are not convinced themselves."

INJURIES AND FORGIVENESS.

"Forgiveness of injuries in general draws on the forgiver a repetition of wrongs—as people reason thus: as he has forgiven so much, he can forgive more."

"If we thought only of others, we might be tempted never to pardon injuries; but when we wish to preserve our own peace, it is a most essential step toward insuring it."

"It is easier to pardon the faults than the virtues of our friends, because the first excite feelings of self-complacency in us, the second a sense of humiliation."

"Great injuries pardoned preclude the enjoyment of friendship on the same happy terms of equality of benefits received and conferred, and of kindly feelings that subsisted previously to the interruption of amity between the parties who had been linked together in the bonds of mutual love. The friend who pardons a great wrong acquires a superiority that wounds the self-love of the pardoned man; and however the latter may admire the generosity of the forgiver, he can love as he had previously done—no more."

AMBITION.—CHANGE.

"Those who are content to follow are not formed to lead; for the ambition which excites a man to put himself forward is, in general, the attribute of the strong mind, however beset by difficulties, resolved to effect an object much desired."

"Time and change, what are they but the same?
For change is but for time another name."

"Nos liens s'elongent quelquefois, mais
Ils ne se rompent jamais."

"How like Goldsmith's line:

"'And drags at each remove a lengthening chain.'"

"The tide of life is continually ebbing and flowing, and myriads of human beings pass away to the ocean of eternity, succeeded by others, as do the ripples of a stream that flows on to the sea, continually disappearing and renewed."

Unfinished lines of Lady Blessington in a memorandum-book:

"The snow-drop looks as if it were a tear of winter,
Shed before it parts, touched by its icy breath,
Which doth become a flower,
Springing from snow—as souls emerge from death."

THE FLOWER TO THE STARS.

"Despise us not; we are the stars of earth,
And though we homage pay to you on high,
Lifting our fragile heads to view your brightness,
Are ye not forced to let your shining eyes
Dwell on us denizens of the favored earth?
Formed by the same Almighty cause of all,
Ye look down on us from your azure fields,
And we from ours of green look up to you."

"And thou art gone from earth, like some fair dream
Beheld in slumber, leaving naught behind
But memory, to tell that thou hast been,
And there for evermore to be enshrined.

"As ships that sail upon the boundless deep,
Yet leave no trace; or onward in their flight,
As birds which cleave the blue and ambient air,
Leave no impress, and soon are lost to sight,

"So those who to eternity do pass,
Like shadows disappear, and naught remains
To tell us they have been, but aching hearts
And pallid traits which memory retains."

UNEQUAL MARRIAGES.

"Oh wise was he, the first who taught
This lesson of observant thought,
That equal fates alone may dress
The bowers of nuptial happiness:
That never where ancestral pride
Inflames, or affluence rolls its tide,
Should love's ill-omened bond entwine
The offspring of an humble line."

To Sir William Massy Stanley, Baronet, on receiving a present of woodcocks:

"At a season when dunning the mind with dread fills,
You send me the only acceptable bills,
And their length, unlike others, no gloom can inspire,
Though, like many long bills, they're consigned to the fire;
And we never discuss them unless with a toast,
Washed down by a bumper to Hoolen's good host."

Lines in penciling in a commonplace book of Lady Blessington:

"Ye gods, what is it that I see?
Oh, who a grandfather would be!
Behold the treasure-store of years,
Sole objects of my hopes and fears,
Collected from far distant lands,
Become a prey to vandal hands;
Rare manuscripts that none could read,
Symbols of each religious creed;
Missals with reddest colors bright,
Black-lettered tomes long shut from light;
Medals defaced, with scarce a trace
Of aught resembling human face;
All in chaotic ruin hurled,
The fragments of a by-gone world.
And you, unpitying girl, who knew
The mischief of this urchin crew,
How could you let them thus destroy
What to collect did years employ?
Away, ye wicked elves! Ah me!
Who e'er a grandfather would be?"

TRIALS AND AFFLICTIONS.

"My heart is like a frozen fountain, over which the ice is too hard to allow of the stream beneath flowing with vigor, though enough of vitality remains to make the chilling rampart that divides its waters from light and air insupportable."*

"A knowledge of the nothingness of life is seldom attained except by those of superior minds."

* This entry is in the early part of the Night Thought Book, dated 21st of October, 1834.

"The first heavy affliction that falls on us rends the veil of life, and lets us see all its darkness."

"Desperate is the grief of him whom prosperity has hardened, and who feels the first arrow of affliction strike at his heart through the life of an object dearest to him on earth."

"The separation of death is less terrible than the moral divorce of two hearts which have loved, but have ceased to sympathize, with memory recalling what they once were to each other."

"Religion converts despair, which destroys, into resignation, which submits."

"Sorrow in its exaltation seems to have an instinctive sympathy with the sufferings of others. Brisset observes: 'L'ame exaltée par la douleur se monte au diapason d'une autre ame blessée, aussi facilement que le violon qui, sans être touché se met à l'accord de l'instrument qu'on fait vibrer loin de lui.'"

"How many errors do we confess to our Creator which we dare not discover to the most fallible of our fellow-creatures!"

"Fatality is another name for misconduct."

CHAPTER XII.

LINES ADDRESSED TO LADY BLESSINGTON BY VARIOUS PERSONS.

Lines written by Walter Savage Landor to Lady Blessington:

"What language, let me think, is meet
For you, well called the Marguerite.
The Tuscan has too weak a tone,
Too rough and rigid is our own;
The Latin—no, it will not do,
The Attic is alone for you."

"February 28th, 1848.

"Dear Lady Blessington,—The earthquake that has shaken all Italy and Sicily has alone been able to shake a few cindery verses out of me. Yesterday there was glorious intelligence from France, and you will find, on the other side, the effect is produced on me within the hour. No! there will not be room for it. Here are some lines that I wrote when I was rather a younger man—date them fifty years back.

"Ever yours most truly, W. S. Landor."

"The fault is not mine if I love you too much—
I loved you too little too long;
Such ever your graces, your tenderness such,
The music so sweet of your tongue.

"The time is now coming when love must be gone,
Though he never abandoned me yet;
Acknowledge our friendship, our passion disown,
Not even our follies forget."

Lines of Walter Savage Landor on a postscript of a letter from Florence, dated April 25th, 1835:

"Out of thy books, O Beauty! I had been
For many a year,
Till she who reigns on earth thy lawful queen
Replaced me there."

In one of the letters addressed to Lady Blessington are the following beautiful lines, written by W. Savage Landor after perusing a passage in a letter:

"*I have not forgotten your favorite old tune: will you hear it?*"

"Come sprinkle me that music on the breast,
Bring me the varied colors into light,
That now obscurely on its marble rest;
Show me its flowers and figures fresh and bright.

"Waked at thy voice and touch, again the chords
Restore what envious years had moved away;
Restore the glowing cheeks, the tender words,
Youth's vernal noon, and pleasure's summer day."

TO THE COUNTESS OF BLESSINGTON.

"Since in the terrace-bower we sate,
While Arno gleamed below,
And over sylvan Massa late
Hung Cynthia's slender bow,

"Years after years have passed away,
Less light and gladsome! Why
Do those we most implore to stay,
Run ever swiftly by?"

Not signed, but in the handwriting of W. S. Landor.

The reply of an octogenarian (the elder D'Israeli) to a beautiful lady who wrote him some verses on his birth-day, May 11, 1845:

"A wreath from a muse, a flower from a grace,
Are visions of fancy which memory can trace.
Though sightless, and braving my dungeon around me,
How is it vain phantoms of glory surround me?
The enchantress with flattery's thrice potent rhyme
Reopens the hours which I loved in my prime;
From my eightieth dull year to my fortieth I rise,
And cherish the shadows her genius supplies."

Addressed to Lady Blessington at Genoa by Lord Byron:

"You have asked for a verse: the request
In a rhymer 'twere strange to deny;
But my Hippocrene was but my breast,
And my feelings (its fountain) are dry.

"Were I now as I was, I had sung
What Lawrence has penciled so well;
But the strain would expire on my tongue,
And the theme is too soft for my shell.

"I am ashes where once I was fire,
And the bard in my bosom is dead;
What I loved I now merely admire,
And my heart is as gray as my head.

"My life is not dated by years—
There are moments which act as a plow;
And there is not a furrow appears
But is deep in my heart as my brow.

"Let the young and the brilliant aspire
To sing, while I gaze on in vain;
For sorrow has torn from my lyre
The string which was worthy the strain."

Answer by Lady Blessington:

"When I asked for a verse, pray believe
'Twas not vanity urged the desire;
For no more can my mirror deceive,
No more can I poets inspire.

"Time has touched with rude fingers my brow,
And the roses have fled from my cheek,
And it surely were folly if now
I the praise due to beauty should seek.

"And as pilgrims who visit the shrine
Of some saint bear a relic away,

I sought a memorial of thine,
As a treasure when distant I stray.

"Oh! say not that lyre is unstrung,
Whose chords can such rapture bestow,
Or that mute is that magical tongue
From which music and poetry flow.

"And though sorrow, ere youth yet has fled,
May have altered thy locks' jetty hue,
The rays that encircle thy head
Hide the ravaging marks from our *view*."

Lines of Lord Erskine for an inscription for a collar of a lap-dog of the Countess of Blessington:

"Whoever finds and don't forsake me,
Shall have naught in way of gains;
But let him to my mistress take me,
And he shall see her for his pains."

Note accompanying lines to Lady Blessington, by Thomas Moore:

"Sloperton, February 19th, 1834.

"MY DEAR LADY BLESSINGTON,—When persons like you condescend *so* to ask, how are poor poets to refuse? At the same time, I confess I have a horror of *albumizing*, *annualizing*, *periodicalizing*, which my *one* inglorious surrender (and for base money too) to that Triton of literature, Marryatt, has but the more confirmed me in. At present, what with the weather and my history, I am chilled into a man of mere prose. But as July approaches, who knows but I may thaw into song? and though—as O'Connell has a vow registered in heaven against pistols, so *I* have against periodicals, yet there are few, I must say, who could be more likely to make a man break this (or any other) vow than yourself, if you thought it worth your while.

"And so, with this gallant speech, which, from a friend of a quarter of a century's date, is not, I flatter myself, to be despised, I am, my dear Lady Blessington, most truly yours, THOMAS MOORE."

"What shall I sing thee? Shall I tell
Of that bright hour, remember'd well
As though it shone but yesterday,
When, as I loitered in the ray
Of the warm sun, I heard o'erhead
My name, as by some spirit, said,
And looking up, saw two bright eyes
Above me from a casement shine,

"Dazzling the heart with such surprise
As they who sail beyond the Line
Feel, when new stars above them rise?
And it was thine—the voice that spoke,
Like Ariel's, in the blue air then;
And thine the eyes, whose lustre broke,
Never to be forgot again!

"What shall I sing thee? Shall I weave
A song of that sweet summer eve
(Summer, of which the sunniest part
Was that which each had in the heart),
When thou, and I, and one like thee
In life and beauty, to the sound
Of our own breathless minstrelsy,*
Danced till the sunlight faded round,
Ourselves the whole ideal ball—
Lights, music, company, and all?"

Verses for an album, written at the request of the Countess of Blessington, by George Colman.

1.

"How have I sworn—and sworn so deep,
No more to put my friends to sleep
By writing crambo for 'em!
Rhymes my amusement once I made,
When Youth and Folly gave me aid,
But since they have become *my trade*,
I must, of course, abhor 'em.

2.

"Entirely generous Mr. Thrale,
Who sold brown stout, and haply ale,
Was always fond of giving,
Of whom Sam Johnson said one day,
'Thrale would give any thing away,
Rather than porter, I dare say,
By which he makes his living.'

3.

"Yet the allusion holds not here—
Mine is but Poetry's small beer,
And every line will show it:
Thrale brewed more potent stuff, I ween,

* "I believe it was to a piper; but it sounds more poetical to say, to our own singing."

From Thames, than I from Hippocrene,
So there's no parallel between
The brewer and the poet.

4.

"Still, why again be scribbling! List!
There is a pair I *can't* resist,
'Tis now no drudging duty,
The *Blessingtons* demand my strain,
And who records against the grain,
His sparkling converse and champagne,
And her more sparkling beauty?

5.

"But hold! I fear my prudence sleeps,
Her ladyship an Album keeps,
Whose leaves, though I ne'er spied 'em,
Are graced with verse from wits profess'd,
Bards by Apollo highly bless'd;
No doubt they've done their very best,
How shall I look beside 'em?

6.

"Dare I, in lame and silly pride,
Hobble where Rogers loves to glide?
Whose sweetly simple measure
Make enviers of Genius mad,
Delight the moral, soothe the sad,
Give *human life* a zest, and add
To *Memory's* greatest *pleasures.*

7.

"Or if I venture, cheek by jowl,
With the Anacreontic soul,
That master, to a tittle,
Of elegant erotic lore,
Then they, who *my* weak page explore,
Will reckon me much less than More,
Not half so Great as Little.

8.

"Well, well, no matter; still, I feel
My talent's dearth supplied by zeal;
Away, then, base dejection!
This scrawl, whate'er its want of wit,
If Lady Blessington think fit,
So very much to honor it,
May rest in her collection." 1st August, 1819.

Note accompanying lines to Lady Blessington, by F. Mills, Esq.:

"57 Audley Street.

"My dear Lady Blessington,—I send you my verses; they were written *for you*, but I was unwilling to present them, in the fear that you would not pass the threshold of the title. That you may not do now; but still, as they are registered in my book as having been composed at your request, I think it right that you should see them. I have no better excuse for myself. If you will not read them, nobody else will.

"Ever yours sincerely, F. Mills."

CHARACTERISTIC—THE ROSE OR THE VIOLET.

A cause pleaded in Italy.

"I saw a violet droop its head;
'Tis strange, and yet it seem'd in grief,
And there, from nature's book, I read
A tale of sorrow in the leaf.

"A tear as in the eye would stand,
The cheek was of a livid hue;
The form was bow'd by some rude hand,
And for its fragrance bruised too.

"There was a canker in that cell,
The secret source of many a woe,
Of deep remorse those lips would tell,
Or—never had they quiver'd so.

"She loved, 'twas in the soil or clime,
In every flower, in every field—
Her earliest lesson, only crime;
And one so soft was form'd to yield.

"But near her, late transplanted there,
A rose was glittering in the light;
It grew not in its native air,
And yet it seemed to bloom as bright.

"And though it played with every wind
As willing as the blushing morn,
Who thought to gather it would find
'Twas always guarded by a thorn.

"'Twas Anglia's boast, and well I trow,
A badge for which her sons had bled,
Had many a life's spring caused to flow,
And widow'd many a bridal bed.

"And though its bloom may pass away,
Or fade beneath the coming hour,
'Twill still be fragrant in decay,
Not rankle, like that bruised *flower*."

A note, rather idolatrously complimentary, addressed to Lady Blessington. No signature, no date, with lines written on leaving Naples, and said to be "translated into French:"

TRADUCTION.

"Si ce n'etait pas un culte uniquement reservé au Dieu que nous adorons, de bruler de l'encens sur ses autels; l'univers s'empresserait de t'offrir ces honneurs. Alors nuit et jour j'entretiendrais ce feu de mes mains, et un nuage épais de parfum s'eleverait jusqu'aux cieux. Mais puisque cela m'est interdit, que je puisse, au moins t'offrir cet encens sacré, que je brulerais pour toi, si j'etais payen.

TRADUCTION.

"Adieu terre classique, adieu ciel sans nuages,
Adieu dignes amis, vous dont le souvenir
Vient s'unir dans mon cœur aux charmes de ses rivages,
Je songe avec douleur! hélas! qu'il faut partir
Doux amis! doux climat que j'aime et que j'admire.
Quel enivrant tableau vous formiez reunis
L'un et l'autre à l'envi sembliez me sourire;
Mais le sort me l'ordonne . . il le faut . . je vous fuis
La Syrene, disais-je, un moment abregée
Vit Naples et mourut, et j'envirais son sort
Mais plaignons la plutôt, jamais après sa mort
A-t-elle peut trouver un plus doux Elisée?
Vous enchantez encore les sens du voyageur,
Parthenopé en ce jour a plus d'une Syréne,
Que de fois les accens de Lisette et d'Iréne,
Ont charmé mes instants, ont enivré mon cœur.
Adieu tendres amis! dans ma froide patrie
L'image du bonheur qu'en ces tems j'ai gouté
Viendra toujours s'offrir à mon ame attendrie
Avec le pur éclat de ce ciel enchanté."

Lines by James Smith, in a letter addressed to Lady Blessington, dated November 10, 1836:

GORE HOUSE—AN IMPROMPTU.

"Mild Wilberforce, by all beloved,
Once own'd this hallow'd spot,

Whose zealous eloquence improved
  The fetter'd Negro's lot;
Yet here still slavery attacks
  When Blessington invites;
The chains from which he freed the Blacks,
  She rivets on the Whites.

"27 Craven Street, Tuesday."

Note accompanying lines to Lady Blessington, by Jas. Smith:

"27 Craven Street, Friday, December 9, 1836.

"DEAR LADY BLESSINGTON,—'Gore House' has awakened another (anonymous) muse; I wonder who it can be.

"Your ladyship's faithful and devoted servant, JAMES SMITH."

A more deliberate reply to the Impromptu:

"No, not the chains which erst he broke
  Does Blessington impose,
Light is her burden, soft her yoke,
  No pain her captive knows.

"The slave by galling fetters bruised,
  By force his will subdued;
Obedience of the mind refused,
  With haste his tyrant viewed.

"On willing hearts her bonds are thrown,
  Her charms her empire prove;
Pleased with their fate, the captives own
  No power but that of love."

Lines to the Countess of Blessington, by James Smith:

"July 11, 1832.

"The Bird of Paradise, that flies
  O'er blest Arabia's plains,
Devoid of feet, forbears to rise,
  And where she rests, remains.

"Like her of footing reft, I fain
  Would seek your bless'd dominions,
And there content, till death, remain,
  But ah! I lack the pinions."

"Admiralty, May 6, 1820.

"DEAR LADY BLESSINGTON,—I have received from Lord Blessington your commands for the third time. I beg pardon for having been so tardy; but the inclosed will show that I have, at last, implicitly and literally obeyed you.

"I have the honor to be, dear Lady Blessington, your very faithful servant, J. W. CROKER."

"You've asked me three times
For four lines with two rhymes;
Too long I've delayed,
But at last you're obeyed!"

Letter of T. Stewart, Esq., inclosing lines written in Naples, addressed to Lady Blessington:

"Palais Belvidere, Naples, Monday.

"MY DEAR MADAM,—Although these lines can only prove the good wishes and intentions of their author, I hope you will not be displeased at receiving them.

"My uncle* refused your kind invitation with great regret yesterday, but he is so lame at present that he can scarcely walk. He is likewise, in some degree, alarmed about himself.

"With my best wishes to Miss Power and to D'Orsay, I remain your ladyship's, most sincerely, T. STEWART."

Lines addressed to Marguerite, Countess of Blessington, on her leaving Naples, spring, 1826, in consequence of the climate injuring her health:

1.

"'Tis vain that the rose and the myrtle are twining
In wreaths that the Graces intended for thee;
For thou wilt be far when their blossom is pining,
Unseen in the grove, and unculled on the tree.

2.

"The light step of spring o'er the mountains is bounding,
The nymphs are returned to the fountains again;
The woods with the nightingale's notes are resounding,
Yet sadness through all thy lone precincts shall reign.

3.

"Though forests of citron the mountains are shading,
Though hues like the rainbow's enamel the vale,
The flower that is fairest is secretly fading,
For sickness is wafted to thee on the gale.

4.

"Alas! that in climes where all nature is gladdest,
Her charms, like the visions of youth, should deceive;
Of the tears at thy parting, those tears will be saddest,
That, grieving for thee, we for nature must grieve."

* Sir William Gell.

Lines inclosed in a letter of Mr. N. P. Willis to Lady Blessington, April 2, 1840 :

"The music of the waken'd lyre
Dies not within the quivering strings,
Nor burn'd alone the minstrel's fire
Upon the lip that trembling sings;
Nor shines the moon in heaven unseen,
Nor shuts the flower its fragrant cells,
Nor sleeps the fountain's wealth, I ween;
Forever in its sparry wells
The charms of the enchanter lie,
Not in his own lone heart, his own rapt ear and eye.

"I gaze upon a face as fair
As ever made a lip of heaven
Falter amid its music—prayer;
The first lit star of summer even
Springs scarce so softly on the eye,
Nor grows with watching half so bright,
Nor mid its sisters of the sky
So seems of heaven the dearest light.
Men murmur where that shape is seen,
'My youth's angelic dream was of that form and mien.'

"Yet, though we deem the stars are bless'd,
And envy in our grief the flower
That bears but sweetness in its breast,
And praise the enchanter for his power,
And love the minstrel for the spell
He winds from out his lyre so well;
The starlight doth the wanderer bless,
The lyre the listener's tears beguile,
And, lady, in the loveliness
Doth light to-day that radiant smile,
A lamp is lit in beauty's eye,
That souls, else lost on earth, remember angels by!"

Copy of verses, signed Fitzgerald. Addressed to Lady Blessington, on Literary Taste.

"Dec. 19, 1818.

"Through wide creation's ample round,
Where'er her varying forms are found,
The landscape deck'd with nature's dyes,
The boundless sea, o'er-arching skies,
The waving wood, the winding shore,
The tranquil lake or torrent's roar,

The modest valley, far withdrawn,
Or the proud cliff or laughing lawn;
These all can please, yet none to me
Such soothing charm conveys as minds refined and free.

"Let goblets shine on festal board,
And lavish art exhaust her hoard
To raise the soul or warm the heart,
And a new zest to life impart;
How vain the pomp, the wealth how poor,
Worthless as gold on Indian floor,
Unless the grace of mind preside,
To soften down the glare of pride;
With magic touch the feast refine,
Wreathe bays round pleasure's cup, to nectar turn his wine.

"'Mid darker scenes, in sorrow's hour,
Taste comes with softly soothing pow'r;
Sheds a mild radiance through the gloom,
And shades with silver wings the tomb!
Strews roses o'er the waste of time,
And lulls the anguish of his crime
'Gainst love and hope, whose precious buds
He cuts, and casts them on the floods!
So drops an anodyne t' endure
Those deep and trenchant wounds which it can never cure!

"Oh! thus amid the dream of joy,
Or trance of grief, can taste employ
Those hours that else to riot run,
Or waste in sadness with each sun!
Should Beauty lend her smile to Wit,
And Learning by her star be lit,
As gems beneath the solar ray
Are ripened and enriched with day;
How bless'd the happy pow'r we prove!
Then bright Minerva shines in *Blessington* with love."

Verses inclosed in a letter of John Kenyon, Esq., to Lady Blessington, Paris, 15th June, 1840:

ITALY.

"Fair blows the breeze: depart! depart!
And tread with me the Italian shore,
And feed thy soul with glorious art,
And drink again of classic lore.

"Nor haply wilt thou deem it wrong,
When not in mood too gravely wise,
At idle length to lie along,
And quaff a bliss from bluest skies.

"Or pleased more pensive joy to woo,
At falling eve, by ruin gray,
Move o'er the generations who
Have passed, as we must pass, away.

"Or mark, o'er olive-tree and vine,
Steep towns uphung, to win from them
Some thought of Southern Palestine,
Some dream of old Jerusalem. J. K."

Lines written by R. Bernal, Esq.:

TO LADY BLESSINGTON.

"When wintry winds in wild career
Howl requiems for the by-gone year,
And thought, responding to the blast,
With sighs reviews the gloomy past;
Where every sorrow leaves its trace,
And joy obtains no resting-place;
When, sickening from the dull survey,
Hope, warmth, and energy decay,
What mortal charm can then impart
A ray of sunshine to the heart,
And by its healing balm dispense
New vigor to each failing sense?
On one bright charm alone depend,
The feeling of a genuine friend,
Whose ready sympathy sincere,
The graces of her mind endear
To those who are allowed to share
Her kindly thoughts, her gen'rous care
Dear lady! cruel time, I feel,
May from my pen refinement steal:
Should language fail me to express
The grateful thanks I would confess,
Believe me that the words of truth
Bear in themselves perpetual youth."

R. Bernal, January 2d, 1849.

From J. H. Jesse, Esq., 20th March, 1840:

"In your gay favored leaves I am ordered to write,
Where wit on poetical verdure reposes;
But I fear I shall prove, in those pages so bright,
To use the count's phrase, like a pig among roses.

"Should this lay, in your book, with the verses entwine
Of painters, bards, sculptors, blue-ribbons, and earls,
Instead of the pearls being thrown among swine,
I fear that the *swine* will be thrown among pearls.

"But should you find room in your splendid parterre
Of fancy and wit for a slave so devout,
Though a pig among flow'rs is a sight rather rare,
At least he's an excellent hand at a *rout*.

"In pity accept this nonsensical lay
Instead of my promised historical lore;
I but wish to escape from the grave to the gay,
Lest the pig, to your sorrow, should turn out a *boar*.

"But your 'wonderful pig' must give over his feats,
And endeavor to quench his poetical fire,
Lest, striving to enter a garden of sweets,
In the end he should find himself sunk in the mire.

"J. H. JESSE."

THE COUNTESS OF BLESSINGTON'S SOIREE.

"By genius enlivened, here splendidly bright
Are the rays which adorn and embellish her 'night!'
While 'the nine' shed their influence down from above,
To unite taste and wit with the charms of 'the grove.'

"OCTOGENARIUS.*

"Mount Radford, Exeter."

IMPROMPTU.—ON A SMALL VOLUME OF POEMS BEING PLACED IN THE LIBRARY OF LADY BLESSINGTON.

"What 'earthly' was before, is now 'divine;'
Minerva's priestess placed it in her *shrine*.

"OCTOGENARIUS.

"Exeter, September 16th, 1842."

Lines addressed to Lady Blessington (no name or date):

"Some dear friend a present has made me
Of an instrument armed like a dart;
But the warning of witches forbade me
To use it secundum the art.

* The writer occasionally signed his letters to Lady Blessington, and his numerous poetical effusions, "Pilgrim." Mount Radford, I think, near Exeter, was the name of a property of one of the Barings some thirty years ago.

"It may be by some fairy designed,
A blow aimed through my lips at my heart;
Ah! my heart has already resigned,
And my lips claimed their share of the smart!"

Inclosed in a letter of Dr. W. Beattie:

THE CLOSING YEAR.

"Cosi trapassa—a'l trapassar' d'un giorno."

"Could time contract the heart
As time contracts our years,
I'd weep, to see my days depart,
In undissembled tears.

"But no! the mind expands
As time pursues its flight,
And sheds upon our ebbing sands
A sweeter, holier light.

"If time could steel the breast
To human weal or woe,
Then would I long to be at rest,
And deem it time to go.

"But no! while I can cheer
One sad or stricken heart,
Unreckoned let my days appear,
Unmourned let them depart.

"Time, reckoned by our deeds,
And not by length of days,
Is often blessed where it speeds—
Unbless'd where it delays.

"But oh! when deaf to human sighs,
When dead to human woes,
Then drop the curtain! close my eyes,
And leave me to repose!

"December 30, 1840."

P.S.

"Such, lady, is the creed
Thy gifted pen has taught,
And well the daily-practiced deed
Gives body to the thought.

"Thy mind's an intellectual fount
Where genius plumes her wing,
And fancy's flowers, like Eden's bowers,
Enjoy perennial spring!"

Lines of Dr. Wm. Beattie to the Countess of Blessington, on perusing "The Book of Beauty" for 1839:

"As Dian, 'mid yon isles of light,
With starry train illumes the region,
So, lady, here, with eyes as bright,
Thou lead'st abroad thy starry legion.
All marshaled in thy brilliant book,
What fascinations fix the reader!
Ah! when had stars so bright a look,
Or when had beauty such a leader?

"And gazing on that starry train,
In each methinks I see the token
Of conquests won, of suitors slain,
Of heads they've turned, and hearts they've broken.
Lady, thy task is nobly done;
Who else could have performed the duty?
Where find, unless in Blessington,
The synonym for wit and beauty?

"Nov. 7th, 1838."

Lines "'A l'Arabe," to Lady Blessington, by an Eastern traveler:

"If e'er the price of tinder rise,
To smoking as I'm given,
I'll light my pipe at your bright eyes,
And steal my fire from heaven.

"In Paynim climes, when forced to sip
Cold water through devotion,
I'd think the cup had touched your lip,
To nectarize my potion.

"If dread simoom swept o'er my tent,
I'd call back scenes enchanting:
On blissful hours in Naples spent,
And your abode descanting.

"In that eclipse which lately threw
Half Naples into terror,
When it was very clear that you
Had breathed upon your mirror;

"In antres vast and desert wild,
With jackals screaming round me,
I'd dream of you when toil and fright
'In slumber's chain had bound me.'

"I'd fancy beauty's queen, arrayed
In smiles, was watching o'er me;
And, waking, find the picture laid
Of Lady B—— before me. R. R. M.

"Rome, Feb., 1828."

From Mrs. P——s to Lady Blessington, St. James's Square:

"In this frigid season of stupefied spleen,
October, when nothing goes down but the queen*
(Though lately her majesty seems to get up),
So oft is the slip 'twixt the lip and the cup,
Methinks it were proper, of one of my trips
By sea, in the steam vessel call'd the Eclipse,
I with pen, ink, and paper, and table and chair,
Indite to my ——— who lives in the square.
"Oh say what philosopher found out in steam,
That wonderful property stemming a stream:
It could not be Locke, for a lock dams the splasher;
It could not be *Bacon*, that makes sailors *rasher*.
It is not *Sir Isaac* the vessel that urges,
Though certainly *eyes ache* when looking on surges:
Descartes sounds more like it; for Gallican art
Moves over the waves by assistance *des cartes:*
No! now I remember: the man who by toil
Of noddle, and midnight consumption of oil,
First hit upon steam, was Philosopher *Boyle*.
"This learned discussion has made me forget:
Proceed we to sing of our voyage from Margate.
As the clock sounded eight, I myself and my maiden
(Having coffee'd at Broadstairs), with bandboxes laden,
Both spurning the pier, and the coast out of reach of
(If spurning a Peer should be privilege breach of,
Keep this to yourself, and if sworn on the Bible,
Lest the Lords, in a rage, should commit for the libel),
Embark'd on the main, which, erst tranquil and steady,
Soon heaved, like the tragical chest of Macready.
One Mr. MacDonald on board also came
(Related, I'm told, to the lord of that name),
And Smith, christened James: of the whole of the crew,
These twain were the only two people I knew.

* The Queen Caroline. This poetical epistle is not dated; but, as Lady Blessington was not living in St. James's Square after 1822, nor previous to 1816, the epistle must have been written in the interval.

I straight introduced both these voyagers with
'Mr. Smith, Mr. Mac—Mr. Mac, Mr. Smith;'
We then talk'd a trio, harmonious together,
Of Naples, and Spain, and the queen, and the weather,
Of Margate, its windmills, its balls, and of raffles,
Of misses in curls, and of donkeys in snaffles:
In gay sprightly pace, though I sing it in dull verse,
Then pass'd the two steeples they call the Reculvers,
When, finding Dan Phœbus preparing to unshine,
We entered the cabin and ordered a luncheon.
But ere we went down, I forgot to inform
Your ladyship, Jupiter pour'd down a storm.
Smith raised his umbrella, my kid leather shoes,
Unused to such scenes, were beginning to ooze,
When a German, who look'd at me, all in a float,
Most civilly lent me his wrapping great-coat.
Thus muffled, while Iris poured rain from her window,
I looked like a sylph keeping watch on Belinda.
I laugh'd at the tempest this tunic of drab in,
But laid it aside when we enter'd the cabin.
There hanging my straw bonnet up on a peg,
Sitting down on a stool with a rickety leg,
And doffing my shawl to sit down to my meal,
I flatter myself I look'd rather genteel.
Smith sat with each leg on the side of a column,
Which check'd him in eating, and made him look solemn.
So, hastily quitting our seats when we all had
Sufficient cold lamb, beef, potatoes, and salad,
I went upon deck, and when seated upon it,
I put on again my drab wrapper and bonnet.
A woman and daughter had borrowed the streamer
That floats, red and white, from the stern of the steamer;
This form'd a *deck-tent*, and from Jupiter's thunder it
Guarded us safely; 'twas nothing to wonder at,
For 'non mi ricordo' that any slept under it!
When qualms (not of conscience) seized one of the crew,
To a berth near the chimney I quickly withdrew,
And beat with my right foot the devil's tattoo.
Of one of our minstrels, an Irish Pandæan,
I asked if that ocean was call'd the Ægean;
If it was not, old Guthrie was born to confound me,
For *I'll* swear that the *cyc-lades** circled around me.
We pass'd on our left the four hanging Lascars,
Who peep at the moon and keep watch at the stars;

* Two sick ladies.

Just opposite South-end we plump'd on a porpoise,
Uncommonly like Stephen Kemble in corpus;
In temper like Gerard, whose surname is Noel,
In swimming like Twiss, and in color like Powell.
And when we were properly soak'd, at the hour
Of five, anchored safely athwart of the Tower.
"The scene that ensued when we swung by a cable,
The mixture of voices out-babeling Babel—
What scrambling for bandboxes, handkerchiefs, caskets,
Trunks, carpet bags, brown paper parcels, and baskets,
While the captain stood quietly wetting his whistle,
Must all be reserved for another epistle,
For my paper scrawled o'er is of no further service.
"Adieu, your affectionate ever, E. P——s."

CHAPTER XIII.

NOTICE OF COUNT ALFRED D'ORSAY: HIS ORIGIN.—SOME ACCOUNT OF HIS EARLY LIFE, THE CLOSE OF HIS CAREER, AND OBSERVATIONS ON HIS TALENTS AND THE APPLICATION OF THEM.*

ALFRED GUILLAUME GABRIEL COMTE D'ORSAY was born the 4th of September, 1801. His father, Albert Comte D'Orsay, who was considered one of the finest-looking men of his time, early entered the army, and served with great distinction under Napoleon, who was wont to say of him that he was "*aussi brave que beau.*" His mother, a woman no less remarkable for her wit, and noble and generous disposition, than for her beauty, was a daughter of the King of Wurtemberg by a marriage which was good in religion, though not in law. The family of D'Orsay was a very ancient one, and formerly held large possessions both in Paris and in the provinces. The grandfather of the late Comte D'Orsay was one of the most liberal patrons of art of his day. His collection of pictures and statues was singularly fine and valuable. Several of the latter, which were seized in the first revolution, that disastrous period when he lost nearly the whole of his fortune, now form a part of the statuary which decorates

* For a large portion of the details of this memoir, extending to the period of D'Orsay's last sojourn in Paris, I am indebted to a lady very intimately acquainted with the count in his brighter days, as well as in his latest moments.

the Place Louis Quinze and the gardens of the Tuilleries. The fact of their belonging to the house of D'Orsay was admitted by subsequent governments. Louis Philippe, only a short time before his expulsion from France, was in treaty with Comte D'Orsay to pay an annual sum to retain the statues in their present places, having refused to restore them. After the abdication of Napoleon, General D'Orsay entered the service of the Bourbons.

The eldest son of the general having died in infancy, the family consisted of two children—Alfred and a daughter, Ida, the present Duchesse de Grammont, a year younger than her brother. From his earliest infancy, Alfred D'Orsay gave token of the remarkable physical and mental superiority which distinguished his manhood. As a child and boy, his remarkable comeliness, strength, and adroitness in all exercises, ready wit and intelligence, facility of acquiring knowledge, high spirit, the frankness of his nature, the chivalrous generosity of his disposition, made him a general favorite with young and old.

At a very early age he entered the army, and somewhat later, very unwillingly, the *garde du corps* of the restored Bourbon sovereign. All his sympathies during the whole of his life were with the Bonaparte family. The ardent enthusiasm inspired in his boyish mind by Napoleon (whose page he was to have been) kept possession of his mind in after years. So far was the feeling carried, that at the entrance of the Bourbons into Paris, though but a mere boy, he betook himself to a retired part of the house, that he might not see or hear the rejoicings that were made for the downfall of Napoleon and his empire, and gave vent to his feelings in tears and strong expressions of repugnance to the new regime. When in the army, he was greatly beloved by the men, whose comforts and interests he looked to with the utmost care. Their affection for his person was equaled only by the admiration excited by his feats of strength and superiority over his comrades in all manly exercises.

Some of the traits of his garrison life, though trifling in themselves, are too characteristic to be left unnoticed. At the provincial balls, where his repute as a man of fashion, of family, and of various accomplishments had made itself known, and rendered him a leading object of attention; he used to be jeered by his brother officers for his apparent predilection for persons not remarkable for their personal attractions, as he made it a practice to single out the plainest girls present to dance with, and to pay the greatest attention to those who seemed most neglected or unnoticed. There was no affectation of any kind about him; whatever he did that appeared considerate or amiable was done simply from natural kindness of disposition.

On one occasion, living out of barracks, he lodged at the house of a widow with a son and two daughters; the son, a young, robust man of a violent temper and of considerable bodily strength, was in the habit of treating his mother and sisters with brutality. Comte D'Orsay, one day while in his room, hearing a loud noise and tumult in the apartments of his hostess and her daughters on the ground floor, descended to ascertain the cause, and finding the young man offering acts of violence to his mother, fell upon him, and notwithstanding the powerful resistance of his formidable opponent, whose rage had been turned against him, inflicted such severe chastisement on him that quarter was soon called for. The count then, with his characteristic quietude of manner in the midst of any excitement or turmoil, ended the scene by assuring the subdued bully that any repetition of his violence on his family would meet with punishment far exceeding in severity that which he had the trouble of bestowing on that occasion.

Comte D'Orsay's first visit to England was in the year 1821 or 1822. He came in company with his sister and her husband, then Duc de Guiche, who, in the previous emigration, had been educated and brought up in England, had served in an English regiment (of dragoons), and who had a sister married to the Viscount Ossulston, now Earl of Tankerville; consequently, the Duke de Guiche already held a position in English society calculated to insure the best reception for his brother-in-law in the first circles of London society.

In that visit, which was but brief, the young count, accustomed to manners and customs of a world of fashion differing very materially from that of London, formed that hasty judgment of English society, erroneous in the main, but in its application to a portion of it not without a certain basis of truth. Byron's eulogistic expressions on the perusal of the journal could not fail to be very gratifying to the writer of it. But the riper judgment and later experience of the count led to the formation of other opinions, and induced him to destroy the diary, and the reason given for its destruction was "lest at any time the ideas there expressed should be put forth as his matured opinions." Byron, in a letter to Moore, dated April 2, 1823, thus refers to the arrival at Genoa of the Blessingtons and the Count D'Orsay, a French count, "who has all the air of a *cupidon déchainé*, and is one of the few specimens I have ever seen of our ideal of a Frenchman before the Revolution."

To Lord Blessington his lordship writes:

"April 5th, 1823.

"My dear Lord,—How is your gout? or, rather, how are you? I return the Count D'Orsay's journal, which is a very extraordinary production, and of a most melancholy truth in all that regards high life in England. I know, or knew personally, most of the personages and societies which he describes; and after reading his remarks, have the sensation fresh upon me as if I had seen them yesterday. I would, however, plead in behalf of some few exceptions, which I will mention by-and-by. The most singular thing is, *how* he should have penetrated, *not* the *facts*, but the *mystery* of the English *ennui*, at two-and-twenty. I was about the same age when I made the same discovery, in almost precisely the same circles—for there is scarcely a person whom I did not see nightly or daily, and was acquainted more or less intimately with most of them—but I never could have discovered it so well, *Il faut être Français* to effect this. But he ought also to have been in the country during the hunting season, with a 'select party of distinguished guests,' as the papers term it. He ought to have seen the gentlemen after dinner (on the hunting days), and the soirée ensuing thereupon, and the women looking as if they had hunted, or rather been hunted; and I could have wished that he had been at a dinner in town, which I recollect at Lord Cowper's—small, but select, and composed of the most amusing people . . . . . Altogether, your friend's journal is a very formidable production. Alas! our dearly beloved countrymen have only discovered that they are tired, and not that they are tiresome; and I suspect that the communication of the latter unpleasant verity will not be better received than truths usually are. I have read the whole with great attention and instruction—I am too good a patriot to say *pleasure*—at least I won't say so, whatever I may think. I showed it (I hope no breach of confidence) to a young Italian lady of rank, *tres instruite* also; and who passes, or passed, for being one of the most celebrated belles in the district of Italy where her family and connections resided in less troublesome times as to politics (which is not Genoa, by-the-way), and she was delighted with it, and says that she has derived a better notion of English society from it than from all Madame de Staël's metaphysical disputations on the same subject in her work on the Revolution. I beg that you will thank the young philosopher, and make my compliments to Lady B—— and her sister.

"Believe me, your very obliged and faithful, BYRON."

In subsequent letters to Lord Blessington, Byron repeatedly returns to the subject of the count's English journal. One written on the 6th of April (the very day after that before quoted), to condole with the Earl of Blessington on the death of his only son, thus concludes: "I beg my compliments to Lady Blessington, Miss Power, and to *your Alfred*. I think, since his majesty of the same name, there has not been such a learned surveyor of our Saxon society." Again, on the 9th, "I salute the illustrious Chevalier Count D'Orsay, who, I hope, will continue his History of His Own Times. There are some strange coincidences between a part of his remarks and a certain work of mine now in MS. in England (I do not mean the hermetically-sealed memoirs, but a continuation of certain cantos of a certain poem), especially in what a man may do in London with impunity while he is *à la mode*." And in a letter which Mr. Moore did not print at length, Byron said of D'Orsay, "He seems to have all the qualities requisite to have figured in his brother-in-law's ancestor's Memoirs"—alluding to the famous Memoirs of Grammont.

Byron's approbation of D'Orsay's diary was given in the following characteristic terms:

"April 22, 1823.—My dear Count D'Orsay (if you will permit me to address you so familiarly), you should be content with writing in your own language, like Grammont, and succeeding in London as nobody has succeeded since the days of Charles the Second, and the records of Antonio Hamilton, without deviating into our barbarous language, which you understand and write, however, much better than it deserves. 'My approbation,' as you are pleased to term it, was very sincere, but perhaps not very impartial; for, though I love my country, I do not love my countrymen—at least, such as they now are. And besides the seduction of talent and wit in your work, I fear that to me there was the attraction of vengeance. I have *seen* and *felt* much of what you have described so well. I have known the persons and the réunions described (many of them, that is to say), and the portraits are so like, that I can not but admire the painter no less than his performance. But I am sorry for you; for if you are so well acquainted with life at your age, what will become of you when the illusion is still more dissipated?"

The illusion was wholly dissipated, but only a few months before D'Orsay's death.

On the 6th of May following, his lordship writes to Lady Blessington:

"I have a request to make my friend Alfred (since he has not disdained the title), viz., that he would condescend to add a cap to the gentleman in the jacket—it would complete his costume, and smooth his brow, which is somewhat too inveterate a likeness of the original, God help me!"

The diary of Count D'Orsay, illustrative of London fashionable life, which was pronounced by such competent authority to be equal to any thing Count de Grammont has left us about contemporary frivolity, is said by others to have surpassed the memoirs of the latter in genuine wit and humor.

The Duchesse de Grammont has the papers of Count D'Orsay, and a portion of the effects; most of the latter were sold to pay debts. His journal was burned by himself some years back.

It was on the occasion of D'Orsay's first visit to London that he made the acquaintance of Lord and Lady Blessington, not in garrison in France, as has generally but erroneously been stated; neither is the assertion true that it was to accompany them to Italy that he abandoned the intention of joining the expedition to Spain, there being no question of his doing so at the period of that visit.

At the earnest desire of Lord and Lady Blessington, the young Frenchman became one of the party in their tour through France and Italy. During their journey and prolonged sojourn in the latter country, the companionable qualities, and that peculiar power of making himself agreeable, which he possessed to a degree almost unequaled, so endeared him to his English friends, that a union was at length proposed by Lord Blessington between the count and one of his daughters, both of whom were then in Ireland with Lady Harriet Gardiner, the sister of Lord Blessington.

This proposition meeting the approval of the count's family, it was finally decided that Lady Harriette, the younger daughter, should become his wife, and she was accordingly sent for to Italy, where the marriage was celebrated.*

After a long Continental tour, and a sojourn of some years in Italy, Lord and Lady Blessington, with the Count and Countess D'Orsay, came to reside in Paris, where, in 1829, Lord Blessington died of apoplexy.

During the Revolution of 1830, the events of which are related by Lady Blessington in the "Idler in France," Count D'Orsay, during the most dangerous moments, was constantly abroad in the streets; and on more than one occasion, when recognized, though known to be the brother-in-law of the Duc de Guiche, one of the staunchest of the Legitimists, he was greeted by the people with shouts of "*Vive le Comte D'Orsay!*" Such was the influence which his mere presence produced. One of the proofs of the effect on others of his insinuating manners and prepossessing appearance was the extreme affection and confidence he inspired in children, of whom he was very fond, but who usually seemed as if they were irresistibly drawn toward him, even before he attempted to win them. The shyest and most reserved were no more proof against this influence than the

* We find in the "Annual Register" for 1827 an account of the marriage ceremony having been performed at Naples by the chaplain of the British embassador. "At Naples, in December 1827, Count Alfred D'Orsay, only son of General Count D'Orsay, to the Lady Harriette Anne Frances Gardiner, daughter of the Right Hon. the Earl of Blessington." Of this unhappy marriage an account has been given in the preceding memoir, and the sentiments of the author in regard to it have been expressed there. Of the greatness of the calamity of that union, and the grievous wrong done by it to one almost a child in years, experience, and understanding, the author has nothing more to say than has been already said by him on that painful subject.—R. R. M.

most confiding. Children who in general would hardly venture to look at a stranger, would steal to his side, take his hand, and seem to be quite happy and at ease when they were near him. The same power of setting others perfectly at their ease in his presence extended to his influence over grown-up persons.

In society he was agreeable, attentive, kind, and considerate to all; no one was too humble, too retiring, too little *au fait* in the modes of living, acting, and thinking of those among whom he might be accidentally thrown, to be beneath his notice, or beyond the reach of his extraordinary power of finding out merit, devising means of drawing out any peculiar talent the person might possess, or of discovering some topic of interest to the party on which he could get into conversation with him. Men of all opinions, classes, and positions, found themselves at home with him on some particular question or other; and this not from any effort or any unworthy concession on his part, but from a natural facility of adapting himself to the peculiarities of those around him. His active mind sought and found abundant occupation in such conversational exercise. He often said that "he had never known the meaning of the word *ennui*."

No matter where or with whom he might be, he found means to employ his mind and his time more or less usefully or agreeably. The dullest country-town had for him as many resources as Paris or London. Wherever he went, he was disposed to find every thing interesting and good in its way, and every body capable of being made amusing and agreeable. To the last, when time, grief, and disappointment, the loss of fortune, friends, and nearly all he loved best on earth, might well be supposed to have soured his disposition, this happy turn of mind yet remained unimpaired as in his early youth.

Arrogance, and affectation, and purse-proud insolence alone found him severe and satirical: on these his keen wit and remarkable powers of raillery were not unfrequently set, and perhaps his only enemies were those who had fallen under his lash, or who were jealous of the superiority of his talents.

Some months after the death of Lord Blessington, Lady Blessington and the Count and Countess D'Orsay returned to England.

Shortly before the death of Count D'Orsay's mother, who entertained feelings of strong attachment for Lady Blessington, the former had spoken with great earnestness of her apprehensions for her son, on account of his tendency to extravagance, and of her desire that Lady Blessington would advise and counsel him, and do her utmost to counteract those propensities which had already been attended with embarrassments, and had occasioned her great fears for his welfare. The promise that was given on that occasion was often alluded to by Lady Blessington, and, after her death, by Count D'Orsay.

A variety of painful circumstances, which have no place in the present memoir, led to a break-up of the establishment of Lady Blessington in Paris, after the death of Lord Blessington. On her return to London, Lady Blessington took a house in Seamore Place, and Count D'Orsay one in Curzon Street; from thence they removed to Kensington Gore—Lady Blessington to Gore House, Count D'Orsay to a small dwelling adjoining it; but finally they both occupied the former place of abode till the break-up of that establishment in April, 1849.

The count returned to his native country after a residence of nineteen years in London. In Paris he was joined by Lady Blessington and her nieces, the Misses Power, shortly after his arrival; and in the following month of June he met, in her loss, an affliction, from the effects of which he never thoroughly recovered.

The ensuing year he realized a plan he had formed and often spoken of in happier days. He hired an immense studio, with some smaller rooms connected with it, attached to the house of M. Gerdin, the celebrated marine painter. Here he transported all his possessions (consisting chiefly of his own works of art, easels, brushes, paints, &c.), and with the extraordinary taste and talent for arrangement that constituted one of his gifts, a large waste room, with naked loft, became transformed into one of the most elegantly fitted up and admirably disposed studios of Paris, and, at the same time, a habitable salon of great beauty, combining requisites for a museum *en miniature*, and objects of *virtù* and art sufficient to furnish a small gallery. In this salon he might be said to be domiciled. Here he lived, here he daily received the visits of some of the greatest celebrities of Europe; statesmen, politicians, diplomatists, men of letters, and artists, were his constant visitors and frequent guests.

The *ex-roi* Jerome continued to be one of the most faithful and attached of his friends. The paternal affection of the good old man, with the warm regard of his son, the Prince Napoleon, formed a remarkable contrast to the conduct of others, which fully bore out the observation, "There are some benefits so great that they can only be paid by the blackest ingratitude." The ex-king Jerome never swerved in his affection for Count D'Orsay, and his earnest desire was to see him elevated to a post worthy of his position and talents. This hope, however, was destined to be defeated. The President of the Republic had nothing in common with the exile and prisoner of Ham; he who had long and largely served, counseled, and aided in various ways the latter, through good report and evil report had been a faithful friend to him, was looked on with coldness and aversion when he proved too independent and high-spirited to be a mere servile, opinionless partisan of the most astute as well as successful conspirator of modern times; and as his presence recalled obligations in private life, he became an object of jealousy, his services a disagreeable souvenir. The poor count pined away, long expecting an appointment, but expecting it in vain. His health broke down, and when it was completely broken down, Louis Napoleon conferred on his friend of former days, already struck by the hand of death, the nominal post of Director of Fine Arts, the duties of which office he was no longer able to perform. The prince imagined, by the tardy act of gratitude, he had screened himself from the just reproaches of all who knew their former connection.

Count D'Orsay was struck to the heart by the ingratitude of Louis Napoleon, but his generous nature was incapable of bitterness, and no sentiment of animosity was engendered by it; he suffered deeply and long in silence, but the wound festered, and at times it was evident enough how much it galled him.

From the period of Lady Blessington's death, the count had

given up general society, and during the last two years of his life he confined himself almost altogether to the house, receiving in his studio-salon morning visits of his family and a very small circle of intimate friends. Lady Blessington's nieces, the companions of his happy and prosperous days, his attendants in those of sickness and sorrow, some members of his family, his beloved sister, the *ex-roi* Jerome and his son, Emile de Girardin, Dr. Cabarrus, his school-fellow, the son of the celebrated Madam Tallien, and the well-known Monsieur Ouvrard, Madam de C——, the Comtesse of D——, were among the last in whose constant society he found repose and pleasure when that of others had lost its charm.

In the spring of 1852, the spinal malady which finally proved fatal declared itself, and then commenced a long series of sufferings, which ended but with his life—sufferings endured with fortitude, patience, uncomplaining gentleness, a manifest absence of all selfishness, and consideration for those attending on him, which none but those whose painful task it was to watch by his couch could form any idea of.

In the month of July he was ordered to Dieppe as a last resource, and thither he was accompanied by Lady Blessington's nieces. From the time of his arrival in Dieppe he sunk rapidly; at the end of the month he returned to Paris dying, and on the 4th of August, 1852, breathed his last, surrounded by those whose unremitting care had been the last consolation of his declining days.

During his illness he had more than once been visited by the excellent Archbishop of Paris, though a comparatively late acquaintance, who entertained for him a warm regard.

Two days previous to his decease, the archbishop had a long conversation with him, and at parting embraced him, assuring him of his friendship and affectionate regard.* The following day, the last of his existence, he received the consolations of religion from the *curé* of Chambourcy. For the church of this good priest he had done a great deal: he had restored many

* "J'ai pour vous plus que de l'amitié, j'ai de l'affection," were the archbishop's words.

of the pictures, and bestowed the original picture of the *Mater Dolorosa*, which had been painted by himself expressly for the church, the lithograph of which is well known, and is sold under the title of the Magdalen, though why thus called it would be difficult to say.

Thus terminated, at the age of fifty-one years, the existence of this highly-gifted man, when hardly beyond the prime of life.

An innate love of all that was beautiful in nature and excellent in art, a generous, chivalrous nature, strong sympathies with suffering, ardent feelings, a kindly disposition, elegant tastes, and fine talents, capable of being turned in almost any pursuit to an excellent account, these were the distinguishing characteristics of Count Alfred D'Orsay.

Many gifts and advantages, natural and intellectual, were united in him. To remarkable personal comeliness were added great strength and courage, which nothing could daunt, and an adroitness which enabled him to excel in every thing he attempted. He was one of the best horsemen, the best shots, the best fencers, and the best boxers of his day. His talents as a painter and sculptor, though wanting cultivation and study, were of the first order; he had an excellent ear, and some taste for music, with a tolerable tenor voice, which, however, he very rarely exercised. His wit was keen and brilliant, his taste in all matters of dress, furniture, and equipage, as well as in art, excellent. In his mind and his manners there was a singular mixture of refinement, simplicity, warmth, and frankness, very productive of strongly pleasing impressions. Generous to lavishness, frank to indiscretion, unsuspicious to credulity, disinterested to imprudence, his defects were, in the eyes of his ardent friends, the excesses of his noble qualities. He has been often heard to say that he would prefer being deceived a hundred times rather than suspect another unjustly. He had a great horror of scandal, and possessed chivalrous feelings, which led him always to take the part of those who were violently assailed, absent or present, known to him or utter strangers.

During his residence at Gore House he was a generous benefactor to those of his nation who required alms, encouragement, assistance, introductions, hospitality. From Louis Napoleon to the poorest exile, his services were rendered with a frank, earnest good-will, and a considerate delicacy and sympathy for misfortune, that increased the value of his assistance. He founded the *Société de Bienfaisance*, still existing in London, for the benefit of his distressed countrymen, nor was his aid ever withheld from the poor or suffering of his adopted country, for his admiration for England ended only with his life.

In his temper, either in sickness or in health, he was never irritable nor morose. Those who were about him and in attendance on him said, "They never knew any one so easy to live with, so little given to find fault."

But there was one thing in his demeanor and carriage of a very marked and distinguished character; the high bearing, proud spirit, and strong energy of a nobly constituted man were mingled with the gentleness, the sensibility, self-devotion, and tenderness of a woman's nature. Frank and open in all his dealings, the idea of deceiving or condescending to stoop to any sophistry in conversation never entered his mind. This ingenuousness of mind and natural excellence of disposition were admirably associated with external advantages, and set off by an appearance of no ordinary comeliness, which in its perfections united excellence of form, coloring, and expression. Wit, genius, and generosity, thus gracefully presented, and graciously recommended in his person to observation, it may not be much wondered at, were admired; nor need we doubt that Alfred D'Orsay was regarded by many with sentiments of regard and esteem, and by some with stronger feelings of affection than may be easily reconcilable with the prevailing opinion of his faults and his defects.

Many of the preceding observations have been written by one most intimately acquainted with Count D'Orsay, and devoted in her attentions to him in his last illness, and up to his last moments; one who had known him long and well in the full force and vigor of life and health in happier times, in the brilliant circle in which he moved, "the glass of fashion and the mould of form;" who had seen him in gay salons, the delight of all around him, and in splendid equipages, witching also the world of fashion in Hyde Park "with noble horsemanship," "the observed of all observers," there and every where he came. They were written by one who had seen him in a few months reduced from a high position, surrounded with all the luxuries of life, from health and happiness to comparative obscurity and indigence, to wretchedness and weariness of life, utterly broken down in health and spirits. They were written with the warm feelings of elevated kindness and of unfailing friendship of a woman's heart, ever most true and faithful when the object of its solicitude stands most in need of pity and of care.

In this notice we must not look for a close and scrutinizing search for frailties and errors; and we may fairly presume, however truthful the account may be which is given to us of the many excellent qualities of this gifted man, that he had his faults and imperfections; and happy may it be for him and most men if the amount of evil is counterbalanced to some extent by that of good.

The nearest and dearest living relation of Count D'Orsay, who cherishes his memory as one of the objects in this world most precious to her, makes no concealment of her conviction that Count D'Orsay's ignorance of the value of money—the profuse expenditure into which he was led by that ignorance, the temptation to play arising from it, the reckless extravagance into which he entered, not so much to minister to his own pleasures as to gratify the feelings of an inordinate generosity of disposition, that prompted him to give whenever he was called on, and to forget the obligations he contracted for the sake of others, and the heavy penalties imposed on his friends by his frequent appeals for pecuniary assistance, were very grievous faults, and great defects in his character. In other respects, it can not be denied that great wrongs were inflicted on one entitled to protection from him; that public opinion was outraged by that career in London which furnished slander with so many plausible themes; and, however groundless may be the innumerable rumors prejudicial to character that had been industriously propagated in relation to them, that great imprudence had been committed, and grave suspicions had been incurred by that imprudence.

Those who deal rigorously with the defects of other people may be very conscious of being exempt from the failings they discover in eminent persons filling a large space in the public view like the late Count D'Orsay; but before they exult overmuch in the fullness of their sense of superiority over others less perfect than themselves, and in the abundance of their self-complacency give thanks to God they are not like those other frail and erring people, let them be well satisfied they have no frailties themselves of a different description, and that they are in possession of all the good qualities that may belong even to their erring brothers; let them be well assured that, had their own position in early life, and at the commencement of their career in society, been surrounded by unfavorable circumstances and evil influences, as those of the persons who are condemned by them may have been, their own virtue was of such exalted excellence that it would have triumphed over all those unfortunate circumstances and influences which had militated against the happiness and good repute of others.

The following facts need no comments, and render any further statements unnecessary on the subject I have referred to, of lavish extravagance.

Soon after the count separated from his wife, an agreement was executed, in 1838, whereby he relinquished all his interest in the Blessington estates, in consideration of certain annuities amounting to £2467 being redeemed, or allowed to remain charged upon the estates (the sum then necessary to redeem them was calculated at £23,500), and also in consideration of a sum of £55,000 to be paid to him; £13,000, part thereof, as soon as it could be raised, and the remaining £42,000 within ten years. These latter sums were not paid until the estates had been sold, namely, in 1851, when with interest they amounted to about £80,000, and that entire amount was paid to parties to whom the count had given securities on the estates; so that with the annuities, the actual amount paid to his creditors out of the estates was upward of £103,500. During his residence in England he had an allowance from the Court of Chancery in Ireland of £550, and Lady Harriet £400 a year.

D'Orsay's embarrassments, from the years 1837 and 1838 to the close of his career, were continuous. In 1841, some efforts were made by his friends to extricate him from them. It was the honorable motive of turning his talents to a profitable account which subsequently led him to devote himself to art with the idea of ultimately increasing his income by his pursuits as a sculptor and a painter, and to cultivate the friendship of artists, with the view of deriving advantage from their several excellences in their pursuits.

Most of his works of art are well known. His portrait of Wellington, who had so great a regard for him that it was sufficient to mention Count D'Orsay's name to insure his attention and interest even when otherwise occupied, was, he believes, the last for which the duke ever sat. At its completion his grace warmly shook hands with the noble artist, exclaiming, "At last I have been painted like a gentleman! I'll never sit to any one else." In Paris he executed a splendid bust of Lamartine, on which the poet wrote some fine verses; one of Emile de Girardin, the boldest, the ablest, and the last open supporter of liberty against oppression; one of Napoleon Bonaparte, the son of Jerome; a picture of Sir Robert Peel; various other sketches and medallions; and, shortly before his death, he had completed the small model of a full-sized statue of the ex-king Jerome, ordered by government for the Salle des Maréchaux de France, and had commenced a colossal statue of Napoleon.

The following article respecting the merits of Count D'Orsay as an artist appeared in the "Presse" newspaper of the 10th of November, 1850 (written by Monsieur de la Guerronniere), on the occasion of the exhibition of a bust of Lamartine executed by the count. The lines which follow the article, composed by Lamartine, are not the least admirable of the celebrated poet.

LE BUSTE DE M. DE LAMARTINE, VERS A. M. LE COMTE D'ORSAY.

"M. le Comte D'Orsay est un amateur de l'art plutôt qu'un artiste. Mais qu'est-ce qu'un amateur? C'est un volontaire parmi les artistes ; ce sont souvent les volontaires qui font les coups d'eclat dans l'atelier comme sur les champs de bataille. Qu'est ce qu'un amateur ? C'est un artiste dont le génie seul fait la vocation. Il est vrai qu'il ne reçoit pas dans son enfance et pendant les premières années de sa vie cette éducation du metier d'où sort Michel Ange, d'où sort Raphaél. Il suit moins les procèdés, les traditions, les secrets pratiques de son art ; mais s'il doit moins au maître, il doit plus à la nature. Il est son œuvre. C'est elle qui a mis le ciseau et le maillet du sculpteur entre les mains élègantes et aristocratiques de Mme. de Lamartine, de Sernesie, de M. de Nerewerkerke et de M. le Comte D'Orsay.

"M. D'Orsay est d'une famille où l'on doit avoir, plus que dans toute autre, le culte du beau dans l'art. Il est le fils d'un général de nos années héroiques, aussi célèbre par sa beauté que par ses faits d'armées. Il est le frère de cette belle Duchesse de Grammont, dont le nom rappelle toutes les graces et toutes les délicatesses d'esprit de la cour de Louis XIV. Lui-même, avant d'avoir la célébrité d'artiste et d'homme lettré, eut l'illustration de la nature : il fut un type de noblesse et de dignité dans les traits. Il exerça dans les salons de Paris et de Londres la dictature Athénienne du goût et de l'élégance. C'est un de ces hommes qu'on aurait cru préoccupé de succês futiles—parce que la nature semble les avoir créés uniquement pour son plaisir —mais qui trompent la nature, et qui, après avoir recueilli les légères admirations des jeunes gens et des femmes de leur âge, échappent à cette atmosphère de légèreté avant le temps où ils laissent ses idoles dans le vide, et se transforment par l'étude et par le travail en hommes nouveaux, en hommes de mérite acquis et serieux. M. D'Orsay a habité longtemps l'Angleterre ou il donnait l'exemple et le ton à cette société aristocratique, un peu raide et deforme, qui admire surtout ce qui lui manque, la grace et l'abandon des manières. Mais il s'y était rendu recommandable aussi et surtout par le patronage intelligent et infatigable qu'il exerçait envers les Français de toutes les classes dénués de ressources dans ce dèsert de Londres. Une des plus admirables institutions de sécours pour les Français ses compatriotes, lui doit son nom et sa prospérité.

"De cette époque, il commença à jouer avec l'argile, le marbre, le ciseau. Liè par un attachement devenu une parenté d'esprit, avec une des plus belles et des plus splendides femmes de son époque, il fit son buste pendant qu'elle vivait ; il le fit idéal et plus touchant après sa mort. Il moule en formes après, rudes, sauvages, de grandeur fruste, les traits paysanesques d'O'Connell. Il sculpta la viellesse toujours verte et calme de Lord Wellington. Ces bustes furent a l'instant vulgarises en millieres d'exemplaires en Angleterre et à Paris. C'étaint des créations neuves. Rien de factice ; rien de convenu ; rien de l'art, excepté le souverain art, celui qu'on ne sent pas et qui ne laisse sentir que l'homme.

"Ces premiers succès lui en presageaient de plus complets. Il cherchait un visage. Il en trouva un. Lord Byron, dont il fut l'ami et avec lequel il voyagea pendant deux ans en Italie, n'était plus qu'un souvenir aimé dans son cœur. Il retrouva ailleurs le génie de la poésie uni a la grandeur du caractère et à la noblesse du courage. Il fit le buste de Lamartine. Il le fit de mémoire, sans que le modèle lui-même en fut instruit. C'est devant ce buste, bientôt exposé au salon, que nous écrivons ces lignes, en demandant pardon à M. Theophile Gautier, notre spirituel collaborateur, d'anticiper sur sa critique, et de venir dans son gracieux domaine, nous profanes, qui sommes des pionniers de la politique dans un champ si rude à labourer.....

"Le buste de Lamartine était très difficile a sculpter, selon nous dira t-on. Ses traits sont simples, regulières, calmes, vastes ; cela est vrai. Mais c'est que, dans leur simplicité, dans leur regularité, dans leur calme, ils ont des expressions fugitives et très diverses. Or, comment être à la fois *un* et *divers*, pour un artiste qui se donne la tâche de reproduire ce type ? Là était le problème. Le Comte D'Orsay l'a résolu.

"La nature, qui ne se plie pas à nos dissections, fait quelquefois des hommes que nous pourrions appeler des hommes multiples. Elle en faisait bien davantage dans l'antiquité, qui n'avait pas nos sottes jalousies, nos ridicules préjugés à cet êgard, et qui permettait à un homme d'être à la fois—si Dieu l'avait fait tel — un poète, un orateur, un soldat, un homme d'etat, un historien, un philosophe, un homme de lettres. Athènes et Rome sont remplies de ces hommes-là, depuis Solon, jusqu'à Périclès et Alcibiade, depuis Cicéron jusqu'à César. Il n'y avait point alors ce système de caste dans l'intelligence et dans le caractère, qui défend aujourd'hui en France, comme cela est défendu dans l'Inde, d'exorcer plusieurs metiers, ou plusieurs génies, ou plusieurs caractêres à la fois. Cette castration morale de l'homme n'était pas inventée. Voilà pourquoi les hommes de ces temps nous paraissent si grands. C'est qu'ils sont entiers? Aujourd'hui ce n'est plus cela. Si vous avez touchè une lyre dans votre jeunesse, il vous sera defendu de toucher à une épée plus tard. Vous serez rangé, bon gré mal gré, dans la caste des poètes. Si vous avez revètu un uniforme, il vous sera interdit d'être un écrivain. Si vous avez été un orateur, il vous sera impossible de revêtir un uniforme et de commander une armée. Si vous avez écrit l'histoire, il vous sera reproché de toucher aux choses qui seront l'histoire à écrire par d'autres un jour. C'est notre loi. C'est ce que nous appelons *la division du travail.* C'est ce j'appellerai plus justement la mutilation des facultés humaines. Mais enfin, il n'y a rien à dire à cela chez nous. C'est un fait; c'est convenu.

"Or, il arrive quelquefois que la nature se révolte contre ces distinctions arbitraires de notre société et de notre temps, et qu'elle donne à un même homme des facultés très diverses quoique très complètes.

"Voici Lamartine posant devant M. D'Orsay! Evidemment il y a la plusieurs Lamartine. Lequel choisira le sculpteur? Est-ce le Lamartine des *Méditations poétiques*, des *Harmonies religieuses* et de *Jocelyn?* Est-ce Lamartine de la tribune? Est-ce le Lamartine de l'Hôtel de Ville haranguant les multitudes pour désarmer la Révolution du drapeau de la Terreur, la poitrine découverte, haletant, les habits déchirés? Est-ce le Lamartine écrivant *l'Histoire des Girondins?* Est-ce le Lamartine à cheval et au feu des journées de mai et de juin, marchant à la tête des colonnes de la garde mobile et de la garde nationale, contre la Place de Grève ou contre les barricades des faubourgs insurgés? Est-ce Lamartine vaincu, désarmé de son pouvoir et de sa popularité, se refugiant de la politique dans les lettres, et demandant à son travail solitaire et à la lampe de ses nuits des travaux qui épuisent la jeunesse d'un écrivain? Eh bien! non, ce n'est ni celui-ci, ni celui-la que M. le Comte D'Orsay a voulu choisir. Il n'a pas choisi; il a mieux fait: il a fait le Lamartine de la nature, le Lamartine tout entier. Celui des poésies, celui de la tribune, celui de l'histoire, celui de l'Hôtel de Ville et celui de la rue, celui de la retraite et du travail.

"Voilà pour nous et pour l'avenir l'incomparable supériorité de cette œuvre. Ce n'est pas tel ou tel homme, telle ou telle partie de la vie de cet homme, c'est l'homme, l'homme divers, l'homme multiple, l'homme comme la nature et le hasard des circonstances l'ont fait.

"On jugera de cette œuvre de vie au salon. On pourra critiquer tel ou tel coup de ciseau, tel ou tel muscle, telle ou telle ligne du bronze ou du marbre. Mais on verra vivre un homme. On dira ce qu'un de nos amis a dit en voyant pour la première fois cette epreuve: *C'est le buste de feu sacré.* Béranger, si grand juge, est sorti plein d'admiration de cet atelier. Ami du modèle il lui appartenait plus qu'à personne de prononcer sur le talent du sculpteur.

"Au reste, il paraît que le modèle lui-même a été pressionné par son image, car cette impression lui a rendu sa voix de poète qui s'est tue dupuis si longtemps au tumulte d'autres pensées et d'autres actes. En recevant à Mâcon, il y a quelques jours ce buste qui lui était envoyé par le statuaire, il a adressé, et comme improvisé dans l'instant même à M. le Comte D'Orsay, les strophes suivantes que nous devons à l'obligeance de celui qui les a reçues. Nos lectures y retrouveront la voix qui nous remuait dans notre jeunesse, et que le temps, au lieu de la briser, a rendu plus virile, plus grave et plus pénétrante que jamais:

"A MONSIEUR LE COMTE D'ORSAY.

I.

"Quand le bronze ecumant dans ton moule d'argile,
Léguera par ta main mon image fragile
A l'œil indifférent des hommes qui naîtront,
Et que, passant leurs doigts sur ces tempes ridées,

Comme un lit dévasté du torrent des idées,
Pleins de doute, ils diront entre eux: De qui ce front?

II.

"Est-ce un soldat debout frappé pour la patrie?
Un poète qui chante, un pontife qui prie?
Un orateur qui parle aux flots seditieux?
Est-ce un tribun de paix soulevé par la houlle,
Offrant, le cœur gonflé, sa poitrine à la foule,
Pour que sa libertè remontât pure aux cieux?

III.

"Car dans ce pied qui lutte, et dans ce front qui vibre,
Dans ces lueurs de feu qu'entr'ouvre un souffle libre,
Dans ce cœur qui bondit, dans ce geste serein,
Dans cette arche du flanc que l'extase soulève,
Dans ce bras qui commande et dans cet œil qui rêve,
Phidias a pétri sept ames dans l'airain.

IV.

"Sept ames, Phidias! et je n'en ai plus une!
De tout ce qui vécut je subis la fortune.
Arme cent fois brisée entre les mains du temps,
Je sème des trames dans ma route vers la tombeaux
Et le siècle hébété dit: 'Voyez comme tombe
A moitié du combat chacun des combattans!'

V.

"Celui-là chanta Dieu, les idoles le tuent!
Au mépris des petits, les grands le prostituent:
Notre sang, disent-ils pourquoi l'epargnas-tu?
Nous en aurions tachè la griffe populaire!
Et le lion couché lui dit avec colère:
Pourquoi m'as-tu calmè? Ma force est ma vertu.

VI.

"Va, brise, ô Phidias, ta dangereuse épreuve;
Jettes-en les débris, dans le feu, dans le fleuve,
De peur qu'un foible cœur, de doute confondu,
Ne dise en contemplant ces affronts sur ma joue,
'Laissons aller le monde à son courant de boue,
Et que faut d'un cœur un siècle soit perdu!'

VII.

"Oui, brise, ô Phidias! dérobe ce visage
A la postérité, qui ballotte une image
De l'Olympe à l'égout, de la gloire à l'oubli.
Au pilori du temps n'expose pas mon ombre!
Je suis las des soleils, laisse mon urne à l'ombre.
Le bonheur de la mort, c'est d'être enseveli!

VIII.

"Que la feuille d'hiver au vent des nuits semée,
Que du coteau natal l'argile encore aimée
Couvrent vite mon front moulé sous son linceul!
Je ne veux de vos bruits qu'un souffle dans la brise,
Un nom inachevé dans un cœur qui se brise;
J'ai vécu pour la foule, et jé veux dormir seul.

"A. DE LAMARTINE."

"Il y a encore une strophe plus touchante et aussi grave que les autres. Mais nous ne nous croyons pas permis de la copièr. L'auteur ne les écrivait pas pour le public, mais pour un cœur. Nous obéissons à la discretion qu'il nous aurait sans doute demandée.

"On est heureux de pouvoir inspirer de pareils vers! Plus heureux sans doute d'avoir pu les écrire en quelques minutes, au milieu des préoccupations des affaires et des difficultés du temps. Nous en félicitons M. D'Orsay et M. de Lamartine. L'un a une belle page en vers; l'autre a une belle page en marbre. Ils sont quittes l'une envers l'autre. Mais nous ne le sommes pas envers eux, car nous leur devons une double émotion, et nos lecteurs la partageront avec nous.

"A. DE LA GUERONNIERE."

There are some excellent remarks on D'Orsay's talents as an artist, though a little too eulogistic perhaps, in an article in "The New Monthly Magazine" for August, 1845.

"Whatever Count D'Orsay undertakes seems invariably to be well done. As the arbiter elegantiarum, he has reigned supreme in matters of taste and fashion, confirming the attempts of others by his approbation, or gratifying them by his example. To dress or drive, to shine in the gay world like Count D'Orsay, was once the ambition of the youth of England, who then discovered in this model no higher attributes. But if time, who 'steals our years away,' steals also our pleasures, he replaces them with others, or substitutes a better thing; and thus it has befallen with Count D'Orsay.

"If the gay equipage or the well-appareled man be less frequently seen than formerly, that which causes more lasting satisfaction, and leaves an impression of a far more exalted nature, comes day by day into higher relief, awakening only the regret that it should have been concealed so long. When we see what Count D'Orsay's productions are, we are tempted to ask, with Malvolio's feigned correspondent, 'Why were these things hid?'

"But we are glad to see that they are hidden no more, and the accomplished count seems disposed to show the world of how much he is really capable. His *croquis de société* had long charmed his friends, and his great skill in modeling was bruited abroad, when the world began to ask, 'Is it true that in the man of fashion exists the genius of the sculptor and the painter?' Evidence was soon given that such surmises were true.

"Count D'Orsay's statuettes of Napoleon and the Duke of Wellington, and his portraits of Dwarkanauth Tagore and Lord Lyndhurst, exhibited capabilities of the first order, and satisfied every inquiry. Additional proof of his powers has been afforded by the publication of the engraving of his portrait of Lord Byron.

"It is certainly a highly interesting work of art, and, in point of resemblance, we are assured that one who knew him, perhaps best of all, has declared that, until now, there never existed a likeness which completely satisfied the mind. Certain traits of that thoughtful and intelligent countenance were wanting in other portraits, but in this they are all happily united.

"Count D'Orsay has represented the noble bard where most he loved to be, on the deck of his own vessel. He is sitting in sailor's costume, leaning on the rudder, with his right hand under his chin, and his head elevated. In his fine large eyes is an expression of deep thought, and a pensive character marks his firm, but femininely-cut mouth. His noble expanse of forehead and fine contour of head are drawn with a free and vigorous pencil. If we did not know whose likeness was intended, we should still call this portrait an exceedingly fine study; but our interest in it is increased by the fidelity of the resemblance. The portrait is well engraved by Lewis.

"We understand that his grace the Duke of Wellington is so well pleased with the statuettes to which we have alluded, copies of which he has given an order to be executed in silver, that he is now sitting to the count for his portrait also. We therefore look forward with a very pleasant anticipation to another likeness of the hero of a hundred fights—and pictures too."

Haydon, in his Diary, 31st of June, 1838, makes mention of D'Orsay: "About seven D'Orsay called, whom I had not seen for long. He was much improved, and looking the glass of fashion and the mould of form; really a complete Adonis, not made up at all. He made some capital remarks, all of which must be attended to. They were sound impressions and grand. He bounded into his cab, and drove off like a young Apollo with a fiery Pegasus. I looked after him. I like to see such specimens."*

Again, in his Diary, 10th of July, 1839, Haydon observes: "D'Orsay called and pointed out several things to correct in the horse (the Duke of Wellington's charger), verifiying Lord Fitzroy's criticism of Sunday last. I did them, and he took my brush in his dandy gloves, which made my heart ache, and lowered the hind-quarters by bringing over a bit of the sky. Such a dress—white greatcoat, blue satin cravat, hair oiled and curling, hat of the primest curve and purest water, gloves scented with eau de Cologne or eau de jasmine, primrose in tint, skin in tightness. In this prime of dandyism he took up a nasty, oily, dirty hog-tool, and immortalized Copenhagen (the charger) by touching the sky."†

A friend of D'Orsay's, in a notice of the count's death in the "Globe" newspaper, has truly observed:

"Unquestionably one of the celebrities of our day, the deceased man of fashion, claims more than the usual curt obituary. It were unjust to class him with the mere Brummels, Mildmays, Alvanleys, or Pierreponts of the Regency, with whom, in his early life, he associated, much less the modern men about town who have succeeded him; equally idle were the attempt to rank him with a Prince de Ligne, an Admirable Crichton, or an Alcibiades; yet was he a singularly gifted and brilliantly accomplished personage."

* Memoirs of B. R. Haydon, vol. iii., p. 86.

† Ibid., vol. iii., p. 105.

A writer in the "Annual Register," in another notice of the count's death, thus speaks of his talents and acquirements:

"Few men in his position have shown greater accomplishments. His literary compositions were lively and imaginative. His profile portraits of his friends (of which many have been published in lithography) are felicitous and characteristic, and his statuettes are not only graceful, but possess greater originality of conception than is evinced by the majority of professional artists. In his general intercourse with society, Count D'Orsay was distinguished not merely by true politeness, but by great amiability. He was kind and charitable to his distressed countrymen, and one of the most assiduous supporters of the Societé de Bienfaisance.

"In England the count became acquainted with Prince Louis Napoleon, and soon after the arrival of the prince in France, he fixed his own residence in Paris. His name was designated several times for diplomatic office, but it was rumored, and generally believed, that the prince was too dependent upon his personal advice and assistance to spare his society. We are now told (by M. Girardin, in 'La Presse') that, before the 2d of December, nobody made greater or more reiterated efforts for a policy of a different course and of the highest aspirations; after the 2d of December, no man exerted himself more to assuage the stroke of proscription. The President of the Republic had not a more devoted and sincere friend than the Count D'Orsay, and it is at a moment when the prince had attached him to his person by the title and functions of Superintendent of the Beaux Arts that he has lost him forever."*

Count D'Orsay's connections with English families of distinction, and relations with eminent persons of his country residing in England, had made him well acquainted with London and its society before his intimacy with the Blessingtons.

In 1828, Lady Blessington speaks of the General and Countess D'Orsay as having taken up their abode in Paris, and their recent arrival from their *chateau* in *Franche Comté*.

No mention, however, is made in that portion of her journal,

* This appointment was announced only a few days before his death.

nor, indeed, in any previous part of the "Idler in France," of their son Count Alfred D'Orsay. "The Countess D'Orsay," Lady Blessington observes, "had been a celebrated beauty, and though a grandmother, still retains considerable traces of it. Her countenance is so *spirituelle* and piquant that it gives additional point to the clever things she perpetually utters; and what greatly enhances her attractions is the perfect freedom from any of the airs of a *belle esprit*, and the total exemption from affectation that distinguishes her.

"General D'Orsay, known from his youth as Le Beau D'Orsay, still justifies the appellation, for he is the handsomest man of his age that I ever beheld. It is said that when the emperor first saw him, he observed that 'he would make an admirable model for a Jupiter,' so noble and commanding was the character of his beauty. There is a calm and dignified simplicity in the manner of General D'Orsay that harmonizes with his lofty bearing."*

Elsewhere Lady Blessington observes, "I know no such brilliant talker as she (the Countess D'Orsay) is. No matter what may be the subject of conversation, her wit flashes brightly on all, and without the slightest appearance of effort or pretension. She speaks from a mind overflowing with general information, made available by a retentive memory, a ready wit, and inexhaustible good spirits."†

The customary transmission of intellectual power in the maternal line, and of striking traits of physical conformation from sire to children, were not deviated from in the case of the children of the brilliant countess and the beau D'Orsay.

The mother of the Countess D'Orsay, Madame Crawford, was a person of singular endowments. The King of Wurtemberg had been privately married to this lady; but on the legal marriage of the king with a royal personage, which his former wife considered as an act of injustice to herself and her children (a son who died young, though grown up, and a daughter, afterward Madame D'Orsay), she went to France, and fixed her abode there. She subsequently married a Mr. O'Sullivan, an Irishman

* The Idler in France, vol. i., p. 238. † Ibid., vol. ii., p. 33.

of large fortune in India, and after his death, Mr. Crawford, a member of an ancient Scotch family, and also possessed of large property. She survived him, and died at the age of eighty-four.

In India, the personal attractions of this lady obtained for her the title of "La Belle Sullivan." On her return, one of her countrymen addressed the following *jeu d'esprit:*

ON SENDING A SMALL BOTTLE OF OTTO OF ROSES TO MRS. SULLIVAN.

"Quand la 'belle Sulivan,' quitta l'Asie,
La Rose, amoureuse de ses charmes,
Pleura le depart de sa belle amie,
Et ce flacon contient ses larmes."

Madame Crawford, in 1828, was residing in Paris. "Her hotel," says Lady Blessington in her diary, "is a charming one, *entre Cour et Jardin;* and she is the most extraordinary person of her age I have ever seen. In her eightieth year, she does not look to be more than fifty-five, and possesses all the vivacity and good humor peculiar only to youth. Scrupulously exact in her person, and dressed with the utmost care as well as good taste, she gives me a notion of the appearance which the celebrated Ninon de l'Enclos must have presented at the same age, and has much of the charm of manner said to have belonged to that remarkable woman. It was an interesting sight to see her surrounded by her grandchildren and great-grandchildren, all remarkable for their good looks, and affectionately attached to her, while she appears not a little proud of them."

Lady Blessington, in referring to the fascinating powers of this elderly gentlewoman, and comparing them with those of Ninon de l'Enclos some seven-and-twenty years later, might have found an elderly gentlewoman verging on sixty, nearer home, possessing the extraordinary attractions she alluded to in the case of the old French lady, who had a violent attack of youth every spring for upward of half a century.

Ninon de l'Enclos, at the age of fifty-six, inspired the Marquis of Sevignè with the tender passion.

Bordering on her seventieth year, she inspired a Swedish nobleman, a bold baron, with feelings of admiration and affection.

Her last conquest was at the age of eighty: "Monsieur l'Abbé Gedouin fut la derniere passion."

But the last-named abbé, it would appear, was not the first abbé who had felt the power of her attractions, even in her mature years. The Abbé Chaulieu, descanting on the loveliness of this remarkable old woman, said, "L'amour s'est retirè jusque dans les rides de son front."

Ninon preserved not only her beauty, but her sprightliness of fancy in her advanced years. She had the art of saying good things promptly and appropriately on proper occasions in a natural manner, and the good sense never to violate the decencies of life in conversation. She made no affectation of prudery, however, and even declaimed much against prudes. "Elles etoient les Jansenistes de l'amour."*

The late Duke de Grammont, father of the present duke (brother-in-law of Count Alfred D'Orsay), is described by Lady Blessington as "a fine old man, who has seen much of the world, without having been soured by its trials. Faithful to his sovereign during adversity, he is affectionately cherished by the whole of the present royal family, who respect and love him, and his old age is cheered by the unceasing devotion of his children, the Duke and Duchesse de Guiche, who are fondly attached to him."†

* Lettres de Ninon de l'Enclos, &c., avec sa Vie, 16mo, London, 1782, tome i., p. 31.

† The celebrated Duchesse de Grammont, who perished on the scaffold in the French Revolution, was the sister of the famous minister, the Duke de Choiseul. In 1751 we find the Duchesse de Grammont thus described by one of her cotemporaries: "She never dissembles her contempt or dislike of any man, in whatever degree of elevation. It is said she might have supplied the place of Madame de Pompadour if she had pleased. She treats the ceremonies and pageants of courts as things beneath her. She possesses a most uncommon share of understanding, and has very high notions of honor and reputation." This celebrated lady possessed a very uncommon share of courage and magnanimity, which she was called on some thirty years later to exhibit—not in gilded salons or brilliant circles of wit and fashion, but before the Revolutionary tribunal and on the scaffold. The duchesse, when brought before the judges of that murderous tribunal, with an energy and eloquence that even struck the judicial assassins of that iniquitous court with surprise, pleaded for the life of her dear friend, the Duchesse de Chatelet, but plead for it in vain. They died on the same scaffold.

The parents of the present Duke of Grammont accompanied the royal family in their exile to Scotland. The mother of the duke died in Holyrood House in 1803.

In October, 1825, "the remains of the Duchess of Grammont, which had lain in the royal vault of the chapel of Holyrood since the year 1803, were transported in a hearse from the palace to Newhaven, to be embarked on board a French corvette at anchor in the roads. The lord provost and magistrates, the lord advocate, the lord chief baron, Sir Patrick Walker, Sir Henry Jardine, &c., attended, and followed the hearse in mourning coaches to the place of embarkation, as a testimony of respect for the memory of the illustrious lady, who died while sharing the exile of the royal family of France. The original shell had previously been inclosed in a coffin of a very superb description, covered with crimson velvet, and gorgeously ornamented. The plate bore the following inscription:

"Louise Françoise Gabrielle Aglae
De Polignac,
Duchesse de Grammont,
née à Paris le 7 Mai,
1763;
morte le 30 Mars,
1803."*

Lady Tankerville, sister of the present Duke of Grammont, is a native of Paris. Her position in early life, belonging to one of the first families in France, and one of those the most devoted to the Bourbons, added to her great beauty, rendered her in the old régime an object of general attention and attraction at court. The Duke de Berri, before his alliance with a Neapolitan princess, wished much to marry Mademoiselle de Grammont. On the downfall of the elder branch of the Bourbons, her family having suffered severely in the Revolution, she came to England, and during her residence in this country in quasi exile, married the Earl of Tankerville. This lady possesses all the vivacity of her nation, and graceful, sprightly manners.

Charles Augustus, Lord Ossulston, the present Earl of Tank-

* Annual Register, 1825, p. 148.

erville, the 28th of July, 1826, married Corisande de Grammont, daughter of Antoine, Duc de Grammont, and Aglae de Polignac.

Another sister of the present Duke de Grammont married General, afterward Marshal, Sebastiani, who, though an habitual invalid, was sagaciously chosen by the King of the Barricades to represent the armed majesty of France at the court of St. James, immediately after the "three glorious days" of 1830.*

He was a man of profound reflection, though of no *pretensions* to talent of any kind. He had the art of exerting influence without exciting envy or raising opposition. At an interval of thirty years he married two ladies of the highest rank in France—a Coigny and a Grammont.

In a letter of the Duc de Grammont, then Duc de Guiche (without date), to Lady Blessington, he says, "My sister is gone to London as embassadrice de Ls. Pe. Is it not strange? But what will appear to you still more so is, that this extraordinary change at their time of life is the operation of love, by which influence no couple of sixteen have been ever more subdued. I, who feel daily old age creeping on, I hope that some like occurrence will in twenty years' time set me up again. I, however, trust that, through our numerous acquaintances and connections with English society, she will be *bien reçue*, and that people will remember the *Comtesse Sebastiani est née* Grammont. Believe me, my dear Lady Blessington, ever faithfully your attached friend, (Signed), GUICHE."

Count D'Orsay was a year younger than his sister, the present Duchess of Grammont. Shortly after the death of the count, by the desire of that lady I visited her at her seat at Chambourcy, near St. Germain en Laye. Her resemblance to her brother is striking. A more dignified and commanding, but, withal, amiable-looking lady I have seldom met. Though her face and noble form had been touched but recently by the hand of sorrow and of sickness, the remains were still there of surpassing loveliness and beauty, and in her conversation there were ample evi-

* Byron speaks of meeting General Count Sebastiani, "a cousin of Napoleon," in London, in 1816. "Sebastiani," he observes, is "a fine, foreign, villainous-looking, intelligent, and very agreeable man."

dences of a high order of intellect, and of exalted sentiments of a religious kind. Five-and-twenty years previously she was described by Lady Blessington as the most striking-looking woman she ever beheld. Tall and graceful, her commanding figure, at once dignified and perfectly symmetrical, was in harmony with her noble features, their lofty expression of superior intelligence, and the imposing character of her conversational powers.

With respect to Count D'Orsay's sentiments on the subject of religion in the latter part of his life, I have a few words to add.

I visited my poor friend a few weeks before his death, and found him evidently sinking, in the last stage of disease of the kidneys, complicated with spinal complaint. The wreck only of the *beau* D'Orsay was there.

He was able to sit up and to walk, though with difficulty and evidently with pain, about his room, which was at once his studio, reception room, and sleeping apartment. He burst out crying when I entered the room, and continued for a length of time so much affected that he could hardly speak to me. Gradually he became composed, and talked about Lady Blessington's death, but all the time with tears pouring down his pale, wan face, for even then his features were death-stricken.

He said with marked emphasis, "*In losing her I lost every thing in this world—she was to me a mother! a dear, dear mother! a true, loving mother to me!*" While he uttered these words, he sobbed and cried like a child. And referring to them, he again said, "*You understand me, Madden.*" I understood him to be speaking what he felt, and there was nothing in his accents, in his position, or his expressions (for his words sounded in my ears like those of a dying man) which led me to believe he was seeking to deceive himself or me.

I turned his attention to the subject I thought most important to him. I said, among the many objects which caught my attention in the room, I was very glad to see a crucifix placed over the head of his bed; men living in the world, as he had done, were so much in the habit of forgetting all early religious feelings. D'Orsay seemed hurt at the observation. I then plainly said to him, "The fact is, I imagined, or rather I supposed, you had followed Lady Blessington's example, if not in giving up your own religion, in seeming to conform to another more in vogue in England." D'Orsay rose up with considerable energy, and stood erect and firm with obvious exertion for a few seconds, looking like himself again, and pointing to the head of the bed, he said, "Do you see those two swords?" pointing to two small-swords (which were hung over the crucifix crosswise); "do you see that sword to the right? With that sword I fought in defense of my religion. I had only joined my regiment a few days, when an officer at the mess-table used disgusting and impious language in speaking of the Blessed Virgin. I called on him to desist; he repeated the foul language he had used; I threw a plate of spinach across the table in his face; a challenge ensued; we fought that evening on the rampart of the town, and I have kept that sword ever since."

Whatever we may think of the false notions of honor, or the erroneous ones of religion which may have prompted the encounter, I think there is evidence in it of early impressions of a religious nature having been made on the mind of this singular man, and of some remains of them still existing at the period above named, however strangely presented.

On this occasion, Count D'Orsay informed me that Lady Blessington never ceased "in her heart" to be a Catholic, although she occasionally attended the church of another persuasion; and that while she was in Paris, she went every Sunday to the Madeleine, in company with some member of his family.

And here I may observe, that on one occasion, when I visited Lady Blessington on a Sunday, after her return from church, I found her with several visitors, discussing the merits of the sermon she had just heard preached. Her ladyship inveighed strongly against the sermon, and the style of preaching in England.

A young man observed, he should hardly have expected such severe censures on their pulpit from a person of such high church principles as her ladyship.

Lady Blessington said, very calmly, and more deliberately than usual, "The doctrines of the Protestant Church never appeared to me better than those of the Catholic Church. I was educated in the doctrines of that church. When I married I got into the habit of accompanying my husband to his church, and I continued to go there from the force of habit and for convenience, but never from conviction of its doctrines being better than those of the Catholic Church."

I think there were seven or eight persons present when this startling avowal was made.

But perhaps I ought to have observed, fully two or three years before that period, I had taken the liberty of an old and privileged friend to write a letter to her ladyship, venturing to remind her of the faith she had been born in, to point out the hollowness of the pleasures of that society in which she moved, of the insufficiency of them for her true happiness, of the day that must come, when it would be found that religion was of more importance than all the fame, or glory, or delight that ever was obtained by intellectual powers, or enjoyed in brilliant circles. And though that letter has no place among her papers, I have reason to know it did not pass altogether out of her memory.

The death of D'Orsay was thus noticed by "La Presse," edited by Emile Girardin, of the 5th of August, 1852:

"Le Comte Alfred D'Orsay est mort ce matin à trois heures.

"La douleur et le vide de cette mort seront vivement ressentis par tous les amis qu'il comptait en si grand nombre en France et en Angleterre, dans tous les rangs de la société, et sous tous les drapeaux de la politique.

"A Londres, les salons de Gore House furent toujours ouverts à tous les proscrits politiques, qu'ils s'appelassent Louis Bonaparte ou Louis Blanc, à tous les naufragés de la fortune et à toutes les illustrations de l'art et de la science.

"A Paris, il n'avait qu'un vaste atelier, mais ou quiconque allait frapper au nom d'un malheur à secourir ou d'un progrès à encourager, était toujours assuré du plus affable accueil et du plus cordial concours.

"Avant le 2 Décembre, nul ne fit d'efforts plus réitérés pour que la politique suivît un autre cours et s'élevât aux plus hautes aspirations

"Après le 2 Décembre, nul ne s'employa plus activement pour amortir les coups de la proscription: Pierre Dupont le sait et peut le certifier.

"Le Président de la République n'avait pas d'ami à la fois plus dévoué et plus sincère que le Comte D'Orsay; et c'est quand il venait de la rapprocher de lui par le titre et les fonctions de surintendant des beaux-arts qu'il le perd pour toujours.

"C'est une perte irréparable pour l'art et pour les artistes, mais c'est une perte plus irréparable encore pour la vérité et pour le Président de la République, car les palais n'ont que deux portes ouvertes à la vérité: la porte de l'amitié et la porte de l'adversité, de l'amitié qui est à l'adversité ce que l'éclair est à la foudre.

"La justice indivisible, la justice égale pour tous, la justice dont la mort tient les balances compte les jours quand elle ne mesure pas les dons. Alfred D'Orsay avait été comblé de trop de dons—grand cœur, esprit, un goût pur, beauté antique, force athlétique, adresse incomparable à tous les exercices du corps, aptitude incontestable à tous les arts auxquels il s'était adonné: dessin, peinture, sculpture—Alfred D'Orsay avait été comblé de trop de dons pour que ses jours ne fussent pas parcimonieusement comptés. La mort été a inexorable, mais elle a été juste. Elle ne l'a pas traité en homme vulgaire. Elle ne l'a pas pris, elle l'a choisi."

Among those who attended the funeral of Count D'Orsay were Prince Napoleon Bonaparte, Count de Montaubon, Count de Latour du Pin, the Marquis du Pradt, M. Emile de Girardin, M. Clesinger, the sculptor; M. Charles Lafitte, M. Bixio, M. Alexandre Dumas, Jun., M. Hughes Ball, and several other English gentlemen. The Duke de Grammont, brother-in-law of Count D'Orsay, being confined to his bed by illness, Count Alfred de Grammont and the Duke de Lespare, nephews of the deceased, were the chief mourners. No funeral oration was pronounced over the body, but the emotion of the persons present was great, and the sadness of the scene was increased by the appearance of the Duchess de Grammont, sister of the deceased, who, with her husband, had assiduously attended him during his illness.

"The Bulletin de Paris says, 'When the news of the death of Count D'Orsay was communicated to the Prince President, he exclaimed that he had lost "his best friend."' The same journal states that the large model of the statue of Napoleon, which Count D'Orsay was making from a small one, executed by Mortimer, which was seen at the London Exhibition, was nearly terminated at the time of his death, and that M. Clesinger was formally charged by him to finish his marble statue of the ex-king Jerome."*

The Prince President, we are told, exclaimed, when he heard of the death of Count D'Orsay, that he had lost "his best friend." The Prince President may have said these words, and the day may come when he will feel that Count D'Orsay was one of his very best and truest friends, when he raised his voice, not once or twice, but frequently, it is asserted, against the meditated act of treason to the government he, the Prince President, had sworn to maintain.

The relations that existed at Gore House between Count D'Orsay—something more than a mere leader of fashion in London—the intimate friend of statesmen of all parties, of political people of great eminence in Parliament, of editors of newspapers, mighty men of influence of "the fifth estate of the realm;" of the foreign ministers at the court of St. James's, and the secretaries of the several legations; and though last, not least in importance, the intimate and confidential friend of the lady at whose réunions in Gore House of the celebrities of all political parties and of all intellectual pursuits in London—and the proscribed Prince Louis Napoleon, the twice discomfited conspirator, and still conspiring refugee in England, were such as might have been expected; they were most intimate, cordial, and confiding. To those relations, it may be truly said, without exaggeration or fear of contradiction, the proscribed conspirator was indebted for the position in society, the opportunities of acquiring influence, of obtaining an early and timely knowledge of passing events in foreign courts, and especially in the court of France, and in the diplomatic circles in London; and also of

* Gentleman's Magazine, September, 1852, p. 308.

promoting his views in France by the co-operation of Count D'Orsay's immediate friends and influential connections, which ultimately secured for him the presidency of the French Republic.*

But the *coup d'état*, which was accomplished at the expense of personal honor, and the cost of perjury and blood, put an end to the relations of amity that had subsisted hitherto between Count D'Orsay and Prince Louis Napoleon. D'Orsay, with all his faults, was a man of chivalrous notions as to the obligations of solemn promises and sacred oaths; he believed the President of the Republic had violated those obligations, and D'Orsay was not a man, for any consideration on earth, to refrain from expressing his opinion of the dishonor of such a violation. Very shortly after the *coup d'état*, a friend of mine, Monsieur du P——, dined in Paris at the house of a French nobleman of the highest rank, where Count D'Orsay was present. There were about twenty or two-and-twenty persons present, persons of distinction and of various political sentiments. The all-important topic of the *coup d'état* was discussed for some time with all due prudence and reserve. D'Orsay at length coming out with one of

* On the 9th of April, 1849, the Duke of Wellington wrote a letter to the Count D'Orsay, in which the following passage occurs: "Je me rejouis de la prosperité de la France et du succès de M. le Président de la République. Tout tend vers la permanence de la paix de l'Europe qui est necessaire pour le bonheur de chacun. Votre ami très devoué. WELLINGTON."

This singular letter of one of the most clear-sighted, far-seeing men of modern times, was written after the election of Louis Napoleon to the presidency of the republic. *Not after the coup d'état of December*, 1851. A few dates of remarkable occurrences in the latter part of the career of Louis Napoleon will enable us to form a better idea of the views expressed in the communication above referred to.

Louis Napoleon was elected President of the Republic the 10th of December, 1848. His coup d'état, the arrest of the leading members of the Chamber of Deputies, and the downfall of the republic, took place the 2d of December, 1851. His presidential powers were prolonged for ten years the 20th of December, 1851. He was proclaimed emperor the 2d of December, 1852, then in his forty-third year, being born the 20th of April, 1808.

From the time of the Chartist demonstration in London in 1848, when the Prince Louis Napoleon (then in exile) was sworn in as a special constable for the preservation of the peace in the metropolis of England, to the period when he was proclaimed Emperor of the French in December, 1852, there was an interval of about four years and a half.

his customary notes of preparation, "*à bas!*" made short work of the reserve and prudence of the discussion. He expressed his opinion in English in a deliberate manner, speaking in a loud tone, but emphatically and distinctly, these words: "*It is the greatest political swindle that has ever been practiced in the world!*"

My friend, who was deeply interested in the welfare of D'Orsay, was dismayed at "the indiscretion of this explosion of opinion." It was like a bomb-shell in the circle. There were persons present who might be supposed to have to advance their fortunes by the prince's favor; there were several servants in the room at the time, moreover, and it might be reasonably feared at that period the police were not remiss in making themselves acquainted with the servants of all persons of political influence and importance in Paris.

It must be borne in mind that D'Orsay at that time was wholly dependent on the favor of the prince for his future position in his own country. He had left England utterly ruined in his circumstances, and came to France counting on the friendship and gratitude of his former friend at the head of the French republic, to whose elevation he had certainly very largely contributed. He was well received by the prince, and proffers of public employment adequate to his expectations and his talents were made to him. But after the period of the *coup d'état* and the dinner above referred to—*post* or *propter* that entertainment—the friendship of the prince for the count cooled down from blood heat to the freezing point, and eventually to zero. The man with the heavy eyelids, and the leaden hand of care and calculation pressing them down, when he imposed on himself the weight of empire, could not see his former friends without looking down on them, and D'Orsay was not a man to be looked down on, or coldly at, even by an emperor. For eighteen months before his death his relations with Louis Napoleon had wholly ceased.

The prince at last, when D'Orsay was laboring under the illness which soon after consigned him to an early grave, allowed himself to be persuaded, by urgent and pressing friends of the poor count, that his former friend had some claim on him. The emperor deigned to recognize the claim. His imperial majesty appointed Count Alfred D'Orsay "Director of Fine Arts." Of all things it can not be said truly "better late than never." This thing, that was meant to look like an act of kindness and of gratitude, was too late to be of any use. No one was bettered or deceived by it.

I spoke with some surprise of similar acts of the same exalted personage to Lamennais, not long before his death; the abbé, with the quiet look, the cold, unimpassioned expression of the bright, clear gray eyes of his, observed, "Voyez vous mon cher Monsieur Madden, cette homme là, n'a pas le sentiment ni du bien, ni du mal—il n'a pas de sentiment que de soi même." English history, as well as French, will yet have to ratify the opinion of the Abbé Lamennais.

Among the papers of Lady Blessington I find some very remarkable lines by a very remarkable man, one of the master spirits of original mind of his age—lines which might be read with advantage by all "swimmers in the stream of politics."

"SOME ADDITIONAL LINES FOR A POEM, ONE OF THE THEMES OF WHICH IS THE QUEST OF HONOR.

"The swimmers in the stream of politics,
That keep each other down where none float high
But who are rotten, shouted in my ear,
'Come hither! here is honor, on this side;
He hates the other.'
I passed on, nor look'd,
Knowing the voices well: they troubled me
Vociferating: I searched for willow wand
To scourge and silence the importunates,
And turned me round: lo! they were all upon
The farther bank, and, basking in the sun,
Mowed at me, and defied me to cross o'er,
And broke their cakes, and gave their curs the crumbs,
Weary with wanderings."

In bringing this sketch of the career of Count Alfred D'Orsay to a close, a summary notice of his most remarkable qualities, his talents, and the application of them, is given, that the reader may be able to form a just estimate of his character and abilities.

One was reminded not unfrequently, by the wit combats at

Gore House, of the days of the Chevalier de Grammont, when Dorset, Sedley, Ethelridge, Denham, Killigrew, " and all the whole band of wits"* diverted the beau monde with *bon mots*, sarcastic repartees, quaint observations, humorous sallies, and sharply-pointed epigrams, brought to bear on striking peculiarities of absent acquaintances, or well-known persons of quality within the category of " precieuses ridicules."

" The wits" of the age of Horace Walpole were pretty much the same as those of the times of Holland House and Kensington Gore intellectual gladiatorship. The wit combatants of both in the arena of fashionable literary circles are composed of various grades of competitors for celebrity and pretenders to distinction, and success in sprightly conversation, in lively correspondence, and occasional written drolleries in prose and verse; the efforts of all are to amuse and to be distinguished, and for these ends they must exhibit a keen perception of the ridiculous, a facility for catching salient points in conversation, and combining apparent similitudes of things ludicrous in themselves with ideas of subjects naturally grave or serious; they must evince a strong sense of the obligations imposed on vivacity of mind and liveliness of imagination by the patronage of people *à la mode* or a favored position in society; they must submit to the necessity, in short, of amusing its magnates by a felicitous expression of quaint, jocund, and striking thoughts opportunely brought forth and without apparent effort. In this strife of highly-excited intellectuality, mere pleasant conversationalists jostle against story-tellers and retailers of anecdotes of more or less celebrity, humorists at table after the cloth is taken away, and only then at home in broad and farcical jests, and in impromptu *double entendres* come in contact with the pet poets of the salons, who figure in albums, and compose *vers de société* on the spur of the occasion, previously expected or anticipated, furnish parodies and burlesques to order, conveyed in an invitation to dinner, and sit down deliberately to load their memories in private, and with malice in their wit aforethought, and come charged into company with sarcastic epigrams, to be fired off in public

* Memoirs of Grammont, p. 189.

at the peculiarities of absent friends, or the failings or absurdities of the celebrities of other circles. In this sharp encounter of keen wits, the mere punster, endowed with great natural powers of impudence, and a large stock of animal spirits, whose whole laborious leisure is devoted to the amusement of playing upon words, is to be met cheek by jowl at the same tournament with one like Curran, not always, however, to be found in the most brilliant circles of fashion, or salons of ladies of literature *à la mode*, whose wit is "as keen as his sword, but as polished as the scabbard," which relies on its success neither on flippant sarcasms, or vulgar scoffing in society at high principles or heroic actions, or sneering humorous observations on sacred or on serious subjects, but on its own bright light of intellectuality, condensed and capable, when called into action, of irradiating every subject on which it glances even for a moment.

When the mind of genius is charged with intellectual electricity, we have sparkles of intelligence flashing from the assimilation of dissimilar ideas, which have been suddenly, and apparently accidentally, brought into collision; and these fitful gleams of bright thoughts, felicitously expressed, constitute what is called wit.

But we have as many kinds of these bright emanations of intellectuality as we have of atmospheric meteors in all the varied forms of electrical phenomena.

Perhaps the highest order of wit exhibited in our times (the keenest wit combined with the greatest powers of eloquence) was that which was displayed by Curran in public and in private.

Of Curran's conversational powers, Byron, in his memorandum-book, has spoken in terms of no stinted praise: "Curran! Curran! the man who struck me most. Such imagination! There never was any thing like it that I ever saw or heard of. His published life—his published speeches, give you no idea of the man—none at all. He was a machine of imagination; as some one said of Piron, that he was an epigrammatic machine."*

Elsewhere in his memoranda he said, "The riches of his

* Moore's Life of Byron, p. 304, 8vo ed., 1838.

(Curran's) Irish imagination were exhaustless. I have heard that man speak more poetry than I have ever seen written, though I saw him seldom, and but occasionally. I saw him presented to Madam de Staël. It was the great confluence between the Rhone and the Saone."

The wits of Horace Walpole's day, Sir George Selwyn, Sir Hanbury Williams, Bubb Doddington, Charles Townsend, and their associates, it is difficult to judge of at the distance of a century from their times. But it would appear their wit was of the social, unpremeditated, conversational character, in which Sydney Smith, Talleyrand, Hook, and Barham particularly excelled in our times.

For conversational humor and drollery in the composition of quizzical verses, Sir Charles Hanbury Williams, the protegé of Sir Robert Walpole (if his contemporaries speak truly of him), can hardly have been excelled by any modern humorist. The social character of the clubs, taverns, or coffee-houses of those days was favorable to the development of conversational talent.*

Selwyn, the man renowned for social wit, was utterly deficient in the gift of oratory. He sat forty years in Parliament for Gloucester, and never spoke on any question. He was always torpid as well as silent in the House.

Sir Hanbury Williams, the celebrated sayer also of *bon mots*, and composer of pointed epigrams, a man of astounding audacity in turning sacred subjects into ridicule, and treating the most solemn subjects with flippant jocularity and revolting levity, sat in the House of Commons a silent member, rapt in gloom, which terminated in insanity and suicide.

"Sayers of good things," in general, are not men of great powers of eloquence. Wits who can set the table in a roar, and give utterance to *bon mots* of remarkable drollery, may be incapable of delivering twenty consecutive sentences on any serious subject before a number of people prepared to listen to them.

* Count D'Orsay was a member of Crockford's as long as it lasted, and afterward of the Coventry. An attempt was made to get him into "White's," but it was discovered there were some parties who were determined to exclude him, and consequently his friends withdrew his name before the ballot took place.

D'Orsay was no exception to the rule. He abounded in rich humor, and excelled in repartee. There was an air of aristocratic nonchalance in the grave irony of his conversational sallies. He gave vent to his wit in the quietest tone, and with the most immovable features possible. He was an adept in the art of quizzing people who were at all ridiculous with singular composure of mien and manner. His performances in this line were gone through with ease and elegance, but the gift of eloquence was not bestowed on him.

Of D'Orsay's rich humor and repartee, it might be said, like Selwyn's:

> "*His* social wit, which, never kindling strife,
> Blazed in the small, sweet courtesies of life;
> Those little sapphires round the diamond shone,
> Lending soft radiance to the richer stone."

It would be difficult to convey in words any precise idea of D'Orsay's wit and powers of facetiousness in conversation. A mere report would be in vain of the *bon mots* he uttered, without a faithful representation of his quiet, imperturbable manner, his arch look, the command of varied emphasis in his utterance, the anticipatory indications of coming drollery in the expression of his countenance, the power of making his *entourage* enter into his thoughts, and his success in prefacing his *jeu d'esprit* by significant glances and gestures, suggestive of ridiculous ideas.

The literary artist who could describe these peculiarities must be no ordinary word-painter.

D'Orsay had made a study of the wit of Talleyrand, and he became a proficient in that species of refined conversational *esprit*, combining terseness of language, and neatness of expression, and certitude of aim, with the polish of the shaft and the sharpness of the point of an intellectual weapon of rare excellence.

The *macaronis* of a century ago, the *bucks*, *bloods*, and *beaus* of a later period, represented by the *fops*, *exquisites*, or *dandies* —the inane exclusives—the ephemeral *petits maîtres* of our times, are not the tribe which furnish men of fashion of D'Orsay's stamp. D'Orsay was a fop in attire and appearance, but his foppery was only a spice of vanity, superadded to superior intellectual powers, which condescended at times to assume a dandyish character.

D'Orsay's fine taste was particularly exhibited in the construction and turn-out of those well-known, elegant vehicles of his and Lady Blessington, which used to attract so much attention in Hyde Park a few years ago. D'Orsay, like Grammont, has left reminiscences of promenade achievements—"*à cheval et en voiture*"—in that favored locality, but of a very different character.

In the time of Grammont, "Hyde Park, as every one knows, was the promenade of London." In 1659 it was thus described to a nobleman of France:

"I did frequently, in the spring, accompany my Lord N—— into a field near the town, which they call Hide Park; the place not unpleasant, and which they use as our course, but with nothing of that order, equipage, and splendor; being such an assembly of wretched jades and hackney-coaches, as, next a regiment of carr men, there is nothing approaching the resemblance. The Park was, it seems, used by the late king and nobility for the freshness of the air and the goodly prospect,"* &c. . . . .

In these latter days Hyde Park makes a different figure in the pages of Mr. Patmore. The scene he describes is the ring, and the writer of the sketch is supposed to be lounging there, gazing at the brilliant equipages as they pass, and the celebrities of fashion who figure there.

"Observe that green chariot, just making the turn of the unbroken line of equipages. Though it is now advancing toward us, with at least a dozen carriages between, it is to be distinguished from the throng by the elevation of its driver and footman above the ordinary level of the line. As it comes nearer, we can observe the particular points which give it that perfectly *distingué* appearance which it bears above all others in the throng. They consist of the *white* wheels, lightly picked out

* A Character of England, as it was lately presented to a Nobleman of France, 12mo, 1659, p. 54. Ap. Grammont's Mem.

with green and crimson; the high-stepping action, blood-like shape, and brilliant *manège* of its dark bay horses; the perfect *style* of its driver; the height (six feet two) of its slim, spider-limbed, powdered footman, perked up at least three feet above the roof of the carriage, and occupying his eminence with that peculiar air of accidental superiority, half *petit maître*, half plow-boy, which we take to be the ideal of footman perfection; and, finally, the exceedingly light, airy, and (if we may so speak) the intellectual character of the whole set-out. The arms and supporters blazoned on the centre panels, and the small coronet beneath the window, indicate the nobility of station; and if ever the nobility of nature was blazoned on the 'complement extern' of humanity, it is on the lovely face within—lovely as ever, though it has been loveliest among the lovely for a longer time than we dare call to our own recollection, much less to that of the fair being before us.

"But, see! what is this vision of the age of chivalry, that comes careering toward us, on horseback, in the form of a stately cavalier, than whom nothing has been witnessed in modern times more noble in air and bearing, more splendid in person, more *distingué* in dress, more consummate in equestrian skill, more radiant in intellectual expression, and altogether more worthy and fitting to represent one of those knights of the olden time, who warred for truth and beauty beneath the banner of Cœur de Lion. It is Count D'Orsay, son-in-law of the late Lord Blessington, and brother to the beautiful Duchesse de Guiche. Those who have the pleasure of being personally intimate with this accomplished foreigner will confirm our testimony that no man has ever been more popular in the upper circles, or has better deserved to be so. His inexhaustible good spirits and good nature, his lively wit, his generous disposition, and his varied acquirements, make him the favorite companion of his own sex; while his unrivaled personal pretensions render him, to say the least, 'the observed of all observers' of the other sex. Indeed, since the loss of poor William Locke, there has been nobody to even dispute the palm of female admiration with Count D'Orsay."*

* My Friends and Acquaintances, &c., vol. i., p. 104.

D'Orsay's position in English fashionable society was not due to rank, wealth, or connections, or to his generally admitted excellence of taste in all matters appertaining to attire, equipage, the adornment of saloons, "the getting up" of liveries, the training of his tigers, or the turning out of cabs, tilburies, chariots, and other vehicles remarkable for elegance of form or lightness of construction.

It is very evident that the individual was something more than a mere fop and man of fashion, or "a compound even of Hercules and Adonis," who could count among his friends the Duke of Wellington, Marquis Wellesley, the Lords Brougham, Lyndhurst, and Byron; and such men as Landor, Forster, D'Israeli, the Bulwers, &c.

The foreigner could be no ordinary person who figured in the society of the most eminent men of England for nearly twenty years, and who, in circles where genius, as well as *haut ton*, had its shrines, "claimed kindred there, and had his claim allowed."

D'Orsay's celebrity was undisputed as a man of fashion—a noble-looking, classically-moulded, English-mannered young Frenchman "of the *vielle cour*"—a *beau monde* gentleman, at once graceful, dignified, frank, and *debonnaire*, full of life, wit, humor, and originality—an "*exquisite*" of the first water in brilliant circles—an admirable rider, fit "to witch the world" of the Parks of London "with noble horsemanship;" a keen sportsman, a capital boxer for an amateur, a good swimmer, an excellent swordsman, a famous shot, a celebrated cricket-player; at one time a great collector of classical rarities, "far gone (like Horace Walpole in his youth) in medals, lamps, idols, prints, and all the small commodities of antiquity;" at another time a zealous partisan of a great conspirator, and great promoter of his plans to effect a revolution.

Alfred D'Orsay figured, in his day, in all these characters; but, alas! of what avail to his memory is the celebrity he obtained in any of them?

All the celebrity which his true friends may desire to be coupled with his name is that which he derived from the exercise of his fine talents as an artist, and of his kindly feelings as a man naturally disposed to be benevolent, generous, and open-hearted.

In Dickens's "Household Words" (No. 176, p. 536) there are a few kind words spoken of poor D'Orsay, in some allusions made to the former occupants of "the little stuccoed houses" of Kensington Gore, contiguous to Lady Blessington's: "At number 5 lived Count D'Orsay, whose name is publicly synonymous with elegant and graceful accomplishments; and who, by those who knew him well, is affectionately remembered and regretted as a man whose great abilities might have raised him to any distinction, and whose gentle heart even a world of fashion left unspoiled."

Mr. Patmore, in his recent work, "My Friends and Acquaintances" (vol. i., p. 230), alluding to one of the chief difficulties of Count D'Orsay's social position in England, and the anomalies in the constitution of fashionable society there, says: "And yet it was in England that Count D'Orsay, while a mere boy, made the fatal mistake of marrying one beautiful woman, while he was, without daring to confess it even to himself, madly in love with another still more beautiful, whom he could not marry—because, I say, under these circumstances, and discovering his fatal error when too late, he separated himself from his wife almost at the church door, he was, during the greatest part of his social career in England, cut off from the advantages of the more fastidious portion of high female society by the indignant fiat of its heads and leaders."

A man in his twenty-seventh year can hardly be designated as a mere boy, nor can the circumstance of his separation from his wife "almost at the church door" be accounted for in any manner that will appear excusable to the friends of the young deserted wife, or the fastidious portion of high female society in England or elsewhere. This marriage was not only a great misfortune for those who were married, but a great crime on the part of those who promoted that marriage, and were consenting to it.

If any comment must be made on this unfortunate union and its results, might it not be better to summon courage, and, taking counsel of Montesquieu, to speak out a solemn truth on an occasion that can be best served by its enumeration?

"*Religion, good or bad, is the only test we have for the probity of men.*"

There is no dependence to be placed in probity or purity of life without the protection of religion. Human honor is inadequate to the security of either. There is an amount of indigence at which honor, long resisting, will stagger in the end; there is a degree of temptation at which honor will suffer vice to approach her in the mask of innocent freedom, and will dally with it till infamy itself becomes familiar to her bosom. But respectable folks, who figure in good society, solemn-faced sages and literary celebrities, will say it is false: honor is alone sufficient to regulate the minds of educated men, and to prevent all disorders in society. It is to libel honor to say that it is sufficiently strong to bind respectable members without religion, and that the latter is only needful for the happiness of people in another world. Nevertheless, there is not one of those people who does not know in his own breast that such is not the case—that in his own character and conduct the assertion does not hold good, and in very few of those of the individuals with whom he is best acquainted. There is no dependence on any man's probity or any woman's virtue whose reliance is not placed in religion.

Nothing more can be said with profit or advantage on this subject, except that it is deeply to be lamented this marriage was forced on Count D'Orsay, and that he consented to contract a marriage with a young lady for whom he entertained no sentiments of love or kindness.

It would be very unjust to D'Orsay, with all his errors, to place him in the same category with his profligate countryman De Grammont, and still more unjust to set him down on the same list with the Dukes of Buckingham, Wharton, and Queensberry, and the more modern antiquated libertine of exalted rank and vast possessions, the Marquis of Hertford.

In one very essential matter he differed from most of them. Though practically not living in the world of fashion under the restraints of religion, all the influences of an early recollection of its sacred character were not lost, and these, which, in the midst of a wild and thoughtless career, sufficed at least to show that all respect for that character had not been wholly abandoned, and that they were still faintly perceptible in some of the noble qualities possessed by him, at the close of life were strongly manifested, and made the mode of his departure from it the best, the only consolation taken that could be given to a sister eminently good and spiritually minded.

The close of that career, and the ministrations on it, form a strong contrast with the termination of a life of an English duke, and the attendance on a death-bed, of which Sir N. Wraxall, in his Memoirs, has left a remarkable description.

"When Queensberry lay dying, in December, 1810, his bed was covered with billets and letters to the number of at least seventy, mostly, indeed, addressed to him by females of every description and of every rank, from duchesses down to ladies of easiest virtue. Unable, from his attenuated state, to open or peruse them, he ordered them, as they arrived, to be laid on his bed, where they remained, the seals unbroken, till he expired."

If the sordid homage paid to the wealth of the expiring debauchée had been offered only by the ladies of easiest virtue, there might be little to be surprised at; but what is to be said or thought of the ladies of reputed virtue, of exalted rank, who manifested so much sympathy for the old libertine of enormous wealth, and still more enormous wickedness?

Society suffers little from charity toward its erring members, but morality suffers a great deal when habitual vice and dissoluteness of life of persons in high places or regal station, which never has been abandoned or repented of, find sycophants and slaves to pander to them, and people, forgetful of the dignity of their position or their pursuits, to lend their services to palliate them.

Count Alfred D'Orsay died in Paris, the 4th of August, 1852, in his fifty-second year, having survived the Countess of Blessington three years and two months. His remains were laid in the same sepulchral chamber in which hers were deposited.

The monument erected to her memory at Chambourcy had been hardly finished, when it became the resting-place of all that is left of the accomplished, highly-gifted, generous-hearted Alfred D'Orsay:

"Pulvis et umbra, nomen, nihil."

CHAPTER XIV.

PRELIMINARY NOTICE OF THE CORRESPONDENCE OF LADY BLESSINGTON.

THERE is one thing well worthy of observation, and that must strike every person who looks over the extensive correspondence of Lady Blessington, namely, the implicit trust that was put in her judgment and integrity by the most eminent men of her time in politics, literature, and art. Statesmen of great renown for wisdom, judges and grave lawyers, men of letters and science devoted to philosophical pursuits, seem to have had entire confidence in her honor, discretion, and common sense and kindness of heart. They communicated with her with the utmost freedom, and evidently with a firm conviction that their confidence would never be abused. In their letters it is plainly to be seen how fully sensible they were the only account that confidence would be ever turned to by Lady Blessington would be to promote peace where strife had sprung up; to make people who had been estranged think less unkindly of one another; and those who were at variance disposed to consider that the state of nature in their several pursuits was not a state of war.

Lady Blessington's correspondents were not of one class, or country, or profession, or pursuit; they were of all orders of high intelligence, of all lands, of all positions ennobled by genius, of every science, art, or walk in literature, or in public life distinguished for talent, or deserving in her opinion to attain any distinction in it, and there were to be found among them likewise persons who had no pretensions to intellectual gifts, or remarkable abilities of any kind, but who possessed amiable qualities, honorable principles and kindly feelings, bookish people not pedantic, amateurs of art without the airs of *dilettanti*, travelers more at home in a desert than a drawing-room, who had seen outlandish places, and could be drawn out a little on the subject of their peregrinations on rare occasions.

Among the correspondents of her ladyship we find princes and princesses, authors and authoresses of all lands, rich and poor, generals and critics, poets and politicians, publishers and diplomatists, play-actors, novelists, and ministers of state, lord chancellors and literary ladies, peers of the realm, nabobs of India, natives of Hindostan, hidalgos of Spain of "thirteen grandfathers," descendants of ancient Irish kings, and gentlemen, in fine, of no ancestors at all, renowned in literature, art, or science.

The lady who was engaged in this extensive correspondence could be no ordinary person. It was carried on for a long series of years with many of the master-spirits, not only of England, but of the world.

The qualities of mind and of disposition of this gifted lady, the influence of that goodness of heart that was diffused over every act and word of hers, the fascination of her manners, and all the collateral allurements of her external beauty, could surely be of no common order, that could procure for her not only the admiration and esteem of passing observation, but such long-enduring friendship and affectionate regard as we see, by this correspondence, she enjoyed to the close of life at the hands of many of the most eminent persons of our age.

There are many difficulties of an editorial kind to be dealt with in the present undertaking; and one of the most serious that presented itself was that of the arrangement of the correspondence.

The natural and usual course would be to introduce the letters generally in the order of their dates, and not those of each correspondent consecutively There was, however, a disadvantage in such a course as this to be considered, and a very great difficulty to be surmounted.

Lady Blessington's intercourse with eminent persons distinguished in literature, art, science, and politics, and her literary career, had three phases: one of these was included in the period between her marriage and her departure for the Continent—her early London life from 1818 to 1822; another was the period of her Continental tour and sojourn chiefly in Naples—her Italian life from 1823 to 1829; and, lastly, that which includes the period between her return to England, her residence in Seamore Place, and the break-up of her establishment at Gore House, from the end of 1831 to the spring of 1849, a few weeks before her decease in Paris—the period of her second London career of nearly nineteen years.

Each of these phases in the life of Lady Blessington was distinct from the other, in the composition of the society in which she moved, in the development of literary tastes, the progress of intellectual culture, the nature of her literary pursuits, at one time engaged in solely on account of the delight taken in them, at another for sake of distinction, and finally with a view to gain.

Her correspondence partook of the nature of those differences and distinctions, and the value of it seemed to consist, to a great extent, in that distinct individualism which belonged to the letters, and the style and subjects of them in such numerous instances, that to separate and scatter the several letters of each writer over different portions of the work would have been to break up the interest taken in the several subjects, and the connection between matters frequently referred to in the letters of the same writers.

The difficulty above referred to, in the way of arrangement according to dates, was, in fact, insuperable. Literary men and artists are singularly prone to forgetfulness in regard to dates and addresses in their correspondence. A vast number of the letters addressed to Lady Blessington are without date or place of residence; a great many have the date of the week specified but not of the month, and where both are to be found the year is seldom mentioned. In many cases the dates are determined by the post-marks, but in many more, where the letters have been written prior to the general use of envelopes, there is no clew whatever to the date, and the period can only be approximately arrived at by knowledge of the place where Lady Blessington was residing at the time such letters were received by her, or derived from matters referred to in them.

For the above-mentioned reasons, and some others which may readily suggest themselves to the reader, I have, as a general rule, inserted the letters of the different correspondents consecutively, as they appear to have been addressed by Lady Blessington.

In the notices prefixed to the letters, I have endeavored to bring before the readers of these volumes the correspondents and friends of Lady Blessington, and the acquaintances especially of her ladyship during her sojourn in Naples and Rome, in a way to make them recognizable, and to recall the particular traits of character which belonged to them.*

In the letters of Lady Blessington, it will be in vain to seek for those excellencies in the art of epistolary correspondence, graces of style and composition, vivacity, esprit, and epigrammatic power of expression which are to be found in the correspondence of Madame de Sevigné, and more or less in that of the Marquise du Deffand, Madame Geoffrin, our own Lady Mary Wortley Montague, or Madame D'Arblay.

But, in one respect, the letters of Lady Blessington were not inferior to those of any of the above-mentioned letter-writing celebrities, namely, the manifestation in her letters of kindly feelings, as ardently expressed, as generously and unselfishly entertained. The best actions of mankind are the worst recorded facts of history and biography. Of the many generous acts of Lady Blessington, we find few records in her correspondence, but we shall find in her letters evidences enough (undesignedly furnished by her) of that natural and unaffected goodness of heart, which manifested itself in an affectionate interest in the welfare of her friends, an enduring, unselfish regard, that was never influenced by any change in their position or accident of

* The want of a slight thread of descriptive illustration of the position, character, or peculiarities of persons whose correspondence is introduced into the biographies of well-known persons has been often felt and complained of. A brief notice of the principal productions or characteristics, traits of originality or remarkable qualities of many of those whose letters form a part of this correspondence, will be found prefixed to the letters of several of the writers.

fortune. It mattered not to her an iota, in her estimation of their worth and merits, however altered for the worse might be the condition of friends she had known long and well, however depressed by adverse circumstances, and fallen on that account in the opinion of the world, they were never forsaken by her—the feelings of Lady Blessington toward them were unaffected by any change in their fortunes. There was no "feigning of generosity" in the uniform kindness of this steadfast friendship—the same in adversity as in prosperity—no affectation of benevolence in this manifestation of genial feelings—these were part and parcel of a noble disposition naturally turned to goodness.

It has been truly observed that, "in addressing even a common acquaintance (in a letter), there is a kindlier feeling, a courtesy, which tends to endear and to familiarize; but in addressing a friend, there is evidence that one never loves one's friends half so well as when writing to them! Every act of kindness, every amiable quality, rushes on the memory and the imagination, softened by the real absence, and heightened by an ideal presence.

"*This constant sense of the presence of her correspondent is the greatest charm of that queen of letter-writers, Madame de Sevigné.* We feel throughout that every thought, every word, is addressed to one individual, and to one only—the daughter, the idolized daughter, who filled that warm heart."*

Lady Blessington did not write to her friends for effect—she reserved that object for her conversation. She sat down in her dressing-room to talk on paper naturally and familiarly with good-natured familiar friends, as if it was a relief to her to give expression unreservedly to thoughts *en deshabille*, and to feelings for which no domino of affectation was required. She wrote to those friends carelessly and affectionately, as if she felt that every trifle would interest, every slight allusion would be understood, every sprightly fancy would amuse, every word of kindness would be appreciated, and every expression of pain or sorrow, or reference to her own cares or anxieties, would meet with sympathy.

* New Monthly Magazine, vol. ii., 1821, p. 143.

No attempt at fine writing is to be met with in the letters of Lady Blessington. There was too much heart in her epistolary correspondence, and too little disposition to enter into discussions in letters to her friends on any topics but those which related to her own immediate affairs, and which concerned the interests or happiness of others, to give a literary character to her correspondence in general that would interest the public in it.

For this reason, out of a vast number of the letters, or rather notes of Lady Blessington, none have been selected for publication except those which came within the limits of the last-named category. The number of her ladyship's letters is not large, but the few that are presented to the public will be found to give a favorable opinion of the writer's sound common sense, clear conception, kindly feelings, and amiable disposition.

I have rejected a vast number of letters of mere compliment on ordinary subjects of correspondence between friends, inquiries after health, references to private matters, intimations of intended visits, and apologies for long silence, non-appearance at parties, &c.

Sir William Jones, in one of his lectures, said, "For what I have produced I claim only your indulgence: it is for what I have suppressed that I am entitled to your thanks."

CHAPTER XV.

SIR WILLIAM GELL.

The name of Gell will recall to many minds very pleasing reminiscences of Rome and Naples—his small classic house at Rome, fitted for a scholar's home, that might have served for the abode of Petrarch, with its adornments far from costly, but its arrangements elaborately tasteful, with its pleasant gardens and trellised walks; his place of residence, too, at Naples in the latter years of his life—its picturesque locality, his drawing-room, library, studio, museum, all combined in one very moderately-sized apartment, with such a store of rarities, old folios in vellum, modern topography, and illustrated travels richly bound, caricatures, charts, maps, and drawings; the light guitar, which he had recourse to so often, in moments of torture, and for whose sweet remedial influences he had "thrown physic to the dogs"—not, however, to the well-bred animals of the canine species who had the entrée of his salon, and the privilege of his best chairs and sofas—so many models, too, of ancient structures, so many curious things in so small a space,

> "that still folks wondered Gell
> Had one small room could hold so much so well."

In 1814, when her royal highness, the Princess of Wales, left England, and proceeded to Milan, via Brunswick, her establishment consisted of Lady Charlotte Lindsay and Lady Elizabeth Forbes, maids of honor; Mr. St. Leger, Sir William Gell, and the Honorable Keppel Craven, chamberlains; Captain Hesse, equerry, and Dr. Holland, physician. Mr. St. Leger remained at Brunswick. Shortly after her royal higness's arrival in Milan, Bartholomew Bergami was taken into her service as courier and valet. The princess and her suite set out for Rome and Naples the latter end of October, and arrived in the latter city on the 8th of November, 1814. King Joachim Murat was then sovereign of Naples. Her royal highness gave a fancy ball to his Neapolitan majesty, in which she appeared in three characters; first as a Neapolitan peasant, secondly as "The Genius of History," and thirdly as a Turkish peasant, in costumes by no means cumbersome, though not quite in accordance with the notions of some persons of her English suite. The princess remained in Naples till March, 1815. She then took her departure for Rome, Genoa, and Milan, leaving four of her suite, Lady E. Forbes, Sir W. Gell, Mr. Craven, and Captain Hesse, in Naples. Lady Charlotte Lindsay had previously left her royal highness at Leghorn. At Genoa she was joined by Lady Charlotte Campbell, who remained with her only two or three months. After her return from Palestine, Sir William Gell accompanied her from Naples to Rome, and continued with her there in attendance upon her as chamberlain while she remained in Rome.

The following year he was again about three months in attendance on her at Frascati and Rufinellé; and again, on the occasion of her last visit to Rome, he attended her for some days.

In his evidence on the trial before the House of Lords, Sir William swore that it was on account of an attack of gout he had quitted her royal highness's service; and, "notwithstanding the opportunities he had of observing the conduct of the queen and Bergami toward each other, never saw any impropriety pass between them upon any occasion."

Nevertheless, the opinion of Sir William of his royal mistress's habits, modes, and manners was not more favorable than those of Lord Malmesbury, of which he has left a curious record in his diary.

In 1815 and 1816, we find Gell, in his letters, under various signatures—"Blue Beard," "Adonis," "Anacharsis," "Gellius (Aulus)," and while still retaining the title, and occasionally filling the office, of chamberlain to the Princess of Wales, indulging in his sarcastic propensities—playing the part of a male gossip, conveying little bits of scandal in humorous passages, and making fun of his royal mistress for the sport of the fair Philistines who had once been maids of honor and friends of her royal highness.

But even at that time Sir William was a martyr to gout and rheumatism. In December, 1816, he wrote from Bologna that he was then reduced to the necessity of confining himself to his fireside; but, in giving the account of his ailments, he could not help having a fling at his royal lady's orthography:

"To a person of my romantic disposition, *reduit* by *di dizette* of legs and now of arms to the fireside, it is a great comfort to have escaped from the land of wine, houses, and carts, and wooden shoes, and neckless children (France), and to find one's self once more in Italy, and to be able to leave my painful leg or arm for a moment out of bed without finding it frostbitten."*

Sir W. Gell and the Honorable Keppel Craven are mentioned in Moore's diary of August, 1820, as being "on the way from Naples to England as witnesses for the queen." "Gell still a coxcomb, but rather amusing—said the Constitution of Naples

* Diary and Times of George the Fourth, vol. iv., p. 129.

came in a gig (*corricolo*)—told some ludicrous things about the Duchess of Devonshire's sway at Rome: her passion for Gonsalvo, her admiration for the purity of the Roman government." (Memoirs, vol. iii., p. 137.) Moore's compendious opinion of Gell as "a *coxcomb, rather amusing*," if relied on, would give not only a very unfavorable, but a very incorrect notion of his character and his acquirements. He was a man of much erudition and artistic talents, and of great humor. Sir William Gell's literary tastes were chiefly devoted to antiquarian researches.

For the last twenty years, Naples was his head-quarters. There he was universally known and respected, and terminated his earthly career.

Sir William Gell was a man of very amiable character, extremely amusing and lively, fond of the society of young people, with much singularity of mind, and originality of character, manners, and ideas.

His indolent easiness of temper had something in it of a philosophical calmness of an Epicurean character. The common objects of men's ambition to him were not worth the trouble of the pursuit. He was at once indifferent, apathetic, and unimpassioned in the society of men struggling for wealth, glory, or exalted dignities. He smiled serenely at the inordinate trouble they gave themselves, at all their great cares for little ends, at all the great weaknesses of little men of large desires. And yet this pococurante gentleman had many difficulties to encounter to secure for himself "les douceurs d'une vie privée et oisive," and many little harmless vanities and weaknesses of his own to make him singular and eccentric, of which, however, he was entirely unconscious.

All his tastes were of a literary and artistic turn, and all were of a refined, scholar-like, and some of them rather of a Sybaritic kind. Like Sir William Temple, "he loved painting, and music, and statuary, and gardening," and *embellishing buildings*. Health, and ease, and fine weather were the constituents of his happiness: Temple wrote, "Le seul homme que j'envie dans le monde c'est Milord Falconbridge, que son embassade va conduire dans un si beau climat, ou il va gouter tous les charmes attachés aux delicates et spirituelles conversations d'Italié. Il trouvera les jours et les esprits egalemens purs et brillants."

Though a martyr to gout, Sir William Gell's natural gayety and good humor were little affected by his natural sufferings; and with the most profound knowledge and information he combined the utmost simplicity and playfulness.

Some of his topographical books were illustrated by himself, as, for instance, his Pompeii, Greece, and other descriptive productions of an antiquarian kind—works acknowledged to be the best of their several sorts and classes.

In June, 1834, referring to a conversation at Lady Blessington's, Willis, in his "Pencilings by the Way," 3d edition, London, 1849, refers to some valuable notices of Sir William Gell, illustrative of an interesting portion of the latter part of Sir Walter Scott's career:

"She (Lady B.) had received from Sir William Gell, at Naples, the manuscript of a volume upon the last days of Sir Walter Scott. It was a melancholy chronicle of weakened intellect and ruined health, and the book was suppressed; but there were two or three circumstances narrated in its pages which were interesting. Soon after his arrival at Naples, Sir Walter went with his physician and one or two friends to the great museum. It happened that on the same day a large collection of students and Italian literati were assembled in one of the rooms to discuss some newly-discovered manuscripts. It was soon known that the 'Wizard of the North' was there, and a deputation was sent immediately to request him to honor them by presiding at their session. At this time Scott was a wreck, with a memory that retained nothing for a moment, and limbs almost as helpless as an infant's. He was dragging about among the relics of Pompeii, taking no interest in any thing he saw, when their request was made known to him through his physician. 'No, no,' said he, 'I know nothing of their lingo. Tell them I am not well enough to come.' He loitered on, and in about half an hour after he turned to Dr. H. and said, 'Who was that you said wanted to see me?' The doctor explained. 'I'll go,' said he; 'they shall see me, if they wish it;' and, against the advice of his friends, who feared it would be too much for his strength, he mounted the staircase, and made his appearance at the door. A burst of enthusiastic cheers welcomed him on the threshold; and forming in two lines, many of them on their knees, they seized his hands as he passed, kissed them, thanked him in their passionate language for the delight with which he had filled the world, and placed him in the chair with the most fervent expressions of gratitude for his condescension. The discussion went on; but, not understanding a syllable of their language, Scott was soon wearied, and his friends, observing it, pleaded the state of his health as an apology, and he rose to take his leave. These enthusiastic children of the South crowded once more around him, and, with exclamations of affection and even tears, kissed his hands once more, assisted his tottering steps, and sent after him a confused murmur of blessings as the door closed on his retiring form."

The scene is described by Sir W. Gell as one of the most affecting he had ever witnessed

His career of authorship commenced so early as 1804, when he published "The Topography of Troy," folio. Subsequently appeared "The Geography and Antiquities of Ithaca," 4to, 1808, "The Itinerary of Greece"—"Travels in the Morea"—"The Topography of Rome"—and, finally, his "Pompeiana," the most interesting and extensively known of all his works.

Sir William resided in Italy since 1820; occasionally at Rome, but chiefly at his beautifully situated and elegantly arranged villa in Naples, in the society of his erudite friend, Sir William Drummond, and that of his old friend and amiable companion, the Hon. Keppel Craven. After the death of Sir William Drummond at Rome in 1828, his friendship with Craven appeared to have become more closely cemented than ever, and it went on increasing in strength to the period of his death.

Gell's notions of authorship were of a very aristocratic nature. All his works were brought out on so large and extensive a scale as to be out of the reach of that class of readers for whom his topographical and antiquarian researches would have been especially useful—for travelers in those countries whose remains were described by him. But it was the misfortune of this enlightened and accomplished man to be an aristocrat in all things, and to mar his attainments by *hankering* after great people—"patricians born to greatness," or parvenus having "greatness thrust upon them"—thrust on "good society," and admitted there par droit de richesses ou lieu de naissance.

Sir William Gell, it must be admitted, frittered away his time and talents for upward of twenty years on the fashionable fribbles of the little coteries of English traveling aristocracy that customarily wintered in Rome, and passed the spring or autumn in Naples or its vicinity.

Every one delighted in his society; in his conversation and correspondence he was equally amusing and agreeable.

When Sir William Gell died, Lady Blessington might have truly said, "J'ai perdu en lui mon meilleur causeur."

There is an admirable sketch of Gell in a letter of James Ramsay, Esq., a resident merchant of Naples, an old and valued friend of mine, addressed to the Hon. Richard Keppel Craven in the spring of 1836, soon after the death of Sir William Gell, urging on Mr. Craven the task of composing a biographical sketch of his deceased friend, and eventually signifying his intention of writing such a memoir:

"I frequently urged," says Mr. Ramsay, "our inestimable friend to compose his biographical memoirs; to bequeath to posterity the 'personal narrative' of a career in which the pursuits of science were so happily blended with the lighter occupations and brilliant attractions [distractions] of society. I said it would be a great pity if the rich fund of observation and anecdote which he had accumulated should be lost with him, and that it might be screened from public view until the writer should be 'removed beyond the reach of criticism or of ridicule.' He sometimes appeared to be half inclined to adopt my suggestion, and owned that he possessed materials sufficiently 'piquant,' if he should determine to employ them. Will you forgive me for insinuating that the task which he failed, or rather neglected to accomplish, seems naturally and gracefully, when time shall have in some degree moderated the more poignant emotions of regret, to devolve upon you? upon you, his juvenile companion, the friend and fellow-traveler of maturer years, the depositary of his inmost sentiments, and probably of many of a series of letters in which events and opinions have been faithfully recorded.

"Though enjoying Sir William's acquaintance and intimacy during a considerable period, I can not presume to hope that I could furnish any important contributions toward such an undertaking, otherwise I should be most ready to co-operate with those who are so much better qualified. His correspondents would, I dare say, willingly communicate his letters, or extracts from them, and the names of these correspondents are doubtless known to you.

"There is a peculiar charm in the unguarded effusions of eminent persons, when, casting off the artificial garb with which rank or other adventitious circumstances may have invested them, they paint their natural character and feelings without any other reserve or restraint than those which discretion prescribes.

"Hume and Gibbon have left us interesting, though very different memorials of this description, and the familiar letters of Munro, of Collingwood, of Mackintosh, and of such as resemble them, will be fondly cherished when their public achievements are perused with historical indifference. But I beg pardon for detaining you with remarks so obvious.

"If, on the one hand, it is to be regretted that Sir William did not finish his novel of 'Julia di Gonzaga,' it may, on the other, be permitted to doubt whether or how far such a work would have added to his literary fame. Of his powers of imagination and invention I had no adequate opportunity of judging; but, though the novel might have contained some lively scenes, some striking descriptions, some sparkling dialogue, I should be inclined to question—yet by no means conclusively—whether a profound knowledge of the human heart, of the intricate mazes and complicated workings of passion, and feeling, and sentiment, were among his distinguishing attributes.

"He had not made a *study* of *composition*, and, in the confusion of foreign languages, the purity of his own had still become considerably impaired. These observations, dictated by an affectionate and jealous attachment to his memory, are hazarded with diffidence, as they are with deference submitted to your taste and judgment.

"I am aware that the scope of the memoir would be chiefly limited to private circulation; and at a time when the novel and the romance usurp, if not the honors, at least the emoluments of literature, the noble-minded author would seek and find his reward in another disinterested offering on the altar of friendship. I am, &c. J. R."

A SKETCH OF THE CHARACTER OF SIR WILLIAM GELL, BY JAMES RAMSAY, ESQ.

"The merits of Sir William Gell as an author, chiefly on subjects of antiquity and topography, are already sufficiently known and appreciated by the public. The fruits of much patient research, of ingenious conjecture, of great personal activity and industry, with admirable graphic illustrations, his works are valuable helps to the student, and an accurate guide for the traveler. In attempting the more difficult task of delineating his general and private character, as deduced from an intercourse of many years, if I am conscious of any bias, it must be in favor of one with whom I have spent so many delightful hours, unalloyed by the recollection of even a passing cloud; for to me he was uniformly kind and attentive. Yet I will endeavor to be impartial, though at the hazard of incurring the reproach of being rather severe.

"Sir William started in life with the advantages of a handsome person—of a fine, open, placid countenance—of a prepossessing manner—of a remote ancestry, and of an extensive connection with the best society. He traveled at a period when travelers were rare, and thus early acquired a distinction which he continued to maintain. Possessing general, though superficial information, both literary and scientific, including some acquaintance with the Oriental languages and hieroglyphics, he sketched beautifully, had a taste for and some knowledge of music, and excelled as an easy, off-hand, unaffected correspondent; indifferent, indeed insensible, to the graces of composition, yet universally courted for a style of *naïveté* 'beyond the reach of art.' Although, however, led by the course of his studies into classical inquiry and reference, the character of a profound scholar will not be assigned to him, notwithstanding his general reading; he had little taste for literature, and never seemed to feel the beauties of poetry. I should say, indeed, that, in other respects, his taste—meaning by this term a delicate and just perception of the beautiful—was far from being refined, and that that defect was apparent in all, even his personal decorations, by a preference for gay, gaudy colors, striking contrasts, and meretricious ornament.

"To depth of thought Sir William would have no just pretensions. He rarely made a general reflection or observation; all his conclusions were particular. On many of the important questions by which the world is now agitated, he had no steady, fixed opinions; he had neither the boldness to form, nor the courage to avow his sentiments, which were very liable to be temporarily influenced by the last speaker, the last writer.

"In his political principles he was decidedly aristocratical, with a strong predilection for 'rank, fortune, and fashion,' our besetting sin!

"But it is in a companionable, sociable point of view that the memory of Sir William Gell will be most fondly cherished, his loss most deeply lamented by his surviving friends and acquaintances; for there he shone without a rival, with a charm peculiarly his own. To a considerable share of wit and humor—to a natural tact and penetration, improved by a long intercourse with the great world, to the habits and bearing of a 'high-bred gentleman,' Sir William added an unceasing flow of lively, playful language, sparkling dialogue, and brilliant repartee upon every topic which formed the subject of conversation, and this, his great forte both in company and *tête-à-tête*, was endless. Placing people of all classes on a footing of easy familiarity, and thus unlocking their confidence, he drew from them a perpetual supply of materials for his own combination — 'toujours varièes toujours renaissantes'—his house became the resort of all ranks, ages, and sexes, and his mornings one continued levee. The equanimity of his temper under the pressure of bodily infirmity, often of acute suffering, enhanced the value of a cheerful, humane, benevolent, charitable disposition, and even the shafts of sarcasm and of ridicule, in which he occasionally indulged, left no sting, because it was felt that they were the offspring of no malignant spirit. With all his resources, however, Sir William languished in solitude; he breathed only in the atmosphere of society; even his literary and other occupations were sometimes carried on in company, while conversing with those around him.

"He was fond of being looked up to as a patron and protector, and somewhat jealous of the ascendency which he thus sought to preserve.

"It has been said that, as in thinking, so in feeling, he was a stranger to any great depth; and certainly he seldom betrayed much emotion, or even expressed much interest in the fate of others. It is a remark of his friend, Lady Blessington, in one of her books, that 'persons the most remarkable for general kindness are those who have the least feeling.'

"Emulous of fame, he aspired after notoriety and display; and the latter was sometimes evinced by introducing subjects with which his auditors were very imperfectly conversant, in order, as it seemed, that he might excite their surprise and command their applause.

"In an argument he was easily vanquished; in a forward remark as easily checked; by superior powers painfully eclipsed. Sir William liked to be the presiding genius. In his acquaintances, visitors, guests, with a few exceptions, he preferred variety, novelty; and when these had lost the power of pleasing, he willingly resigned them, 'like the last month's magazine,' for others more attractive.

"Hence he was deemed by some people rather selfish, not quite sincere, and not sufficiently mindful of past favors; but in endeavoring to exhibit the various traits of a distinguished character, we ought always to bear in mind that they include many from which no human being is entirely exempt.

"Amid a boundless acquaintance, it may be questioned whether Sir William Gell had many really and truly attached friends. his affections were infinitely subdivided, frittered away; but he was a kind and indulgent master.

"He seemed to be a great favorite with the fair sex. They gathered—flocked around him; they confided in—they confessed to—they consulted him as a superior being! Yet all the youth, beauty, grace, accomplishments, whose homage he was constantly receiving, did rarely, in my hearing, call forth an admiring, never one enthusiastic, one impassioned sentiment. They might be 'well-looking,' 'well-mannered,' 'a pleasing person,' that was all. I often asked him *who* was the most beautiful woman he remembered to have met with? He replied that 'he thought he should say Lady Blessington.' Still, his behavior, attentions to, correspondence with ladies, were excellent, polite, and kind. In estimating character, we judge partly from what people do and say, and, *which frequently escapes them*, from what they do *not* do and say!

"In these peculiarities and other foibles we have, alas! only to recognize the imperfections from which none are free; but the verdict of an immense majority will decide in favor of the amiability, the charms of the character of Sir William Gell, and will confess he has left a blank which it will be difficult, if possible, to supply."

*** There are several busts of Sir William Gell, but none of them a good likeness. With the exception of a less aquiline nose, he bore a strong resemblance to the statue, said to be of Aristides, in the museum of Naples.

CHAPTER XVI.

LETTERS OF SIR WILLIAM GELL TO LADY BLESSINGTON.*

"Naples.

"My dear Lady Blessington,—A most horrid affair has taken place at Pæstum, Mr. Hunt and his wife having been murdered by robbers. Three

* The Blessingtons arrived in Naples in July, 1823. They established themselves at the Villa Belvidere, on the Vomero, about the 23d of the same month.

parties were at Pæstum—Mrs. Benzon and daughter, the Hunts, and a party of officers from 'The Revenge.' Mrs. Benzon was returning to Naples, and about two miles from Pæstum met four robbers, who with threats demanded and took all their money. They seem not to have ill treated them otherwise. Mrs. Benzon gave the alarm at Salerno, and sent *gens d'armes.* About a quarter of an hour after came Mr. and Mrs. Hunt by the same place. They tore off the vetturino and the servant from the box, and were ill treating the servant for having no more money while Mr. Hunt was descending from the carriage. Mr. Hunt seems to have remonstrated in violent terms at this, and one of the thieves said he would shoot him if he continued. Mr. Hunt seems to have continued, and to have said he dared not shoot him: this the enraged thief did with two balls, both of which passed through his body, and he fell from the step. One of the balls took a side slant, and went through the body and lungs of Mrs. Hunt also. The thieves, seeing what they had done, immediately fled without any booty. The husband and wife, the first almost insensible, were carried back to Pæstum. The husband died at half past seven o'clock of the same day. The act took place about one. Mrs. Hunt was carried to Mr. Belelli's, a decent house, and seemed for some time better, and the officers, sending Mr. Thompson here for assistance, remained with her. Dr. Watson went last night, about twelve o'clock, to see if he could do any good. It is almost certain Mrs. Hunt can not live. I have written this in a great hurry, having merely had time to give you an outline, but a correct one, of the facts, which I heard from Mr. Thompson himself. I have sent certain documents to Lord Blessington about Lady Falkiner, which the judge wishes you to see, because he says you are the person who knows most about the business. With kindest regards to the count and the 'Lady Julia,'* believe me most truly yours, dear Lady Blessington, W. GELL.

"A sua Eccellenza la Contessa di Blessington, Villa Belvidere, Vomero."

"Naples.

"Do your excellencies dine at home to-day? If you do, I purpose an ascent to the Belvidere. You are in danger of being rivaled with the archbishop† by Mrs. Beaumont and her three daughters, for whom he has conceived a passion. Most truly yours, WILLIAM GELL."

"Naples.

"When I had read Lord Byron, which I found very interesting, but most particularly the revengeful poem, which must have been written after some conversation with you about his wife, I found myself rather forlorn; but, recollecting my charge of the letters, I thought for some time what I should do

They remained there till March, 1825, and about the 25th of the latter month removed to the Villa Gallo, where they remained till February, 1826, when they left Naples for Rome.—R. R. M.

* The Lady Julia was Lady Blessington's sister, Miss Mary Anne Power.—R. R. M.

† The venerable Archbishop of Tarento.—R. R. M.

with them, so I took the liberty of going into the drawing-room, and, after some consideration, I put them carefully into a large red portfolio on the count's table, with a red ribbon, where pray go and take them, having made my apology for taking such a liberty with him. I am sorry Miss Power is angry with me, but I have nothing on my conscience. No Casorano came. I kiss your feet, and am ever yours, W. GELL."

"Naples.

"The devil has upset his inkstand in the clouds, and I think it therefore better to postpone my visit, as you were kind enough to say I might, if the world went upside down. Dr. Doratt, having engaged me to write, sent also yesterday to say he had forgotten his engagement to the Hamiltons, brute that he is for his pains. I will come when the weather changes, and, not to disturb you, will send the same morning to ask if it suits you. Kind compliments to your party. Perhaps you have got another Museum or other book. WILLIAM GELL."

"Naples.

"I lost no time in consulting the doctor, all the way down the hill, and as far as he goes there would be no difficulty, except his engagement with Sir William Drummond. He said, at the same time, what a fool he should look like if Sir William D. died in ten years, and he found himself without a shilling. It was resolved, therefore, to talk to Sir William, and the consequence was, a declaration that five years was to him the same as his whole life; that he would give the other hundred a year which I stated to be necessary for the present, and that he had left Dr. Watson £200 and some other things.*

"He said at the same time, that if Dr. Watson wished it, he was at liberty, and such a resolution should have no effect in changing his good intentions toward him.

"However, of course, seeing that Sir William listened to the reason of the case (which he always does when properly explained), the doctor would be very unwilling to give him any pain on the subject.

"You see you have been the cause of good, so let us console ourselves, and pray believe me, most truly and affectionately, W. GELL."

"Naples.

"According to your orders, I have told Mr. Craven that he has to appoint an early day to go to the Belvidere, and he will come on Wednesday.

"That being fixed, I have to inform your ladyship that the weather seemingly consenting to relent, Dr. Watson and I have an idea of a trip to Pompeii to-morrow, and having had a sort of half agreement with your amiable party, I think perhaps you may not be disinclined to the excursion.

* Dr. Watson, the medical attendant of Sir W. Drummond, one of the most eminent linguists of Europe.—R. R. M.

"Suppose we say we will meet there at or about twelve, and bring our dinners in our pockets, and dine either in the quarters at the great table, or any where else about three or four, for later it may be cold, but about three will be very agreeable, the place being sunny and sheltered. You can dine either in the villa at the end of the tombs, in the Triclinium of the tombs, or on that of the Actæon, in the centre of the town, or in the Forum, which last will be sunny and warm, just as you please. If you accede to these propositions, let me know what dish or dishes I shall bring in my pocket for the public good.

"Would you be so good as to ask Count D'Orsay to let me have my camera lucida, as without that I am not fitted out for my labors.

"WILLIAM GELL.

"I think I myself will begin at the soldiers' quarters, and so ramble by degrees toward the Forum and the new excavations there. Thus we shall meet without doubt or difficulty, even if you begin from the tombs, which is much the most striking, and consequently the best beginning.

"A. S. E. Madamigella M. A. P. à casa del Conti di Blessington, Palazzo Negroni."

"Naples.

"If I waited longer I might get a better piece of paper, but I have no patience, so this is just to let you know, madam, that your carnival pranks have all been watched, and that I have observed your tricks for the last five days.

"Tremble, then, when you see the handwriting of your jealous

"LAWFUL."

"Rome, April 5th, 1824.

"I really did arrive at Rome on the 12th of last month, having quitted your city on the 8th, and having experienced on the way every possible misfortune except being overturned or carried into the mountains. In short, I know nothing to equal my journey except the ninety-nine misfortunes of Pulicinella in a Neapolitan puppet-show. I set out without my cloak in an open carriage; my only hope of getting warmer at St. Agata was destroyed by an English family, who had got possession of the only chimney. I had a dreadful headache, which, by-the-by, recollecting to have lost at your house by eating an orange, I tried again with almost immediate effect. Next morning one of my horses fell ill at the moment of being put to the carriage, and has continued so ever since, so that I have had to buy another, which is so very (what they call) good that it is nearly as useless as the other, so that I never go out without risking my neck. When, at length, I got to Rome in a storm of sleet, I found a bill of one hundred and fifty dollars against me for protecting useless lemon-trees against the frost of the winter, which, added to the expense of the new horse and the old one, have ever since caused the horrors of a jail to interpose themselves between me and every enjoyment, and so much for the ugly side of the question.

"In other respects I am in very good health and spirits, and go out every day to dinners, of which the chief givers have hitherto been Lady Mary Deerhurst, Mr. Morritt, of Rokeby, Lord Dudley, Lord Kinnaird, Torlonia, Mrs. Beaumont and Co., and others, besides the same company, Mr. Irving or Irvine, Mr. and Lady Selina Robinson, Lord C. Fitzroy, Lord Ashley, Captain Southill, His Highness the Prince of Mecklenburgh, Dr. Wilson, a most agreeable Scot, fresh from Egypt, Jerusalem, and all the East, and very talkative, Mr. Hare, Mr. Dodwell, and your humble servant, to which lately we add Sir William Drummond and Dr. Quin. Do not, therefore, imagine that in dinners or dinner company we are at all behind you at Naples, though all the strangers are supposed to have left this place, the Lord rest their souls. Since my arrival we have had nothing but misfortunes; first, the sad affair of Miss Bathurst,* and, secondly, the death of the Duchess of Devonshire. Miss Bathurst's death really made every body unhappy, having been one of the principal delights of the society here while living, and really beloved by every body. Lord Aylmer does not appear to be recovered yet as to spirits, and it seems that the idea still recurs to him every instant: at first his exertions in the water, and the agitation he underwent, seemed to threaten his senses for some days.

"Mr. Mills has been of the greatest use to him, having at length succeeded in persuading him to talk about the fatal business till he acquired by degrees a little calmness and fortitude. Mills eats his breakfast as usual, and desires your ladyship may be informed of the circumstance, adding, he will give you a breakfast at the Vigna Palatina, as he has done to Lord and Lady Aylmer almost every morning for the last fortnight. They go away in a day or two to meet the unhappy Mr. Bathurst at Genoa.

"The poor duchess had every possible consolation at her death. By the most lucky chance, the duke and Mrs. Ellis were here, and Dr. Quin, coming here for a frolic, sat up with her eight nights, so as to have hurt his own health. He describes her as dying in the most calm and amiable manner possible, and the physicians having permitted her to see her friends when they had no longer any hope, the duke, Mr. Ellis, the Duc de Laval, and Mr. Artaud went to see her, to take leave of her, as well as Dr. Nott or Knott, who had a conversation with her very satisfactory to him on matters of religion, showing that she did not die a Catholic, and would have taken the sacrament, but the doctors would not permit it on account of her weakness. Dr. Quin had been desired by the Duke of Devonshire to be present at the embalming of the body, which is to go by land to England. It was discovered that an ossification of the arteries had commenced, so that in a short time she would probably have died from that cause, had not an accidental cold, neglected by herself for too long a period, thus destroyed her. And now I will give you no more of the miseries of this life. I hope you have at length had better weather. Mr. Morritt says that for two months the thermometer has been seven degrees higher in London than Rome this winter. What will Lord

* The lamentable death of Miss Bathurst, who was drowned in the Tiber in February, 1824.—R. R. M.

Blessington say to an Italian climate after this? but when I recollect that I have been able to breakfast in my loggia, in a hot sun every morning, except, perhaps, ten during the winter, I shall not be easily persuaded that we are not better off. I found two letters from Lady Westmoreland, who has already got at Malta £300 worth of things prepared for her voyage to and in Egypt, where she will probably never go. I have answered her with my own projects, but do not build much on the negotiation.

"In the mean time, they say the Pacha of Egypt has declared himself independent; and others state that he is going in person to attack the Morea, which last is a folly he never will be guilty of, as the government of Constantinople would then catch him in a trap. If he quits the country, adieu to traveling there, and so says Mr. Wilkinson at Cairo, from whom I have another letter, saying the pasha has now 30,000 men armed and disciplined in the European manner, with which certainly he might bid defiance to the Porte, if the opinion or religion of the multitude be sufficiently changed for them to resist an imperial order to lay down their arms before the standard of the Prophet.

"Lord Dudley will set out for Naples the first fine day. I don't know whether Dr. Watson has had any success with the volume of Dr. Richardson lent to Sir William Drummond; his illness and his usual carelessness seem to have been our great enemies. I don't know what to do about it, except to pray that as Lord Blessington had the goodness to send for a copy for me, he will possess himself of that, and leave the other at Naples. I am so much ashamed of my neighbor's conduct, that I never will be responsible for him again. Alas! he is so accustomed to losing and destroying books, that he feels no shame himself on the occasion, and swears, though he conversed frequently about the book, he never saw it in his life. Indeed, he never does read a book except for the first five minutes. He seems in very good health and spirits, and his trip to Rome has already done him good. I am quite sorry you all hate this place so much, for I find myself better amused in general than at Naples, where there is nothing but eternal Toledo, Chiaja, and San Carlo. There can be no doubt that this is preferable for society; but for me, I think one great motive of preference is a large and shady garden, where I can hobble among and under my own trees of my own planting. I have already been on one, and I intend to go on several excursions to different parts of the country, where I make observations for the making of a map of the neighborhood. Every body seems inclined to go on these excursions, so my researches appear as if they would become the fashion in the shape of morning rides and drives, with cold dinners brought to the point of rendezvous. I fear you see little or nothing of Craven, who seemed to me, when I left him, as if he was established for life, tacked to his mamma's apron, without benefit of clergy.

"I hope you will let me hear how you all go on, and what you are all doing, and that you have given up that tour in Sicily, where you will have more than the inconvenience of Egypt, with very little of the entertainment or profit. If the Egyptian journeys can not be contrived, I have a sort of faint idea of a tour to Como, and the northern Italian lakes. I kiss your hand and feet; and with the kindest regards to the count and the great Mathews, believe me, my dear Lady Blessington, your affectionate and faithful

"William Gell."

CHAPTER XVII.

LETTERS OF SIR WILLIAM GELL TO LADY BLESSINGTON.

"Rome, 4th July, 1824.

"I was going on in much too flourishing a state of health and jack-ass riding when I received an unlucky letter from Dr. Watson, congratulating me on the same, and singing the praises of Dr. Neiker, who he says has cured him of his infamous headache.

"This was a sort of triumph old Nick could not allow, so the same day, having invited Dodwell to dine under the trees in my garden in order to concert an expedition to Soracte, &c., which would have taken up three days, after which I meant immediately to throw myself at your feet, I was obliged to be carried to my post, and have never, since the 27th of June, made a single pace on my own feet, nor till this evening in any other manner. In the mean time I have really very little pain, though I have been so bewildered that I could not even sit up for two days—a great inconvenience, as it deprives one of so many amusements. At present I am better, or the scene is shifting, which it makes no scruple of doing between both feet, both knees, and a dozen or two of the elbows and fingers; and thus you have had a long and dull account of my enemy and myself.

"I have been, since I wrote last to your ladyship, doing nothing but living in the country houses of the Romans. We had a week at Tivoli, at the Villa Santa Croce, after we returned from Bracciano. We next borrowed the palace of the Duke of Tagerolo of that ilk, and thought that though the thieves were already strong in the field, a population of four or five thousand souls, with the ducal palace in the centre, would render the neighborhood safer for us; and indeed so we found it, having the good fortune to *assify* all over the country in all directions unassailed. Lady Mary Deerhurst, who is the lady of the castle on all these excursions, carries the whole household, children, tutor, governess, dogs, and the rest of the royal family, so that we made some show even in the largest of these mansions, that at Zagarolo being really a magnificent pile, and the place where the pope of those days sent the learned men to consult on the best Catholic edition of the Bible, since published, and called the Vulgate. Here we were joined for some days by Lords Kinnaird and Dudley, and Mr. Hare, to say nothing of Mrs. Dalton, and two beaux, Mr. Bacon and Mr. Stevenson, whom Lady Mary found out one day by chance as she was riding through Valmontone, the whole party and I believe three carriages having only mistaken their way a little, and traveled through the whole territory of the thieves by Monte Casino, thinking they were going by the Terracina road, much as the lovely Bess Caldwell went half way to Vienna in her way from Brussels to Paris.

"When we had seen every thing in that country we returned again to Rome, whence we fitted out several little expeditions for the day, and discovered several cities with good old Greek-looking walls of large blocks, which the wags and antiquaries had no idea of.

"Probably the lost cities taken by Romulus and the Tarquins will all be found in time, if we all live and are well, which, as you very wisely observe, is doubtful.

"I shall only give you one more of our tours in search of Cures, the ancient city of the Sabines, whence came Mr. Smith's cousin, King Tatius, and all the Quirites to Rome. We found the place, though there are but few remains, near the modern village and river Correse, a charming trout stream, running through the most beautiful country we had ever seen. Between the high range of Monte Gennaro (Lucretili according to Mathews) and the Tiber is a country perhaps eight miles in width, interspersed with villages at short distances, perched on the most romantic spots, perfectly defended by nature, but beautifully picturesque, with the remains of the ancient fortifications of the baronial houses. We had the palace of Prince Sierra at Monte Libretti, one of those villages, and though we had it not enough to ourselves to be very comfortable, we managed to make our excursions with effect. Nothing can give you an idea of the infinite beauty of the country, which, generally speaking, seems an eternal forest of oaks and spina Christi; yet every now and then, and just when you wish it, opening into a little cultivation, either in corn, flax, or gardens. Every half mile, in crossing the direction of the great mountains which bound the whole, you have a descent by a precipice into a deep woody dell, with its little stream, sometimes with a patch of cultivation, and forcing its way through the rocks; but I will say no more, lest you should think the gout is got into my head. How sorry you will all have been for Lord Byron. We have a little medal here of him, but it might as well have been of Cæsar, to my eye. They should have sent to Count D'Orsay for a profile. It is really a sad loss to literature, and an immense deficit of interest from the Greek cause. I am afraid the said cause is not very flourishing, as we begin to receive letters from ruined families of the Greeks, saying that, having lost almost all they had by the revolution, and no law existing, they fled with the little remainder, and now solicit your excellency's support. In the mean time, Lady Westmoreland, who had been nearly famished during the late scarcity of 'cases,' is quite set up again by Mr. Battier's case, and the death of Lord Byron before he had time to reform; and with these two she is now exercising her eloquence, first at Venice, and since at Vicenza, and other towns in the north of Italy, where Mr. Craven met her. Craven writes from the Lake of Wallensee on the 16th, and Munich the 17th of June. He finds no attempt at pease, or even salad. At Wallensee several patches of snow down to the water's edge. The elder flowers not come out. The apple-trees yet in early bloom, and a sharp frost every evening. Two days before, he was eating over-ripe cherries in Italy.

"I wish I could send you a good account of the robbers, but nothing has been heard of them lately, except that they are living like fifty prodigal sons at Montellano on the product of the last ransom. When that is spent, of course they will send for more; and if I get well by the time they begin to infest the road, I must really take the liberty to escape by sea, for to be beaten to death because I can not walk into the mountains, or, being taken on an ass, to have to pay the greater part of my fortune for a ransom, would neither of them be advisable cases. I hope, at least, the earl now likes the Belvidere better than in the winter, when the window curtains sometimes insisted on becoming part of the dinner company at the table. Speaking of a gun, do any of you want a groom, named Crispin, who has been all over this country with Lady Mary, but which Lady Mary is now gone to Leghorn with only an English groom for her riding-horses, and, in consequence, the man is left in my hands to dispose of? Now for a description. Crispin is of middle stature, slim, active, intelligent, and much in appearance like a real slang English groom; in feature like a baddish caricature of K—— C—— put into an oven till his hair was singed. Born at Viterbo, aged about thirty, and I suspect concerned in divers serenades, sung in a high key, and not remarkable for precision, which I sometimes hear in the street. If any of the family of Belvidere want for themselves, or can dispose to their neighbors of a person so eminently qualified, he is now to be had cheap. I hope you will be able to read my writing, as it has only just occurred to me that I am obliged to sit in a posture which I can not do myself, with my feet in the air. I have no news from England. A friend wrote to me in the greatest haste to help him to a peerage, that of Darcy of ———.* I gave him his answer, and told him Darcy of Navan was what he had a claim to, and no other of that name. Yet I have had no answer, so conclude he has died of it, as it is now above three months ago. They say the Aberdeens are coming here, instigated, if true, I suppose, by Captain Gordon. We have long been without a single milord of any sort or kind, but I believe there yet remain many of a tribe of both sexes, who are in want of money to go away the next day to England with a very pitiful story, which they take round every winter, without ever quitting for an instant the Holy City.

"We have yet had not a hint on the subject of the learned 'Faustus.' I hope and trust she has been exorcised long ago, and does not mean to be ill any more, but to be a nice little neat sort of a tidy discreet old sort of a body as usual, when fate allows me to come clumping like a parrot into her pres-

* Word illegible.—R. R. M.

ence. I kiss the hems of your garments. I salute the whole company, and am most affectionately and faithfully, W. G."

"Rome, October 2d, 1824.

"I am sitting in my garden, under the shade of my own vines and figs, my dear Lady Blessington, where I have been looking at the people gathering the grapes, which are to produce six barrels of what I suspect will prove very bad wine; and all this sounds very well till I tell you that I am positively sitting in a wheelbarrow, which I found the only means of conveying my crazy person into the garden. Don't laugh, Miss Power. The fact is, that all those feelings which I had for two days at your house most kindly contrived to resolve themselves into a fit of the gout on the very morning of my departure, so that I got into the carriage in torture, and was obliged to be borne out by two porters at Capua, since which time till to-day I have never put a foot to the ground. I considered, at Capua, that if I let Sir W. Drummond turn back, as he wanted to do, it was most probable he would fall ill before I was well, and he would be thus disappointed of his tour, so I was carried again to the coach, and, after a drive of thirty-five miles to San Germano with the same horses, through a most beautiful country, and not very bad road, we found ourselves compelled at sunset to mount two wretched asses, and climb by a steep zigzag road for an hour and a half to the monastery of Monte Casino. All this, with a fit of the gout, was certainly rather an undertaking, but I was carried by some very good people of the jackasses up five hundred steps and forty corridors, and laid upon a bed, where the holy fathers, the very nicest of Thingumberrys in the world, were so kind to me that I could have been nowhere better. They gave us a fine supper in the next room, as I found by the number of good plates they brought, and tried to persuade me to eat. Sir William Drummond seemed quite pleased with them, and talked till a late hour, and they, on their parts, seemed equally delighted with him. The next morning, Tuesday, they took him to see their library, which is very good, and their archivio, or room of manuscripts; and finding I was not in a movable state, they were so kind as to send five or six of their most curious MSS. to me. Among them was the MS. Virgil, which has all the lines filled up (by the Lord knows who) which Virgil had left unfinished in his hurry to die. We remained there till Saturday, when I descended the mountain in a sedan chair, and we renewed our journey. On Friday, the fathers insisted on my seeing their wonders in the said sedan; and I went into the church to hear the celebrated organ, which, in the shattered state of my nerves, only served to make me cry. The church is really the most beautiful thing ever seen. It is entirely incrusted with the finest marbles, and neither stone nor mortar appears in any part of it. The pilasters are inlaid in beautiful arabesques of verd-antique, porphyry, and serpentino; and the whole so clean, so new, and so polished, that, till I had seen it, I had no idea of the effect which might be produced by colored marbles. The floor is also equally beautiful and simple, and the ceiling gilt and painted in the gayest and most elegant manner. Under the dome is the abbot's throne, and in the chancel the stalls are of carved oak, of the most elaborate and astonishing workmanship. When the first effect of the organ had passed off, I found it was really more like an orchestra than any thing I had ever heard, and the organist was never tired of playing, and of setting it off to the *best* advantage. These people are really learned monks, and we found, out of ten, three or four who were good scholars, and had even got as far as the Hebrew. In former times they had great revenues, and more than one hundred residents. They have now 16,000 ducats, or about £3000 per annum. Nothing could exceed their kindness to us, and we did our best to repay it, by showing them the sextant, camera lucida, and all we possessed, which might be new to them in science or literature. Quitting these good souls, we began our adventures, intending to go to Rome by the nearest way. We set out, therefore, with a vetturino for Ceprano, the first town in the Roman States. We found, near St. Germano, the remains of an amphitheatre; and we spun along a fine new road, past Aquino to below Rocca Secca, for two hours or more, with the greatest success, and there met with the River Melfa, almost dry, but at the bottom of a deep, rocky dell, over which a bridge is building—to get over the stream; it was therefore necessary to diverge to the right, and in about twenty minutes we regained the good road, only to quit it forever on the left, and wander for the rest of the day in the wilds and vineyards, without roads or any fixed direction. It appears that, if ever five miles of the road be made, there will be no difficulty in reaching Ceprano in a direct line. As it is, however, the fine road runs to the right to Sara, and we were condemned to hunt our fortune in a large coach and four, and at last to make nine or ten miles out of the five. There were few absolute dangers, particularly as the weather had been dry, but it began to rain in the afternoon, and we passed a sort of devil's bridge between two precipices of slippery earth, which was not quite agreeable. We reached at length the little village of Isolatta, and soon after got into the Roman States, where we found a road, and a very good new bridge over the Liris, by which we entered the little town of Ceprano. Here we lodged at the house of a surgeon, to whom our friends of Monte Casino had recommended us, and we were treated as well as, under a very humble roof, we could expect. In the morning of Sunday we set out again, and, passing by a very decent but tiresome road, eternally mounting and descending, but in a well-cultivated and pretty country, through Frosinone, Ferentino, and Anagni, cities of Latium, with great remains of antiquity, we arrived at night at Valmontane, having gone forty-four miles with the same horses from Ceprano. As we came late, though the inn is very large, it was occupied, and, after a good deal of waiting and trouble, we got two corn-chambers, with damp beds to sleep in. Sir William could not sleep, but in the morning we proceeded to the Holy City, twenty-five miles, and arrived at two o'clock, having performed our journey through the whole of the thieves' country without any sinister accident. Lord Kinnaird we saw on our arrival, and Mr. Mills came the same day. Mr. Millingen was also here, and is gone on to Paris. Lady Mary Deerhurst came yesterday, and I expect her in my garden every minute. Craven arrives to-morrow, and the margravine is hourly expected: a most wonderful coincidence of travelers. My companion voted me too crazy to accompany him to Albano, where he thinks he is going to ride about on the mountain, so I am sent to grass for a few days at my own casino on the Quirinal. I expect in less than a week to be summoned to Albano, and so to return to Naples, when, as I already begin to hobble, I expect to be quite well—in my way, and where I hope to hear of you on my arrival; for I will not let you write, as I am most uncertain in my motions. I think I am the only person who sets out at the beginning of a fit of the gout on a party of pleasure, but I think it has succeeded, as I should not have been well any where; and I can say that, except starting, the pain of the gout seems to have very much worn itself out, or to have been conquered by Dr. Neiker. You will know poor Miss Bathurst's body was found the day we arrived. A flood seems to have removed the sandbank which had covered it, near the scene of the accident. Having been always under water, the flesh had become like spermaceti, and the hat, veil, &c., were perfect; even the mouth was recognizable. I beg my kindest regards to the earl, count, Mousey, Mathews, and all your party. W. GELL."

"Naples (1824).

"'The doughty Douglass' could not come because he was going away so soon, but will wait upon you in St. James's Square.

"I intend to come to-day, and will bring a specimen of the Royal Letters, and Mademoiselle Demont's journal, if you will be at home.* Your slave,

"W. GELL."

* On the queen's trial in 1820, Louisa Demont was examined. Said she was a native of Switzerland, of the Pays de Vaud, a Protestant; engaged with her royal highness as first *femme de chambre* at Lausanne. Her testimony was the most damaging to the princess of all the evidence of the crown witnesses. September 1st, 1820, on her cross-examination, said she had been in England thirteen months, and could not speak English. Was discharged by the princess in 1817 for saying something which was, in fact, untrue. Did not go into other service, because in Switzerland she had funds of her own sufficient to live upon.

A letter of hers, after her departure, was read to her sister, another servant of the princess, named Mariette, dated 8th Feb., 1818, in which this passage occurs: "You can not think, Mariette, what a noise *my little journal* has made." In this letter she says she spoke in her journal in the highest terms of the princess. The whole evidence of this witness showed her to be a very unscrupulous, intriguing, cunning, clever person, not deficient in education. Lord Brougham said of her, "This woman was the most perfect specimen, the most finished model of the complete waiting-maid."—R. R. M.

"Naples.

"I have been thinking of your learning Italian, and think at last I could teach you in two hours to read; and as you are professor of Pausanias already, would willingly have a set-to at a little bit of it with you; there can be no doubt that no modern language is equal to it, and when you have it, Latin, Spanish, and Portuguese (to read) will be easy. I shall therefore bring Pausanias on Sunday and hope you will not have company who will prevent my lesson. With kindest regards to the count and Lady Julia,

"William Gell."

In a letter of Sir William Gell's, addressed to Lady Blessington, 1824, at the Villa Belvidere, the following observations on mythological emblems, ornaments, instruments, and vesture are inserted, in the hand-writing, I think, of Mr. Craven, probably transmitted in compliance with the wishes of Lady Blessington, communicated to Gell:

"Certain wreaths were peculiarly given as rewards to the winners in particular games. Wild olive was the recompense in the Olympic games, laurel in the Pythian, parsley in the Nemean, and pine twigs in the Isthmic games. The diadem or fillet, called Credemnon, was among the gods reserved for Jupiter, Neptune, Apollo, and Bacchus, and among men it was regarded as the peculiar mark of royalty. The radiated crown, formed of long sharp spikes, emblematic of the sun, and represented as issuing from the head of that deity, was first worn only on the tiaras of the Armenian and Parthian kings, and afterward became adopted by the Greek sovereigns of Egypt and of Syria. A wreath of olive-branches was worn by ordinary men at the birth of a son, and a garland of flowers at weddings, on festivals, and at feasts; in order that the scent might be more fully enjoyed, the wreath was often worn round the neck. As a symbol of power, gods, sovereigns, and heralds carried the sceptre, or *hasta*, terminated by the representation of some animal or flower instead of a point. As the emblem of their mission, Mercury and all messengers bore the caduceus twined round the serpent.

"The car of each Grecian deity was drawn by some peculiar kind of animal or bird: that of Juno by peacocks, of Apollo by griffins, of Diana by stags, of Venus by swans or turtle-doves, of Mercury by rams, of Minerva by owls, of Cybele by lions, of Bacchus by panthers, of Neptune by sea-horses. The Gorgon's head, with its round chaps, wide mouth, and tongue drawn out, emblematic of the full moon, was regarded as an amulet against incantations and spells, and is for that reason found not only on the formidable ægis of Jupiter and of Minerva, as well as on cinerary urns and in tombs, but on Grecian shields and breast-plates, at the pole-ends of chariots, and in the most conspicuous parts of every other instrument of defense or protection to the living or the dead. The prows of Greek galleys or ships of war were ornamented with the *cheniscus*, frequently formed like the head and neck of an aquatic bird, and the poop with the *aplustrum*, shaped like a sort of honeysuckle. Two large eyes were generally represented near the prow, as if to make the vessel like a fish, to see its way through the waves. In religious processions of the Greeks, masks were used as well as in their theatres, and in order to represent the attendants of the god who was worshiped. Thus, in Bacchanalian processions (the endless subjects of ancient bas-reliefs and paintings), the fauns, satyrs, and other monstrous beings are only human individuals masked; and in initiations and mysteries, the winged genii are in the same predicament; and the deception must have been the greater, as the ancient masks were made to cover the whole head. Of these masks, which, together with all else that belonged to the theatre, were consecrated to Bacchus, there was an infinite variety. Some represented abstract feelings or characters, such as joy, grief, laughter, dignity, vulgarity, masked in the comic, tragic, and satyric masks, others offered portraits of real individuals, living or dead. The thyrsus, so frequently introduced, was only a spear, of which the point was stuck in a pine cone, or wound round with ivy leaves. Afterward, to render the blows given with it during drunkenness harmless, it was made of the reed called *ferula*.

"Of musical instruments, the *phorminx*, or large lyre, was dedicated to Apollo, and was played upon with an ivory instrument called *plectrum*. It was usually fastened to a belt hung across the shoulder, and sometimes suspended from the wrist of the left hand, while played upon with the right. The *cithara*, or smaller lyre, was dedicated to Mercury, and when the body was formed of tortoise-shell, and the arms composed of a goat's horns, it was called *chelys*. This was played upon by the fingers. The *barbitos* was a much longer instrument, and emitted a graver sound. The *trigonium*, or triangle, an instrument borrowed by the Greeks from Eastern nations, much resembled the harp. Besides these instruments with chords, the Greeks had several wind instruments, principally the double flute and the *syrinx*, or Pan's flute. To these may be added a certain instrument for producing noise, the *tympanon*, or tambourine, chiefly used in the festival of Bacchus and of Cybele: the *crembala*, or cymbals, formed of metal cups, and the *crotals*, or castanets, formed of wood, shaped like shells.

"In attire, the *chlamys*, a short cloak, was a garment of gods and heroes, fastened over the shoulder or upon the chest. Such is the mantle of the Apollo Belvidere, and many of the statues of Mercury. Wreaths of oak leaves were consecrated to Jupiter, laurel leaves to Apollo, ivy and vine to Bacchus, poplar to Hercules, wheat ears to Ceres, gold or myrtle to Venus, fir twigs to the fauns and sylvans, and reeds to the river gods.

"The *peplum* was a sort of mantle worn by the Greeks; the tunic a loose robe. Venus is the only one of the goddesses that is represented without a peplum, and Diana is generally represented with hers furled, and drawn tight over the shoulders and round the waist, forming a girdle, with the ends falling down in front. The peplum had small metal points attached to its corners, in order to make them hang more straight and even."

"Rome, 23d March, 1825.

"I shall never have the pleasure of 'whipping the family all round most severely' again, if it be true that poor old Parr is really dead, as I see it announced in the newspapers. I am always for those living longest who contrive to be content with the world, and endeavor to make the best of it; and he was really one of those. I conclude he was by no means young, but it is a pity that two such scholars as he and Porson should have departed without having left something of more consequence behind them to perpetuate their fame. I continued to mend in my hobbling as I approached the Holy City, and for some days after my arrival; but, as fate would have it, all my friends lived up one hundred and fifty stairs, and I ruined myself by my premature activity so effectually, that, though without pain, I have been forced to be carried by two people, one of whom is the great Pasquale, till three days ago. It would be natural that I should have therefore seen very few persons, but the good Lady Manvers, who protects me most especially, is so popular, that, seated in her wheeling chair, I have seen almost all the good company at Rome, Lady Bute excepted, who threatens me with a visit in my garden to-day, as she does not attempt stairs. I have no doubt Dr. Neiker could cure her of that also. We have Sir George Talbot, who gives great and good dinners as I am told, for I was not well enough to go when invited. We have Lady Davy, who lives in the right horn of the moon, in the Valdombrino palace, up five hundred steps, who gives agreeable little dinners neither great nor good. We have Anna Maria Starke, who gives parties and misereres, if you are fond of music; Lady George Seymour, who has a very pretty daughter, and a very nice girl; Mr. Rose, the man of Greek inscriptions; a rich Mr. Ferguson, with one or two others, last from Persepolis and Bagdat; a Baron Uxscull or Oxscull, from Finland, last from Egypt and Syria, with a collection of drawings; William Burrell, with a new waistcoat and neck-handkerchief of real Cashmere (or do you spell it Cashemire) shawl for every day in the year, and a gold toilet; Mr. Dodwell, who has just cut open a mummy in public, and found it to be a lady of fashion three thousand years old, and his pretty wife, who has a party every Sunday, and I dine with them to remain at it; Mrs. Singleton, née Upton, and Miss Upton, unmarried; Mr. and Mrs. Lucas, very nice people, from Ireland; Dr. and Mrs. and Miss Hall, the Dean of Durham, from Naples, who seem good people, and a variety of others, fathers and mothers unknown. A little while ago, every body was engaged in companies, like Anglo-Mexican miners, to make excavations in secret; as nobody got any good by these speculations, the taste seems at present all gone into the *miserere* line, and there really are arrived many pilgrims, and even prelates, who do penance, much as I think I could do it myself, by arriving here in a coach-and-four, and under their oil-cloth dress and cockle-shells are clothed in real cloth of gold and fine linen. I believe the Duke of Lucca is also a pilgrim, and, in short, from what I understand, the plot begins to thicken, and the desert of Rome to be peopled. I can not help thinking it would entertain you all exceedingly to make a trip for a week, particularly as holy years do not occur every day of one's life, and we shall end with an illumination and fireworks of the most brilliant kind.

"I wish I could say I would lodge, clothe, and feed you if you would come; but for amusement, the people, the quaintness of every thing, and the air of general decadence, are, after the bustle of Naples, things to ponder upon, and could not fail to strike you at the time, and to prove a source of recollections and reflections afterward, not to mention the queer things you would pick up for the adventures in your new romance. I wish you would engage me in that to-be-celebrated work. Have you read the 'Travelers,' a book with some such name, with anecdotes of all the robberies, real or supposed, in the way between Rome and Naples? Have you got 'the Inheritance,' by the author of 'Marriage?' It is excellent, and very interesting. Think of poor Colonel S—— hanging himself, and the shocking affair of Lord Shaftesbury's son at Eton. The world is gone crazy. Lady Mary Deerhurst I see often, and she will come to Naples in May. She wants to send her son to school in England. Our spring is very backward, but nevertheless I find my garden, which is full of evergreens, in considerable beauty. When the weather is warmer I shall begin my geographic excursions with Lady Mary and Messrs. Graham and Dodwell. We purpose going up Mount Soracte among other things, and to hire all the diligence, and go in it to Civita Vecchia, and thence to Corneto or Tarquinium. You will most likely think us all very crazy, but as Lady Charlotte Campbell said, if it be not right, it is at least very agreeable. Lord Kinnaird is by no means well, and it is supposed he must quit Rome. I hope Mesdames Lucrezia and Letizia continue to be the ornaments of their profession, and to draw the great coach with success. I beg to be most kindly remembered to my lord and 'Lady Julia.' Pray tell the count his particular friend Dr. Wilson has sent Lady Mary also some oranges, so he must not think the protection exclusive. I don't hear whether he called her 'Mary' in his letter, or added her title. I kiss your hands. WILLIAM GELL."

"Drummond has given his word of honor to close his gates to the abbot,* and told Craven and Scarfe to announce it to the world. Captain Scarfe was a witness, and Craven says, quite eloquent, and without compliments.

"There does not appear to be any sympathy for the abbot at present any where. Reilly seems a sort of helper, and S—— in the worst scrape as to the figure he makes, for he has unsaid and has to reunsay. Most truly and sincerely, W. GELL."

* The well-known Abbé Campbell.—R. R. M.

"Naples.

"I could not answer your last kind letter, as I was wofully beset by banker's business at the moment, but I intended to have sent a letter this morning, when your man arrived. I must come to-morrow, as I don't like to refuse Craven at this moment, just after the tidings of Lord Craven's death. I will come on Wednesday to dinner, and at seven, if I do not hear that your hour is changed, if you can see me, and think then, with assistance, I shall be able to do without my chair, as to-day I can stand alone. I am quite well, but with such legs (in their best state), I am long in recovering the little use of them which remains.

"A nasty man, Mr. R——: he has gone and bought a house in Piccadilly, on which I had £4000, or rather an annuity of £400 a year, which has thrown my money, or rather the interest of it, into a sad state.

"With kind regards to the Lady Julia and the count,

"WILLIAM GELL."

"Naples.

"How do you do after your star-gazing? and have you got your treasures safe, and has the count been angry at me for slipping them into his portfolio? for I am anxious to know all these circumstances. After waiting some time, I recollected that Lord Blessington said you were to wait for the moon, and that I might have remained many centuries listening for the wheels of your chariot; so I departed, hoping that I should meet you somewhere on the road to the studio, where you turned off to the observatory. I doubled up my note as curiously as I could, that no one might dare to open it, and learn where I had placed the letters, and I hope I succeeded.

"VERSES BY PAYNE KNIGHT'S GHOST TO MR. SOTHEBY:

"Dear Botherby, let me alone,
For as asses still scratch one another,
Every mortal that hears of your moan
Will imagine that I was a brother.
Bad verses I wrote, but no cant;
Was a scholar and wit, as you know it;
While, in spite of pretension and rant,
You're a quack and a prig, but no poet.

"Most truly yours, W. GELL."

"Naples.

"It is so many centuries since I heard of you from yourself, that I have thought it better to write than to go on longer in darkness. I have heard, however, that poor Miss Faustus* is going on well, from Dr. Doratt; pray let me hear how she is to-day. It is so cold for the last three days that I think of giving up the ghost myself, and Sir William Drummond is not yet quite

* One of the numerous appellations Sir William was in the habit of giving his fair friend Miss Power.—R. R. M.

recovered. I fear you will have also suffered from the winter, which, in your exposed situation, must have been more serious than here. Nevertheless, I have always breakfasted on my terrace, for the abominable wind does not blow here till twelve or one. I expect Craven to-morrow evening, who has escaped with difficulty from his constituents, the actors at Rome, for they are quite ruined by his departure, and expect no more good benefits. Lady Drummond threatens us with a masked ball, and Mrs. Hamilton with another, at the end of the month. M. De Serre gives a ball this evening, and Count Jeniseo, who is just as fat as ever after the *liquidation* of his blood, according to Bess Caldwell, gives another in a few days. I shall certainly be danced quite off my legs. What do you think of my dining with the archbishop yesterday, at what he calls three, and not ending till seven, which made nine at night appear like twelve? He had two new dandy counts from Sweden, one of which was a Count Hamilton, to dinner, and I took the Angell* with me to show his precious sculptures. The archbishop says you are all most cruel people to come like an apparition, and then, after swearing eternal friendship, to come no more; however, he has turned off the Beaumont girls, and says he will deliver himself up to you, body and soul, if you are inclined to return to his embraces and charities. In the middle of dinner the Angell put down his hand by accident, which was immediately seized and scratched by the great black cat 'Othello,' who lies watching for such opportunities. He only climbed upon my knee once by setting his claws into my pantaloons.

"I fear we shall end by falling into the arms of Mr. and Mrs. Montefiore, Mr. Rothschild's brother and sister-in-law, for our Egyptian voyage. They are now waiting at Rome, and mean to get a ship from England in September.

"Pray let me hear how you all do; and with best regards to the earl, the count, and all the party, WILLIAM GELL."

"Naples, August 6th.

"I really don't think it would be fair to attack you a third time by the post, having already, as you ordered, first addressed you at Turin, and then at Geneva, particularly as, before this arrives at Florence, you will probably be in Ireland. First, his lordship was very kind and very gracious about the map, which I wrote him word I accepted with pleasure, and his name, as the Mecænas, is already inscribed in the title; and I wrote by the same post to put off Lady Ruthven, who was likely to have been the map's protectress. Moreover, I wrote to his lordship again to say that, as he told me, I had, through Torlonia, made a sort of draft on Messrs. Ransom at a long date—I think three months—as the map was almost finished. I have put down in the title at once that his munificence was the cause of the publication, for it seems better to write the real truth. So it begins, 'Munificentia Exc. Viri Carolus Johannes Comitis Blessington,' and set forth properly in capitals.

* Mr. Angell was an eminent English architect.—R. R. M.

Nobody can be offended at the puff, and his lordship's modesty will not, and can not be alarmed. I have also twice written to say my d—d £1000, which I have in London, is not yet cleared from certain houses on which it is secured; and since then I have from Craven a letter, to say the time is by no means fixed when it will be forthcoming.

"Ye gods, how hot it is! Mr. Lambton's vessel is here, and the sailors wanted to take the Neapolitan frigate, where it was launched the other day, because the English flag was placed the lowest, except the Algerine. There is spirit for you! W. G."

"Naples, 15th April, 1826.

"It was very silly of me not to ask one of you to send me one line from Florence, as I have been thinking ever since of the displeasure I should receive from losing a letter to you. However, I will proceed on the supposition that you are really gone on to Venice, unseduced by the wiles of Messrs. Strangways and Co. to detain you at Florence. Oh, what pens and paper one meets with in Dodwell's house! but I have mended it, for there I am waiting for dinner at four o'clock on the 15th day of April, 1826.

"You left us in great tribulation at your departure, and the next day it seemed as if you had been gone a week, so heavily did the time pass. I immediately fell to map-making with great vigor, and it is positively engraving on a great plate of copper weighing thirty-six pounds, and costing the Lord knows what. The said plate arrived when I was out, and Squintibus, to whom I had mentioned my wish to put a metal plate behind the fire, mistook it for that, and was on the point of sacrificing my new copper to that purpose. I made the tour proposed with Messrs. Dodwell and Nibby, and the Conte di Monte Vecchio, last Monday; but, having wisely selected the only rainy day ever seen, we did nothing but fence off the bad weather with umbrellas, and after getting up at five to set out at seven, we dined at twelve in a cottage, at a place called Buccea, twelve miles from Rome, and returned without being much the wiser for our pains.

"On Tuesday next we set out for Antium—that is, Dodwell, Mills, and I, in two carriages; as Mills goes on a plant expedition only, and we go to flatter ourselves in vain, we shall find Corrioli with Caius Marcius and John Kemble on the wall. Sir William Dry arrived the day before yesterday, having deluded Lady D—— to stay a fortnight longer in Naples. I have not seen him yet, but go to-night at eight, after dining at Dodwell's. He has brought Dr. Watson to take care of him, for he is by no means right, having a hind leg out of order; but he is getting well. They don't know how long they stay, or whither they are bound, except that they think Paris will be somewhere in their journey. I have a letter to-day from Champollion, who has found treasures at Leghorn, in Salt's collection, which the French government have sent him to examine and pack up. He has found, among other things, the great Queen of Egypt, Nitocris—not that of Babylon—and is very ingenious on the subject, having really a splendid talent at making silken purses out of sows' ears. Manetho, or Eratosthenes, I forget which, says the name Nitocris meant the victorious Minerva; so Champollion's queen begins with the signs of Neith, the goddess answering to Minerva, and of the rest of the characters after Neit or Neith he makes the word victory in Coptic, of which I believe every word (like a goose, you will say), and quite worship the knowledge united with the talent he possesses. He says he will come here on the 15th of May, and certainly will be a great acquisition to me—

"'The Strabo informs us.'

"Miss Power has long ago left the room, I conclude; but, as she does not yet know Champollion, she can only call him a bore. Moore is really gone to Naples, and so is every body I ever heard of, except the licentious people who go by a vetturino to Vienna to meet 'my lawful.' My nasty friend has ended by declaring that he can not give the £400 he promised me two years ago, and I have yet £1500 of my capital which my friends have not disposed of at Naples, and which grieveth the financial boss of my cerebellum full sore.

"I was sent for by Princess Geracè as I quitted your house, and she told me ——— was restored to Nelly; but I fear 'not no good won't come of it.' The Sagan woman was most uncommonly civil to Nelly, and last Saturday set out for Vienna with the Potocka girl. I saw for a moment the margravine's memoirs at Torlonia's. In the middle of them is a long essay on Etruscan art, written by the editor, Mr. Brett, out of Winkleman, a book I have often seen in his hands. The said lady has ordered C—— never to invite Luttrell to dinner again, because he never spoke to her. Mills says he is glad the *receipt* is at last discovered. Please to tell Miss Power that the Mr. Demetri, her friend, I have at last found out to be a person whom I never saw but once in my life for a moment, and not a bit a certain Athenian that I really did know. Mrs. Dodwell has agreed to take a box at the Theatre de Buratini, or Theatre of Puppets, next Saturday. This has long been a fashionable amusement at Rome; but they have now got up, with splendid scenery and dresses, Iphigenie in Tauris, and other heroic pieces, which are said to be very entertaining, particularly when the machinery goes wrong, and the heroes, instead of striking a blow with their swords, thrust them through the train of their own robes. This operation is so long deferred on account of their journey to Antium, about which you have heard so much, and probably care so little. This letter is concluded the 16th of April, when I have had a long tea-party with Sir William Drummond, and very long discussions on divers points of history, and particularly that of Rome, by Niebuhr, the ex-Prussian minister here, which if you ever meet with in French, pray get it, as it is very curious. You have probably been overtaken by 'Puss in Boots' at Florence; at all events, last Friday he determined to set off, but I think my letter may overtake him yet, as he goes by a vetturino. The world is grown very wide—I mean, there is quite room enough for those remaining in Rome—and to-day I have seen no one but Dr. Watson, Nibby, Mr. Petre, and Mr. Sykes, the first bound for Naples, and the latter for England, where Pussey will wend for the sake of buying horses.

"I have now sent you a very long and very ugly letter; but Lady Westmoreland says little queer letters are the only ones which arrive safe. I have neither announced myself in France or Portugal yet, in the persons of their embassadors, not having had time, or perhaps the courage which sound legs inspire; but I will do so next week, that I may not be in that dinnerless condition described by Hare at Florence, which, in the present dearth of company, seems not impossible. By this time Miss Power may be returned, hoping my dull letter may be finished; but no, you have yet the loves of the Contessina Dodwell, who says you are all sympathetic—sympatica; of Mills, who loves you tenderly; and Dodwell, who eagerly asks every day for information I can not give him. Pray let me hear from you ere long, not a letter, but a line to say how you all are, and whither bound. Dr. Robertson came a day or two after you went, and seemed sorry not to have caught you. I salute you all with a kiss a little warmer than Dr. Parr's holy kiss on the stairs.

"Your ladyship's slave, W. Gell."

"Rome, June 7, 1827.

"I am gone to bed at nine, having a dozen gouts and as many agues, besides swelled glands, and every other species of agreeable sensation. It rained yesterday furiously, on account of which Lady Westmoreland gave a fête in a villa at Rome. Now I had no idea that Lord B—— was with the rest of the family, imagining that he had departed some fortnight ago for the purpose of appearing in Parliament; and, on this supposition, I ventured to ask the count whether the mention of the map would be an imprudence or not. His lordship has solved my doubts in a very agreeable manner; so I shall, according to his order, consider him as the Mecænas of my map, and he must figure away with arms, coronet, and supporters, with a sort, I think, of Latin dedication in one corner, according to the custom of the modern Medes and Persians, which altereth not. Depend upon it I will contrive the thing in a few words, saying the truth, that his lordship is the cause of its appearance, by his munificent protection of the engraving. What I wish him to do is to tell the Ransoms to answer my drafts for a sum not exceeding 400 dollars (and I hope not 300), which was the way settled with Lord Kinnaird by his own desire; and let me beg of him not to think of dying as he did, for it puts me in a fright, now the map is nearly engraved, quite indescribable. The next thing is the business of the £1000. Last year I was in high quest of a person to whom I might lend on annuity that or somewhat a larger sum; but it was disposed of to a certain Signore Pietro, lord of the manor of Porto, and, after Torlonia, the greatest proprietor here, who pays one twelve per cent. for the same; and £500 more I lent to a friend on the same terms, that is, when I die, adieu to my rent. Now I have another £1000 in London, settled on houses for three lives at ten per cent., but I can leave that in my will; moreover, the owner of the houses has delayed payment ever since the Fauntleroy affair—that is, he owes me £300 at this moment, and my lawyer has ordered the rents to be paid to him instead of to the said proprietor, and it is probable I am to expect my arrears and my principal soon.

"All the people here pay on the first of every month, which is very convenient, and they pawn their lands and houses. Moreover, there is an office in which you examine whether the said houses and lands have been pawned before; and if the thing be not registered there, the engagement would be the last to be discharged. If the money should be forthcoming, I will immediately let his lordship know; and as Craven is in London, it is not impossible that I should hear something shortly. It is true we talked about Mr. Galt, and Lord B—— thought that at his instigation he might be able to dispose of the work on the Alhambra, but I am afraid he is gone to America; and by what I hear, the trade of bookselling and making, except in novels and plays, is quite finished in London. As to lithography, I am told no publisher can afford any thing else, and that nothing else appears. Lord B——'s belle, the margravine, goes to Naples to-morrow, and Lady D—— is retired to the Villa Ricciardi, in spite of Sir William, who wrote to her not to come because it was so dull. The rest of the Neapolitan world are gone to Castelamare.

"Rocca Romano is, I believe, constant, but has made up matters with ———. He lives a good deal in the country. Caserano is still at Palermo. Mrs. Dodwell not quite so handsome, but more severe; and having heard of what that book contained against her, vowed she would never again enter an English house. She and her husband, who has the gout in his toe, desire kind remembrances to all your family, and they say they love them merely through fear. You will be gone when Mills arrives, though he hastened his journey on purpose. Lord B—— should come here as embassador, not to Florence, which I believe is *infra dig.* for you, though not to an eldest son.

"The Pope will now be content to receive him as deputed to a temporal monarch, without talking of his divinity. Manage that, and you shall be my Magnus Apollo.

"Dr. Goodall, the Provost of Eton, is here, and we are such friends that he sends me Latin verses on myself, which I shall put I don't know where to be seen, they are so flattering. When you see the Galt, do ask him what he can do about books, and when you have time let me know. W. GELL."

"Rome, 29th June.

"MOST ILLUSTRIOUS,—I wrote according to your orders to Turin, but as it is by no means impossible that by delaying your journey, or changing your route, you may forget that my letter exists at Turin for you, so I shall recapitulate the marrow and pith of the same. First, I have caused his excellency's name to be inscribed on the map in a way that can not offend his modesty, being only the simple truth in classical language, which runs somehow thus:

MUNIFICENTIA EXC. VIRI.
Comitis Blessington,
Hoc Tentamen Geographicum,
Exhibens
Latium Vetus Et Hodiernum, &c., &c., &c.
Romæ Kal. Sexti Anno. MDCCCXXVII.,

showing that his lordship's munificence is the cause of the production of the map. Please to tell Messrs. Ransom about it as soon as you can, so that when I draw through Torlonia, it may be all right. Now for the second proposition about the £1000 and the annuity. I have no money at this moment not disposed of, but I expect £1000 to be paid me by a certain Mr. Baxter, settled on houses in Carmarthen Street. Whenever it comes, I will fire you a line; but I am not at all certain when that may be, yet I should say soon. Most truly and affectionately yours, W. GELL."

"Rome, June 6th, 1828.

"Any decent person—I mean, any person with decent legs—would have got up and got a good sheet of paper, instead of writing to you on two leaves of a book of MS. sermons. But I have given my people so much trouble in setting out the breakfast for two German professors, who have just brought me a diploma, creating me member of the Academy of Thuringia, that I don't wish to call them again.

"Where the deuce is Thuringia? say you. Why, I hardly know myself, except that in the diploma I see it is in Saxony, and, if literally translated, it would seem the employment of the society should be digging up the graves of their ancestors, to see what sort of fellows they were. I beg you would have and feel a proper respect, in common with 'my lawful,' for my new and budding honors. Moreover, the Prussian Academy has sent to say they thank me for my book on Walls, and will take care it shall be published with due care and honor.

"Now what have you all been doing in the mean time? I have been twice or thrice ill, and between the acts to the Torlonias, at Castell Gandolfo, and the Comptons at Frescati.

"I have got by Cavaliere Bunsen, the Prussian minister, just returned (and worth all the rest put together), the Hare and the Thirlwall's translation of Niebuhr's History of Rome. There is a good deal of information in the work, and several jokes and vulgarities not proper for history; but that is the author's fault; the translators seem to have been two Frenchmen. What think you of this? 'It were a great thing if I might be able to scatter, for those who read me, the cloud that lies on this most excellent portion of ancient story, and to spread a clear light over it.' Pray set 'my lawful' to turn it into English, with her well-known grammatical accuracy. One can make out what it means, but scatter instead of disperse is not pretty, and Julius Hirsutus* can never have revised his work.

* Mr. Julius Hare.—R. R. M.

"Poor Mrs. B—— has lost her son, which I fear will go nigh to lose her, poor soul! She got the news before she reached England, where or whither she was going post haste. Lady Mary is going on the 10th to Naples, over the mountains—of China; so that Dodwell and I shall have the town to ourselves, as well as the Villa Borghese. But Bess Caldwell, by the way, who has been to see an old place which she calls by a name which she mistakes for castellated, is to replace all deserters. Craven writes that he leaves England soon.

"I have a letter from Black Fox, at Naples, to-day; he has been hunting antiquities in Samnium with great success. I wish, when you get to Paris, you would desire the count to send for Champollion, in my name, to dine with you. He may say, by way of introduction, that I have charged him to announce that I have received from Cairo for him Burton's 'Excerpta Hieroglyphica,' which I will send by the first opportunity. He is a great friend of mine, certainly one of the most marked men of the time, and agreeable in many ways, and lively in society, and I know they will be mutually glad to have seen each other. I never know whether my letters reach you. Cover the people with affectionate kisses for me, not forgetting my dear tormentor, who I am sure will find no one to make such silly faces, say such foolish things, or sing without knowing the words or having a voice, so readily as their slave in the Negroni, W. G.

"P.S.—I have found a great resource in Mr. Manning, the Chinese scholar, since you went; he knows every thing by sheer study. Imagine that he does not know a note on any instrument, but has studied music out of a book —Chambers' Dictionary. I make him sing from the notes backward and forward, base and treble, at sight. I tried him in a difficult canzon, and he sung it all right the first time, singing la la instead of words, which he had never tried—a most curious instance of application; but he must have a good ear. The Barings at Florence have brought him for the summer. I hope with him I shall have concluded the Chinese museum for Naples. Since you went also, I have entirely painted my room, and you will think me crazy when I tell you that people really come to see it—I mean, people I don't know. I have done it in all the bright staring colors I could get, a sort of thing between Etruscan and Pompeii; and the son of the Duca di Sermoneta, much the most clever and agreeable person in Rome, but whom I never got an opportunity of introducing at Blessington Castle, has had the patience, kindness, and ability to come and stand on the steps of a ladder till he had finished, with much spirit, a frieze of one hundred men, women, horses, and chariots round the apartment.

"I beg to say few people possess rooms adorned by the hands of a duke, descended from the Lombard conquerors of Italy, or with an estate ten miles long by fifteen, producing twopence a year. 'Adieu, my duck,' says the Moore; love to you all.

"Once more, ever yours, W. G."

The following letter, signed E., inclosed in a letter of Sir W. Gell to Lady Blessington, is thus addressed:

"FROM THE BEST BERKELY HUNDRED CHEESEMAKER.

"Naples, 4th April.

"LA DEA CONSOLATRICE,—Your poetry is the best I have ever seen, and made us all laugh, while I admired the style. I am much better than I was, but not quite well, nor shall I be till these barbarous March winds are over, and I have taken some baths. Keppel has a bad cold. It is quite a disagreeable thing to have you at Rome while I am here. I heard last night at the Opera that Baily goes off for Rome to-morrow, and so I shall send this. I hope you have better health than we have, and better pens; this is the sixth new one I try to write with. Yours most affectionately, E."*

"Naples, July 5th (1828).

"I am resolved to write to you, though my hand refuse its office, and will probably be shared by its less practiced fellow before I have filled my sheet. I have been attacked with an abominable rheumatism, beginning in the shoulder, and, having well established itself in the neck, so as to produce the most excruciating pains, sending a colony to establish itself in the elbow, wrist, and hand in the shape of the gout, that I have passed an entire week in purgatory, whence I am now only beginning to escape, with the loss of the little remaining hair, known by its 'couleur *mouchicide*,' as the count used to say of it. Let 'my lawful,' therefore, prepare her spirits for the reception of her bald admirer, and no longer expect those beautiful ringlets which Lord Blessington so well remembers. Bless me! I have given you a whole page of my own misfortunes, when I only intended to say I have been and still am ill, but in the mean time have taken the measures for removing the remains of my person to the Holy City, to partake of the corner of the heterodox at the pyramid of Caius Cestius.

"So I have stolen from myself, therefore, the necessary money for the journey, and in wishing to lend my house to a most excellent person and friend of mine, Miss Whyte, in my absence, have found a tenant who insists upon paying rent whether I will or not, and with whom I can leave my goods and chattels all at sixes and sevens, just as they are, without any trouble or preparation. The gentleman Lord Blessington calls the training groom has the politeness to be just as ill, or rather worse than I am, all the time; so that, having been forced to give up going out, we are obliged to dine at home, much assisted by the frequent appearance of Fox, who, having found out that the groom knows a trick or two besides training, has long courted his society.

"I am sometimes astonished by the wonderful knowledge of my companion

* It is possible this letter, signed E., in the hand-writing of a very aged person, is the production of the Margravine of Anspach, whose Christian name was Elizabeth.—R. R. M.

on all political subjects, and do not depend on my own judgment, which has not been exercised that way, but on that of Fox, who is in every respect capable. I fear I shall lose my said friend at Rome, and then Lord Blessington will not have the trouble of being civil, though, if you continue to repeat the kind things the groom has said of Lord B——, that may perhaps effect a change. The news here is, that the Holy City is so full of factious and fractious John and Mary Bulls, that the whole herd is split into four or five sections, and one party abjures the other. The universal complaint is, however, that there are two houses so much more pleasant than the rest, that the gentlemen of taste and intellect won't go to the others, which are comparatively deserted, and these houses are yours and Lady Mary's.* Here you have the sum and substance of all the letters from Rome to friends at Naples, and perhaps this may give you the first idea of what you are doing, which I dare say you were not aware of. I have a letter from Miss Agnes Berry at Paris, with snow and sleet, and the other 'agremens' of the season, and they return to England to be with poor Mrs. Dorner, whom they think failing, and who wants them, otherwise they would have been at Rome with the Hardwickes. They write that they mean to be at Lucca baths with Lady Charlotte Lindsay in the summer, and vow I shall go, whether I will or not; while I, like a goose, feel more than half inclined.

"Matthias desires kind things to you—'God bless my soul!'† I have just got a letter from Egypt, where my friend Wilkinson has found at Thebes a whole list of *kings* not yet known, painted and carved on three sides of the room. He announces twenty-seven queens, ladies of high fashion in their time, two of whom were black, and one very ill-tempered. How he finds out their disposition I can not tell. My nephew is, I find, arrived at Rome, and I conclude will be in scrapes, if he can not get some body to take care of him. I fear he would be of little use to you; but if you should feel compassion for his youth and innocence, order him to wait upon you, and say I did it, but I will not force him on your charities. When I have settled my affairs, I shall let you know the day when, after breakfasting at Albano, I shall hope to rejoice in the sunshine of your eyes once more. W. GELL.

"'A sua Eccellenza la Signora Contessa di Blessington, Palazzo Negroni, Roma."

"Naples, December 29th, 1829.

"I have put off writing to you so long, day after day, that I almost feel ashamed at last of addressing you. One of the causes was the delay of 'my unfaithful spouse,' who has been for six months in my debt a letter; and another, that where no good can be done, one feels averse to mentioning the many subjects you must have encountered of an unpleasant and afflicting nature. I beg only to assure you that, though absent and distant, I have never ceased to think of you with regard and affection, and to have most anxious-

* The house of Lady Mary Deerhurst.—R. R. M.

† A favorite exclamation of poor old Matthias, the author of the Pursuits of Literature.—R. R. M.

ly inquired of all travelers from France concerning your welfare and proceedings.

"Nevertheless, till the unexpected arrival of Colonel Stewart, I had never been able to make out any thing satisfactory about you; for, though Mills seems to have known, yet a tour which he made to England seemed to put an end to his power of writing; and even Craven, who was in the habit of hearing from him, heard no more. Lately, I have an account of you from Mr. Hamilton, who sent me a Mr. Chester, to whom I was to give certain introductions to persons in Egypt. Since I saw you, I have, I think, written two or three books, none of which have as yet appeared in public. One is a little treatise on the walls and military architecture of the Greeks, with a view to the question about Cyclopean walls, with about thirty plates, which I have dedicated and given to the Royal Society of Berlin, out of gratitude for their unsought protection and election of myself when I was as yet young and unknown.

"This, I believe, they are publishing at Berlin. The other is a second series of Pompeiana, which was thought of when you were in Italy, but which is now enlarged to more than eighty plates, and is in the hands of Mr. Jennings, a bookseller in London, who begins to publish it in the spring. In the mean time, I recommended to him the propriety of sending me £500, which he says he was very glad to do, and which I regret is now in a fair way of dissipation, having, however, stopped in its progress the mouths of my creditors, occasioned by Mr. Fauntleroy. I shall request that you will accept a copy of the new work on Pompeii, as a companion to that which used to be on your table.

"I suppose we shall soon hear some advertisement on the subject, so pray do not send for it if you feel so disposed, as I will order you to be served with one of my own copies. I did not much like the account I sent Count D'Orsay about his Sicilian money. The people are such thorough-bred cheats, that they have made a roundabout plot to throw it upon the shoulders of the government, who are not troubled with a propensity to payment. We have fewer milords than usual this year, and at Rome there is also a deficiency.

"The Normanby plays at Florence seem to make that place the favored residence. Here we have the Langford, Brookes, and Townley Parkers of Cheshire, very admirable people, and I don't know that I ever remember the society so pleasant as it has been for the last two years. Bess Caldwell was at Rome last year, and she seemed very much taken up with going every day to examine the Duke of Buckingham's exhalations. It is supposed she meant excavations. When she heard of poor Sir William Drummond's death, she asked whether that was not the man that died writing a history of oranges; by which she meant 'Origines.' She is a great loss, but I suppose you will have her at Paris this year. I was pleased and displeased to see by the papers that the count had won a race. I am always in a fright at all sorts of sporting for money; and often one small sum won causes the loss of thousands.

"I fear you will none of you ever come into Italy again, unless you can contrive to ruin yourselves. The Roman disturbances are ended, and even Lady Sandwich has been to dine with Lady Mary. What geese people are, to say no worse of the trying to pull all one's neighbors down to get into their places. The poor archbishop is by no means right; he has lost his favorite Annette, which is a severe blow to him, poor man! in his eighty-sixth year. Otherwise, I don't think he was more changed than his age would warrant. He always asks very kindly about you all.

"I saw the Filangieré the other night; he told me his wounds were breaking out afresh, and giving him pain. The Ricciardis spend their lives in getting up plays, but as it has rained three months, and now begins to snow, who can go to them? I must apologize for my horrid paper, the baseness of which I did not detect till it was too late to retract. Do you know old Le Chevalier, the author of the voyage to the Troad? He was formerly a great friend of mine, as was Barbia de Bocage, the Barber of the Grove, but he is dead, and, I fear, Le Chevalier is by this time grown old; but he is a very good man, and of the old school.

"My health is, I think, much the same, or perhaps, on the whole, improved. Pray let me hear all about yourself, and remember me most kindly to the fat doctor, Sir Manly, and the count—most kindly, poor little souls! to those two children. W. GELL."

"Sir William Drummond's book goes on slowly, on account of the writing. As to such drawings as you are kind enough to admire, they cost but little trouble, and have no value; but being taken from the antique, or being of places difficult of access, as you say, we shall be bound in calf together, with great éclat. Speaking of art, M. Ternite has at length seen the new pictures at Pompeii, and says of that of Achilles and Briseis, 'Ah, c'est unique.' Moreover, he swears that, compared to it, all that modern painters have ever done are, in comparison, daubs. I really believe I shall be old fool enough to see it before I go to Rome, which must take place, whether I will or no. I fear the poor abbé has lost £500 by the failure of B—— and Company.

"W. GELL."

"Naples, March 20th, 1832.

"You have been on my conscience for at least the last six months, that is, I have been purposing to myself to write to you for at least so long a time; but I have been so much occupied in writing like a steam-engine for my bread, that I have been obliged to neglect every thing else, till I could finish a work on the Roman Topography, in which there is nothing about Rome, but a great deal about the country, and which the Society of Dilettanti are undertaking, and for which I now expect, perhaps in vain, at least £500, to satisfy the claims of the Torlonias, who give one enough of credit to be one's ruin.

"Among the misfortunes of the age, cholera, reform, and rebellion, the poor dear old Countess Ricciardi, of Camaldoli, has been a terrible loss to her family and friends; she had the measles (which the Italian doctors do not know how to treat, when of the kind called confluent); and just as the poor Princess of Butera died a year ago, our poor friend was killed, by the disease being thrown inward by some imprudent exposure to air, and the total want of knowledge of the doctors. She died about two days ago. The unhappy husband left the house, and retired to that of Coriati, whose daughter married one of the Ricciardi's sons. I can not tell you any more of the consequences, but every body was sorry for her, poor soul! and regretted her loss. You remember Mr. H——'s sudden attachment to her, and they have continued great friends ever since, and seen one another often, as he lives at the Belvidere. He is only yesterday returned from Persano, where he was pretending to shoot, by way of getting over the fêtes of the Carnival. We have had a very bad winter—that is, it has never been very cold, but always too cold, and it has rained much more than usual. Even now it is not at all the climate for enjoyment, and the spring is three weeks later than it is in general. I hope you got, and continue to get, the new work on Pompeii; if not, let me know, I beg, that I may arm you with full powers against the publisher, Mr. Jennings.

"The world here is much altered since you left it. I should say, the society last year was better than ever, but I was prevented, by the probability of the *Trastoverini* sacking Rome, from going there. I intend to go this year, if they do not get up another riot between the French and Austrians, which seems not unlikely. In the mean time, the world is grown much more luxurious and expensive, for one is asked every day to dinners of sixteen and twenty, instead of ten and twelve, and there seems to be a ball, even in Lent, nearly every night, only not with fiddles.

"Yesterday I was invited to three dinners, Lord Hertford, Lady Drummond, and Sir George Talbot, and to an assembly at the two first, and another at Count Lebrettern's, the Austrian minister, so that the world here is really going on swimmingly. We are to have an omnibus expedition to Pompeii on Monday next, under the auspices of Lord Hertford. It carries twenty-four, and I think so great will be its fall, that I intend going in a carriage of my own, if I can. You know we have Sir Walter, and he is in much better health; in short, I should say recovered, and all the better since his arrival here. I took him to Miss Whyte's, in the way to Pæstum, and I see him almost every day, and dine with him to-morrow. He is very agreeable in a drive or *tête-à-tête*, but lost in parties of twenty, to which he is invited. I took him to the archbishop's* to dine, and am to go again this week. The archbishop is quite well, except an inflamed eye, which Dr. Hogg says they are treating ill, and which might be cured in a few hours; but he has recommended a proper cure to the canonico, who will, I hope, persuade the Neapolitan doctor to apply it. Sir Granville Temple told me last night Champollion was dead. It is a great loss, as I believe he has no successor, unless Rosellini of

* The Archbishop of Tarento.

Pisa may be so called. Our last accounts of your London cholera are alarming, but I trust untrue. Pray remember me kindly to the count, and all who are faithful to you—to your sister of the long eyelashes, the Contessa ——, for I never can remember the name, pray also remember me. On the whole, Italy is quiet and uncholeric for the present, and I can not but think you would be at least as happy here as among the turbulencies of Lord Grey and Co.

"W. G.

"P.S.—Among the curiosities, I was delighted to see Miss Skeene, who is the 'Miss Pratt' of the novel called 'Inheritance.' You remember, she comes to Lord ——'s house in a hearse. I asked Sir Walter, before I saw her, if the character was like. He said, 'Well, I believe it may be, with a little ill nature added to her.' She seems the very person. I was near calling her Miss Pratt twenty times."

CHAPTER XVIII.

LETTERS OF SIR WILLIAM GELL TO LADY BLESSINGTON.

"Naples, October 26th, 1832.

"I am become so much of a coffee-house, that I really have been two days beginning to write to you, and even now I begin with two people talking to me, so that it is not likely I should indite any thing coherent. You are right in saying I have been long obeying your order to write. The besetting vice, after vanity of this world, is putting off, just as hell is said to be paved with good intentions. I have certainly put off writing for the last three months, having all the time suffered my duty to sit as an incubus upon my conscience. I have now, however, received your kind present and your beautiful picture. Without compliment, it is a most lovely portrait, and, except the expression, is like you; there is something about the mouth which is not you; and what is singular is, that most of the people who see it on my table exclaim at the likeness to Lady Augusta Coventry, who is grown up into a beautiful girl, and makes many conquests among the heathen. The picture by Mr. Uwins is, I think, like me, but it is a little more unhappy than the original. Nevertheless, I must have a melancholy cast of countenance, for a Mr. Uwins, at Rome, has taken a small waxen profile of me, which has the same character; and it would not be extraordinary, after thirty-two years of illness, if some twinges had taken a permanent lodging in some of my features. I am, however, except the loss of most of my hair, not so much worse than when you quitted Italy as might have been expected, and Lord Hertford's plan has saved me for the last eighteen months from the same degree of torment which I have suffered for the last ten years. I was in hopes your letter would have told me when you intended to revisit these countries; but your house, as Craven tells me, is so exquisite in all respects, that he thinks it impossible any thing can ever tempt you to move again. Mr. Powell, who seems a most agreeable person, I have already seen twice, and am to meet to-morrow at dinner at Craven's. He gives a good account of yourself, and tells me that the affairs of Count Alfred will soon be arranged to his satisfaction. I am delighted to see that the spirit of order which you always possessed, and which has done so much good on other occasions, has enabled you to take care of such of your friends as have less foresight than yourself. My preaching has the peculiar advantage of coming from a person who is always in debt, and always in the last stage of poverty himself. Either the cholera or the reform has so fettered the booksellers in London, that, though the Dilettanti Society have engraved a map for me at their own expense, yet £300, which I want to get for the book accompanying it, from a bookseller, do not seem at the moment to be easily forthcoming. You say Mr. Uwins has given you my picture. Do you mean that you have not got my last Pompeiana, second series? If not, it is not my fault, but your own, for decidedly Messrs. Chaplin and Jennings, in Fleet Street, have long ago put down your name as one of my copies *sent*. Pray send immediately about it, for I dare say all the booksellers will fail on the first opportunity. I am sure I sent you the order very long ago. By-the-by, I wish there were any means of seeing your *Byroniana* here, where nothing ever arrives till five years after its birth. You are probably, by this time, an arbiter of the fate of more than one bookseller. Jennings told Craven that nothing sold but what would go into one of the annuals. It is very disagreeable to a poor author to write without a certain way of disposing of his works. I have at present about seventy paintings from Pompeii, &c., which are colored from the originals, and form a very beautiful and useful history of the art among the ancients. I wish I could find a bookseller to undertake it. Should you see any means of furthering my interest with your man of books, pray nail the said bookseller, if you can do it without inconvenience to yourself. I think I could make an interesting work on the Arabs of Spain, interspersed with translations of some of their poetry, which would suit one or any of the annuals, but I must have introduced some views of the Alhambra, to make it more interesting.

"If I ever *come of age*, and am not obliged to write for money, I shall certainly, at all events, give the public an account of the Moors, with the Alhambra as an embellishment, as the last and most exquisite of their works. I have got notes without end on the subject, which I think would make a very interesting book. Our mountain goes on burning, and, I think, seems inclined to continue ejecting lava, till a little cone, which has grown out of the centre of the crater, you remember, shall be as high as the highest peak of the hill.

"*November 2d.* I dined at Craven's with Mr. Powell and his companion, Mr. Harcourt. They are going, under the protection of Lord William Fitzgerald, to Cumæ, on Saturday, and I was asked to meet them at dinner on their return. In short, they go about sight-seeing, and they seem to have little occasion for any assistance from me. I shall try to get them a footing at Lady Coventry's, who keeps open house every evening both here and at

Rome, and under whose auspices they may see all the world without trouble. I have already told you Lady Augusta is grown up one of the prettiest girls possible, and one of the best-educated and well-informed, and mamma has taken her to court; and, in short, she is come out, and the house is on a better footing, and has more company in consequence. We have Lord Ponsonby arrived as minister, but Mr. Hill is yet at the Belvidere on the Vomero, for Lord Berwick is expected not to survive twenty-four hours. It is true he rallies perpetually, but by the time this reaches you, you may consider Mr. Hill to have become Lord Berwick. You were very kind in remembering my servants, and they were very much struck with your goodness when I told them, and desired to kiss your hand. Craven desires also a thousand kind remembrances. He is in bad humor, as he thinks he is more deaf than usual, but I think it only imagination. Nevertheless, he would soon become a sort of hermit if he had not some one to keep him always in agitation. The young captain seems disposed to keep him in hot water every now and then; but it is a very agreeable, genteel youth, and he acts quite without a rival both in French and English. We are to have private theatricals this winter, and I dare say shall do very well for company, though the characters supposed to be coming from England are, as yet, not named. A family of Colonel Vyse have settled in the Palazzo Paterno, one of the most agreeable that ever came to Naples, in my opinion. They are numerous, but seem to be rich, so as to have all in due proportion. It is said many are come to Rome, but I can learn no names. The Torlonias go on just as usual. You would scarcely know the father was defunct, except that you don't hear his tremendous cough when you go there. I suspect my finances are, however, arrived at that state which will render my visits to Rome more rare and more difficult. Mrs. Dodwell is at last by no means so ill off as we feared; in short, every thing considered, I hope she will be in a better state of finance than nine tenths of the Roman nobility. Mr. Mills, who is gone to Sicily, and myself, were left her trustees, and I think, between coaxing and scolding, her affairs are in a fair way of being settled, insomuch that we have relinquished the business, our agency being no longer required. Pray remember me most kindly to Colonel Stewart, who has been expected here for the last three years by many. For my part, I conceive that Dr. Potter, who hates Naples, will not bring him here again. I hear of the ex-Lady Gell, La Comtessa di St. Marsault,* sitting with a disdainful air in a high fly-cap in a corner of the room. My blessing upon her. The archbishop, who has got your picture, and is delighted with it, has been ill, but is now flourishing, aged ninety. Matthias is younger than ever, and more discontented.

"The Ricciardis I will see or send your message to, with all speed. They have not recovered their loss. My dog family consists of *Ticati*, who is my companion, his son and heir, *Monsu Qua*, a youth of promising talents. I

* The countess was the youngest sister of Lady Blessington, lately the Miss Mary Anne Power whom Gell used to call "my lawful."—R. R. M.

have also a white terrier, *Monsu Bo*, of Craven breed. My house is really become quite pretty at the expense of £100 two years ago, and when finished, and I called for the account, I found it had been paid by Lord de Ros; Sir Charles Monck also gave me a fine organ, so you would not know the place. My kind regards to Count Alfred, and pray continue to believe me very affectionately yours, W. G.

"P.S.—Ladies are so used to writing criss-cross, that perhaps you will not be displeased at this for your Byronian, and may put it in your own terms if my short note suits you. Lord Byron had once a vis-a-vis; I used frequently to drive out with him in it. One day, passing the Alfred Club, he asked if I were a member. I said some one had put me down, but as I had never been there, I was going to take my name out. 'Oh,' says he, 'on no account take out your name.' 'Why?' said I. 'Because there are nine hundred candidates waiting for admission, and I should have taken out my own name, but that I found it would make one of these expectants happy. Only imagine,' said he, 'if you took yours off also, there would be two of these wretches delighted, and that would be really too much.' He then, as we had no auditors, laughed at his own affected misanthropy, which was only put on for the purpose of making the world in general believe there was something extraordinary about him, and which he found for many years a great recommendation in that sort of highly-refined society, which is in perpetual want of new and extraordinary excitation. I believe I mean excitement. Adieu. W. G.

"I fear my letter is stupid, and has too much parish business, but I hope my next will be more entertaining."

"Naples, April 4th, 1833.

"I scarcely know why I have been so long in answering your amiable letter, and thanking you for your kind attention about books and booksellers; for, though I have been frequently ill, and have passed the winter, which has been here remarkably cold, rather comfortably, I have somehow or other written a great deal, and when your letter arrived had just been employing myself, by the desire of the family, in writing those very same memoirs of Sir Walter Scott's residence in Italy which you recommended to my attention. I have made use of the letter from the bookseller you had spoken to so far as to direct Mr. Hamilton's attention to him with regard to the disposal of my 'Roman Topography,' but I have not as yet heard the result. Not that I have, indeed, any great hopes of any thing favorable, for he writes that the booksellers are absolutely ruined, and that even [———] has been twice in danger of bankruptcy. M——, however, offers to print my book, and to give me half the profits, which is not what I want, as such profits, though guaranteed by the Society of Dilettanti, are never likely to be great to an author abroad. The odd circumstance is, that though the book was written at the desire of the said society, and they profess high satisfaction at its execution, they do not offer me the £300 which I want, and take the profits to themselves as they arise. Miss Scott wrote to me, by the desire of Mr. Lockhart, to beg I would send him my reminiscences of Sir Walter, because I was 'the last of his friends.' The fact is, that I had generally the care of him while he was in Italy, and though I thought I was going to write only a page or two, I soon found myself writing my twentieth and thirtieth pages, without approaching the end of my materials, which finally reached a fiftieth page, and, considering all circumstances, the whole is by no means so barren of interest as I thought it would have been when I begun the narrative. It contains, even to a certain degree, information as to his future literary projects, which could not have been recorded, I believe, by any other means.

"I shall send you a little bit of it with regard to Lord Byron, which I forgot to send you before, and you can mention it or not, as it suits your purpose. Your house at the Belvidere is just become vacant by the retreat of Lord Berwick, who is going to England. He wishes to buy it, and the price is only about £3000, so it is quite wonderful it is not already sold, as the windows have been renewed. The dowager queen has bought and beautifully fitted up your Villa Gallo, and the Duke of Gallo himself died some two months ago, having left his family not ill provided for. It is hoped Diego Pignatelli will marry the widow. Of the Ricciardis, there is nothing new; they are well, and always ask most kindly about you. Naples has the advantage of Rome this year in point of company; but after the Holy Week we are to change sets. To-day is the holy Thursday, when carriages are not permitted in Naples, so I am going on an ass to dine with Lord Hertford at the next house to the Paterna, and I hear he has either juggles or phantasmagoria at night. My pension as vice-chamberlain seems about to be granted, under the protection of the lord chancellor—that is, it would seem so, for the claim is established, and he promises his assistance; but I am not to be deluded by appearances, and Lady Charlotte Lindsay, who says she backed her application with a roasted turkey and a bottle of well-iced champagne, says she is aware, like Lord Duberley, that 'fine words butter no parsnips.' The acknowledgment of my claim proves that I ought to have arrears, and if they did not acknowledge my claims, it might in the end be worse for their own people, and would serve as a precedent to cut them off. Nevertheless, I shall only believe in my pension when I see it. I have written all this while obliged to talk to company, who *sit* upon me, a penance to which I am very much subjected; and my house is really become so pretty by the expenditure of only £100 upon it, which has built a portico, and made all the rooms communicate in a suite, besides a fine organ which Sir Charles Monck gave me, that I am become a sort of coffee-house for the idle and the *nothing-to-doarians* of the place. I believe I shall not get to Rome this year, as my journey depended on the £300 for my book arriving, and that seems cut off.

"Now for Sir Walter: I accompanied him to the convent of La Trinita della Cava, and in going he repeated to me the poem or ballad of Jock of Hazledean. In returning I desired him to let me hear it again, and on expressing my surprise at the clearness of his recollection, he told me he had a most remarkable memory, and had astonished many by it. On his first introduction to Lord Byron, some one (whose name I forget) was looking on with wonder at the apparent correctness with which he spoke, and the singular changes in Lord Byron's countenance as he proceeded. He was repeating to the great poet the whole of the poem of Hardyknute, which he then knew by heart, and which proved so highly interesting to his lordship. My notes also refer to a conversation I had with Sir Walter as to why he had left off writing poetry. When I asked this question, he said, 'Because I found Byron beat me; but I shall now try again.' These anecdotes, which may amuse some, are all found in my contribution, which I have sent to Hamilton to give to Mr. Lockhart; for as the family had requested them of me, I could not well dispose of them to my own advantage, which I was told I might easily do.

"I keep a copy, however; and if Mr. Lockhart does not use my materials, which I think he can hardly reject, as I have taken care to give due honor to his hero, they may appear hereafter separately. I have lately been very idle as to writing; for the penny magazines afford no encouragement to booksellers, nor they, in consequence, to me. I hear I am made a member of the French Institute, and so is Millingen, who is just come into my room, and sends his best respects to you. I hear of Count Alfred in the newspapers as hunting in Leicestershire: pray give my kindest regards to him. I have also lately seen a print of him on horseback, which is good. Lady Augusta Coventry and Henry Fox are to be united in the holy bands of matrimony immediately, at Florence, whence they proceed northward. She is become a very pretty girl, and he has at present a very bad fit of the gout at Rome. The houses at Castelamare are already taken for the summer. Lord Ponsonby was on the point of embarking for Constantinople in the Actæon, when, the day before yesterday, so violent a storm arose that he is yet on shore.

"My servants, who all cherish your memory, hearing me ask about the means of sending this letter to you, desire to kiss your hands, according to the custom of the country. My dogs, horses, and every thing else, remain just as you left them, except that I inherited the margravine's landau, which is more convenient for my disabled legs. My kind regards to the Contessa de St. M——, whom I have heard of sitting silent in a corner in a high cap.

"William Gell."

"Naples, Nov. 19th, 1833.

"Your friend, Mr. Bulwer, I have received safe, with his friends; but not so your book, which, in a box with several things of their own, they have contrived to lose on the way; so I must put off the gratification I should have had in reading it till somebody here gets it, which may not be for months to come, for books are ages before they arrive in this country. Mr. Bulwer seems, indeed, all you have described; for, though he has only been here some three or four days, yet we have contrived to get very well acquainted in a very short time. I asked them to breakfast the morning after I received your letter, and they brought me one at the same time from Lady S—— at Rome, by which I found they were fond of dogs; so that the first thing I heard in my outer room, and before I saw any person, was the exclamation, 'Oh, you dear creature!' addressed to my dog, who went to see who was come. We got on very well, and they ate maccaroni with great success, and positively bought a dog of the same species as mine before they went home, of a black color, which they christened Lusio, and carried off to their lodgings. I have had a note from each of them since, and on Sunday I am to meet them at dinner at Mr. Craven's, for whom I believe you gave them also a letter. I have also told Lady Drummond to invite them to dinner, which she has promised to do; and thus, so far, I hope they will feel satisfied with my little attentions, bestowed according to your order.

"I have made every inquiry as to the sale of books by a bookseller here, and, not trusting to my own exertions, I have employed such of my friends as are most fitted for the purpose. There is nothing in the shape of bookselling in this town; the libraries are only just tolerated, and their owners can hardly exist. No bookseller here has a correspondent in London, that I can find; nor do I hear of any purchase of such a book as yours, except the Duke of Cassorano, in the whole city. He immediately thought of making such a book himself, and filling it with princesses of Centola, Tre Cose, Monte Yago, &c., &c.; but he could give me no assistance, and certainly Naples is not a place for the advancement of literature, so I am unable to execute your commands. You had heard that I was in bad health, and so I am certainly; but I think not much worse than when you were in Italy, only that my hair is fallen off, and I shall be reduced to baldness or a wig in the course of another year, if I live so long. Here is Terrick Hamilton just arrived, but going shortly to Rome. He is well and merry; but when I meet him at dinners, where I die of cold, he is always complaining of heat, and is very amiable. Here, also, is Dr. M'G——, author of the last novel I read, called 'The Parson's Daughter.' At this moment I received a little work of a few pages from the archbishop upon cats, on the occasion of a cat's mummy brought for him from Egypt by a friend of mine, Dr. Hogg, who is just come from that country. The good old soul is really very little altered since you saw him, though he is now ninety-two; but I can not imagine how the machine is to go on much longer. He desires one thousand loves to you, and I am to take the Bulwer to dine with him shortly, though I fear, if he is not quick at Italian, he will scarcely become very intimate, as I observed Walter Scott and Monsignore did not make it out very well together, for the archbishop will not take the trouble to talk much or long together in French. By-the-by, I observed to you that my life of Walter Scott in Italy, which I wrote by the desire of Miss Scott, was very entertaining in its way, and I sent it to Mr. L. by Mr. Hamilton. He has never, however, thanked me for it, nor even acknowledged the receipt of it, nor sent me Sir Walter's works, which he ordered for me with almost the last sentence he uttered that was intelligible; and if it does not appear in the work, it will be really worth publishing, and I shall send it to you.

"*November 27th.* I went with the Bulwer to the archbishop's to dine yesterday. The good old man would be very polite, which I told him to submit to. He showed us several curiosities, and put off the dinner till four by so doing. We coaxed his cats, and Bulwer seemed much pleased with him, as he seemed with Bulwer. There was nobody but Cavaliere Venorio, the chief of the botanists here; and he seemed, also, to get on very well with the Bulwer, who is this day gone to Pompeii, luckily with fine weather. At this moment, in comes the Baron de Billing, the French secretary of embassy, who wishes to know Mr. Bulwer, and I have given him a note of introduction, as I promised. The Baron de Billing has been ten years in London, and is a very clever person, and I think it probable you know him. The Craven's mother has bought and fitted up beautifully your old Villa Gallo, but your other house, the Belvidere, remains untenanted since Lord Berwick departed, and will want repairs, as I hear, before it can be habitable again. It is to be sold for only £3000, and Lady Drummond has given over £10,000 for the villa, or cake house, of Mr. Dupont, on the Capo di Monte. We have three or four of the Yacht Club here, with their ships, which help to enliven the scene, and we expect Lord Anglesey with his. I have seen Lady Harriet and her sister, as also, another day, her aunt; she is so altered since I knew her as a girl that I really should not have known her. They live at Brettagna, but in such retirement that I have never seen any of them out. The Acton Palace is so far finished that they receive company, and give dinners and balls with great success. It is quite astonishing how many people come to Naples, and how the people, whom I knew when I was a young man in London, appear yet unexhausted, so that I have very often my whole morning taken up by visitors. Matthias, aged eighty-one, is rather younger than ever, but complains that he sees nobody. Craven had him to dinner, and remarked how clever he was at contriving to ask questions without ceasing, yet never to profit in the least by the answer. The canonico is well and merry, and the Ricciardi in a good state. Cariati and Casarano desire *mille choses* to you.

"W. G."

"Naples, January 22, 1834.

"I am now roasting myself close to a large fire in my own house, waiting dinner for Dr. Hogg, a portentous name, you will say, but belonging to an exceedingly benevolent and amiable physician, who, after residing here for some years, is just returned from a tour in Syria and Egypt, with your friend Mr. Baillie. Though I am roasting, the necessity for it is only produced by my own cold nature, for a finer summer's day was never seen than this has been, and Doctor Watson, who is just arrived from Paris, where he has been five or six years, says he had no idea of the difference till he found himself again in Italy. He says that, except the three 'glorious days,' he has never seen the weather so fine since he left Naples. But that was not at all the thing I intended to say. My first object was to tell you that my man, Gennarino, who is only just saved by the English doctors from death, has been twice to see the boy in question, and that he is quite well and happy. He has fine, light-colored hair, which could scarcely be seen for the magnificent cap, made ornamental, which he wore on his head. He appears about six or seven years old, and is very lively, and they say very clever, and learns every thing with quickness. He is, moreover, remarkably clean and well clothed, and, as Gennarino says, is treated quite like a *signore di qualita e parla Francese*, and is so well satisfied with his present treatment, and with those who have the care of him, that he ran away and hid himself when he found the inquiries were made for himself, for fear that my man might be sent to take him away. There is always a drawback to every story, and it appears that the little boy has some sort of defect in one leg, which may be perhaps in the hip joint, but is called in the foot, and it is said that Ischia waters will cure him. I confess, from the account, the cure seems to me doubtful, but in the mean time the boy is perfectly well in health, and by means of a shoe with a thicker sole, 'fatto dal meglio scarpayo di Napoli con molta cura,' he runs about just as well as any other boy of his age. As far as care goes, therefore, he has all you can wish, and his health is perfect. A letter is just arrived for his mother from the family, which I shall direct and send, as the letters sent before had probably failed from want of superscription.

"So much, therefore, for your commission, which I hope you will find satisfactory. I have consulted Casarano about the sale of your book here, and I find any attempt would be quite useless, as nobody has any money for books in the whole kingdom, nor will any one buy a book of any kind. I have heard only of four persons any where who read or buy. Two live in the mountains of the frontier, and thus smuggle into the state the few books they can obtain; the third is a Neapolitan cavaliere, who receives books of classic learning from Germany; and the fourth is the prefect of a provincial town, who longs in vain for books, but is forced to go without them. I shall keep a sharp look-out for Colonel Hughes, who, I suppose, is one of Lord Dinorben's family.

"You have done me a great kindness by sending me the 'Conversations,' of which I have hitherto seen only detached portions, which, by-the-by, are so full of talent and of shrewd observation, that I can not help congratulating the memory of Lord Byron on the fortunate circumstance which left his ideas in such good keeping, that they have been matured and perfected before they saw the light. There were brave men before, as a Roman poet observes, but no Homer to celebrate them. The truth is, you see things in a much better, and fairer, and juster light yourself than Byron; you know more of the world than he did; and, moreover, it is not part of your system to make yourself seem in ill humor when you are not so.

"I beg to observe that, in 'The Conversations,' I reverence you infinitely more than the poet; indeed, as I have more respect for Homer than for *Agamemnon*, I have had this in my mind whensoever I have read the extracts from your work, but you have probably had the same feeling repeated many times, and better explained by a hundred literary admirers. As to Mr. L——, I fear much that he is not good for much, and I am certain he got the work, for I sent it to Mr. William Hamilton, who gave it with a request that he would not omit a word of it in printing. I kept a copy of it, however, and I will send it to you. There are no remarks except such as tend to explain away and render less ridiculous the total want of classical taste and knowledge of the hero, in a situation full of classical recollections, and which I have added, that I might not seem insensible to his real merits. They were written for the family, and by the desire of Miss Scott herself, and therefore nothing offensive could have been inserted; and when I had finished the anecdotes, I was surprised myself at the number of circumstances I had recollected, and perceived that the account of the last days of so distinguished a person was really interesting, when told with strict regard to truth. The circumstances of his illness having changed his mind, or deprived it of its consistency, which I myself much doubt, might be judged of from his way of treating the subjects of conversation which presented themselves, and this alone would be of consequence to his numerous friends.

"I think it scarcely possible that any of those most attached to him could be displeased at my manner of representing him, and, at all events, I have repeated what he said, and related what he did in Italy, in a way that satisfied every one here who was the witness of his sayings and doings. However, I shall send the copy to you, and if the Life is published by the said L——, without use and acknowledgment of my papers, the best way will be to sell it to the bookseller, and to let it come before the public. I will affix, or rather prefix, Miss S——'s request that I would write it, and will suppose that the original has been lost or mislaid, in consequence of her premature decease. In this case, I shall beg of you to make the most advantageous bargain you can for a poor author under your protection.

"My book on Roman Topography, which will, I am persuaded, if it ever sees the light, gain me credit, still continues unsold and unprinted. M—— is calculating the expense, Hamilton and Co. and Vyse are interesting themselves, and the University of Cambridge offers to take one hundred copies, but I hear of no results at present. Mr. Bulwer has written to his man of bookselling in London, after having read my work, to recommend it, but the answer is not yet returned. The times are bad, or, as my royal mistress would have expressed it, 'O trumpery, O Moses,' for 'O tempora,' &c. I go on scribbling at you to the end of my paper, which you must rejoice to see arrived.

"I dine with the archbishop to-day, who is well and merry, and sends his love. Lady H—— is leaving Naples for Rome immediately. I suppose, at the end of March, I shall see her again at Rome. WILLIAM GELL.

"Mrs. Dodwell is really become Countess Spaw, or Spanker, and is Bavarian *Incaricato,* and is to be minister at Rome. She will now have a fair chance in life; her last husband was quite crazy during the latter part of his life."

"Naples, 30th January, 1834.

"I have scarcely had time to overlook a copy of my Scottiana before Mr. Bulwer sets out for England. It is written by the Sticchini mentioned therein, who does not understand English, and therefore I fear blunders may have escaped me and him. I have an abominable headache, so that I can scarcely sit up to write, and I can say little more than what occurs to me as right.

"With regard to the MS., if Mr. L—— has got the original, and has used it entirely in his Life of Sir Walter, nothing is to be done, I suppose; but if he has not got it, has lost it, and does not publish it instanter, I am for selling it to the highest bidder. In my own copy I have the portrait, most luckily like, in a good sense, and two Roman caricatures mentioned.

"The Galera, which I took when there with you; a view of the Castle of Bracciano, which I took while sitting talking with Lord Blessington; a view from the window of the lake, which I took while talking with Sir Walter; and the stair-case in the court, which I did for him: but these I do not send, as I hear London booksellers can no longer deal with plates.

"I am too headachy to write more. WILLIAM GELL.

"Lady Harriet is gone to Rome."

"Naples, March 9th, 1834.

"I feel as if I were going to write you a long letter, and to become very troublesome. Since you wrote to me on the 17th of February, you will have received from Mr. Bulwer the MS. of the notes on Sir Walter Scott, and may have, perhaps, disposed of it to some bookseller in London, so that it no longer rests with me to decide on what should be its fate. I was asked, on the day I sent the original, why I sent it to Mr. L——? and I answered, because Miss S—— had asked me to write it; but that I was totally unacquainted with the gentleman, or he with me, and we had no friend in common.

"The truth is, that he ought to have been thankful for the information, and as the conversations chiefly took place in a carriage, these circumstances can not possibly have been learned from any other quarter. I dare say he thanked Mr. Hamilton, but as he thinks he has better information elsewhere, it is doing him no harm to keep my information for my own use; and when I consider that the whole about Rhodes can only have been said to me, and that I am the only person who could have given Sir Walter the information he wanted on that subject, I must think that interesting, and I could mention many other things in the MS. that could only be related by myself.

"However, I will beg of you to make a few changes, which I will write on a separate sheet, for I do not wish to offend any body, begging of you to wafer into the MS. at the proper places the few words about the publication at the beginning and end, and a few anecdotes which have recurred to my memory since the notes were written. I can not but imagine that you will be disappointed on reading the work, because it will be found so much shorter than you expected, the whole being purposely as much condensed as possible. You will therefore not be surprised if it does not produce in the market the respectable sum you have imagined as its value. I am not at all surprised at the wish to print it as if from another supposed hand, for I have seldom, out of the sixteen or seventeen publications I have made of maps and books, succeeded in securing to myself the fame of any merit they may possess.

"You would be surprised at the catalogue of literary thefts by which I have suffered. Yet, 'per grazia del cielo,' I find myself very frequently cited, both in England and on the Continent, wherever the subjects I have discussed are touched upon; and so much for that business. One shall be a great man among the little boys some years after one's death.

"Mr. Craven, with whom and the *Paterno*, and the Satriano Filangieris, &c., I have been to dine with Miss Whyte to-day at Portici, says he will get ready for you by the time appointed a story for your 'Book of Beauty.' Pray tell me whether a translation of a very queer old Portuguese book, 'The Travels of the Infante Don Pedro to the Seven Quarters of the Globe,' would not do for your work? It is very strange, and quite original, and the prince goes, among other places, to the court of Prester John of Abyssinia. It might be divided, perhaps, into two or three parts, if it be too long, which I really think it is. Would you like some of the old Spanish Moorish ballads translated? for example, any addressed to the 'beautiful Zayda,' as yours is a 'Book of Beauty?'

"I had once an idea of publishing such things when I was younger and more romantic, before age and infirmity had put an end to all poetic illusions.

"Mr. Rothwell, by-the-by, the great painter who was sent to me by Lord S——, and whom I have sent in a letter to you this morning, says, on looking over my book of the Alhambra, that a Moorish Annual or Album would be one of the prettiest things in the world, and might, with good engravings, become a successful work; and in such a case, the Moorish ballads would come in well. Nothing, certainly, would be half so picturesque or so beautiful; but, like every thing of the kind, it could not be carried on with interest for more than two or three years. I shall see, in your 'Book of Beauty,' what sorts of subjects are fitted for it, and hope to be able to do something in some way or other to suit it. A little bit of an adventure, a journey in Asia Minor, would perhaps not be amiss; but we shall see. I don't think myself capable of exciting much interest without having recourse to the pencil to aid my muse, whether poetic or historic. Lady H—— is gone, but it is possible I may see her at Rome, where I think of being on the 1st of April, and of remaining till the 1st of June. My house there is let to the 25th of March to Mr. Brooke Greville, who is perhaps known to you. We have floods of company, and sometimes, between Lady Strachan and Lady Acton, two private plays in a week. We had three Italian comedies, like the French vaudevilles, last night at Lady Acton's, and they were got up by Neapolitans with very great success.

"The young Duke of St. Theodoro, as a shy lover, won great applause, and Donna Olympia Colonna, and the mistress of the house, the Duchess of Miranda, and the Duchess of Cajanello, with many others, showed much talent in the French plays. Craven is the only Englishman engaged, but his son is expected soon. The family of La Feronays, as usual, form the heroes and heroines of all the French pieces, and sing and act in perfection.

"The king and all the court generally come to all these great entertainments, and, besides being very expensive, they last till about two hours after midnight. Besides those amusements, we have tremendous dinners at Lady Drummond's and Lord Hertford's, with assemblies in the evening, to most of which I go in my wheeling chair, by way of seeing the world in my old age, and must say I find every one as kind and compassionate as one can have either right or hopes to expect in these hard times. Craven, as you know, has bought a large convent in the mountains, near Salerno, which he has fitted up with every sort of convenience, and where he receives in the summer all comers, four or five ladies at a time, with gentlemen to match, and is really very hospitable both to strangers and natives. If you ever return to this country, you will be amused by a trip to his valley.

"I have sent you, as I said before, Mr. Rothwell, the new Sir Thomas Lawrence, and I think a very clever person; so much so, that he is quite big enough to help himself in the world. But I mean to send you a most benevolent and good sort of person, not much known to fame, with the ugly name of Dr. Hogg, who has been here some years, and is just returned from Egypt and the Holy Land, 'where saints did live and die.' He makes the most wonderful faces, and has the strongest action with his hands you ever saw, and Mr. Hill used to ask him to dinner to witness them; but he will tell you how the world goes on here better than most people, and as you have round you many men of rank and fashion, you will not dislike, for a change, to see a traveler without pretensions, whose merit consists in a kind heart, and a very benevolent disposition to do all he can for the benefit of his fellow-creatures. Speaking of which, Gennarino is become a great friend of the family, and the child in Strada di Chiaja, and sees them almost every day. He says they are all very well, and seem pleased at his coming to see how well the boy is taken care of. I forgot to say that Doctor Hogg will not torment you much, as he is only going to England for a short time on business. Our Duke of Derbyshire is in Sicily, and very much recovered from his lameness. He is very kind-hearted, and is the only person I have seen for years who knows any thing of my family, which I don't believe flourishing. My nephew, that hopeful youth, is at Milan, and, as Count Metri told me at the archbishop's (who is quite well, and salutes you), he is not very flourishing. How glad you must be my paper is ended, for curiosity will lead you to read the whole of my letter. So, with kind regards to the count, and thanks to Lord Durham, &c.,

"ANACHARSIS.

"Lady Blessington is requested to insert in my MS., after the last of the notes on Rhodes, the following record of a conversation with Sir Walter respecting the Stone of Odin:

"On our return to the Palazzo Caramanico, we passed Mr. Laing Mason in the street, and this brought to Sir Walter's mind the refutation of the antiquity of Macpherson's Ossian by Mr. Laing, who had shown that the names of the heroes were taken from the map, I think, of the channel between the Isle of Skye and the main land. 'One of these names,' said he, 'happens to have been given in the last century, and the date of that is well known.' Mr. Laing knew those countries well, and his proof was striking and satisfactory. I think he said Mr. Laing came originally from Orkney, and he added, 'I once went to see him, and carried over in my boat a fagot of sticks for the peas in his garden, which were reckoned there a great curiosity.' He said, however, that elders would grow, and that the face of the country might be improved by them. From this he was led to compare the once flourishing state of those islands with their present forlorn appearance, and observed that, 'to a people from the farthest north, these might perhaps have seemed the abodes of the blessed. They were certainly,' said he, 'esteemed holy, and there was a great circular building like Stonehenge not far from Kirkwall, which proved the importance of the place.' Saying this, he searched for and presented to me a pencil drawing of the temple, which I preserve, and highly value. It is entitled, 'Standing Stones of Stenhouse in Orkney,' and has on the back inscribed the name of J. Keene, Esq., by whom it was probably drawn. Sir Walter mentioned another pillar, called the Stone of Odin, which is perforated, and afterward descanted on the ordeal by which persons accused of crime were deemed innocent if capable of passing through this species of aperture in very remote ages.

"Lady B. is requested to insert the following passage where Sir Walter has been speaking of his acquaintance here:

"Before Sir Walter Scott quitted Naples, he made the acquaintance of Mr. Ball, a gentleman advantageously known to the society of that city as the author of two poems, of which the baronet was pleased to express his approbation. His amiable feeling, on every occasion, led him to assist and encourage all younger authors, and he seemed totally devoid of every spark of that littleness and jealousy which sometimes actuates even the most illustrious and established literati."

"March 10 (1834).

"I have just received a letter from Mr. Bulwer, who writes that his first visit in London was to Ottley and Saunders, booksellers, and that he has succeeded in selling them my work, called 'Roman Topography.' How very good-natured of him to have attended to my wants before he had settled himself, and rested from the fatigues of his journey. He writes me a kind letter to thank me for my little attentions at Naples. I did for him what you ordered—that is, set him a going, by presenting him to the best people, or praising him as he deserved; after which he made his own way, of course, with success. I wish my means permitted me to be more useful. By-the-by, a Mr. Reynolds sent by you seems very angry with me, but I can not help it. I have no legs to go a visiting, and never go out but borne by two servants. So, if you send me any one in a letter, pray tell them that I am a cripple, and can only be useful to them if they will take the trouble of coming to my house, as I can not make calls. It only makes enemies, if the people will not recollect that I am lame. I have got another passage, which, I think, ought not to be omitted, about Sir Walter, and don't be angry at all the trouble I give you. I believe I can say that Craven has already begun something in verse for your work. He will, I have no doubt, do it well as to execution, and as to story, he knows the history of all the odd things which have happened in Italy from the most remote period of the darkest ages. I have just discovered that I must have a little separate slip of paper for my last Scott anecdote, as the list about Odin's Stone does not come at the end.

"*March* 12. Your maid's child is well and merry, but is to be taken to Ischia in the summer for this defect in the joints; he is very well taken care of, and delighted to see Gennaro. The archbishop is quite well, and not a day older than when you left him. W. G."

"Naples, June 2d, 1834.

"Here I am again, just returned from Rome, and agreeably surprised to find a long letter from you, which I expected the less, as I had not answered that which Messrs. Errington and Lyne Stevens, or Stephens, brought for me to the Holy City; for there I have done all that could be done under the existing circumstances, when all the 'milords' and 'my ladies' were disappearing, and leaving Rome and the Colosseum to their own resources. The best thing I could do for them was to sell them to Lady Coventry, with a request that they might be treated on a par with the most favored nations, and to see that she executed her part of the treaty. I believe they will tell you I was as good as a grandmother to them, and I think it ended by their becoming guests 'at Coventry' almost every day in the week. Moreover, I dare say Lady Goodwin will arrive at Naples in a few days, and take them again under her protection here, and as she keeps open house at both places, they find her a very useful and a very agreeable acquaintance.

"I told you it had not rained for three months at Rome, and till the last few days I spent there, every thing was as yellow and burned up as if it had been August instead of May.

"I find this kingdom quite green, and every thing in a most flourishing condition, after that worn-out, misgoverned, unfortunate representative of the mistress of the world. I found here Craven, on the point of setting out for his convent of Penta; and I have scarcely seen any of my acquaintance yet, though Mr. Temple invited me for to-day, and I shall dine with the archbishop to-morrow. I have been so perpetually ill at Rome, that I am inclined to desert it, and as books will no longer sell in my line, it will be quite as well for my finances.

"You have had a great deal of trouble in fishing for a decent escape from the business of Mr. L——, and I thank you for it. I do not wish myself to do any thing disagreeable to the family, but I think it very ill-judged of them not to place every thing in its true light, especially when I had suppressed every thing which might have been put in a ludicrous light, out of respect and regard to Sir Walter. They can not revoke his two last novels, so it will be out of their power to get rid of the facts, while they lose all the merit they might claim for stating the case as it was. Besides, the whole philosophy of the business becomes tainted by that want of candor which spoils their book, without hiding the truth. They have shown the man as he was in his glory (we will suppose); it was equally their duty to the public and to posterity to show him in his decline. The whole is a dull piece of affected piety, which vitiates whatever they may publish of him; but, as far as I am concerned, I only care about it as having taken the trouble to recollect and write down what was so little worth recollecting or writing, except as the sequel to something of more consequence, and the winding up of the story. I believe I discovered, during the time I was writing, that any biography of any contemporary must be amusing. And this brings to my mind your recommendation to write an autobiography of Sir William Gell. There is no doubt, if one dared to write all one knew and all one had witnessed, the book would indeed sell, and be a great favorite for a time; but I doubt whether the author would find himself in a very agreeable position in society after the publication. By living partly in London and partly abroad, I have certainly met with, and have known a great variety of personages, not to mention Dr. Parr, and the queen, of whose life and manners I could certainly make very good fun and much amusement; but I must treat them in a very different manner to that which I measured my account of Sir Walter for the inspection of his family. I have a neighbor who often desires me, and urges me, to write my life, but I really do not see the possibility of making it true and entertaining without committing half my acquaintance. I have some sixty or seventy letters of her most gracious majesty, Queen Caroline; and, 'Mein Gott!' what curious things they are, and how rightly it would serve the royal family, supposing they had not quarreled with her, to publish their wife and cousin's correspondence, as they have cheated me out of my pension. By no means, however, publish my 'Scottiana,' as you seem to think that L—— is inclined to behave well about it, though his reasoning is poor, and false, and inconclusive, as a history of Rome would be which finished at the Antonius's, or one of Bonaparte which ended at the taking of Berlin. Speaking of which, I dined in company with the Prince of Musignano, at Rome, the other day, who married a cousin, a Miss Bonaparte, which wife seemed as dull as the prince himself seemed animated and interested in every subject. And so my paper is ending before I have finished my story. I will find a Spanish, or Arabian-Moorish historico-romantic ballad for you, and I will set about Matthias to-morrow, who will disclaim all knowledge of poetry in Italian, but who will most probably end by sending you what you want. I forgot to tell you that Mr. Errington and Co. are here, for they overtook me at Mola, as they traveled post, and I with my own horses. So we dined together, and set out together the next morning; but as my said horses had only been at Naples some twelve hours before, they have been indulged in rest, and I have not seen your friends here yet. Mr. Errington said he had written to you. Lady H—— I saw at Rome with Lord B——'s aunt. Our warlike king has taken the city by capitulation, and has spared the sacking of it, which would have taken place had it been taken by storm. Mr. Mills I left at Rome, but going to the lakes of Lombardy. Not a soul, except William Petre, will be left at Rome.

"The Torlonias are well. Kind regards to the count, and pray believe me affectionately yours, AULUS (GELLIUS).

"P.S.—I don't know whether you knew poor Mr. Coote, a young man of Wiltshire, and son of Sir Eyre. He had a yacht here, and is just returned from a voyage to Greece. After this, he would steer his ship in a storm of rain to Pæstum, and then dine in his wet clothes; the consequence of which was, that he died in a few days."

"Naples, July, 1834.

"Your two books of Byron and of Beauty are at length arrived, and I return you my most hearty thanks for the kind present.

"I see by the book that the ladies are sometimes only very slenderly attached to the letter-press, like the unpaid attachés of an embassy, so that as far as that goes, one of my Arab or Spanish ballads may be attached to the next lady you have in an Oriental costume, who may be called Zayda, as well as by any other name equally sweet-smelling. This reflection gives me some hopes that what I have written may be of use to you, though it is terribly prosaic, because I want to prove that the world is deceived in calling the whole of that a romance which is in great part true, and of which the circumstances are very peculiar. I think I have proved what I wished, and that, as it all ends in specimens of Spanish and Arab poetry, it is not too heavy for your work. It is also very poor in style; but if you knew how many people that have nothing to do call upon me in a day, so that the prose is all written in talkative company, and the verse with a pencil, as one takes an evening drive in a carriage on the *Strada Nuova*, you would pity rather than condemn the most humble of your slaves. Besides this, I am scarcely a day in tolerable health between gout and headache, though my spirits keep up most marvelously, and I am just as merry as my more fortunate neighbors. I know not when my letter was begun, but this day, July 15th, I have finished all I mean to write for you, and given three or four romances in limping verse, and I end with an anecdote about a king who sent his enemy with a letter of recommendation, which authorized the receiver to cut off the bearer's hands and feet, and to bury him alive.

"If I had thought it sufficiently serious, I would have terminated by a parallel passage in my own life which I suggested. I received a letter thus: 'Dear Gell, I send you my friend Mr. ——; you will find him the greatest bore and the most disputatious brute you ever knew. Pray ask him to dinner, and get any one you know of the same character to meet him.' This was brought me by the man himself, and I found him in every way answering to the character. Pray add or subtract any thing you like from what I send you. I see plainly that it is not quite right, though the intention is good, and I have given a full proportion of love, mixed with a proper degree of bloodshed, which the genius of the time requires. Pray also correct in the verse, according to the fashion of the day, the words opprest or oppress'd, and such like words, to your taste, and if you think it all a bore, as very likely you may find it, you may put it in the fire altogether, with my compliments.

"I have no doubt, however, Craven will send you some sort of Italian story of the Middle Ages worth having. He is at Penta, his country house, and can have nothing else to do, when tired of gardening. I have written to him to have it ready, and my chief object in writing this, and sending it by the post, is, that you may know that you are sure of some thirty pages of my little scribble, and something from Craven also.

"Mr. Temple being with the count for some days at Palermo, I have no means of sending you so large a packet as my Arabo-Spanish lucubrations will make, so I only send this to apprise you that we have executed your commands. Young Craven vows a contribution from himself or his wife, Mdlle. Pauline la Feronays, but he is so much engaged in making love that I dare say he will write nothing. They are to be married in September, or sooner, if possible. As to that gay man, Matthias, now in his ninety-third year, he is as obstinate as twenty pigs, and vows he will never write another line, as it is time, he says, to leave off making himself a fool in public. I thought at first I could persuade or bully him into it, but he is too resolved for the present. If he relents, he will put his sonnet into the 'Book of Beauty' for the year 1867, when Mr. Irving says the millennium is to begin. Here is my neighbor Mr. Ramsay, who writes much, but it is all on the corn-laws and political economy, so he can not help us much. They say Don Miguel is coming here, but in the mean time is consoling himself by feasting and making merry with the Duke of Lucca. I have been forced to give up my Roman establishment, as I could afford it no longer, and I believe Dr. Watson is going to live there instead of at Paris. You remember how it amused you that I had begun to take the necessary steps when I thought I was ruined by the hanging of Fauntleroy, since which my finances have always kept me in a state of alarm.

"Mr. Mills is gone toward Switzerland for the summer, and Mrs. Dodwell, now Countess Spaw, and Bavarian minister at Rome, is just brought to bed with a fine boy at Albano. I beg you will remember me most kindly to the count, who, I hope, did not lose his own money, but that of his neighbor, at a shooting match, which I saw an account of the other day in the newspaper. I can not make out as yet who brought your two books, for which I thank you. Mr. Lyne Stephens is gone, but has left Mr. E—— in the good graces of Miss M——, so that they go gallivanting all over the country. I have not seen them lately. I hope your friends will tell you that I set them a going with all my might when they first appeared. They are very amiable children. Love to your sister the contessina. W. GELL."

"Naples, August 6, 1834.

"I have written to you so often lately that you will begin to think me a nuisance. But I now write on business, to introduce to you my little Essay on the 'Romantic History of Spain,' which will, I believe, be presented by my friend John Auldjo, Esq., celebrated for his excursion to the summit of Mont Blanc, and as much celebrated for the interesting and unaffected account which he has published of his ascent and descent, which makes you think you know the mountain as well as he does. He will give you an account of all that is going on at Naples, what we are doing, and who is going to be married. The Ricciardi send their loves to you. I saw the two girls at old mother R——'s, at the Villa Rugina, on the Vomero, the other night, where they sang, and two nights ago I saw them again, and had a long conversation with their father at a ball, concert, and supper, given by Dominico Catalano, the great lawyer, on St. Dominic's day, at which all Naples was present. There Madame Nicolas, who yet seemed to retain all her beauty, sang, but with perhaps less voice than formerly. The other sister has become a regular large dowager, and did not sing; so I conclude her voice has departed like a mist on the hills of Morven. The whole world came from Palermo the other day—the St. Theodoros, Actons, kings, princes, and queen; so that Naples, which had been deserted, begins to be inhabited again; and at Catalano's there seemed to be between three and four hundred persons, many of whom jigged away just as if the thermometer had not been up to eighty, and afterward ate as if there had been no fear of an hereafter. Coriali, Pepe, Filangieri, are well and merry.

"Torlonia, now Duca di Ceri, was to have been married to a granddaughter of the Paterno, a Mdlle. de Moncada, but they quarreled, and broke off the match. Craven is living at Penta, and receiving company, having established a house with twenty beds, stables, and all that tends to reception. I have been there once this summer, and am going again with Lady Coventry. The archbishop is very well, perhaps better than usual, but paler and more bent, and desires loves to you. I go and dine there about once in ten days.

"The Actons have finished their house, and live very hospitably and agreeably in it, and give balls, dinners, and plays. Young Craven marries Mdlle.

Pauline la Feronays on the 28th of August. The happy couple have each a rent-roll of trois mille francs, but K. Craven will give £600 a year, so they will have about £900 to begin with, and I hope they will contrive and be prudent with it. Your old Belvidere is to be sold, and the queen will, if you like also, sell you the Villa Gallo: the Belvidere for about £3000. I could find no earlier method of sending you the Spanish Arabic article, but I hope it will be in time. I have got a most beautiful lady really, the Princess of Monte Vago, in Sicily, who would do for Zayda's picture, if you wanted a new face for your book, and if you are in want I would contrive to send it for engraving. Mr. Auldjo has in his Constantinople journal a beauty or two of that country, whose faces he copied with an instrument, and they are not only good in themselves, but very different from any thing European, and might consequently be very useful in your book, and prevent a sort of nationality that will be observed when all the artists are from one country. Lady Coventry gave the archbishop a copy of your 'Book of Beauty,' which delighted him much.

"You may cut down my dissertation or print it all, just as you like; change, burn, or otherwise destroy what you don't like, or the whole together, and put my name, or that of any one else, just as you find it convenient. I lent it to Captain Basil Hall to review, and he says it should have my name; but judge for yourself. Craven has got an Italian story for you, and I am sure you will have it soon. Augustus Craven has something else, and I should not wonder if one of the Stewarts sent you something also. *What is become of that most amiable Stewart, the colonel of Killymoon?* Not to intrude more on your time, and having the gout myself, I must stop, but with love to La Comtessa de St. Marsault and Count Alfred. Yours, &c., WILLIAM GELL.

"Gennaro sees your maid's child very often, and he is well."

"Penta, June 23d, 1835.

"It was not so much because I had been ill myself, as because I had heard that you were ill, that I have delayed writing so long. I trusted that I should get some fresh intelligence about you, and from day to day put off writing accordingly. I conclude, from your silence on the subject, that you have not been much indisposed; though it is not for me, who have been six months laid up, to glory in the strength of my constitution, which broke up, like the ice on the Neva, about the middle of November last, and left me a prey to all the diseases into which gout has been known to resolve itself when it is fairly tired out with the common symptoms and pains. Among these, dropsy is generally the most prominent and the most fatal; and the next is asthma, with which two agreeable companions I have, since November, passed my time; sometimes suffering from one, and often both the complaints united.

"I found my talent for sleeping in company much improved, and I can give you no better specimen of it than these two last lines, where you will observe the —— words united and very much disguised by having fallen asleep three times while I was writing the following sentence: 'I had turned up the shortest road to Penta.'

"I will let it stand as it is, for it will explain to you why I could not write before, and why I might as well not have written now. I cease writing, or write nonsense, or the pen goes on scribbling, but I can not guide it. I will now begin again, three hours later. Well, the symptoms of asthma and dropsy continued, and I could not lie down horizontally for fear of suffocation. Nevertheless, with four doctors—Dr. Strange, Dr. Heath, Dr. Knight, and Dr. Watson—I am alive, and one might almost say recovering, as fast as possible, from the physic and the disease. The most curious symptoms are the going dead asleep all at once, and the dreaming, when wide awake, about eating, and helping my friends to eatables. I gave Lord Aberdeen a large slice of cold ham this morning about five o'clock, but when I came to repeat it, I found he had no plate. I rung the bell, and by the time the servant really came, I was sensible there was neither ham nor any other eatable in the bed. This sort of thing happens twenty times in the twenty-four hours, and sometimes produces the most ridiculous combinations. However, the other day I was alone at Mr. Temple's, looking, as I believed, at some prints in a book, when, falling asleep, I pulled over my chair in trying to save myself, and fell on the pavement in a manner which makes the idea of a repetition of my gambols frightful. Not having had time to save myself with my hands, I fell with my weight on the floor—a most abominable crash—and the hip-bone, of course, and all that side, suffered most severely; nor am I well of that accident, which has much retarded the cure of the original illness. The only wonder was that it was no worse.

"I was ordered to move about a little, which I do with grief and pain; and am now at Craven's, at Penta, thirty-five miles from Naples, to which place I came on a sort of trading voyage, beginning with a visit of four days to Lady Barbara, who is at Castelamare. I stay here four days, and then take two more with the Ponsonbys, and then, after some four days at Naples, shall do the same over again, changing Lady F. Barbara for Mrs. Locke or her daughter, ... perhaps at Castelamare. I give you the history of my life, as it is a good way of letting you judge of my health. You see that I might do tolerably well were my one hundred and forty diseases curable. Dr. Heath, who is with the Ponsonbys, seems, I think, to be satisfied that I shall shortly be better, and possibly much better than usual; and that my grand climacteric, which usually falls at the age of sixty-three, has been hastened by length of illness, and fallen upon me at fifty-eight instead, after which the constitution might change for the better. I thought, till now, that the age of sixty-three was required for the change, but he says no. So you see, my dear Lady Blessington, I have given you a long statement of my case, and the results, as far as we know them. You tell me of your bad weather, and if this be in due proportion, you ought yet to be in Siberia, for I have at this moment a tolerable fire, by which I am too cold; and without, it is raining cats and dogs, and seems likely to continue to do so. The consequence is, the most wonderful verdure I ever beheld, the vines in unusually large leaf, and the Indian corn, flax, and hemp shooting into thickets below them. I never saw any thing so verdant as the world is here, whenever we have an hour or two of sun to enjoy so green and beautiful a scene. What is become of the English I know not; the spring was forgotten, the season for summer is half over, and the winter yet remains, and the milords seem to have forgotten to come to Italy. There may be three families of no note at Sorrento, and about as many threaten to come to Castelamare for the month of July, so that the houses are for the present empty. The Salsa has, however, worked herself into Dorchester House, as the papers say; and as far as her own account of things goes, she finds no difference, but all goes on well; at all events, she is not the person to cry stinking fish, and would say that harmony existed as long as possible.

"We have at Craven's a tremendous large old convent, with cells for as many as can be got to fill them; and Craven himself, out of perverseness, is as hospitable and as open to all comers here, as he sometimes appears the contrary at Naples, where society might be had without the trouble or expense of maintaining it. I am glad you have seen Dr. Hogg; he writes remarkably well, and will, I doubt not, make a pretty book from very scanty materials. When he was here he used to go crazy on the subject, which, I hope, will not be the case in London. Pray order him to return here directly, and tell him that he would find plenty of room to practice, if so disposed.

"Mr. Wilkinson I am glad you admire, for he must by this time be one of the most learned men in Christendom.

"You say people speak kindly of me. I assure you, since I have been so ill, I have found great consolation in observing how far the world in general exceeds in kindness what one had any right to expect from it.

"As to that ugly old abbot, I suppose he had imbibed a false impression, and never could get rid of it.*

"My romance has not advanced a step. I thought, during my illness, I could at least have written that; but that is *historia*, and requires facts and dates; and I never could guide my pen, as you will have said many times before you get to the end of this long and dull letter. A thousand kindnesses to Count Alfred, and the young lady, your sister. I hope your young friend will return pleased with Naples. Faithfully yours, W. Gell.

"I got both your novels by Mr. Stanley, and thank you much. I think I was most entertained with the 'Repealers,' and you certainly speak out. Poor Matthias is very well, but is querulous and old, and thinks himself deserted—so much so, that nobody can undertake his society, he is so discontented and curious.

"The archbishop is as well as ever, and dined with me a few days ago when he laughed and was as gay as ever.

* The Abbé Campbell, I presume, is alluded to.—R. R. M

"The Ricciardis are doing well also."*

* This remarkable letter was the last, I believe, which Sir William Gell addressed to Lady Blessington. The date of it is about nine months before his death. The singular account of the breaking up of his mental powers, of the consciousness of their failure, and of those waking dreams of his—when he imagined himself in the society of old friends then far distant, and fancied himself discoursing with them as if they were present—is painfully interesting. Before taking leave of poor Gell, perhaps a letter of introduction, addressed to the Admiral of the Egyptian fleet, of his, and one very characteristic of him, which he furnished me with when I was setting out for the East in 1824, will not be found misplaced in this collection.

FROM SIR W. GELL TO THE GRAND ADMIRAL OF THE EGYPTIAN FLEET:

"Napoli, 16 Agosto, 1824.

"MIO CARO AMICO GRAND' AMMIRAGLIO DI' EGITTO,—Con questa V. mando un amico mio, il Signore Madden, chirurgo, di gran talento, il quale va viaggiare in Turchia, per osservare tutto quello che si trova di bello o di nuovo nella sua arte, e por mostrare quanto e bravo se stesso nella operazione di chirurgio. Trovarete se avete l'occazzione assai capace, e forse, siccome ve ne sono tanti medici ma pochissimi di veri chirurgi sera questo signore di grande utilita a sua Altezza il Pasha o el armata per terra o mare. Dunque vi prego asser quanto potete utile durante la sua dimora nella terra dei Mussulman.

"Pensai tutto quest' anno fare il viaggio d'Egitto, ma fra l'incertezza della guerra con Algieri, la guerra Greca, ed il non avere bastimento sicuro per trasportasmi ad Alessandria di Misir, sono qui per ora, e veramente non vedo mezzi, al momento, a fare il tragetto con commodo e siccurezza, ad essendo Zoppo, ed alquanto in vecchiato doppo il nostro celebre viaggio nella vostra fregata L'Africa, non vale per me la pena viaggiare se non con commodo e siccurezza. Ho gran desiderio andare per qualche giorne a Gerusalemme ed a passare l'inverno in Egitto se abou Gosh ed il Diavolo me permettessero, ma quando questo sara non so.

"Se avete l'occaggione e sapeta di qualche bastimento che viene in questi paesi vi prego scrivermi e far me sapere como vanno gli affari vostri e quelli d'Egitto perché da vero qui ve ne sono certe volte delle conte ed istorie falsi, che non ci permettono sapere il vero.

"Non so se il figlio resta anchora in Malta altrimentri da lui potrei Io recevere una vostra lettera. Spero che voi riuscite in ogni cosa che vi tocca personalmente, e che sarete gia diventato il piu ricco della famiglia di Giblachtar. Non so se avete in compagnia fin ora il vostro fedele Turcomanno, ma supponzo che il Tenente Osman non resta piu in vorta equipaggio. Hassan Bey di Rhodi sento esser morto. Mi fara grandissimo piacere quel giorno che posso rivedersi.

"Spero al fine vederui, un altra volta in questo mondo, siccome non essendo Turco il vostro grand Profeta non permette che Io andarse al settimo cielo nel altro.

"Wilkinson ha fetto grande progressi nello studio delle antichita d'Egitto. Sento che la povera città di Atene e tutta distrutta e tutti quanti gli amici miei morti tanti Greci quanti Turchi, Osman Mollah Ibrahim Aga e Compagnia. Vi prego fatta la pace e non mazzata piu gente, e trattata i vostri prigioneri con clemenza per l'amor di Dio e su Profeta.

"Credetemi sempre, carissimo Amaraglio, amico e servitore vostro fedelissimo,

"GELL."

CHAPTER XIX.

In the preceding letters of Sir William Gell there are some persons referred to, of whom a more detailed account may be desirable than can be given in the limits of foot-notes. Of some of these persons, moreover, frequent mention is made in the Diaries and Letters of Lady Blessington, which have reference to her sojourn in Naples, and the acquaintances she formed there and in Rome.

The brief notices now introduced will enable the reader to comprehend more easily and fully observations on passing occurrences, only slightly glanced at in those letters, and allusions to persons which may only suffice to excite curiosity, and leave a desire to know something more in relation to them.

SIR WILLIAM DRUMMOND.

The Right Honorable Sir William Drummond, a Privy Councilor, formerly H. B. M.'s Envoy Extraordinary and Minister Plenipotentiary to the King of the Two Sicilies, and subsequently at the Ottoman Porte, died at Rome the 29th of March, 1828.

His first work was published in 1794, "A Review of the Governments of Sparta and Athens," 8vo. In 1798 he published "The Satires of Persius," translated; in 1805, "Academical Questions," 4to; in 1810, in conjunction with Robert Walpole, "Herculanensia," &c., containing a MS. found at Pompeii; in 1811, in 4to, "An Essay on a Punic Inscription found in the Island of Malta;" in 1818, in 4to, "Odin," a Poem; and in 1824, "Origines, or Remarks on the Origin of several Empires, States, and Cities," 2 vols. 8vo. He also printed, but not for sale, a remarkable work, entitled "Œdipus Judaicus," of very anti-Christian tendencies, reducing Scriptural histories to mere astronomical allegories.

In 1811, Byron, in a letter to his friend Hodgson, says: "I have gotten a book by Sir William Drummond, printed but not published, entitled 'Œdipus Judaicus,' in which he attempts to prove the greater part of the Old Testament an allegory, particularly Genesis and Joshua. He professes himself a Theist in the preface, and handles the literal interpretation very roughly."*

Byron was then in his twenty-third year, and no doubt the veteran Theist's erudition was not thrown away on the young, impressible mind of Byron. How much unhappiness may not the author of the erudite infidel work of this accomplished writer have to answer for, even in the single instance I refer to?

Lady Blessington makes frequent mention in her letters and diaries of Sir William Drummond as a profound scholar, whose classical lore was united with scientific knowledge of various kinds in modern literature, mineralogy, chemistry, and astronomy. His conversation was not only erudite, but brilliant and playful. He had the imagination of a man of original poetical genius; a capacity fit for a philosopher, a statesman, or a metaphysician. He was a polished, high-minded gentleman, moreover, with all the *politesse de la vielle cour*.

Sir William Drummond and his lady were of very opposite tastes. He passed his days, and the greater portion of his nights, in reading or writing. The tables, chairs, sofas, and even the floors were loaded with books. "He seldom saw Lady Drummond except at dinner," says Lady Blessington, "surrounded by a large party. She passed, as she passes still, her time in the duties of an elaborate toilet, paying or receiving visits, and playing with her lap-dog. A strange wife for one of the most intellectual men of his day! and yet this dissimilarity produced no discord between them; for she was proud of his acquirements, and he was indulgent to her less *spirituelle tastes*."†

It might be a question difficult to answer whether "the most intellectual man of Europe" benefited his species more by erudition turned against Christianity, than the lady "of less spirituelle tastes," though occupied occasionally with the duties of an elaborate toilet, but habitually devoted to works of charity, profuse in her liberality, and making use of her vast wealth, as she

* Moore's Life of Lord Byron, p. 157, 8vo ed., 1838.

† The Idler in France, vol. i., p. 148.

did in Naples, for the relief of the poor and the distressed, served her fellow-creatures.

When Lady Blessington met Sir William for the last time at Rome, he was then evidently verging fast toward the close of his career. Ill as he was, however, he came to see her at her hotel. His death-stricken, pallid features, the utter feebleness and extraordinary emaciation of his frame, shocked her. He was taken from his carriage in a chair by his servants; and as he was thus conveyed into her *salon*, she was forcibly reminded of the sitting statue of Voltaire, executed shortly before his death, which is placed in the vestibule of the Theatre Français at Paris. His mental faculties remained unimpaired. His conversation was the same as ever—delightful to listen to.

"He is conscious," says her ladyship, "that the King of Terrors is fast approaching, and awaits his presence *with all the dignified composure of a philosopher of old.* He spoke to me of his approaching end with calmness; said he should have liked to have had time to finish the work in which he is engaged; and observed that it was a blessing for which he was penetrated with gratitude to the Most High, that his mind still survived the wreck of his body, and enabled him to bear, if not to forget, the physical sufferings entailed by disease.

"Speaking of his approaching end, he said, 'There is something in Rome, with its ruins, and the recollections with which it is fraught, that reconciles one to decay and death. The inevitable lot of all things seems here so strongly brought before one, that the destiny of an individual is merged in that of the scene around him.'"*

It was not long before Lady Blessington's fears for her friend were realized. In May, 1828, she visited his grave in the English burying-ground in Rome. The massive pyramid of Caius Sextus cast its shadows over the resting-places of Shelley, Keats, and Drummond; but the remains of Drummond were to be removed to Scotland in the course of a few months. The fair pilgrim who visited his grave thought of the happy hours passed in his society, the brilliant conversation of that highly-gifted

* The Idler in Italy, Par. ed., 1839, p. 391.

man, the deep reflections she had heard from those lips that were now silent forever.

THE ABBÉ CAMPBELL.

"The English in Italy," from 1820 to 1829, acquainted with Naples, the resident *Inglesi* of Naples especially, can not fail to remember the celebrated *abbatè*, an ecclesiastic not renowned for his learning, remarkable for amenity of manners, or agreeableness of appearance or address; not venerated much for sanctity, or sought after for the excellence of his example, the purity of his morals, and the influence of his life and conversation before men in his spiritual character, but distinguished for a sort of mysterious *prestige*—an apprehension of his power over people in high places, in several courts, and in various Continental capitals—a nondescript influence seldom exercised for any good-natured purpose, and courted even in the best society on account of the fear with which the unbridled license of his tongue inspired it. The abbé had to be petted, caressed, abundantly fed, and propitiated with good dinners by all new-comers of distinction and of discretion.

In Naples particularly, and in some other Continental courts of absolute princes, he was without a rival among *parvenus* and hangers-on of great men in power or authority.

There was nothing in his education, his natural position, his antecedents, or his habits, to conciliate men's favorable opinion of his companionable qualities. In the latter part of 1821, when I first met him, he was, I think, upward of sixty-eight years of age, low of stature, exceedingly bulky, unwieldy, and ungainly in his movements. His features were large and heavy, coarse and vulgar; his complexion was of an obfuscated, lurid red, with a predominance of the purple of the grape in it. The expression of his face was all animal. His look was cunning, and there was a leering, frolicksome twinkle always in it after dinner, that contrasted unpleasantly with his age and dilapidated appearance. His head was enormously large; and his neck, extremely short and thick, was always buried in a profuse quantity of cravat of a dingy hue. The head and trunk merging into one, with so little of intervening neck, reminded one of the conformation of some of the larger lizards. His clothes, generally bedaubed with snuff, hung on his large person as if they had been pitched about him casually and carelessly by an old servant of his—Pococurantè, as great an oddity as his master.

In Naples, his intimate relations of friendship with the minister Medici, and the terms of acquaintance on which he was with the old king Ferdinand, gave an importance to his "undefined and undefinable position in society," which contributed very much to an influence exercised over it by him that was certainly one more of fear than love. The abbé was said to have a pension from the Neapolitan government, and an annual stipend also from some official source in England, and for some public services that were of a very private nature.

He had been, at a very early age, a chaplain to a Neapolitan embassador in London about the time of the marriage of the Prince Regent with Mrs. Fitzherbert, and rumor assigned the perilous duty of the performance of the marriage ceremony to the young chaplain of the Neapolitan embassador.

I have heard this rumor mentioned in the presence of the abbé, and it remained not only uncontradicted by him, but so far acquiesced in, at least, as to leave an impression that he knew the priest by whom the marriage was celebrated.*

In the second volume of "The Memorials and Correspondence of Charles James Fox," by Lord John Russell, we have the principal circumstances related of the Prince of Wales's marriage with Mrs. Fitzherbert. First comes a letter of Mr. Fox to the prince, in the strongest terms dissuading him from the rumored intention of the marriage, dated Dec. 10, 1785; next follows a reply of "the true prince" and truth-loving heir-apparent, dated the 19th of the same month, solemnly denying the rumor that "*there not only is, but never was, any ground for these reports which have of late been so maliciously circulated.*" Then comes Lord John Russell's statement, that ten days only after this solemn averment his royal highness had married Mrs. Fitzherbert.

* When Mrs. Fitzherbert was married in 1785, the abbé, who was born about 1754, must have been rather more than thirty years of age.

The marriage, it is stated by Lord John, was performed in private by a clergyman of the Church of England, in the manner prescribed by the Book of Common Prayer, and the certificate, dated December 21, 1785, was attested by two witnesses. This is only half the truth. It would have been no satisfaction to Mrs. Fitzherbert's scruples to have had the marriage ceremony performed by a clergyman not belonging to her church, unless the ceremony had been previously performed by a Roman Catholic clergyman; and I have been assured by the late Mr. Thomas Savory, of Sussex Place, Regent's Park, the confidential and long-loved friend of the Duke of Sussex, that he knew of a certainty that the ceremony had been performed by a Roman Catholic priest who was connected with one of the foreign embassies in London, and who thought it prudent to fly the country after the marriage ceremony had been performed.

Lord Brougham, in his "Historical Sketches" (George IV.), says, "Mrs. Fitzherbert was a Roman Catholic; sincerely attached to the religion of her forefathers, she refused to purchase a crown by conforming to any other; and the law declared that whoever married a Catholic should forfeit all right to the crown of these realms, as if he were naturally dead. This law, however, was unknown to her, and, blinded by various pretenses, she was induced to consent to a clandestine marriage, which is supposed to have been solemnized between her and the prince beyond the limits of the English dominions, in the silly belief, perhaps, entertained by him, that he escaped the penalty to which his reckless conduct exposed him, and that the forfeiture of his succession to the crown was only denounced against such a marriage if contracted within the realm."

And his lordship adds, in a note, "Some affirm that it was performed in London at the house of her uncle."*

The abbé's recollections were no less vivid than entertaining, and some gravely interesting, of Lord Nelson and of Lady Hamilton, of his social intercourse with the latter, and of the admirable old port (rarely to be met with in Naples), which gave a particular charm to her dinners, the pleasures of which were

* Historical Sketches of Statesmen of the Time of George III., p. 222.

generally of a prolonged description, and extended sometimes far into the night.

The abbé was at Naples at the time of the execution of Carraccioli and his associates, and was cognizant of many of the circumstances relating to that infamy — the court intrigues, the connection with them of Lady Hamilton, and the unhappy influence that lady brought to bear on Nelson.*

The abbé stated that some days after the execution (which he spoke of, to his credit, with reprehension, though all his sympathies were with Cardinal Ruffo and his party), the body of one of the persons executed, said to have been that of Carraccioli, was found floating under the stern of Nelson's frigate, and was visible to the admiral from his cabin windows. On one occasion of a controversy on this subject, the abbé said, *He knew for a certainty that Nelson had seen one of the bodies of the executed men, some days after the execution, floating near the stern of his ship, with the face upward, and he knew that Nelson was shocked at the spectacle, and well he might be.*

The abbé was on terms of close intimacy with the late King of Hanover and with the Duke of Cumberland, and seldom visited England that he did not enjoy the duke's hospitality.

It was something more than amusing to hear this old man, of an obscure origin and humble rank, of no very prepossessing appearance or courtly manners, vaunting of his intimacy and terms of familiar intercourse with kings, and princes, and ministers of state: "My friend Cumberland;" "My old acquaintance, the King of Sardinia;" "Mio Caro Amico Medici," &c.

In Naples, after the abortive attempts at revolution in 1821, there was a very strict surveillance of the police over foreigners, especially the English, in Naples. Their letters were opened

* "The 20th of April, 1799, Cardinal Ruffo, at the head of the Neapolitan Royalists and some Russian auxiliaries, entered Naples. Soon after, a confederate force of English, Russians, Italians, Portuguese, and Turks, entered the port under a convoy of Lord Nelson, and invested the Castle of St. Elmo; Capua and Gaeta were afterward taken by the assistance of the English. A severe vengeance was afterward inflicted, in contravention of a solemn treaty, on the Neapolitan patriots, with the culpable connivance of Nelson, acting under the influence of the profligate wife of the English embassador, Sir William Hamilton."—*British Chronology*, by Wade, ed. 1839, p. 615.

and examined at the post-office by authority. The services of an Englishman, or of some one well acquainted with the English language, were required for this private duty of foreign correspondence examination, and on more than one occasion the abbé was openly charged with the performance of this duty. Secrets became known to him which could only be obtained from this source of information. They might certainly have been communicated to him by his confidential friend Medici, and the direct duty of opening the letters might have been performed by some other person. My own opinion is that such was the case.

Sir William Gell for some time adopted a formula for the more speedy transmission of his letters through the post-office; the following words, in larger characters than the rest, were usually written at the top of the page of every letter of his: "*When the Abbé Campbell has read this private communication, and replaced the broken seal, he is requested to send on the letter to its destination.*"

This was a dear joke to Gell; it was the cause of a deadly feud in English society in Naples, a feud in which, on one side, was ranged the redoubtable abbé, and occasionally, and at a convenient distance, an ally worthy of a better cause, Charles Reilly, the well-known surgeon of the Chiaga; and, on the other, Sir William Drummond, Sir William Gell, Keppel Craven, the Count D'Orsay, Dr. Watson, the celebrated linguist, and, on the confines of the field of battle, Ridgeway, the secretary of Sir William, and "the Master of the Horse" of Lady Drummond.

Ridgeway was a man of worth and integrity, of a remarkably staid and solemn aspect. He had the soul of a "gentleman usher of the time of Elizabeth," penetrated with solemn conviction of the grave importance of old ceremonials, and set formulas, and stately etiquettes.

In flinging dirt, the Abbé Campbell was an incomparable belligerent. There was nothing in the shape of an offensive missile too foul or too heavy for his hands. The abbé was a ferocious hater, savagely sarcastic, and strangely jocular in his furibond movements. There was something terrible in his rancor when he was drunk with passion, and in his revelry, when he was inebriated, as he was "wont to be of an afternoon," with wine.

Few people could tell the place of birth, parentage, or antecedents of the abbé. He passed for an Englishman with Englishmen, a Scotchman with Scotchmen, and any thing but an Irishman with Irishmen in general. To Reilly and myself, Dr. Quin, and one or two more, he was known to be an Irishman, a native of the north of Ireland.

He was pleased to promise me, on divers occasions, when in "the superior condition," the inheritance of his papers, and, among the rest, some fragments of a Memoir of his Life, which he had written some years previously, and had condemned to the flames—no doubt very judiciously, when the Carbonari had got the upper hand in Naples.

In attempting to destroy the MS. in a place suitable enough for it, a sudden puff of wind scattered the burning papers about the abbé, and, according to his humorous account of this *auto-da-fé* of his Memoirs, he was in danger of suffering death by his own life.

The few pages that were unconsumed the abbé was obliged to carry off, and to take beyond the frontier with his own valuable person.

Lady Blessington observes, "It is not easy to imagine how the abbé's influence is acquired, for his talents are of a very mediocre kind, his manners coarse, and his reputation not honorable; mais n'importe, he preserves his ground, and is received, though abused, in every great house in Naples.

"This is one of the many extraordinary instances one often witnesses of a man rising from a low station without one quality to justify his ascent or maintain it, yet whose presence is tolerated by those who decry him."*

The "German prince," Puckler Muskau, whose travels in Germany, Holland, and England were published in 1831, makes mention of a celebrated wit of a sarcastic turn, "once a patentee of puns," whom he had met in one of the first circles of fashion-

* The Idler in Italy.

able life in London, whose every word was extravagantly admired and extolled, though the liking for the facetious cynic was feigned and pretended to, out of fear of the waspish tongue of the sarcastic humorist. "I have a mortal hate," says the prince, "for the whole tribe of such wits, especially when, like this person, they combine a repulsive exterior with gall and sarcasm unredeemed by grace of any kind. In human society they appear as poisonous insects, whom people, out of a pitiful weakness, help to nourish with the blood of others to save their own."*

The abbé's head-quarters at Naples, in the latter years of his life, were on an eminence called Capo di Monte, and occasionally at the Albergo di Crocelle, in the Chiatamone. He made yearly journeys to England, and sometimes more frequently visited London, and during his stay there (often a very prolonged one) installed himself in the house of my old friend, Thomas Field Savory, in Sussex Place, Regent's Park. On one occasion of a visitation there he had dined out, and done ample justice to the viands and the wines of his entertainer. He sallied forth at a late hour, after some unsuccessful attempts to procure a hackney-coach for him. He had ordered a vehicle, which was not to be found. There was a large party at a house adjoining his entertainer's, and there was a long line of carriages in front of the house, and among them a solitary sedan chair, of large dimensions. The drivers of the coaches and the bearers of the sedan chair were probably regaling themselves. It was a wet night in every sense of the term. The unfortunate abbé no sooner espied the sedan chair than some unaccountable impulse sent his great bulk of body bundling into the ancient vehicle, and no sooner had he plopped down and was seated than he fell fast asleep, snoring loudly.

The bearers, on their return, found a fat snoring gentleman in the sedan, whom it was impossible to rouse or to eject by any exertion of their lungs or efforts of their arms. A crowd collected: among them, some mischievously-minded individual, an anticipator of the hydropathic system, pointed to a spout, from which torrents of water were pouring down from the roof of a

* Travels of a German Prince.

neighboring house. In an instant the poles were thrust into their places ; the sedan chair, with its enormous burden, was uplifted, borne to the spot, and placed under the spout; the head was then lifted, and the abbé was suddenly awakened, drenched, bewildered, and dismayed, imagining the end of the world was come, and another deluge was taking place.

A compassionate jarvey, seeing the prospect of getting a good fare, contrived to elicit from the thoroughly-soaked gentleman his address. He was conveyed home, cool, but not comfortable, and not in a very seraphic state of mind.

The abbé, on various occasions, had given Savory to understand that nearly all he possessed should go to him (Savory) at his death. He held out solemn promises also to the nephew of that gentleman, Mr. John Savory, that he would find his name had not been forgotten in the disposition of the property of Henry Campbell.

He broke all his promises to the elder Savory, to whom, for many years, he had given a vast deal of trouble about his pecuniary and other private affairs; but he kept faith with Mr. John Savory (the present head of the firm of Savory and Moore, of Bond Street). A short time before he left London for the last time, and about three or four months previous to his death, in the early part of 1830, having made some arrangement of his affairs, he called on Mrs. Savory, and with some signs of emotion, and marked solemnity of manner, placed a small package in her hands, and spoke of his tender regards for her husband. He went away very much affected, and never was seen more by his kind friends. The small but precious package was opened with all due care when he was gone, and some twenty yards of old Mechlin lace were taken from the paper and laid on the table.

The next news from Naples brought the intelligence of the abbé's death ; and a very lamentable account it was of the close of a career that was in keeping with the whole of its bad course. While the wealthy, friendless, dying man was still conscious of what was passing around him, his servants were plundering his house, ransacking the room, even where he lay dying, for objects of any value that he kept there.

At his death, his money was found lodged in several hands, with bankers and others. He had left no regular account, showing how his property was placed. Mr. Thomas Field Savory discovered that there were several thousand pounds of his lodged in the bank of Messrs. Wright, of Henrietta Street, which his representatives had no knowledge of. A young gentleman who had been acknowledged by the abbé to be his nephew inherited the whole of his property—about £16,000—and in a few years managed, I believe, to get through the greater portion of it.

CHAPTER XX.

CHARLES REILLY, ESQ., SURGEON, R. N.

OF all the medical men in Naples of the *forestieri*, Charles Reilly, a native of Ireland, a retired medical surgeon, who had accompanied the Oxford family to Naples in the capacity of traveling medical attendant, and had settled down in practice in that city in the time of King Joachim, was in the highest repute when I was there, in the latter part of 1821, 1822, and 1823, and the spring of 1824.

Reilly was, in every sense of the term but one, a thorough Irishman. He was full of humor, jocose, good natured, with something of a lachrymose expression in his serious, business-like, corrugated features, till some odd fancy would flash across his mind, or some ridiculous object present itself to his eye, or droll expression meet his ear, and then that lugubrious physiognomy, with all its deep traces of worldliness, would brighten up as if by magic, and beam with hilarity, that literally made every feature of his face glow with joyousness. Reilly's humor and gayety were peculiarly Irish, and as "racy of the soil" he had abandoned some twenty or thirty years previously to the period I refer to as if he had only quitted it the day before.

Reilly was not only funny himself, but he was the cause of fun in others. He was as essential to the jollity of the old Abbé Campbell as the jolly abbé was indispensable to Reilly whenever he exercised the rights of hospitality, which was seldom less than twice a week. On these festive occasions, Reilly was to the abbé what Boswell was to Johnson, in some respects. He tickled the great bear, and jumped with his humor. He bore with an odd growl from him, and an occasional cuff of his big paw, as if he was complimented by the notice of the great animal he had the care of.

The abbé loved Reilly as much as it was in his nature to love any body. He never failed to perform his awkward gambols at those weekly entertainments. Gulosity and gayety went hand in hand at them.

Some years before Reilly's arrival in Naples with Lady Oxford's family, while serving as assistant surgeon on board a vessel of war at Lisbon, an adventure occurred in the vicinity of that city of a very profligate nature, which was attended with calamitous results. A first lieutenant, of the name of S——, and the surgeon of the ship, made the acquaintance of two ladies in a convent at Belem, adjoining the city, who consented to leave their nunnery, the means of escape having previously been devised and prepared for them.

The first lady, who descended from a window by a rope ladder to the street beneath, reached the ground without accident, and was carried off by the lieutenant. That lady I was in company with about ten years later, at a ball in Naples, the wife of the officer just referred to—then a post-captain in the navy; and Mrs. S——, the mother, at that time, of three or four children, bore the character of a most exemplary wife and mother.

But the other lady, who attempted escape on the same night, had fallen from the frail ladder to the ground from a considerable height and broken her leg. The cries of the unfortunate person were heard in the convent; people came to the spot; she was discovered, and carried back to the convent. The gentlemen who had occasioned this disaster fled to the boat that was in waiting for them, a little way below the convent, and effected their escape, leaving the wretched victim to her doom, whatever it might be.

Reilly's acquaintance with Naples in the time of Murat, when

Lady Oxford and her lovely daughters* were the bright stars round which revolved, not only the fashion, but the political intrigues of King Joachim's court, was fraught with reminiscences highly interesting, and was a never-failing subject of conversation with him.

Having ceased to be the traveling medical attendant of the Oxford family, he commenced practice in Naples, and proved so eminently successful in it as to have realized a very large fortune so early even as 1821.

He had married in Naples an English woman in affluent circumstances, a very thrifty and money-making person, but withal amiable and kindly disposed, the widow of the maître d'hôtel of the Duke de Gallo. This lady, far advanced in years, had two children—a son named Marzio, a young man of good talents, a fiery temperament, and ungovernable disposition, and a daughter, an amiable and pretty girl, who grew up to womanhood a highly-accomplished and attractive person (the belle of the Chiaja), who eventually became the bride of a young English surgeon, the successor of Reilly in his professional business.

Reilly and his wife (and his daughter, I believe), a second wife also, whom he had married about ten years ago, all have passed away; and of the English, Irish, and Scotch—not a few remarkable persons, I may add—whom I remember in the habit of frequenting that pleasant and hospitable house of his, with two exceptions—those of Dr. Quin, now established in his profession in London, and my worthy old friend, Mr. Ramsay, living in Mordaunt College, Blackheath—none, I believe, are in being.

* The Right Hon. Edmund Harley, fifth earl of Oxford, born in 1773, married, in 1794, a daughter of the Rev. J. Scott, vicar of Ichen, near Southampton, and had issue three sons and four daughters. 1. Edmund, Lord Harley, born in 1800, died in 1828. 2. Alfred, Lord Harley (the present earl), born in 1809, married Miss Nugent in 1831. 3. Jane Elizabeth, married, in 1835, to Henry Bickersteth, now Lord Langdon. 4. Charlotte Mary, married to Colonel (now General) Bacon, a distinguished officer in the service of Don Pedro, of Portugal. 5. Anne, married, in 1835, to an Italian gentleman, the Cavaliere San Giorgio. 6. Frances, married, the same year, Henry Vernon Harcourt, Esq. 7. Madeleine, who died in infancy.

DR. QUIN.

In 1821 my acquaintance with Dr. Quin commenced in Naples. He was then a young, rising medical practitioner, in great vogue with all fashionable English visitors and sojourners in Naples, full of life and spirits, of excellent address, with a keen perception of the ridiculous, and a great zest for merriment. But Quin had solid worth and good sound sense to bring to the aid of his professional talents, though some of the invalids of Naples, accustomed to grave, lugubrious doctors, seemed to think the philosophy of Heraclitus was more becoming physicians than that of Democritus. We are told by old Burton, that when Hippocrates came to Abdera, he found Democritus "busy in cutting up several beasts to find out the cause of madness and melancholy." And while he pursued his studies, he laughed ever and anon, and the public thought he was mad. But when Hippocrates conversed with him, he discovered there was a great deal of philosophy in his laughter. And he told the Abderites, though the little man laughed more profusely than other people, "that Abdera had not a wiser, a more learned, a more honest man, and they were much deceived to say that he was mad."

"Thus Democritus was esteemed (drolly) of the world in his time; and this was the cause of his laughter, and good cause he had.

> "Olim jure quidem, nunc plus Democrite, ride
> *Quin* rides uita hæc nunc mage ridicula est."*

Three-and-thirty years have had little effect in subduing Dr. Quin's high spirits, or making inroads on his vigor of body or vivacity of mind. The same quickness of apprehension and observation, unfailing humor, ready wit and repartee, characterize the most eminent homœopathic physician of London of the present day, that distinguished the young traveling physician of the Duchess of Devonshire in those early days of his and mine, which I look back to with feelings of pleasure, and

* Burton's Anatomy of Melancholy, ed. 1827, vol. i., p. 34.

recall among the reminiscences of times and scenes the most agreeable of my life.

In his profession Dr. Quin is zealous and discreet, mindful of the sanctity of the sick chamber, and of the obligations it imposes on the physician. In private life he wins and retains the confidence and esteem of those with whom he becomes acquainted. His practice is chiefly among the aristocracy. The present King of the Belgians reposed the highest confidence in his skill. The late Duke of Cambridge left no means untried to induce him to accept the post of physician to his family on allopathic principles, but those efforts were in vain. Yet I remember when the doctor made a *burla* of Hahnemann and the infinitesimal dose system. At an early period of his career in Naples, professing to write against homœopathy, he went to Germany to inquire into the system; and he who went to scoff remained to study, and to become a convert to the new theory of medicine.

Those persons are not likely to forget Dr. Quin who remember Naples and its society in the time of Sir William Drummond, Sir William Gell, the Honorable Keppel Craven, Sir Frederick Faulkner, the Margravine of Anspach, the well-known Abbé Campbell, the Blessingtons, Sir Richard Acton and his lady; Dr. Watson, the celebrated linguist; Ramsay, the Scotch merchant, with his elegant tastes and classic lore; Cottrell, the wine merchant, of Falernian celebrity, renowned for his *lachrymachristi*, and his efforts to rival Francis, and to render Horace into better English than all previous translators; Reilly, the true Hibernian; Dr. Milne, the skillful Scot and accomplished gentleman of the Chiatamone; old Walker, of the Largo Castello, the expatriated Manchester reformer, who, in the good old times of William Pitt and George III., was tried for sedition, and narrowly escaped the fate of his reforming brethren, Muir and Palmer; and, though last, not least deserving of remembrance and of honorable mention in the list of worthies from foreign lands who figured in Neapolitan society some thirty years ago, the venerable commandant of the Castello D'Ovo, General Wade, the old Irish warrior, one of the brave old souls of the Brigade, renowned for his hospitality, and beloved by all who knew him, English, Irish, and Italian.* Maurice Quill should have lived in Naples in those days, and Lever should have recorded all the extraordinary scenes and ridiculous occurrences, the reminiscences of which are connected with the names of Reilly and the abbé, Quin, Mahon, the redoubtable Milesian; Thornton, the Irish tutor of the Duchess of Eboli; Ridgeway, the secretary of Lady Drummond; young Edward Molyneux and his friend, the incipient surgeon, in those days of nature not unfit for scenes of gayety and humor, nor unfamiliar with them.

SIR FERDINAND RICHARD E. D. ACTON.

One of "the celebrities" of Neapolitan society in 1823 and 1824 was Sir Ferdinand Richard Edward Dalberg Acton, the seventh baronet of Aldenham Hall, in Salop. He was the eldest son of Sir John Francis Edward, the sixth baronet, for some years prime minister of the King of Naples, by Mary Anne, daughter of Joseph Edward Acton, Esq. Sir Ferdinand Richard, in his tenth year, succeeded to the title in 1811 (in which year his father died at Palermo). He married in Paris, in 1832, the only child and heiress of the Duc de Dalberg, by which marriage he obtained large possessions in Austria. He died in Paris, aged thirty-five, in January, 1837.

SIR FREDERICK FAULKNER.

Those who were acquainted with Naples about thirty years

* General Wade, in all probability, was a member of a Westmeath family of that name, which gave a field marshal to the British army in the reign of King William. That distinguished officer had gained his first military honors at the battle of Aughrim, in 1691, and commanded in the Highlands, as a general officer, from 1726 to 1737, during which period he had caused roads to be made through mountainous districts previously impassable for troops, for which works he was immortalized by a Scotch poet in the verse,

"Had you traveled these roads before they were made,
You'd lift up your hands and bless General Wade."

The grandfather of the field marshal had considerable grants of land in the neighborhood of Tyrrell's Pass, conferred on him by Cromwell in 1653. The field marshal of Westmeath, who died in 1748, aged seventy-five, reposes in Westminster Abbey. The field marshal of Meath, who died in 1852, rests, after the labors of eighty-four years, in St. Paul's.

ago will remember an Irish gentleman, tall and portly, a fine specimen of one of the old school of Hibernian gentility, of prepossessing appearance and elegant manners, *degagées et debonnaires*, and free from all restraint; who was exceedingly poor, and might have been extremely rich; who lived from day to day by borrowing from all his friends, and yet made an appearance in society; dined out a great deal, and passed for an Irish landlord ever on the brink of prosperity, sure to get rents which never came to hand, and in daily expectation of remittances which were always coming, but, alas! which came not. Sir Frederick Faulkner was this unhappy gentleman — a person abounding in anecdote, most agreeable in society, and singularly inconsistent in his character.

Gell talked of founding a hospital at Rome for genteel persons of decayed purses, and discontented, disappointed, agreeable people.

Sir Frederick would have been a most agreeable inmate of such an institution.

Nothing could induce Sir Frederick to violate his public principles, but in private life his principles were violated every day; his poverty, but not his will, consented to the violation. He borrowed daily, without any prospect of being able to pay what was lent him. He made solemn promises day after day, which were invariably broken by him.

For many years previous to the Union this gentleman was a member for the county of Dublin,* and one of the most strenuous opponents of that measure, though in very straitened circumstances, and having had divers overtures made to him of a very tempting nature for his support. He terminated a career rendered miserable by pecuniary embarrassments, in Naples, by suicide, in 1822. Sir Frederick married, in 1798, Miss Anne Frances Gardiner, daughter of Sackville Gardiner, second son of the Right Hon. Luke Gardiner, the grandfather of the late Earl of Blessington.

* In 1807, at the general election, we read in the papers of Mr. Frederick John Faulkner, the former member for the county of Dublin, being defeated by Mr. Talbot, of Malahide.

THE DUKE DE LAVAL MONTMORENCI.

This antique remnant of the ancient aristocracy of France was embassador at the court of Rome in 1825, when Lady Blessington had taken up her abode in the Palazzo Negrone. The duke, whom I had subsequently met in Rome, on several occasions, at their abode, was a remarkable person in society. Occasionally lively and spiritual, frequently and suddenly somnolent, and always, when awake, extremely gallant and complimentary to the ladies. But his compliments and eulogies were generally *mal-apropos.* All his senses, and a few of his faculties, were defective; some impaired by age, one naturally imperfect. In these particulars he resembled an old Chancery barrister, Bell, whom Lord Eldon used to commend, though he could neither talk, walk, think, or write like any other man.

The duke's talent for diplomacy was said to have outlived all his other capabilities. He was respected, however, by all who knew him, for his sterling worth and his generous conduct, especially to Pius VII. when in France, whose wants were liberally supplied by him.

The name of this gentleman is connected with a very melancholy occurrence, frequently referred to in Lady Blessington's Journal and Correspondence, which took place in Rome in the month of February, 1824.

MISS BATHURST.

Miss Bathurst was a granddaughter of the late venerable and excellent Bishop of Norwich. Her father, some years previously to the calamity above referred to, in his travels in Germany, unaccompanied by his family, had disappeared, and was never more heard of by them, leaving a young widow and two infant daughters to deplore his loss. Miss Bathurst, the subject of this brief notice, grew up to womanhood—a lovely girl, strikingly beautiful. She was traveling in Italy, and sojourning in Rome, in 1824, with her uncle and aunt, Lord and Lady Aylmer. She had gone out, on one occasion, on horseback, escorted by Lord and Lady Aylmer and the French embassador, the Duke de

Laval Montmorenci. The groom of Miss Bathurst had been sent back to Lord Aylmer's on some message, and when they approached the Pont Motte, over the Tiber, the Duke de Laval took them by a path he was in the habit of riding along on the banks of the Tiber. Finding this path difficult, the party were in the act of retracing their steps, when Miss Bathurst, in turning her horse, approached too near the edge of the bank, and, in an instant, horse and rider were plunged into the river. Lord Aylmer made two ineffectual attempts, though unable to swim, to rescue the young lady.* The Duke de Laval was incapable of affording any assistance. Miss Bathurst managed to keep her seat after the horse fell into the river till his violent plunging caused the girths to burst, and then she lost her seat and sunk, but rose once more to the surface, and then disappeared to rise no more. The remains were not discovered for months; they were interred in the English place of burial in Rome, where the ashes of Shelley and of Keats are deposited. The vast sepulchral pile that stands there in honor of the memory of Caius Cestius excites less interest than the small marble monument, of snowy whiteness, well fitted to recall the purity of that fair creature, whose melancholy fate it commemorates. The monument erected to the memory of Miss Bathurst is the work of Sir Richard Westmacott, and alike worthy of the mournful subject and of the skillful sculptor.

From W. S. Landor, in relation to the death of Miss Bathurst:

"Dear Lady Blessington,—I have just requested Mrs. Paynter to let me send your ladyship what Lord Aylmer says about the drowning of Miss Bathurst, which shows that Mills is not quite correct. Lord Aylmer is remarkably so on all occasions, and is a most amiable and most intelligent man, greatly (of course) hated and injured by the people in power.

"W. S. Landor.

"Kindest regards to Miss Power and Count D'Orsay."

EXTRACT FROM A LETTER OF LORD AYLMER REGARDING THE DEATH OF MISS BATHURST.

"When at Bath, it did not occur to me to mention to Mr. Landor an error,

* Lord Aylmer died in 1850, in his seventy-fifth year.

into which Lady Blessington has been led, in her 'Idler in Italy,' when describing a certain dreadful event at which Louisa and I were present at Rome.

"She says that I was prevented by Louisa from rendering any assistance to that poor girl who there perished, to our indescribable anguish; whereas you know I made *two* distinct attempts to save her, and was very nearly drowned myself in doing so, more especially in the last, when I gave myself up as lost. Do you think it worth while to mention this to Mr. Landor, who is, I believe, in habits of intimacy with Lady Blessington? AYLMER."

PIAZZI,

THE DISCOVERER OF THE PLANET CERES.

Joseph Piazzi, President of the Royal Society of Sciences of Naples, of whom mention is made in Lady Blessington's Italian Journals, died at Naples in July, 1825, in his eightieth year. He was born in the Valteline in 1746. He entered into the order of Theatines in 1764; and after enjoying the professorship of Astronomy at Malta, he was made professor at Palermo in 1781. In 1787 he made several observations, in conjunction with Lalande, at the Parisian observatory; and afterward he visited England to purchase instruments. It was on the 1st of January, 1801, that he discovered the planet Ceres, which led to the discovery of Pallas, Juno, and Vesta. In 1814 he printed a catalogue of 7500 stars, a work which gained for him the medal founded by Lalande. In 1816 he published at Milan the first volume of the "History of Sicilian Astronomy," and completed his "Elements of Astronomy."*

SIR AUGUSTUS D'ESTE.

The Duke of Sussex, in 1793, married the Lady Augusta Murray in Rome. A few months later, the marriage was resolemnized in London, and the year following, in 1794, it was declared invalid in the Court of Arches, being contrary to the Royal Marriage Act. The union, however, was uninterrupted till the year 1806, when a separation took place, and the ill-used lady took the name of Madame de Ameland, and the two children by this marriage took the name of D'Este, after that of the

* Annual Register, Appen., 1826, p. 269.

illustrious family of Ferrara, which was nearly connected with the house of Brunswick.

The eldest child, Sir Augustus D'Este, entered the army, and obtained a commission in the Royal Fusileers; he served at New Orleans in 1814, and at length obtained the rank of colonel. He retired on half pay in 1824. In 1830 he was appointed Knight Commander of the Bath by King William, and in the same year he claimed succession to the titles and honors of his father, the Duke of Sussex. He had previously memorialized the king on the subject. The matter was brought before the House of Lords, and a judicial committee finally decided against his claim. Sir Augustus traveled extensively on the Continent, and in 1828 was sojourning in Florence, in very impaired health, where I had the honor of making his acquaintance. He died, unmarried, in 1849.

His sister, Miss Ellen Augusta D'Este, married Sergeant Wilde in 1845.

CAPTAIN HESSE.

The following account is given by Lady Blessington of a young military officer, of much notoriety in Naples, as a man of gallantry and extraordinary adventures in royal circles, at the period of my residence there some thirty years ago.

This account is taken verbatim from one of the commonplace books of Lady Blessington, entitled "Night Thoughts," which I have had occasion already to refer to.

It may be well to observe that Captain Hesse was one of the gentlemen attached to the household of Queen Caroline, who left her majesty's service and remained in Naples after the departure of the queen in 1820.

"Captain Hesse," says Lady Blessington, "was the son of a Prussian merchant, who acquired great wealth by various contracts, and more especially for clothing the Russian army.

"When a youth he was sent to England, to be educated under the auspices of the Margrave of Anspach, then residing in this country. Being a good-looking, lively youth, he was taken much notice of by the margrave and margravine (formerly the celebrated Lady Craven), and was invited to pass his short vacation with them. His education being completed, he returned to Berlin, where his father, then become a banker, lived in considerable splendor, and was expected to leave his son a large fortune. Napoleon's campaign against Prussia blighted these prospects; for the banker Hesse having contracted to clothe the Prussian army, their defeat, and its consequent result, precluded the king from paying Hesse, and occasioned his ruin. Under these circumstances, young Hesse was sent to England, in the hope that, through the influence of the margravine (the margrave was then dead), some situation or provision could be obtained for him. A letter, detailing the ruin of the family, and entreating the commiseration of the margravine, was dispatched to her; and, with great good-nature, she received young Hesse beneath her roof, and so successfully used her influence in his favor, that the Duke of York granted him a cornetcy in a dragoon regiment (I think the 18th), and the margravine and her son, the Honorable Keppel Craven, fitted him out for joining his regiment in a suitable manner.

"The Duchess of York, herself a Prussian, and knowing his family, felt interested for her youthful countryman, and spoke in his favor to her kind-hearted husband. Meeting, at the margravine's, the most distinguished persons, young Hesse was received into good society. Gay, amusing, good-looking, a good horseman, and with an easy address and manner, he soon rendered himself conspicuous by a certain coxcombry in dress, originating in his besetting and only sin—vanity. This weakness induced him, when scandalous reports assisted to account for his good fortune in England, to allow it to be believed that he was the son of the margrave and the margravine previous to their marriage, rather to encourage than discountenance the rumors. The calibre of his mind could not be better proved than by his preferring to have it believed that he was the illegitimate child of persons of high rank rather than the legitimate son of a respectable banker at Berlin. His dashing appearance, and his desire to attract the attention of the fair sex, drew him into notice; and when sent with a portion of his regiment to the neighborhood of Bognor, where the Princess Charlotte of Wales was then staying, he attracted her attention by riding constantly in front of her window, until the youthful and self-willed girl, captivated by his appearance and horsemanship, condescended first to bow to him, and then to write to him. The correspondence was supposed to be carried on through the medium of the Countess de F——, then Miss M. E., though afterward several letters were conveyed to the princess through General Garth, who was imposed on, and led to believe they were from the mother of the princess. Portraits were exchanged, and young Hesse, vain and elevated, was perhaps less cautious than he ought to have been, and the matter got talked of, and reached the ears of the royal family.

"The princess was scolded, watched, and guarded. Hesse was sent to Spain with his regiment, where he was wounded; and it being discovered that he still possessed the letters and portrait of the princess, an awkward thing, when her marriage with some princely suitor might soon be looked for, the margravine and Mr. Keppel Craven were applied to to use their influence with Mr. Hesse to have the letters and portrait returned: the application came from the princess. The margravine and Mr. Keppel Craven, justly offended at Hesse's having encouraged the false reports of his being the son of the former—a report which their great kindness had given a color to—had marked their displeasure to him, and more especially as the romantic interest attached to his position as the supposed son of a prince and an English countess had greatly influenced the girlish fancy of the Princess Charlotte in his favor. Hesse, when applied to, was very reluctant to return the letters and portrait, but at length yielded to the representation of Mr. Keppel Craven on the impropriety of retaining letters which the writer reclaimed; he sent Mr. Craven an order to have the sealed box containing them (which had been left with a friend, with injunctions that, should Hesse die, the box and its contents, unopened, should be consigned to the flames) delivered to Mr. Craven. The latter gentleman living out of England, the box was transferred to the Countess de F——, in whose possession the letters still are, as that lady assured Mr. K. Craven a year ago.

"Gratified by Hesse's surrender of the letters, the margravine and Mr. K. Craven, when he returned from Spain, overlooked his former folly, and received him into favor. The Princess Charlotte, at a ball at Carlton House, saw the unmarried sister of Mr. K. Craven, whom she had never previously met, and walking up close to her, said, 'I am glad of an opportunity of seeing you, and I request you will tell your brother, Mr. Keppel Craven, how truly obliged I feel to him. He will know to what my obligation refers.'

"This, with Hesse's after-scrapes at Naples in royal circles, was told me at my house, on the evening of the 31st of August, 1846, by the Honorable Keppel Craven. M. B."

CAPTAIN GARTH.

General Garth, the father of Captain Thomas Garth, Colonel of the 1st or Royal Regiment of Dragoons, was a grand-nephew of the celebrated Sir Samuel Garth, physician in ordinary to George the First. Some unfortunate circumstances, about thirty years ago, made the marriage of General Garth with a royal princess of the house of Hanover a matter of notoriety. The issue of that marriage was Captain Thomas Garth. The general died in London in 1830, in his eighty-fifth year.

Captain Garth was one of the foreign celebrities of Naples about 1821 and 1822, and made his sojourn there sufficiently remarkable.

CHAPTER XXI.

THE HONORABLE RICHARD KEPPEL CRAVEN, AND MARGRAVINE OF ANSPACH.

Mr. R. K. Craven was the third son of William, sixth Baron Craven, by his marriage, on the 18th of May, 1767, with Elizabeth, daughter of Augustus, fourth Earl of Berkeley (born in 1750), by whom he had issue several children.

Lady Craven separated from her husband in 1781. In the "Dictionary of Living Authors," published in 1816, it is stated that Lady Craven had been so cruelly treated by her husband that her friends were obliged to interfere to effect a separation. This event took place in 1781. The succeeding ten years were spent by Lady Craven on the Continent and in the Levant. In 1789 she published, in 4to, "A Journey through the Crimea to Constantinople."

Horace Walpole, in November, 1786, wrote to Lady Craven, then scouring the Continent and the Levant, *skurrying* over Italy, Germany, Poland, Russia, Turkey, and Greece, on the difficulties she had occasioned her friends by the rapidity of her movements, and the impossibility of finding out "in what quarter of the known or unknown world she might be resident or existent at any particular time." On receiving a note from her at Strawberry Hill, offering to call on her for a moment, he tells her, " A whirlwind, I suppose, was waiting at your door to carry you to Japan, and as balloons have not yet any settled post-office in the air, you could not, at least did not, give me any direction where to address you, though you did kindly reproach me with my silence." In his justification he observes, "I heard from you from Venice, then from Poland, and then, having whisked through Tartary, from Petersburgh, but still no directions. I said to myself, I will write to Constantinople, which will probably be her next stage. Nor was I totally in the wrong, for there came a letter from Constantinople with a design mentioned in it of going to the Greek Islands, and orders to you at Vienna, but with no banker or other address specified.......You had been in the tent of the Cham of Tartary! and in the harem of the Captain Pacha, and, during the navigation of the Ægean, were possibly in the terrible power of corsairs. How could I suppose that so many despotic infidels would part with your charms?"

Shortly after Lord Craven's decease, his lady, in 1791, married the Margravine of Anspach and Bayreuth. This prince, some years after he had gained the hand of the English lady, disposed of his German principality to the King of Prussia, and retired to England, where he died in 1806, at Brandenburg House, Hammersmith. The festivities and fashionable *divertissemens follatres* of Brandenburg House attracted no little notice in their day.* A private theatre was fitted up in this palace of pleasure, and many dramatic pieces, written by the margravine, were produced on this stage. Some of these had been written previously to her separation from Lord Craven.

"The Sleepwalker," a comedy, printed at the Strawberry Hill press in 1778, and "The Miniature Picture," a comedy, written in 1781. "Nourjad," a French comedy, was written by her ladyship during her residence in Anspach, and printed there in 1787. She published a translation of Cibber's comedy of "She would and she would not." Also a very singular composition, a satirical piece, in 1779, in 12mo, entitled "Modern Anecdotes of the Family of Kinkvervantotsdarsprakengotchderns," a tale.

The letters of Lady Craven addressed to her son, translated into French, are noticed in Grimm's Memoirs (of the year 1788.)† Grimm observes that "a superior intelligence, and sentiments the most just and delicate, are obvious in the lessons which this enlightened mother gave to her son, with regard to the consideration due to the sensibility of the sex."

In 1802 she published also "The Soldier of Dierstein," an Austrian story, in 8vo.

Boswell speaks of Johnson's "dining with the beautiful, gay, and fascinating Lady Craven." Ah! if the admiring lexicographer could have looked at the same lady through a telescope of sixty years' power of looking into futurity, how he would have been astounded at the haggard old woman, wrinkled and withered as she was in her latter days, retaining nothing of the former belle but the sprightliness of her nature, and that vivacity contrasting very painfully with the wreck of pristine beauty and comeliness.

During the latter years of her life the margravine resided altogether in Naples.

* The margravine, in her Autobiography, alluding to the magnificence of her establishment at Brandenburg House, says, "We had thirty servants in livery, with grooms, and a set of sixty horses. Our expenses were enormous, though I curtailed them with all possible economy."

† Memoires par le Baron le Grimm, vol. iv., p. 164, 8vo, London, 1813.

Her well-known villa in the vicinity of Pausilippo, on the Strada Nuova, was furnished with taste and elegance; the grounds were laid out with great care under the immediate direction of the margravine.

I have seen her, a few years before her death, working in her garden, spade in hand, in very coarse and singular attire, a desiccated, antiquated piece of mortality, remarkable for vivacity, realizing the idea of a galvanized Egyptian mummy, or one of the weird sisters working at "a charm of powerful trouble." She died in Naples in June, 1828, in the seventy-ninth year of her age.

Lord Charles Murray, who had known the margravine in England, was in Naples in 1822. A short time previously to my first acquaintance with him in that year, he had been seized with fever in Sicily, which malady was followed by temporary insanity. He was brought to Naples, and there a great improvement took place in his health of mind and body. When his lordship was beginning to recover, he was in the habit of making excursions, suitably attended, in the vicinity of the city.

Lord Charles, on one occasion, had begged me to accompany him to the residence of the Margravine of Anspach, as he was desirous of paying his respects to the old lady, whom he had formerly known in London. Unfortunately, the margravine did not receive us in her house, or in such costume as ladies usually receive visits in. Indeed, her costume and appearance would have suited admirably for the character of one of the weird sisters in the scene of Macbeth, where the witches are introduced performing incantations dire.

We were conducted to her in the garden, where she was in the act of digging, and we found her attired in a manner not calculated to encourage gravity, or keep an excited person's mind long in an undisturbed condition. For a few minutes after introduction and recognition, things went on very agreeably. The margravine made many inquiries after old friends, and Lord Charles answered them with all possible courtesy.

But at length a cloud began to gather on his brow, when he surveyed the poor old lady, in her singular costume, from head to foot. I endeavored to hasten our departure for Naples, but all my efforts were in vain; Lord Charles burst out into a perfect hurricane of reprehension, calling up reminiscences of a disagreeable nature, rumors of strange occurrences in various quarters of the globe, on which he enlarged with extraordinary vehemence and volubility, to the great amazement of the margravine, till such time as I found an opportunity of explaining the unhappy illness under which his lordship had been lately laboring. It was with no small difficulty I brought the unpleasant interview, at length, to a termination.

The margravine accompanied us to the gate of the villa, and there a new scene was in store for her. Lord Charles insisted on showing her a new mode of entering a carriage, which he recommended her particularly to adopt; he then made a rush toward the carriage door, and, putting his hand on the window frame, made a jump of that kind which harlequins and clowns are wont to make in pantomimes, through panels representing clocks, and fairly launched the upper part of his body through the window, leaving his long legs on the outside, kicking furiously in all directions.

The consternation and astonishment of the margravine was beyond description. I succeeded, with a great deal of trouble, by opening the opposite door of the carriage, to get his lordship's legs dragged in where the rest of his person was sprawling; and, not without a great deal of violence on his part, ending in the demolition of all the glass in the vehicle, managed to get him back to Naples.

That access of mania appeared to me to have been produced mainly by the margravine's strange aspect and apparel. I thought I could read Banquo's inquiry in poor Lord Charles's searching gaze when he first set his eyes on her:

> "What are these, so withered, and so wild in their attire,
> That look not like the inhabitants of earth,
> And yet are on't? Live you, or are you aught
> That man may question? You seem to understand me
> By each at once her chapping fingers lying
> Upon her skinny lips."*

* Poor Lord Charles perfectly recovered his reason; about two years later I

The present Dowager Duchess of Athol was the mother of two children, Lady Catherine, who died young, and Lord Charles Murray, who, having volunteered in the cause of Greek independence, died at Gastonini, in Greece, August 11th, 1824, aged twenty-five. The circumstances of his decease are recorded in vol. xciv., p. 465, of the "New Monthly Magazine." The following particulars are taken from a later number of the same periodical.

"Lord Charles Murray, an amiable and benevolent young man, who had been bred up in luxury and ease, underwent every species of fatigue, and submitted to every possible privation, in order to encourage the Greeks by his example, and to be able to furnish them with means from his far too limited income. Nothing seemed to him degrading that could contribute a mite to the cause, and the noble son of a lofty Scottish Thane has been seen, day after day, giving lessons of the broad-sword to a pack of ragged Greeks! So active was this young nobleman's charity, so little did he care for self, that, after an inflammatory disorder, brought on by his constant exposure to an unhealthy climate, and under a burning sun, he expired on a solitary pallet, far from all his friends and connections. An Englishman, who had arrived just in time to close his eyes, on taking an inventory of his effects, found them to consist of nothing more than two old shirts, a pair or two of stockings, a brace of pistols, a sabre, and a Bible. Every thing had gone to assist the impoverished Greeks and the distressed Frank volunteers in their ranks. The gentleman who had paid him the last sad offices had, a few months before, owed him his life. Lord Charles, though at the time a perfect stranger, waited unremittingly, with the care of an affectionate brother, at his bedside, until he saw him rise from it with recovered health."

Some interesting particulars of Mr. Craven's early history are given in a publication to which literary men who have to treat of their contemporaries are more largely indebted than to all other periodicals of their times—"The Gentleman's Magazine."

met him at Marseilles, quite restored. He was then about to embark for Greece where he died a little later.

"When Keppel Craven was about three years old, his father took leave of Lady Craven, never to see her more; and when she shortly afterward returned to France, she was allowed to take Keppel (being her youngest child) with her, but it was under a promise to return him to his father when he was eight years of age. This condition was not fulfilled; but she afterward placed him at Harrow, under a feigned name.

"'While Keppel was at Harrow,' says his mother, 'a lady saw him in the master's private library, and when she was stepping into her coach, she asked the master who the boy was. He answered, "A German." "It is the image of Lady Craven," she said. Keppel, who at this time was about thirteen years old, spoke English perfectly, without any accent, although he had been so much abroad. The lady's remark struck the master forcibly, who went back to the child immediately, and told him he suspected he was Lord Craven's son, and it was better that his uncle, Lord Berkeley, who was left to direct his brother, then at Eton, should know where he was; and, after his first confusion was over, the child consented to it.' In consequence, Keppel passed the next vacation with his brother Berkeley, in Dorsetshire.

"Mr. Keppel Craven, however, was not, by this incident, permanently estranged from his mother, who shortly after came to reside in this country with the Margrave of Anspach, to whom she had been married in 1799. After the margrave's death in 1805, he fixed his residence with her at Naples."*

When her royal highness, the Princess of Wales, set out in 1814 on her foreign tour, she was accompanied by several English gentlemen and two English ladies in her suite. The princess quitted Naples in March, 1815; her two chamberlains, Sir William Gell and Mr. Craven, and her only remaining maid of honor, Lady Elizabeth Forbes, stayed behind, as did likewise her royal highness's equerry, Captain Hesse.

Mr. Craven, in his examination on the queen's trial in 1820, said he was in the queen's service as one of her chamberlains in 1814, but left it at the expiration of six months, in conformity

* The Gentleman's Magazine, October, 1851, p. 492.

with previous arrangements; was aware of the presence of a spy from England, whose business it was to watch the conduct of the queen. He saw no impropriety in the conduct of the queen at Milan or Naples, or improper familiarity on the part of Bergami. He (witness) left her at Naples, and proceeded to England.

Mr. Craven, having fixed his abode in Naples, became intimately acquainted with Sir William Gell.

Their tastes, habits, pursuits, and inclinations were identical. There never were friends more united in sentiment and affection.

Mr. Craven was a good classical scholar, had an excellent taste for drawing, was a great lover of books, and had all the feelings, refined manners, and the gentle, winning, easy address of an accomplished gentleman.

One of the earliest and most highly-esteemed acquaintances made by Lady Blessington on her arrival in Naples in July, 1823, was the Honorable R. Keppel Craven.

Mr. Craven (says Lady Blessington) possesses a highly-cultivated mind, manners at once dignified and graceful, and exercises an elegant hospitality, that renders his house the most attractive here.

She speaks of him in her letters and diaries of 1823 and 1824 as "one of the most agreeable persons in Naples," "a person of the greatest versatility of knowledge," "a scholar," "a musician," "a draughtsman of much merit," "a comic actor of considerable ability."

In 1821, Mr. Craven published in 4to, "A Tour through the Southern Provinces of the Kingdom of Naples," to which is subjoined an Account of the Revolution. This work is embellished with views from his own sketches.

Mr. Craven's principal work is "Excursions in the Abruzzi and the Northern Provinces of Naples," in 2 vols., published in 1837. In that excellent work, worthy of the taste for art and antiquarian lore of his old friend and companion, Sir William Gell, there is one description, which alone would render the "Excursions" of no ordinary value; the detailed and most interesting account of the Benedictine monastery of Monte Casino (the original foundation of St. Benedict), and its valuable library, and precious archives, diplomas, chronicles, and monastic records, and its innumerable documents illustrative of the early history in those regions of the Lombards and Normans; the original copies of Leo Ostienses and Richard of San Germano, as well as rare manuscripts of the works of Homer, Virgil, and Dante; and, lastly, the celebrated vision of Alberica, a monk of this fraternity, from which that poet is supposed to have taken the first idea of the "*Divina Commedia.*"

Mr. Craven died at Naples in June, 1851, aged seventy-two, the last of a triumvirate of English literati, scholars, and gentlemen of refined taste in art and excellence in antiquarian pursuits, who resided for so many years in Naples in the closest bonds of friendship—Drummond, Gell, and Craven.

The respect and affectionate care paid by Mr. Craven throughout his whole life to his mother was one of the most remarkable and amiable traits in his character. No amount of eccentricity, or waywardness, or restlessness on the part of the margravine made the slightest difference in the undeviating and uniform dutifulness and tender devotion to her of this favorite child of hers.

She was fully sensible of this kindness, and returned her son's affection to some extent. I have never observed, except in a single instance—that of the filial homage, affectionate regard, and dutifulness of Sir Moses Montefiore to his venerable mother—the same deference, honor, and child-like love shown by a man advanced in years to a parent, as was exhibited by Keppel Craven to his mother. And in this particular case the merit of the son's conduct was certainly enhanced by a great deal of eccentricity on the part of her whose happiness and comfort were the chief objects of his care.

Mr. Augustus Craven, the only son of the Honorable R. Keppel Craven, was attached to the mission at Naples in the latter part of 1830, and to that at Frankfort in 1833; was appointed paid attaché at Lisbon in 1836, at Brussels in 1839; was made secretary of legation at Stuttgardt in 1843.* He acted, for a

* Foreign Office List for 1854, p. 54.

short time, as private secretary to the Marquis of Normanby at Paris in 1846, and resigned his post at Stuttgardt in 1852. A little later, he was a candidate, on the liberal interest, for the representation of the county of Dublin, and was defeated.

LETTERS TO LADY BLESSINGTON FROM THE HON. KEPPEL CRAVEN.

"Pente, near Salerno, August 29th, 1835.

"Your last kind letter, and the very flattering expressions it contained, ought to have received an earlier answer than I have bestowed upon it, but I am not the less grateful; and you will admit the validity of an excuse for silence when I inform you that it has been protracted from a desire of giving you a better account of our friend Gell than I could have done two months ago. Then, indeed, his state of health was such as to excite considerable alarm, but about the beginning of August a crisis appears to have taken place, and a considerable improvement has been the consequence; he is now here, where he has been staying a week; but that would prove nothing in favor of his amended condition, as even at its worst period his courage and activity of mind never drooped, and he went out just as usual.

"I wish I could add to this that I am free from all apprehension; but as long as a tendency to somnolency continues, the only symptom which has not disappeared, I feel uneasy. This affection is considerably diminished, that is, modified in its form and periods, but still it exists to a degree that must undergo great alteration before his friends can find their minds totally reassured with regard to the consequences; that this may occur I am assured by his physicians is probable, and Heaven knows I am but too well disposed to believe them. In addition to this fund of uneasiness, I have had some occupations of an annoying nature in the uncertainty which arose and hung over my son's departure, who, with his wife, is gone to France for some months. This had been decided some time back, but the approach of the cholera southward urged them to anticipate their intended departure, for fear of finding themselves shut in to the north of Italy, and surrounded on all sides with sanitary cordons.

"I have just heard from them in date of Milan, and there seemed no obstacle to their having reached Switzerland in safety, so their difficulties are at an end. With regard to the malady itself, there seems no doubt that it has declared itself at Nice, Genoa, Corsi, and Leghorn, but it has not been very violent, and seems just now to be suspended. Measures are taking in this kingdom to present obstacles (if that is possible) to its approach, and to attend to it in the most effectual manner if it does come; but the panic it had caused at first appears to have subsided, and its effects seem confined to the innkeepers and laquais de places, who foresee a sterile winter for them, as it is not probable that, as long as any lurking remains of the malady are supposed to exist in any part of Italy, strangers will voluntarily select it for their next winter's residence; at present there are very few, who will most likely soon depart. I have been staying here ever since the beginning of June, occupied much as usual, with additions and improvements, which, however, have somewhat changed their form, as I begin to reap the enjoyments of past labors instead of undertaking new ones. I have had some visitors, enough to break upon the unwearied tenor of my usual habits, but not too frequently to prevent the resumption of them. The summer has been variable, therefore, for this climate, cool; and now, heavy rains and thunder-storms seem to give us a foretaste of the equinox a month before its natural time.

"I ought before this to have thanked you for your offer of assistance with regard to the publication of my last journey, a proposal which I should most gratefully avail myself of should circumstances favor its appearance; it is now completed, and copied out in a fair, legible hand, therefore accessible to the inspection of any bookseller, who, of course, will choose to examine it before any stipulations are made. I will seek an opportunity of forwarding it to England, and if I find one, will take the liberty of addressing it to you as its guardian; in the mean while, I may as well state the nature of the work and its contents, which are the result of various excursions in the northern provinces of this kingdom, that is, the Abruzzi; to these are added others less extended, in the district of Samnium and Basilicata, and other less remote parts, but certainly not better known. The whole would form a quarto volume about the size of the last I published relative to the South, and, as far as I can judge, written in the same manner—that is, in that of an Itinerary, principally useful to such as are inclined to examine those regions, but not arriving at any details of science or statistics. There are some drawings annexed, but I would leave the expediency of adding them to the work to the publisher's decision, though I think they would add considerably to the effect, as they are selected from many, represent spots entirely unknown, and of some interest, as well from their locality as their picturesque accompaniments, all which I state, in case any previous inquiry should be made as to the general nature of the work. Gell, in whose room I am now writing, requests his kindest regards to you; may I beg you will add mine to Count D'Orsay, and believe me, dear Lady Blessington, yours most obliged and sincerely,

"R. Keppel Craven."

"Naples, April 17, 1836.

"I hope you will not judge of the impression your last kind letter produced upon me by the tardiness I have observed in replying to it; but for this I shall offer no apology; acquiescing in all your friendly expressions regarding the loss I have sustained* is but a poor way of denoting my thanks, and I deferred offering them till I could at the same time inform you with some certainty of my intended movements for the summer, which I now can do, hav-

* The death of Sir William Gell.—R. R. M.

ng determined to leave this very early in the ensuing month, and to proceed as rapidly as a weary-spent and not a very robust state of health will allow me, resting only a few weeks at Paris, so that I hope to be in London in the first week of June, when I need not say you will be very shortly apprised of my arrival. I have been very busy in arranging the memorials I preserve of our excellent friend, so as to have them constantly under my inspection. You know that there are various ways of finding relief, which differ according to the disposition and habits of the sufferer in similar cases, and I own that flying from, or destroying every record which recalls the person lamented, does not appear (to me at least) an efficacious mode of obtaining consolation; for surely it does not require such tangible mementoes of departed excellence to remind one of an irreparable loss, the conviction of which will intrude itself at all times, and through every circumstance of social or solitary life. I have, therefore, amalgamated the books of which I have possession with my own, in a manner that no eye but mine can detect; and they serve to adorn, and give additional value to, the apartment I always inhabit. The drawings I have placed in two cabinets, in drawers, except those forming a series of his 'Travels in Greece,' which I knew he wished to be finally bestowed upon the British Museum; these are all in one case, with his initials, and at my death shall be removed to that destination, more worthy, perhaps, of their merits than their present position, but not more honored by the owner.

"We had a beautiful month of March, which has been followed by an April reminding us of January, the rigor of which still endures in the shape of cold winds, stormy showers, melted snow, and other irregularities, as ill suited to the season as to the latitude.

"There are numerous arrivals from Rome, but few of name or note. S. Carlo is closed altogether, and the season more than usually dull in every respect. I fear your friend, Count Matuschewitz must be singularly struck with it, but he seems in high good humor, and does not complain; he has favored me with his company to dinner a few times, and I find him every thing you describe; he has taken the Palazzo Fernandina, and is getting it up. There could not be a better selection, and I have no doubt he will find it so; but he is still at the inn, the house not being yet ready for him. The king is at present enjoying the honors of a camp composed of about a third of his forces, near Salerno; this is an amusement he was much inclined to in his early days of celibacy, but latterly his growing attachment to his poor young wife appeared to have absorbed his attention; however, after three months' mourning, he has had recourse to this object, either to resume his bachelor's avocations, or perhaps by way only of a little dissipation. There are already reports of his having the intention of traveling to seek a worthy successor of the late queen; and they are not without probability. To the questions you put, and which appear to me but too natural, respecting Gell's last days, or rather weeks, I find it rather difficult to return a positive answer, more especially as to his own feelings respecting his state. I think that at times he was quite aware that his system had received a blow from which it could never recover, and that as far back as this time twelvemonth; but he had continued so many months under the impression of repeated somnolence, of somnolence totally free from bodily suffering, that I don't apprehend he considered himself worse at the end of the year than last spring. He was not aware of his increasing debility; and as the functions of his stomach continued unimpaired until within but two days before the sad event, when a general and rapid decay of all the vital functions occurred, I don't think that his reflections dwelt upon his dissolution as being very near. Nevertheless, his last will, about which he was very anxious, was executed little more than a week before his decease, and occasionally he would allude to the event itself in an indirect manner; for on receiving some books about a month before it happened, and my asking him to lend some to me, he said, 'You had better read them when they are your own—and you are not likely to wait long.' I find in his daily journal, in which he noted observations on his health, about Christmas, these words—'*May consider myself well.*' He had rallied to what appeared a very improved condition about three weeks before the catastrophe; but it was principally in the suspension of the lethargic affections which had so long oppressed him that this was evident, and the consequence was, that, having much longer intervals of clear consciousness and reflection, he was undoubtedly more awake to his situation, both morally and physically; for he then complained of bodily ailings much more than during his whole malady, though to all appearance they had ceased. He never ceased, I don't say for an hour, but an *instant*, to have a book open before him; and though he sometimes could not fix his eyes for two minutes at a time on its contents, he nevertheless understood it, and could afterward talk of the work in a manner which proved that, while his mental powers were awake, they were as strong as ever—more especially his memory; but the state he was in caused much confusion in his ideas of time and distance, of which he was aware, and complained of.

"I cannot end my letter without thanking you for your very kind offer of receiving me at Gore House, and conferring on me the many advantages such a residence must insure; but I fear my stay in England will be too short to allow me to accept them more extendedly than in as frequent visits as it will allow me to pay. Toward these I look forward with real satisfaction and anticipated gratitude. R. K. Craven."

"Monday evening, June 27th, 1836.

"You have my best thanks for the two numbers of the 'Athenæum' you were so good as to send me; the article you so obligingly bestowed is the same I had read in its most valuable parts; the other having only some additions relative to our friend's descendants and family. I feel very thankful for what you have stated of me, though I flatter myself it is no more than the strict truth in all that regards my affection for one so deserving of it. By what you say of him, I am still more grateful, for it does justice to his exalted qualities in the most concise and yet the most elegant manner.

"R. KEPPEL CRAVEN."

CHAPTER XXII.

THOMAS JAMES MATTHIAS, ESQ., F.R.S., F.S.A.

MR. MATTHIAS took the degree of B.A. in Trinity College, Cambridge, in 1774. The following year he gained the members' prize for the best dissertation in Latin prose; the next year he gained one of the prizes as senior bachelor. Shortly after taking the degree of M.A., he quitted college, and obtained an office at the court, that of clerk to the queen's treasurer, and subsequently that of treasurer of her majesty's household. The rampant Toryism which prevailed about the court of George the Third soon and strongly infected the young Cantab official. He became a political satirist and a poetical politician, and devoted to party the noble talents which were given for mankind.

In 1781 he published "Runic Odes," imitated from the Norse tongue, in 4to.

In the controversy concerning the authenticity of the Rowley poems, assisted by Dr. Glynn, he espoused the cause of Chatterton, and expended a great deal of energy in vindicating the young literary impostor in a brochure "On the Evidences, internal and external, relating to the Poems attributed to Thomas Rowley," in 8vo, in 1783.

In 1794 he published the first part of an anonymous poem, "The Pursuits of Literature," which was eventually compiled in four parts.

This work attracted universal notice, chiefly on account of the extensive and erudite notes, which abounded with evidences of varied learning and scholastic attainments, combined with a bitter spirit of sarcastic criticism, arrayed against every thing liberal in politics or religion, under the guise of a constitutional and Christian zeal against revolutionary principles, and infidel or unorthodox opinions.

The leading Whigs of the times were castigated by Mr. Matthias with merciless rancor, but with signal ability. The chiefs of Toryism, on the other hand, were incensed, till the atmosphere around them reeked with eulogistic vapor, and the swing of the censer became monotonously wearisome and *ennuyant*. Several other works appeared in succession from 1794 to 1832.*

Matthias had some peculiarities of an amusing character, or *petits ridicules*, which Lady Blessington has duly recorded in her Italian diaries. His memory was peculiarly tenacious at dinner-time in regard to dates, of early productions of vegetables, the first appearance of certain meats in the season; he was reminded, at the first sight of green peas on the table, of the particular day on which he had partaken of them the preceding year. It was the same with spring fowl, game, asparagus; and as each *entremet* was offered to him, he invariably exclaimed, "God bless my soul! what a delicious dish! God bless my soul!"

Another of poor Mr. Matthias's peculiarities was a terror that had got possession of his mind of being driven over by the corricolos which dash along the streets of Naples.

He has been often seen posted at the corners of streets for a considerable time, anxiously looking out for a favorable opportunity to make a dart across the street with security to his person, trying to muster courage to make the dreaded rush, or waiting for some charitable passenger to give an arm to him; and frequently, when half across, he has been known to make a sud-

* In 1794 he published anonymously, "The Imperial Epistle from Kien Long to George the Third;" in 1795, "The Political Dramatist of the House of Commons;" in 1796, "Letter to the Marquis of Buckingham, chiefly on the subject of the numerous French Emigrant Priests," by a Layman; in 1798, "The Shade of Alexander Pope on the Banks of the Thames," a satirical poem, occasioned chiefly, but not wholly, by the residence there of the Right Honorable Henry Grattan; in 1798, "Odes, English and Latin" (new edition); in 1802, "Componimenti lyrici di piu illustri Poetici d'Italia," in 3 vols. 12mo; in 1802, "Commentari intorno all' Istoria della Poesia Italiani," per Crescimbeni, 3 vols. 12mo; in 1805, "Canzoni e prosa Toscane;" in 1808, "Agguinta al componimenti lyrici de pue illustri Poeti d'Italia," 3 vols. small 8vo; in 1809, "Saffa—Drama lyrica tradotto dell' Inglese de Mason," in 8vo; in 1812, "Licidi, de Giovanni Milton, tradotta dal Inglese," in 8vo. Mr. Matthias edited in 1803, Tiraboschi, "Storia della Poesia Italiana;" in 1806, "Della Ragion Poetica, di Gravina;" in 1814, "The Works of Thomas Gray, with his Life, and additions."

den retrograde movement, and to have run back to the refuge of his corner, exclaiming, "God bless my soul!"

To Sir William Gell the *petits ridicules* of Matthias were invaluable foundations for ludicrous anecdotes. On one occasion he dined in a restaurateur's in company with Matthias, when a very heavy shower of rain was pattering against the Venetian blinds; and observing a cat and a dog making their appearance in the salon, Gell exclaimed, "It is raining cats and dogs!" Whereupon Matthias, catching a glimpse of the animals that had just entered, said gravely, "God bless my soul! so it does! so it does! S'il n'etait pas vrai au moins c'est bien trouvé."

The author of the "Pursuits of Literature," the translator of several of the pieces of our first authors into Italian, the composer of many original Italian sonnets, and author finally of the elegant little collection of poems entitled "Lyric Poetry" (a new edition), privately printed in 1832, comprising the latest of his compositions, for the last twenty years of his life resided wholly in Naples. Those who remember that city in 1821, 1822, 1823, and 1824, as the writer of these notices remembers it in those years, will not readily forget the literary recluse of the old palace of the Pizzofalcone, the distinguished scholar and elegant writer, then verging on old age, not yet absolutely in the sear and yellow leaf of life, but with that air and aspect of senility which bookish habits of an inveterate nature, and their influence on health, seldom fail to impart to mien and manner of men of literary pursuits.

Mr. Matthias was a man of small stature, of fine, intelligent features, but of a sarcastic expression. Had he been more attenuated, more animated, yet somewhat paler and more thoughtful, his eyes larger and more fit for reserving light to flash out in the excitement of animated conversation, he might be said to resemble Lamennais—at least, as the abbé looked for the last ten or twelve years of his life.

The climate and the literature of Italy had become indispensable enjoyments to Mr. Matthias; he lived by himself and for himself in those enjoyments. Those who knew him well held him in something approaching to esteem; those who did not, looked on him, in the literary and elegant foreign society of Naples, in which he allowed himself occasionally to be drawn from his old Italian books and poetic reveries, as an ungenial old man (for he had the look of age at fifty), with no kindness in his nature, and no sympathies with his fellow-men who were not devoted to Italian literature, and familiar with his "pursuits" in it.

Mr. Matthias died in Naples in August, 1835.

LETTERS OF THOMAS JAMES MATTHIAS, ESQ., TO LADY BLESSINGTON.

"74 Monte d'Iddio, Pizzo Falcone, May 13, 1825.

"My dear Madam,—As I have heard lately that you have given much application to the language of Italy, I am induced to hope that you will oblige me by accepting a little volume lately printed in Naples. You are well acquainted with 'The Minstrel' of Dr. Beattie, and he is now desirous of claiming your ladyship's attention in a Tuscan instead of his Highland dress.

"Believe me, my dear madam, your ladyship's sincere and obedient servant, T. J. Matthias."

"Naples, November 3.

"I hope to do myself the pleasure of accompanying Sir W. Gell, on Sunday next, to dine with you. I should have written before, but I understood that you would have the goodness to expect me if I said nothing to the contrary. I am sorry, however, that I did not write. T. J. Matthias."

"Naples, Feburary 7.

"The inclosed little volume has just been printed in Naples, and I have a pleasure in thinking that your ladyship will do me the favor to accept it as a mark of the regard with which I am, my dear madam, &c.,

"T. J. Matthias."

JAMES MILLINGEN, ESQ.

This celebrated classical antiquary died at Florence the 1st of October, 1845. Mr. Millingen was the eldest son of Mr. M. Millingen, formerly of Queen's Square, Westminster. From early life he distinguished himself among archæologists, and was particularly fitted for his antiquarian pursuits by his intimate acquaintance with Greek literature and history, his critical acumen, and refined taste, and solid judgment. He published numerous works on fictile vases—" Ancient Unedited Monuments,"

"Painted Greek Vases," "The Medallic History of Napoleon," and on "Numismatic Subjects connected with Rome," "Etruria," "Græcia Magna," &c. Mr. Millingen enjoyed a small pension of £100 a year from the British government. He left two sons; one of them, formerly physician to Lord Byron at Missolonghi, was recently physician to the Sultan; the other is on the retired list of the medical department of the East India Company.

For several years this eminent antiquarian carried on his favorite pursuits in Rome, Naples, and Florence. His profound knowledge of numismatics, and of antique gems, and Etruscan vases, had rendered him the first authority in his day in these matters. When I had the pleasure of knowing him in Naples, in 1821 and 1822, he was far advanced in years—a mild, gentlemanly, accomplished person, courted in all circles of literary and refined people, whether English or Italian.

LETTERS FROM JAMES MILLINGEN, ESQ.

"Florence, October 24, 1834.

"I met with an accident on the road, and escaped being robbed and carried up to the mountains. Though safe for a time, I should advise, however, any person to take great precaution between Naples and Rome, as the banditti, who are now desperate, and concealed very much, make an attack when least expected.

"You have heard, without doubt, of the discovery of the unfortunate Miss Bathurst's body; it was the general subject of conversation for two or three days, and one not at all calculated to dispel my disposition to gloominess.

"What a contrast between its state at the moment of the fatal accident, and that to which it was reduced by remaining so long in the water—six months and ten days! It would, perhaps, have been better for her parents and friends if the discovery had not been made, as it renews all their grief.

"It is surprising how much interest the Romans of all classes expressed on the occasion. It was, in fact, an event highly deplorable and tragical.

"Pray tell Alfred that I saw Mr. A—— at Rome, who will be most happy to show him every possible attention on his arrival; he recollects having seen him, when a very fine child, at his grandmother's.

"With regard to your books, he says that the best mode would be to take those that are prohibited in your carriage, and to send the others, especially the English, to Mr. C——, by the *procaccio* wagon.

"Previously to my quitting Rome, I left with Mr. Freeborn a copy of my work on vases, which I beg you will have the goodness to accept, and honor with a place in your library. I hope the label on the book may sometimes catch your eye, and recall me to your recollection.

"I never can express to you, my dear lady, how much I am sensible of all the kindness which I have received from you since I had the happiness to make your acquaintance, nor can I ever forget the agreeable moments I passed in your society. I regret much that I could not enjoy them longer. I must go to England: I have hopes of seeing you. J. MILLINGEN."

"Palazzo Calabrella, Friday morning.

"I do not know how to thank your ladyship sufficiently for your kind note, and for the interest you are so good as to take in my convalescence.

"I am quite confused at your eulogies of my productions, and must ascribe them solely to your indulgence and kindness. As such, they are highly grateful to me. J. MILLINGEN."

EDWARD DODWELL, ESQ.

This eminent and erudite topographer and traveler, having spent a large portion of his life in traveling, took up his permanent abode in Rome, and in 1826 was enjoying there his literary ease and leisure in a very dignified manner, surrounded with all the elegances of modern luxury, and a great many of the rarities of ancient art. Mr. Dodwell is known principally in the literary world by his "Travels in Greece," a work of considerable erudition and research.

Mr. Dodwell, at about the age of sixty, married a young Roman lady of a noble family, of great beauty, who was young enough, in common parlance, to be his daughter. The old English antiquarian and his blooming Italian bride were no less disproportioned in age than dissimilar in tastes; but they lived most happily together. Lady B——, on one occasion, when he was descanting with enthusiastic ardor on the rare perfections of an Egyptian mummy of some princess, whose flesh had blood in it, and her bones marrow in them upward of three thousand years ago, could not help giving a glance at his beautiful young wife standing by him, "offering in her own person one of the most faultless models of loveliness ever beheld, while the arch smile that played round her lips seemed to say that living beauties might be found to compete with the dead ones."

Mr. Dodwell ended his career in Rome in 1832, while engaged in his favorite archæological pursuits, making researches among the ruins of the Eternal City on the subject of Cyclopean architecture.

LETTER FROM EDWARD DODWELL, ESQ., TO LADY BLESSINGTON.

"Friday morning.

"MY DEAR LADY BLESSINGTON,—I am very sorry I shall not be able to have the pleasure of dining with you to-day, as I have got an eruption of Vesuvius on my forehead, which is not only painful, but unseemly, and Miss Power would never admire my beauty again, were she to see me with such a patch, and in such a plight.

"Believe me, most truly and faithfully yours, EDWARD DODWELL."

THE ARCHBISHOP OF TARENTO.

This venerable prelate is well described by Mr. Willis in his "Pencilings by the Way:"

"A friend, whom I met at the same house, took me to see the Archbishop of Tarento yesterday. This venerable man, it is well known, lost his gown for his participation in the cause of the Carbonari (the revolutionary conspirators of Italy). He has always played a conspicuous part in the politics of his time, and now, at the age of ninety, unlike the usual fate of meddlers in troubled waters, he is a healthy, happy, venerated old man, surrounded in his palace with all that luxury can give him. The lady who presented me took the privilege of intimate friendship to call at an unusual hour, and we found the old churchman in his slippers, over his breakfast, with two immense tortoise-shell cats, upon stools, watching his hand for bits of bread, and purring most affectionately. He looks like one of Titian's pictures. His face is a wreck of commanding features, and his eye seems less to have lost its fire than to slumber in its deep socket. His hair is snowy white; his forehead of prodigious breadth and height; and his skin has that calm, settled, and yet healthy paleness, which carries with it the history of a whole life of temperance and thought.

"The old man rose from his chair with a smile, and came forward with a stoop and a feeble step, and took my two hands as my friend mentioned my name, and looked me in the face very earnestly. 'Your country,' said he, in Italian, 'has sprung into existence like Minerva, full-grown and armed. We look for the result.' He went on with some comments upon the dangers of republics, and then sent me to look at a portrait of Queen Giovanna, of Naples, by Leonardo da Vinci, while he sat down to talk with the lady who brought me. His secretary accompanied me as a cicerone. Five or six rooms, communicating with each other, were filled with choice pictures, every one a gift from some distinguished individual. The present King of France had sent him his portrait; Queen Adelaide had sent a splendid set of Sevres china, with the portraits of her family; the Queen of Belgium had presented him with her miniature and that of Leopold; the King and Queen of Naples had half furnished his house; and so the catalogue went on. It seemed as if the whole Continent had united to honor the old man."*

Lady Blessington speaks in enthusiastic terms of the archbishop's comeliness of person, the imposing aspect of this beau ideal of a venerable father of the Church—his pallid, thoughtful face; his eyes soft, and full of sensibility, like those of a woman; his long white hair and attenuated figure; the suavity of countenance and address, benevolence of disposition, attractiveness of manner, and refined politeness.

He appeared to regard Gell with the affection of a brother. He took the warmest interest in his antiquarian pursuits, and in all matters relating to literary or scientific subjects.

This venerable prelate died about 1839.

LETTERS FROM THE ARCHBISHOP OF TARENTO TO LADY BLESSINGTON.

"Potrei sperare, mia cara contessa, di festeggiare l'anno novello *Giovedi prossimo?* La mia gran festa sarebbe di pranzare colle due sorelle, e col mio Alfredo, e se vi piasesse anche col bravo medico. L'ora destinata sarebbe la vostra solita, cio e dopo le cinque, poiche io prendo qualche doze medicinale con una zuppa verso il mezzo giorno e quindi nulla soffro fino a quel momento. Che ne dite? Volete sellevare—Il vostra VECCHIO TARENTO.

"Dal Vecchio Tarento."

"Io son sicuro mia cara contessa, che voi mi amate e per cio vi direi che la mia salute potrebbe risentirne danno nel venire al Vomero con questo caldo, *non voglio,* direste, *non voglio.*

* Willis's Pencilings, &c., p. 46.

"Dunque per non oppormi al vostro comando vi auguro salute e felicità nella ricorrenzà della vostra nascita e vi prego di gradire l'offerta di un vecchio poiché un vecchio non può dar cose nuove: Vi prego soltanto di ricordarvi di me allorché la distanza ci avrà divisi. A colei che ama i sorci, al mio caro conte al grazioso ospite ed all' amabile D'Orsay, il bacio sincero della vera amicizia L'ANTICO PASTOR TARRAS.

"Napoli, il prmo. 7bre, del 1824."

"Resposta

"La salute dell' antico Tarento si sostiene a fronte dall' oblio della Madonna Il canonico va meglio ma sempre fra le tenebre. Il Conto Alfredo e pregato di rimettere il Volume del Viaggio Pittoresco, poiché per la morte dell' ottimo *Denon* si deve diriggere à Parigi una notizia di qual travaglio, nel quale ebbe parte quel bravo litterato.

"Napoli, li 16 Maggio, 1825."

CHAPTER XXIII.

COUNT MATUSCHEWITZ.

COUNT MATUSCHEWITZ played an important part in the great diplomatic performances of the northern powers some thirty years ago. He was a brother actor of Count Pozzo di Borgo, Prince Paul Esterhazy, Metternich, and the Baron Bulow, on some memorable occasions at a later period.

On the accomplishment of the French Revolution of 1830, which came like a thunder-clap on the courts of Europe, the capital of England became the head-quarters of the councils of the diplomatic representations of the principal great powers With a view to the restoration of the balance of power, or the regulation at least of the recent disturbance of the European system, Talleyrand, Pozzo di Borgo, Esterhazy, Matuschewitz, and others, occasionally met at Baron Bulow's, whose opinions, it is said, ultimately prevailed in the diplomatic councils, which a little later took the title of the Hollando-Belgian Conferences.

Count Matuschewitz was a native of Poland, of noble birth, who had been educated in France, and was a distinguished pupil of the Polytechnic School. When the Emperor Alexander and Napoleon were on terms of amity, the former requested the services of two of the pupils of the Polytechnic of most merit.

Matuschewitz was one of the two pupils chosen by Napoleon to correspond to the wishes of the autocrat.

In the Russian civil service he bore out fully the high reputation he had gained at the Polytechnic, not only as a distinguished scholar and proficient especially in the abstract sciences, but in diplomacy. But he was a lover of pleasure, and his ruling passion is said to have been for the chase. He sometimes, at the seat even of diplomatic conferences, made his appearance on horseback, uniting in his costume and character the modern Nimrod with the Russian Nestor of diplomacy.

In the diplomatic career which this gentleman pursued in the service of the Emperor of Russia at the court of Stockholm, his reputation for astuteness, penetration, tact, and ability stood extremely high with the other European ministers. He had spent much time in England, and acquired the tastes, habits, and manners of an Englishman. He is said to have largely enjoyed the confidence of the Emperor of Russia, to have been deeply versed in the secrets of Russian policy, and in all great emergencies of state in which relations with foreign powers were concerned to have been consulted by the autocrat. Bearing in mind the position he occupied, and the advantages it bestowed on him, his letters will be read with interest. The high character of the count for honorable principles and integrity, his easy manners and gentlemanlike deportment, his cultivated mind and tastes, made him a welcome guest in the best society of every country he visited.

LETTERS FROM COUNT MATUSCHEWITZ TO LADY BLESSINGTON.

"Stockholm, Nov. 5, 1839.

"How kind and amiable of you not to have allowed Alfred's letter to depart without the addition of a few lines in your hand-writing, to satisfy me that I still live in your friendly recollection. Depend upon it, your remembrance is not thrown away on me. I should consider it the climax of ingratitude were I not most anxious and impatient to revisit good old England, and to find myself once more under the roof of Gore House, that hospitable roof, under which I am certain to receive a hearty welcome, and to meet a most instructive variety of eminent characters, who move round you as it were by magic, each happy, each communicative, each contributing his quota to a general conversation and harmony which, I believe, was never known to exist among them except at your house and under your influence. I hope spring will restore me, for a time at least, if not yet for good, to those friends from whom I grieve now so sincerely to be separated, and to those social enjoyments to which I am here a perfect stranger. There never was a country (though not uninteresting in some respects) so devoid of society as this one. I live all but in solitude, and my happiness, if happiness it is to be called, is only that which any rational being *ought to carry with and within himself.* Under those circumstances, it is real Christian charity in my friends to do occasionally what you have done now with so much kindness. Well may I say that the smallest donation will be gratefully received. If, therefore, you ever have this winter a few minutes to spare, let me hope that I will hear once more from you. Another year will not be ushered in without some charming publication to appear under your patronage. A copy of it would beguile my solitude, and if inscribed with your name, it will prove, of course, doubly valuable. Your political news are gloomy. Some of my friends appear more sanguine, but others are of the same opinion with you. I, for one, perceive in the highest quarters a turn of mind which I can not sufficiently deplore.

"Now, my dear Lady Blessington, I have most unscrupulously transgressed on your time and indulgence; but I know you will forgive me, and readily believe that I will always remain yours very sincerely,

"MATUSCHEWITZ.

"When you see Lord Lyndhurst and Mr. *Bear* Ellice, will you be so good as to remember me particularly to both?"

"Stockholm, February 8th, 1840.

"I can not tell you how fond I am of your 'Belle of the Season.' The engravings are beautiful, the poetry charming. If I was Prince Albert, I would have offered to the queen, on the day of my marriage, those delightful lines, in which you have contrived, though in one of your richest veins, not to overdraw her picture, and, keeping as near as possible to reality, you have only clothed it in admirable language. I have not finished yet your 'Governess,' but it is *une excellente peinture de mœurs* in every room and story of a London house. Now that you have delineated to life, and with such success, Ireland in your 'Repealers,' and England in your 'Governess,' Scotland is awaiting your pencil. You really ought to make an excursion north of the Tweed in the course of this autumn. It will amply repay your trouble, and, being drawn from a recent and personal observation of nature on the spot, your description will be, if possible, still more graphic and vivid.

"Now for a word or two of politics. We have here the English papers only to January. Poor Prince A——! What an inauspicious political start he has made! The Commons curtail his allowance with an overwhelming majority against him; the Lords seem determined to take away from him unanimously the precedency he was to have obtained. Upon my word, I don't know that I would have ventured to C—— under similar circumstances, and left the little island and its ministers to hunt out a more popular prince.

"When you wrote to me in the latter end of December, appearances were so much against the government, that no one could have insured its existence at any price for another month; but it strikes me that since the opening of Parliament they look rather stronger. The last elections had turned against the Conservatives, and some unaccountable 'presentiment' whispers into my ear that the government majority on the motion of want of confidence will have been such as to enable them to live on. Next post will enlighten us on this most important subject. You have no idea how anxiously I do expect that post. The privilege question is also a very curious one. I hope that, acting with the wisdom of the Romans and the Albans of old, the Commons and the court of justice will contribute three champions to fight out their quarrel in mortal combat, Eglinton presiding over the lists. Fancy our having here a Parliament annulled, and a triumphant opposition, and a little political crisis. Old Bernadotte is at great discount just now, and will have a hard time of it. No greater misfortune in this world than to live too long.

"Adieu, my dear Lady Blessington. My kindest remembrances to Alfred. If ever you have another minute to spare, let me hear again from you. You have no idea what pleasure it is in a remote corner of Europe, and with such feelings as those. MATUSCHEWITZ."

"Naples, May 1st, 1834.

"I will not allow Mr. Keppel Craven to leave Naples for good old England without availing myself of his kind offer to take over a letter to you. Indeed, I can not mention his name, and not return you once more my most sincere thanks for the way in which you have been so kind as to recommend me to him. He is no less agreeable than well-informed, no less obliging and indulgent than interesting and instructive in his conversation. You will have undoubtedly the greatest pleasure in seeing him in England, but we can not well spare him here; and as you abound in resources of pleasant society, which are extremely scanty at Naples, I trust you will not charge me with egotistical cant and unfriendly feelings if I candidly declare that, upon this occasion, what will give you satisfaction gives me unfeigned regret. I have found Naples in mourning for the young queen, without any thing like social amusements, or even social spirit—without even St. Charles's Theatre, which is shut up, or the usual mildness and beauty of the climate; added to which, my bankers here have failed, and stripped me of a good sum of money; part of my establishment has been shipwrecked, and at the moment I am writing to you, reminiscences of yours come again upon me. It is not consistent, therefore, with human nature that I should feel the least prepossessed in favor of Naples. Still, I have experienced considerable pleasure in admiring its beautiful situation, in visiting its very picturesque environs, and especially in examining those wonderful monuments of antiquity, which, independent of their magnificence and exquisite taste, carry one two thousand years back so completely and so magically as to make one fancy one's self a contemporary of the most powerful nation that ruled the world in ancient times. Hence I shall always maintain a journey to Naples to be a delightful one, and some stay in that country not only to be pleasant, but necessary to complete one's classical education, and one's notions of former grandeur with all its peculiarities, customs, and usages. But, much as I esteem and delight in Craven, I could not, like him, fix myself at Naples. There is no native society to be found; one is therefore thrown back forcibly upon foreigners, and too often obliged to live, as it were, in a sort of anteroom to London, Paris, Vienna, or Petersburgh. Even in the best years, good society is but transient; and it stands to reason, that when one has to associate with strangers to the country, it is next to impossible to form long friendships or durable connections. Under these circumstances, you will not be surprised to hear of my not intending to take root among the Lazarones, and though I don't know yet how long I shall stay with them, I feel much more inclined to shorten than to protract my sojourn in the south.

With you the Whigs seem to have it all their own way; I could never understand upon what foundations the Conservative papers had foretold, about three months ago, the present administration's immediate downfall; and I verily think the Conservatives, since they can not upset it, had much better try, by a timely coalition, to rescue the ministers from the necessity of looking for occasional support to the Radicals, and of framing some measure for that purpose. Every danger might be averted from the country by such a course; too disinterested, perhaps, to be expected from any political party, but still, in my humble opinion, the safest and wisest to follow. There is a great deal of natural conservatism growing out from the possession of power, and growing the more as that possession is lengthened and confirmed. Besides which, except upon one question, the real differences of opinion do not seem to be very considerable, and though no ministerialist, I can not help thinking the ministers would not hesitate between Peel and O'Connell, Stanley and Hume, and feel much more inclined to come to a rational compromise with the former, than to endanger perpetually their own authority by yielding to the destructive impulses of the latter. However, you will perhaps consider my observations as the mere effect of the distance at which I am writing, and not the least applicable to the actual state of affairs. I shall therefore drop the subject, not without begging you to remember me to E. Ellice, with whom I got more thoroughly acquainted in Paris, and whose kindness to me I shall always most gratefully recollect. Will you tell Alfred that I do shake him by the hand most sincerely? MATUSCHEWITZ."

Copy of a letter from Count Matuschewitz, under the signature of Matthew:

"Stockholm, March 6th, 1840.

"When I wrote to you last, I had just only gone over the two first chapters of the 'Governess,' and was yet a stranger to many of its best characters, and not aware of the sympathy and interest these characters, as well as the very natural and simple, but extremely attaching progress of the story would excite in me. When I resumed the book, I found it impossible to lay it down without having read the last words in the last page; and I can assure you, that for many a day, ay, many a year, I have not been so thoroughly charmed with a novel, to say nothing of the governess herself, who will impress every one with a strong feeling of love and regard. I dote upon the old Quaker, I am excessively partial to Lord Oxminster. You have extricated your heroine very cleverly from the toils of a 'wicked earl,' who gets baffled, as the real one invariably is; added to which, the infusion of humor in several parts of the novel is excellent, the picture of manners, high and low, to the life, and the language remarkable for vivacity, purity of taste, and elegance.

"The Conservative opposition have at last published a missive war manifesto against the government. The sole fact of such a declaration of uncompromising hostility must prove a considerable addition to the cabinet's previous and constitutional weakness. I doubt more than ever that, situated and assailed as they are now, the ministers should pull through the session; but whether their downfall will be productive of good or evil in the first instance, at least with the evident bias of the court and its personal feelings, is more than I can venture an opinion upon at so great a distance. I wonder what our friend the *Bear* says to all this? Will you be so kind as to remember me most friendly to him, and to give my best love to Alfred? MATTHEW."

THE PRINCE SCHWARTZENBERG.

The Prince Schwartzenberg, whose correspondence with Lady Blessington shows the intimate terms of friendship which subsisted between him and her ladyship, was the person who figures in the correspondence under the "nom du guerre" of Capitaine Wolff. That he was an Austrian nobleman, had been employed in most important diplomatic situations, had an accurate knowledge of passing political events in Italy, was not a great admirer of the Metternich régime, may be inferred from his letters. There can be very little doubt that the prince stands in the same relation to a recent prime minister of Austria that Capitaine Wolff did to the prince some fifteen or sixteen years ago.

Schwartzenberg is supposed to have been in early life initiated in the mysteries of the secret political societies (Burschenschaften), which promulgated political ideas with sufficient astuteness, while violating existing laws, to propagate their opinions in spite of all despots, and to have abandoned his early opinions.

The Prince Jean Adolphe Frederick C. Schwartzenberg, Landgrave of Klegau, chamberlain of the Emperor of Austria, succeeded his father, the Prince Joseph, who died December 19th, 1833. He married, in 1830, a daughter of the Prince of Lichtenstein, by whom he had two children.* I presume this person is the brother of the correspondent of Lady Blessington.

Mr. Charles Pridham, in his "Kossuth and Magyar Land" (London, 1851, page 38), in his account of an interview with the prince in 1849, when prime minister, says, "If you search Europe through, you will scarcely find a man of nobler bearing or a more majestic mien. To say that he is the first gentleman of the Continent is only his due, for out of England such men are seldom or never to be met with; in fact, his aspect is essentially English, perhaps from his having so long dwelt among us. He is now far advanced in years, yet he is scarcely less energetic than ever; and, judging from his remaining attractions, you cease to wonder at the love conquests of his prime."

In April, 1852, a stroke of apoplexy deprived the Emperor of Austria of the most able, gifted, and devoted of ministers. None greater than Prince Schwartzenberg ever wielded with a master-hand the destinies of the Austrian empire, or influenced, by the superiority of his genius and the purity of his principles, the political condition of Europe.

Prince Schwartzenberg was a most successful minister. An article appeared in the "Times" shortly after his death, acknowledging his great merits as a minister, and stating that from the depths of the disasters of 1848–9 he had rescued the German empire, and replaced it on a secure basis. He was almost the only man fitted to uphold the dignity of the state. But the prince, according to the "Times," was of an overbearing and arrogant temper, and he relied, to an absurd extent, on military force as the mainspring of his government.

* Almanach de Gotha pour l'Année 1854, p. 178.

Another writer, perhaps more intimately acquainted with German state matters (Mr. W. B. Maccabe) than most foreigners, speaking of the prince, observes:

"From the days of the imperial despot and irreligious 'reformer,' Joseph II., the Catholic Church in Austria had been in a most degraded condition. It was hampered by the state in every way. When power was placed in the hands of Prince Schwartzenberg, he saw the demoralizing, infidelity-spreading results of the *Josephian* system upon the great masses of the population. The Prince Schwartzenberg, as prime minister of the Austrian empire, was invested with absolute power, and the first use, it may be said, that he made of that absolute power was to free the Church from the shackles which the Emperor Joseph had imposed upon it — to make it free — to separate Church and state."

To no Austrian minister is the liberty more indebted which allows men to worship God according to their conscience than to Prince Schwartzenberg.

FROM THE PRINCE SCHWARTZENBERG (UNDER THE SIGNATURE OF CAPT. WOLFF).

"Constantinople, August 25, 1835.

"Vous serez etonnée, madame, de récévoir cette lettre des côtes du Bosphore, du coin opposé de l'Europe. Elle portera l'empreinte incontestable de son origine Orientale par les marques des précautions sanitaires que l'on aura prisés, et en cela elle rappellera le caractère et la teinte locale de ce beau pays, ou les femmes sont voilées, et ou il n'est permis qu'a la *peste* de montrer sa face cadavereuse et découverte. Il faut qu'il soit bien beau ce pays, ce climat, ces souvenirs, pour que l'on parvienne à oublier ce qui l'habite. Eh bien, malgré peste, chats, chiens, rats, punaisses, et mosquites, malgré absurdités de tout genre, on s'attache à cette contrée, et l'on prend un interet veritable à sa destinée.

"Depuis le massacre des Janissaires, catastrophe d'un tragique sublime, l'Orient est refoulé en Asié. C'est là qu'il existe encore avec sa poesie, ses pompes, ses mœurs patriarchales, poetiques, ses opinions, ses traditions, tantôt sublimes, tantôt absurdes.

"Ici au porte des redingotes bleus, on fait l'exercise à l'Européenne, et l'on n'a gardè de l'Orient que la coutume de noyer les femmes quand elles sont trop sensibles, et l'insouisance quand on doit mourir de la peste.

"Toutefois cette existence est completement differente de la vie d'une capitale Européenne, et elle exerce une influence marquée sur nos gouts et nos dispositions. Je passe une partie de ma vie à cheval ou sur la mer; et il y a toujours une scene teinte d'aventure en tout ce que l'on entrepend. Car ou vous allez est au risque de vous noyer; à *pied* en évitant chaque passant à crainte da rapporter le peste; et si vous sortez à *cheval* pour vous éloigner dans les compagnes, je vous conseille d'oublier plus tôt votre mouchoir que vos pistolets.

"J'ai vu en un marché d'esclaves, une jolie femme couter entre 4–5000 piastres; à peu près 1000 francs. A Paris elles sont meilleurs marchées. Ce sont des marchandes qui les aménent ordinairement, de Trebisonde, j'en ai vu arriver avec leur cargaison.

"Au reste l'esclavage n'est nullement odieux en Orient. C'est le moyen de devenir grand fonctionnaire au sultane. En Orient l'esclave devient membre de la famille, en Amérique il est animal domestique.

"J'ai vu le grand seigneur entouré d'une nombre de soldats habillés à moitié à l'Européenne. C'est une figure ordinaire, quoique assez expressive, l'exterminateur des Janissaires a même une sorte de sourire bienveillant.

"Du reste, un pays ou chaque intrigue d'amour fait encourir la bastonnade, et ou l'on ne boit le vin que par contrebande, ne saurait être de mon gout. Je voulais continuer mon voyage en Syria et en Egypte, mais pour cette fois je me contente de ce que j'ai vu, et me depecherais d'autant plus de rétourner en Europe, ou ils preparent des événements qui sont d'un grand interet.

"J'espère milady, peut être avoir le bonheur de vous voir cet hiver, et certainement, en touchant le sol de l'Angleterre, cela sera pour moi une des felicités les plus grandes. Gardez moi un peu de votre souvenirs, ayez de l'indulgence si je ne puis cesser de le reclamer. Si vous saviez comme il est difficile de vous oublier! Si vous saviez comme il est penible de se croire oublié de vous!

"Dans quelques jours mon cheval, mon Tartare, pistolets, seront prêts et je parcourrais le Roumélie et le Servie. Je rencontrerais peut être dans cette course aventareuse quelque tableau digne de vous fournir une esquisse. En tout cas je ferais usage de mon privilège, qui me permet de vous ecrire en comptant sur votre indulgence. Ici, dans ce pays, ou les souvenirs agissent si puissamment, ou les étoiles brillent sur en firmament d'azure comme les heures de bonheur se réflêchissent de l'imagination, ou les vagues de Bosphore se brisent sur le rivage comme l'écho des sensations évanouies, ici, ou on est pour ainsi dire au milieu de deux mondes, entre deux siecles, et entre deux générations, ou, bien des fois j'ai fait passé devant le lanterne magique de ma mémoire, les impressions de ma vie, et toujours votre image est venue, entre toutes ces apparitions, comme une fée gracieuse, comme un bel astre, me concilier avec le reste de cette fantasmagorie qui me répresentait une foule de caracteres ridicules, de faces insipides ou de fantomes hideux!

"Milady! je baise, et vous me l'avez permis, cette main charmante que vous me tendites à mon depart! Envoyez moi de grace, celle de marbre, peut être le rechaufferais-je avec mes lèvres ! Daignez m'ecrire, si ce n'est que deux mots, car quelquefois j'ai peur de vous avoir trop ennuyée en abusant de votre indulgence. Sans être par trop timide, j'avoue que vous m'avez toujours imposé. Daignez vous ressouvenir avec bonté et amitié de votre devoué

CAPITAINE WOLFF."

"Quarantine de la tour rouge et Transylvanie, ce 1er Nov., 1833–35.

"Permittez vous, milady, qu'un de vos admirateurs les plus sinceres vienne, du fond des gorges et des abymes de la Transylvanie, se representer à votre souvenir? Oui je suis certain que vous l'accueillerez avec bonté, car vous savez combien il vous aime.

"Avez vous reçu ma lettre que je vous ecrivis le 2 Mai, une autre que j'expédiais par Mr. Trager à Vienne le 29 Mai, et une troisieme de Constantinople du 26 Août? Je désirerais pour cause qu'elles ne fussent pas egarées.

"Voila un mois que j'ai quitté Constantinople. J'ai dit adieu à l'Orient, pays de voiles et de mystêres, aux fleurs et au ciel d'azur. J'ai vu le grand seigneur et la peste; j'ai nagé dans le Bosphore et parcouru les montagnes de l'Anatolie, et pour le moment j'en ai assez. J'ai encore un *Fez*, bonnet Turc sur la tête, les cheveux rasés, je m'asseois par terre avec une longue pipe et une tasse de café sans sucre mais j'aimerais tout autant être assis sur une chaise sur le boulevard des Italiens à Paris, fumer mon cegare, manger des glaces et voir passer des femmes *sans* voiles.

"Pourtant cette existence Orientale a un certain charme qui agit sur beaucoup de monde qui y a vécu, et qui parfois la fait regretter au milieu de notre monde Européen, ou touts les ressorts de la vie sont agités et usés par les passions et les differents interets, comme par une mécanique à vapeur, et ou la vie ne se balance pas, comme en Orient, comme une barque sur une rivière, mais roule comme une voiture à vapeur sur une route de fer artificielle; monde ou il n'y a plus ni individus, ni actions, mais societés et principes; ou l'absolu a engloutè toute specialité, ou l'homme individuel disparait de l'interet de la masse; monde ou il n'y a plus ni amour ni religion ni poesie; monde essentiellement industriel, et qui est en train de remplacer même le bon Dieu par quelque machine electrique, calorifique, galvanique!

"J'ai traversé à cheval les plaines de Roumélie, les montagnes de la Bulgarie, les steppes de la Valachie. Je me suis arreté à Adrianople, j'ai visité les positions militaires de Balkan et du Danube, et enfin me voilà. Malade et fatigué je subis l'emprisonnement de la quarantaine avec resignation. C'est un sacrifice qu'il faut porter au bien être de la societé Européenne, un prison comme tout d'autres, ou l'on se trouve au cachet sans trop bien savoir pourquoi.

"Au milieu de cette solitude, au fond d'un gorge et montagnes ou je n'apperçois que deux pieds gravès de ciel je vis avec mes souvenirs donc en excellente societé, et vous, madame, venez bien souvent, sans le savoir, me visiter dans mon isolement et me consoler dans ma captivité. Oui! j'aime à me rappeler votre apparition ravissante, et les heures que j'ai passées près de vous me semblent quelquefois un rêve! Je serais bien heureux de vous revoir un jour!

"Ma quarantaine finira le 4me. Alors j'croise à Hermanstadt, et poursuiverais ma route par Arad, &c.

"Peste et Vienne, voyage fatiguant, ennuyant et long. Daignez me donner de vos nouvelles ne serait ce qu'avec dix lignes qui m'autorissent à vous écrire plus souvent. J'ai aussi quelques *griffonages* qui me retracent quelques scenes de la vie aventureuse que je menais autrefois, et pour laquelle vous avez bien voulu prendre quelque interet. Si vous le voulez je vous les remettrais.

"Deux lignes, avec une troisieme qui dit—Marguerite—me rendront bien heureux. Que le ciel vous protége, chère dame, et que même le diable vous donne un petit coup de main, si vous en avez besoin. CAPITAINE WOLFF."

"Qui je vous suis reconnaissant, madame, de votre bonne lettre du mois d'Avril. Enfin, en voila une, qui parle pourtant un peu de vous même. Il y a un siècle que je vive aussi eloigné de vous, comme si vous viviez en Perou et moi à Japon, et pourtant il y a des instants ou je me sens si près de vous qu'il me semble que mon ame pourrait toucher la votre.

"Je vous ai envoyé quelques pages contenant l'histoire de ce voleur nommé Habacuk, dont une fois je vous contais l'exécution. Je me suis seulement tenu aux faits et l'ai traduit litteralement de mon journal. Pardonnez les defauts du style, en faveur de la couleur locale. Pour celle là, elle en porte l'empreinte. Davantage que j'avance en âge, je vois ressortir les impressions de ma jeunesse un peu agitée à la verité, mais riche en emotions vives. Bien des illusions depuis ce temps là ont éte tués et ensevelis dans ma poitrine, et s'il y a du repos c'est celui d'un cemetière.

"Il fut un temps où une carabine à la main, la croix sur le *scheko*, les airs de Korner à la bouche je croyais combattre pour une belle idèe, je voyais renaitre de ces cendres une nation Germanique! Qu'en est il resulté; une diete de Francfort, MM. Rothschild, des Princes de Coburg, Rioss, *Schlig*,* des petites conversations tracassieres et des chambres que presentent plutôt l'interieur d'une maison de mauvais *gaugots* qu'une representation national. Voila mon rêve de liberté et de patrie realisé en trente deux, petites portions, si infiniment petites qu'il faut beaucoup d'erudition geographique pour savoir le nom de la nation, à laqu'elle on appartenait et pour l'independance de la quelle on combattait à Lutzen, à Leipzig, à Brienne, &c., &c., &c. Voila pour le politique!

"En amour c'etait encore pire. La digne dame etait si belle qu'elle m'oubliait, et je crus voir au ciel ouvert, dont elle était l'ange guardien. A peine osais-je approcher du seuil de ce paradis. Heureusement pour moi et heureusement pour elle, j'avais un ami que j'aimais beaucoup, qui est fort beau

* Name hardly legible.—R. R. M.

garçon, et qui avait le regard plus clair que moi; lui ne s'arrete pas sur le marchepied, et un beau jour je perds mon ange, et mon ami. Voila pour l'amour et l'amitié ! ! !

"Enfin je crois encore, à un avenir et à un bon Dieu indulgent, puisque il a eu la patience de ne pas nous noyer vingt fois depuis le Deluge, et de se contenter du destruction exécuté à Sodome et Gomorrha; même à un ciel, où ceux et celles qui ont quelque chose d'angelique de leur nature retrouveront leurs ailes, qu'on leur a coupé sur cette terre, et je suis curieux si ces rêves et espèrances là s'accompliront davantage que les autres.

"Je ne suis pas encore decidé comment je disposerais de cet été, si l'on ne dispose pas de moi, ce qui m'eviterait l'embarras du choix. Croyez que par tout où je suis, votre souvenir me restera toujours bien chère. Daignez m'ecrire quelques lignes qui me prouvent que l'absence et le temps ne brisent contre votre caractère si noble et si vrai! Vous n'êtes pas comme les autres femmes!

"Quand vous voulez bien m'envoyer votre belle main en *effigie*, je le baiserais avec tout l'enthousiasme de souvenir, malgré que être pendu reellement est autre chose que de l'être en effigie. Veuillez l'adresser à l'embassade à Londres, d'où on me le fait toujours parvenir. Bientôt, madame, je vous ecrirais quelques folies et reveries. Vous savez que vous m'avez permis de pleurer et de rire devant vous. Continuez à m'y autoriser en me justifiant de temps en temps par quelques bonnes lignes. CAPITAINE WOLFF."

"Presburg, 25th June, 1840.

"MILADY,—Après un si long silence puis j'ai encore esperé ne pas être entièrement effacé de nos bons souvenirs? Je n'osai au milieu d'une vie agitée et orageuse vous importuner du recit de mes aventures, que n'aurait servi qu'à troubler les images calmes et paisibles qui vous entourent; et depuis rentré dans ma existence douce et tranquille mais monotone, je voudrais encore moins vous ennuyer par la description de mes simples et pacifiques occupations, après une époque poetique mais sombre de ma vie à une prose tranquille et raisonnable.

"J'espere, milady, vous retrouver un jour encore, j'en compte sur la dure de vos bons souvenirs, et si au coin de votre fin hospitalier vous daignez m'ecouter en balançant votre belle main sur ces beaux cheveux que j'admirais tant, je vous raconterais ma vie et mes aventures.

"Toutefois je n'ai pu me priver de l'occasion qui se presente de me rappeler de votre memoire par la personne qui vous porte cette lettre. C'est le Compte A. Deperffy un de mes amis les plus intimes que j'ose vous recommander instamment, et qui m'a demandè expressement cette lettre, desirant particulièrement être introduit chez une dont le genie et la beauté ont rendu le nom celebre jusqu'au Monts Raipaths et auxrives de la ——* comme au

* Word illegible.

T 2

Rocky Mountains, et aux bouches de l'Oronoco. Je l'envie trop pour ne pas acceder à sa demande, et j'espère ne pas abuser de la permission que vous milady donnez en vous le presentant. C'est un des membres les plus influents de notre Diête, et il a joué un rôle éminent au derniers sessions de notre Parlement. Ses Conversations sur la Litterature Européenne vous interesseront. Il voyage en Angleterre pour observer et examiner quelques institutions administratives que l'on veut imiter en Hongrie, et en outre veut etudier parmi les habitans de votre patrie milady, qui est le pays modêle, et serait le ciel pour moi, si il etait habité pas beaucoup d'anges comme vous.

"Mais je ne veux pas vous enrager en vous repétant ce que tant d'autres vous auront certainement deja dit, mais ce que je crois sentir plus, ou au moins aussi profondement qu'aucune autre. Je finis donc en vous recommandant mon ami, qui, j'espère, aura le bonheur, de vous convenir sous touts les rapports, et en vous priant, milady, de me conserver vos bons sentiments que je crois meriter parceque je vous admire, aime et cheris dans l'absence comme tous ceux qui vous voyent sans cesse! FREDERICK SCHWARTZENBERG."

CHAPTER XXIV.

THE DUKE D'OSSUNA.

THE present and the former Duc D'Ossuna were both intimately known to the Countess of Blessington. The family of D'Ossuna is one of the oldest, noblest, and richest in Spain. There, and likewise in Belgium, their territorial possessions are very great. The late duke, an accomplished, intelligent, and amiable young man, died seven or eight years ago, in Belgium, about the age of thirty. The present duke has inherited all that was his brother's except his intelligence. This duke bears the title also of Count de Arcos, de Gandia, de Lerma, Marquis de Terra Nova, &c., &c.

LETTERS OF THE DUKE D'OSSUNA.

"Paris, 24th Janvier, 1844.

"Je vois avec le plus grand plaisir que le petit cadeau que j'ai remit pour vous à M. le Comte D'Orsay vous a été agréable et c'est à moi maintenant à vous temoigner toute ma reconnaissance de tant de choses aimables, comme vous voulez bien me prodiguer dans votre charmante lettre, et surtout pour l'assurance d'une amitié à la quelle j'attache le plus grand prix.

"On a dit, il est vrai, dans le monde, que j'etais nommé embassadeur à Naples, et même à Paris et à Londres, mais il n'en est rien, et jusqu'à present je me suis toujours refusé à representer le gouvernement Espagnol, qui à mon avis, n'est pas encore *representable.*

"L'Espagne est menacée de grands boulversements, et je suis convaincu que pour lui rendre une tranquilité durable, et pour y etablir un gouvernement solide, national, et completement independant des influences de la France, il n'y a qu'un seul moyen, c'est de marier notre jeune Reyne Ysabelle avec le fils ainé de Don Carlos, qui pourraient regner ensemble tous deux comme en temps de Ferdinand et Ysabelle la Catholique dans nos beaux jours de gloire.

"J'ai l'intention d'aller faire un voyage en Ytalie pour revenir à Paris au mois d'Avril et rentrer en Espagne à la fin de Mai.

"Veuillez milady dire bien de choses aimables à vos charmantes nieces, et agréer je vous prie l'assurance de tous mes sentimens sinceres et devoués.

"D'OSSUNA."

"Vendredi Chateau de Esabek, par Tubise, Belgique.

"Permettez moi, milady, de rappelér à votre souvenir un pauvre ami pour lequel votre aimable accueil a été si précieux cette année, il y est certes en premier rang dans les bons souvenirs que je garde de l'Angleterre. J'ai revu mon pauvre pays. J'ai failli meme aller passer une semaine à Paris, les Provinces sont loin d'etre aussi animé que la capitale, à Lille même dans une si grande ville ou ne se croirait pas au milieu d'une si ardente revolution.

"Je suis ici dans un château au milieu des terres à cinq lieu de Bruxelles, chez un ancien militaire Français, entouré de ses enfants que j'ai presque vus naitre.

"Je ne puis que foiblement vous donner idée de la vie calme et de la bonne humeur de tout ce monde là. Outre le père et la mère, la famille se compose de quatre filles et d'un garçon, l'une d'elles à vingt-un ans, est veuve, et a la tête d'une grande fortune, elle est receuillé chez son père ; la seconde sœur est aux environs, nous la voyons toutes les semaines, au este deux jeunes filles et un garçon de vingt ans ; ces bonnes petites personnes sont chargés des pauvres du pays, et je n'exagere pas en vous disant qu'elles ont chaque jour affaires à plus de vingt individus. Les pensions de chacune, l'argent destiné à mille petits choses de luxe, tout y passe, et tout cela si gaiement et si naturellement.

"Je crois en verité qu' une long tems passé dans pareil séjour de paix pourrait me rendre meilleur. Nous dessinons toute la journée. Même le soir à neuf heures la prière avec les domestiques, à dix heures tout le monde se couche : à cette heure qu'il est (onze heures) ma bougie que est sur ma table est certainement la seule lumiere de toute la maison.

"Nous allons souvent diner à deux lieus chez le gendre du aître de la maison, là dans un vieux salon devant une grande cheminée ou l'on met presque des arbres entiers, nous causons chasses et chevaux en bonne compagnie d'excellents cigarres. Je me demande quelquefois s'il n'est pas coupable de se laisser être si heureux quand à cent lieux de distances ses pauvres amis et ses compatriotes, sont livrés à toutes les angoisses de l'inquiètude et du désespoir.

"Voulez vous bien, milady, vous charger des plus aimables souvenirs pour cette charmante Miss Power. J'ai parlé souvent à mes petites amies d'ici de votre bonne hospitalité, à force de me questionner elles sont tout à fait au courant de ma vie de Londres, aussi si l'on voit mon front desempeser un peu on dit aussitôt, il pense à Gore House, à Lady Blessington et à ses jolies nièces.

"Adieu, milady, je me fais une grande fête d'aller bientôt vous faire ma course. J'espere être libre avant la fin du mois.

"Agreez le nouvel hommage de mes sentiments le plus respectueux et les plus devoués. AUG. LERMA."

"Madrid, ce 2 Septembre, 1844.

"A Madame la Comtesse de Blessington:

"MADAME LA COMTESSE,—La douleur qui m'accable est si affreusse que je reclame toute votre indulgence pour m'excuser de ne pas vous annoncer de ma propre main la mort prematurée de mon pauvre frère ainé, le Duc D'Ossuna arrivé le 29 Aôut dernier à 9 heures du matin.

"Je suis persuadé Madame la Comtesse de l'affectieusse amitié dont je vous suis redevable, et sais d'avance la part que vous prendrez à ma peine.

"Veuillez agréer Madame la Comtesse l'hommage de mes sentimens distingués avec les quels j'ai l'honneur d'être, MARQUIS DE TERRANOVA."

"Monsieur le Duc D'Ossuna Comte Duc de Benavente et de l'Infantado de Arcos de Bejar de Gandia de Lerma de Pastrana de Medina Comte d'Ureña, Marquis de Terranova de Peñafiel et autres titres Grand d'Espagne de la première eclasse, Colonel de Cavalerie, Chevalier de l'Ordre Militaire de Calatrava, &ª., &ª., &ª.,

"A l'honneur de vous faire part de la perte douloureuse qu'il vient defaire en la personne de Monsieur le Duc D'Ossuna, Comte Duc de Benavente et de l'Infantado, &ª., &ª., &ª., son frère, décédé à Madrid le 29 Aôut, 1844, à 5 heures du matin, à l'age de 35 ans muni des sacrements de l'Eglise.

"DE PROFUNDIS."

"Madrid, el 17 Octobre, 1844.

"CHÈRE COMTESSE,—Vos deux aimables lettres datées du 18 et 25 Septembre, m'ont fait un bien sensible plaisir, comme toutes celles que vous voulez bien m'addresser, et qui dans les circonstances ou je me trouve m'ont apporté une bien douce emulation, et un grand adoucissement à ma douleur: je viens m'informer dans toutes vos aimables lettres les sentiments si affectueux et si sincere que vous portiez à mon malheureux et très cher frère, et que vous voulez bien me presenter à moi meme. Je veux donc vous exprimer dans ces lignes, toute ma reconnaissance pour tentes vos bontés infinies envers moi, mais j'espere que bientôt je pauvais de parole vous temoigner ce que ma plume me suffit de faire, et je suis persuadé que seulement auprès de si bons et si chers amis, je pourrois trouvér les soulagements dont j'ai tant besoin dans une grande douleur.

"J'ai été bien reconnaissant à l'extreme bonté de vos aimables et charmantes nièces, Mesdemoiselles Power, d'avoir bien voulu se rappeler de moi en m'adressent les deux aimable lettres que vous avez en la bonté de me faire parvenir, et aux quelles je prend la liberté de repondre, en vous prient de vouloir bien leur remettre les ci jointes lettres.

"Les occupations graves et nombreusses qui m'ont occupèes pendant ces derniers jours, m'ont empeché de pouvoir repondre aussitôt que je la voulois à vos deux dernières et aimables lettres. Je compte sur votre indulgence Madame la Comtesse, pour me pardonner cette faute involontaire.

"Je vous remercie mille fois, Madame la Comtesse, pour tout l'interêt et le soin que voulez bien prendre pour ma santé qui est toute aussi bonne qu'elle peut l'être après tants et si graves desagremens que j'ai epreuvé depuis le jour ou j'ai quitté Londres. La reflexion, et les consolations de l'amitié, sont les seuls soulagements que je peux recevoir dans ce moment et si parmi cela que tout autre graves affaires me le permettaient je compte partir de Madrid, et aller à Londres, ou je trouverois auprès de vous et de votre aimable et si chérie famille toutes les consolations qu'ici je ne penserois avoir jamais.

"Je vous prie chère comtesse, quand vous écrivez à Lady Canterbury, de vouloir bien lui presenter mes respects, et de lui dire combien je suis reconnaissant à son bon et aimable souvenir pour moi.

"Je ne puis encore vous dire pour quelle epoque je pouvois me trouver à Londres, mais je compte m'y rendre le plutôt possible, et dans l'etat ou je me trouve, mon esprit a bien besoin de trouvér quelque soulagement, et aussi de ceremettre un peu de tout ce travail qui presse sur moi, et qui à peine me laisse libre de la journée, et bien de fois le soir aussi je suis obligé de travailler presque sans retache dans la nuit; mais tout cela j'espere finira bientôt.

"Permittez moi, chère comtesse, de terminer cettre lettre, ma prochaine sera plus longue, et en attendant veuillez quelque fois me faire l'honneur de m'adresser de vos nouvelles, ainsi que de votre chère famille si aimable et si chère de la quelle je vous prie de vouloir me rappeler en vous assurant qu'aucune consolation peut m' être plus agreable, que celle de recevoir vos aimables lettres.

"Veuillez chère comtesse assurer mes sinceres amitiés à vos aimables et charmantes nièces, ainsi qu'à Monsieur le Comte D'Orsay.

"Le Duc D'Ossuna."

"Paris, ce Lundi, Novembre 24, 1845.

"Ma chère Comtesse,—J'ai appris l'affreuse malheur qui vient de nous arriver, et qui comme à vous à frappé de douleur toute notre chère famille. Je n'essayerais de vous adresser des consolations, car malheureusement je sais par une bien triste et recente experience que pour cette douleur il n'y a point de soulagement. Vous devez être persuadé ma chère et aimable comtesse de toute la part si sincère que je prend à votre malheur, car vous savez tout l'interêt et reconnaissante amitié que je vous porte.

"J'ai pensée avoir en le bonheur de vous revoir cet automne, mais malheureusement il m'a été impossible d'avoir ce plaisir toujours si grand pour moi par ma santé qui a été bien chancelante tout ce derniers temps, et par un nomination.

"Je me suis obligè à aller en Espagne pour quelque temps ; mais je compte avoir ce plaisir au printemps prochain, car je me propose d'aller à Londres vers cette epoque, et avant si je le peux.

"Je ne veux pas abusér de notre bonté plus long temps, car je me figure bien toute la tristesse de vos moments: et ma prochaine lettre sera plus longue.

"Veuillez en attendant offrir mes humbles hommages à vos aimables et charmantes nièces Misses Power, et mes amitiés sinceres pour le cher Comte D'Orsay, et vous Madame la Comtesse assurez vous je vous prie du respect, et sincere attachement que vous porterer pour la vie.

"Votre tout devoué et reconnaissant serviteur et ami,

"Duc D'Ossuna et D'Arcos."

CHAPTER XXV.

MONSIEUR EUGENE SUE.

Monsieur Eugene Sue, a native of Paris, the author of "Les Mystères de Paris," "Mathilde," "Le Juif Errant," "Mémoires d'un Valet-de-Chambre," "L'Art de Plaire," "Deleytar," "La Vegre de Hoat-ven," "Therese Dunoyer," "L'Institutrice," &c., is a strange compound of credulity and imposition; a man of strong Republican principles, united with the most luxurious tastes. His manners in society, like those of many keen observers, are reserved, and generally retiring. His sentiments are, for the most part, generous, and, in many cases, his judgments are just, but, like many of his order, not guided by fixed principles of religion and morality. He sees clearly, and describes graphically, the evils and disorders of a corrupt state of society, without being able to discern the true cause of the evil, or to indicate a remedy for them. He ever dallies, however, with some new political theory, that is ultimately found to be impracticable and Utopian. To human will and human wisdom alone he looks for the removal of all the ills that belong to poor humanity. For some years he held the first place in public opinion among the novel-writers of his day and nation. His "Mystères de Paris" and "Juif Errant" abound with evidences of genius, but, unfortunately, with evidences also of another kind; the first-mentioned work with ample proofs of tendencies to inflame and to excite the passions, while pretending to promote philanthropical objects of reform, social and administrative; while the obvious aim and settled purpose of the other production is to foster the prevailing opinions of two large classes of his countrymen, the literary and philosophical Radicals and the Socialists, against religion and its members generally, and the members of one of the religious orders in particular.

Though still in the prime of life, his latter works, strange to say, are below mediocrity. The character and peculiarities of the Count D'Orsay furnished the author with the idea of the hero of his production, "Le Viscomte de Letocère, ou L'Art de Plaire." He has entirely abandoned Paris, where he formerly resided with great extravagance, and now lives wholly retired from the world, in the territory called La Soligne, near the Lake d'Annesy. The descriptions in Sue's "Mystères de Paris," like the scenes in "The Monk," by Lewis, "ought to have been written by Tiberius, at Caprea; they are forced—the filtered ideas of a jaded voluptuary."*

Before he commenced the *metier* of a literary social reformer—substituting *sensualisme effrenèe* for liberty of conscience, and the rant of an infidel philosophy for religion—Monsieur Sue wrote some stupid books, which no one read or bought; and among these a "History of the French Navy," which nearly ruined his bookseller. The Socialists, in 1848 and 1849, foolishly imagined they had found a powerful ally, and sincere adherent to their cause, in the author of "The Mysteries of Paris" and "The Wandering Jew." Some clap-trap passages in those works in favor of Communist doctrines procured him a seat, in 1849, in the French National Assembly. Universal suffrage was at once dishonored and deceived by the selection of the sensualist literati in the domino of a Socialist. Monsieur Sue

* Byron's Diary, December 6, 1813.

had promulgated a doctrine which rendered him extremely popular: "No one had any right to superfluity while any one was in want of necessaries."

A theory so plausible and so plainly enunciated it was imagined must be a practical truth, demonstrated by the propounder in the frugal simplicity of his mode of life. The poor Socialists were deceived by the author of "Les Mystères de Paris." The sensualist had mystified the Socialists.

Monsieur Auguste Johanet, in a brochure entitled "Verités Sociales, Inconnues ou Meconnues," has given us a description of Eugene Sue's mode of living, and of his mansion in the manor and park of Des Bordes:

"It is impossible to convey an idea of this luxury, of the sumptuousness of those caprices, of those whims of all kinds: here a dining-room, where the sideboards display plate, porcelain, and crystal, with pictures and flowers, to add to the pleasures of the table all the pleasures of the eyes; then an inner gallery, where pictures, statuettes, drawings, and engravings reproduce subjects the most calculated to excite the imagination. Here is a library full of antiquities, whose book-cases contain works bound with unheard-of luxury, where objects of art are multiplied with an absence of calculated affectation, which appears as if wishing to say they came there naturally. A daylight, shaded by the painted glass windows, and curtains of the richest stuff, gives to this place an air of mystery, invites to silence and to study, and produces those eccentric inspirations which M. Sue gives to the public. A desk, richly carved, receives sundry manuscripts of the romance-writer, the numerous homages sent to Monsieur, as the valet expresses himself, from all the corners of the globe, and which the faithful servant enumerates with the most scrupulous care. Every where may be seen gold, silver, silk, velvet, and soft carpets. Every where taste and art tax their ingenuity in a thousand ways to produce effect, ornament, and domestic enjoyments. A vast drawing-room, furnished and decorated with all imaginable care, exactly reproduces that of one of the heroines of romance of Monsieur Eugene Sue; and there have been carved on the woodwork of a Gothic mantel-piece medallions representing the Madeleine falling at the feet of our Savior, who tells her that her sins will be forgiven her because her love has been strong. An immense looking-glass connects this *salon* with a greenhouse, filled with exotic shrubs and trees, and it is lighted at night with magnificent lustres. The walls are highly decorated, and gold and silver fish are seen swimming in marble basins. In addition to the lustres, there are candelabra for *bougies*, mixed with the foliage of the trees and plants, to increase the effect when the place is lighted up. A small gallery, lined with odoriferous plants, leads to a circular walk, which surrounds a garden cultivated in the most expensive manner, and there is a fine piece of water, with numerous swans on it.

"The walk is a *chef d'œuvre* of comfort, for it is alike protected from the wind and the rain, being covered with a dome. It is inclosed with balustrades, covered with creeping plants of the choicest nature. It is a sort of a terrestrial paradise in the bosom of the Salogne, and beyond it is a park, admirably laid out with kiosques, rustic cottages, elegant bridges, and a preserve for pheasants, which secures myriads of birds for the shooting excursions of the illustrious communist, whose keepers exercise a severe look-out to prevent any person from touching the game. The out-buildings show the same elegance. There is a splendid court-yard leading to the stables for carriage-horses, one of which has his name, 'Paradox,' marked over his stall. The woodwork is richly painted and varnished, with an infinity of brass ornaments. Near this place is a box, exclusively devoted to the favorite mare of citizen Eugene Sue, the famous 'Good Lady;' it is furnished with even more elegance. The harness is kept in the finest order, and there is a communication from the harness-room to the green-houses. The dog-kennels are in the same luxurious style as the stables. Many workmen would think themselves happy to have such habitations. In a walk round the reserved grounds, we convinced ourselves that the walks were carefully kept, and here and there are banks of moss for the author to repose upon in his meditations; but the tenants of the environs do not appear to derive any advantage from the vicinity of the great apostle of progress and amelioration. Several of the houses are badly roofed, and the walls are cracked, and the houses are on a level with the marshy soil, covered with manure, which gives the inhabitants the ague during two thirds of the year. On the other hand, however, there is a profuse distribution of little books, such as the 'Berger de Kravan,' and other Socialist publications."*

Madame de Staël's observation to a lady on visiting her in a villa very much decorated, and rather too sumptuously furnished, " Ma chère, vous avez trop de luxe," might have been addressed to Eugene Sue on entering his splendid mansion, and likewise to Lady Blessington in every abode of hers, from the period of her second marriage to the time of the break-up at Gore House.

The poor Socialists and true Republicans who had applauded the generous sentiment of Monsieur Eugene Sue, " No one had any right to superfluity while any one was in want of necessaries," might well say to their theoretical champion, " Mon cher Sue, vous avez trop de luxe: donnez nous qui sont en la misère, de ces superfluites, à lesquelles vous n'avez aucune titre."

LETTERS FROM MONSIEUR EUGENE SUE.

" Je ne saurais vous dire, madame, combien j'ai été touché, non seulement de les trop aimables lettres que vous m'avez bien voulu écrire, mais encore de ce que vous avez pris la peine de me l'écrire en Français. Sous ce rapport elle m'a été doublement precieuse. Croyez, madame, que je sais trop la valeur de vos encouragements et de votre approbation pour la demeriter, et que je tiendrai desormais en bride une assez mauvaise tendance à la licence qui en effet m'a bien souvent et trop souvent privé d'une foule de charmantes *connaissances* et cela à mon grand regret, car je ne sais rien de plus ravissant au monde que de songer à cette espece de communion ou vous met votre cœur avec de pures et fraiches ames de candides jeunes filles—mais Helas! souvent le diable me tente et je succombe. Heureusement votre lettre, madame, me sera une infaillible talisman pour ne plus retomber dans les ecarts. Mille fois merci encore, madame, de vos bontés pour mon ami Pleyel que vous avez je vous assure bien jugé et qui est digne de tout ce que vous avez daigné faire pour lui, du moins par sa profonde reconnaissance. Adieu, madame, croyez je vous prie à mon respectueux dévouement. EUGENE SUE."

* Men of the Time, p. 401. London, 1853.

"Mille et mille pardons, madame, de ne pas vous envoyer comme j'esperais par notre cher Alfred la petite nouvelle que vous m'avez permis de vous adresser. 'Ouvre Poètes' c'est plutôt une biographie vrai qu'aura peut etre assez d'interêt, comme contenant, au milieu d'une si elegante composition de livres charmant qui emprunte son plus grand beauté au reflet de votre nom. J'avais l'honneur de vous faire parvenir le manuscrit au plus tard le trois ou quatre Juillet, il est terminé; mais j'ai beaucoup à revoir et à corriger. C'est une si bonne et belle fortune pour moi de paraître sous vos auspices, madame, que vous m'excuserez de ce petit retard occasioné par le soin que je met à revoir ce travail. Je quitte Alfred avec une vraie tristesse, plus je le connais, plus j'apprecie ce bon ce vaillant cœur, si chaud, si génereux pour ceux qu'il aime. Tout mon espoir est de le revoir bientôt, avec vous, madame, et de pouvoir enfin vous dire, combien je suis profondement touché de vos bontés pour moi.

"Agreez, madame, l'assurance d'une estime la plus respectueuse, &c.

"Eugene Sue."

"Madame,—Ce sont de nouveaux remercîments que j'ai encore à vous adresser, pour les deux livres merveilleux que vous m'avez fait l'honneur de m'envoyer, et surtout pour les lignes si flatteuses qui les accompagne. Ma seule ambition (et elle est grande) serait de meritér ces eloges accordés avec une grace bienveilleuse, et un esprit, qui doublent encore le prix.

"Notre excellent ami me rassure un peu en me disant que vous êtes, madame, satisfait de mon pauvre *Voyageur Eternel* qui se voit à peu près exilé de tous les pays Catholiques, ce qui reduit singulièrement sa promenade de *touriste.* Heureuse pour lui l'Angleterre est plus hospitable, et cela j'aime à la croire, guidèe à l'exemple de Gore House, qui a souffert pour lui donner droit de cité. Merci donc encore, madame, au nom de mon pauvre proscrit, excommunié, damné, que l'autorité de votre nom et de votre grand esprit a si genereusement defendu et protégé.

"J'ai ecrit à Alfred, et je tiens à avoir l'honneur de vous le repeter, madame, que d'après l'an prochain, pouvoir vous adresser quelques pages plus dignes de vos admirable livres, c'est presque un droit que j'ai acquis, et je m'en montrerai toujours tres jaloux.

"Adieu, madame, veuillez croire à l'assurance de mon respectueux dévouement.

Eugene Sue."

"Madame,—Je suis sure davance que vous daignez accepter ce livre avec cette bienveillante indulgence que vous m'avez toujours témoigné. C'est donc seulement une occasion que je saisis avec empressement de me rappeler à votre bon souvenir.

"Agreez, madame, l'assurance de mon respectueux dévouement.

"Eugene Sue."

MONSIEUR LE VICOMTE D'ARLINCOURT.

Vicomte D'Arlincourt (Victor Prevost) was born in 1789, at his father's chateau, De Merantais, near Versailles. His father, Charles (*Fermier General*), perished on the scaffold, as did likewise his grandfather, Adrian, in 1794. They had lent the enormous sum of four millions of francs to the royal family in 1792: a million and a half to the aunts of Louis the Sixteenth, then in Rome; half a million to the brothers of the king, emigrants in Germany; and two millions to the king himself, previously to the disastrous 10th of August.

The present viscount commenced his literary career in 1818, by the publication of his poem, "La Caroleide," of which Charlemagne is the hero. "Le Solitaire" appeared in 1821; "Le Renegat," in 1822; "Ibsibo," in 1823; "L'Etrangère," in 1825; "Le Siege de Paris," in 1826, which was performed thirty nights consecutively at the Theatre Français; "Les Rebelles sous Charles V.," in 1831, a romance in verse; "Les Ecorcheurs, ou l'Usurpation et la Peste," published in 1833; "Le Brasseur Roi," in 1834; "Le Double Règne," in 1835; "L'Herbagère," in 1836; "Les trois Châteaux," in 1840; "Ida," in 1841; "Le Pelerin," in 1842; "L'Etoile Polaire," in 1843; and his great work (if the author's opinion of its merits be well founded), "Les Trois Royaumes," of a later date. The Viscount D'Arlincourt made a starring tour of Europe in 1840, 1841, 1842, providing for the translation of his works, and attributing to his success "les riches cadeaux des puissances du Nord."*

The viscount has traveled much over Europe, and wherever he has been, his position in society, in literature, and the political affairs of the elder branch of the French Bourbons has obtained for him a flattering reception. He was much about the court (and in the councils, he gives us to understand) of Louis the Eighteenth and Charles the Tenth. Their dynasty went down, but the attachment to it of the viscount remained unchanged, and the light of his loyalty he has not allowed to remain hid under a bushel, or, indeed, any of the shining lights

* Annuaire Biographique Descriptif, p. 5, Paris ed., 1843.

which adorn his intellectual character. The viscount has written many works, feeling impelled to write by the cravings of an appetite quite insatiable for praise. He is the author of several ephemeral articles, literary and political, and some dramas, which are dead and d—d.

In principles the viscount is an uncompromising legitimist; in literature he is a sort of La Bruyère. He mingles the characteristics of both in his works rather successfully. He possesses considerable shrewdness and finesse, sarcastic wit, and a natural penchant for romantic incidents. The intensity of his vanity, personal and literary, does not prevent his according praise liberally, or rather profusely, to others in the upper regions of literary society. His works have a certain interest, derived, perhaps, to a great extent, from the combination of a taste for imaginative fiction and romance, remarkable astuteness, and wisdom of a worldly kind, advantageously exhibited in them. This was particularly the case in his earlier productions, at a time when light and imaginative literature in France was much rarer than it now is, and possessed also less vigor than at present. His works generally, if they made their appearance now, would hardly obtain the character they have acquired. The viscount, however, it must be admitted, is a graceful writer, with a great facility of expression, and an epigrammatic turn that gives a terseness to his descriptions and observations. In conversation he is amusing, and if pointed in his remarks, polished at the same time in his delivery and manner. He possesses an immense fund of anecdote, and relates well. Altogether, the viscount is looked upon by those intimately acquainted with him as a good and rare specimen of the accomplished gentleman of the old French school, of amenity dignified by mental culture and enlightened by liberal pursuits.

From Vicomte D'Arlincourt:*

"Aix-la-Chapelle, Oct. 22, 1843.

"Aimable et excellente Amie,—J'ai reçu votre charmante lettre du 16 Octobre, qui m'a prouvé que la bonté et le talent sont inseparable chez vous. Combien je suis reconnaissant des peines que vous vous êtes donnés pour

* I doubt if there is in any language a more remarkable specimen of intense literary vanity and consummate self-conceit than these letters afford.—R. R. M.

moi. Pourquoi faut il que votre eloquence ait en si peu de prise auprès de celui que vous daignez appeler vous entendre.

"Ses propositions me paraissent rudes. Soumettre mon livre à l'acceptation ou au véto d'un libraire, à son éloge, ou à son blame me parait trop inconcevable! Il me semble que je ne saurais m'y repondre. Ce monsieur, est il apte à juger du style d'un écrivain Français? En comprendrait il les pensées? J'avoue que s'il me renvoyait mes pages après les avoir parcourus, sans vouloir faire affaire avec moi, cela me paraitrait une singulière humiliation. Est-ce que je peux, est-ce que je dois m'y exposer? Qu'en dit le Comte D'Orsay, la vie de la grace et du goût? Qu'en dites vous genie protecteur? Une ———* doit être un *oracle*.

"Avant tout je desirerais savoir quel prix *il* donnerait de mes deux volumes, en admettant le cas qu'*il* daigne en être satisfait. Je parle de monseigneur le libraire.

"Puis: dites moi s'il entend par *édition Anglaise* une traduction; je suppose que cela veut dire, une edition publié à Londres en Français. Cependant il faut s'expliquier.

"Enfin, si je me déterminais à envoyer un *specimen* je demande *imperieusement* qu'il ne se compose plus que d'un tiers de volume. Ce sera bien assez pour juger: surtout si *ce monsieur* a une intelligence en harmonie avec ses prétensions, et à la hauteur de ses *arrets*.

"Conseillez moi, aimable dame! Pensez vous qu'il puisse être prudent d'envoyer courir un manuscrit *par mer* et par terre? C'est plus que *par monts et par vallées:* de quelle façon faudroit il s'y prendre pour qu il ne lui arrivât pas mal-aventure?

"Pardon de tout de détails ennuyeux: mais c'est à un sœur que je les adresse, et cela me rassure un peu.

"Votre jolie nièce, a t'elle pensée ou petit travail que j'attends de son obligeance? la nomenclature de vos charmants ouvrages. Je lui demande aussi le titre des principales celebrités litteraires et artistiques de Londres, et avec un mot sur le merite et les succès de chacun d'eux. Sont-elle connu pour y songer!

"Sur le petit note qu'elle m'a donnée, il y a un nom que je ne lis pas bien: c'est celui d'un peintre: est-ce bien Edwin Landseer? je n'en suis pas sur.

"Adieu chère et belle comtesse! je vous adresse ici une lettre bien matérielle, une lettre à fastidieux détails, mais votre génie repliera ses ailes un instant pour reprendre après un plus brillant essor.

"Mille amitiés á mon bon Comte D'Orsay; et croyez moi tous deux pour la vie. Votre tout devoué, LE VICOMTE D'ARLINCOURT.

"P.S.—Tout reflexions faite, s'il faut se resoudre à envoyer un *specimen*, autant vaut un demi volume qu'un tiers. C'est à quoi il faut s'arreter c'est à la manière de l'envoyer, puis, avant tout, il faut savoir si le *prix* qu'il pourrait donner vaut le *sacrifice* qu'il exige."

* Word illegible.

"Janvier 19, 1844.

"AIMABLE SŒUR EN APOLLON!—Voyez combien je compte sur vos bontés pour moi. Voici une 50aine de prospectus des Trois Voyageurs que mon éditeur de France me supplie de vous adresser pour les donner à Monsieur Murray, et à les confrères en librairie (sans oubliér Monsieur Dulon.)

"Me pardonnerez vous cette importunité? Oh oui: car vous êtes la grace et l'obligeance même, mais c'est un frère qui en appele à l'affection et au génie.

"D'ici a peu de jours, chère milady (vous me permettez ce doux nom: n'est-ce pas)? Je vous enverrais plusieurs beaux feuilles de mon premier volume pour remettre à Mr. Murray comme *specimen*, après les avoir lus, il vous dira quels sont ses offres? Je desire vivement qu'elles soient avantageuses. Arrangez cela pour moi, comme si c'était pour vous, et croyez à ma vive reconnaissance.

"J'ai ici un traducteur (le gendre de M. Kenyon) qui a du vous écrire. Il offre de traduire mon livre, et sous mes yeux, de manière à être pret le jour même ou je paraîtrais à Paris.

"Vous pouvez dire à Mr. Murray que je retarderais ma publication, pour que le traduction Anglaise soit en vente à Londres lorsque l'edition Française paraîtra à Paris. *Mais il faut que Mr. Murray m'offre un prix convenable. Je compte à cet egard sur vos bons offices.*

"Il faudrait faire mettre s'il est possible, un extrait du prospectus dans quelques Journaux Anglais notamment dans le 'Morning Post' et le 'Courier de l'Europe.'

"Il faudrait aussi en envoyer à Dublin et à Edinburg.

"Je vous en adresserai encore par l'ambassadeur d'Sardaigne. Mais en vérité je suis honteux et confus de tous les egoismes de cette lettre. Je ne vous parle que de moi. Vous m'y avez autorisé, et cependant je ne saurais me le pardonner.

"Mille amitiés à mon cher Comte D'Orsay. Je regrette bien de ne l'avoir pas vu à Paris quand il y a passé. J'ai pris une vive part à la perte qu'il a faite, et ou chagrin qu'il a du ce rapporter.

"Vous savez sans doute le brillant cadeau que m'a fait l'Empereur de Russie, après avoir lu l'Etoile.

"Veuillez ma aimable sœur agréer les expressions bien senties de ma tendre dévouement, et de ma profonde gratitude. Votre tres humble et tres obeissant serviteur,

LE VICOMTE D'ARLINCOURT."

"29 Mai, 1844.

"CHÈRE CONTESSA,—Voici une petite nouvelle qui, si l'affair vous sera agréable, et pourra plaire à vos lecteurs *in the Book of Beauty:* lorsque vous l'aurez traduite, et que vous l'aurez revêtue des charmes de votre style, elle aura un mérite de plaire: Vous lui donnerez un nouveau charme.

"Je suis vraiment heureux de trouver une occasion de vous être agréable.

Disposez de moi en toute occasion, et croyez à mon dévouement inalterable; il vous est acquis pour la vie.

"Mille remercîmens de votre charmant article du *Court Journal.* Mon livre '*Les Trois Royaumes,*' est sans doute, en ce moment publié à Londres. Il aura commencé sa carrière, et, protégé par vous, il a du faire son entrée dans le monde avec de grandes chances de succès. Continuez lui votre secours, aimable sœur! Soutenez ses pas sur la terre étrangere, et tenez moi au courant de ses destinées.

"J'attends impatiemment les journaux qui en rendent compte à Londres. Quant à ceux de Paris, ils l'ont comblé d'eloges.

"Mes *Trois Royaumes* obtiennent ici en ce moment un grand succès de vogue. C'est le livre à la mode, et il me donne ici de vive jouissances. Dieu veuille qu'il en soit de même à Londres; et à cet effort je compte sur la brillante ——* qui a bien voulu être son ange tutelaire.

"Adieu, ma bonne sœur, dites au Comte D'Orsay les choses les plus affectueuses pour moi; je me recommande toujours à lui, et je suis à tout,

"Votre tendre et reconnaissant, VICOMTE D'ARLINCOURT."

"Paris, ce 12 Mai, 1844.

"CHÈRE ET EXCELLENTE AMIE,—J'ai enfin terminé avec Monsieur B——, mais non pas comme je l'avais desiré, néanmoins si son edition Anglaise a de succès, et *s'il est honnete homme,* mon traité pourra me rapporter quelques bénéfices.

"Voici ce qui a été convenu. Mr. B—— paye tous les frais de traduction, d'impression et de publication, paye tous les frais nombreuses, il partage avec moi les bénéfices de la vente. Le livre paraîtra à Londres en même temps qu'à Paris.

"Il résulte de cet arrangement, que je puis n'avoir pas grand chose, mais qu'il y a chance de gain s'il y a *succès.*

"Or donc, c'est un succès qu'il faut obtenir; et qui mieux que vous, aimable sœur! peut y contribuer? Parlez du livre! faites en parler! protégé par vous, il aura de la vogue.

"Dès que l'edition Française sera prete je me haterai de vous envoyer un joli petit exemplaire, hommage de dévouement et de reconnaissance.

"Mille tendresses à mon cher Comte d'Orsay, je me recommande à lui aussi pour mettre mes *Trois Royaumes* à la mode, *Le Morning Post, Le Courier de l'Europe,* et tous les journaux qui vous admirent devraient bien m'accorder quelques lignes de bienveillance à votre sollicitation.

"J'aime à y compter; car il me sera bien doux de vous exprimer ma gratitude et mon affection. Laissez tomber quelques rayons de votre gloire sur mon humble ouvrage en ce moment à vos pieds; et sa route sera brillante, et son pere vous benira.

"Veuillez agréer, chère sœur, les nouvelles expressions d'amitié fidèle de votre tout dévoué, LE VICOMTE D'ARLINCOURT.

* Word illegible.

"Oserai je vous prier de revoir Mr. B——, et de vous concerter avec lui pour le succès des 'Trois Royaumes.'

"Le Baron D'Haussez m'a dit qu'il avait été fort content de Mr. B——, lorsque celui-ci édita la traduction Anglaise de son livre.

"Si je le sais aussi, Mr. B—— et moi, nous pourrons parler ——* d'autres affaires : le tout depende de succès."

"12 Fevrier, 1844.

"Aimable et chère Comtesse,—Je ne saurais vous exprimer combien je suis touché de votre bonté. J'ai vu le 'Court Journal,' et je l'ai lu avec une vive reconnaissance. M. M. doit avoir pris maintenant une decision ; et grâce à l'interêt que vous me portez, je ne doute pas qu'elle ne soit convenable. On m'a dit qu'il avait fait deja annoncer dans les journaux que le livre paraîtra chez lui. On m'a aussi assuré que C—— était désolé de ne s'en être pas rendu acquireur. Tout cela promet une heureuse fin et c'est à vous que je le devrais.

"J'ai reçu la jolie petite lettre de votre charmante nièce, et je le remercie vivement. Je corrigerai les erreurs que vous me signalez.....

"A mon traducteur Monsieur M—— travaille toujours avec activité. Je vous envoye par une occasion sure huit feuilles qu'il vient de terminer. Si Mr. Murray s'arrange avec vous il pourra commencer de suite à imprimer la traduction ; car on attend impatiemment mes '*Trois Royaumes*' et il serait facheuse de trop retarder la publication.

"Laissez-moi vous repeter ici les expressions de ma gratitude. Je serai heureux d'aller vous les porter moi même à Londres, et si je puis ici vous être utile, disposéz de moi, comme le frère le plus tendre et le plus devoué.

"Mille amitiés à mon bon Comte D'Orsay. Quel regret j'ai eu de ne pas le voir à Paris pendant son court sejour ; je compte aussi sur vos soins et son affection.

"Croyez moi toujours pour la vie, tout à vous de plume et de cœur,

"Le Vicomte D'Arlincourt."

"Rue Canmartin, Paris, 17th Mai.

"Aimable et chère Sœur,—Mes *Trois Voyageurs* veut paraitre à Londres et à Paris, en deux, trois ou quatre jours. Soutenez les! protégéz les! Qu'une des palmes qui ceignent votre front s'etende sur eux comme un talisman de protection. Son plus grande gloire aura été d'être sous votre égide.

"Les journaux vous les parleront sans doute de mon livre. Surtout s'il a un beau succès. Je voudrais bien avoir quelques un de vos articles pour le faire reproduire dans les Gazettes Français.

"Les dernières pages du 2e volume sont toutes politiques : Elles parlent de Mr. le Duc de B——, et vous comprenez la colère que j'aurais de y mettre. Tachez d'en faire parler, *dans notre opinion*, par *le Morning Post, le*

* Word illegible.

Court Journal, &c., et toutes les gazettes qui sympathisent avec la cause. Je ferais repondre ici leurs articles et leurs reflexions politiques, et cela pourrait être utile *ici* à moi et aux notres. Je regarde cela comme important de bien des choses et sous bien des rapports.

"J'espere vous envoyer prochainement l'exémplaire Français qui vous est destiné, accueillez le avec votre bonté accoutumé ; et cet hommage de reconnaissance vous dira combien je suis heureux et fier de votre illustre patronage.

"Je n'ai pas besoin de vous recommander mes interêts sous le rapport pecuniaire. Je ne doute pas que vous soyez bonne à cet egard comme en tout le reste ; esperons que Monsieur B—— montre de l'honneur propre à en agir noblement avec moi ; nous pourrons faire quelques autres affaires ensemble, si je suis content de lui.

"Adieu, ma excellente amie. Je vais attendre impatiemment des nouvelles de Londres, le moment décisif est venu.

"Croyez moi pour le vie chère sœur, votre reconnaissant et dévoué serviteur,
VICOMTE D'ARLINCOURT.

"Mille tendresses à mon bon Comte D'Orsay, je compte aussi sur son amitié, sur ses soins, sur son credit, et sur son talent, il a, à la fois tant d'obligeance et tant de bonté," &c.

CHAPTER XXVI.

CASIMIR DELAVIGNE.

LADY BLESSINGTON made the acquaintance of this distinguished writer in Naples. She speaks in high terms, in her letters, of the simplicity and naïveté of his character. His unaffected manners and amiable disposition made a strong impression on her mind. His conversation appeared to her interesting, full of poetry, but devoid of all manifestations of morbid sensitiveness and vanity.

Casimir Delavigne died at Lyons, in his fiftieth year, in December, 1843.

For a considerable time he had been in delicate health, the result of his unremitting literary labors for many years. Monsieur Jules Janin published an interesting memoir of this eminent poet and dramatist in the Debats newspaper. His dramatic productions have long kept possession of the French stage, and still retain all their original popularity. He died without pain or suffering, in the full possession of all his faculties, and unconscious, it would appear, of any immediate danger. When he breathed his last, his wife was in the act of reading to him Scott's novel of "Guy Mannering;" and living in illusions, the poet died in them. His son, a boy of ten years of age, was present when he expired.

LETTERS FROM CASIMIR DELAVIGNE TO LADY BLESSINGTON.

"MADAME,—Je ne saurais trop vous remercier du présent que vous avez bien voulu me faire. Vous demandez en revanche des vers de moi; après ceux que je viens de lire. J'ai quelque honte d'envoyer les miens cependant je dois obeir, ils n'auront d'autre merite que de vous rappeler très imparfaitement dans une imitation Française une des plus sublimes images du 'Giaour.' Je vous dois de nouveaux remerciéments pour l'espérance que vous nous avez donnée de vous revoir en France. C'est alors que mieux inspiré dans ma patrie je pourrai vous adresser à vous même des vers qui par le sujet seront moins indignes de l'honneur que vous voulez leur faire en les plaçant près de ceux de vos grands poetes.

"Recevez, madame, l'hommage de mon respect.

"CASIMIR DELAVIGNE.

"En quittant Napoli, 22 Janvier.

"Je prie Monsieur le Comte D'Orsay d'agréer mes complimens les plus affectueux."

"Contemplez une femme avant que le linceuil
En tombant sur son front brise notre espérance
Le jour de son trépas, ce premier jour du deuil
Où le danger finit, où le néant commence:
Quelle triste douceur! quel charme attendrissant!
Que de mélancolie et pourtant que de grace.
Dans ses levres sans vie où la frâleur descend!
Comme votre œil aride admire en fremissant.
Le calme de ses traits dont la forme s'éffacе,
La morne volupté de son sein palissant!
Du corps inanimé l'aspect glase votre âme.
Pour vous même attendri, vous lisez vos destins
Dans l'immobilité de ses beaux yeux éteints
Ils ont séduit, pleuré, lancé des traits de flamme,
Et les voila sans feux, sans larmes, sans regard!
Pour qu'il vous reste une doute il est déjâ trop tard;
Mais l'espoir un moment suspendit votre crainte,
Tant sa tête repose avec sérénité!
Tant la main de la mort s'est doucement empreinte

Sur ce paisible front par elle respecté,
Où la vie fuyant a laissé la beauté !* CASIMIR DELAVIGNE."

COMTE ALFRED DE VIGNY.

The name of this gentleman stands high in French literature. His popularity as a poet, a novelist, and miscellaneous writer, a few years ago, was hardly surpassed by that of any other French author. His "Cinque Mars," an historical novel, possesses great interest and merit.

His "Chatterton" also was greatly admired in its day, and several of his minor tales and poems still maintain a high place in public opinion.

I have met this gentleman in the best literary society in Paris about ten years ago. His highly-cultivated mind, elegant tastes, polished manners, and amiable disposition, were not more worthy of observation than his remarkable modesty and simplicity of character.

"Alfred de Vigny," observes Lady Blessington, "is a man of fine feelings as well as genius, but were they ever distinct? I like to think they can not be, for my theory is, that the feelings are to genius what the chords are to a musical instrument—they must be touched to produce effect."

FROM COUNT ALFRED DE VIGNY TO LADY BLESSINGTON.

"18ieme ——, [1840], Paris.

"Moi qui me souviens, milady, de vous avoir trouvé une soir si profondement affecté de la mort d'une amie, je puis mesurer tout la peine que vous avez éprouvée à la perte de Lord Durham. J'aimais toujours à me figurer que je le retrouverai à Gore House à coté de vous, et je ne puis croire encore qu'en si peu de tems il ait été enlevé à ses amis. Je ne crains point avec vous de parler d'une chose deja ancienne, comme ou dirait à Paris, car je sais quel religieux souvenir vous gardez à ceux qui ne sont plus, et qui vous furent chers.

"Je regrette dans Lord Durham tout l'avenir que je me promettais de sa vie politique, et le developpement des idées saines et larges, que, chez vous il m'avait montrée. Si je ne me suis trompé sur lui, l'alliance de la France lui semblait précieuse à plus d'un titre, et il connaissait profondement les vues de

* These lines would have served well to describe the marvelous beauty that supervened on death, the revived loveliness of Lady Blessington, as it was in the bloom of youth, that manifested itself in the remains of that lady a few hours after her decease.—R. R. M.

la Russie. S'il tenait à cette géneration de vos hommes d'etat qui prirent part aux plus grandes luttes, il était pourtant jeune d'esprit et de cœur, et un homme de passé et d'avenir à la fois sont bien rares.

"Vous pensez à voyager in Italy, y songez vous encore, milady, je le voudrais puisque Paris est sur le chemin, et je suis assurè par tout la grace avec laquelle vous m'avez ouvert Gore House, que vous ne seriez point affligée de me voir vous porter en France l'assurance du plus sincére et du plus durable dévouement. ALFRED DE VIGNY."

From Signore Luigi Chiave, on the death of the Duke Torlonia:

"Rome, March 14, 1829.

"DEAR LADY BLESSINGTON,—We were all in the deepest affliction for the severe loss of our dear Duke Torlonia when your letter from Paris of the 14th ult. reached me; you will, therefore, excuse my delay in answering the same, and the slowness of my reply.

"The duke's death is a great loss to our family, although he had made his will, providing for every one of his family very magnificently, and for Alexander in particular. The house of commerce goes on just the same as before; just now all are very busy, which causes to us some distraction; but my poor mother, who has not the same advantage, feels the loss still more, and has experienced a great blow.

"I am sure, Lady Blessington, that you and all your party will sympathize with us in our profound grief, and will take a kind interest in our situation.

"This has been a dreadful winter—deaths without end: more than the half of the Roman society is in mourning, not for the Pope, for whom nobody has mourned either exteriorly or internally. His death puts an end to all the gayeties of the Carnival, and then the others followed, till our own calamity befell us, and every thing was at an end. There were all the appearances for a most brilliant Carnival, and the day on which the poor duke died was to be our bal masqué. What a change! I see that all the world is not equally unfortunate. I rejoice with Count D'Orsay for the happy accouchement of his sister the Duchesse de Guiche, which I have seen in the newspaper, as also with you for your sister's marriage.*

"I remain, dear Lady Blessington, ever yours sincerely,

"LUIGI CHIAVE."

* In 1815, the authoress of the Diary of the Times of George the Fourth, referring to the assembly at Torlonia's in Rome, and his two palaces, the old for his banking business and his money-bags, the new for his festas, observes, "It would be unjust not to acknowledge that the Duc de Torlonia, though purse-proud and a parvenu, is a very useful and hospitable person, and his family render themselves equally serviceable and agreeable to all strangers who visit Rome, especially to the English."—*Diary of the Times of George the Fourth*, vol. iii., p. 7.

The writer goes on to say, that the wealthy banker, whom Bonaparte made a

THE BABOO DWARKANAUTH TAJORE.

This enlightened and opulent Hindoo claimed descent from one of the five renowned Brahmins of Bengal, who settled in that country many centuries ago. He inherited vast estates in Cuttach, and property in houses and land in and adjoining Calcutta. At an early age he showed a strong predilection for European society and manners, and commercial enterprise. He built indigo factories, bought and chartered ships, and obtained from government a high office, that of the head Dewan of the salt department. His munificence was unbounded to all the charitable and scientific institutions of Calcutta. He first visited England in 1842 for a few months. He proceeded to the Continent, studied the language and institutions of that country, and again returned to England, but much impaired in health.

Among the many friendships he formed in London with distinguished persons, that in which he seemed to take most pleasure was the close intimacy he had contracted with Lady Blessington and the Count D'Orsay. Some proofs were given of the value he set on their acquaintance in the shape of Cashmere shawls and other precious objects of great value.

Count D'Orsay's portrait of his Hindoo friend was one of the happiest efforts of his pencil. The Baboo died at his residence, St. George's Hotel, Albermarle Street, on the 1st of August, 1846, aged fifty-one. His remains were interred in Kensal Green cemetery, in the unconsecrated portion of the ground. No religious service was performed over the body. The son of the deceased attended the funeral, attired in an Indian costume, composed wholly of black cloth.

LETTER FROM THE HINDOOSTANEE PRINCE, DWARKANAUTH TAJORE.

"Calcutta, 15th February, 1844.

"MY DEAR LADY BLESSINGTON,—Your highly esteemed favor of the 16th of December, 1842, with the no less esteemed gift which accompanied it, reach-

duke, purchased the Princess of Wales's most valuable jewels; and that some pearls of priceless value, which belonged to her royal highness, decorated the ample bosom of the citizen's wife.—R. R. M.

ed me only on the 8th instant, after wandering for upward of a year in the wide world, and visiting Mauritius, Madras, &c., where the ship was subjected to many detentions.

"An unlooked-for gift, however, is never too late to be thankfully received; and I only regretted the circumstance, because my not acknowledging the favor within a reasonable period must have made me appear very ungrateful in your eyes. I now lose not a moment to assure you that the sight of your hand-writing was truly acceptable, and, according to our Eastern notions, as much as half a visit.

"The two Annuals I have perused with great pleasure, more especially the contribution by yourself, and others of the highly-gifted circle with whom I have passed so many pleasant hours at Gore House.

"You remind me of my promise to revisit England—a promise which I can never lose sight of so long as its many attractions continue, and which would have been fulfilled ere now, had I not considered it necessary, in the first instance, to make myself better acquainted with such objects of interest in my own country as I had not before visited. This I have now accomplished, having but lately returned from an extensive tour in the upper part of India, in the course of which I visited the Holy City of Benares, Agra, Delhi, and many others, abounding with works of art far surpassing my most sanguine expectations, and presenting, at the same time, the most romantic associations, which would be better suited for your poetical genius than my prosaic pen.

"The Tai Mehal of Agra, built upward of 200 years ago by the Emperor Sha Jebaun, as a tomb for his beloved wife, Noor Mehal (the 'light of the harem'), is a work which has no equal in the world, and is truly beyond description. No words, no idea, no drawing, no model, nothing indeed but the Tai itself, can show what the Tai really is. The symmetry of the whole, and the proportions of the component parts, the materials of which it is built, the mosaics, and the endless variety of detail in the friezes, screens, pavements, and balustrades, are all alike worthy of the highest admiration, and in so perfect a state, that one can scarcely believe that they were not the work of yesterday.

"The pure white marble of which the tomb is built is still as transparent and beautiful as it was at the time of the erection, and the exquisitely-finished inlaid work, composed of precious stones, and representing the most beautiful flowers, is in no less perfect a state of preservation.

"I must, however, conclude my letter, and defer giving you any further description of the many palaces and other works I have visited until we again meet in England, which I hope will be at no very distant period.

"Kindly present the inclosed letter to Count D'Orsay, and remember me to your fair niece, and the other kind friends who have been inquiring after me, and believe me, my dear Lady Blessington, ever most sincerely yours

"DWARKANAUTH TAJORE."

LETTERS FROM HASSUNA D'GHIES TO LADY BLESSINGTON.

"33 Albemarle Street, ———, 1822.

"Hassuna D'Ghies presente ses complimens respectueuses à my Lord et my Lady Blessington, et leur temoigne ses regrets de ne pouvoir pas avoir l'honneur d'accepter leur aimable invitation pour aujourd'hui, parceque il se trouve engagè, et leur doit la même obligation.

"D'Ghies les prie de recevoir de nouveaux l'assurance de son parfait consideration.

"Mercredi à quatre heures."

"33 Albemarle Street, 4th July, 1822.

"My Lady,—Having received a small shawl from my country, I take the liberty of sending it to your ladyship, in hopes you will favor me by accepting it; though not sufficient for your merit, neither for my gratitude, yet as a mark of esteem for all the civilities I have received from your ladyship.

"Receive, my lady, the expression of my high consideration.

"I have the honor to be, your obedient servant, Hassuna D'Ghies."

LETTER FROM NAMIZ PACHA TO LADY BLESSINGTON.

"Carlton Hotel, 16th May, 1835.

"My Lady,—Je regrette infinement de ne pouvoir pas me rendre chez vous pour prendre congé. Depuis ce jour dernier, que je dois quiter l'Angleterre un indisposition me tiens dens le chambre.

"Je vous remette un livre sur medecine, et la note de music que sa hautesse le sultan a composè que je vous prie d'accepter, en attendant et dans l'espoir de revoir l'angleterre bientôt à fin de pouvoir vous exprimer de nouveau madame tout l'estime et la sincere amitié que je vous porte, je veux que vous m'envoyez aussi, madame, le portrait charmant qui m'a été gratuitement offert.

"Agreez, madame, l'assurance de ma sincere amitié, Namiz."

LETTER FROM GENERAL COUNT D'ORSAY TO LADY BLESSINGTON.

"Rue de Bourbon, Paris.

"Chère Lady Blessington, ma femme m'a dit qu'un bureau, pareille à celui que j'ai donné à Alfred conviendrait à Lord Blessington : faitez moi le plaisir de lui offrir celui ci de ma part et de le prier de l'accepter comme souvenir de son ami.

"Ce petit cadeau en passant par vos mains ne peut que devenir plus agreeable, vous savez si bien en votre amabilitè s'accoutumèe faire valoir les plus petites choses, que vous saurez mettre un nouveau prix à cette bagatelle et malgré les rarétes que possede le cher lord daignez le faire entendre que les souvenirs de l'amitié ne doivent point être appreciès par le magnificence.

"Homages et amitiés sinceres. A. Comte D'Orsay."

ROBERT WESTMACOTT, JUN., ESQ.

The "young sculptor of much promise," who made the acquaintance of Lady Blessington at Naples in 1824, had been studying in Rome, and had already executed, during his residence there, several works of great merit. Lord Dudley and Ward had been one of his earliest and most zealous patrons.

Few artists were held in higher regard by Lady Blessington and Count D'Orsay than this eminent sculptor, and accomplished and amiable gentleman. To his professional talents, refined taste, and judgment, he added literary abilities far above mediocrity. He wrote prose and verse with grace and facility, and conversed with ease and effect. His high moral character and worth, mental culture, and amiable disposition, made him an estimable member of society, and an especial favorite of Lady Blessington, both in Italy and at home.

LETTERS FROM ROBERT WESTMACOTT, ESQ., TO LADY BLESSINGTON.

"Mr. R. Westmacott presents his compliments to Lady Blessington, and does himself the pleasure to inclose a copy of the lines of Mrs. Hemans he spoke of last evening.

"He hopes Lady Blessington will think as well of them as he does. He is quite vain for the share he has had in calling forth so sweet a song.

"He takes advantage of being in good company to send some wildish lines, written 'on the spot,' as authors say, that is, in a storm literally.

"Monday evening."

"Thursday.

"I only returned to town last night, or I should have had the pleasure to answer your ladyship's inquiry sooner, or, rather, to acknowledge your note, for, I am sorry to say, neither my Italian nor I can remember the date of Miss Bathurst's death, and I fear I have destroyed every memorandum (excepting a cast of the *relievo* I executed in Rome) connected with the event.

"RICHARD WESTMACOTT."

LETTER FROM SIR WILLIAM DRUMMOND TO LADY BLESSINGTON.

"Capo di Naplis (Naples).

"I am ashamed of having been so long answering your ladyship's kind letter, but I could not get the decision of Prince Stiliano Colonna till the night before last, and the death of one of my own horses yesterday made me uncertain whether I could go to Capo di Monte or not to-morrow. It is, however, now settled that we are to have the honor of waiting on you. I have taken the liberty of asking the prince's brother, who lives with him.

"W. Drummond."

CHAPTER XXVII.

FROM JOHN AULDJO, ESQ., TO LADY BLESSINGTON.

"Naples, September 25, 1835.

"My dear Lady Blessington,—I have been somewhat remiss in not answering you kind letter sooner, but the wish to see the end of a story of Bonuccio's in 'The Omnibus' (a weekly publication), in which you are one of the principal characters, has kept me from writing to you till I could tell you what you do and say at Pompeii, in company with Scott, Byron, and many other great persons of this great era. This end has not yet appeared; but I can no longer delay in thanking you for your kindness to my humble self, and I am much afraid that it is owing to your good nature that you have read my trivial tour with an eye closed to its defects, and praised what you ought to have condemned. Nevertheless, I am extremely flattered by your good opinion, which, in truth, I value more than the accumulated encomiums of a thousand critics, could so many of those dread arbiters of an author's fate be found to give me a favoring word. Besides, I feel honored by your promise of the Book of Beauty, which I look forward to with anticipations of no little pleasure. If you will direct it to be sent to Messrs. Bingham and Richards, King's Arms Yard, Coleman Street, addressed to me, it will be forwarded to me by the very first opportunity.

"I am glad to find that Mrs. Torre Holmes's poem meets your approbation. I am certain she will feel delighted by your attention, and will be tempted to place at your disposal many such offerings, even of greater beauty than the present one: her address is, Mrs. Torre Holmes, care of F. Mangles, Esq., Down Farm, near Guildford, Surrey. With regard to any contribution of my own, I am almost afraid to tempt my fate among the beautiful and well-wrought tales which your magic wand calls forth; yet I fain would answer the spell, and will send you, before the end of January, one, the scene of which is in Naples, in the stormy times of the 'conspiracy of the barons,' and if it should not meet with approbation, you will only have to treat it with a short process and throw it into the fire. And now let me analyze Signor Bonuccio's curious story. You are accused of visiting Pompeii by moonlight, with Scott, Byron, Madame Recamier; and the author, Bonuccio, describes himself as waiting for your arrival, sitting on the steps of the Temple of Fortune—the moon, rising in all its southern beauty and softness from behind the mountains over Amalfa and Salerno, Vesuvius, with the red glare of an eruption on its summit, strives to contend with its silver rays for possession of the sacred spot, and illumines one side of the temples and statues of the Forum with its murky red, while the other is under the dominion of the silver tint of the glorious orb. On one side the sky is darkly, deeply blue; on the other, thick volumes of sulphuric smoke roll up and shroud the face of heaven. Of course he is in a reverie, from which a well-dressed page startles him, and announces the arrival of his expected guests; he hurries toward the entrance, and meets you by the Theatre; but he observes that the Dey of Algiers, with a vast train of odalisques, a beautiful sultana, almehs, and singers, was reposing under the weeping willow of the Forum, and can not be stirred from his pipe, his dances, and his songs, rapt up in their enjoyment, and with true Eastern feeling, heedless of the treasures of Pompeii and the beauty of the ladies of your society. He leaves the dey to his pleasure, and with you under his care, leads the party through the city of the dead. Walter Scott hobbles for a time, and is then accommodated with a crutch; he speaks *cattivo Inglese,* because il facile e gentile idioma glia era affatto ignota.

"He was sulky because he was Zoppo, like Byron, Bulwer (what will he say to this libel?), Chateaubriand, and Canning. However, poor Sir Walter takes little notice of any thing, being buried, as it were, in his own past dreams, and was as one called from the grave, and only kept with them by the enchanting smiles of the beautiful genius who hung upon his, the delighted author's arm! Well, you wander about till near dawn, but, faith! not a word does he repeat of what you said, or indeed any of the party. But you do wander about till near dawn, and arrive at the Basilica, where the first rays of the rising god of day disclose a beautiful sight—the whole Bay of Naples. Naples, Castelamare, the coast of Sorrento, the plain all awakening into life under the warm influence, and all are struck with the amazing loveliness of the scene. But these first rays disclose another sight still more enchanting—a table covered with the rarest flowers, and spread with all the delicacies of the season, from India, Persia, America; the dishes of gold and silver. What fairy has done this? 'Tis by the munificence of the Duke of Casarano, who, as the darkness cleared away, was discovered at the head of the table, waiting to do the honors of the feast. Your ladyship sits on his right hand; the attendants hand round the flowers and fruits, when lo! they are found to be all *sorbetti,* and you the queen of beauty, after a long conversation about the ancients and the moderns too (but all of which instructive conversation is unfortunately suppressed), conclude by declaring that Italia was ever the classic land of taste, of the arts, of politeness, and that the Duke of Casarano is the great representative of all three! Here the story stops, and I anxiously look for the next paper, when I hope we shall learn how you got home after this dainty feast. It would be a pity to deprive you of the end of so beautiful a tale, and I shall take an opportunity of transmitting it to you when it appears. But now I suspect you will be sadly tired of all this nonsense; yet I trust you will excuse my obliging you to wade through this short abstract, instead of sending you several sheets, had I transcribed the whole.

"It was with great pain that I received an invitation from Ellice to join Lord Durham and himself at Malta, and go to Constantinople, Odessa, and Moscow; but, unfortunately for me, Ellice wrote so shortly before they left London, and the process our letters undergo at various frontiers to keep cholera out of them delay them so long on the road, that I only got it in time to be disappointed, for I could not have reached Malta by any contrivance before they got there, and luckily decided on not trying to do so, for I have since learned that they did pass before I could have got to Messina.

"Poor Sir William Gell is very far from being in a convalescent state, and I am afraid the approach of winter will be too much for him. Instead of rallying, as we expected, with the summer, he gradually grows weaker, and, ere long, the fitful dream must be over; he is in good spirits, and is very grateful for any attention. The archbishop, though so much older, is likely to live much longer than his friend, and the Ricciardis are the great supporters of a new singing, acting, dancing society called the *Filarmonica*. The second son is liberated, but is very little seen in society. JOHN AULDJO."

DR. JOHN WILLIAM POLIDORI, M.D.

In April, 1816, when Byron set out on his second tour, he was accompanied by a young Italian physician in the capacity of his traveling medical attendant. Polidori was a young man of considerable talents, wild and ill-regulated, exceedingly eccentric, vain, capricious, and irascible, but of honorable principles, an outspeaking, original, independent thinker. He was the son of a person of high character and respectability, who had been in early life a secretary of the poet Alfieri. Had his abilities been well directed, and time given for the exercise of them and the cooling down of his excessive ardor and enthusiasm, he might have become very eminent in his profession or in the pursuits of literature. He took a pleasure in provoking his indulgent patron, Lord Byron, sometimes even practicing acts of rudeness which another might not have ventured to attempt with impunity.

In 1816, Mr. and Mrs. Shelley were living at Secheron, on the borders of the Lake of Geneva, with Lord Byron, and some time after, when Byron removed to Diodati, the Shelleys were again guests of his lordship. On each occasion Polidori was an inmate of his lordship's abode.

While at Diodati, during a week of rain, the party had agreed to amuse themselves with reading German ghost-stories, and composing pieces in that style.

Polidori commenced his tale of "The Vampire," and repeated one evening the sketch of the story. Mrs. Shelley's wild and powerful romance of "Frankenstein," Moore observes, was "the most memorable result of this story-telling compact." But another remarkable result of it was the transformation of the slight sketch of the story dashed off at Diodati by Polidori, into a strange novel entitled "The Vampire," allowed to go forth, though not avowedly, with all the appearances that could be given to it, to foster the supposition that it was the production of Lord Byron.

In 1817 Byron and Polidori parted. His lordship found it impossible to bear any longer with the annoyances he suffered from the intolerable vanity and extraordinary caprices of this eccentric young man.* Besides, his lordship had quite enough

* One of Polidori's escapades at Milan is referred to in Moore's Diary, in some allusions made to Lord Byron's occasional fits of ungovernable choler:

"Okeden mentions having seen Lord Byron in a state of great excitement. On one occasion he made an effort to restrain himself, and succeeded; on the other, he gave full vent to his violence. The former was at Copet, when, on coming to dinner, he saw unexpectedly among the guests Mrs. Harvey (Beckford's sister), whom he had not seen since the period of his marriage, and who was the person chiefly consulted by Lady Byron, I believe, on the subject of his proposals to her. He stopped short upon seeing her, turned deadly pale, and then clinching his hand, as if with a violent effort of self-restraint, resumed his usual manner. The other occasion was at Milan, when he and Hobhouse were ordered to quit the city in twenty-four hours, in consequence of a scrape which Polidori had brought them into the night before at the Opera, by desiring an officer who sat before them to take off his cap, and on his refusal to do so, attempting to take it off himself. The officer, upon this, coolly desired Polidori to follow him into the street, and the other two followed, ripe for a duel. The officer, however, assured them he had no such thing in his contemplation; that he was the officer of the guard for the night; and that, as to taking off his cap, it was contrary to orders, and he might lose his commission by doing so. Another part of his duty was to carry off Polidori to the guard-house, which he accordingly did, and required the attendance of Byron and Hobhouse in the morning. The consequence of all this was, that the three were obliged to leave Milan immediately, Polidori having, in addition to this punishment, 'bad conduct' assigned as the reason of his dismissal. It was in a few minutes after their receiving this notification that Okeden found Lord Byron storming about the room, and Hobhouse after him, vainly endeavoring to tranquillize his temper. Must ask Hobhouse about this."

to do to manage his own scrapes, without having to be troubled by the police about the escapades of his physician.

Polidori went to England in 1817, well recommended by Byron to his friends in London. The young doctor's intention then was to go to the Brazils, to exercise his profession under the auspices of a Danish consul. This idea, however, was relinquished. Polidori remained in London for a considerable time, published his extraordinary novel, was lionized for a season or two, made the acquaintance of many distinguished persons—among others, of Lady Blessington—fell into pecuniary difficulties, and eventually terminated his existence.

On the subject of Polidori's novel, and the false impression made on the public mind as to the author of it, Moore merely observes, that, "under the supposition of its being Lord Byron's, it was received with much enthusiasm in France," and alludes to some French writer's having asserted that it was this work (believed to be his lordship's) which first attracted attention in France to the genius of Byron, and publishes a letter of Byron to Murray, dated Venice, May 25th, 1819, in which there is the following passage: "A few days ago I sent you all I know of the Vampire. He may do, say, or write what he pleases, but I wish he would not attribute to me his own compositions."*

But Moore makes no mention whatever of a very remarkable letter which Byron addressed to the editor of Galignani's paper, denying the imputed authorship of the Vampire. I am not aware whether that letter was published or not in Galignani's paper, but having obtained a copy of it from a Mr. Armstrong, an acquaintance of Lord Byron's in Italy, who received it from his lordship shortly after it was written, it is here given, as far as I know, for the first time to the public.

LETTER FROM LORD BYRON TO THE EDITOR OF GALIGNANI'S MESSENGER.

"Venice, April 27th, 1819.

"Sir,—In various numbers of your journal I have seen mentioned a work entitled 'The Vampire,' with the addition of my name as that of the author. I am not the author, and never heard of the work in question until now. In

* Moore's Life of Byron, p. 394

a more recent paper I perceive a formal annunciation of 'The Vampire,' with the addition of an account of my residence in 'the island of Mitylene,' an island which I have occasionally sailed by in the course of traveling some years ago through the Levant, and where I should have no objection to reside, but where I have never yet resided. Neither of these performances are mine, and I presume that it is neither unjust nor ungenerous to request that you will favor me by contradicting the advertisement to which I allude. If the book is clever, it would be base to deprive the real author, whoever he may be, of his honors; and if stupid, I desire the responsibility of nobody's dullness but my own.

"You will excuse the trouble I give you; the imputation is of no great importance, and as long as it was confined to surmises and reports, I should have received it, as I have received many others, in silence.

"But the formality of a public advertisement of a book I never wrote, and a residence where I never resided, is a little too much, particularly as I have no notion of the contents of the one nor the incidents of the other. I have, besides, a personal dislike to 'Vampires,' and the little acquaintance I have with them would by no means induce me to divulge their secrets.

"You did me a much less injury by your paragraphs about '*my devotion*,' and 'abandonment of society for the sake of religion,' which appeared in your Messenger during last Lent—all of which are not founded on fact; but you see I do not contradict them, because they are merely personal, whereas the others in some degree concern the reader.

"I know nothing of the work or works in question, and have the honor to be (as the correspondents to magazines say), your constant reader, and very obedient, humble servant, BYRON."

LETTER FROM DR. POLIDORI, THE PHYSICIAN OF LORD BYRON, TO LADY BLESSINGTON.

"SIGNORA CONTESSA,—Chi ha avuto una volta la sorte di conoscerla non può scordarsi di lei. A farne prova à me vengono adesso questi tre piccoli tomi i quali spero ch'ella non sdignerà d'accettare e d'onorarli d'un posto nella sua libreria. Forse s'ella gli trova degni di suoi sguardi, le potrà venir fatto di menzionarli in quelcuno di suoi scritti lo che saria un favore distinto ch'ella mi farebbe ed io le ne sarei infinitamente obbligato.

"Sono Signora Contessa, suo servitore, E. POLIDORI."

LETTER TO LADY BLESSINGTON, FROM THE REV. AUGUSTUS F. HARE, ADDRESSED TO LADY BLESSINGTON WHILE LIVING AT THE PALAZZO NEGRONI IN ROME.

"DEAR LADY BLESSINGTON,—The poem of Wodin, or Odin, is, I hope, a great deal better than the MS. which I have been just perusing, and in which I have taken the liberty of putting a pencil mark opposite the few lines (there are only five of them) that struck me as having some merit. The first line I have marked is picturesque; I think the second and third are neatly expressed; the fourth and fifth are perhaps pretty. All the rest of all the poems I consign to your ladyship's most critical indignation.

"Such is my opinion of the MS., and I write it, though I hardly know why; if it is right, you know it already; if wrong, you had better not hear it at all. The truth is, I wish to say a word on that 'black hole,' which contrasts so strangely with a guess of mine, that the ancients dreaded death; but that we, thanks to Christianity, only dread, if saved, dying. Nothing can be more opposite than Sir William's lines and my remark; and yet, perhaps, all things considered, the first confirms the last. To be sure, the lines on death have an odd appearance, coming so immediately as they do after the Platonist. To be told in one page that boxes are nothing, holes are nothing, the world itself is nothing but a make-believe! and to find the very next page filled with horror (horror so sincere it almost makes one shudder) at the thoughts of what? of an imaginary confinement in one of those imaginary holes, within one of those non-existent boxes! Is not such philosophy as this like a 'sick man's dreams?' Poor Sir William, I would not have such dreams for all his horses and all his learning, nor even for Lady D—— to boot. The truth is, and the more I think, the more thoroughly I am convinced of it, there are but two consistent opinions in the world—Christian* Atheism and Catholic Christianity; and whoever halts between the two must, sooner or later, find unrest. I began with a criticism, and have ended with a sermon.

"You, perhaps, when you see me, will reverse the matter, beginning with a sermon for writing at all, will conclude with a criticism for having written nonsense. Well, be it so—a most clerical conclusion—so long as I may subscribe myself your ladyship's most obliged and very obedient servant,

"AUGUSTUS F. HARE.

"Wednesday."

This admirable letter of a most estimable as well as erudite man, whom I had the pleasure of knowing at the outset of his professional career—unfortunately one too brief for all who came within the sphere of his duties or the circle of his acquaintance—it will be perceived, was in relation to a volume of MS. poems, written by Sir William Drummond, the philosophy of which was, to the Christian mind of Mr. Hare, "like a sick man's dreams," and which he consigned to Lady Blessington's "most critical indignation." How strangely and, it must be added, how sadly, does a letter of Lady Blessington to Sir William Drummond on the same subject contrast with the foregoing communication of Mr. Hare!—R. R. M.

* An almost illegible word, written over another that had been erased.—R. R. M.

LETTER FROM LADY BLESSINGTON TO SIR WILLIAM DRUMMOND.

"Villa Gallo (Naples), April 24th, 1825.

"My dear Sir William Drummond,—The perusal of your beautiful poem, 'Odin,' has delighted me so much, that I can not deny myself the gratification of expressing my thanks to its author, and, at the same time, demanding why so exquisite a poem remains unfinished. It is cruel to your readers and unjust to England to leave such a work incomplete: it is like the unfinished statues of Michael Angelo, which no hand has ever been found hardy enough to touch, for I am persuaded that we have no living poet who could write a sequel to 'Odin.'

"Do not think me presumptuous for venturing to give my opinion on poetry; I have studied it from my infancy, and my admiration for it is so enthusiastic that I feel more strongly than I can reason on the subject. With this passion for poetry, you may more easily imagine than I can describe the delight that 'Odin' gave me. I have copied many, many passages from it into my album, under different heads, such as Contemplation, Love of Country, Liberty, Winter, Morning, Meditation on a future State, Immortality of the Soul, Superstition, Vanity of Life, Jealousy, and many others, too numerous to mention; and they are of such transcendent merit as to be above all comparison, except with Shakspeare and Milton. In the sublimity and harmony of your verses, you have equaled, if not surpassed, the latter; and in originality of ideas and variety, you strikingly resemble the former; but neither can boast of any thing superior to your beautiful episode of 'Skiold and Nora.'

"Hitherto, my dear Sir William Drummond, I have looked on you as one of the first scholars and most elegant prose writers of the present day; permit me to say, that I regard you as *the first poet.* When I have been charmed with the productions of writers who were either personally unknown to me, or, unhappily, dead, how have I regretted I have not been able to pour out my thanks for the pleasure they have afforded me! In this instance, I rejoice that I have the happiness of knowing you, and of being able to express, though feebly, the admiration with which your genius inspires me, and of offering up my private prayers that you may be long spared to adorn and to do honor to the age, which is, and ought to be, proud to claim you. In writing to you, I abandon my pen to the guidance of my heart, which feels with all the warmth for which such hearts are so remarkable. A poet can understand and pardon this Irish warmth, though a philosopher might condemn it; but, in addressing you, I forget that I am writing to one of the most eminent of the last class, and only remember that I am talking of Odin to the most admirable of the first.

"I am at present reading 'Academical Questions,' which, if I dare take possession of, should not again find their way to Chiaja. 'Odin' I shall most *unwillingly* resign, as I find it belongs to Lady Drummond; but if you have any other works by you, will you have the goodness to lend them to me? Pray name what day you will dine with us, accompanied by Mr. Stewart,* to whom I owe my best acknowledgments for having lent me 'Odin.' Believe me, my dear Sir William, to be, with unfeigned esteem, sincerely yours,

"MARGUERITE BLESSINGTON."

* Mr. Thomas Stewart was a nephew of Sir William Drummond, and brother of the present Sir William Drummond Stewart, of Grandtully, County Perth. Shortly after the date of the preceding letter, Mr. Stewart became a Roman Catholic, and eventually a clergyman of that Church, and a dignitary of it in the kingdom of Naples. He was assassinated some years ago, while in the act of bathing—I think on the coast of Calabria; and, as I was informed by an Italian servant who was in attendance on his master at the time of this catastrophe, the murder was committed by some desperadoes for the sake of a valuable gold watch he was known to carry with him.—R. R. M.

APPENDIX.

No. I.—INTRODUCTION, p. 13.

A BRIEF NOTICE OF LORD AND LADY CANTERBURY.

THE Right Honorable Charles Manners Sutton, son of the most Reverend Charles Manners Sutton, Lord Archbishop of Canterbury, was born in 1780. Being destined for the profession of the law, he was placed at an early age at Eton, where he passed some years, and completed his education at Trinity College, Cambridge, and having taken the degree of Bachelor of Arts in 1802, he entered as a student at Lincoln's Inn, and was called to the bar in 1805. For some years he practiced in the Court of King's Bench. He entered Parliament in 1807, for the borough of Scarborough, which he represented till 1832, when he was returned for the University of Cambridge. He was appointed Judge Advocate in 1809. In 1817 he was chosen Speaker of the House of Commons, on the retirement of Mr. Abbott. A perfect knowledge of the forms of the House, admirable capacity for business, fairness in the discharge of his duties, acknowledged by all parties; a noble, prepossessing, and commanding appearance, a fine, clear, sonorous voice, an air of hilarity, and appearance of bonhommie, and excellent temper, were the distinguishing characteristics of the new speaker; and with these advantages, and the possession of the respect and regard of all parties in the House, though chosen by a Tory Parliament on two successive occasions, he was proposed by a Whig administration for the speakership. On November 2, 1830, on the meeting of the new Parliament, the Duke of Wellington being prime minister, the Right Hon. Mr. Manners Sutton was again chosen Speaker of the House of Commons. The celebrated Reform ministry, Lord Grey being first Lord of the Treasury, was installed in office on the 22d of the same month.

Mr. Sutton occupied his office from 1817 till 1835, when Mr. Abercrombie was chosen by a majority of ten.

A little later, he was called to the Upper House, and shortly after appointed to the office of High Commissioner for adjusting the claims of Canada, but resigned the office without entering on its duties.

In 1811, Lord Canterbury married a daughter of John Dennison, Esq., of Ossington, Nottinghamshire (who died in 1815), by whom he had issue,

1. Charles John, the present viscount, born in 1812.

2. John Henry Thomas (formerly Under Secretary of State for the Home Department), born in 1814.

3. Charlotte Matilda (who married Richard Sanderson, Esq., M.P., in 1833).

His lordship married secondly, the 6th of December, 1828, Ellen, daughter of Edmund Power, and widow of John Home Purves, Esq., of Purves Hall, N. B., and by her had issue,

1. Frances Diana, born in 1829.
2. A son, born in 1831, who died in infancy.

His lordship was seized with apoplexy while traveling on the Great Western Railway, and conveyed to Paddington in a state of insensibility. He was removed to the house of his younger son, in Southwick Crescent, where, having lingered in the same unconscious condition for three days, he died, in his sixty-sixth year, in July, 1845. His remains were interred at Addington, with those of his father, the late archbishop.

Probate of the will of the late Viscount Canterbury was granted to his second son, the Hon. H. T. Manners Sutton, one of the executors, on the 16th of February, 1846. His lordship directed, at the death of the viscountess (who survived him only four months), the sum of £20,000, the dividends of which constituted her jointure, should be divided in four parts; his eldest daughter taking first therefrom £1000, appropriating to his two sons one fourth part each, and the remainder to his youngest daughter. He directed also the sum of £75,000, settled on him for life on his first marriage, should be equally divided among his two sons and eldest daughter, the issue of that marriage. All other property not specially disposed of, to be divided into four parts between the viscountess, the two sons, and youngest daughter. Of Lady Canterbury a few words remain to be said.

Ellen, the third daughter of Edmund Power, of Curragheen, and younger sister of Lady Blessington, was born at Knockbrit, in the county of Tipperary, in 1791.

She was one year, at least, younger than her sister Marguerite, and in early life surpassed the latter in beauty and gracefulness, though not in intellectual powers. Miss Ellen Power grew up to womanhood, surrounded by the same unhappy influences and unfavorable circumstances in her father's house as her sister had to contend with, and often spoke of in after-life in terms of regret, and even of reprobation.

In 1806, Mr. Edmund Power having been prosecuted by Mr. Bagwell, of Kilmore, for a libel published in the "Clonmel Gazette," written by Solomon Watson, a Quaker merchant of Clonmel, in favor of the views and interests of Lord Donoughmore, a verdict was given against Power for £500 damages. This occurrence brought the embarrassed affairs of Power to the verge of utter ruin. Ultimately Lord Donoughmore was induced to do something, in conjunction with Watson, toward indemnifying Power. From that period Lord Donoughmore was a constant visitor and a favored guest at the house of the nearly ruined editor of the "Clonmel Gazette."

The necessity of feasting his lordship and his friends led to renewed and augmented extravagance in the way of entertainments.

Mr. Power's house became, in fact, the resort of the young squirearchy of the vicinity, the professional people of Clonmel, who were the adherents of the Hutchinson family and that of Lord Llandaff, and of the military officers stationed in the town.

Miss Ellen Power's personal attractions had rendered her at a very early age an object of general admiration. She was in the habit of accompanying her sister to balls and parties in the town of Clonmel and its vicinity, and to a sort of subscription soirées, which were given at particular seasons in the town of Tipperary, and were called "Coteries." There are persons living who remember meeting the beautiful Misses Power at those parties, and recall the pleasures they experienced in dancing with them.

A Mr. Scully has a vivid and pleasing recollection of the "Coteries," and his fair partners from Clonmel. Miss Margaret Power was an admirable dancer: the excellence of her taste and dress, and the elegance of her costume, were never equaled at the "Coteries," even by her sister. But Miss Ellen Power surpassed all the belles of those parties in the symmetry of her slight form, and the quiet, simple beauty of her calm, marble-like features, which had all the repose and perfection of outline of a finely-sculptured bust of a Grecian divinity.

Yet her sister Margaret, then far less beautiful, had the art of withdrawing attention from surrounding competitors for admiration, of engaging observation, and entertaining as well as retaining admirers.

The difference in the manners of the two fair sisters is described as being remarkable by persons who have a lively recollection of them at the period referred to. Margaret always manifested that desire to please, which gave a piquant character of agreeable coquetry to her *agrèmens* of conversation and deportment in after-life, and which reminds one of a distinction she drew, in one of those aphorisms which she was in the habit of setting down in the "Night Thought" books, between coquetry and a laudable desire to please:

"The desire to please half accomplishes its object, and is in itself praiseworthy, when self-gratification is not the aim or end of it. Yet has it often been mistaken for coquetry, from which it totally differs. The first extends to our own sex as much as the other, while the second is addressed peculiarly to the male. The woman who desires to please spreads a charm over the circle in which she moves; the coquette merely gratifies the vanity of men by evincing her wish to attract them."

And elsewhere, in one of the same MS. books:

"A desire to shine proceeds from vanity, but a desire to please proceeds from *bienveillance*. Without the latter disposition, no woman was ever loved, or man was ever popular."

Ellen Power manifested neither the desire to shine, nor an anxious solicitude to please. She seemed conscious of being entitled to admiration, and in receiving it sometimes seemed as if it would have cost her no great effort to spurn it.

All persons who remember the daughters of Edmund Power from 1804 to 1807 concur in the observation that it was surprising to see girls so little indebted to the advantages of education, rank, and fashion in society, in their manners, carriage, and attire appear on a par with ladies of the highest rank—"there was a natural gentility and refinement about them, which had no air of affectation whatsoever in it."

Miss Ellen Power had no lack of admirers, however, and of offers of marriage, some of which had been declined by her, or by her family, about the period of her sister's separating from her husband.

Among the admirers of Miss Ellen Power was the lieutenant colonel of the Tyrone militia, Colonel William Stewart, of Killymoon, near Cookstown, in the county of Tyrone, who had made her acquaintance between 1806 and 1807. The colonel was a large landed proprietor, an intimate friend of the young Lord Mountjoy, whose Tyrone property was adjacent to the Killymoon estates.* But the colonel was not a marrying man. He lived and died in single blessedness.

When Mrs. Farmer was residing at Fethard, after her separation from her husband, and a residence of some months at her father's in Clonmel, Miss Ellen Power visited her sister, and remained with her at Fethard, but for how long a period I am unable to state.

When Mrs. Farmer went to reside in England, she was also invited there by her sister; and while sojourning with her, about the year 1813, first made the acquaintance of John Home Purves, Esq., a Scotch gentleman of good family, and at one period an expectant of the baronetcy, at the death of his father, during the absence of an elder brother, who had been long absent from his native land.

Mr. John Home was the son of Sir Alexander Purves, of Purves Hall, county Berwick, who succeeded to the baronetcy in 1761. Sir Alexander married four times; by his first marriage he had issue one son and three daughters. By his second marriage he had issue four sons and four daughters. By his third marriage he had issue two sons and one daughter. By his fourth marriage he had issue an only son.

Sir Alexander Purves died in 1813, and was succeeded by his eldest son, Sir William, born in 1767 (the step-brother of John Home Purves, Esq.). Sir William, who had assumed the additional surname of Campbell, died in 1833, leaving an only child, the present baronet, Sir Hugh Hume Campbell.

Persons who have a remembrance of Mr. John Home Purves when on a visit at Mountjoy Forest, in the county of Tyrone, in 1816, speak of this gentleman as "Major Purves," and several have an impression in their minds that he held that rank in the Scots Greys, which I believe to be erroneous. The

* The same fate was reserved for the large properties of Colonel Stewart as for those of the Earl of Blessington. The estates of both have passed into the hands of strangers. The Colonel died in 1850. Killymoon and its noble mansion were sold in the Encumbered Estates' Court.

acquaintance of Mr. Purves* with Miss Ellen Power was probably not anterior to the year 1813.

Circumstances led to Mr. Purves separating himself from his family in the year 1823. He obtained the office of British Consul at Pensacola, and there he died, from the effects of the climate, in 1827.

In the "Gentleman's Magazine" for that year, part ii., p. 573, we find the following notice of his death:

"At Pensacola, on the 20th of September, 1827, aged forty-two, John Home Purves, Esq., for the last four years British Consul at that place. He was eldest son of Sir Alexander Purves, the fifth and late baronet of Purves Hall, in Berwickshire, by his second wife, Mary, daughter of Sir James Home, of Blackadder, and was consequently half-brother to Sir William, the present baronet of the Purves family, who assumed the names of Hume Campbell on the death of the late Earl of Marchmont."

Mrs. Purves, who had remained in England, was left with five children:

1. Louisa, married to J. Fairlie, Esq., died in April, 1843, aged about thirty-three.
2. Mary, died unmarried at Cheveley.
3. Margaret, married Augustus Tollemache, Esq.
4. John, an only son, unmarried.
5. Ellen, married —— Arkwright, Esq.

In the latter part of 1828, Mrs. Purves married the Speaker of the House of Commons. The "Annual Register" for that year thus records the marriage: "The 6th of December, 1828, at St. George's Church, Hanover Square, Mrs. Home Purves, widow of the late John Purves, Esq., to the Right Honorable Charles Manners Sutton, Speaker of the House of Commons."

Moore, in his "Diary," speaks of Mrs. Manners Sutton and the speaker's residence at Westminster: "Amused to see her, in all her state, the same hearty, lively Irishwoman still. Walked with her in the garden, the moonlight on the river, the boats gliding along it, the towers of Lambeth on the opposite bank, the lights of Westminster bridge gleaming on the left, and then, when one turned round to the house, that beautiful Gothic structure, illuminated from within, and at that moment containing within it the council of the nation, all was most picturesque and striking."†

The same ruin that at a later period came on the fortunes of the proprietors of Gore House, was destined for those of the mistress of the establishment, with all its state, at Westminster, which Moore refers to.

Lord Canterbury held the office of speaker for eighteen years. When he retired in 1835, on his retiring pension of £4000 a year, his circumstances were involved in difficulties of an extensive nature, and a very large portion of them were not created by him.

* A Lieutenant John Purves (Adjutant), of the Royal Wagon Train, appears in the Army Lists from 1804 to 1809, when he appears to have been promoted, and continued in the rank of captain in that corps till 1812.

† Moore's Memoirs, vol. vi., p. 32.

The loss of the speakership was poorly compensated by the pension and the peerage in 1835. Lord Canterbury's difficulties in a short time became overwhelming. The latter years of Lady Canterbury's life were disquieted and seriously troubled by those embarrassments, and the very straitened circumstances which were the result of the loss of the speaker's office and its large emoluments. But, to the honor of this lady be it stated, no effort was left untried by her to adapt her mode of life to the altered circumstances of her husband, and with the utmost cheerfulness she gave up all those luxuries to which she had been accustomed; nay, even comforts that people in middle life deem almost necessary in their families. She laid down her carriage, parted with ornaments of value, and objects precious in themselves or from the recollection of those from whom they had been received, and lived only to cheer the drooping spirits and to watch over the impaired health of her amiable and kind-hearted husband.

Lady Canterbury survived her husband only four months; after a brief residence on the Continent, she had returned to England, quite broken down in health and spirits. Her sister, Lady Blessington, by whom she was tenderly loved, was frequently with her in her last illness, and at the moment of her death. An attached servant of Lady Blessington, a person of respectability, excellent character, and superior intelligence, who had lived with her Ladyship fifteen years, Mrs. Cooper, was also in attendance on Lady Canterbury in her last illness. She states that her ladyship's strong sense of religion was manifested in the most edifying manner through her entire illness, and on many occasions by earnest and fervent prayers that her sister Marguerite might be turned to the consideration of the things of eternity, and that her thoughts might be taken away from the turmoil of the things of time, and the vanities of life by which she was surrounded. This amiable and once beautiful woman died at Clifton, in the fifty-fourth year of her age, on the 16th of November, 1845. The remains of Lady Canterbury were interred with those of her husband in the crypt of Clifton church.

The late Viscountess Canterbury by her will left a valuable service of porcelain china, formerly belonging to Archbishop Sutton, to the present viscount; to her son, Captain J. Home Purves, of the Guards, all her plate which had belonged to her previous to her marriage with the late viscount; and to her daughters Mary and Ellen, all the furniture and books, and to her daughter Frances the contents of her two jewel boxes deposited at her banker's. Bequests to the amount of £6000 she left between her three daughters, Margaret Home Purves, Ellen Home Purves, and Frances D. Manners Sutton. The residue of her property, real and personal, she left to the same parties. Specific bequests were made to the Honorable Mrs. Sanderson, Lord Auckland, and her ladyship's sister, the Countess of Blessington.

MRS. FAIRLIE.

The favorite niece of Lady Blessington—the eldest daughter of her sister Ellen, can not fail to be well and most advantageously known to the correspondents of Lady Blessington, and those who enjoyed the friendship of that lady. Lady Blessington seemed to take a particular delight in speaking of Louisa Fairlie and her interesting child, "the beautiful mute," whose mind it was the greatest of all Lady Blessington's enjoyments to see gradually developed.

Mrs. Fairlie had married at an early age a gentleman not of large fortune, John Fairlie, Esq. She endeavored to add to those scanty resources by literary labors, and it is to be feared she impaired her delicate health by them.

Mrs. Fairlie was a contributor to Lady Blessington's Annual, "the Keepsake," and to other similar periodicals, and eventually became the editor of one of them, entitled "The Children of the Nobility." Many of her poetical pieces evince considerable talent, and all her compositions singular purity of mind and unaffected religiousness of feeling. This disposition to piety was manifested in her whole life and conversation; and in the few letters of hers which are given to the public, the feeling will be found expressed in such amiable, gentle, and graceful language, in all simplicity and naturalness, as can not fail to render devotional sentiments powerful in influence and effect. A few months before her decease she lost a child of extraordinary intellectual powers, though deaf and dumb from her birth. This interesting little girl was well known to the distinguished literary people who frequented Mrs. Fairlie's and Gore House some twenty years ago, and was the theme of many admirable verses in praise of the loveliness and mental qualities of the beautiful mute.

LINES OF B. D'ISRAELI, Esq.,

TO A BEAUTIFUL MUTE,

THE ELDEST CHILD OF MRS. FAIRLIE.

1.

"Tell me the star from which she fell,
Oh! name the flower
From out whose wild and perfumed bell,
At witching hour,
Sprang forth this fair and fairy maiden,
Like a bee with honey laden.

2.

"They say that those sweet lips of thine
Breathe not to speak;
Thy very ears, that seem so fine,
No sound can seek.
And yet thy face beams with emotion,
Restless as the waves of ocean.

3.

"'Tis well; thy face and form agree,
And both are fair.
I would not that this child should be
As others are;
I love to mark her in derision
Smiling with seraphic vision

4.

"At our poor gifts of vulgar sense,
That can not stain
Nor mar her mystic innocence,
Nor cloud her brain
With all the dreams of worldly folly,
And its creature melancholy.

5.

"To thee I dedicate these lines,
Yet read them not.
Cursed be the art that e'er refines
Thy natural lot;
Read the bright stars, and read the flowers,
And hold converse with the bowers."

Lady Blessington was greatly attached to her sister Lady Canterbury and her children, but her affection for Mrs. Fairlie was stronger perhaps than for any member of her family, and the interest she took in that lady's eldest daughter Isabella, the singularly intellectually gifted child, though deprived of the faculties of speech and hearing, can only be imagined by those who have heard her speak of her "darling Isabella."

The following letters and lines of Mrs. Fairlie will give some idea of the amiable character and spiritual mind of this accomplished and most excellent lady.

Letter from Mrs. Fairlie, on the last illness of her daughter Isabella, the subject of D'Israeli's lines, "the Beautiful Mute."

"My dearest Aunt,—How much longer it will last, God only knows; she is very patient, and she looks like herself. I have been with her all day yesterday. I said on my fingers, 'Jesus wants you! will you go?' she nodded.

"To-day she turned and said, 'I want to die.' I fancy she will live till near Thursday. Oh, this is indeed a trial! but God be praised, he supports me, as he promised in his holy word. God bless you! and do, dear aunt, think seriously, and turn to the Lord while he may be found!"

From Mrs. Fairlie:

"My dearest Aunt,—I was in her room till near five yesterday, from ten in the morning. I came in to tea, and we saw no change; she dozed. At seven, being sadly fatigued, I went to bed, hearing she was the same. At about twenty minutes past seven, she told White she wished to be moved from the bed to the sofa, and John assisted to do this. Two minutes after, she was dying; John came and carried me in, and I saw my first-born die peacefully—no groan, no struggle. She had lived to show forth the power and glory of God, and she died, knowing that but for Jesus she could not be saved.

"On Saturday morning, at five, John and Somerset purpose leaving this, and the funeral will be at Marylebone Church at twelve, and they return by the half past three train.

"I cut off Isabella's plaits, and send you one just as it is. Oh, how mercifully God supports me! May you, my own darling aunt, learn to feel the power of religion.

"Your fond Louisa."

From Mrs. Fairlie:

"———, 1843.

"My dearest dear Aunt,—I was glad you were where I fain would have been yesterday; you were mistaken in thinking I wished to deprive you wholly of the dear little note. I return it. I only wanted it yesterday; the day week it was written. I have borne this wonderfully; but God promises his strength, and he gives it.

"I am not so well as I have been; but still, no one could expect me to be half so well as I am.

"If you knew all the worry about the coffins, and the outer one—such an affair at last, only ready on Friday. But it matters not. The inner one (under the lead), so large, and long and deep, we had to use a mattress pillow, sheet, and wadding to fill it and keep the body from moving.

"Auckland tells me he wanted to attend the funeral, and was at the church, but missed the hour, which we understand, as you were there an hour or more behind time.

"How I bless God for the loan of that precious child, and for his aid in enabling me to train her in the ways of piety. How boldly she ever rebuked sin. Do you remember how it pained her that you should, in any way, profane the Lord's day by visitors or driving out? At her baptism she was 'signed with the cross, in token that she should not be ashamed to confess the faith of Christ crucified, but manfully fight under his banner against the devil, the world, and sin, and continue his faithful soldier and servant unto death.' She did so continue, God be praised!!!

"If Johnnie comes this week, could you spare dear Elly for a few days? Her address I inclose. That will be but a very short visit, but then, perhaps, Mag giewill come and visit me. I am very tired now, so end all in a hurry.

"Your own fond and most anxious Louisa.

"I hope you will read the book I sent by White."

The note of the dear child referred to in the preceding letter of Mrs. Fairlie:

"My dear Aunt,—I am so pain in my breast, and cough a deal. I thank you for a barley-sugar and large cake. Papa gave me a flower paper. I am writing in bed, at night: how kind you are to bring what I want. Mamma send me large round barley-sugar, not like you give me. Give my love to Alfred, Margery, Ellen, from I. L. F."

ENDORSED.

"Written by my blessed grand-niece, Isabella Louisa Fairlie, on Saturday night, the 28th of January, 1843. She expired on the 31st, at twenty minutes before eight in the evening, resigning her pure spirit without a groan or struggle. M. B."

LINES WRITTEN BY MRS. FAIRLIE.

"May 12, 1842.

"I used to place my happiness
In scenes of youthful mirth,
And think that I could never tire
Of this small speck of earth.

"Then years flew on: I placed my heart
On one well worth its love;

He and my babes had every thought,
  Instead of God above.

"But now, O thou long-suffering God!
  Thou truly art ador'd;
Husband and babes are fondly loved,
  But more I love thee, Lord. L. F."

DIALOGUE.

BY MRS. FAIRLIE.

"Old man, thou art poor, and thy house of clay
Must soon fall to ruin: Oh hast thou, say,
  No friend who will cheer thy gloom?"
"Oh yes, gentle maid. I've a pow'rful friend,
His patient affection will never end,
  It will last beyond the tomb."

"Then why does he never thy cottage cheer?
Old man, I have never seen him here.
  Does he give thee fire or food?"
"Oh, lady, my friend is my constant guest;
He counsels, upholds me, and gives me rest;
  He's long-suffering, gentle, good.

"If I eat his food I shall never die,
It will nourish me eternally;
  And in his bless'd abode
A place is prepared for me, and I long
To join the blissful and ransom'd throng,
  Who surround the throne of God."

"Old man, it now is made plain to me,
What ever has been a mystery;
  The cheerful look amid pain.
I'll call on this friend, I will seek the Lord—"
"Do, lady, and trust thy Redeemer's word,
  That none shall seek in vain." L. F., May 12, 1842.

Mrs. Fairlie died at Cheveley, near Newmarket, in April, 1843, after a protracted illness. She survived her beautiful and interesting child little more than two months. That sweet child had gone before her angelic mother to a fitting home on high, the 31st of January, 1843.

No. II.—INTRODUCTION, p. 13.

THE FATE OF THE SHEEHYS IN 1765 AND 1766.

THE maternal grandfather of the Countess of Blessington, a Roman Catholic gentleman of an ancient family in Tipperary, and in comfortable circumstances, Edmund Sheehy, Esq., was one of the victims of the murderous spirit of religious rancor which prevailed about the middle of the eighteenth century. Young Mr. Sheehy was persecuted to the death by the Terrorists of Tipperary of those times, on a charge of White Boyism, and executed at Clogheen, near Clonmel, on that charge, the 3d of May, 1766. A cousin of his, the Rev. Nicholas Sheehy, was likewise sacrificed at the same period, on a charge of White Boyism, with one of murder superadded.

The Rev. Mr. Sheehy was a man of unblemished character; a pious, zealous clergyman, earnest in his endeavors to promote religion and justice in his parish, and to protect his parishioners from the extortions of tithe proctors and church-rate collectors. In the parish of Newcastle, he had denounced some rapacious proceedings of the extortionist farmers of these imposts; and for this crime of interference between the people and their exacting masters, he was soon "a marked man," and in due time a persecuted one.

"The Dublin Gazette" of the 16th of March, 1765, announces that, "About eight o'clock on Wednesday night, Nicholas Sheehy, a popish priest, charged with being concerned in several treasonable practices to raise a rebellion in this kingdom, for the apprehending of whom government offered a reward of £300, was brought to town guarded by a party of light horse, and lodged by the Provost in the Lower Castle Yard." It was not till the 10th of February, in the following year, that he was brought to trial in the Court of King's Bench. The Lord Chief Justice of the King's Bench, then, was the Right Honorable John Gore; second justice, Mr. Christopher Robinson; third justice, William Scott, Esq. The indictment charged the prisoner with acting as a leader in a treasonable conspiracy, exercising men under arms, swearing them to allegiance to the French king, and inciting them to rebellion. The witnesses produced were a man of the name of John Toohy, a prisoner in Kilkenny jail, committed on a charge of horse-stealing; a woman of the name of Mary Butler, and a vagrant boy named Lonergan.

It would be difficult to comprehend the nature or extent of the wickedness exhibited in these proceedings, without referring to the circumstances which rendered Sheehy and others more obnoxious to the magisterial conspirators than other persons of his persuasion in the neighborhood, who had the good fortune to escape being similarly implicated. The inclosing of commonage in the neighborhood of Clogheen in the winter of 1761–2 had inflicted much injury on the parishioners of Father Sheehy.

About that time, the tithes of two Protestant clergymen, Messrs. Foulkes and Sutton, in the vicinity of Ballyporeen, were rented to a tithe proctor of the name of Dobbyn. The tithe farmer instituted in 1762 a new claim on the Roman Catholic people in this district, of five shillings for every marriage celebrated by a priest. This new impost was resisted by the people, and as it fell heavily on the poor of the parish of Father Sheehy, it was publicly denounced by him. The first "risings" in his neighborhood were connected with their resistance to this odious tax.

The various informations and indictments framed against the obnoxious priest show plainly enough, differing as they do in the most material particulars, yet concurring in one point, the influence of Sheehy over his parishioners, that his persecutors were casting about them at random for evidence of any kind or character that might rid them of the annoyance of a man of an independent mind, and, by his implication, give additional color to the pretended popish plot.

For several months previously to Mr. Sheehy's surrender, he had been in concealment, flying from house to house of such of his parishioners as he could confide in. He had been frequently obliged to change his abode to avoid the rigorous searches that were almost daily made for him. At length, terror and corruption had exerted such an influence over his own flock, that he hardly knew whom to trust, or in whose house to seek an asylum. Indeed, it is impossible to wade through the mass of informations sworn to against him by persons of various grades, without wondering at the extent and successfulness of the villainy that was practiced against him. His last place of refuge at Clogheen was in the house of a small farmer, a Protestant, of the name of Griffiths, adjoining the church-yard of Shandrahan, where his remains now lie. The windows of his house open into the church-yard, and there Father Sheehy was concealed for three days, hid during the day in a vault in the latter place, and during the night in the house, when it was necessary to keep up a large fire, so benumbed with cold he used to be when brought at nightfall from the place that was, indeed, his living tomb. The house is still standing, and inhabited by the grandson of his faithful friend, and one not of his own creed, it is to be remembered.

The last service rendered to him at Clogheen was likewise by a Protestant, a gentleman in the commission of the peace, Mr. Cornelius O'Callaghan, and to whom he surrendered himself. This gentleman gave him one of his horses to convey him to Dublin, and the sum of ten guineas to bear his expenses.

Mr. O'Callaghan's high rank, his character for loyalty, his position in society, were not sufficient to secure him from the malignity of the magisterial conspirators. Mr. O'Callaghan was denounced by Justice Bagwell as a suspected person; Lord James Cahir, the ancestor of Lord Glengall, was likewise declared to be on the black list of this gentleman, and of his associate, the Rev. J. Hewetson. Both these gentlemen had to fly the country to save their lives, and the noblemen who are their successors would do well to remember how necessary it is to keep the administration of justice in pure hands, that rapacious villainy may be discomfited in its attempts to promote its interests by the inculpation of men who have broad lands and local influence to be deprived of by convictions and confiscations.

One of the earliest charges of White Boyism brought against Father Sheehy stands thus recorded in the indictment and information book in the Crown Office:*

* The above document, and all the others of a similar kind, which are here given, were

"Nicholas Sheehy, bailed in £2000; Dennis Keane, £1000; Nicholas Dogherty, £1000. A true bill. Clonmel General Assizes, May 23, 1763, before Right Hon. Warden Flood and Hon. William Scott. Nicholas Sheehy, a popish priest, bound over in court last assizes, trial then put off by the court, indicted for that he, with divers others, ill-disposed persons and disturbers of the peace, on the second day of March, in the second year of the reign of George III., at Scarlap, did unlawfully assemble and assault William Ross, and did wickedly compel him to swear that he would never discover any thing to the prejudice of the White Boys, &c. William Ross bound over in £100, estreated; James Ross, £100, estreated."

At Clonmel Summer Assizes of 1764, Nicholas Sheehy was again indicted, and seven other persons, out on bail, were included in the same indictment, wherein it set forth, "That they on the 6th of January, in the fourth year of the king's reign, at Shanbally, did assault John Bridge, against the peace."

At the same assizes, a true bill was found against Edward Meehan, Nicholas Sheehan, Nicholas Lee, John Magan, John Butler, and Edmund Burke, charging them with "compassing rebellion at Clogheen, on the 7th of March and 6th of October, second year of the king, and unlawfully assembling in white shirts, in arms, when they did traitorously prepare, ordain, and levy war against the king;" and bound to appear as witnesses, Michael Guynan, Thomas Lonergan, and Mary Butler.

On the 19th of November, 1764, Denis Brien, of Ballyporeen, was bound over before Mr. Cornelius O'Callaghan, to appear at the following assizes, "to answer *all things brought against him* by Michael Guynan, John Bridge, *or any other person, concerning the late disturbances.*"

The number of informations sworn to against all the leading Catholic gentry of the county, by the Lonergans, Guynan, Toohy, a horse-stealer, and two abandoned women, of the names of Butler and Dunlay, between the years 1763 and 1767, would fill a good-sized volume. The names of the magistrates before whom these informations, in almost every instance, were sworn, were John Bagwell, Thomas Maude, and the Rev. J. Hewetson.

At the general assizes held at Clonmel, the 16th of March, 1765, before Chief Baron Willes and Mr. Justice Tennison, the following bills, found at the former assizes, were brought before the grand jury. Some of the trials were put off, all the parties admitted to bail, or allowed to stand out on heavy recognizances; and the names of the persons who bailed the prisoners are deserving of notice, for it will be found that to enter into sureties for a man marked out for ruin by the Clonmel conspirators was to draw down the vengeance of these conspirators on those who dared to come forward as witnesses, and stand between the victims and their persecutors.

I doubt if anything more terribly iniquitous than the proceedings which I have traced in these official records is to be met with in the history of any modern conspiracy.

collected by myself, and copied from the original official documents in the Crown Office of Clonmel, many years ago.

The high sheriff in 1765 was Sir Thomas Maude ; the foreman of the grand jury, Richard Pennefeather, Esq. The following are the persons named as having been formerly indicted and held to bail :

"Edmund Burke, of Tullow, bail £500 ; his sureties, John Hogan and Thomas Hickey, of Frehans.

"John Butler, innkeeper, Clogheen, bail £500 ; his sureties, George Everard, of Lisheenanoul, and James Butler, of Gurranne, county Cork.

"Edward Meehan, Clogheen, £500 ; his sureties, Pierce Nagle, of Flemingstown ; John Butler, of Mitchelstown ; James Hickey, of Frehans ; John Bourk, of Rouska.

"Nicholas Sheehy, surrendered ; James Buxton, Patrick Condon, and Patrick Boar, out."

The preceding details sufficiently explain the views and objects of the prosecutors, and their temporary defeat by the terms entered into by Father Sheehy with government, by which a trial in Dublin was secured to him.

The trial, which took place on the 10th of February, 1766, in the Court of King's Bench, was impartially conducted ; the conduct of the "managers," who got up the evidence, at every turn of the testimony, bore on its face the evident marks of subornation of perjury. The vile witnesses broke down, and after a trial of fourteen hours' duration, the persecuted priest was honorably acquitted. He had redeemed his pledge to the government, he had given himself up, stood his trial, and proved his innocence. But no sooner was the verdict pronounced, than the faith of government was broken with him. The unfortunate man was informed by the chief justice that a charge of murder was brought against him, and on this charge he must be committed to Newgate. He was accordingly taken from the dock, removed to the prison, and, after two or three days' imprisonment, was put into the hands of his merciless persecutors, to be forthwith conveyed to Clonmel.

The first intimation of the new charge against him was given to him in Dublin, a few days previously to his trial, by a person named O'Brien, who had accompanied him from Clogheen. Martin O'Brien, on account of his intelligence and prudence, had been chosen by the friends of the priest to accompany him to Dublin, and he gave some proof of his fitness for his appointment by strongly urging on him, a few days previously to his trial, to quit the kingdom. Father Sheehy was then at large ; he had been confined for a few days after his surrender in the provost in the castle-yard. He was placed under the charge of Major Joseph Sirr, then town-major, and father to the person of less enviable notoriety in the same office at a later period. His innocence was so manifest to Mr. Secretary Waite and to Major Sirr, that he was relieved from all restraint, and the latter held himself responsible for his appearance at the time appointed for his trial.

While he was at large, he was informed by O'Brien that a person had brought him an account from Clonmel, that no sooner had the news of Father Sheehy's surrender been received, than a rumor got abroad that a charge of murder was to be brought against him. He recommended Father Sheehy not to lose a moment in getting out of the kingdom, and urgently pressed him to put himself the same day on board a packet for England.

O'Brien several years afterward stated to my informant, that Sheehy smiled at the proposal. He said, "The rumor of Bridge's death was raised only to frighten him out of the country, but he would not gratify his enemies, and if they brought such a monstrous charge against him, he could easily disprove it. Sheehy's arrival in Dublin, it is to be borne in mind, was only five months after the alleged murder, and at the time of his departure from Clogheen, it is positively affirmed by Magrath, on the authority of O'Brien, that Father Sheehy had then no knowledge of the murder; and the probability is, that it was in Dublin a fugitive named Mahony, when about quitting the kingdom, had made the revelations to him.

Sheehy was conveyed on horseback, under a strong military escort, to Clonmel, his arms pinioned, and his feet tied under the horse's belly. While in confinement in the jail of Clonmel, he was double bolted, and treated in every respect with the utmost rigor. In this condition he was seen by one of his old friends, and while this gentleman was condoling with him on his unfortunate condition, he pointed to his legs, which were ulcerated by the cords he had been bound with on his way from Dublin. He said, laughing, "Never mind, we will defeat these fellows;" and he began humming a verse of the old Irish song of "*Shaun na guira.*"

On the 12th of March, 1766, Sheehy was put on his trial at Clonmel for the murder of John Bridge. Most of the witnesses who gave evidence on the former trial were produced on this occasion.

Nicholas Sheehy was indicted on the charge of having been present at and aiding and abetting Edmund Meighan in the murder of John Bridge. Mr. Sheehy had a sister, Mrs. Green, who resided at Shanbally, in the vicinity of Clogheen; and at this place, according to the evidence, the murder of Bridge, Lord Carrick, Mr. John Bagnell, Mr. William Bagnell, and other persons obnoxious to them, was first proposed by Mr. Sheehy to a numerous assemblage of White Boys; and by him, all those present were sworn to secrecy, fidelity to the French king, and the commission of the proposed murders, and subsequently the murder was committed by one of the party, named Edmund Meighan, of Grange, in the month of October, 1764.

Sheehy and Meighan were tried separately. The same evidence for the prosecution was produced on both trials. The notes of one of the jurors, taken at the trial of the latter, were communicated to the editor of "The Gentleman's and London Magazine," with a view to establish the guilt of the accused parties; and, therefore, the account is to be taken as one, the leaning of which was certainly toward the prosecutors, and in support of the finding of the jury.* There is evidence, however, on the face of this report, of the innocence of the prisoners. John Bridge, the man alleged to have been

* Gentleman's and London Magazine, June, 1766, page 370.

murdered, was a simple, harmless creature of weak intellect, and was accustomed to go about the country among the small farmers, with whom he was a favorite, and was looked on by them as a good-natured poor fellow, who, having no friend or relatives, had some claim to their kindness. When the head-quarters of the Earl of Drogheda were at Clogheen, he had been taken up on suspicion of White Boyism, or for the purpose of obtaining information from him ; he was flogged with great severity, and under that torture made disclosures which were supposed sufficient to implicate several persons in the neighborhood of Clogheen.

The discovery of the remains of a man alleged to have been murdered, on the trial of the persons charged with his murder, it might have been imagined, would have been a matter of some importance. But the fact of the parties who swore they had been present at the murder and interment of the body having failed to substantiate the latter part of their statement by the discovery of his remains was of no advantage to the accused.

Dr. Curry, in his pamphlet, the "Candid Inquiry," alludes to a letter which Sheehy wrote to Major Sirr the day before his execution, wherein he admitted that the murder of Bridge had been revealed to him in a manner he could not avail himself of for his own preservation ; and that the murder had been committed by two persons, not by those sworn to by the witnesses, and in a different manner to that described by them. Curry admits this letter was written by Sheehy, but he does not insert it ; and in his subsequent work, "The Review of the Civil Wars," there is no mention at all made of it in his account of these proceedings. Having obtained a copy of this letter, the first point to ascertain was, if the letter was written by Sheehy, or fabricated by his enemies. The result of my inquiries was to convince me that the letter was genuine. It was declared to be so by the successor of Father Sheehy, in the parish of Clogheen (Mr. Keating), to Mr. Flannery, another clergyman, living in the same place, at a later period. Dr. Egan, who then administered the diocese, had likewise declared it to be genuine. The present parish priest of Clogheen, a relative of Edmund Sheehy, believes it to be genuine. One of the Roman Catholic clergymen of Clonmel, who takes the deepest interest in the fate of Father Sheehy, has no doubt of its authenticity. Every surviving relative of either of the Sheehys with whom I have communicated entertains the same opinion ; and lastly, I may observe, the document bears the internal evidence of authenticity in its style and tone.

The following is a literal copy of this document:

"TO JOSEPH SIRR, ESQ., DUBLIN.

"Clonmel, Friday morning, March 14, 1766.

"DEAR SIR,—To-morrow I am to be executed, thanks be to the Almighty God, with whom I hope to be for evermore: I would not change my lot with the highest now in the kingdom. I die innocent of the facts for which I am sentenced. The Lord have mercy on my soul! I beseech the great Creator that for your benevolence to me he will grant you grace to make such use of your time here that you may see and enjoy him hereafter. Remember me to Mr. Waite, the lord chancellor, speaker, and the judges of the King's

Bench; may God bless them! Recommend to them, all under the same charge with me; they are innocent of the murder; the prosecutors swore wrongfully and falsely; God forgive them. The accusers and the accused are equally ignorant of the fact, as I have been informed, but after such a manner I received the information that I can not make use of it for my own preservation; the fact is, that John Bridge was destroyed by two alone, who strangled him on Wednesday night, the 24th of October, 1764. I was then from home, and only returned home the 28th, and heard that he had disappeared. Various were the reports, which to believe I could not pretend to, until in the discharge of my duty one accused himself of the said fact. May God grant the guilty true repentance, and preserve the innocent! I recommend them to your care. I have relied very much on Mr. Waite's promise. I hope no more priests will be distressed for their religion, and that the Roman Catholics of this kingdom will be countenanced by the government, as I was promised by Mr. Waite would be the case if I proved my innocence. I am now to appear before the Divine tribunal, and declare that I was unacquainted with Mary Butler, *alias* Casey, and John Toohy, never having spoken to or seen either of them, to the best of my memory, before I saw them in the King's Bench last February. May God forgive them, and bless them, you, and all mankind, are the earnest and fervent prayers of, dear sir, your most obliged, humble servant,

"NICHOLAS SHEEHY."

The witnesses stated that the murder was committed the 28th of October, 1764. Father Sheehy says it was on the 24th. The number of persons implicated in it by the former was considerable; by the latter, only two were concerned in it. In the mode of committing it, the discrepancy of the accounts is no less obvious.

The question arises, When was this confession made to Father Sheehy, and with what object? Amyas Griffith speaks of the disclosure thus made under the veil of confession as "no new method of entrapping credulous priests."

Curry treats the disclosure as a snare laid by the enemies of Sheehy for their own purposes. The purposes to be served by having recourse to the infamous proceeding of deceiving the unwary priest, and of making the functions of his sacred office subservient to the designs of his enemies, could only be the following. If resorted to previously to trial, by the disclosure of the alleged murder to deter him from adducing evidence of the man's existence; or, if subsequently to it, to leave it out of his power to make any declaration of his ignorance of the fact of his alleged death.

The attempt for the accomplishment of either object was not too unimportant for the character of the prosecutors; nor can it be deemed too infamous to be beyond the compass of their wickedness when we find them holding out offers of pardon to their three next victims, on condition of their making a declaration that "the priest," in his last solemn protestation of innocence, "had died with a lie in his mouth."

Bridge had been sought out, at the commencement of the persecution of the Sheehys, as a fit person to be worked upon by the influence of terror and the infliction of corporal judgment.

This man, having been tortured, made whatever disclosures were suggested to him or required of him; and he was bound over to appear as a witness when called on. He made no secret of the punishment he had received or the disclosures he had made, and some of the people implicated by him were desirous to get him out of the country; others, in his own rank in life, there is reason to believe, distrusted his intention to leave the country, and contrived a nefarious plot to get rid of his testimony, by implicating him in felony.

The church plate, chalice, &c., of a small Roman Catholic place of worship *at Carrigvistail, near Ballyporeen, usually kept for better security at the house* of an inn-keeper of the name of Sherlock,* adjoining the chapel, were stolen, or said to be so, and concealed on the premises, with the knowledge, it is alleged, of the owner of the house. The facts now mentioned have not been published heretofore, and the importance of their bearing on the character of these proceedings rendered it necessary to be well assured of the grounds there were for attaching credit to them before coming to a determination to give them publicity. The authority on which they are now given there are good grounds for relying on. The result of these inquiries as to the truth of the statement of one main fact respecting the fate of Bridge coincides with the opinion of every surviving friend and relative of the Sheehys, and the other innocent men who suffered in this business, with whom I have communicated on the subject.

The rumor of the stolen church plate was soon circulated in the country, and Bridge, being in the habit of frequenting Sherlock's house, was pointed out as the person suspected of having stolen it. The double infamy now attached to Bridge's character of being an informer and a sacrilegious person. He was advised to leave the country; and at length he made preparations to do so. On their completion, he took leave of his acquaintance; and the last time he was seen by them was on his way to the house of an old friend of his, named Francis Bier, for the purpose of taking leave of him. It was known that he intended calling on another of his acquaintances, named Timothy Sullivan, a slater. Sullivan and a man of the name of Michael Mahony, better known in his neighborhood by the name, in Irish, for "wicked Michael," lived at Knockaughrim bridge; *he fell into their hands, and was murdered by them.* No other human being had act or part in this foul deed. Mahony's flight, and his reasons for it, were known for a long time only to his friends. The body of the murdered man was thrown into a pond at Shanbally.

Mahony fled the country; Sullivan remained, and lived and died unsuspected by the authorities, though not unknown as the murderer to one individual at Clogheen—an inn-keeper of the name of Magrath, who had been one of the innocent persons sworn against by Mary Dunlea, and had undergone a long imprisonment in Clonmel jail. On his liberation, Magrath, then suffering under a rheumatic complaint, the effect of his confinement, seeing Sullivan passing his door, said to a person who stood by him, "There goes the man to whom I am indebted for these aching bones." Sullivan turned pale as ashes, quickened his pace, and took no notice of the words, which had been spoken sufficiently loud, and with the intention that they should be heard by him.

* The name of Sherlock occurs in some of the informations against the White Boys, sworn to by Toohy and Bier.

The persons by whom this account was given appeared to be ignorant of any communication respecting the murder made by Father Sheehy to Major Sirr. The circumstance of the coincidence of both accounts, with respect to two persons only having been engaged in the commission of the crime, deserves attention. By one of those guilty persons, Sheehy says the statement was made to him.

Sullivan was a Protestant, Mahony a Catholic. If the crime was perpetrated and revealed by either, the disclosure must have been made by Mahony.

From the time of Bridge's disappearance till this disclosure in the confessional, Father Sheehy states that various rumors were afloat, but which of them to believe he knew not. In concluding this part of the subject, I have only to observe, if the shadow of a doubt remains respecting the fate of Bridge, none whatever can be entertained of the innocence of those who were the victims of one of the foulest conspiracies on record.

"On the day of his (Sheehy's) trial," we are told, "a party of horse surrounded the court, admitting and excluding whom they thought proper; while others of them, with a certain baronet (Sir Thomas Maude) at their head, scampered the streets in a formidable manner; forcing into inns and private lodgings in the town; challenging and questioning all new comers; menacing the friends, and encouraging the enemies of the priest. Even after sentence of death was pronounced against him, which one would think might have fully satisfied his enemies, Mr. S——w (Sparrow), his attorney, declares that he found it necessary, for his safety, to steal out of the town by night, and with all possible speed to escape to Dublin."*

The prisoner was found guilty of the murder of John Bridge, and sentenced to be hanged, drawn, and quartered, and on the 15th the sentence was carried into execution at Clonmel. The head of the persecuted priest was stuck on a spike, and placed over the porch of the old jail, and there it was allowed to remain for upward of twenty years, till at length his sister was allowed to take it away, and bury it with his remains at Shandraghan.

Beside the ruins of the old church of Shandraghan, the grave of Father Sheehy is distinguished by the beaten path, which reminds us of the hold which his memory has to this day on the affections of the people. The inscriptions on the adjoining tombs are effaced by the footsteps of the pilgrims who stand beside his grave, not rarely or at stated festivals, but day after day, as I was informed on the spot, while the neglected tomb of the ancestors of the proud persecutor, William Bagnell, lies at a little distance unhonored and unnoticed by them. The inscription on the tomb of Father Sheehy is in the following terms: "Here lieth the remains of the Rev. Nicholas Sheehy, parish priest of Shandraghan, Ballysheehan, and Templeheny. He died March 15th, 1766, aged 38 years. Erected by his sister, Catherine Burke, alias Sheehy."

An attempt on a large scale was now made to implicate the leading Roman

* Candid Inquiry, &c., p. 9 and 10.

Catholic gentry of Tipperary in the alleged popish plot of 1766, after the necessary arrangements had been completed for the disposal of Father Sheehy.

The rescue of some prisoners in the county of Kilkenny, and the murder of a soldier (as in Keating's case, at a previous period), was the principal charge on which Edmund Sheehy, James Farrell, and James Buxton were first arrested. They were sent to Kilkenny, to be tried at the assizes; but after they had been arraigned, the nature of the evidence affording no grounds for expecting a conviction, the proceedings were stopped, and they were sent back to Clonmel jail on the 4th of April, where new charges were to be preferred against them at the special assizes, which opened on the 8th of May, 1766.

Edmund Sheehy, a second or third cousin of Father Sheehy, was a gentleman of moderate independence, connected with several of the most respectable Catholic families in the county, of a generous disposition, of social habits, and had lived on good terms with the Protestant gentry of his neighborhood. His personal appearance was remarkably prepossessing. Persons still living have a vivid recollection of his frank, expressive features, his fine, athletic form, of his intrepid demeanor on his trial; and on his way to execution, they speak of his personal appearance as that of a man in the prime of life, and the maturity of manly vigor. He was a married man, and had five children, the youngest under two years of age. He was well known in the country as "Buck Sheehy," a term which at that time was commonly applied to young men of figure, whose means were good, and who were looked on in the country as sporting characters.

Buxton was a man in good circumstances, the poor man's friend in his neighborhood, popular with the lower orders, and, as a matter of course, disliked by their oppressors.

Farrell was a young gentleman in affluent circumstances, who moved in the best society, and, on his mother's side, was connected with Lord Cahir. He was about thirty years of age, had been recently married, and, like his friend Sheehy, his taste for field-sports had procured for him the appellation of one of the bucks of Tipperary.

The friends and relatives of the unfortunate priest, Sheehy, appear to have been especially marked out for ruin. The design of corroborating the guilt of Father Sheehy, by involving his immediate friends and relatives in the crime they laid to his charge, is evident, not only in these proceedings, but in others which were adopted at a later period.

True bills having been found against Edmund Sheehy, James Farrell, and James Buxton, they were put on their trials, before the Right Honorable Chief Justice Clayton and two assistant judges. They were tried separately.

Edmund Sheehy was tried on the 11th of April, on a similar indictment to that on which Buxton and Farrell were tried on the two following days.

The substance of the indictment, which I have taken from the crown book, contains six counts. The first sets forth that Edmund Sheehy, James Buxton, and James Farrell were present at, and aided and abetted in, the murder of John Bridge; and that Pierce Byrne, Darbey Tierney, Dan Coleman, John Walsh, Peter Magrath, Thomas Magrath, John Butler, Thomas Sherlock, Roger Sheehy, John Coughlan, John Cruttie, Hugh Kean, John Byrne, John Springhill, William Flynn, J. Dwyer, John Bier, S. Howard, Michael Landregan, John and Edward Bourke, Edward Prendergast, Philip Magrath, Michael Quinlan, William O'Connor, and James Highland, being also present, aided and abetted likewise in the murder. The second count sets forth their swearing in John Toohy, to be true to "Shaune Meskell" and her children, meaning the White Boys. The third count charges them with tumultuously assembling at Dromlemman, leveling fences, waging rebellion, &c. The fourth and fifth count, with the same offense, at Cashel and Ballyporeen. The sixth, with taking arms from soldiers.

The same wretches who were produced on the former trial, John Toohy, Mary Brady, *alias* Dunlea, and John Lonergan, were brought forward on their trials; and two new approvers, Thomas Bier and James Herbert, to support the sinking credit of the old witnesses.* Herbert was the man who had come to the former assizes to give evidence for the priest, and who, to prevent his appearance, had been arrested on a charge of high treason, lodged in jail, and, by the dextrous management of the prosecutors, was now transformed into a crown witness.

Bier was included in the indictment of the prisoners, but had saved his life by turning approver. Previously to the arrests of Edmund Sheehy, Buxton, and Farrell, he sent notice to them that their lives were in danger, and he recommended their making their escape. They had the temerity, however, to rely on their innocence, and they paid, with their lives, the penalty of their folly. The evidence for the prosecution in no material respect differs from that brought forward on the trials of Meehan and Nicholas Sheehy. A detailed narrative of it will be found in the "Gentleman's and London Magazine" for April, 1766. It is needless to weary the reader with its fabrications. It is sufficient to say, the evidence of these witnesses was all of a piece, a tissue of perjuries clumsily interwoven, without a particle of truth, or a pretext for regarding the reception of it as the result of an imposition practiced on the understanding of the jurors.

The principal witness, whose testimony Mr. Sheehy relied on for his defense, was a Protestant gentleman, Mr. James Prendergast, "perfectly unexceptionable," says Curry, "in point of character, fortune, and religion."† This gentleman deposed, "That on the day and hour on which the murder was sworn to have been committed—about or between the hours of ten or eleven o'clock

* 13th of August, 1768, at Clonmel assizes, Bier, up to that time retained in the service of the Tipperary persecutors, was called to plead to the indictment preferred against him several years before, for the murder of John Bridge, when he pleaded the king's pardon, and being used out as a witness, he was paid off. This unfortunate man, driven by terror into the commission of so many crimes against innocent men, died a natural death at Bruges.

† Review of the Civil Wars.—Curry, vol. ii., p. 279.

on the night of the 28th of October, 1764—Edmund Sheehy, the prisoner, was with him and others, in a distant part of the country. That they and their wives had, on the aforesaid 28th of October, dined at the house of Mr. Joseph Tennison, where they continued till after supper, which was about eleven o'clock, when he and the prisoner left the house of Mr. Tennison, and rode a considerable way together, on their return to their respective homes. That the prisoner had his wife behind him, and when they parted, he (Mr. Prendergast) rode direct home, where, on his arrival, he had looked at the clock, and found it was twelve exactly. That as to the day of their dining with Mr. Tennison (Sunday, the 28th), he was positive, from this circumstance, that the day following was to be the fair of Clogheen, where he requested that Mr. Sheehy would dispose of some bullocks for him, he (Mr. Prendergast) not being able to attend the fair."* This was the evidence of Mr. Prendergast. Another witness for the prisoner, Paul Webber, of Cork, butcher, swore that he saw Mr. Sheehy at the fair of Clogheen on the 29th of October, 1764, and conversed with him respecting Mr. Prendergast's bullocks, which he subsequently bought of Mr. Prendergast, in consequence of this conversation with Mr. Edmund Sheehy. Another witness, Thomas Mason, shepherd to the prisoner, confirmed the particulars sworn to by Mr. Prendergast as to the night and the hour of Mr. Sheehy's return home from Mr. Tennison's house.

Bartholomew Griffith swore that John Toohy, his nephew, had falsely sworn on the trial that the clothes he wore on the trial had been given to him by him (Griffith); that Toohy, on the 28th and 29th of October, 1764, was at his house at Cullen.

One of the grand jury, Chadwick, volunteered his evidence to blunt the testimony of Griffith. He swore that Griffith, "on that occasion, was not to be believed on his oath." The next witness swore that Toohy lived with his master, Brooke Brazier, Esq., six weeks, where he behaved very ill. Mr. Brazier, another of the grand jury, was then called, and he declared that Toohy was not known to him, but that a person was in his family for that time, and was of a very bad character. The managers of the prosecution had Mr. Tennison then examined by a crown lawyer. This gentleman swore "that Sheehy had dined at his house in October, 1764;" but "he was inclined to think it was earlier in the month than the 28th." This evidence was received as a triumphant contradiction of Prendergast's testimony.

Now, as far as character was concerned, that of Sheehy's witness stood fully as high as that of Mr. Tennison. But with respect to the statement of the particular fact of the prisoner having dined on the particular day specified by Sheehy's witness with Tennison, the evidence of Prendergast went positive to the affirmative, while that of Tennison amounted only to a supposition that it was on an earlier day in the month than that specified that the prisoners dined at his house. "He was" only "inclined to think" that it was earlier in the month, but Prendergast "was positive," from a particular circumstance,

* A Candid Inquiry, p. 13.

that it was on the Sunday, the day before the fair at Clogheen, he dined there. There was no other witness produced to corroborate the supposition of Mr. Tennison. There were two witnesses called to confirm the positive statement of Prendergast with regard to the particular night and hour of Sheehy's return from Tennison's house. So much for the evidence. It is now necessary to show that it was not relied on alone for the conviction of the prisoners.

The managers who had on the previous trial surrounded the court with a military force, on this occasion crammed it with their adherents, whose minds had been inflamed by public advertisements previous to the trial, in which the leniency of the former measures of government was reprobated.

"The baronet (Sir Thomas Maude) before mentioned published an advertisement, wherein he presumed to censure the wise and vigilant administration of our last chief governors, and even to charge them with the destruction of many of his majesty's subjects for not having countenanced such measures with respect to these rioters as were manifestly repugnant to all the rules of prudence, justice, and humanity. Nor did his boldness stop here; for, naming a certain day in said advertisement, when the following persons of credit and substance, namely, Sheehy, Buxton, and Farrell, and others, were to be tried by commission at Clonmel for the aforesaid murder, as if he meant to intimidate their judges into lawless rigor and severity, he sent forth an authoritative kind of summons 'to every gentleman of the county to attend that commisson.'"* With such arrangements for inflaming the public mind, for influencing the jury, for intimidating the judges, the doom of the prisoners was sealed before they were put into the dock.

The unfortunate Edmund Sheehy was convicted, and sentence of death, with its usual barbarous concomitants in these cases, drawing and quartering, was pronounced upon him. His wife was in the court when that dreadful sentence was pronounced, and was carried from it in a swoon. The two other acts of the judicial drama were duly performed; the packed juries discharged the duties required or expected of them by the managers of the prosecutions. Buxton and Farrell were found guilty, and were sentenced, with Sheehy, to be executed on the 3d of May.

Eight other persons were placed at the bar, who were charged with the same crime as the prisoners who had been convicted. Another Sheehy was on the list of the managers, but the jury was instructed to acquit the prisoners, Roger Sheehy, Edmund Burke, John Burke, John Butler, B. Kennelly, William Flynn, and Thomas Magrath; but no sooner were they acquitted, than several of them were called on to give bail to appear at the ensuing assizes, to answer to other charges of high treason.

A memorial was drawn up by Edmund Sheehy, and addressed to the judges who presided at the trial; and the following copy is taken from the original draught:

* A Candid Inquiry, &c., p. 10.

"To the Right Honorable Lord Chief Justice Clayton, the Honorable Edmund Malone, and Godfrey Hill, Esq.,

"The humble petition of Edmund Sheehy, an unhappy prisoner, under sentence of death, in his majesty's jail at Clonmel,

"Most humbly showeth,

"That at the last commission of Oyer and Terminer and jail delivery, held at Clonmel the 11th of April inst., your petitioner was convicted of the murder of John Bridge, and accordingly received sentence to be executed on the 3d of May next.

"That your petitioner was transmitted from the city of Kilkenny to Clonmel on Friday, the 4th of April inst., four days only before the said commission of jail delivery was opened.

"That from the short time your petitioner had to prepare for his trial, which he apprehended was by order postponed until the next summer assizes, and the confusion he was in, he was not able to procure all his material witnesses to attend on said trial, or to make that just defense that he would have been able to make if he had had more time to prepare for it, which is manifest from the want of recollection in Travers, the butcher, produced on behalf of your petitioner, who, on the very next day after the trial, perfectly recollected, and is now ready to swear he saw your petitioner and the bullocks at the fair of Clogheen. Nor had Mr. Tennison sufficient time to recollect himself, supposing him quite free from the influence of those who managed the prosecution, who were the said Tennison's allies; circumstances that did not appear to your lordship and honors, of whose mercy, humanity, and justice your petitioner has a due sense, which he shall retain unto death, whatever his fate may be.

"That your petitioner has a wife and five small children, the eldest about nine years old, who, together with an aged father and three sisters, principally depend upon your petitioner's industry as a farmer for support.

"That your petitioner forbears stating the nature and circumstances of the evidence which appeared upon your petitioner's trial, but refers to your lordship and honors' recollection thereof. However, from the nature of your petitioner's defense, in part supported by the positive evidence of James Prendergast, Esq., who is a gentleman of unexceptionable good character and of a considerable fortune, notwithstanding the prejudices that were entertained by some against the persons who were to be tried, your petitioner, from the evidence and a consciousness of his own innocence, entertained hopes that he would have been acquitted. But in regard that he was found guilty,

"Your petitioner most humbly implores your lordship and honors to take his unhappy case and the character of the several witnesses into consideration, and to make such favorable report of your petitioner and his family's case to his excellency the lord lieutenant as to your lordship and honors shall seem meet.

"And he will pray, EDMUND SHEEHY."

"Notwithstanding," Curry states, "that frequent and earnest solicitations were made by several persons of quality in favor of the prisoners, who, being persuaded of their innocence, hoped to obtain for them, if not a pardon, at least some mitigation of their punishment, by transportation or reprieve—the chief and most active of these worthy personages was the Right Honorable Lord Taafe, whose great goodness of heart, and unwearied endeavors, on all occasions, to save his poor countrymen, add new lustre to his nobility, and will be forever remembered by them with the warmest and most respectful gratitude—it is no wonder that their solicitations were vain, for the knight (baronet) so often mentioned (Sir Thomas Maude), Mr. ——, &c., had been before with the lord lieutenant, and declared that, if any favor were shown to these people, they would follow the example of a noble peer, and quit the kingdom in a body. The behavior of the prisoners at the place of execution was cheerful, but devout, and modest, though resolute. It was impossible for any one in their circumstances to counterfeit that resignation, serenity, and pleasing hope which appeared so strikingly in all their countenances and gestures. Conscious of their innocence, they seemed to hasten to receive the reward prepared in the next life for those who suffer patiently for its sake in this."*

In the "Gentleman's and London Magazine" of May, 1766, there is "an authentic narration of the death and execution of Messrs. Sheehy, Buxton, and Farrell, with their declarations attested and carefully compared with those in the hand of Mr. Butler, sub-sheriff of the county Tipperary, who received them from these unfortunate people at the place of execution."

These documents I have likewise compared with copies of the same declarations, furnished me by some of the surviving friends of these unfortunate gentlemen; and, except in the omission of a few names, I find no material difference.

The following is the narrative given in the "Gentleman's Magazine" for May, 1766, Appendix, p. 113:

"The sheriff, who proceeded with decency, called upon the prisoners early in the morning of the 3d instant, so as to leave the jail of Clonmel for Clogheen about six o'clock, to which place he was attended by the regiment of light dragoons, commanded by Lieutenant Colonel Harcourt, and two companies of Armiger's foot: these the commander had previously made ready for the purpose by an order from government. Edmund Sheehy and James Buxton were put on the same car, James Farrell on the next, and the executioner on another, with his apparatus, and the gallows so contrived as to be immediately put together; they thus proceeded in awful procession to Clogheen, where they arrived about twelve o'clock, the distance being above eleven miles.

"In the most open part of the village the gallows was erected, and that in a very short time, while the prisoners remained at a small distance in devotion with their priest for about two hours, when it was thought necessary to exe-

* A Candid Inquiry, p. 13, 14.

cute the sentence the law of their country had doomed them to suffer. They were then all three put upon one car, and drawn under the gallows, where, after remaining some time, they were tied up, and in that situation each read his declaration, and afterward handed it to the sheriff.

"Sheehy met his fate with the most undaunted courage, and delivered his declaration with as much composure of mind as if he had been repeating a prayer; when this awful scene was finished, they were turned off, upon a signal given by Sheehy, who seemed in a sort of exultation, and sprung from the car; he was dead immediately; and after the criminals had hung some time, they were cut down, and the executioner severed their heads from their bodies, which were delivered to their respective friends.*

"Sheehy's intrepid behavior, set off by an engaging person, attracted much pity and compassion from all present; but the most oppressive part of this tragic scene yet remains to be told, when I say that Sheehy has left a widow with five children to bemoan his unhappy fate, Buxton three, and Farrell, who had not been married more than three months, has left his wife pregnant. They were all buried the evening of that day, as particularly requested by themselves, where we hope they rest, having made atonement for their crimes; and let not the imputation of the fathers' misfortunes be remembered to the prejudice of their families. Your constant reader, &c.

"Cashel, May 28, 1766."

"THE DYING DECLARATION OF MR. EDMUND SHEEHY:

"As I am shortly to appear before the great tribunal of God, where I expect, through the passion and sufferings of my Redeemer, to be forgiven the many crimes and offenses which I have committed against so great and merciful a God, I sincerely forgive the world, I forgive my judges, jury, prosecutors, and every other who had a hand in spilling my innocent blood; may the great God forgive them, bless them, and may they never leave this world without sincerely repenting, and meriting that felicity which I hope, through the wounds of Christ, soon to enjoy.

"I think it incumbent, as well for the satisfaction of the public as the ease of my own mind, to declare the truth of every crime with which I was impeached, from the beginning to the day of my conviction.

"*First.* As to the meeting at Kilcoran, sworn by James Herbert, and the murder of John Bridge, sworn to by him and the rest of the informers.

"*Second.* The meeting at Ardfinan, sworn by Guinan in October, 1763, and several other meetings and treasonable practices, at all which I was sworn to be present as the principal acting person.

"*Third.* That I had a hand in burning John Fearise's turf, and extirpating his orchard, taking arms from soldiers, *burning Joseph Tennison's corn*, leveling walls, and many other atrocious crimes against the peace and tranquillity of the present happy Constitution.

* The statement is incorrect with respect to the heads of Buxton and Farrel.—R. R. M.

"1st. I now solemnly declare that I did not see a White Boy since the year 1762, and then but once or twice; and that I never was present at the leveling at the Rock of Cashel, or any other wall or commons in my life, nor even gave counsel or advice to have it done, or ever had any previous knowledge of such intentions, nor do I know to this minute any one man that was at the leveling of the said wall.

"2dly. I declare that I never saw Herbert until the day of my trial, and that I never was at a meeting at Kilcoran; never heard an oath of allegiance proposed nor administered in my life to any sovereign, king, or prince; never knew any thing of the murder of Bridge until I heard it publicly mentioned; nor did I know there was any such design on foot, and if I had, I would have hindered it, if in my power.

"3dly. As to the battle of Newmarket, for which I was tried—I declare I never was at Newmarket, nor do I know there was a rescue intended; nor do I believe did any man in the county of Tipperary.

"4thly. I declare that I never meant or intended rebellion, high treason, or massacre, or ever heard any such wicked scheme mentioned or proposed, nor do I believe there was any such matters in view, and if there was, that I am wholly ignorant of them.

"5thly. I declare that I never knew of either French or Spanish officers, commissions, or money, paid to those poor ignorant fools called White Boys, or of a man held in the light of a gentleman being connected with them.

"I was often attacked, during my confinement in Kilkenny, by the Rev. Lawrence Broderick and the Rev. John Hewson, to make useful discoveries, by bringing in men of weight and fortune, that there was an intended rebellion and massacre, French officers, commissions, and money paid, and by so doing, that would procure my pardon, difficult as it was.

"The day after my trial, Edmund Bagwell came to me from the grand jury, and told me that if I would put those matters in a clear light, that I would get my pardon. I made answer that I would declare the truth, which would not be heard. Sir William Barker's son and Mr. Matthew Bunbury came to me the same evening with words to the same purpose, to which I replied as before. Nothing on this occasion would give sufficient content without my proving the above, and that the *priest died with a lie in his mouth*, which was the phrase Mr. Hewson (Hewetson) made use of. I sent for Sir Thomas Maude the day of my sentence, and declared to him the meeting at Drumlemmon, where I saw nothing remarkable, but two or three fellows, who stole hay from Mr. John Keating, were whipped, and sworn never to steal to the value of a shilling during life. I saw Thomas Bier there, which I told Sir Thomas and Mr. Bunbury, and begged of them never to give credit to Herbert, who knew nothing of the matter except what Bier knew.

"I do declare I saw Bier take a voluntary oath more than once, in the jail of Clonmel, that he knew nothing of the murder; nor do I believe he did. May God forgive him, and the rest of those unhappy informers, and all those who had a hand in encouraging them to swear away innocent lives.

"I further declare, that I have endeavored, as much as was in my power, to suppress this spirit of the White Boys, where I thought or suspected the least spark of it to remain.

"The above is a sincere and honest declaration, as I expect to see God; nor would I make any other for the universe, which must be clear to the gentlemen who offered me my life if I would comply. May the great God forgive them, and incline their hearts to truth, and suffer them not to be biased, nor hurried on by party or particular prejudices, to persevere any longer in falsely representing those matters to the best of kings and to the humanest and best of governments, which I pray God may long continue.

"I die, in the 33d year of my age, an unworthy member of the Church of Rome: the Lord have mercy on my soul! Amen! Amen!

"I was informed that Mr. Tennison's corn was burned by one of his own servants, but accidentally, and that since my confinement; I thought so always.

"Signed by me this 2d of May, 1766.

"EDMUND SHEEHY.

"Present—James Buxton, James Farrell."

"A COPY OF THE DYING DECLARATION OF JAMES BUXTON, OF KILCORAN, IN THE COUNTY OF TIPPERARY,

tried for the alleged murder of one John Bridge; John Toohy and Thomas Bier, prosecutors; God forgive them. Whereas I, the said James Buxton, was arraigned at my trial for having aided and assisted, and committed many flagrant crimes against his majesty's law and government since the rise of the White Boys, upon the information of Michael Guinan and John Toohy, I thought it proper to disabuse the public by this declaration, which I make to God and the world concerning my knowledge of these matters.

"First, as to the murder of John Bridge, I solemnly declare, in the presence of God, before whose holy tribunal I shortly expect to appear, that I neither consulted nor advised, aided nor abetted, nor had I the least notion of any one that did, to the killing of John Bridge; nor did my prosecutor, John Toohy, ever serve me an hour since I was born; neither did I ever, to the best of my knowledge, lay my eyes on him but one night, on the 18th of September last, when he lay at my house, and went by the name of Lucius O'Brien. He was pursued next morning by one William O'Brien, of Clonmel, whom he robbed of some clothes two days before, and was taken in Clogheen for the same robbery, and said O'Brien's clothes and other things were found upon him, for which he was committed to jail, and then turned approver.

"As to every other thing that Michael Guinan and said Toohy swore against me, I further solemly declare, in the presence of my great God, that I neither did any such thing, nor was at any such meeting or leveling as they swore against me, except Drumlemmon, and upon the word of a dying man, neither of *them* was there. Nor was any man, upon the same word of a dying man, that was yet apprehended or suffered, in my belief concerned in the murder of Bridge; and that I verily believe and am persuaded that no prosecutor that yet appeared was present, or any way concerned in that murder, though Thomas Bier, God forgive him, swore that he and I were within two yards of John Bridge when he was murdered by Edmund Meehan with a stroke of a bill-hook.

"Secondly. I solemnly declare and protest, in the presence of my great God, that I never heard or ever learned of a rebellion intended in this kingdom, nor never heard of, nor ever saw any French officers, or French money coming into this country, nor ever heard that any merchants supplied or intended to supply any money for the White Boys, or for any other purpose; nor ever saw, heard, or could discover that any allegiance was sworn to any prince or potentate in the world but to his present majesty, King George the Third; and I further declare, on my dying words, that I never knew nor discovered, nor even imagined, that any massacre whatsoever was intended against any person or persons in this kingdom. And I declare, in the presence of the Almighty God, that I positively believe and am persuaded, that if any of the foregoing treacherous or treasonable combinations were to be carried on, I would have learned or heard something of them.

"Thirdly. That last Lent assizes, in Kilkenny, where I stood indicted and was arraigned for the battle of Newmarket, that the Rev. John Hewetson and Rev. Lawrence Broderick tampered with me for six hours and more, setting forth the little chance I had for my life there at Kilkenny; and though I should, that I would have none at all in Clonmel, but that they would write Lord Carrick immediately to procure my freedom if I would turn approver, and swear to an intended rebellion, treasonable conspiracies, and a massacre, against the principal popish clergy and gentlemen of my county, whose names they had set down in a long piece of paper; but wanted me particularly to swear againt Squire Wyse, Philip Long, Dominick Farrell, Martin Murphy, Doctor Creagh, and Michael Lee, and that I should also swear the *Priest Sheehy* died with a lie in his mouth. Likewise, that I was at the battle of Newmarket, and received a letter from one Edmund Tobin to be at said battle, and this in order to corroborate the informer Toohy's oath and the oaths of three of the light-horse, who swore they saw me there. One, in particular, swore he broke his firelock on my head. Now, as I expect salvation from the hands of God, I neither received a message or letter, nor heard or discovered that this battle of Newmarket was to occur, nor any circumstance regarding it until it was advertised. And I further declare, in the presence of my great God, that I never was nearer this place they call Newmarket than the turnpike road that leads from Dublin to Cork, for I never was two yards eastward of that road. As to the schemes of the White Boys, as far as I could find out in the parish of Tubrid, where I lived, I most solemnly declare, before Almighty God, nothing more was meant than the detection of thieves and rogues, which the said parish was of late remarkable for; an agreement to deal for tithes with none but the dean or minister whose tithe was of his or their immediate living; as to leveling, that I never found out any such thing to have been committed in said parish of any consequence but one ditch belonging to John Griffin, of Kilcoran; nor was I ever privy to any wall or ditch that ever was leveled by White Boys in the county of Tipperary or any other county.

"I also declare, that I never approved of the proceedings of levelers, and that my constant admonition to every person whom I thought concerned in such vile practices was to desist, for that the innocent would suffer for the guilty.

"Given under my hand, this 2d day of May, and the year 1766.

"James Buxton.

"Present—Edmund Sheehy, James Farrell."

THE DECLARATION OF JAMES FARRELL.

"As I am shortly to appear before the great God, where I expect, through the passion of our dear Redeemer, to be forgiven the many crimes and offenses which I have committed against so great and just a God, I now sincerely forgive the world in general, and in particular them that have been the cause of wrongfully spilling my blood.

"1st. The crime for which I am to die is the murder of John Bridge, and swearing at Kilcoran.

"2dly. The burning of Joseph Tennison's corn, John Fearise's turf, and all other things that belonged to the White Boys.

"3dly. The battle of Newmarket, which I stood a trial for in Kilkenny—I now declare to the great tribunal that I am as innocent of all the aforesaid facts which I have been impeached with as the child unborn, in either counsel, aiding, assisting, or knowledge of said facts. I therefore think it conscionable to declare what the following gentlemen wanted me to do, in order to spill innocent blood, which was not in the power of any man in the world to perform.

"These are the gentlemen as follow: the Rev. John Hewetson, John Bagwell, Matthew Bunbury, Mr. Toler, William Bagnell, Edmund Bagnell, and some of the light-horse officers. The day I was condemned, they came along with me from the court-house to the jail, where they carried me into a room, and told me it was in my power to save my life. I asked them how. If I swore against the following persons, they told me they could get my pardon.

"The people are as follows: Martyn Murphy and Philip Long, both of Waterford, and some other merchants of Cork; likewise Bishop Creagh and Lord Dunboyne's brother, and a good many other clergymen; likewise James Nagle, Robert Keating, John Purcell, Thomas Doherty, Thomas Long, John Baldwin, Thomas Butler, of Grange, and Nicholas Lee, with a great many others of the gentlemen of the county and responsible farmers, to be encouraging French officers, enlisting men for the French service, to raise a rebellion in this kingdom, and to distribute French money.

"4thly. If in case they should get a person to do all these things, it would not do without swearing to the murder of John Bridge, to corroborate with the rest of the informers, and strengthen their evidence.

"5thly. I solemnly declare to his divine Majesty I was never present at the leveling of a ditch or wall in my life, nor ever was at a meeting belonging to the White Boys in my life.

"6thly. I likewise declare that I had neither hand, act, nor part in bringing James Herbert from the county of Limerick, and also declare, to the best of my knowledge, he swore not one word of truth, and, in particular, what he swore against me was undoubtedly false.

"The great God bless all my prosecutors, and all other persons that had hand, act, or part in spilling my blood innocently, which the Divine tribunal knows to be so.

"Given under my hand, this 30th day of April, 1766.

"James Farrell.

"They also wanted me to swear against Thomas Butler, of Ballyknock, Edmund Doherty, and Philip Hacket.

"In the presence of us: Edmund Sheehy, James Buxton, Catherine Farrell."

The wretched wife of Edmund Sheehy, immediately after his conviction, proceeded to Dublin with the hope of procuring a pardon for her husband. His enemies were, however, beforehand with her. Their pernicious influence was exerted in every department at the Castle to frustrate her efforts. They prevailed, as they had hitherto done there, whenever the favor or the anger of the Moloch of their faction was to be propitiated or appeased, by handing over to them their defenseless persecuted victims. Some idea may be formed of the promptitude with which the foul proceedings against these gentlemen were followed up, when it is borne in mind that their separate trials commenced on the 11th of April; and the following official notice is to be found in the record of these proceedings. "Crown *warrant* for Edmund Sheehy, James Farrell, and James Buxton, given to F. Butler, sub-sheriff, 15th April, 1766."

Mrs. Sheehy, on her return to Clonmel, after a fruitless journey, had not even the melancholy satisfaction of finding her husband in prison. On her arrival there in the morning, she learned that he and his companions had been taken from the jail a short time before, and were then on their way to Clogheen, the place of execution. This wretched woman, worn down with affliction, with the previous conflict between hope and fear, with the shock she had received on her return at finding her last hope frustrated of beholding her beloved husband, and of bidding him farewell, had yet sufficient strength, or the kind of energy which arises from despair, to hurry after that mournful cortège. About half way between Clonmel and Clogheen she overtook it, and, rushing forward, passed through the soldiers, and threw herself into the arms of her husband.

The scene was one which the few surviving friends of this unhappy couple speak of as causing the very soldiers who surrounded them to weep and sob aloud. This scene took place about two hours before the execution. Before they separated, Sheehy resumed his former apparently unmoved demeanor, and addressed a few words, expressive of his last wishes, with extraordinary firmness of tone and manner, to his distracted wife. He told her "*to remember she had duties to perform to her God, to herself, to their children, and to his memory;*" and then praying that heaven might pour down all its blessings on her head, he tore himself from her embrace, and the procession moved on. The officers, soldiers, sub-sheriff, all around them, were in tears during this melancholy interview; and at their separation, Sheehy himself, evidently struggling with his feelings, endeavored to suppress any appearance of emotion, recovered his self-possession, and from that time seemed to be unmoved.

The day before the execution, Mrs. Kearney, an aunt of Edmund Sheehy, applied to one of the officers who was to be on duty the next day to save his unfortunate family the pain of seeing his head placed on a spike, over the entrance of the jail, in the High Street, in which it was situated. Her interference was not ineffectual: he told her he had no power to interfere with the civil authorities; but when the head was separated from the body, if any person were in readiness to bear it off, the soldiers probably would not be overzealous to prevent its removal.

For this act it was wisely thought that the resolution and promptitude of a woman would be likely to prove most successful. Ann Mary Butler, a person devoted to the family, and in her attachment to it incapable of fear and insensible of danger, was selected for this purpose. The head of Edmund Sheehy was no sooner struck from the body, than this woman suddenly forced her way through the soldiers, threw her apron over the head, and fled with it, the soldiers as she approached opening a free passage for her, and again forming in line when the executioner and his attendants made an effort to pursue her, and thus the military prevented their so doing.

The woman, at the place appointed at the cross-roads, near Clogheen, met the funeral (for the mutilated body had been delivered over to the friends for interment), the head was put into the coffin, and was buried at a country church-yard about three or four miles from Clonmel, attended by a vast concourse of people. The executions took place on a temporary scaffold, in an open space called the Cock-pit. The heads of Farrell and Buxton were brought to Clonmel, and, together with those of Father Sheehy and Meehan, were spiked and placed over the entrance to the jail, where, for upward of twenty years, these wretched trophies of the triumphant villainy of the Maudes, Bagwells, Bagnells, and Hewetsons continued to outrage the feelings of humanity and justice, and to shock the sight of the surviving relatives of the murdered men every time they entered the town or departed from it.

The thirst for Catholic blood was not yet appeased. Another batch of Catholic gentlemen, charged with treason, with acting as leaders in the Munster plot, were brought to trial at Clonmel in the month of March the following year (1767). Mr. James Nagle, of Garnavilla, a relative by marriage of the celebrated Edmund Burke, Mr. Robert Keating, of Knocka, Mr. Thomas Dogherty, of Ballynamona, Mr. Edmund Burke, of Tubrid, and Messrs. Meighan, Lee, and Couglan, all charged with high treason, and aiding and abetting White Boyism.* For some of these gentlemen, when first arrested, bail to the amount of several thousand pounds had been offered and refused. They had lain in jail for several months previously to the trial, and the charge that eventually was attempted to be supported against them by the same miscreant who had sworn against Father Sheehy was completely disproved. The "managers" of the prosecution had omitted no means to procure evidence of the right sort. In the middle of July the preceding year (1766), ample encouragement for new perjury was held out in the public papers. It was therein stated that "the reward promised for prosecuting and convicting the other rioters, the sum of £300, had been paid."†

Several of these gentlemen were of the most respectable families in the county. Messrs. Keating and Dogherty were persons who moved in the best circles of society, and whose descendants still hold a prominent station in it. The two latter owed their safety to a circumstance which came to the knowledge of one of the friends of Keating while he was in jail. One of the dismounted dragoon soldiers, then doing duty in the jail, saw the well-known Mary Dunlea privately introduced into the prison by one of the active magistrates in these proceedings, and taken to a window where she had an opportunity of seeing Messrs. Keating and Dogherty without being noticed by them. This was for the purpose of enabling her to swear to persons whom she had never before seen.

On the morning of the trials, the friends of the prisoners, keeping a watchful eye on the movements of the same woman, saw her in a doorway in front of the dock, and Mr. John Bagwell in the act of pointing out the prisoners. The friend of Keating lost no time in hurrying to the dock, and telling them to change their coats. They did so, and the coats were identified, but not the men. The witness, on being asked to point out Keating, singled out Dogherty; and the manifest ignorance of the witness of the persons of those two prisoners was mainly instrumental in causing all to be acquitted.

The trial of these gentlemen, on account of the great number of witnesses examined, lasted from ten o'clock on Wednesday morning until four o'clock on Thursday morning. The jury, after much deliberation, brought in their verdict, "Not Guilty," upon which the prisoners were enlarged. "Not, however, without the factious, bold, and open censures and secret threats against the humane and upright judge who presided at the trial (Baron Mountney), so enraged were they to find the *last* effort to realize this plot entirely frustrated."‡

* Dublin Gazette, April, 1767; and Saunders' Newsletter, July, 1767.

† A Candid Inquiry.

‡ A Parallel between the Plots of 1679 and 1762, p. 39; Saunders' Newsletter, July, 1767.

Curry is mistaken in terming it the last effort. Two other attempts were subsequently made before Judge Edmund Malone and Prime Sergeant Hutchinson. John Sheehy, John Burke, E. Prendergast, and several others, were tried and acquitted on the same charge and evidence. On the 5th of September, 1767, once more, "Mr. Roger Sheehy and six others were tried on an indictment of high treason, for being concerned with the White Boys, on the testimony of Toohy, who, prevaricating, as we are told by Curry, in his testimony from what he had sworn nearly two years before, Mr. Prime Sergeant desired the jury to give no credit thereto, upon which Sheehy was acquitted."*

Thus terminated a most foul conspiracy against the lives of innocent men. The name of Sheehy's jury became a term of reproach in the south of Ireland, that was applied to any inquiry that was conducted on principles at variance with truth and justice, and which made an indictment tantamount to a conviction.

A passage in Sir Richard Musgrave's history throws some light on the implication of Mr. Nagle, whose name is mentioned on the list of prisoners at the former trial in March, 1767. "When the enormities," says Sir Richard, "committed by the White Boys were about to draw on them the vengeance of the law, and some time before Sir Richard Aston proceeded on his mission to try them, Mr. Edmund Burke sent his brother Richard (who died recorder of Bristol), and Mr. Nagle, a relation, on a mission to Munster, to levy money on the popish body for the use of the White Boys, who were exclusively papists." The obvious drift of this passage can hardly be mistaken; but, as Sir Richard Musgrave appears to have had some misgivings as to the success of the attempt to cast suspicion on the loyalty of Edmund Burke, he added the following passage in a note, in type sufficiently small to afford a chance of its escaping observation: "I have no other proof that these gentlemen were employed by Mr. Burke than that they declared it without reserve to the persons from whom they obtained money. In doing so, he might have been actuated by motives of charity and humanity."

The extraordinary judgments which fell on the persons who were instrumental to the death of Father Sheehy are still fresh in the memory of the inhabitants of Clonmel and Clogheen. Several of the jury met with violent deaths, some dragged out a miserable existence, stricken with loathsome and excruciating maladies; madness was the fate of one, beggary the lot of another, recklessness of life and remorse, I believe it may be said with truth, of the majority of them.

This is no overcharged account. On the contrary, it falls short of the reality. One of the jury, named Tuthill, cut his throat; another, named Shaw, was choked; another, named Alexander Hoops, was drowned; the last survivor of them was said to have been accidentally shot by Mr. Sheehy Keating, in Rehill wood, on a sporting excursion. Ferris died mad. One of them dropped dead at his own door. Another, at a gentleman's house,

* Freeman's Journal, September 8, 1767.

where he spent the night in company with Mr. Pierce Meagher, the brother-in-law of Edmund Sheehy, was found dead in a privy. Dumville, by a fall from his horse, was frightfully disfigured. Minchin was reduced to beggary; and of all I have heard only of one, named Dunmead, who died a natural death, that was not signally visited with calamities of some kind or other.

Sir Thomas Maude, the ancestor of a noble lord, died in a state of phrensy, terribly afflicted both in mind and body. In his last moments his ravings were continually about Sheehy, and the repetition of that name became painful to his attendants. Few death-bed scenes, perhaps, ever presented a more appalling spectacle than that of Sir Thomas Maude is described to have been.

Bagwell, of Killmore, was reduced to a state of fatuity for some time before his death. His eldest son shot himself in a packet going over to England; his property became involved, and a miserable remnant of the wreck of it is all that is now left to one of his descendants living in a foreign land.*

No. III.—Introduction, p. 18.

BERNARD WRIGHT, OF CLONMEL.

At the assizes in Clonmel, March 14, 1799, the trial took place of an action brought by Mr. Bernard Wright, a teacher of the French language, against Thomas Judkin Fitzgerald, Esq., late sheriff of the county of Tipperary. The damages were laid at £1000. The trial took place before Lord Yelverton and Judge Chamberlain. The first witness examined, William Nicholson, Esq., deposed that he knew both plaintiff and defendant; plaintiff, on hearing the high sheriff had expressed an intention of arresting him (Wright), immediately went to surrender himself to a magistrate. The magistrate not being at home, witness accompanied plaintiff to the high sheriff. Witness told the latter Wright had come to surrender himself; on which the high sheriff said to Wright, "*Fall on your knees and receive your sentence, for you are a rebel, and you have been a principal in the rebellion: you are to receive five hundred lashes, and then to be shot.*" Whereon "Wright prayed for time, hoped he would get a trial, and if he was not found innocent, he would submit to any punishment." Defendant answered, "What! speak after sentence has been passed!"

(The Hon. Mr. Yelverton, in the House of Commons, in his report of those proceedings, stated the words used by Fitzgerald were, "'What, you Carmelite rascal! do you dare to speak after sentence?' and then struck him, and sent him off to prison; and next day the unhappy man was dragged to a ladder in Clonmel Street to undergo his sentence.")

The witness, Nicholson, swore that he endeavored in vain to persuade the high sheriff to have the plaintiff tried, and to convince him of Wright's innocence, "whom he had known from his childhood, and had always known to be a loyal man."

Solomon Watson, a Quaker, affirmed that on the 29th of May, 1798, the high

* Madden's Introduction to Lives and Times of the United Irishmen, 2d Series.

sheriff told witness he was going to whip a set of rebels. "Saw Wright brought to the ladder under a guard—had his hands to his face, seemed to be praying—saw him on his knees at the ladder. Defendant, the high sheriff, pulled off Wright's hat—stamped on it—dragged him by the hair—struck him with his sword, and kicked him—blood flowed, and then dragged him to the ladder. Selected some strong men, and cried, 'Tie up Citizen Wright! tie up Citizen Wright!'"

Witness further deposed that Wright begged to have a clergyman, but his request was refused; then the flogging began. "Defendant ordered first fifty lashes. He pulled a paper, written in French, out of his pocket, gave it to Major Riall as furnishing his reasons for flogging Wright. Major Riall read the paper, and returned it. Defendant then ordered fifty lashes more, after which he asked how many lashes Wright had received; being answered one hundred, he said, 'Cut the waistband of the rascal's breeches, and give him fifty there.' The lashes were inflicted severely; defendant asked for a rope—was angry there was no rope—desired a rope to be got ready, while he went to the general for an order to hang him. Defendant went down the street toward the general's lodgings. Wright was left tied up during this time, from a quarter to half an hour. Could not say during this time whether the crowd had loosed the cords; if not, he remained tied while defendant was absent. When defendant returned, he ordered Wright back to jail, saying he would flog him again the next day; saw Wright sent back to jail under a guard."

Major Riall being examined, deposed that he did not arrive at the place of carrying the flogging into effect before Wright had received fifty lashes. The high sheriff produced two papers, one of which, being in French, he (the high sheriff) did not understand, but gave it to him to read, as containing matter that furnished ground for the flogging. Witness read the paper, and returned it, saying it was in no wise treasonable; that it was from a French gentleman, the Baron de Clues, making an excuse for not keeping an appointment, being obliged to wait on Sir Lawrence Parsons (subsequently Lord Rosse). Wright, however, was flogged after witness had explained the nature of the letter to the high sheriff. Witness then went away. Next day he accompanied the high sheriff to see Wright in the jail. "Saw him kneeling on his bed while they were speaking to him, being unable to lie down with soreness." Witness further deposed that he knew of three innocent persons being flogged whom he believed to be innocent, of whom Wright was one.

(Solomon Watson had previously deposed, in his evidence, to his knowledge of the defendant having flogged some laborers on account of the kind of waistcoats they wore. He had known defendant knock down an old man in the street for not taking off his hat to him, and he saw a lad of sixteen years of age leap into the river to escape a repetition of a flogging from him.)

The high sheriff, "in an animated speech," which took nearly two hours to deliver, defended the practice of flogging generally, as a means of obtaining discoveries of treasonable secrets; that he had flogged a man named Nipper, alias Dwyer, who confessed that Wright was a secretary of the United Irishmen, "and this information he could not get before the flogging." He insisted on the utility of his efforts to obtain confessions from suspected traitors, when every other means of discovering the truth failed; "*he had a right even to cut off their heads.*"

This mode of arriving at truth rather disturbed the gravity of the court.

The Rev. T. Prior, Fellow of Trinity College, Dublin, being produced to prove the moral and loyal character of plaintiff, deposed that "he had known Bernard Wright from his earliest youth, and that he had always conducted himself as an orderly, loyal, and moral man."

Judge Chamberlain, in charging the jury, said, "The jury were not to imagine the Legislature, by enabling magistrates to justify their acts under the Indemnity Bill, had released them from the feelings of humanity and the obligations of justice in the exercise of power even in putting down rebellion."

The jury retired, and found a verdict for the plaintiff for £500, and 6*d.* costs.

On the 16th of March, 1799, J. Judkin Fitzgerald petitioned the House of Commons, "praying to be indemnified for certain acts done by him in the suppression of the late rebellion." The acts specified were the infliction of corporal punishment, of whipping, on many persons of whose guilt he had secret information, but no public evidence. Petitioner said, not being able to disclose the information on which he acted, "the learned judges who had presided at a late trial (Wright *v.* Fitzgerald) were of opinion, in point of law, that unless petitioner produced information on oath of the ground on which he had acted, that his case could not fall within the provisions of the Indemnity Act passed last session."

Mr. Secretary Cooke bore testimony to "the national services performed by the petitioner."

A Bill of Indemnity was passed in the Irish Parliament, in accordance with the prayer of the petitioner, and immediately after an application was made on the part of Mr. Fitzgerald, in the Court of Exchequer, to set aside the verdict obtained against him by Mr. Wright, which application was dismissed, with full costs.*

In the Parliamentary proceedings, "on the petition of J. J. Fitzgerald, Esq., praying for indemnity for certain acts done by him in the suppression of rebellion," April 6th, 1799, Lord Matthew supported the petition, and bore testimony to the conduct of Mr. Fitzgerald—"he was an extremely active, spirited, and meritorious magistrate."

The Hon. Mr. Yelverton opposed the petition on the ground of "there not being found a scintilla of suspicion against the plaintiff, Wright, to justify the unparalleled cruelties exercised on him."

Mr. Yelverton, in stating the facts of the case, read the letter in the French

* Report of the trial Wright *v.* Fitzgerald.

language which had been shown to Major Riall by the all-mighty sheriff of Tipperary as a justification of the scourging of a respectable gentleman, a peaceable man of literary habits and pursuits, who was designated a scoundrel, whom the sheriff would be justified in flogging to death, and which letter Mr. Yelverton said had been translated in these words to Mr. Fitzgerald by Major Riall on the spot, at the place of execution, in one of the intervals of the flogging:

"SIR,—I am extremely sorry I can not wait on you at the hour appointed, being unavoidably obliged to attend Sir Laurence Parsons. Yours, BARON CLUES.
"To B. Wright, Esq."

The Hon. Mr. Yelverton proceeded to state, that, "notwithstanding this translation, which Major Riall read to Mr. Fitzgerald, he ordered fifty lashes more to be inflicted, and with such peculiar severity, that, horrid to relate, the intestines of the bleeding man could be perceived convulsed through his wounds! Mr. Fitzgerald, finding he could not continue the action of his cat-o'-nine-tails on that part where he was cutting his way into his body, ordered the waistband of his breeches to be cut open, and had fifty more lashes inflicted there. He then left the man bleeding and suspended, while he went to the barracks to demand a file of men to come and shoot him; but being refused by the general, he ordered him back to prison, where he was confined in a small dark room, with no other furniture than a wretched pallet of straw without covering, and there he remained six or seven days, without any medical assistance."*

The Indemnity Bill passed through the Irish houses of Parliament, and received the royal sanction with all due speed, in time to save "the all-mighty sheriff of Tipperary" from the consequences of another action for false imprisonment and ill usage, brought against him by a corn-merchant of Carrick-onsure, of considerable wealth, a Mr. Scott, a man whose large means for a great many years had been freely expended in promoting industry among the lower classes of the community.

Mr. Scott had been dragged from his bed by the high sheriff, charged with being a traitor, heavily ironed, and cast into prison, without any evidence of guilt, and was finally released by General St. John on bail.

The trial, presided over by Judge Yelverton, was going on, when a special courier made his appearance in the court, and delivered a package into the hands of the counsel for Fitzgerald. The counsel handed up a document to the judge—an official notification of the Bill of Indemnity having passed into law. The judge, Baron Yelverton, read the document, tore it, and threw down the fragments, saying to the jury, "Gentlemen, a Bill of Indemnity has been passed, which sets justice at defiance, and makes it incompetent for you to vindicate the present outrage on it."

* Report of the trial

No. IV.—Introduction, p. 27.

COPY OF MARRIAGE CERTIFICATE OF LADY BLESSINGTON WITH CAPTAIN MAURICE FARMER.

Obtained by R. R. Madden from Mr. Legge, Parish Clerk and Registrar of Marriages in Clonmel, the 8th of August, 1854.

1804. Marriage solemnized at the Parish Church, in the Parish of Clonmel, in the County of Tipperary.

When married.	Name and Surname.	Rank or Profession.	Residence at the Time of Marriage.
1804. March 7.	Maurice Farmer. Margaret Power.	Captain 47th Regiment.	Clonmel. Clonmel.

Married in the Parish Church, according to the Rites and Ceremonies of the United Church of England and Ireland, by license, by me,

(*Signed*), Wm. Stephenson.

No. V.—Introduction, p. 29.

CAPTAIN MAURICE FARMER.

Reference has been made in the Introduction to a letter published in a Dublin newspaper by a brother of Captain Farmer, denying certain statements made in a Memoir of Lady Blessington respecting Captain Maurice St. Leger Farmer. In fairness to the friends of that gentleman, I feel myself bound to insert the letter at length, without any omissions whatsoever; although, without calling in question in the slightest degree the veracity of the writer, I must observe there are several statements in that communication of opinions which are entirely at variance with my impressions of facts, and some, I may add, at variance with the impressions of a gentleman who was present at the marriage of Captain Farmer with Miss Power. It is very natural for the brother of that gentleman, actuated as he must be by feelings of fraternal regard and affection, to form favorable opinions of one so nearly connected with him, and to entertain unfavorable sentiments regarding one whose relatives have publicly expressed sentiments which can not be otherwise than disagreeable, and, in his opinion, unjust to the memory of his relative.

But in all matters of this unfortunate kind, it is not from the immediate friends of the persons who have been disunited that we ought to expect a fair and full statement of both sides of the question at issue—one that would do equal justice to each party, to the views of each, and the merits of the case on either side.

I feel once more bound to state my conviction that the following statement is not one which answers to the expectations I have just referred to; and that, if I felt myself at liberty to appeal to the recollections of two very distinguished personages who were present at that marriage, and well acquainted with the parties—one of those persons now commander-in-chief of the British army, and the other commander of the forces in Ireland—that conviction would be confirmed.

"TO THE EDITOR OF THE EVENING PACKET.

"SIR,—I will gratefully feel your kindness if you will give, in your paper, insertion to the accompanying reply to Miss Power's misstatements, in her opening review of Lady Blessington's life, as connected with my brother, the late Captain Farmer, 47th Foot, her first husband.

WALTER FARMER,

"3 Heytsbury Street, lately of Poplar Hall, Ballitore, county of Kildare."

"SIR,—I have seen in your paper of the 11th instant a statement, taken from a Memoir of the Countess of Blessington, contributed in the Preface to 'Country Quarters' by her niece, Miss Power, in which, to exculpate sundry matters in the conduct of her ladyship, gross misrepresentations are made respecting her first husband, Captain Farmer. As the brother of that gentleman, I hope I may be allowed to state my contradictions as follows, and that you will kindly give them equal publicity.

"So far as my brother and Captain Murray having both paid their addresses to the lady, I believe to be true; but that she preferred my brother is an undoubted fact, inasmuch as that it was in every sense a love-match between them, no settlement being made or promised by my brother or his family; for my father, having seven other sons, considered that in the purchase of all his steps he had received his share, but the lady's father promised his daughter a fortune of £1000, a shilling of which was never paid; but, counting on it, the young couple contracted debts, and Captain Farmer, finding his inability to meet them, was obliged to sell his commission to pay said debts. He subsequently accepted a commission in the East India Company's service, and wished his wife to accompany him there, which she declined doing. With a view, however, to her independence and happiness in his absence, he divided with her the surplus amount remaining after paying his debts —namely, £1000, that is, £500 each. Having been my brother's schoolfellow and constant companion, I can assert that, as boy or man, he never showed any symptoms of insanity up to this period; and such I can prove by many parties still alive, and particularly through the very respectable members of the Society of Friends, living in and around Ballitore, in the county of Kildare, his native place, where my father resided. That such a statement might have been made by Captain Murray may be true, though certainly without having had any effect on the lady or her parents, for he at all times evinced great hostility to my brother; and immediately after my brother sold out of the army, having met each other at Blackrock, near Dublin, warm words ensued, which caused Captain Murray, who was in uniform, to draw his sword. My brother, having a stick, quickly disarmed him, and broke the sword; the result was a duel with pistols, when Captain Murray was seriously wounded. A considerable time afterward, my brother went to India, and Mrs. Farmer came to Ballitore. From the reports current as to her misconduct, of which Captain Farmer, from his absence, could not be aware, my father would not see her, and objected to my doing so. I called upon her notwithstanding, when she told me she had letters from my brother, pressing her to go out to India, as he had made comfortable provision for her; but she declined to do so, fearing the climate might disagree with her constitution; thus by her own words disproving the charge now brought up, that their separation was caused by his insanity. I would rather not refer to her conduct from that period, nor do I think the memoir either should go farther; but * * * * It is a notorious fact, that her conduct, coupled with the effects of a *coup de soleil* while in India, often induced my brother, when he went into company, to exceed, as was then too much the custom, and to such was his death to be attributed His host on this occasion, an old brother officer, having unfortunately locked the door on his company in their then state of mind, my brother, in trying to get from the room, endeavored to do so by the window, and fell, which was the cause of his death. A reference to the Times newspaper of that day, containing the report of the coroner's inquest, animadverts strongly on the conduct of his brother officer for so acting, and regrets the loss to the service of a brave officer, who had previously done good service for his country. W. F."

No. VI.—Introduction, p. 22.

PROCEEDINGS ON INQUEST ON THE BODY OF JOSEPH LONERGAN (SHOT BY EDMUND POWER, ESQ., J. P., THE 21st OF APRIL, 1807). EVIDENCE AND FINDING OF JURY—BILL OF INDICTMENT AND SWORN INFORMATIONS:

Copied verbatim from the original documents existing in the Crown Office of Clonmel.

County of Tipperary—to Wit: The names of the jury to try and inquire how, and in what manner, Joseph Lonergan, late of Mullough, in said county, farmer, came by his death. Taken before Richard Needham, Esq., D. Mayor of Clonmel, and Edmund Armstrong, one of the coroners of said county, at the jail of Clonmel, 23d of April, 1807.

Wm. Sargeant,	1.	John Farrell,	7.
John Lindop,	2.	Peter Hinds,	8.
Wm. Harvey,	3.	Dennis Madden,	9.
Patt Phelan,	4.	John Mulcahy,	10.
Joseph Hudson,	5.	James Mara,	11.
Henry Julian,	6.	Bernard Wright,	12.*

Gentlemen, your issue is to try, and inquire how, and in what manner, Joseph Lonergan, now lying dead in the jail of Clonmel, was killed, and by whom, when, and where, and upon what occasion.

We find that Joseph Lonergan came by his death by a gun-shot wound, and from circumstances, we believe that said shot might have been fired by Edmund Power, as magistrate of this county in his own defense, and the execution of his office, and under the authority of the secretary of the lord lieutenant.

Signatures of the jury follow.

Evidence taken on an inquest held on the body of Joseph Lonergan, on the 23d of April, 1807, in the jail of Clonmel.

First witness, John R. Phillips, of Clonmel, surgeon, deposeth and saith that he was called upon, about five or six o'clock on the evening of the 21st of April instant, and saith that in about a quarter of an hour after deponent examined Joseph Lonergan, the deceased, in the jail of Clonmel, and saith he found he had received a gun-shot wound, which wound was the occasion of his death, and saith that the said Lonergan died about eleven o'clock on the ensuing morning.

John R. Phillips, Surgeon.
Richard Needham, D. Lieut. Clonmel.
Edward Armstrong, Coroner.

Second witness: Mary Kirwan deposeth and saith that she saw a shot fired at the deceased Joseph Lonergan, but does not know who fired it, but it was fired by a gentleman on horseback; saith she saw deceased, after the shot was fired, stretched on the ground; saw a good many people gathered at the place

* Bernard Wright was the editor of Mr. Power's paper, "The Clonmel Gazette," the same person who was flogged by Sir John Judkin Fitzgerald.—R. R. M.

where the shot was fired; saith the person who fired the shot was on a small road, and the deceased was at the other side of the ditch; saith the deceased did not throw a stone, and that he could not without deponent seeing him; the gentleman was standing on a ditch at the opposite side of the place where the first shot was fired, when he fired the second shot. Saw a gun in his hand, and saw him charge the gun after the second shot was fired.

MARY KIRWAN, her × mark.
Truly read by me, EDWARD ARMSTRONG, Coroner
RICHARD NEEDHAM, D. L.

Darby Dwyer, of Gananey, third witness, deposeth and saith he knew Joseph Lonergan, the deceased: deponent saith he does think that the person who fired the shot was not on horseback; did not see any one fire the shot, but deponent heard it; saw the above-named Mary Kirwan at the place before deponent went for Mr. Power's horse, and saw Mr. Power there; deponent is not related to the deceased, nor is Mary Kirwan: heard only one shot; does not know who the first shot was fired by; saw a gun in Mr. Power's hand.

DARBY DWYER, his × mark.
Truly read by EDWARD ARMSTRONG.
RICHARD NEEDHAM.

Bridget Hannahan, widow, of Mullough, fourth witness. Deponent saith she heard a shot fired, on which deponent came up and saw a man on the ditch with a gun in his hand, and saw Joseph Lonergan lying on the clay; saith she does not know Mr. Power, and being called upon to identify his person, said she could not do so; saith the person who had the gun in his hand said he would shoot her if she came farther; and saith that the man on the ditch was forty yards from the deceased when deponent came up, and saw no other person with a gun.

BRIDGET HANNAHAN, her × mark.
Truly read by EDWARD ARMSTRONG.
RICHARD NEEDHAM.

John Everard, of Mullough, farmer, fifth witness, deposeth and saith he knew Joseph Lonergan, the deceased: saith he was not present at the beginning of the transaction, but came up a good while afterward, and deponent met Mr. Power, who came up toward the place where deponent was, and deponent and Mr. Power met each other; saith he saw a shot fired by Mr. Power, at which time Joseph Lonergan, the deceased, was running away from Mr. Power, and deponent asked Mr. Power why he fired at the deceased, and he answered witness that the villain had thrown a stone at him, upward of two pounds' weight, which Mr. Power produced to witness, and that he hit him with the stone; the deceased got into the house of Mr. William Lonergan, of Mullough, and Mr. Power asked Lonergan if the second shot he fired had hit him; he, Lonergan, said it did not; on which Mr. Power said, "I am glad of it, for it was at your back I fired, and if it had hit you, it would have killed you." I know that Mr. Power is a magistrate for the county of Tipperary. Heard that after the prisoner was taken away there was a mob collected; saith he believes that Mr. Power, upon the occasion aforesaid, was acting in the capacity of a magistrate for said county.

JOHN EVERARD.
RICHARD NEEDHAM.
EDWARD ARMSTRONG, Coroner.

Mr. Jephson, sixth witness, saith he is a magistrate of the county of Tipperary, and saith there were informations sworn before deponent, as a magistrate of the county of Waterford, against the deceased, for a capital felony, which informations were lodged by a person in the jail of Waterford, who turned approver, and saith that the crime was so very serious, and the parties concerned therein notorious, that deponent wrote to the lord lieutenant and secretary, who by letter informed deponent that he might offer a reward of £100 for the apprehension of any of the gang concerned, and saith the deceased was at the head of that gang; deponent saith that he gave Mr. Power the information to copy, with direction to him to act under them, and to apprehend any one of the said gang, particularly three of them, one of whom was the deceased.

L. H. JEPHSON.
RICHARD NEEDHAM, D. L.
EDWARD ARMSTRONG, Coroner.

COPY OF A BILL OF INDICTMENT AGAINST EDMUND POWER, ESQ., J. P., OF CLONMEL, FOR THE MURDER OF JOSEPH LONERGAN.

County of Tipperary—to Wit: The jurors of our lord the king, upon their oaths do say and present, that Edmund Power, of Clonmel, in the said county, esquire, one of his majesty's justices of the peace for said county, not having the fear of God before his eyes, but being moved and seduced by the instigation of the devil, on the twenty-first day of April, in the forty-seventh year of the reign of our sovereign lord, George the Third, by the grace of God, of the United Kingdom of Great Britain and Ireland, king, defender of the faith, and so forth, with force and arms, at Mullough, in the county of Tipperary, in and upon one Joseph Lonergan, a true and faithful subject of our said lord the king, in the peace of God of our said lord the king then and there being, willfully, feloniously, and of his malice prepense, did make an assault, and the said Edmund Power a certain gun, of the value of five shillings sterling, which he, the said Edmund Power, then and there, in both his hands, had and held, the said gun then and there being charged and loaded with gunpowder and leaden shot, willfully, and feloniously, and of his malice prepense, toward and against the said Joseph Lonergan, did then and there discharge and shoot; by means of the discharging and shooting of which said gun, so charged and loaded as aforesaid, he, the said Edmund Power the said Joseph Lonergan, in and upon the right side of the body, near the right breast of him the said Joseph Lonergan, then and there, with the leaden shot aforesaid, out of the gun aforesaid, so by him, the said Edmund Power, discharged and shot as aforesaid, by force and explosion of the gunpowder aforesaid, so discharged and shot by him, the said Edmund Power, out of the gun aforesaid, then and there willfully, feloniously, and of his malice prepense, did strike, penetrate, and wound, and then and there gave unto the said Joseph Lonergan, with the leaden shot aforesaid, so discharged and shot by him, the said Edmund Power, out of the gun aforesaid, one mortal wound of the length of two inches, and of the depth of three inches, of which said mortal wound he, the said Joseph Lonergan, then and there instantly languished, and, languishing, lived from the said twenty-first day of April until the day next following, and then, that is to say, on the twenty-second day of April, in the said forty-seventh year of the reign of our said lord the king, the said Joseph Lonergan, of the mortal wound aforesaid, at Clonmel, in the county aforesaid, "died;" and so the jurors aforesaid, upon their oaths aforesaid, do say and present, that the said Edmund Power the said Joseph Lonergan, with force and arms aforesaid, at Mullough aforesaid, in the county of Tipperary aforesaid, the day and year aforesaid, in manner and form aforesaid, willfully, feloniously, and of his malice prepense, did kill and murder, against the peace of our said lord the king, his crown and dignity, against the form of the statute in that case made and provided.

True bill for self and fellow-jurors, J. A. Prittie.

INFORMATION OF PATRICK LONERGAN (BROTHER OF THE DECEASED).

County of Tipperary—to Wit: By one of his majesty's justices of the peace for the said county.

The information of Patrick Lonergan, of Mullough, in the western division of the barony of Iffa and Offa, and parish of Mullough, in the said county, farmer, who came before me this day, and being duly sworn and examined on the Holy Evangelists, deponent saith he was in the employment of William Lonergan, of Mullough aforesaid, esquire, on the 21st day of April instant, where deponent's brother, Joseph Lonergan, late of Mullough, deceased, had been, and that he was also on the lands of Mullough aforesaid, and in the actual act of doing the business carefully appointed for him on said day by William Lonergan aforesaid, with this deponent, when then and there Edmund Power, of Clonmel, in said county, esquire, came on horseback, and on seeing the said Joseph Lonergan, deceased, in distance from him about thirty-three yards, did instantly, willfully, and feloniously present a gun directed at the said Joseph Lonergan, deceased, and discharged the contents thereof, with design to kill the said Joseph Lonergan, and did hit him with a ball, which was the cause of the said Joseph Lonergan's death; deponent saith he also saw the said Edmund Power discharge a second shot at the deceased Joseph Lonergan; deponent saith said Edmund Power, Michael Power, and another man, whose name is yet unknown to deponent, did unmercifully take the deceased Joseph Lonergan, and him then bleeding in his wounds, put him on horseback, and carried and guarded him to the jail of Clonmel, in the said county; deponent saith he did not know any cause that commissioned said Edmund Power to kill or murder the deceased, or commit him to the jail of

Clonmel, wherein the said Joseph Lonergan died on the morning of Wednesday, the 22d instant; also saith the said Joseph Lonergan, deceased, made no defense, opposition, resistance, or rescue, against any authority or order then in the hands or power of said Edmund Power against him, the said Joseph Lonergan, deceased; deponent saith it was the aforesaid shot which he, the said Edmund Power, fired on him which caused his death; therefore desires justice, and at trial he will make more fully appear. Sworn before me, this 29th day of April, 1807. THOMAS PRENDERGAST.

Informant bound to the king in the trust sum of £20 to prosecute the above information at the next general assizes, to be holden at Clonmel for said court.

PATRICK LONERGAN,
his × mark.

We certify that the foregoing is a true and correct copy of the information, &c., in the case of the King *v.* Edmund Power, tried at the summer assizes, 1807, for the willful murder of Joseph Lonergan. Dated this 9th day of August, 1854. PEDDER AND CARMICHAEL,

per M. Harvey,
Clerk of the Crown, County Tipperary, L. R.

The long and arduous search for the above-mentioned documents, which led to their discovery, was made in my presence, the 8th of August, 1854, subsequently to the account given in the Introduction of this work of the atrocity they refer to.

On perusing these official documents, it can hardly fail to strike the reader with surprise how little variance there is between the accounts of a transaction which occurred forty-seven years ago, derived from the recollection of various parties, and the judicial records above referred to in relation to it.

The only discrepancies between them of any importance I have to notice, are the following:

By the depositions, it appears that the deceased Joseph Lonergan had a brother, who was present when Mr. Power fired at the former, not once, but twice, taking deliberate aim at him, when he was in the act of running away from his assailant; that no provocation had been given by the deceased, but that he was employed, at the moment he was fired at by Mr. Power, on his lawful business.

By the evidence of Mr. Everard, of Mullough, farmer, it appeared, immediately after he saw the shot fired by Mr. Power at Lonergan, who was in the act of running away, the deponent asked Mr. Power why he fired at the deceased, and Mr. Power replied, "The villain had thrown a stone at him of two pounds' weight."

Mr. Power never said a word about having any warrant for his apprehension; but subsequently the defense of Mr. Power was made on such grounds.

Mr. L. H. Jephson, a brother magistrate of Mr. Power, was produced at the inquest, who deposed "that there were informations sworn before deponent against the deceased for a capital felony" (but Mr. Jephson did not state what the felony was); "that they were lodged by a person in the jail of Waterford, who had turned approver" (but the name of the party was not given); "that the crime was so very serious, and the parties concerned in them so notorious, that deponent wrote to the lord lieutenant and secretary, who by letter informed deponent he might offer a reward *for any of the gang concerned*, and *deponent* saith the deceased was at the head of that gang, and that he gave Mr. Power the information to copy, with directions to him to act under them, and to apprehend any one of the said parties, *particularly three of them*, one of whom was the deceased."

The simple facts of the case were these: Mr. Jephson refers to a communication he made to the government, stating some grave crimes which were said to have been committed in his neighborhood. It is very plain neither he nor the government knew who the offenders were, for the government found it necessary to offer a reward of £100 for the discovery of them, "*for any of the gang concerned.*"

Mr. Jephson having been thus authorized, obtained some information which caused him to instruct Mr. Power to take measures for the arrest of some persons suspected to be of the gang concerned. And Mr. Power's act having rendered it necessary for him to attach suspicion to the unfortunate young man, whom in his phrensied recklessness he shot, had evidently given such reasons for those suspicions to his brother magistrate, that Mr. Jephson, at the period of the inquest, was satisfied that the deceased was one of the suspected parties belonging to the gang concerned in the unspecified outrage he referred to. But it is quite clear, if the evidence of the farmer, Everard, can be relied on, that Power's sole complaint against Lonergan was, that he had thrown a stone at him.

No. VII.—Introduction, p. 19.

PROSECUTION OF EDMUND POWER FOR LIBEL ON JOHN BAGWELL, ESQ.

Extracts from Angell's Report of the Trial, Bagwell *v.* Power, before Lord Norbury and a special jury, at Clonmel, county of Tipperary, Summer Assizes, August 11th, 1804. Published by Edmund Power, Clonmel, printer and publisher of "The Clonmel Gazette, or Munster Mercury."*

The counsel for the plaintiff were the solicitor general, William Lankey, Esq., Charles K. Bushe, Esq., Thomas Prendergast, Esq., Peter Burrowes, Esq., Hon. W. H. Yelverton, John Campbell, Esq., Richard Going, Esq., Edward Pennefeather, Esq., George Grace, Esq., Dennis O'Brien, Esq.

The counsel for the defendant, John Philpot Curran, Esq., Henry Deane Grady, Esq., T. Driscoll, Esq., Morgan Dwyer, Esq., John Lloyd, Esq., Dennis Scully, Esq.

* In one of the preceding references to this trial, there is an error in the date, which is stated 1806 instead of 1804, and in the amount of damages, which is set down at £500 instead of £400.—R. R. M.

The damages were laid at £5000.

Peter Burrowes, Esq., counsel for the plaintiff, stated that his client, John Bagwell, Esq., was colonel of the Tipperary militia; had been mayor of Clonmel, and represented the county in Parliament, and possessed in fee the town of Clonmel, and in virtue of that property had a control and direction over the tolls and customs of the town. The libels were published in the Clonmel Gazette, in December, 1803, in the shape of letters, signed "Cives," "An Inhabitant," "Contrastor," and "Hibernicus." One of them, making allusion to the colonel, not to be mistaken, and mentioning "impositions practiced on the tolls and customs of Clonmel, and in the weights," said,

"Who can expect that the forestaller, the bloodsucker of the poor, and the enemy to every class of society alike, will remain inactive?" Another paragraph speaks of "unprivileged ruffians, who incur the penalties of the law, while the delegated guardians of those laws incurred guilt of a deeper shade."

Another letter, still more outrageously libelous, alluding to Colonel Bagwell, but without naming that gentleman, in his capacity of commanding officer of his regiment, directly charged him with appropriating to his own uses the moneys he had obtained for bounty, intended by the government to be paid to the men enlisting in his regiment. The words of the libel were: "What say the patriot and the soldier? That a person honored by a commission long sought from the most gracious and glorious sovereign in the world, seeks to weaken the loyalty of those under his command by withholding that sovereign's bounty."

In another passage of a letter similarly directed, the following words occur:

"I would direct the enmity, the passions, every known and latent stimulus to hostility, against the common enemy, the indiscriminating desolator."

Thomas Quin, Esq., J. P., examined by plaintiff's counsel, proved that defendant was printer and publisher of the Clonmel Gazette. On cross-examination by Mr. Grady, said, "It was only within these two or three years that Mr. Power commenced the business of a printer. He believed Mr. Power to be a very honest, industrious man, of a respectable family, and had a number of children.

Did not believe him to be a malicious man.

Did not think him capable of telling horrible lies.

Believed him to be of too much integrity to do so.

Did not believe he would set forth any thing in his paper he did not believe to be true.

John Malcolmson, a Quaker (a brewer of Clonmel), made his affirmation. Believed the libels alluded to Colonel Bagwell.

On cross-examination by Counselor O'Driscoll, witness said, "There were reports about two years previously that some (bounty) money had been withheld from the soldiers, and the complaints had been the subject of a court of inquiry, and the result was, that some of complainant's accounts were settled, and the balances due to some of the men were paid."

He did not know who presided over that court.

Did not know whether Lieutenant Colonel Bagwell or Colonel Bagwell.

Knew his own name was Malcolmson. He might be the son of his mother, but may be the *son* of *Malcolm*, or *any other*.

His business was that of a brewer. Counsel observed, then some *grains* of allowance ought to be made for his memory.

Witness considered Power acted in the matter of the publication of these letters free from malice. He believed Power supported Mr. Bagwell in a late contested election, and had accompanied the latter to Dublin relative to his petition to Parliament arising out of the contested election. There had been a great friendship subsisting between them. He knew of one of the defendant's witnesses, Sergeant Hogan, having been at Marlfield, the seat of Colonel Bagwell, some days before the assizes; heard that Hogan had played billiards there.

Counsel asked, Did he hear Hogan had got his *cue* there? Witness said he heard he did.

Counsel asked, Did he hear that Sergeant Hogan *pocketed* the colonel? Witness answered, he heard that one *pocketed* the other, but did not know which. He only knew the colonel *played* with him, but could not say whether the sergeant *played the winning or the losing game.*

The libelous letters were read in evidence, and the plaintiff's case closed.

Henry Deane Grady, Esq., on the part of defendant, proposed to plaintiff's counsel to withdraw a juror, and each party to pay his own costs. The proposal was refused by the solicitor general. Counselor Grady rested his defense on the two pleas put in by the defendant—a denial that the letters complained of as libelous were false and malicious, and justification of the statements made therein. He complained that three of the witnesses, on whom defendant mainly relied to prove the bounty money that they were entitled to on joining the Tipperary militia, had been trepanned into the camp of the enemy at Marlfield by his attorney. It would, however, be proved in evidence, he said, that the colonel did receive £1200 for raising two hundred and forty men, at the rate of £5 each man, and it would be proved the bounty money had been withheld from the men.

(The evidence only in three cases appeared to bear out this allegation.)

Mr. Curran, for the defendant, speaking to evidence, said, when he considered the circumstances of the present time, he felt oppressed and heart-stricken; but he trusted the jury would have some recollection of what they had been, some little remembrance of the spirit of departed liberty, before the few remaining privileges of a free country—those of a free press—were consigned to the grave and extinguished forever. This was an action of a rich man against a poor one, in whose person the liberty of the press was to be punished and put down. Would the jury wish to see its annihilation? Would they walk in procession to the grave of its freedom, at the command of Colonel Bagwell, and, having buried it, then bemoan its non-existence? Was it the wish of the plaintiff to extinguish in Ireland the race of printers? He had seized on one of them—caught him; but having entrapped, he would not destroy him like a rat, although he would burn him in part, singe him on the back, and then send him slinking away among the other terrified creatures of the press, to warn them against publishing in future any similar productions. If the plaintiff's views against the press were to be carried out, there would be an end of all security against wrongs, all disclosures of abuses. Mr. Angell, the reporter, then in court, might cease to take his notes, and at once take his flight to heaven. If the printers of public journals were restricted in their publications, newspapers then would only contain the current prices of fairs and markets, and the arrival and departure of the judges to and from the assize towns, an account of their splendid retinue, and the sheriff's liveries, and the time of high water at Dublin bar.

The solicitor general replied to Mr. Curran at considerable length, arguing that the poverty of the plaintiff should be no bar to the infliction of a heavy punishment in the way of extensive damages for a malignant libel. "No man should come forward with a dagger in one hand and his rags in the other."

Lord Norbury, in summing up the evidence, strongly expressed his opinion that the action was maintainable in point of law, and the jury had a good foundation to find a verdict for the plaintiff. The jury retired at a quarter past three o'clock on *Sunday morning*, and in about a quarter of an hour brought in a verdict for the plaintiff—*four hundred pounds damages and sixpence costs.*

At the Summer Assizes of Clonmel, August 19th, 1806, the extraordinary case of M'Carthy against Watson was tried before Mr. Justice Daly, and lasted three days and a half. The damages laid in the declaration were heavy, but the sum sought to be recovered, on special grounds, was £602 5*s*., being the amount of the execution obtained by Colonel Bagwell against Mr. Power, formerly printer and publisher of the Clonmel Gazette, for a libel in that paper, and which sum it was alleged Mr. Watson had promised to pay a Mr. M'Carthy, of Spring Mount, in consequence of his advancing that sum, in discharge of the execution, and on the ground that Mr. Watson had been the author and instigator of the libel. Some of the family of Mr. Power were examined as witnesses on this trial. The jury brought in a verdict for £316 2*s*. 6*d*., being exactly one half the amount demanded.*

No. VIII.—Page 121.

CERTIFICATE OF BURIALS OF MEMBERS OF THE BLESSINGTON FAMILY.

Diligent search has been made in the Registry Book of Burials in St. Thomas's Parish, Dublin, from 1769 to 1854. The following are recorded:

* Vide Dublin Evening Post, August 19, 1806.

Date.
1769, Nov. 17. Right Hon. Charles Gardiner, Esq., aged 49 years.
1781, Sept. 21. Master Luke Gardiner, an infant.
1783, Nov. 25. Mrs. Elizabeth Gardiner, aged 32 years.
1786, March 20. Florinda Gardiner, aged 12 years.
1791, Feb. 1. Hon. Elizabeth Gardiner, aged 8 years.
1798, June 15. Lord Viscount Mountjoy, aged 52 years.
1814, Sept 17. Right Hon. Mary Campbell, Viscountess Mountjoy, aged 28 years.
1823, March 29. The Hon. Luke Wellington Gardiner, Viscount Mountjoy, aged 9 years and 4 months.
1829, June 20. Charles John, Earl of Blessington, aged 46 years, Gardiner.
1849, March 27. The Hon. Harriet Gardiner, aged 73 years. Rutland Square.

No. IX.—Page 123.

The Annuities, Mortgages, Judgments, and other Debts, Legacies, Sums of Money, and Incumbrances, charged upon or affecting the Estates of the said Charles John, Earl of Blessington, at the time of his Decease.*

Mortgages.

	£	s.	d.
1783, March 1. To Miss Margaret Croft (since deceased), now vested in Michael Lambton Este, Esq.	2,769	4	7
1817, Oct. 31. To Conyngham M'Alpine, Esq. (since deceased), now vested in Lieutenant Colonel James M'Alpine	11,076	18	5
1821, Dec. 1. To the Westminster Insurance Company	25,000	0	0
1825, Dec. 1. Ditto	5,000	0	0
1823, Jan. 1. To Edward Bailey, Richard Saunders, and Executors of Thomas Tatham (balance remaining due)	4,000	0	0
	£47,846	3	0

Legacies.

	£	s.	d.
Emilie Rosalie Hamilton Gardiner, now the wife of Charles Whyte, Esq.	18,461	10	9
To Count D'Orsay, Assignees of	923	1	6½
Luke Norman, Esq., Executors of	923	1	6½
Alexander Worthington, Esq.	923	1	6
Robert Power, Assignees of	923	1	6½
Mary Anne Power, Assignees of	923	1	6
Michael M'Donagh	92	6	2
Isabella Binny	92	6	2
John Bullock	92	6	2
	£23,353	16	11½

* Fourth schedule appended to the act for the sale of the Blessington estates, 9 Vict., cap. 1.

	£	s.	d.
Legacy to the Hon. Harriet Gardiner, principal sum to be raised only in the event of her marriage	9,230	15	4½
1827, Nov. 2. Settlement executed by the Earl of Blesinton on the marriage of his daughter, Lady Harriet Anne Jane Frances Gardiner, with Count D'Orsay	40,000	0	0

Annuities.

	£	s.	d.
1811, March 25. To William James M'Causland. For the Life of Susanna Ellison	36	18	5½
1811, March 25. To Florinda Ellison, now the wife of Wm. Latham, Esq. For her own Life	36	18	5½
1813, Dec. 8. To the Globe Insurance Company. For the Life of George Carr Glynn, son of Sir Richard Carr Glynn, Bart.	526	13	6
1813, Dec. 8. To the same. For the Life of Abraham Mocatta, son of Daniel Mocatta, of Goodman's Fields, London	520	15	0
1813, Dec. 8. To the same. For the Life of William Coles, son of Thomas Coles, of Thornheath, Surry	510	10	0
1813, Dec. 8. To the same. For the Life of David Hunter, son of David Hunter, of East Combe House, Kent	527	10	0
1813, Dec. 8. To the same. For the Life of Maria Blair, daughter of Thomas Blair, of Welbeck Street	517	5	0
1814, July 26. To Anthony Angelo Tremonando. For the Life of Richard Frederick Tremonando	880	0	0
1815, May 2. To Maria Black. For her own Life	46	3	1
1816, Feb. 13. To Alexander Nowell. For the Lives of Francis Stracey, Henry Josias Stracey (since deceased), and the Rev. Thursby Whitaker	1,000	0	0
1816, Mar. 18. To Henry Fauntleroy and John Watson. For the Lives of John Fauntleroy, William Watson, and James Watson	500	0	0
1817. To Martha Anderson. For her own Life	9	4	7½
1817, Sept. 1. To Charles Gardiner (since deceased) and his wife, now Mrs. Hay. For Joint Lives of himself and wife	221	10	9
1829, May 25. To Margaret, Countess of Blessington. For her own Life	2,000	0	0
1829, May 25. To the Hon. Harriet Gardiner. For her own Life	461	10	9
1829, May 25. To Mrs. Isabella M'Dougall. For her own Life	92	6	2
	£7,887	5	9½

Judgments.

1829, Easter Term:	£	s.	d.
George Hill, Assignees of	1,846	3	1
Rev. Claudius Crigan	461	10	9
Robert Power, Assignees of	1,846	3	1
Margaret Viscountess Mountjoy, Executors of	923	1	6½
Ditto	923	1	6½
Ditto	184	12	4
Rev. Joseph Ralph Worthington, Beresford Worthington, Assignee of	276	18	5½
Ditto	1,846	3	1
Ditto	461	10	9
Thomas Worthington	369	4	7½
Owen Lloyd and Alexander Worthington	2,560	7	8
Eleanor Worthington, Alexander Worthington, Executor of	1,107	13	10
The like	369	4	7½
Elizabeth Dudgeon	92	6	2
	£13,268	1	6½

Bond Debts.

	£	s.	d.
1783, June 17. To Miss Margaret Croft, now vested in Michael Lambton Este, Esq.	276	18	5½
1797, August 1. To John M'Evoy, now vested in the Rev. Claudius Crigan	246	3	1
1806, Sept. 12. To John M'Farland	92	6	2
1810, May 14. Marsh, Stracey, and Company, Assignees of	2,233	14	11
——, Nov. 1. To Archibald Johnston, Administrators of	92	6	2
1817, August 15. To William Moore	200	0	0
The like	200	0	0
The like	201	16	1
1819, July 17. To David Ellis, now vested in the Assignees of Henry Fauntleroy	545	14	6
1826, March 4. To James Newton	500	0	0
——, April 1. To Charles Winser, Executrix of, on foot of three several bonds	4,768	9	10
	£10,357	9	2½

Promissory Notes, Letters of Acknowledgment, I. O. U.'s, &c.

	£	s.	d.
1808, April 8. William Scott, Executors of	92	6	2
1816, Nov. 23. John Orr	184	12	4
1825, August 3. George Hill, Assignee of	153	16	11
——, June 1. Count D'Orsay, Assignees of	1,280	0	0
——, Nov. 1. John Cather, Executors of	316	17	8
Carried forward	£2,027	13	1

	£	s.	d.
Brought forward	£2,027	13	1
1825, Nov. 1. John Cather, Executors of	316	17	8
1826, June 21. John Orr	55	7	8
1828, Nov. 1. Hodgkinson and Company	500	0	0
1829, Jan. 1. John Irvine, Executors of	1,800	0	0
——, Jan. 29. Rev. Claudius Crigan	461	10	9
——, April 10. Ditto	461	10	9
——, Sept. 11. Count D'Orsay, Assignee of	4,000	0	0
——, Feb. 6. John Cuffe	500	0	0
	£10,122	19	11

Simple Contract Debts due, or claimed to be due, by the said Charles John, Earl of Blessington.

	£	s.	d.
Robert Power, Esq.	792	19	2
Alexander Campbell, Executor of	38	11	11
Hugh O'Neill, Assignee of	158	10	0
Thomas Branson	40	0	0
Countess of Blessington	518	0	0
John Cather, Executors of	44	8	10
Charles Scott	53	0	6
William Taylor	500	0	0
John Jarman	138	18	0
Smyth and Nephew	710	19	9
Colnaghi and Co.	208	2	0
Benjamin Weale	83	3	0
Barker and Company	437	17	6
Alexander Vincent	44	16	0
Jones and Yarrell	24	8	0
Count D'Orsay	199	1	0
George Barlow	10	5	8
Henry Lees	63	2	3
John Howell	1,723	0	0
Launcelot Burton	100	0	0
Thomas Hodgkinson	349	8	9
George Hill, Assignee of	90	17	6
James Newton	100	1	7
James Andrews	29	6	0
Executors of William Webb	65	9	6
Richard M'Henry	54	0	10
Gallanty Brothers	75	7	6
George Roduart	45	12	10
Madame Theux	79	4	2
Antoinette Valcaringhi	44	5	0
Joseph Hallmarke and William Mason	78	12	0

G. F. Smith.

The Fifth Schedule referred to in the foregoing Act, containing the Mortgages and Sums of Money which have been charged by the Lady Harriet Anne Jane Frances, Countess D'Orsay, upon the Estates comprised in the Second and Third Schedules to this Act:

	£	s.	d.
1837, May 11. Mortgage to Miss Emilie Rosalie Hamilton Gardiner, now the wife of Charles Whyte, Esq.	5,500	0	0
1839, March 30. Mortgage to Simon Jaques Rochard	2,100	0	0
1840, March 25. Ditto to Messrs. Hopkinson and Co.	2,500	0	0
——, August 1. Ditto to John Williamson Fulton	5,000	0	0
1843, April 24. Ditto to John March Case	1,500	0	0
——, August 29. Ditto to Matthew Anderson	1,250	0	0
——, Sept. 1. Ditto to Richard Philip Tighe	434	0	0
1844, July 7. Ditto to Joanna Dowling	600	0	0
1845, July 17. Ditto to Charles Hopkinson	700	0	0
Ditto to James Fiddes	600	0	0

No. X.—Page 123.

RENTAL OF THE BLESSINGTON ESTATES. FROM THE SCHEDULES OF THE ACT OF PARLIAMENT FOR THE SALE OF THE ESTATES, OF THE 18TH OF JUNE, 1846.

Estates situate in the county of Tyrone, in the manors of Newtown Stewart and Rash, situate in the baronies of Strabane and Omagh. Quantity in English acres, 30,221 A., 1 R., 8 P. Present rent (1846), £8265 16*s*. 3*d*.

Estates situate in the barony of Dungannon, held by lease from the crown. Quantity in English acres, 2053 A., 1 R., 32 P. Present rent (1846), £1066 15*s*. 11*d*.

Estates situate in the county and the city of Dublin:

Part 1, comprising the lordship of St. Mary's Abbey, and Grange of Clonliffe, and other parcels of ground, situate in the county and the city of Dublin, held under lease. Present rent, £9730 12*s*. 6*d*.

Part 2, comprising the lordship of St. Mary's Abbey, and Grange of Clonliffe, in the county and the city of Dublin, let to yearly tenants. Present rent, £1764 10*s*. 7*d*.

Part 3, comprising Barrack Street, Tighe Street, George's Quay, Mercer's Dock, Poolbeg Street, and North Strand, the lands of Glasmainogue, and a leasehold interest. Present rent, £1827 15*s*. 7*d*.

SUMMARY OF THE BLESSINGTON ESTATES RENTAL.

All the estates situate in the county and the city of Dublin, comprising parts 1, 2, and 3. Yearly rent, £13,322 18*s*. 8*d*.

Property situate in the city of Kilkenny. Yearly rent, £62 3*s*. 9*d*.

Total of rental of all the properties, including the Tyrone estates above-mentioned, in 1846, estimated at £22,718 14*s*. 7*d*.

No. XI.—Page 180.

GORE HOUSE.

Gore House occupation has had many vicissitudes. The predecessor of Wilberforce was a stingy, money-scraping government contractor, "who would not lay out a penny to keep his gardens" in order. The mammon-worshiper, who meditated in those neglected grounds on the delights of parsimony, was succeeded by "the saint," who thus spoke, in his Diary, of his perambulations in the vicinity of his new residence: "Walked from Hyde Park Corner, repeating the 119th Psalm, in great comfort" (the Psalm of 176 verses); and who thus refers to the house itself: "We are just one mile from the turnpike gate at Hyde Park Corner . . . having about three acres of pleasure-ground around my house, or rather behind it, and several old trees, walnut and mulberry, of thick foliage. I can sit and read under their shade, which I delight in doing, with as much admiration of the beauties of nature (remembering at the same time the words of my favorite poet, 'Nature is but a name for an effect whose cause is God'), as if I were two hundred miles from the great city."*

A new meditator, but not so much on the beauties of nature as those of art and literature, one who was more *spirituelle* in *salons* than spiritual in Wilberforce's sense of the word, "the gorgeous Lady Blessington," became the proprietor of Gore House. Illustrated annuals and fashionable novels were the result of her meditations in "those pleasure grounds" which served Wilberforce for solitudes, for meditations on Psalms.

Lady Blessington was succeeded by Monsieur Soyer. Another species of composition was carried on at Gore House—sauces constituted the chief glory of it. The culinary line had replaced the literary; and every one, during the Great Exhibition, had the *entrée* of those *salons*, once so celebrated for intellectual society, who had a few shillings to expend on a dinner *à la mode*. The glory of Soyer, and his soups and sauces, passed away in a short time, and Gore House was turned into a temporary crowded receptacle of ornamental cabinet-work and studies from the School of Art.

A new destination is now about to be given to Gore House and its pleasure-grounds. "The estate purchased by the commissioners for the site and grounds of the new National Gallery includes those just described, which consists of about twenty acres, and it will probably, when completed, approach to a hundred."

No. XII.—Page 303.

COUNT D'ORSAY AND THE PRINCE LOUIS NAPOLEON.

The intimate relations that subsisted between the present Emperor of the French when a refugee and a proscribed conspirator in England, and the Count D'Orsay in the palmy days of his London fashionable life, may render

* Dickens's Household Words, No. 178, p. 590.

a brief notice of the family and fortunes of Louis Napoleon of some interest in connection with a memoir of the Count D'Orsay.

In March, 1828, Lady Blessington made the acquaintance, at Rome, of Madame Hortense, ex-queen of Holland—the Duchesse de St. Leu.

Josephine Tascher de la Pagerie had two children by her first marriage with General Alexander Vicomte de Beauharnais, who was guillotined in 1794. Of the two children, Prince Eugene, the subsequent Viceroy of Italy, and later Duke of Leuchtenberg, born in 1781, died in Munich in 1824; the second, Hortense—perhaps the only being whom Napoleon could be said to have truly loved—was married to the brother of Napoleon, Louis, King of Holland, and, after many vicissitudes, died in 1838, universally loved and regretted. This excellent lady was highly gifted and accomplished, and, alike on the throne and in private life, her enlightenment, varied talents, and benevolent disposition shed a lustre around her, and rendered her at once the most fascinating and amiable of women. Her marriage, however, was an unhappy one; she lived apart from her husband except, at three very long intervals, for a very short term on each occasion of a sort of reconciliation, that was not destined to be of long duration. They finally separated in 1807.

Lady Blessington while residing in Italy, makes frequent mention of this illustrious lady in her letters.

The time, she says, always passed away rapidly and most delightfully while listening to her conversation and hearing her sing those charming little French romances, which were written and composed by herself. She was equally fascinating in her manners and appearance, though not beautiful. She was of the middle stature, slight and delicate, and well formed; her carriage graceful, and of imposing deportment and address. Her complexion was fair, and the expression of her countenance mild and pensive, but when she entered into conversation her features were full of life and vivacity; she was quick of apprehension, possessed a clear insight into character, and regulated her conversation and bearing toward people in society by the opinions she formed, and usually with excellent judgment and good sense. She was highly accomplished, a good artist, highly skilled in drawing, spoke several languages, was well versed in history and the literature of various countries. But more than for all her accomplishments, Lady Blessington admired the ex-queen of Holland for her kindly disposition, her generous and noble nature. This amiable woman lived much in Italy in her latter years.

The contrast which Lady Blessington drew in some of her letters between the ex-queen Hortense and the ex-queen Maria Louisa was not very favorable to the latter.

The ex-empress Maria Lousia, Archduchess of Parma, formerly wife of the Emperor Napoleon, died at Parma, December 17, 1848, aged fifty-six. In 1810, when this princess was in her nineteenth year, she became the bride of the great soldier-sovereign of France, Italy, Holland, and Belgium.

The scandalous repudiation of the generous-minded, noble-hearted Josephine never appears to have disturbed the apathy of the Austrian princess. Four years of imperial grandeur shared with the Emperor of France—the tie of a child, born to her in that period, and the claims of that child's father on her affection, or the cold feelings even of duty, were matters of no consideration when Napoleon's star was waning. Maria Louisa sought not to share the fortunes of her husband in the mild banishment of Elba. She left her son a hostage in the hands of her father—she left her husband a captive in the hands of his enemies, to entertain his fate alone.

The body of the Archduchess Maria Louisa was conveyed to Vienna, and deposited in the imperial vault, in the church of the Capuchins, by the side of that of her son, the Duke of Reichstadt.

She died without honor, dignity, respect, or esteem.

January the 11th, 1838, the funeral ceremonies in memory of the late Duchesse de St. Leu, ex-queen of Holland, were performed in the church of Reuel, near Paris, with great magnificence and solemnity. Three months later, in April, 1838, the Duke de St. Leu, ex-king of Holland, was married in Florence to the Signora Strozzi. The church of Reuel was crowded to overflowing. Seats were occupied by the Comtesse de Lipona (ex-queen of Naples, the widow of Murat), the Prince of Musignano (son of Lucien Bonaparte), the venerable Marquis de Beauharnais, brother to the first husband of Josephine, General Count Tascher de la Pagerie (once Governor General of Frankfort), cousin to Queen Hortense, and other distinguished persons. A catafalque was raised near the tomb of the deceased's mother, the Empress Josephine, whose statue of marble was covered with a black veil. The pall was borne by the Marquis de Beauharnais and Count de Tascher. The attendance of the clergy was very numerous, and detachments of troops of the line, and national guards of Reuel, added to the pomp of the scene. Many of the persons involved in the prosecution for the attempt at Strasburg were present.*

Louis Bonaparte, ex-king of Holland, bearing the title of Count of St. Leu, the reputed father of the present Emperor of the French, was born at Ajaccio in 1778. He entered the French army at an early age, and accompanied his brother Napoleon to Italy and Egypt. He was aid-de-camp to Napoleon when the latter, seizing a standard, rushed upon the bridge of Arcola, on which occasion Louis placed himself in front of his brother, between him and the fire of the enemy. From that period he was employed by his brother in several diplomatic and confidential employments of high importance to Napoleon's interest and designs. In 1802 he married, "malgre lui," Hortense Fanny de Beauharnais, daughter of the Empress Josephine. After various honors, dignities, and high offices had been conferred on him, in 1806 he was placed, "malgre lui," on the throne of Holland by Napoleon. In 1810 he abdicated his crown from a sense of duty to his subjects, refusing to be the tool of his brother's tyranny in respect to the commerce and trade of the Dutch people. Holland became then united to the empire. Louis retired to

* The Athenæum, Jan. 20, 1838.

Gratz, in Styria, where he resided for three years in honorable self-imposed exile, resisting all pecuniary offers, an apanage, either for himself or his children, made by the Emperor of France.

In 1813, when France was menaced with invasion, he offered his services to the Emperor, by whom they were accepted; but, notwithstanding their acceptance, having proceeded to Switzerland, he remained there unemployed. After the restoration of the Bourbons, he retired to the Papal States, and there devoted himself chiefly to literature and antiquarian pursuits. He published several works—a novel, Historic Documents on Holland, a treatise on Versification, an opera, a tragedy, a collection of Poems, and some comments on Sir W. Scott's History of Napoleon. He died at Leghorn, the 23d of June, 1846, leaving a request that his body and that of his son, who was killed at Forli in 1831, in the insurrection of Romagna, might be taken to France, and buried at St. Leu, near Enghien, with the remains of his father and his first son, who had been buried there, which wish was fulfilled in September, 1847, with great pomp, and an attendance (very significant) of upward of ten thousand persons from Paris, a distance of about eighteen miles from St. Leu, and five hundred of the veteran soldiers of the empire, wearing the uniforms of the Old Guard, and several other corps, *brought together on that occasion* to attend the funeral. Among the attendants were Jerome Bonaparte, ex-king of Westphalia, "and Doctor Conneau, the friend of Louis Napoleon, who was confined in Ham."*

The third son of Louis Bonaparte, King of Holland, the Prince Louis Bonaparte, who died in 1831, left a widow, the Princess Charlotte Bonaparte, daughter of Joseph Bonaparte, ex-king of Spain, who died at Florence the 3d of March, 1839. The sister of this most amiable and highly accomplished lady married Charles Lucien Bonaparte, a son of the Prince de Canino.

In March, 1828, when Lady Blessington made the acquaintance of the ex-queen of Holland, her second son, Prince Louis Napoleon Bonaparte (now Emperor of the French), then living with his mother, was in his twentieth year. Lady Blessington says she never witnessed a more devoted attachment than subsisted between them. "He is a fine, high-spirited youth," she observes in one of her letters, "admirably well educated and finely accomplished, uniting to the gallant bearing of a soldier all the politeness of a *preux* chevalier; but how could he be otherwise, brought up with such a mother? Prince Louis Bonaparte is much beloved and esteemed by all who know him, and is said to resemble his uncle, the Prince Eugene Beauharnais, no less in person than in mind, possessing his generous nature, personal courage, and high sense of honor."

Prince Napoleon Louis was born in Paris in April, 1808. In 1831, both he and his elder brother took part in the Italian insurrection, which had for its aim the establishment of a republic and the downfall of the papal government. His eldest brother was killed, and he himself narrowly escaped the

* Annual Register for 1847, p. 634.

same fate. Five years later, the prince made an attempt to overthrow the government of Louis Philippe—failed, and was captured at Strasburg—was pardoned on account of his supposed imbecility, and conveyed to America. He wrote a letter extolling the generosity of the king, and his gratitude for it. Four years had not elapsed when he made another attempt against Louis Philippe's throne and government. The 6th of August, 1840, he made a descent upon Boulogne with about sixty followers disguised as French soldiers, and very much the worse for excessive tossing the previous night, fired a single shot at an officer, wounded another person, and then fled.

The fugitive prince was taken, tried by the Chamber of Peers, and condemned to perpetual imprisonment. He was confined in the fortress of Ham for five years, and finally escaped from it disguised as a stone-mason, and sought refuge in England in 1845. During his captivity the prince composed some works that manifested sympathy with the laboring classes and the progress of industrial pursuits.

In the various political escapades which made it necessary for the prince to seek a refuge in England, the house of Lady Blessington—her much-needed, but most ill-requited hospitality—her most useful influence in his favor with the persons of the first importance in political circles and in the government—the unfailing friendship of Count D'Orsay—his untiring exertions for the prince and his cause, in the press, in the clubs, in all quarters where an impression was to be made for him, were to be counted on, and were made use of by this refugee. The base return which Louis Napoleon made for these generous services will be found noticed elsewhere in this work; and in the minds of many, his ungrateful and ungracious conduct to D'Orsay in his latter days, when he had lost fortune, friends, health, and spirits, will appear as dark a stain on his private character as any that attaches to his public conduct, except such as have been left by blood.

In February, 1848, Louis Philippe's throne was swept away, the republic substituted for the monarchy of 1830, and among the foremost to hail the young giant of democracy was the Prince Louis Napoleon. In the following September he was elected a deputy, took his seat in the National Assembly, not without much distrust of his intentions, and abundant cause for suspicion in his speeches and public communications.

The 20th of December, 1848, the Constituent Assembly of the French Republic declared Prince Charles Louis Napoleon Bonaparte duly elected President of the Republic from that date until the second Sunday in May, 1852.

On that momentous occasion, a solemn oath was sworn with all due solemnity and sacred form in these words: "IN THE PRESENCE OF GOD AND BEFORE THE FRENCH PEOPLE REPRESENTED BY THE NATIONAL ASSEMBLY, I SWEAR TO REMAIN FAITHFUL TO THE DEMOCRATIC REPUBLIC, ONE AND INDIVISIBLE, AND TO FULFILL ALL THE DUTIES IMPOSED ON ME BY THE CONSTITUTION."

The new president, not content with the oath he had just taken, added to it a voluntary declaration of fealty to the republic. He addressed the Assembly, and the last sentence of his speech was to this effect: "*I shall regard as the enemies of the country all who seek to change, by illegal means, that which entire France has established.*"

The new Constitution, to which the president swore fidelity, guaranteed the inviolability of the persons of representatives of the people, and declared it to be high treason for the president to abrogate, annul, or suspend the privileges and functions of the National Assembly. In three years, less by three weeks or thereabout, on the 2d of December, 1851, the Prince President absolved himself from his oath, dissolved the Assembly and Council of State, arrested the principal deputies, substituted a military government, administered by himself, for that of the republic, under the regime of a popular representation.

Two days later, the Prince President at the Elysée pronounced these decisive words to General Roquet: "*Qu'on execute mes ordres,*" to put an end to all hesitation or remonstrance on the part of his generals; and on the 4th of December, when barricades began to be thrown up in some parts of the city, eight hundred people were butchered by his orders, in cold blood, in the streets of Paris, by the troops of the republic, and the great majority of the slain were persons who had taken no part whatever in the barricades, while a vast number of people were slaughtered in their own houses — old men, women, and children, who were indiscriminately sabred and shot down.

This man-mystery, the depths of whose duplicity no Œdipus has yet sounded, is a problem even to those who surround him. I watched his pale, corpse-like, imperturbable features, not many months since, for a period of three hours. I saw eighty thousand men in arms pass before him, and I never observed a change in his countenance, or an expression in his look which would enable the by-stander to say whether he was pleased or otherwise at the stirring scene that was passing before him, on the very spot where Louis XVI. was put to death. He did not speak to those around him except at very long intervals, and then with an air of *nonchalance*, of ennui, and eternal occupation with self: he rarely spoke a syllable to his uncle, Jerome Bonaparte, who was on horseback somewhat behind him. It was the same with his brilliant staff. All orders came from him—all command seemed centred in him. He gave me the idea of a man who had a perfect reliance on himself, and a feeling of complete control over those around him. But there was a weary look about him, an aspect of excessive watchfulness, an appearance of want of sleep, of over-work, of over-indulgence too, that gives an air of exhaustion to face and form, and leaves an impression on the mind of a close observer that the machine of the body will break down soon, and suddenly, or the mind will give way, under the pressure of pent-up thoughts and energies eternally in action, and never suffered to be observed or noticed by friends or followers.

The man who had the shrewdness and discretion to profit by the stupidity of the democracy when in power, to avoid the blunder of associating republicanism with hatred to priests and hostility to religion, who had the good sense to remember that the masses of the people believed in their religion, that the sacerdotal power was a great element of influence in a state (I do not say who had any sincere regard for the interests of faith or morals, or the ministers of religion), it is in vain to represent as a "vulgar, commonplace personage, puerile, theatrical, and vain," as one "who loves finery, trinkets, feathers, embroidery, spangles, grand words, and grand titles—the sounding, the glittering, all the glass-ware of power."*

I should be more disposed to regard him as a man originally well-intentioned and well-disposed, of good qualities, wrongly directed in his studies, strongly imbued with feelings of veneration for his imperial uncle, taught to conceal them in the times of the reverses of his family; in his tender years, trained to dissimulation; who had grown up to manhood accustomed to silence, secrecy, and self-communion — *peu demonstratif*, an ambitious, moody young man, with a dash of genius in the composition of his mind, and a tinge of superstition in his credence in the connection of his fortune with the dispensations of divine Providence, that give a permanent color of fatalism to his opinions, in keeping with the impulses of an immoderate ambition, which may have perturbed to some extent his imagination.

A man whose life is all interior (not spiritually so, but wholly worldly-minded), who lives for himself, in himself, and by himself, whether in a state prison or on a throne, can not long remain in a state of mind either safe for himself or the confidence that others may place in his stability of purpose, policy, or promises.

The author of "Idées Napoliennes," of a work on artillery, which Victor Hugo even acknowledges "well compiled;" of several treatises, written either in prison or in exile, on "*The Extinction of Pauperism*," "*The Analysis of the Sugar Question*"—"Historical Fragments," "Political Reveries," can not with justice be called "a vulgar, commonplace personage, puerile, theatrical, and vain." He is a man of considerable talent, of measureless ambition, and of no moral principles, of one fixed idea—a belief in the destiny of his elevation to supreme power, and the sufficiency of his own abilities to maintain it—a fatalist working out a destiny that is desired by him — a projector on a grand scale of plans for the promotion of selfish objects, wrapped up in traditions of the empire and its glory, without sympathies with other men, without confidence in any man, a speculator on the meanness, the imbecility, and sordid dispositions of all around him, silent, self-sufficient, self-confident, self-opinioned, self-willed—in the words to me of one of the deepest thinkers and closest observers of France, "A man of no convictions of good or evil —all rapt up in self."

Let us see how he allows himself to be spoken of by an able writer who is within reach of his commissaries of police.

The following is the character of the President of the French Republic, as drawn by M. de la Gueronnière, late editor of "La Presse," and now editor of the "Pays:"

* Napoleon le Petit.

"Louis Napoleon is a superior man, but with that superiority which conceals itself under a doubtful exterior. His life is altogether internal—his words do not indicate his inspiration—his gesture does not show his audacity—his glance does not intimate his ardor—his demeanor does not reveal his resolution. All his moral nature is, in a certain manner, kept under by his physical nature. He thinks, and does not discuss; he decides, and does not deliberate; he acts, and does not make much movement; he pronounces, and does not assign his reasons. His best friends do not know him—he commands confidence, and never seeks it. The day before the expedition to Boulogne, General Montholon had promised him to follow wherever he led. Every day he presides in silence at his council of ministers—he listens to every thing that is said, speaks but little, and never yields—with a phrase, brief and clear as an order of the day, he decides the most disputed questions. And that is the reason why a Parliamentary ministry is almost impossible by his side. A Parliamentary ministry would want to govern, and he would not consent to abdicate. But with that inflexibility of will there is nothing abrupt or absolute in the form. Queen Hortense used to call him the mildly obstinate; and that judgment of the mother is completely true. Louis Napoleon Bonaparte possesses that goodness of heart which tempers and often conceals the workings of the mind. The somewhat English stiffness of his person, manners, and even language, disappears under an affability, which, with him, is only the grace of sentiment. Many are deceived by that appearance, and take his goodness for weakness, and his affability for insincerity. At bottom he is completely master of himself; and his kindest movements enter into his actions only according to the exact measure he has determined on. Easily roused, he can not soon be led away; he calculates every thing, even his enthusiasm and his acts of audacity; his heart is only the vassal of his head. Does that inflexible judgment constitute an active will? I hesitate not to reply no; and it is here that I have to touch on one of the shades the most essential and most delicate of his character. Louis Napoleon Bonaparte is endowed with an incontestable power of resistance—of *vis inertiæ;* but what he wants, in the very highest degree, is the power of initiative. He believes too much that the empire is to be, and is apathetic. He is not sufficiently impressed with the maxim that the head of a government is bound not only to resist the impulse of the parties which desire to lead him away, but that, to properly fulfill all his mission, he ought to have an impulse of his own, to march firmly forward, and to make himself the guide of the public mind. In closely examining the acts of the president of the republic since he has been in power, we perceive that he has freed himself from every one, but led no one after him. It would seem that he must become an instrument in the hands of this man or of that. But he has served no ambition, and has very adroitly withdrawn from all the conjoint responsibilities which impeded or constrained him. All would have been exceedingly well if, after having had sufficient energy to achieve his personal independence, he had possessed sufficient resources to constitute his political importance, and to connect his individuality with a great movement of opinion. It is that which he has not done. Louis Napoleon Bonaparte is at present the free and incontestable head of the government, but he is not the head of public opinion; he has, without doubt, behind him many reminiscences which his name arouses, much enthusiasm which his blood produces, many sympathies generated by his character, and many interests reassured by his government, but he has not under his hand those great currents of opinion which men of real strength produce and direct, which carry their fortune with that of their country. Is that his fault? I am inclined to think it is."

No. XIII.—Page 55.

THEATRICAL TASTES OF LORD BLESSINGTON'S FATHER.

Lord Blessington's passion for theatricals was an hereditary one. His father had his private theatricals in the Phœnix Park, when he filled the office of Ranger. "The Right Honorable Luke Gardiner, member for the county of Dublin, and keeper of the Phœnix Park, had a great love for the stage, and had erected a most elegant theatre in the Park. Captain Jephson's tragedy of Macbeth, and the farce of the Citizen, were thrice performed there in January, 1778, and the character of Macbeth was most brilliantly supported by Captain Jephson." The captain died in 1803; he was the author of "The Count of Narbonne," "Braganza," "The Campaign," an opera; "Love and War," "The Conspiracy," "The Servant with two Masters," "Two Strings to your Bow."

No. XIV.—Page 21.

DUEL BETWEEN MICHAEL POWER, ESQ., AND CAPTAIN KETTLEWELL.

On the 19th of September, 1806, a duel was fought near Two-mile Bridge, in the vicinity of Clonmel, between a Lieutenant Kettlewell (now Colonel Kettlewell) and Michael Power, Esq., the eldest son of Edmund Power, when, after the discharge of two shots each, the affair was amicably settled by the interference of the seconds. Captain Armstrong, of the Artillery, was friend to Lieutenant Kettlewell, and Mr. O'Connell, of Clonmel, was the second of Mr. Power.*

No. XV.—Page 523.

M'CARTHY *v.* WATSON.

"A report of the trial which took place at the Clonmel Assizes, for the county Tipperary, on Thursday, the 4th of August, 1806, wherein *Charles M'Carthy, Esq., was plaintiff, and Solomon Watson, banker, of Clonmel, was*

* The Dublin Evening Post, 23d September, 1806.

defendant," published by Graisberry and Campbell, 10 Back Lane, Dublin, 1807, was, with great difficulty, recently procured for me.*

The following is a summary of the report of those proceedings.

This cause was brought for trial at the Waterford Assizes in the spring of 1806. The jury having differed, a juror was withdrawn by consent. New proceedings were adopted.

The venue was changed to the county of Tipperary on the application of Mr. Watson's counsel, and the case was tried at Clonmel, the 14th of August, 1806, by a special jury, viz., Sir John Craven Carden, Sir Thomas Judkin Fitzgerald, John Palliser, Samuel Perry, Thomas Going, Kingsmille Pennefeather, William Armstrong, William Latham, Thomas Pennefeather, John Roe, William Nicholson, and George Robins, Esqrs.

Counselor Driscol, for the plaintiff, stated the case. His client, Mr. Charles M'Carthy, at the instance and request of Mr. Watson, had advanced a sum of £632, the amount of damages for libel and costs incurred in 1804 by Edmund Power, editor of the Clonmel Gazette, at the suit of Colonel Bagwell. The libels for which Power was prosecuted had been concocted and propagated by Watson, and were printed only on Watson promising to indemnify Power against all consequences.

The execution for the damages was not delivered to the sheriff till 1805. Power, accompanied by Mr. M'Carthy, proceeded to Watson, and demanded the indemnification promised him. Watson made some objection, on the ground of committing himself if the money was paid by him, but suggested Mr. M'Carthy drawing a check for it on his bank, where he had funds, and engaged to make good the amount to M'Carthy. The check was drawn by the latter for £632, and Watson was apprised by M'Carthy, a few days later, of the fact by a letter. In reply, Watson wrote to M'Carthy repudiating altogether the transaction referred to, denied all knowledge of it, and said he never knew of any money transactions which might have occurred between him (M'Carthy) and Mr. Power. The present action was the result of this correspondence.

Defendant and his friends now began to vilify the character of Power "as one of the greatest villains on earth," and a circumstance occurred which had been taken advantage of by them to effect this object. Power had got an order from the foreman of a grand jury upon the county treasurer for the amount of a presentment, without any endorsement on the order, but with the avowed purpose and direction to receive the money and keep it for him.

Power, having occasion to pay the amount of an execution against him,

* This very rare report, one which has evidently been bought up with a view to its suppression, I have only received from J. Luther, Esq., at the request of C. Bianconi, Esq., since a preceding note, in reference to the trial, was printed. I am indebted on the present occasion, as well as on former occasions, for valuable and energetic aid in literary researches to Charles Bianconi, and also to John Luther, Esq., of Clonmel; and I may take this opportunity likewise of returning thanks for similar services to Alderman Hackett of the same place, and to R. Purcell, Esq., of Roan House, county Tipperary.

had endorsed the man's name and received the money. Upon this, Watson had Power arrested on a charge of forgery, from which arrest, however, he was admitted to bail; bills were sent up against him for this offense at the next ensuing assizes, but were thrown out.

Previously to the former trial in Waterford of this case (M'Carthy *v.* Watson), one Reynolds, who had been a printer of Power's at the time of publishing the libels, made an affidavit before a magistrate that Watson was not the author of the libels on Bagwell. This proceeding counsel for M'Carthy said was at the instigation of Watson.

The first witness examined was Edmund Power.

He had known Solomon Watson for fourteen or fifteen years. Watson frequently came to his house at the time of the appearance of the libels "to give the heads of them" to him (Power). He published them at Watson's instance, on receiving promise of indemnification. Reynolds, the printer, used to be present when Watson furnished the materials. Reynolds took them down from Watson's dictation. Mr. Charles M'Carthy paid the amount of the execution for the damages and costs against him on account of those libels.

He (Power) went, on the 4th of June, 1805, with M'Carthy to Watson; he told Watson that M'Carthy, whom he had brought in order to be present at their conversation, was a man of honor; and if he doubted his honor, he (M'Carthy) would pledge himself on oath to keep their conversation secret. Watson, addressing M'Carthy, said that no one could settle that business so well as he could, and prevent any suspicion attaching to him (Watson) as the person paying the damages; and therefore if he (M'Carthy) would be so good as to give an order on the bank for the amount, he (Watson) would give an engagement in writing, if he doubted his word, that he would repay him (M'Carthy) in a day or two. M'Carthy said he would take Watson's word, came away with him (Power), drew a check for the amount, and gave it to the sheriff.

Cross-examined by the attorney general:

Witness said his intimacy with M'Carthy commenced about a fortnight or three weeks, but not a month, before the execution had been laid on. He did not consider himself bound to repay M'Carthy; he (M'Carthy) had executed a release to him for the £632. Watson was at first apprehensive of Reynolds, the printer; but he swore him to secresy in his (Power's) parlor. He had not mentioned that circumstance at the former trial in Waterford.

He (Power) had been once tried for an assault, and wrongfully found guilty. He did not want money at the time of the trial for the libel. He had a family—two daughters and a son grown up, and a younger son and a younger daughter.

He had at the present time (August, 1806) a property of four hundred a year, and had it before his paper stopped, and at that time there was £1400 due to him on it. He applied to Watson for the loan of money to fee lawyers in the libel case. Watson refused to lend money on his (Power's) own note. He (Power) owed Watson, as a banker, money equal to the amount of the damages and costs. He did not call on Watson to indemnify him after the trial, because he did not think Bagwell would press for payment. But Watson, in the interim, issued execution against him for the amount he (Power) owed the bank.

He (witness) was now very intimate with M'Carthy; that gentleman was not domesticated in his family, but was there very frequently; had been much abroad, and was a gentleman of fashion.

George Lidwell, high sheriff, examined:

Said he recollects being in Clonmel immediately previous to the trial for libel. Power, then speaking of the ensuing action, said Watson had agreed to indemnify him on the part of all the Quakers of Clonmel. Believed Power entitled to credit on his oath.

Similar evidence as to the promised indemnification by Watson was given by Counselor O'Dwyer, who had been advocate for Power in the libel case, and also by the Hon. Captain I. H. Hutchinson.

William Duckett (attorney) examined:

Said he was joint attorney of Mr. Power with Mr. Hill, in the case Bagwell *v.* Power. While preparing the briefs, saw Watson come into the office and examine the draughts more than once. He was the only person, except those immediately concerned, who was permitted to see the briefs. He was considered as a friend of Power. He had been previously told, he thinks by Power, that Watson was the author of those libels. Watson on one occasion came in and gave instructions, or rather assistance, by suggestions in making out evidence. He suggested summoning as witness for Power against Bagwell a Lieutenant Garrett, of the Tipperary militia, who, he said, would swear that he raised nearly four hundred men, under a stipulation that he was to enlist the men as cheap as he could, charging government the full bounty allowed for recruits, and that he and Colonel Bagwell were to divide the savings. The effect of Garrett's evidence, however, on the trial was to serve Bagwell rather than Power.

Mrs. Ellen Power examined: Said she is the wife of Edmund Power; remembers the action for libel; met Watson shortly after, and had a conversation with him. Watson came to the house; she received him very coolly. They spoke about the execution being in the hands of the sheriff for the damages. She spoke of interceding with Mrs. Bagwell for her husband. Watson advised her not to do so. Bagwell must be spoken to alone by him and his friends, and they must come upon him unawares, for he was as cute as a fox; but they would soften him, for he was a soft man, after all. Watson told her that before the trial Bagwell cried down salt tears, and said that he had fought three duels, but nothing ever touched him so much as that affair. But when he found there were only three witnesses to be brought against him, he became greatly relieved, as he said he could buy them off. She had spoken to Watson one day when these publications were going on, and when Ned

Power was out, against the attacks on Colonel Bagwell; she did not wish him to be meddled with, he was a man of too much consequence; and in gratitude alone she wished to avoid offending him, as Colonel Bagwell had lately very much served one of her family.

Miss Ellen Power being examined, said:

She was the daughter of Edmund Power; saw Watson with Reynolds very often at her father's house, and together, at the time of the publications against Colonel Bagwell. It was very lately the intimacy took place between Mr. M'Carthy and her father. Mr. M'Carthy was an agreeable, pleasant man.

In reply to the question, Was he not often at evening parties at her father's house with the boys and girls? witness answered yes.

Was he not a good-natured man? Witness answered, I think he is; at least, he showed himself so to Mr. Watson.

On examination by Sir T. Judkin Fitzgerald, witness said she knew none of the compositions referred to—believed Mr. Watson did. Saw him one day take out a paper, and rubbing his hands, he said, "This is the best of all." "The Patriot and the Soldier!" and subsequent to that, the publication of the libel signed "Contrastor" appeared; the words were used on entering the door, and the place is a thoroughfare; her father looked up at her, and shook his head at her. On her coming down, her father met her, and asked her what she heard, and she told him.

Witness being asked by Sir T. Judkin Fitzgerald, Then why did your father not bring you to Waterford? replied, I suppose he forgot it. She never heard from her father that Watson was to indemnify him.

Thomas M'Carthy, Esq., examined: Said he was the brother of Charles M'Carthy, Esq., and was with him at the Globe Hotel, in Clonmel, in June, 1805; met Edmund Power there one day after dinner. He knew Power at that time; his brother did not; spoke to Power of the execution. Power said he had been to Watson that morning, and hoped the matter would be settled. He, Thomas M'Carthy, had advised Power to have a friend present when he next communicated with Watson, and had suggested his brother being that person, having a suspicion of Watson's insincerity.

On cross examination, witness said his brother had been in the habit of visiting frequently at Power's; was there on a friendly, not on a familiar footing. Witness had met them last year at the watering place of Tramore. His brother Charles had spent seventeen or eighteen years in the Imperial service; he had moved in the best society on the Continent, and had been engaged, like other men of fashion, in play, and had won and lost large sums at billiards. He had heard his brother lent Mr. John Denniss money, many years ago, in England, when in deep distress; had won money from him since at billiards, for which he had passed securities; he had now refused to pay, being a gambling transaction.

He thought his brother would as soon poison him (witness) as bring an unjust claim against another.

R. Butler H. Lowe, Esq., examined:

He knew Charles M'Carthy many years, and believes him as little capable as any man in the world of making an unjust claim, and thinks no inducement in the world could bring him to resort to perjury.

William Minchin, Esq., examined, gave similar testimony.

Here the case for the plaintiff closed.

The court adjourned on Tuesday evening, at a late hour, to the next day.

Friday, 15th August, 1806. The court met pursuant to adjournment.

The Attorney General, the Right Hon. W. C. Plunkett, stated the case for defendant.

The question was one formally and nominally for the recovery of £632, but virtually one that involved the fame and character of the defendant. If a verdict should be found against him, Solomon Watson, that verdict would, and must, stamp him with eternal infamy. Watson, at the turn of sixty, knowing the world, does not send to Power's newspaper an anonymous letter, of which no second person on earth could know the author; he, a good husband, a fond father, a mild relative, an honest friend, a moral man in all the relations of life, makes an unnecessary exposure of his malignity against one who believed him to be a bosom friend. He, Watson, is represented as saying of a particular libelous article, "It was the best of all"—that in which the words occurred, "What say the Patriot and Soldier?" If Watson could be such a fool as to make such a proclamation, Providence, at the same time that it robbed him of his honesty, had deprived him of his senses. It was, however, a painful task, but it was a necessary duty, to call upon the jury to say that a fair face and an artless manner could cover a mind capable of flippingly violating the laws of God and man. It led to the reflection, that when ruin of fame and fortune arrives, which penalty Providence has allotted to persons for misconduct and vice, the visitation of the offense was not confined to the offender, but spread itself among his nearest and dearest connections; and the best and kindliest dispositions are pressed into the service, and involved in the consequences of guilt and infamy. When Miss Power was pressed on the inconsistency of selecting two words in the middle of the production, she said, "Oh, no, gentlemen, that is the beginning of the libel." The jury would see the part of the libel set forth in the first part of the declaration, and of course, though in the middle of the publication, when every one took part in the publicity of the transaction, these words were the common topic of conversation, and the daughter, whom you must consider as knowing nothing of the business, was brought forward to tell a ready-made tale, and fastening on two or three words, she spoke as if the name of the production was "The Patriot and the Soldier." This young, volatile, beautiful, and giddy girl tells you that she learns this at the beginning. Did she tell it to her mother? Clearly not; for the mother, when she went to Colonel Bagwell to solicit recompense of his claims, did not know that Watson was the author, and she, Miss Power, knowing that Bagwell would abandon the prosecution on giving up the author, and knowing that Watson was the author, and having heard the declaration of Watson, never appealed to her mother to give up the author. Why, this miraculous behavior betrays a sedateness of intellect fitting her to become prime minister to the potentate in the world most requiring secresy. At the trial in Waterford, where her father and mother went to give evidence, she, who could prove the authorship of the libel and the proclamation of its title by the guilty culprit, never appeared there, and never was heard of in the cause, until that second desperate effort on the credulity of a jury. The jury would consider these matters as an assortment of circumstances so irregular, that in a romance he, the attorney general, would blame the author for combining things so discordant.

The jury were told of Watson going into the office of Power's solicitors during the prosecution for libel, and looking at the briefs on the table. The opinion that he, the attorney general, formed of Watson, was this: that he was a very curious, gossiping kind of man, fair in his dealings, honest in his engagements, but intermeddling, and, as it was observed by one of the solicitors, taking up every brief that he could lay his hands on, cackling over it, and thrusting his nose into every business that did not concern him; and he, the attorney general, candidly owned he did not think that he, Watson, showed that resentment that his friendship for Colonel Bagwell should have made him feel at such a system of slander. . . . I suspect Solomon Watson did not think this article ill written, and I candidly aver to you that I can not say any thing in praise of a man who can relish a pleasure in a malignant libel against a friend. But the question was not whether he was indignant at the libel, and incensed at the libeler, but whether he was the author or instigator of the libel? The jury, in fine, were called on to decide between characters; they had to consider the antecedents of Solomon Watson, and their incompatibility with the sudden adoption of the trade of a libeler; and likewise the peculiarities and refinement of a gentleman of fashion, like Captain M'Carthy, brought up in courts and camps, whose intellect had been sharpened in the frozen climate of the North, and his morality mellowed in the kindlier regions of the South. They had to consider the interest inspired by that gentleman's acquaintance, though very short, with the family of Power. The jury would see the father was a jocose, hospitable, dashing, and probably, what is called in the world, an honest fellow; the mother a good-humored, good-natured, pleasant woman. The gay and gaudy tulip that had been presented to them could not have escaped observation; but flowers of that description might be, and were very often, obtained at a price much too high. [A great deal of similar invective, unwarranted and unwarrantable, was indulged in by Mr. Watson's counsel].

First witness for defendant, James Reynolds, printer, examined.

Witness said he was the conducting printer of Mr. Power when editor of the Clonmel Gazette. He recollected the several libels prosecuted by Colonel Bagwell; Mr. Watson was neither the author nor corrector of them.

None of the facts mentioned in those libels ever came directly from Watson; never was sworn to secresy respecting them by Watson. He knew the author of them—a man of moderate talents. He did not part amicably with Power. He was falsely accused, after he had left Power's employment, of breaking open a lock, that of the printing-office door. The house was a thoroughfare to many people. None of Power's property, not so much as a sheet of paper, was removed by him. He never received any pecuniary consideration from Watson for his evidence. His expenses from Waterford to Clonmel alone were paid. Had no intercourse with Watson till he saw him in Waterford. Knew Miss Power; she was a very young girl when those articles were written.* He never knew any thing of her to her disadvantage. He knew Mrs. Power pretty well. He never thought ill of her at any time. He believed, since the trial at Waterford, Power was not to be believed on his oath. He thought the same now as to Mrs. Power, since her testimony at Waterford.

Witness was asked his opinion of the credibility of Miss Power on her oath. He said,

"When I knew her in Clonmel, my opinion was certainly to her advantage, and I have heard nothing to alter it now."

Witness knew Edmund Dwyer; says he is a bad man. He did not recollect saying in Waterford that Dwyer was a good man; his expression was, when asked if he thought Dwyer would be guilty of perjury, "Not yet." He, witness, had changed his opinion since that trial. He had told Dwyer who the author of the libels was.† The witness, on examination by Sir T. J. Fitzgerald, was pressed to name the author.

Colonel Bagwell, who was in court, engaged, if the author was named, not to prosecute him; whereupon Reynolds said, "*I was the author.*" He had received some information, on which he acted in one of the articles, from persons of the names of Hogan, Murphy, and Mangles

Richard Sparrow, Esq., examined:

Said he knew Watson as long as he can remember; does not believe, if he undertook to indemnify Power, he would decline doing so. Watson was a very wealthy man; derived part of his wealth from a Mr. White. Through Colonel Bagwell's influence, he, Watson, got the office of Clerk of the Peace and Crown. He was of the people called Quakers. He is now a Protestant of the Established Church, and is pretty regular in his attendance at church. He went to the Quaker's meetings for three or four years after getting the appointment of Clerk of the Peace. On the remonstrance of the society as to the incompatibility of his tenure of office with their tenets, he resigned that office. He, witness, did not consider it compatible with Quaker's tenets to

* They were written in 1803; she was then hardly thirteen years of age.—R. R. M.

† There is every reason to believe that the witness, James Reynolds, was the author of the libels, and that some of the facts contained in them had in conversation been given to Power by Watson, and had been communicated to Reynolds by Power.—R. R. M.

keep arms, yet knew that Watson kept them at the time of the rebellion, and was obliged to use them for his defense while living in the country.

Colonel Bagwell examined:

Said he intimately knew Watson three or four-and-twenty years. Had spoken to Watson in 1805 about those libels, and said he thought it incumbent on him (Watson) to exculpate himself, and that if he (witness) were in his place, he would give £1000 to Reynolds to give up the author. He believed Watson utterly incapable of the baseness ascribed to him. Watson had complained to him (witness) of many acts done in the collection of tolls which the corporation highly disapproved of, and which were corrected. As to Power's circumstances, matters had come to his knowledge the winter before last which showed that he was an extremely distressed man. He did not think Mr. M'Carthy capable of extorting a sum of £632, though he did not know him personally, but could not think any gentleman of honor capable of such an act. He had heard Reynolds was a man of good character, and therefore could not be purchased by a sum of £1000.

Dean Bagwell examined:

Said Watson came to him with a letter from Charles M'Carthy, dated 4th of June, for his advice. Watson informed witness of Power and M'Carthy having been at his house, and from circumstances that occurred, he strongly suspected a combination was formed to implicate him in the liabilities of Power. Witness recommended him to write the letter, which he addressed to M'Carthy; on cross-examination, said M'Carthy had got warm and angry, and said that he would pay the money, for reasons of his own; and that he had an utter abhorrence and detestation of Colonel Bagwell and his whole family, because the father of Colonel Bagwell had been the cause of hanging Sheehy,* and had offered, the night before Sheehy's execution, to procure him his pardon, provided he would turn informer against the persons named on a list, at the head of which was M'Carthy's father.

Mr. Burrowes, as counsel for the defendant, spoke to evidence, and was followed by Mr. Hoare at considerable length. In summing up the merits of the evidence on the part of the plaintiff, Mr. Hoare said,

Mr. Power was a gentleman of high descent, independent in property—honored with the commission of the Peace for the counties of Tipperary and Waterford—of a character irreproachable in every respect but one, and in this one only reproachable because of its contact with the impurity of Watson.

He appealed to the jury whether Power's testimony was not, throughout, clear, consistent, and manly; and this after as severe a scrutiny as ever witness endured, in the longest and most trying examination he had ever witnessed. He swore positively to the share Watson had in the manufacture and publication of the libel. Watson's visits and closetings with Power and

* Query: the priest, Father Nicholas, or Edmund Sheehy, the father of Mrs. Power? for both were hanged, in consequence of the measures taken for that end by old John Bagwell. —R. R. M.

Reynolds, during the periods of the publication, were accurately described by Mrs. Power and her daughter. And yet the modest deportment of that respectable matron, the innocence and integrity that marked her clear, consistent testimony, and her conduct in the transactions which she deposed to, yet she could not escape a little gently insinuated animadversion from the counsel of the defendant, suggested, it must be presumed, by Mr. Solomon Watson himself. Did the defendant suppose that his cause was to be benefited by showing the jury that he still delighted in the trade of defamation? that neither venerable age nor artless youth could, even in the face of the court, be protected from his rancor? Did he flatter himself that unfounded insinuations, thrown out with as little regard to decency as to truth, would recommend himself or his cause to such a jury? and that their verdict could be insured by no other means than the unmanly attempt, the scandalous endeavor, the diabolical effort, to blacken with his breath the purity of unsullied innocence, to visit with contumely that which should be cherished by airs from Heaven, to wither the dearest object of man's care and protection, the tenderest of all flowers—female reputation? If he so thinks, he deceives himself—the truth is not in him. Oh! shame to manhood; can he be a man? Oh! disgrace to Ireland; can he be an Irishman? Base in his meditated fraud upon the plaintiff, baser in his information against his best friend, basest of all in his disgusting aspersions upon the loveliest and the most respectable of the softer sex.

Hear this wariest, and at another time weakest of mankind, speak by the admission of his counsel, and by the mouths of his witnesses for himself, and he will use an intelligible and unsophisticated language. . . . . Hear the last speech and dying words of this trader in discount and defamation—as his learned and eloquent advocate bewailed the fate of his client, anticipating your cruel verdict. Will it be deemed too presumptuous of the plaintiff's advocate to add a little to what his learned friend began?

Here lies Watson,
Who perished by the breath of Power;

and many other witnesses, who disclosed to a just judge and an honest jury the not vulgar baseness, though more than common turpitude, of his manifold iniquities. He was dismissed with the ignominious sentence he deserved, and this he survived many years, his heart being alike dead to virtue and insensible to shame.*

The judge, in summing up the evidence, said, in every view of this mysterious case there were difficulties to be met with, and the verdict of the question to be decided by the jury was one which involved the guilt and baseness of one or other of the parties to this suit. If the plaintiff's case could be es-

* Solomon Watson survived this violent and virulent denunciation many years. He died largely engaged in banking concerns, and in the possession of wealth and of a fair reputation.—R. R. M.

tablished, the defendant must be a designing knave—a slanderer of his friend Colonel Bagwell—and intentionally a swindler of Mr. M'Carthy. On the other hand, if it should appear that M'Carthy and Power had conspired to defraud the defendant, then perjury and fraud must be inevitably fastened alike on the plaintiff and Power.

The jury, after a long and protracted deliberation, brought in a verdict for the plaintiff, damages £316 2*s*. 6*d*. (the exact half of the sum of the amount sought).

END OF VOL. I.

www.ingramcontent.com/pod-product-compliance
Lightning Source LLC
LaVergne TN
LVHW021239110826
845150LV00002B/360

* 9 7 8 1 4 2 5 5 6 1 7 4 1 *